GOODNIGHT PUNPUN

1

Story and Art by **INIO ASANO**

GOODNIGHT PUNPUN

Part One

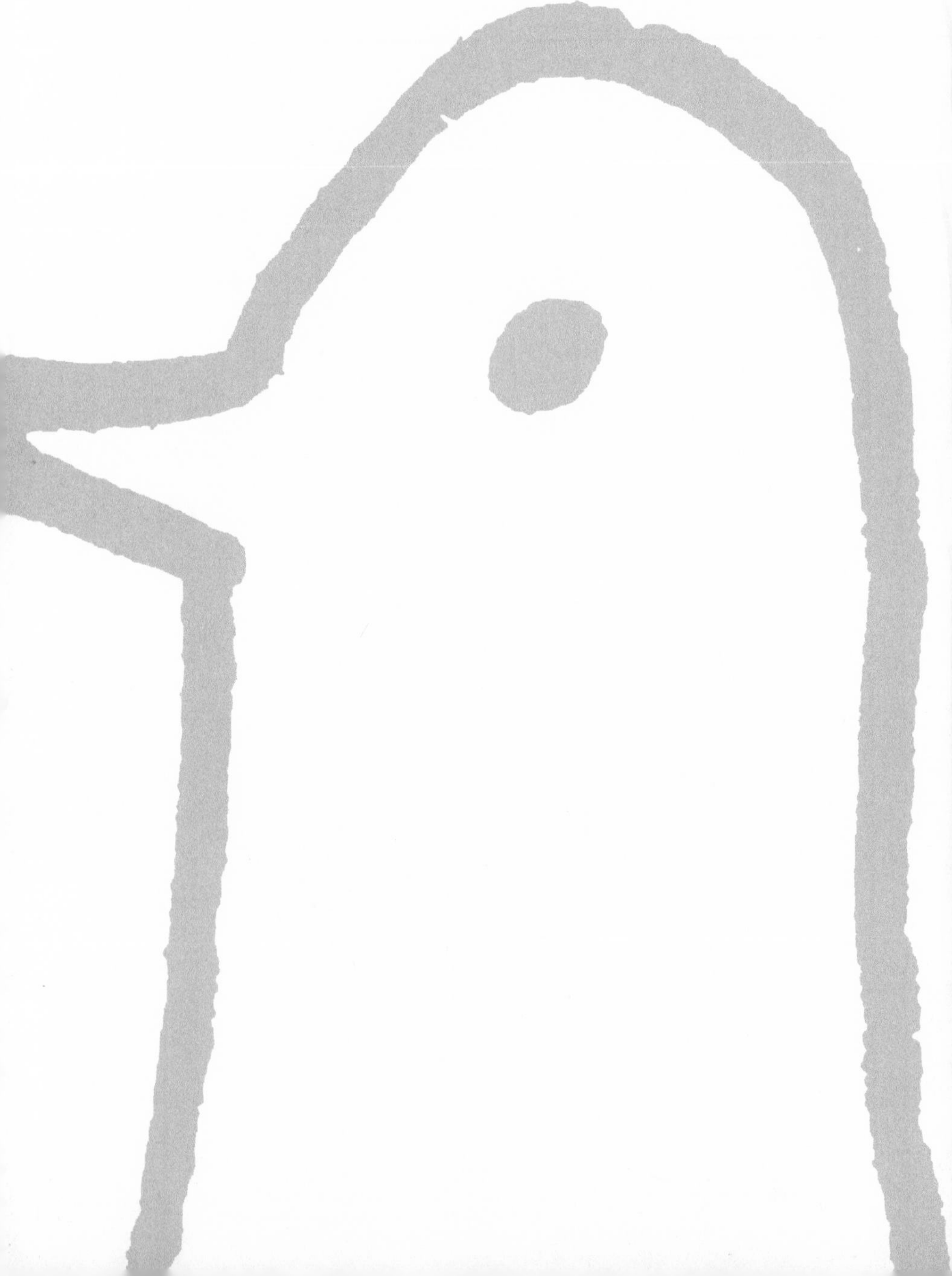

CONTENTS

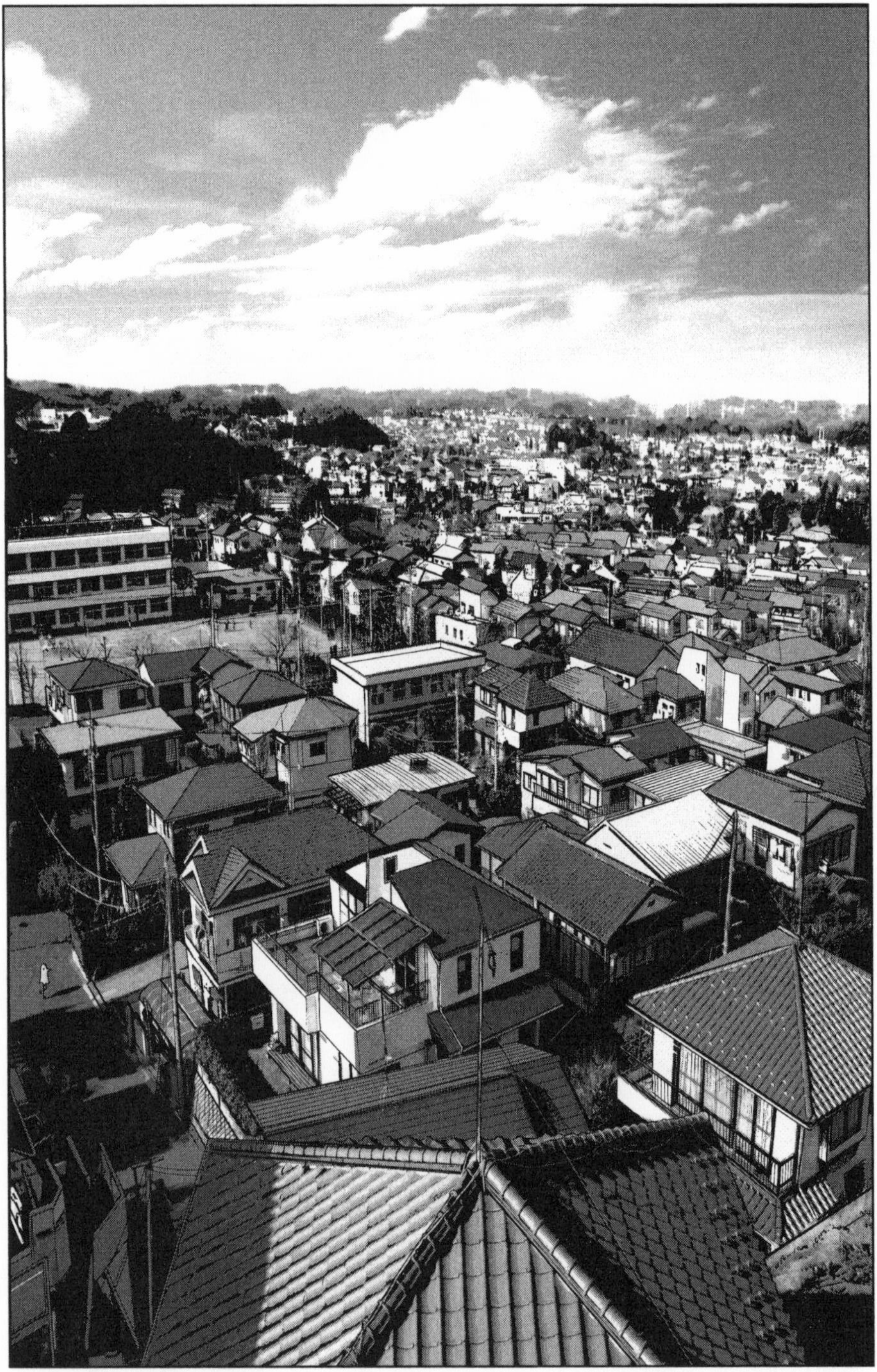

Chapter 1

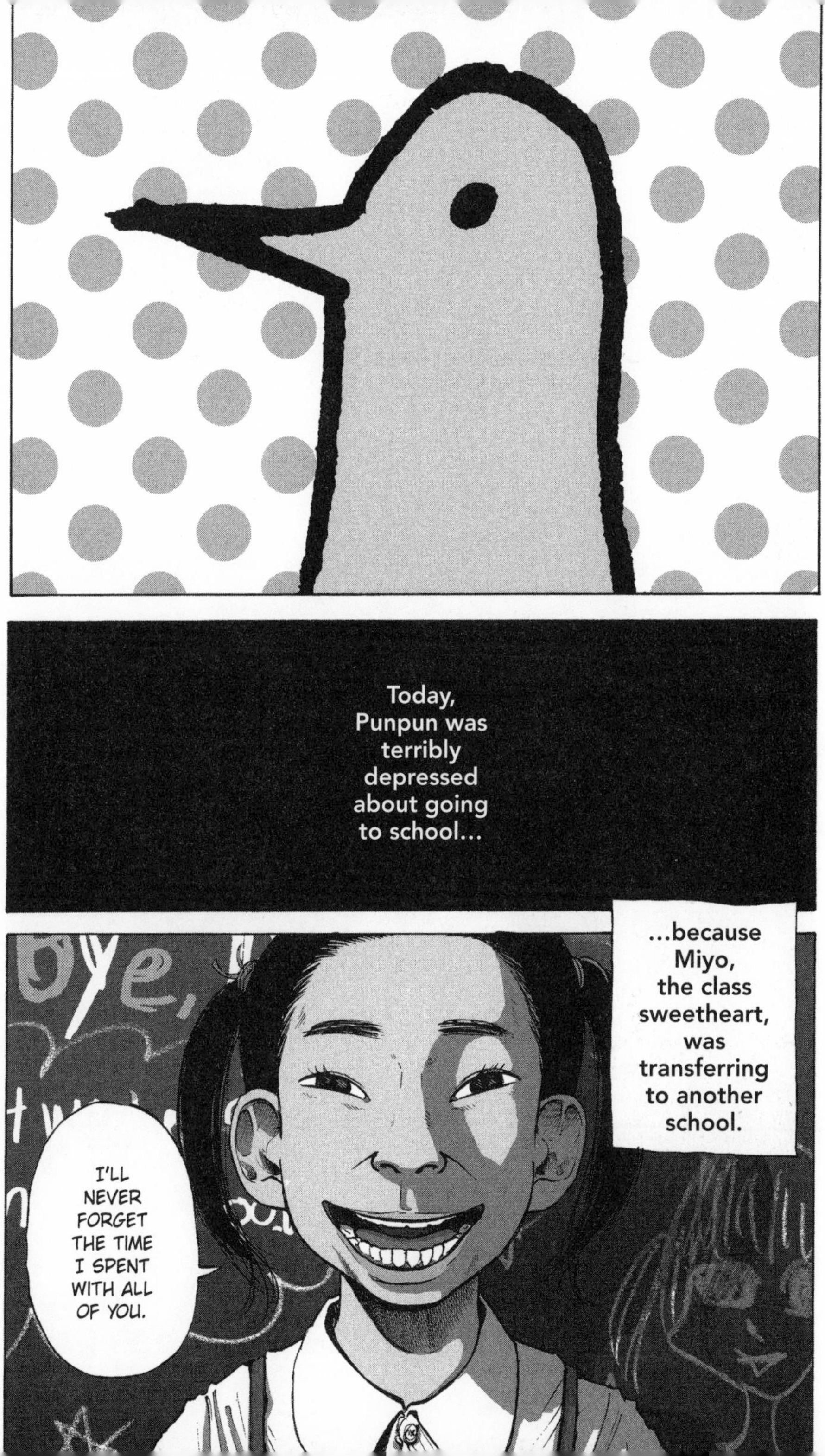
Today, Punpun was terribly depressed about going to school...
...because Miyo, the class sweetheart, was transferring to another school.
I'LL NEVER FORGET THE TIME I SPENT WITH ALL OF YOU.

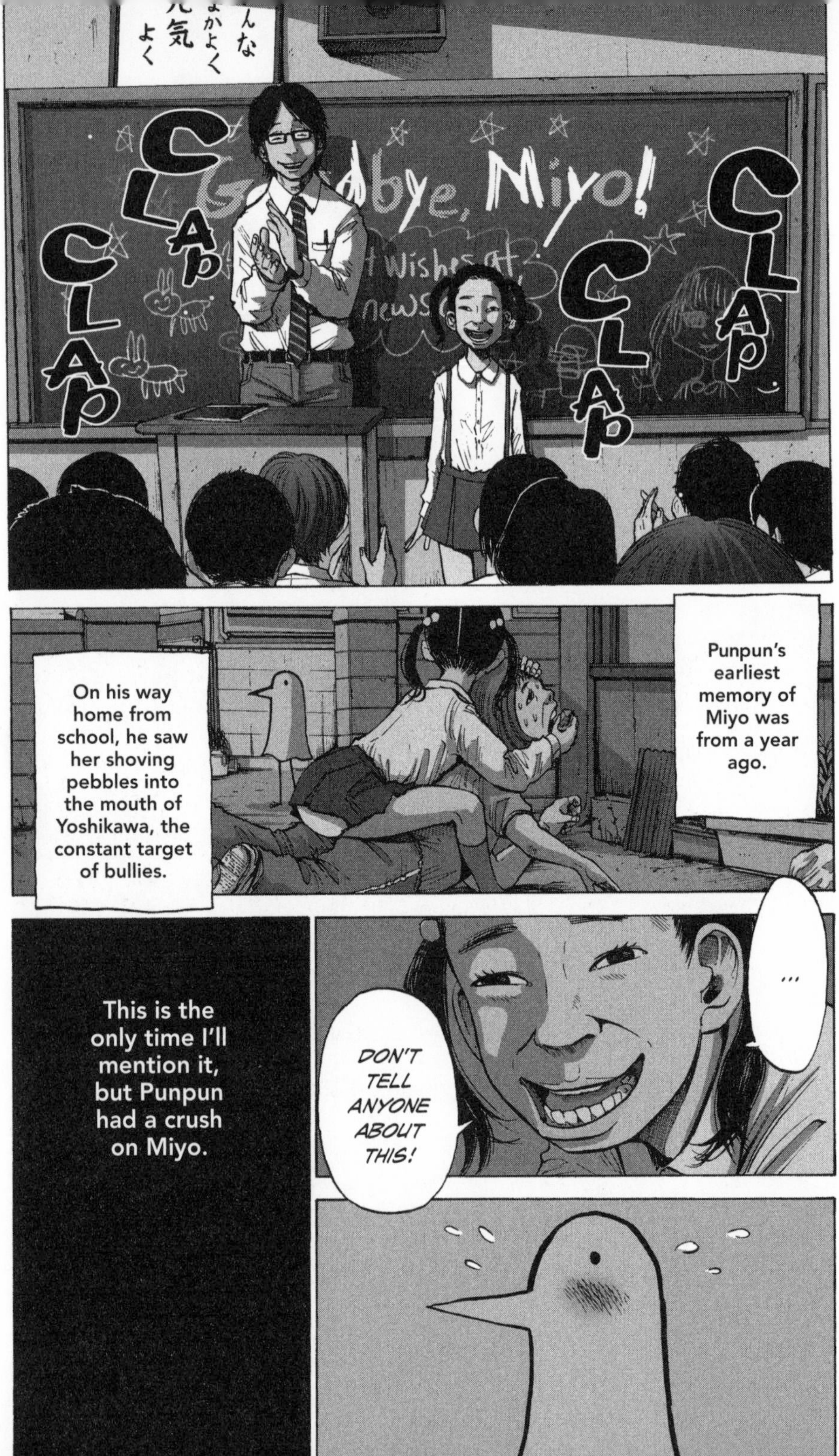
CLAP
CLAP
CLAP
CLAP
Punpun's earliest memory of Miyo was from a year ago.
On his way home from school, he saw her shoving pebbles into the mouth of Yoshikawa, the constant target of bullies.
...
DON'T TELL ANYONE ABOUT THIS!
This is the only time I'll mention it, but Punpun had a crush on Miyo.

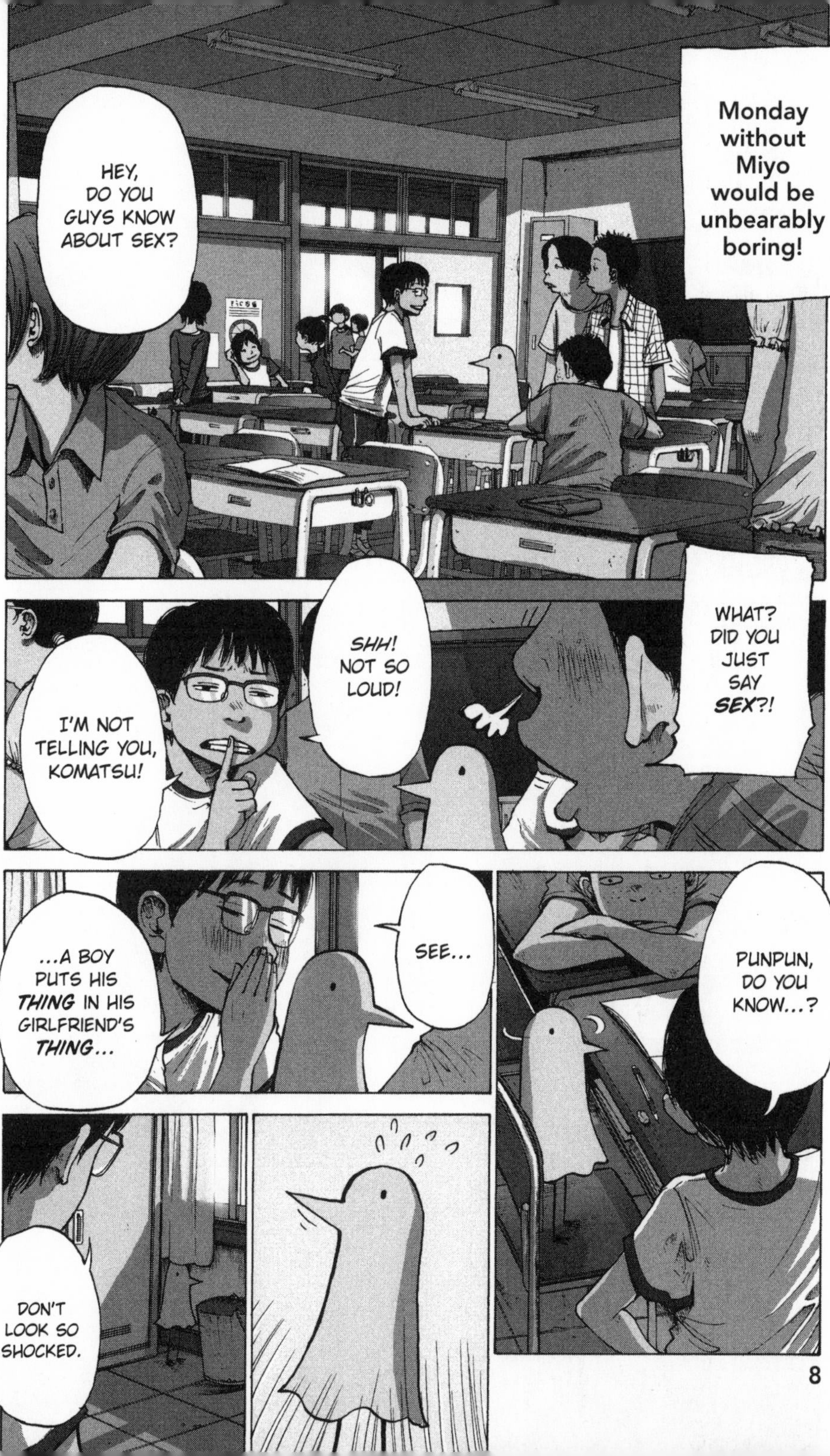

Monday without Miyo would be unbearably boring!
HEY, DO YOU GUYS KNOW ABOUT SEX?
WHAT? DID YOU JUST SAY *SEX*?!
SHH! NOT SO LOUD!
I'M NOT TELLING YOU, KOMATSU!
PUNPUN, DO YOU KNOW...?
SEE...
...A BOY PUTS HIS *THING* IN HIS GIRLFRIEND'S *THING*...
DON'T LOOK SO SHOCKED.

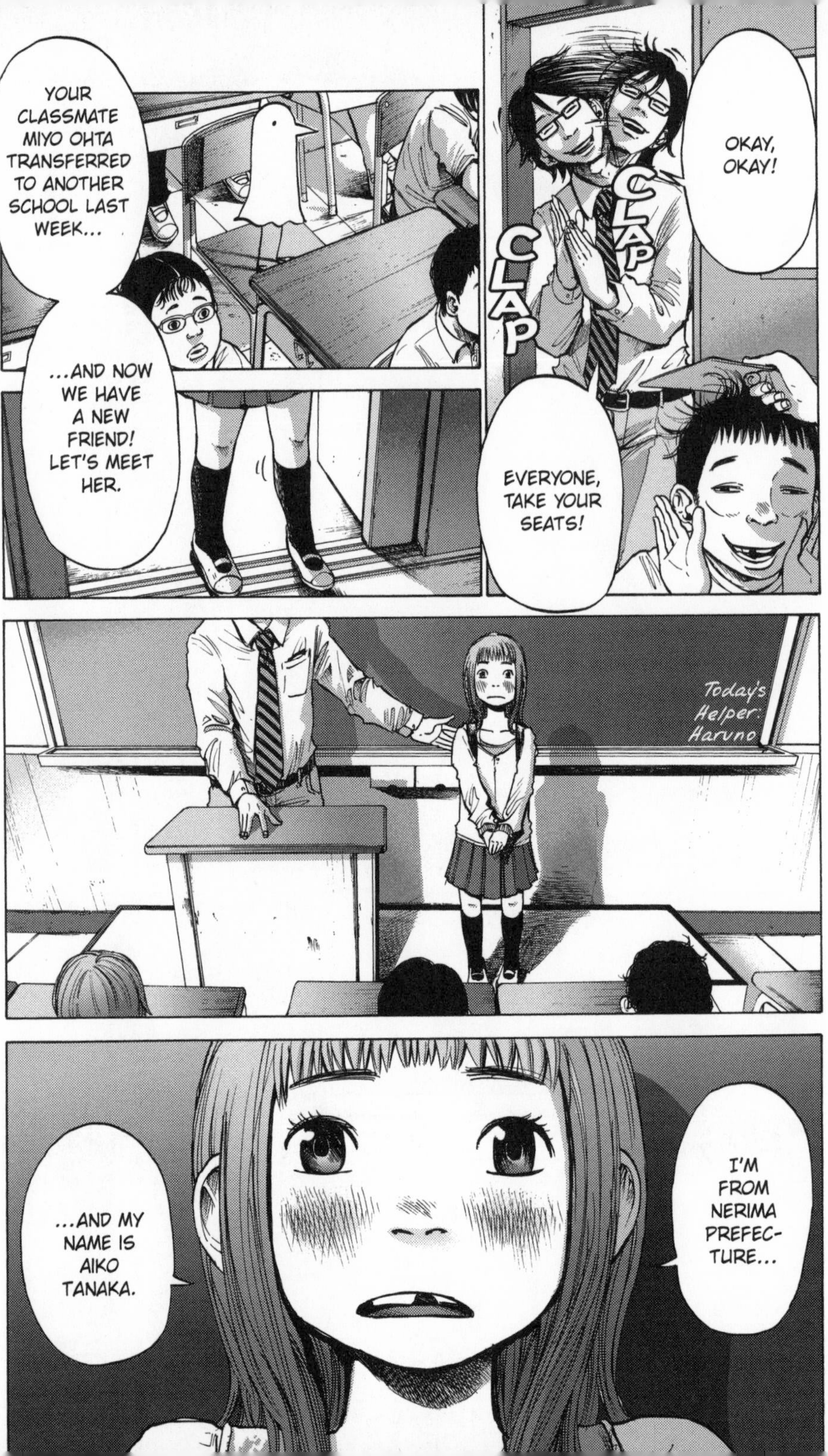
OKAY, OKAY!
CLAP CLAP
CLAP
YOUR CLASSMATE MIYO OHTA TRANSFERRED TO ANOTHER SCHOOL LAST WEEK...
EVERYONE, TAKE YOUR SEATS!
...AND NOW WE HAVE A NEW FRIEND! LET'S MEET HER.
Today's Helper: Haruno
I'M FROM NERIMA PREFEC-TURE...
...AND MY NAME IS AIKO TANAKA.

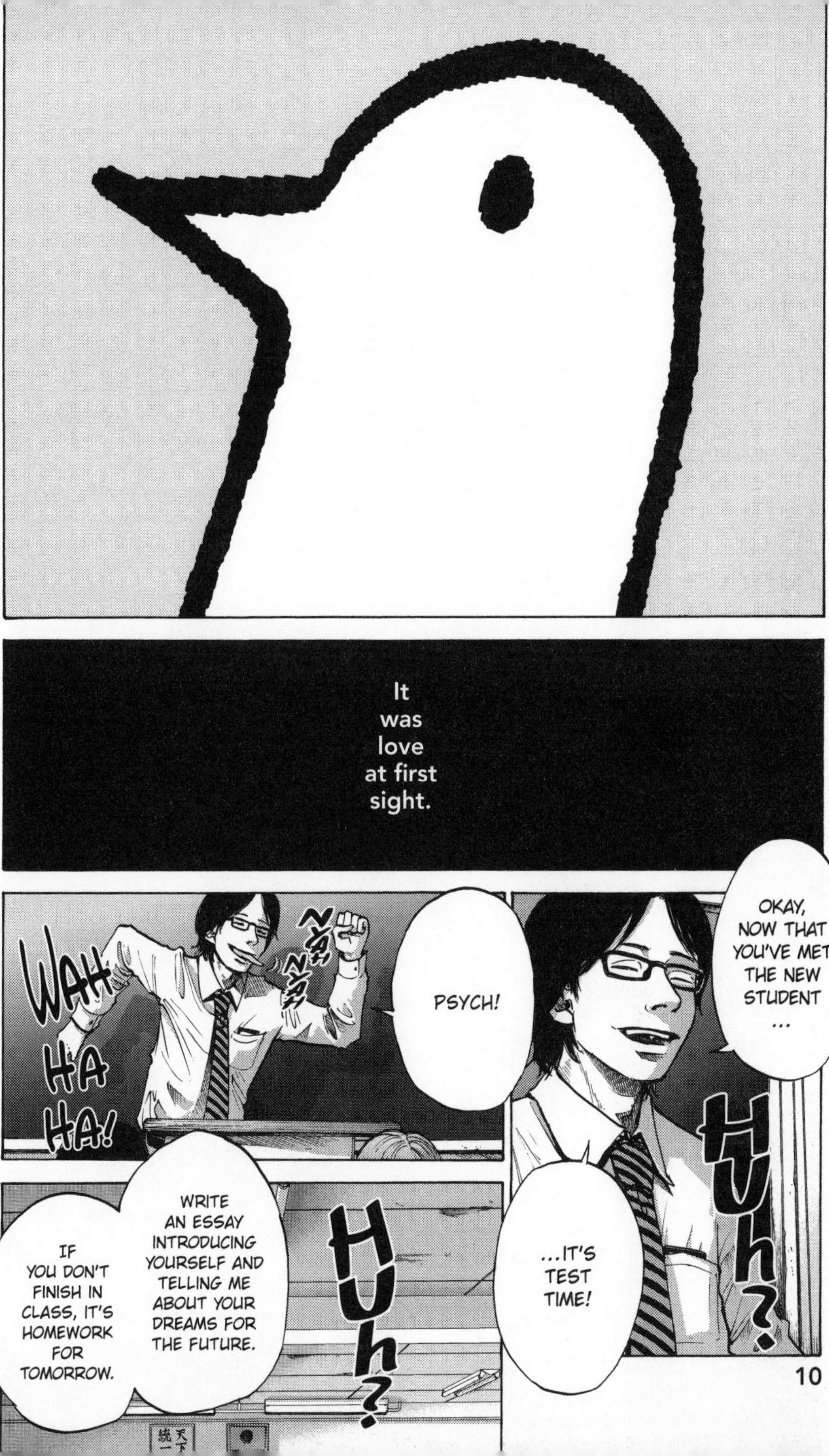
It was love at first sight.
OKAY, NOW THAT YOU'VE MET THE NEW STUDENT ...
HUH?
...IT'S TEST TIME!
PSYCH!
NYAH NYAH
WAH HA HA!
HUH?
WRITE AN ESSAY INTRODUCING YOURSELF AND TELLING ME ABOUT YOUR DREAMS FOR THE FUTURE.
IF YOU DON'T FINISH IN CLASS, IT'S HOMEWORK FOR TOMORROW.

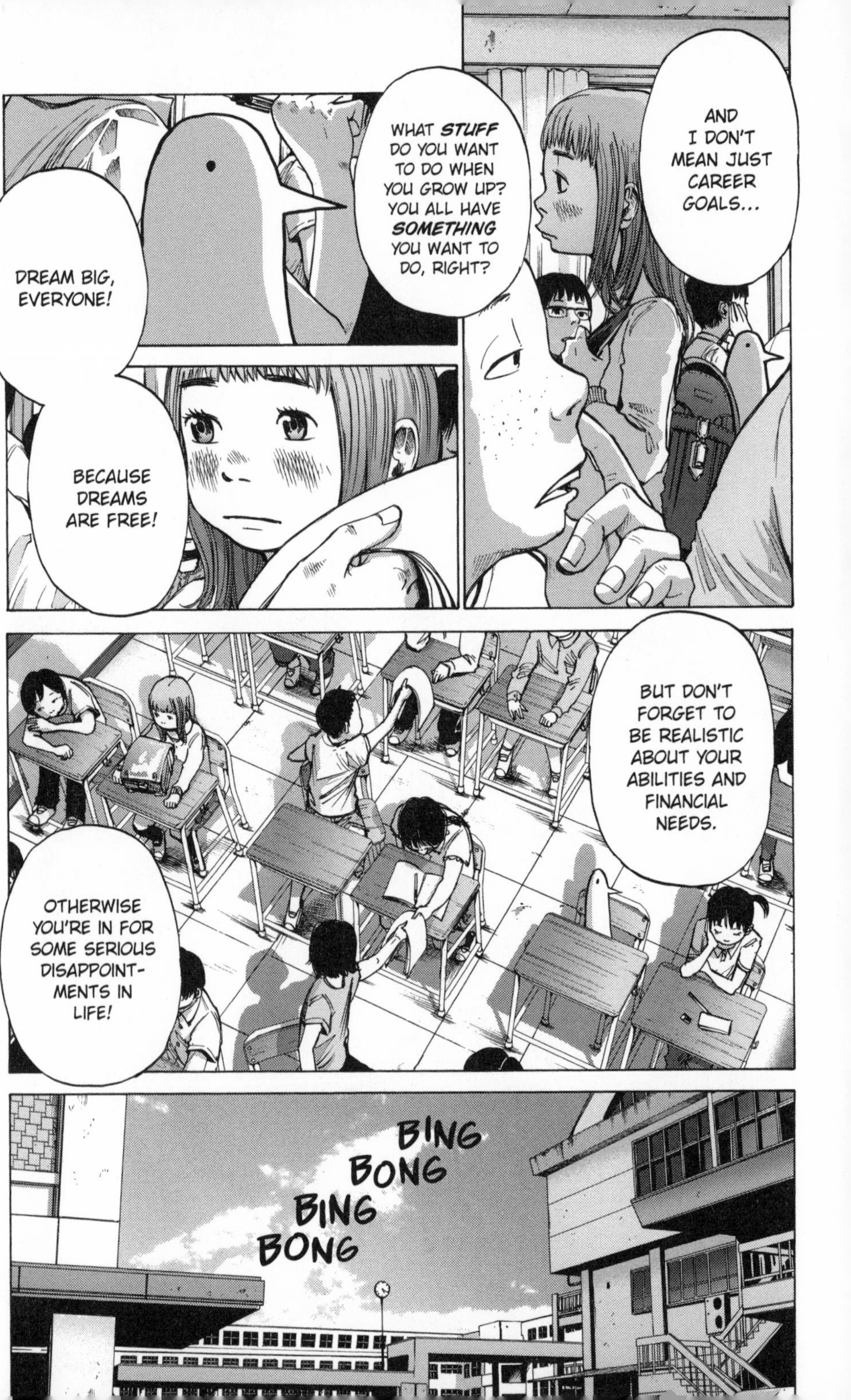
AND I DON'T MEAN JUST CAREER GOALS...
WHAT STUFF DO YOU WANT TO DO WHEN YOU GROW UP? YOU ALL HAVE SOMETHING YOU WANT TO DO, RIGHT?
DREAM BIG, EVERYONE!
BECAUSE DREAMS ARE FREE!
BUT DON'T FORGET TO BE REALISTIC ABOUT YOUR ABILITIES AND FINANCIAL NEEDS.
OTHERWISE YOU'RE IN FOR SOME SERIOUS DISAPPOINT-MENTS IN LIFE!
BING BONG
BING BONG

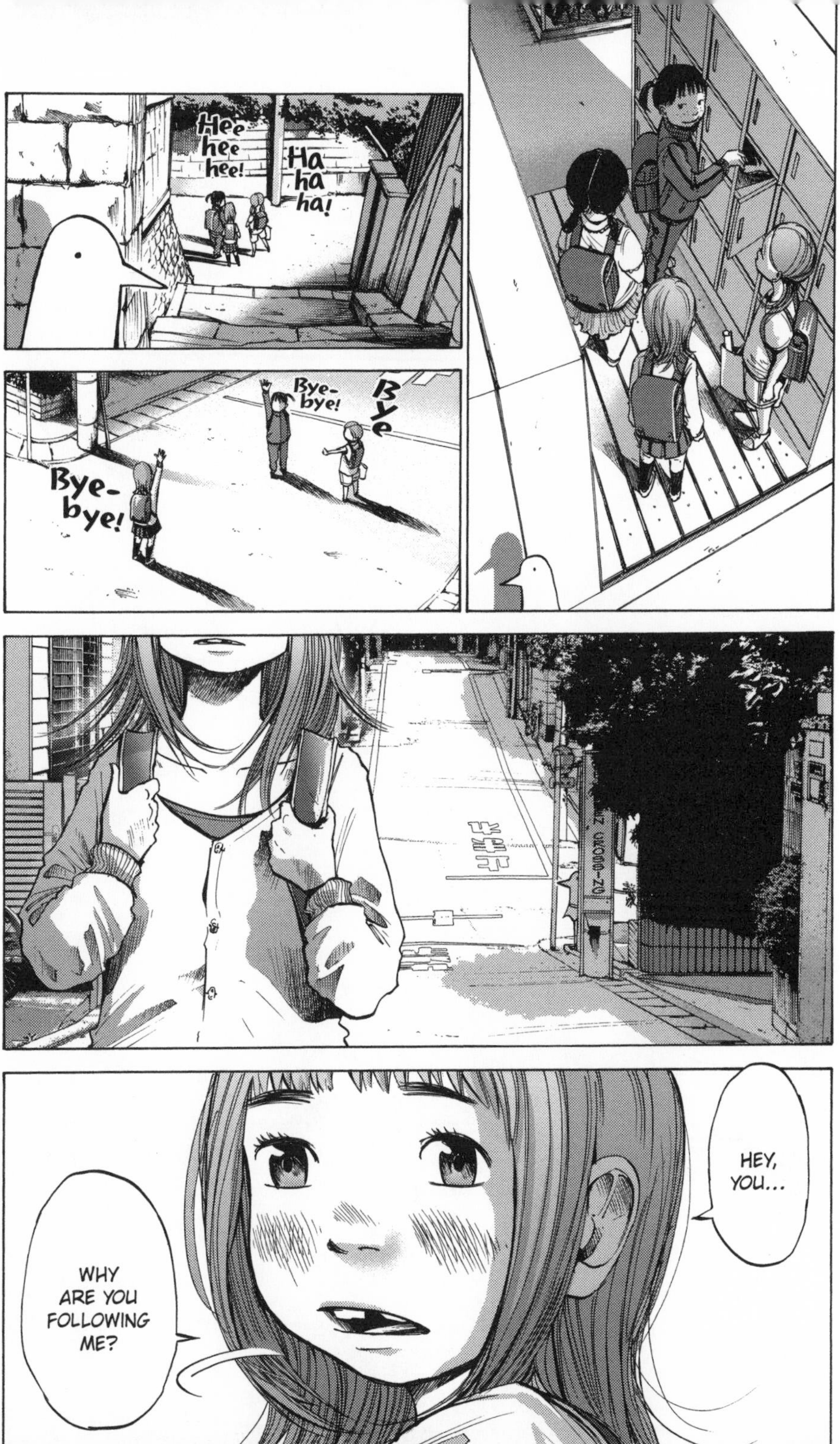

Ha ha ha!
Hee hee hee!
Bye
Bye-bye!
Bye-bye!
HEY, YOU...
WHY ARE YOU FOLLOWING ME?

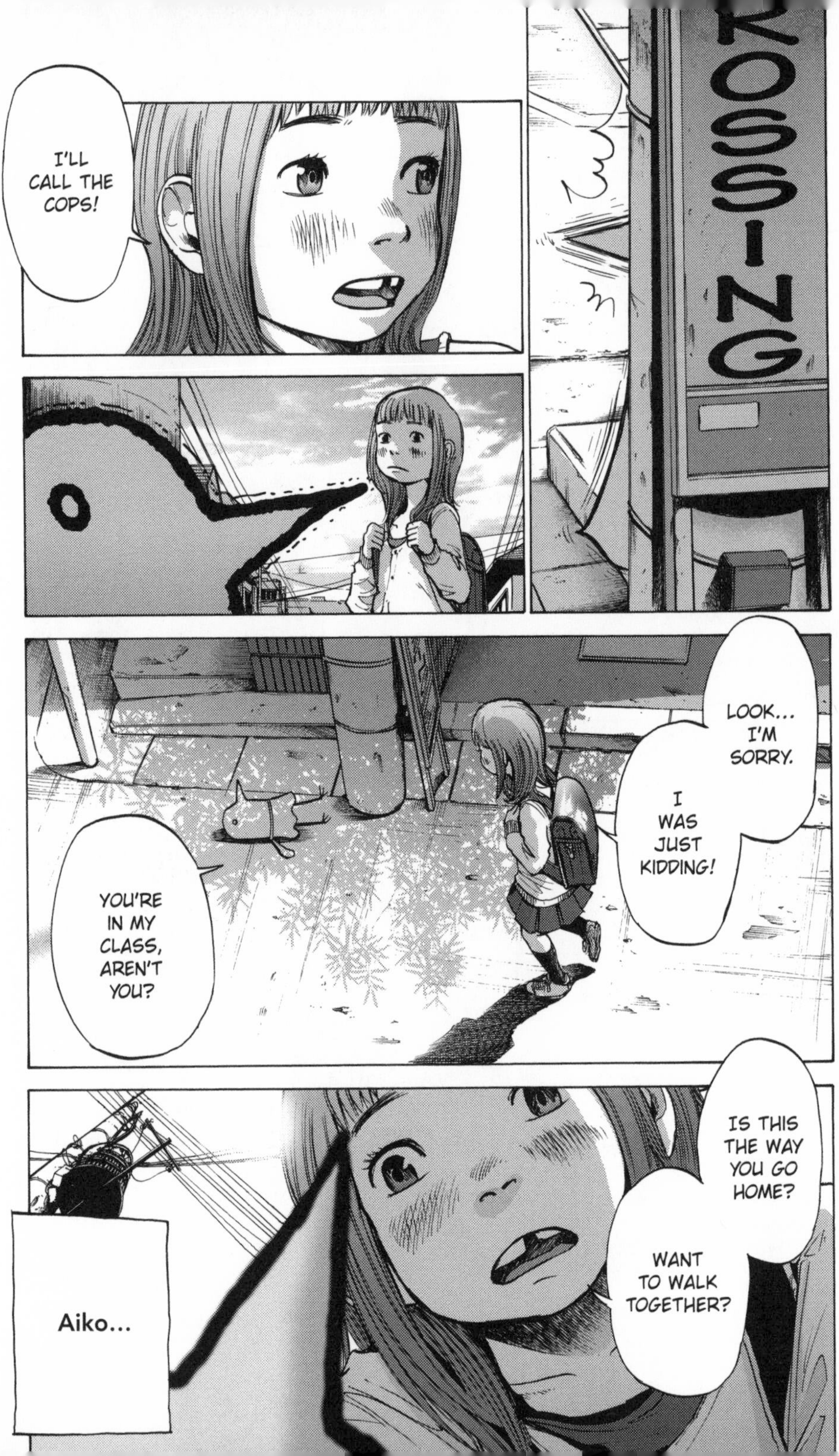
KOSSING
I'LL CALL THE COPS!
LOOK... I'M SORRY.
I WAS JUST KIDDING!
YOU'RE IN MY CLASS, AREN'T YOU?
IS THIS THE WAY YOU GO HOME?
WANT TO WALK TOGETHER?
Aiko...

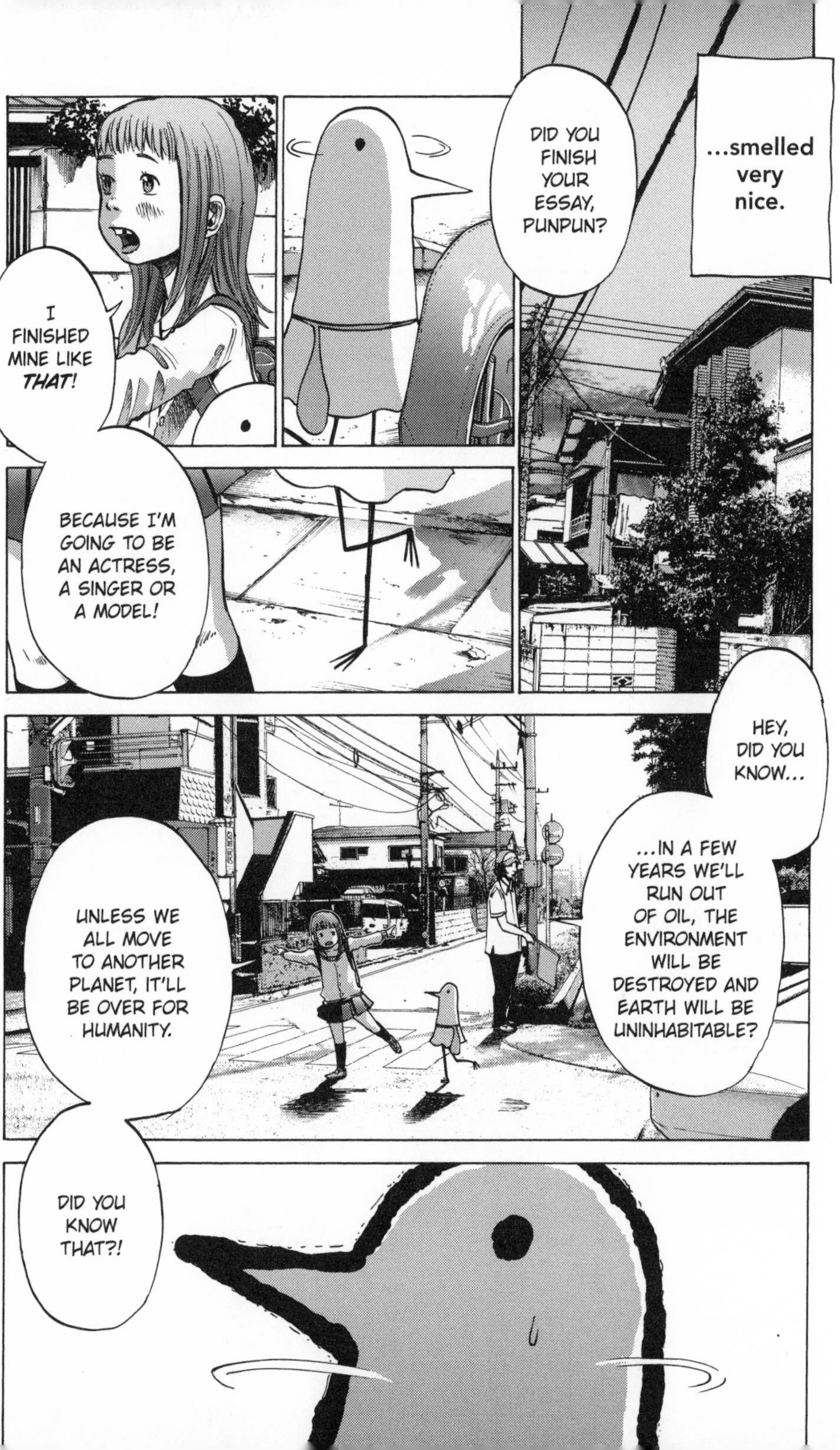
...smelled very nice.
DID YOU FINISH YOUR ESSAY, PUNPUN?
I FINISHED MINE LIKE *THAT*!
BECAUSE I'M GOING TO BE AN ACTRESS, A SINGER OR A MODEL!
HEY, DID YOU KNOW...
...IN A FEW YEARS WE'LL RUN OUT OF OIL, THE ENVIRONMENT WILL BE DESTROYED AND EARTH WILL BE UNINHABITABLE?
UNLESS WE ALL MOVE TO ANOTHER PLANET, IT'LL BE OVER FOR HUMANITY.
DID YOU KNOW THAT?!

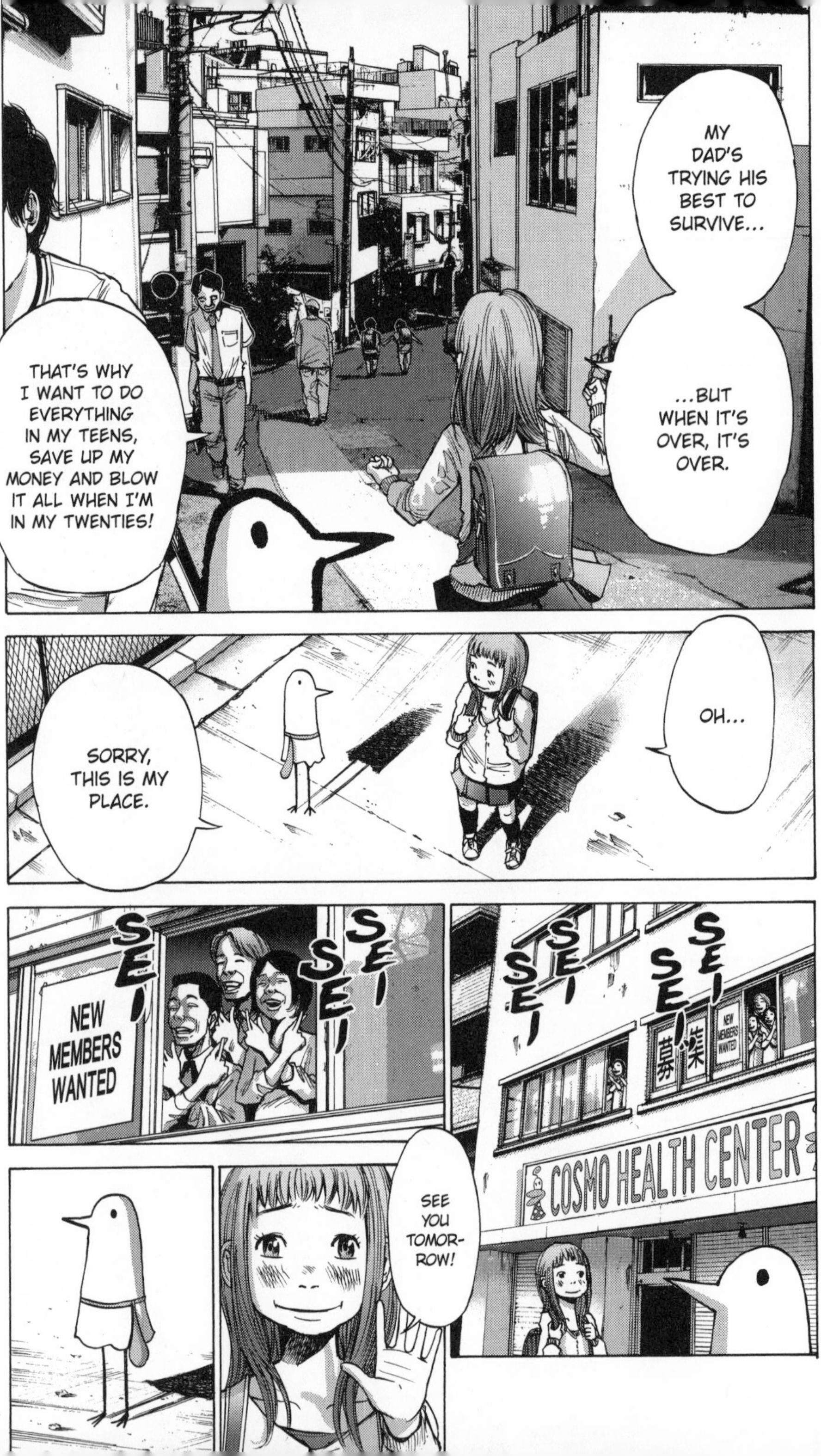
MY DAD'S TRYING HIS BEST TO SURVIVE...
...BUT WHEN IT'S OVER, IT'S OVER.
THAT'S WHY I WANT TO DO EVERYTHING IN MY TEENS, SAVE UP MY MONEY AND BLOW IT ALL WHEN I'M IN MY TWENTIES!
OH...
SORRY, THIS IS MY PLACE.
SE SE SE SE
募集
NEW MEMBERS WANTED
COSMO HEALTH CENTER
SE SE SE
NEW MEMBERS WANTED
SEE YOU TOMOR-ROW!

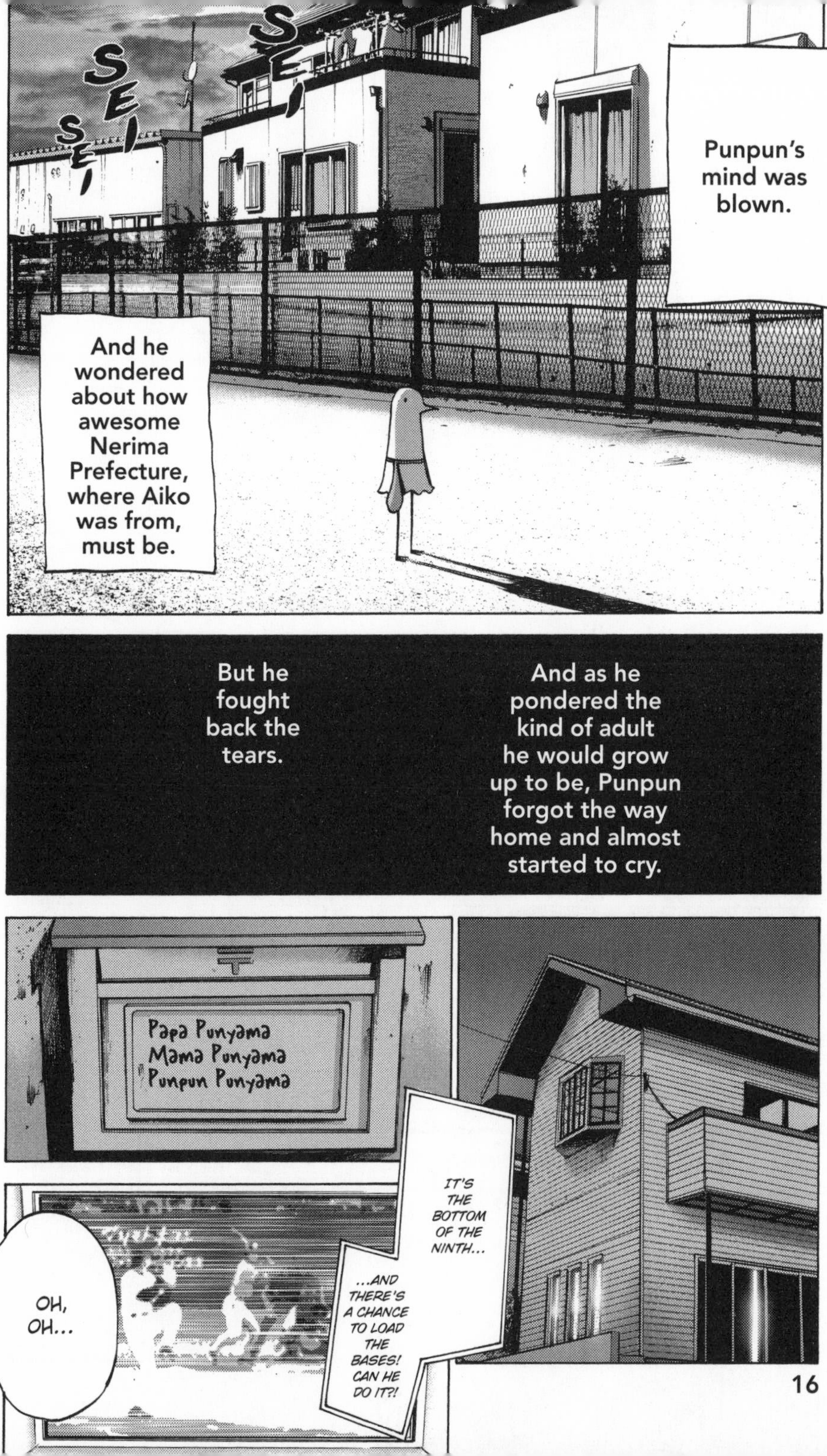
Punpun's mind was blown.
SEI SEI SEI SEI
And he wondered about how awesome Nerima Prefecture, where Aiko was from, must be.
And as he pondered the kind of adult he would grow up to be, Punpun forgot the way home and almost started to cry.
But he fought back the tears.
IT'S THE BOTTOM OF THE NINTH...
...AND THERE'S A CHANCE TO LOAD THE BASES! CAN HE DO IT?!
Papa Punyama
Mama Punyama
Punpun Punyama
OH, OH...

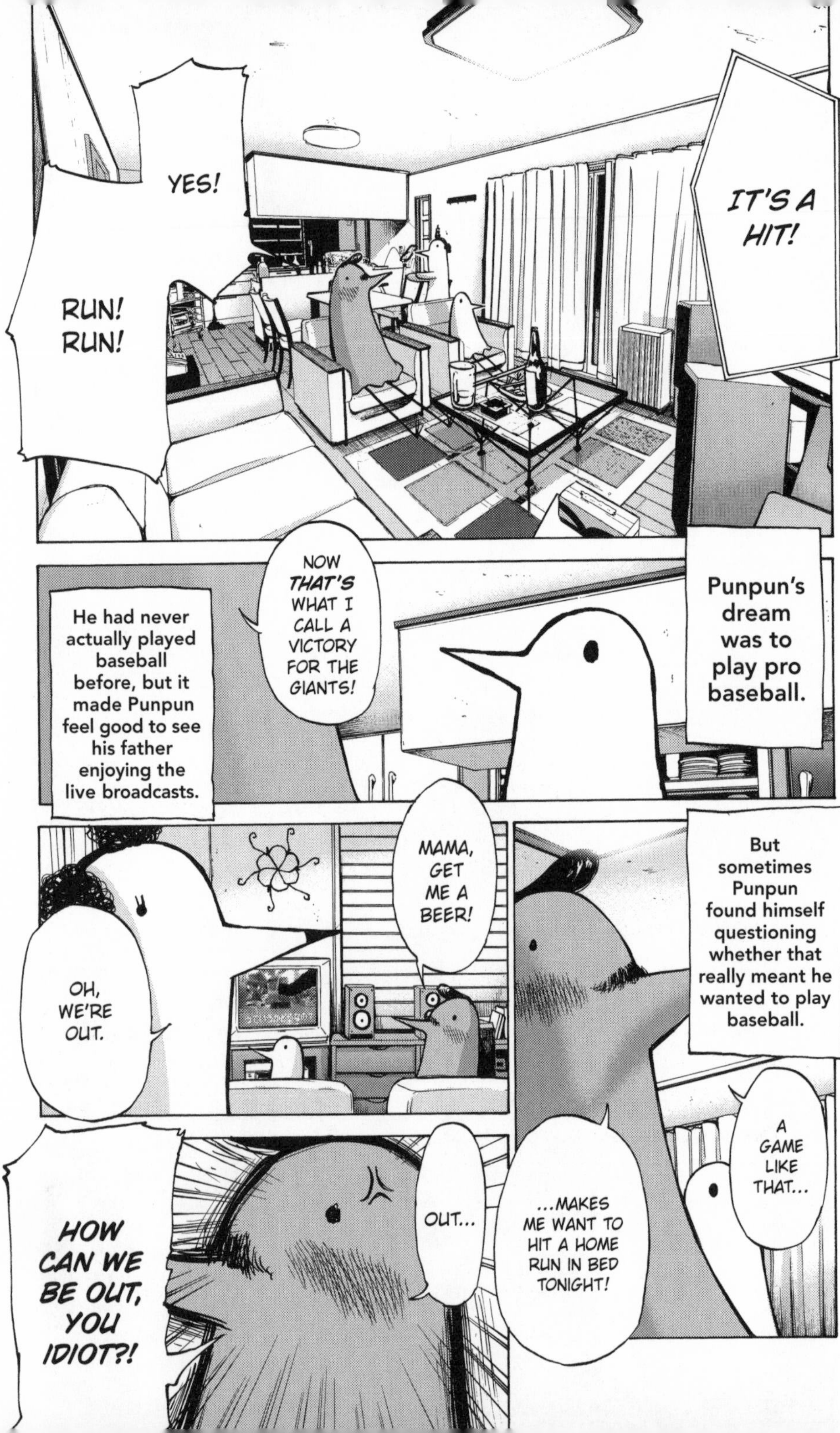
IT'S A HIT!
YES!
RUN! RUN!
Punpun's dream was to play pro baseball.
NOW THAT'S WHAT I CALL A VICTORY FOR THE GIANTS!
He had never actually played baseball before, but it made Punpun feel good to see his father enjoying the live broadcasts.
But sometimes Punpun found himself questioning whether that really meant he wanted to play baseball.
A GAME LIKE THAT...
...MAKES ME WANT TO HIT A HOME RUN IN BED TONIGHT!
MAMA, GET ME A BEER!
OH, WE'RE OUT.
OUT...
HOW CAN WE BE OUT, YOU IDIOT?!

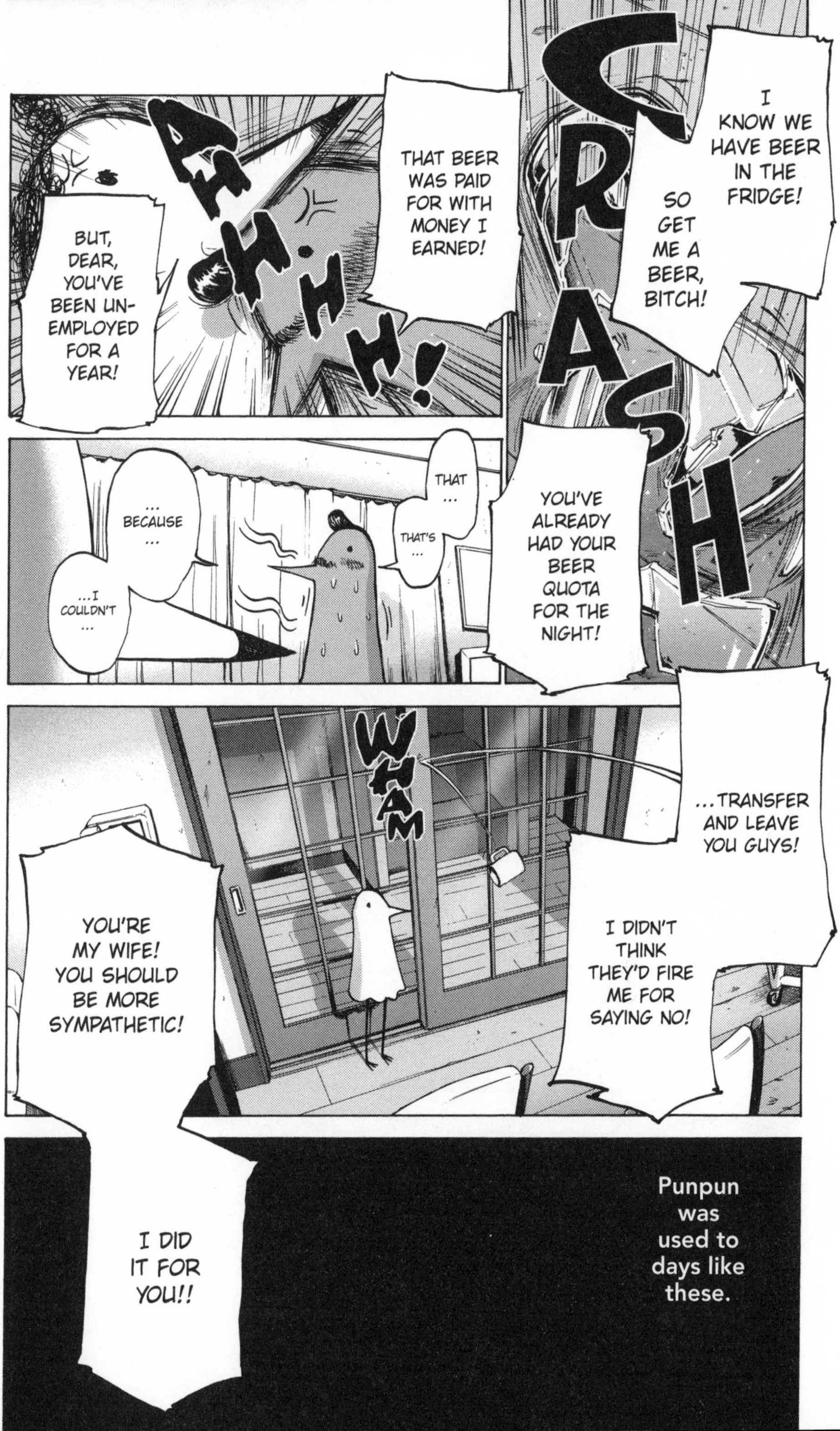
I KNOW WE HAVE BEER IN THE FRIDGE!
SO GET ME A BEER, BITCH!
CRASH
YOU'VE ALREADY HAD YOUR BEER QUOTA FOR THE NIGHT!
THAT BEER WAS PAID FOR WITH MONEY I EARNED!
AHHHHH!
BUT, DEAR, YOU'VE BEEN UN-EMPLOYED FOR A YEAR!
THAT ...
THAT'S ...
... BECAUSE ...
...I COULDN'T ...
...TRANSFER AND LEAVE YOU GUYS!
I DIDN'T THINK THEY'D FIRE ME FOR SAYING NO!
WHAM
YOU'RE MY WIFE! YOU SHOULD BE MORE SYMPATHETIC!
I DID IT FOR YOU!!
Punpun was used to days like these.

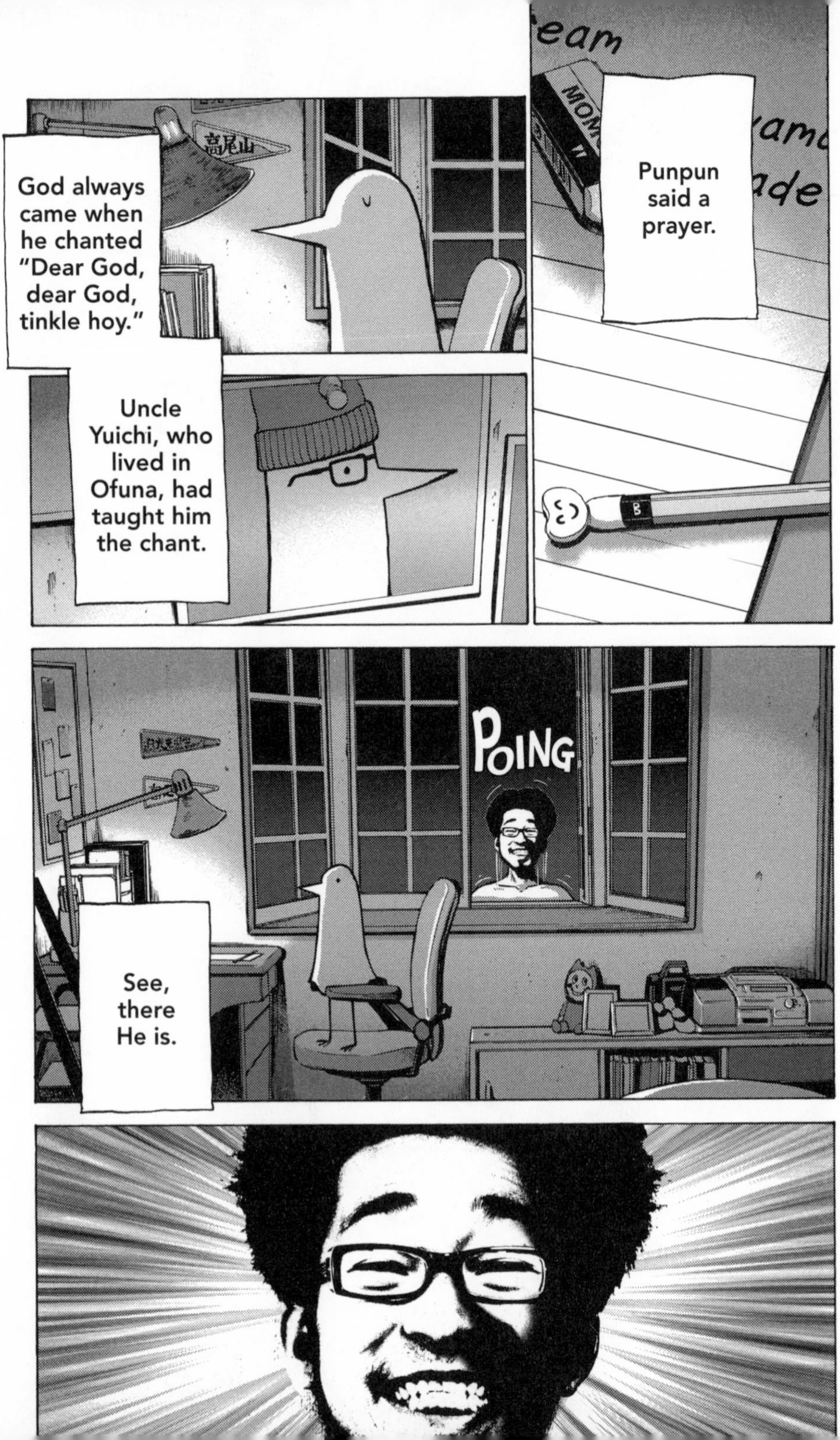
Punpun said a prayer.
God always came when he chanted "Dear God, dear God, tinkle hoy."
高尾山
Uncle Yuichi, who lived in Ofuna, had taught him the chant.
POING
See, there He is.

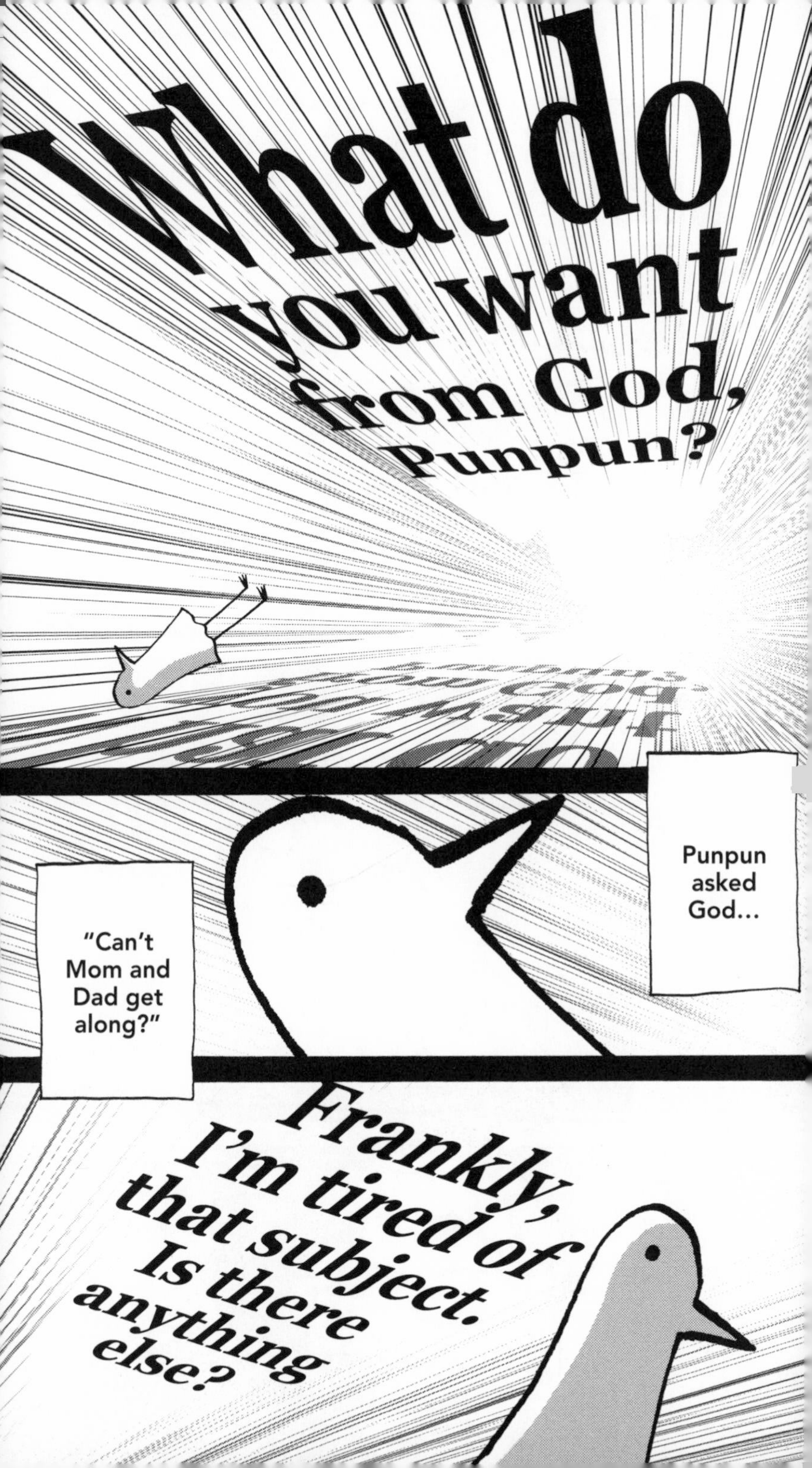
What do you want from God, Punpun?
Punpun asked God…
“Can’t Mom and Dad get along?”
Frankly, I’m tired of that subject. Is there anything else?

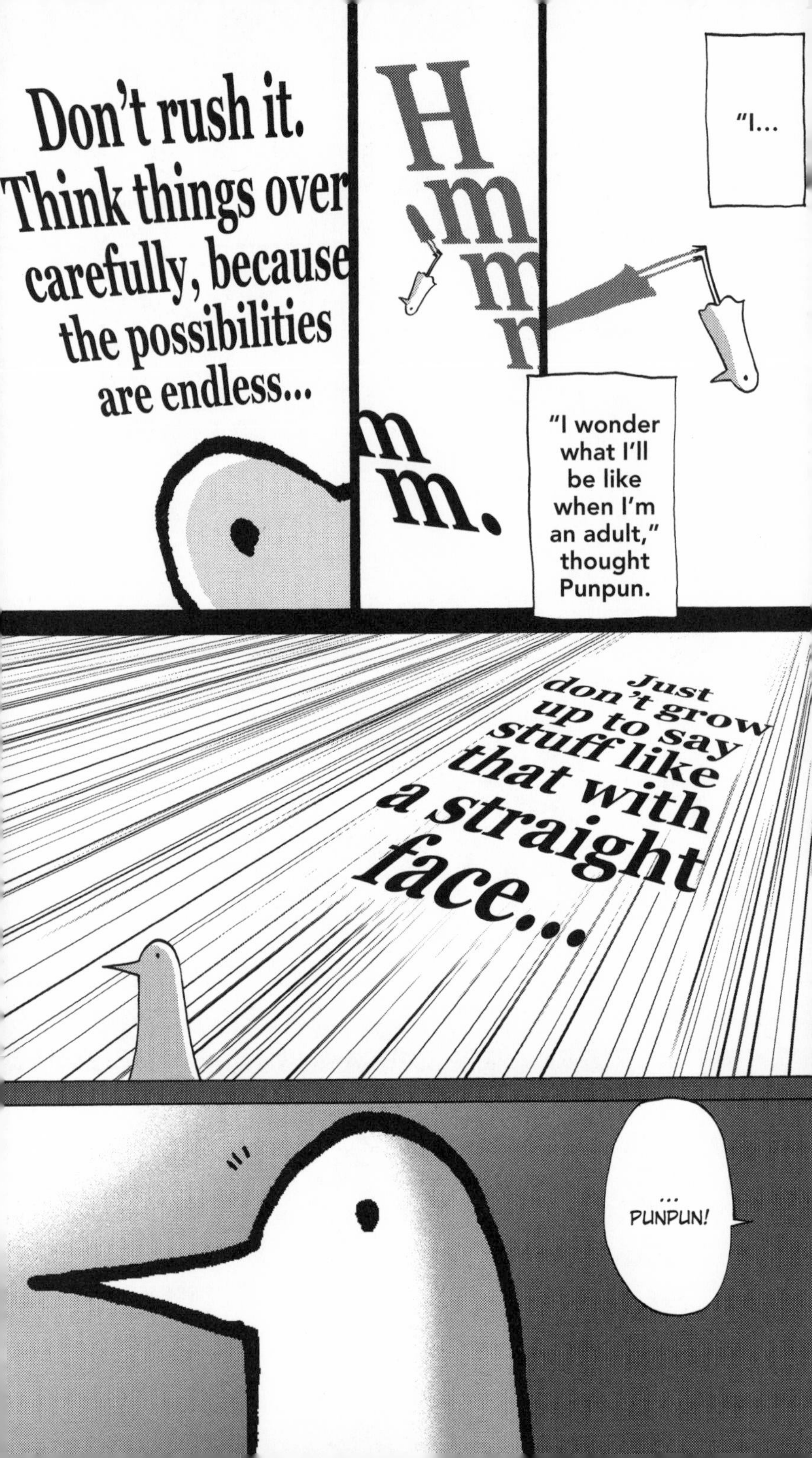
"I...
"I wonder what I'll be like when I'm an adult," thought Punpun.
Hmmmmm.
Don't rush it. Think things over carefully, because the possibilities are endless...
Just don't grow up to say stuff like that with a straight face...
... PUNPUN!

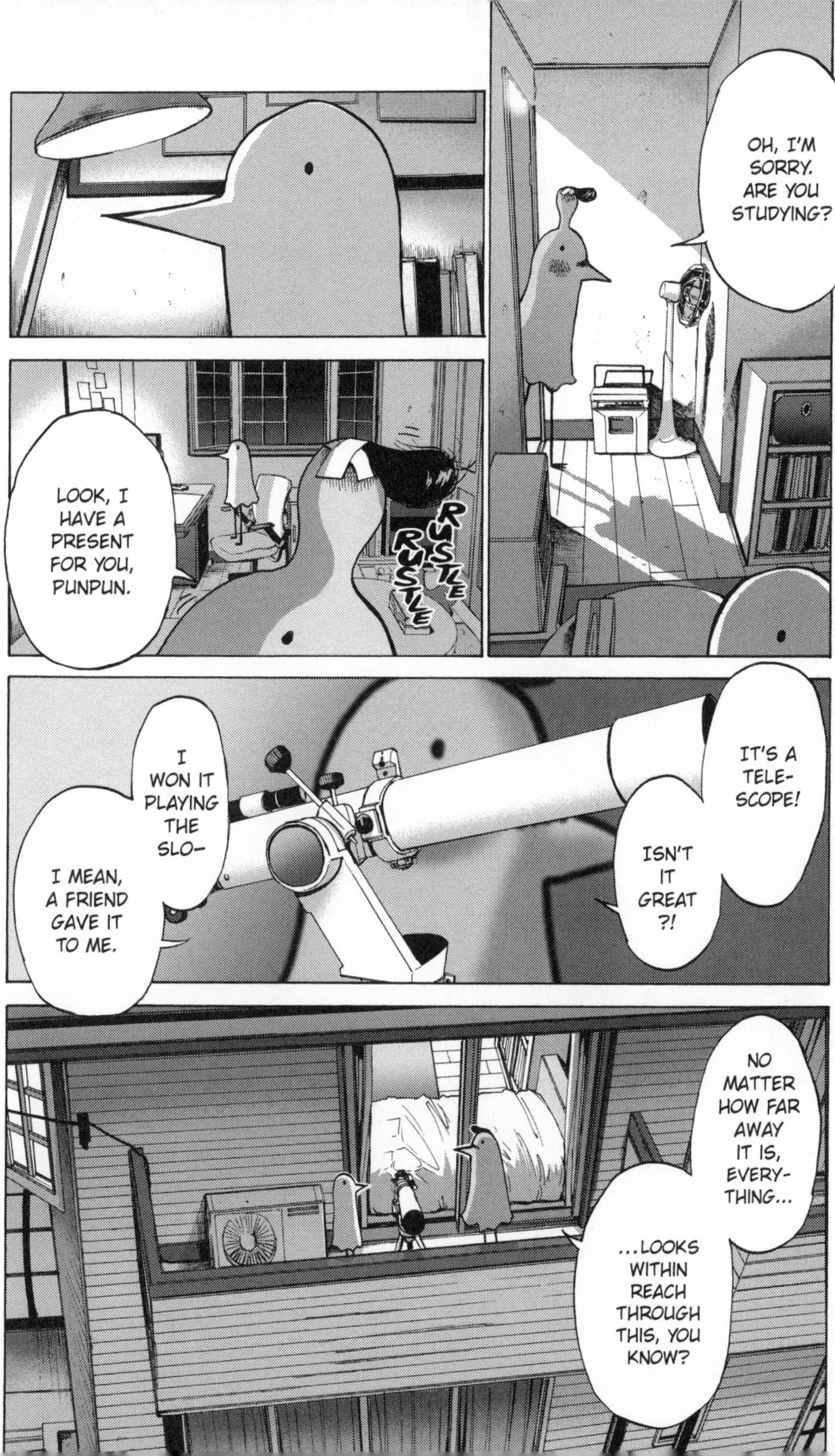
OH, I'M SORRY. ARE YOU STUDYING?
LOOK, I HAVE A PRESENT FOR YOU, PUNPUN.
RUSTLE RUSTLE
IT'S A TELE-SCOPE!
ISN'T IT GREAT ?!
I WON IT PLAYING THE SLO—
I MEAN, A FRIEND GAVE IT TO ME.
NO MATTER HOW FAR AWAY IT IS, EVERY-THING...
...LOOKS WITHIN REACH THROUGH THIS, YOU KNOW?

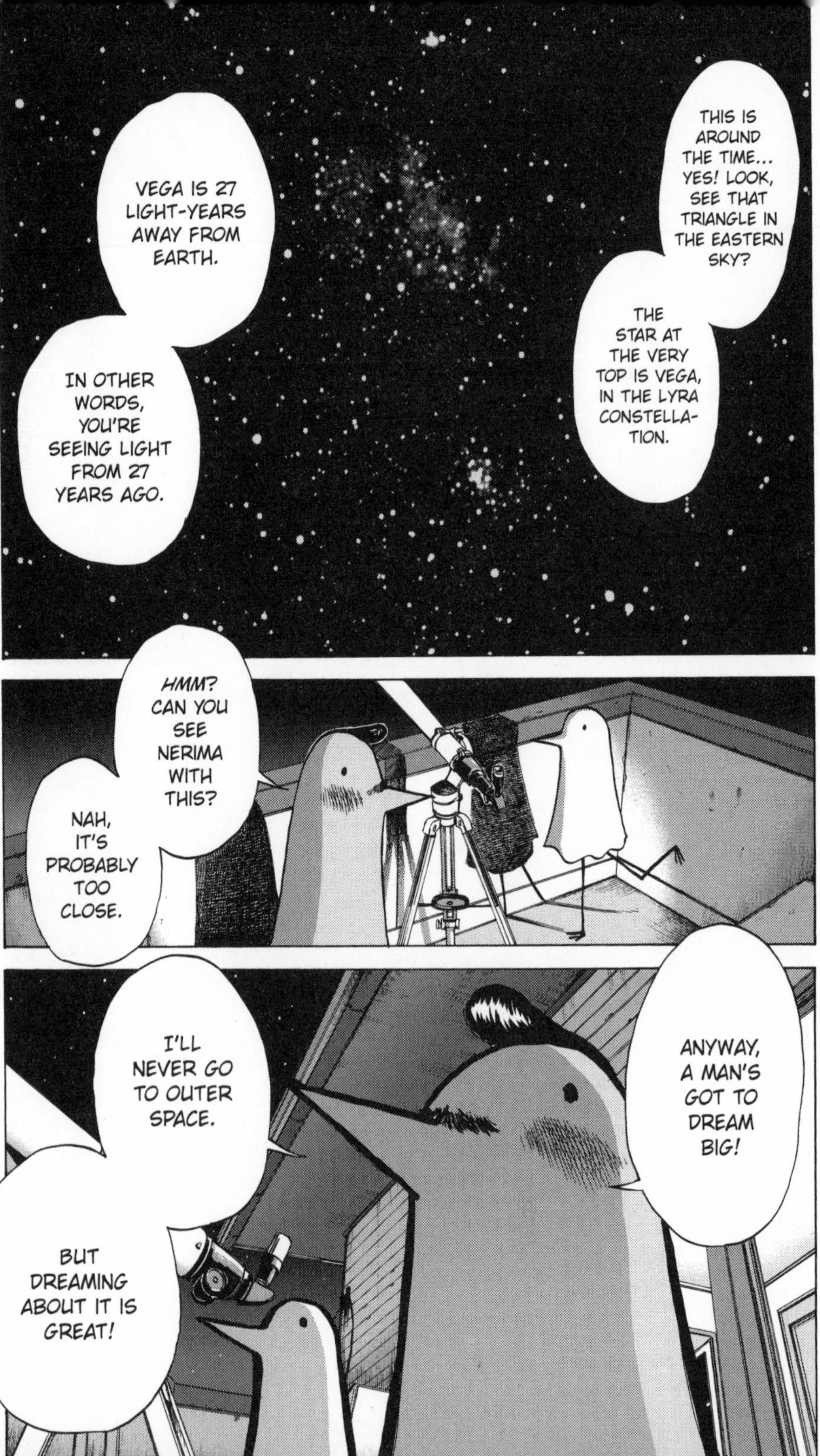
THIS IS AROUND THE TIME... YES! LOOK, SEE THAT TRIANGLE IN THE EASTERN SKY?
THE STAR AT THE VERY TOP IS VEGA, IN THE LYRA CONSTELLATION.
VEGA IS 27 LIGHT-YEARS AWAY FROM EARTH.
IN OTHER WORDS, YOU'RE SEEING LIGHT FROM 27 YEARS AGO.
HMM? CAN YOU SEE NERIMA WITH THIS?
NAH, IT'S PROBABLY TOO CLOSE.
ANYWAY, A MAN'S GOT TO DREAM BIG!
I'LL NEVER GO TO OUTER SPACE.
BUT DREAMING ABOUT IT IS GREAT!

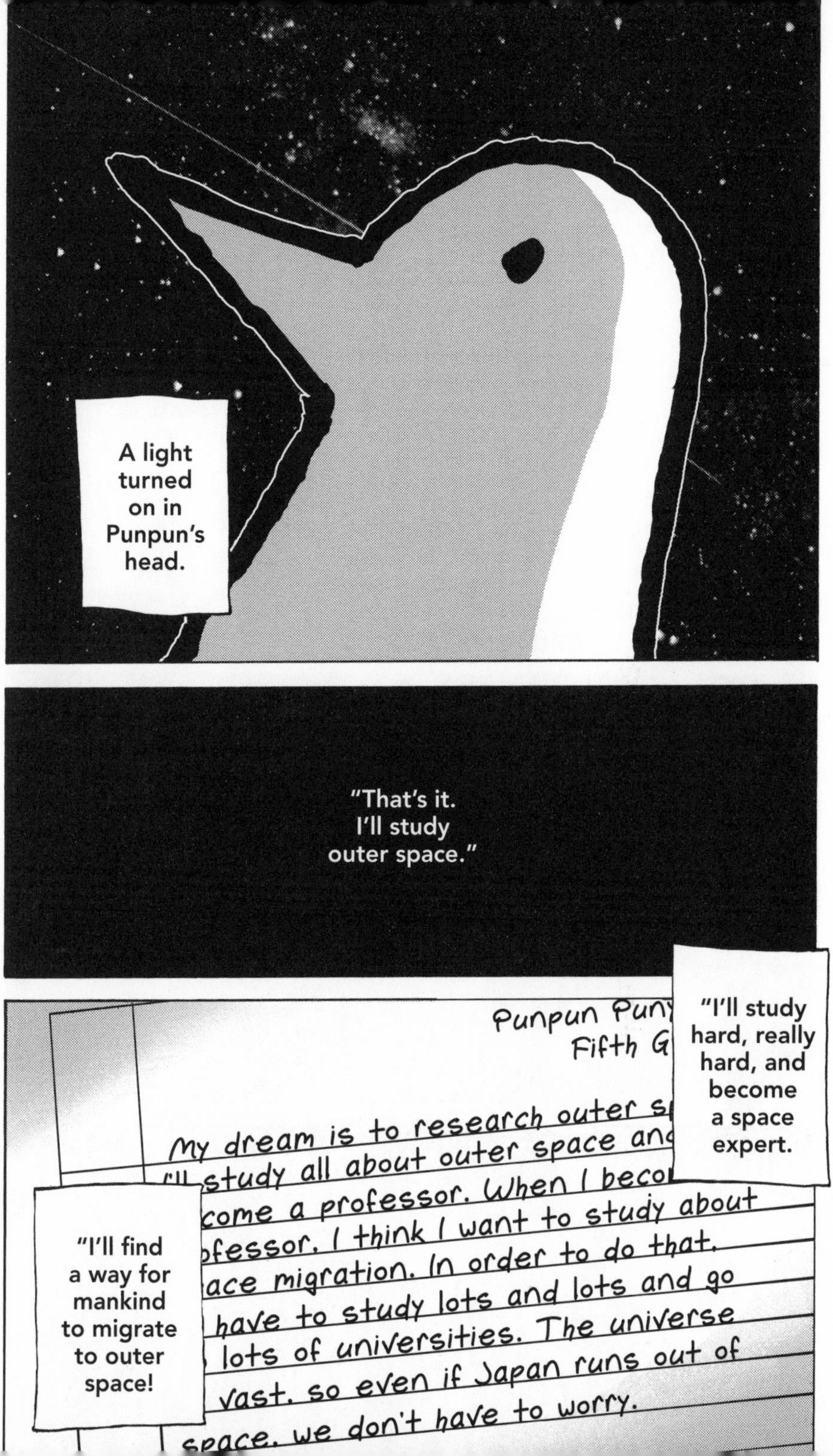
A light turned on in Punpun's head.
"That's it. I'll study outer space."
"I'll study hard, really hard, and become a space expert.
Punpun Pun
Fifth G
My dream is to research outer s
'll study all about outer space an
come a professor. When I beco
ofessor. I think I want to study about
ace migration. In order to do that,
have to study lots and lots and go
lots of universities. The universe
vast, so even if Japan runs out of
space, we don't have to worry.
"I'll find a way for mankind to migrate to outer space!

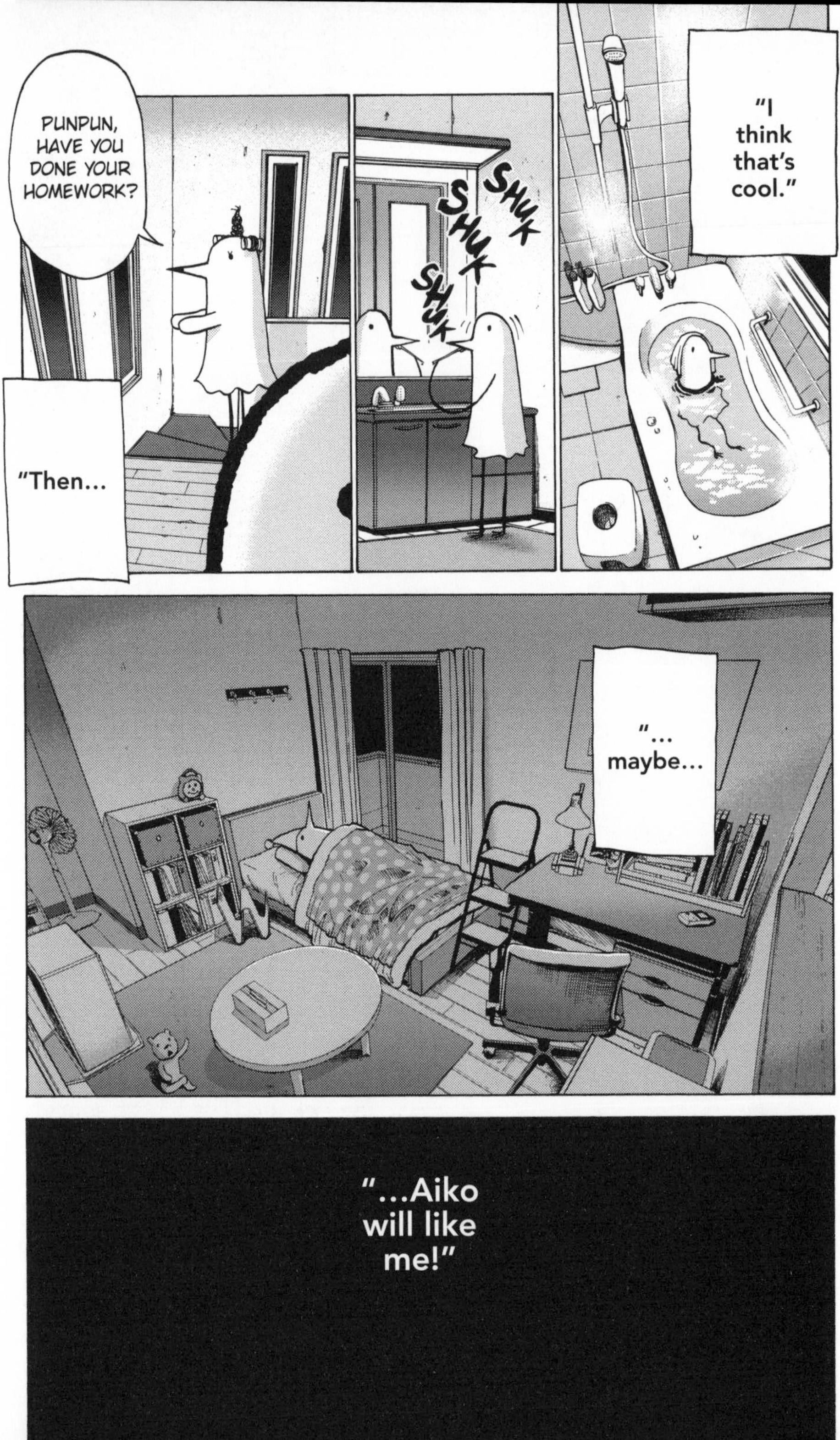
"I think that's cool."
SHUK SHUK SHUK
PUNPUN, HAVE YOU DONE YOUR HOMEWORK?
"Then...
"... maybe...
"...Aiko will like me!"

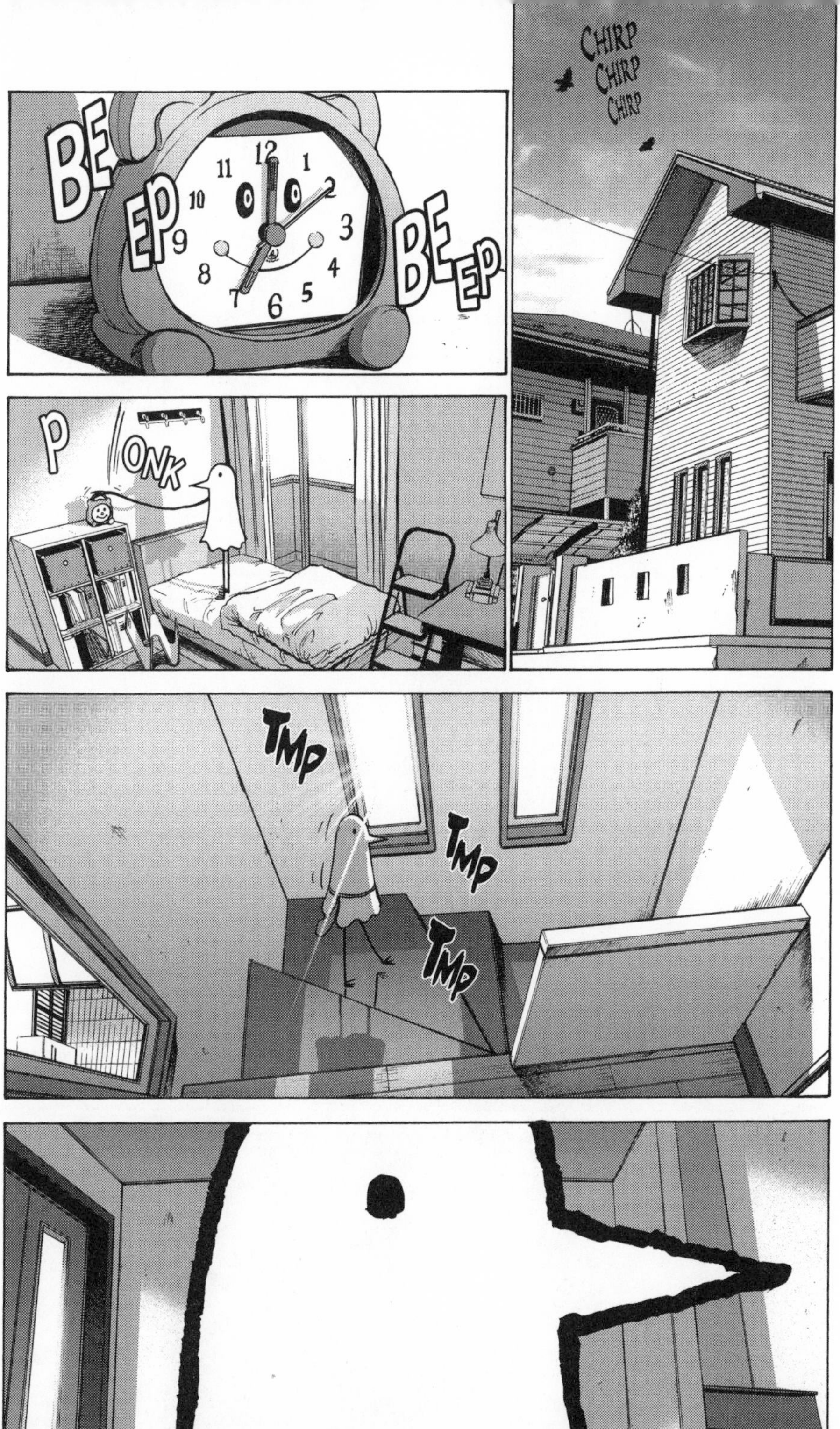
CHIRP
CHIRP
CHIRP
BEEP
BEEP
PONK
TMP
TMP
TMP

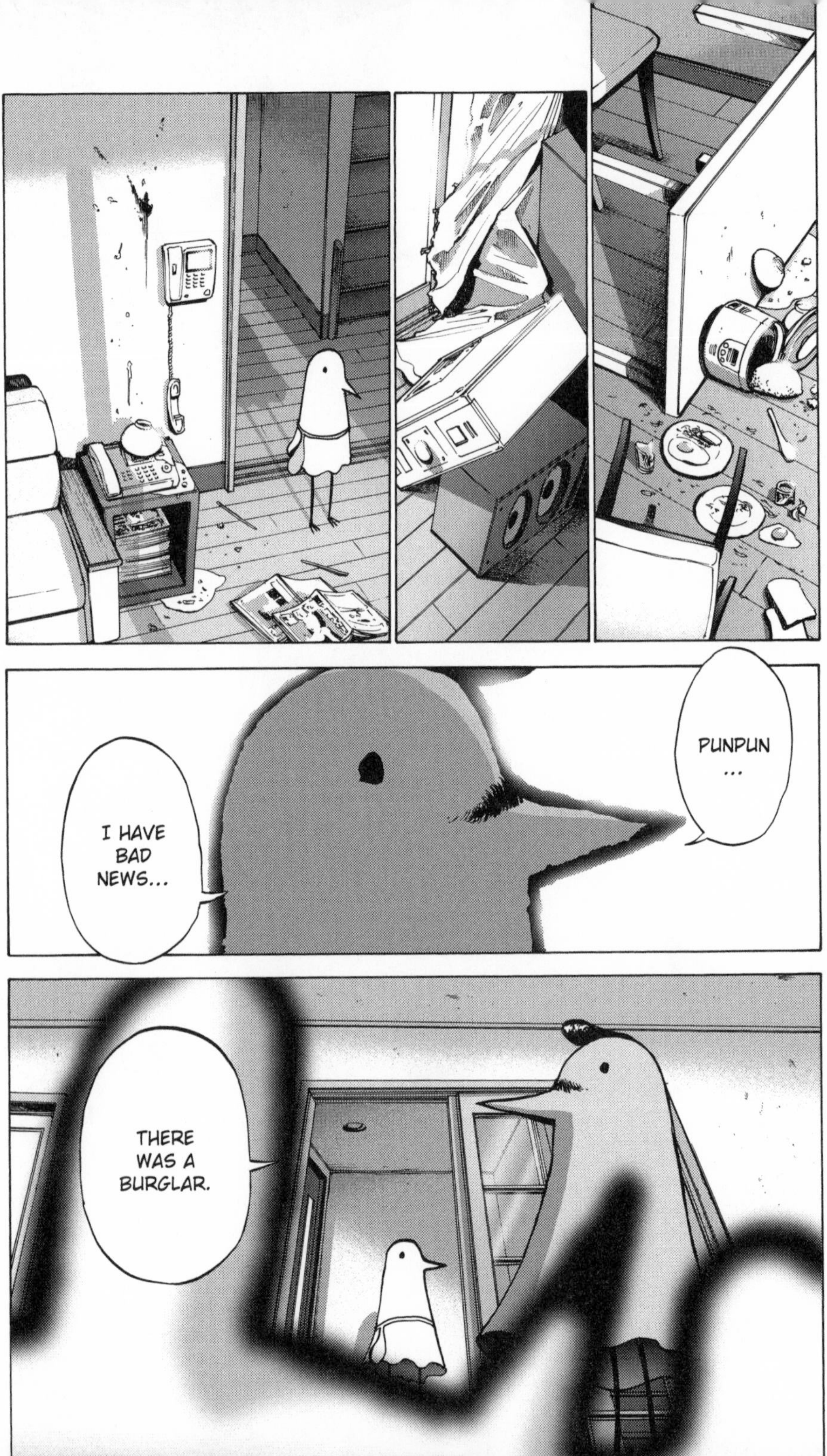
PUNPUN ...
I HAVE BAD NEWS...
THERE WAS A BURGLAR.

PUNPUN
...

IT'S
TRUE.

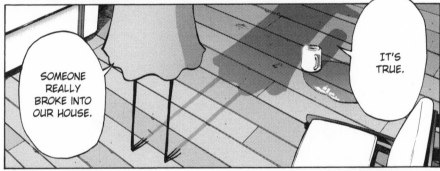

SOMEONE
REALLY
BROKE INTO
OUR HOUSE.

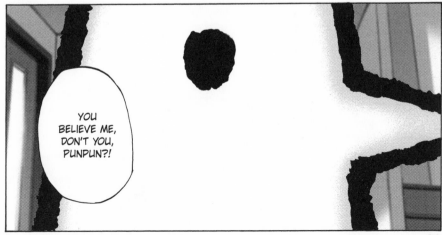

YOU
BELIEVE ME,
DON'T YOU,
PUNPUN?!

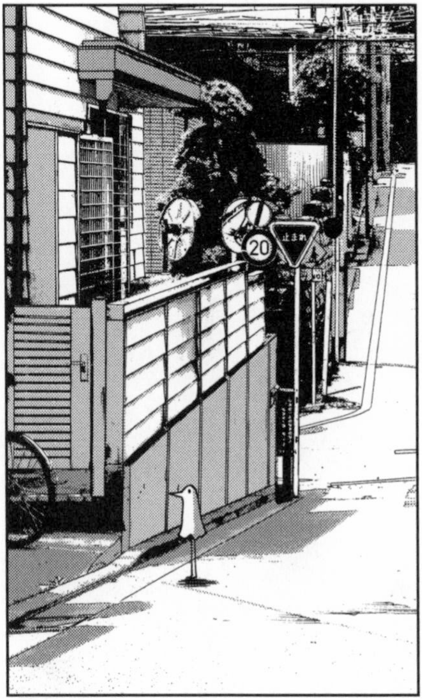
止まれ
20

Chapter 2

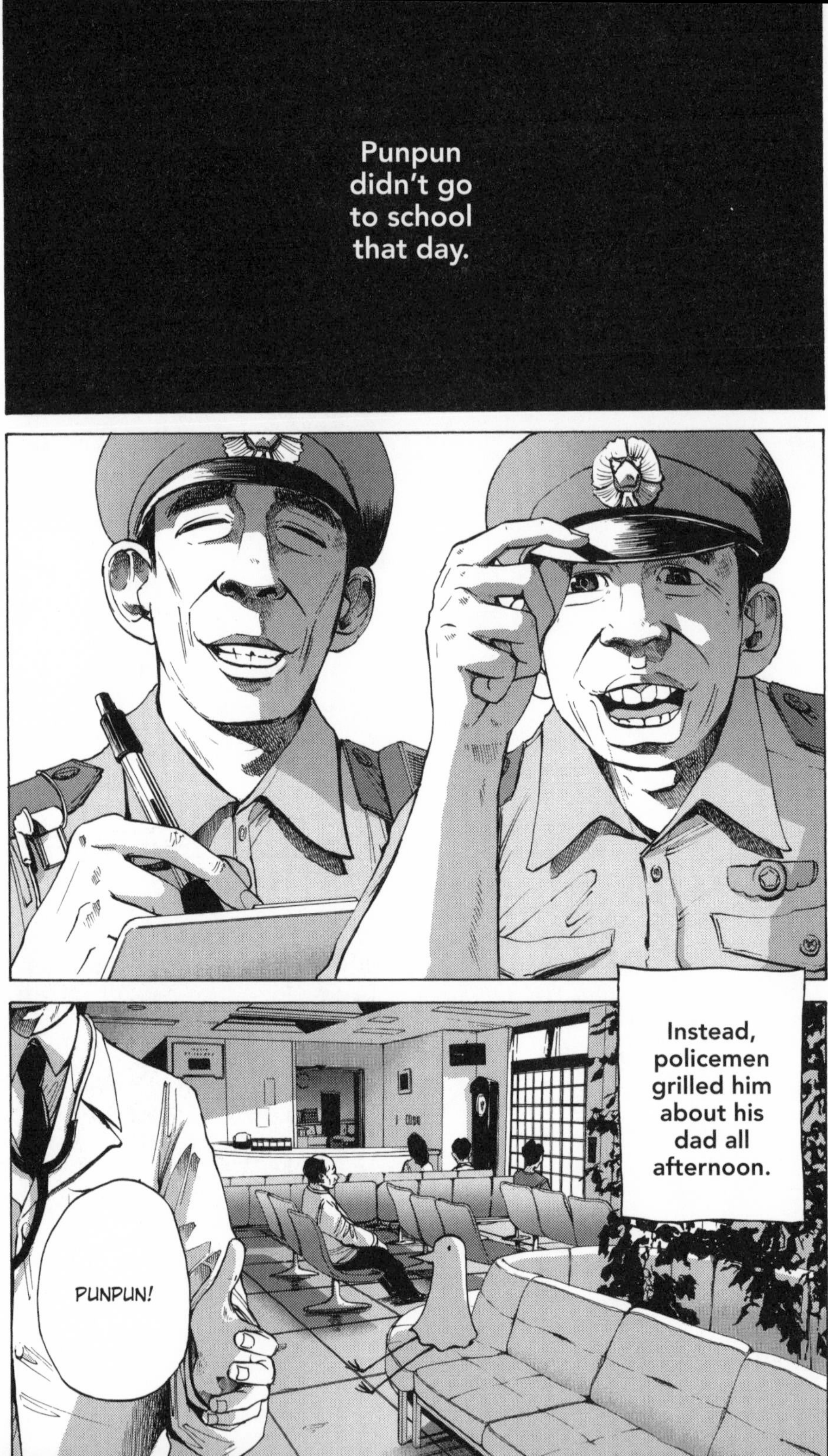
Punpun didn't go to school that day.
Instead, policemen grilled him about his dad all afternoon.
PUNPUN!

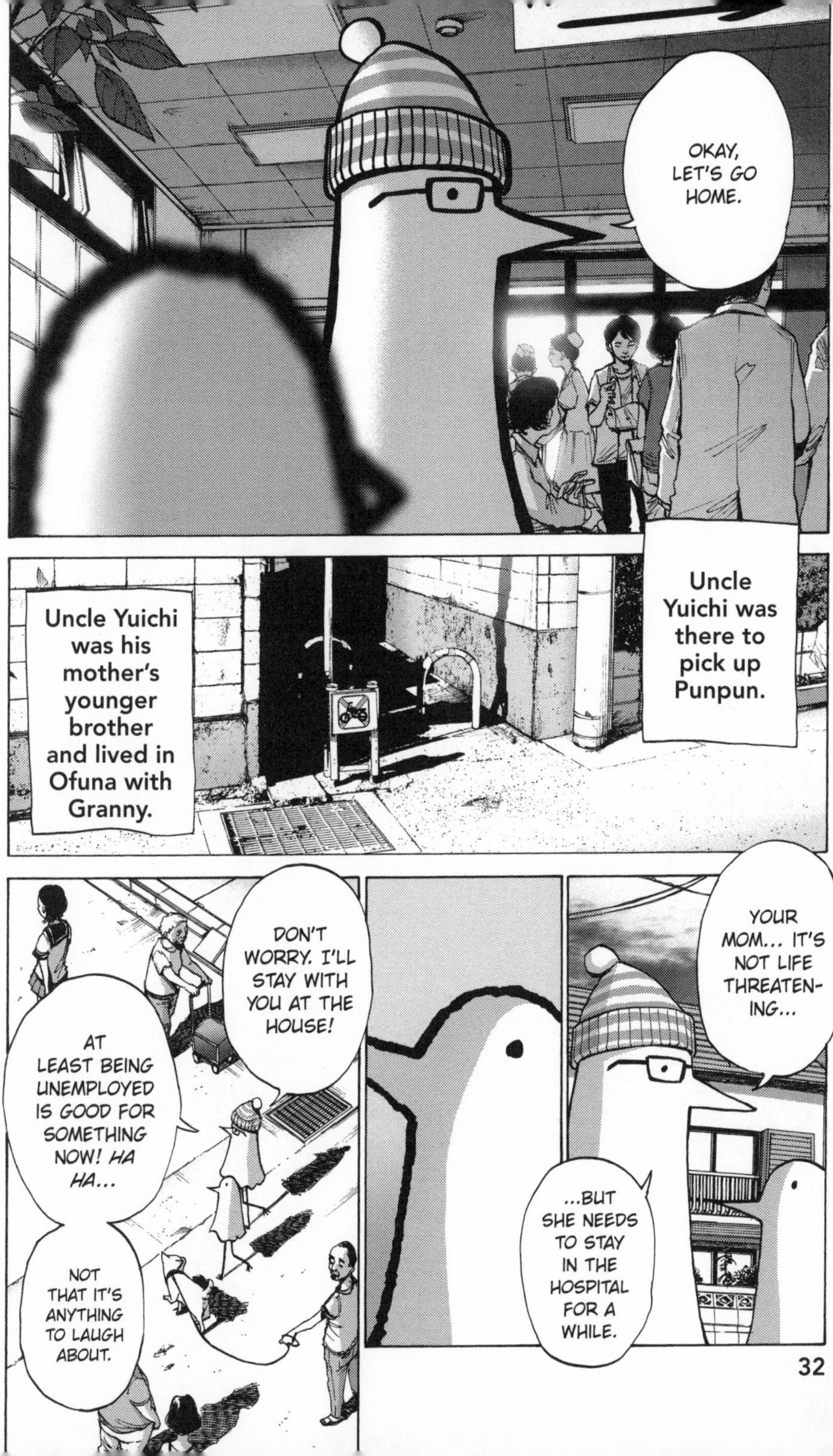
OKAY, LET'S GO HOME.
Uncle Yuichi was there to pick up Punpun.
Uncle Yuichi was his mother's younger brother and lived in Ofuna with Granny.
YOUR MOM... IT'S NOT LIFE THREATEN-ING...
...BUT SHE NEEDS TO STAY IN THE HOSPITAL FOR A WHILE.
DON'T WORRY. I'LL STAY WITH YOU AT THE HOUSE!
AT LEAST BEING UNEMPLOYED IS GOOD FOR SOMETHING NOW! *HA HA...*
NOT THAT IT'S ANYTHING TO LAUGH ABOUT.

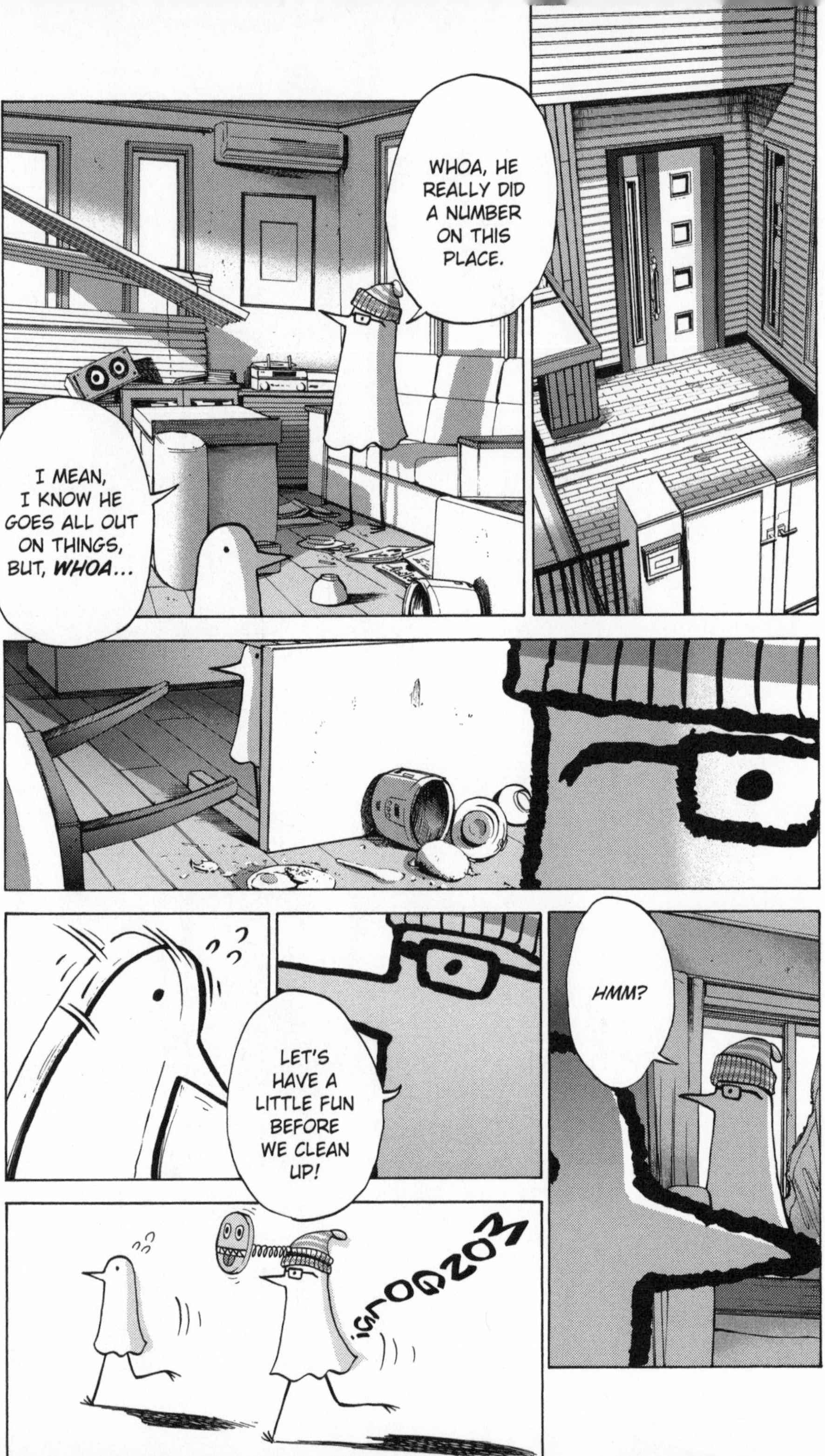
WHOA, HE REALLY DID A NUMBER ON THIS PLACE.
I MEAN, I KNOW HE GOES ALL OUT ON THINGS, BUT, ***WHOA***...
HMM?
LET'S HAVE A LITTLE FUN BEFORE WE CLEAN UP!

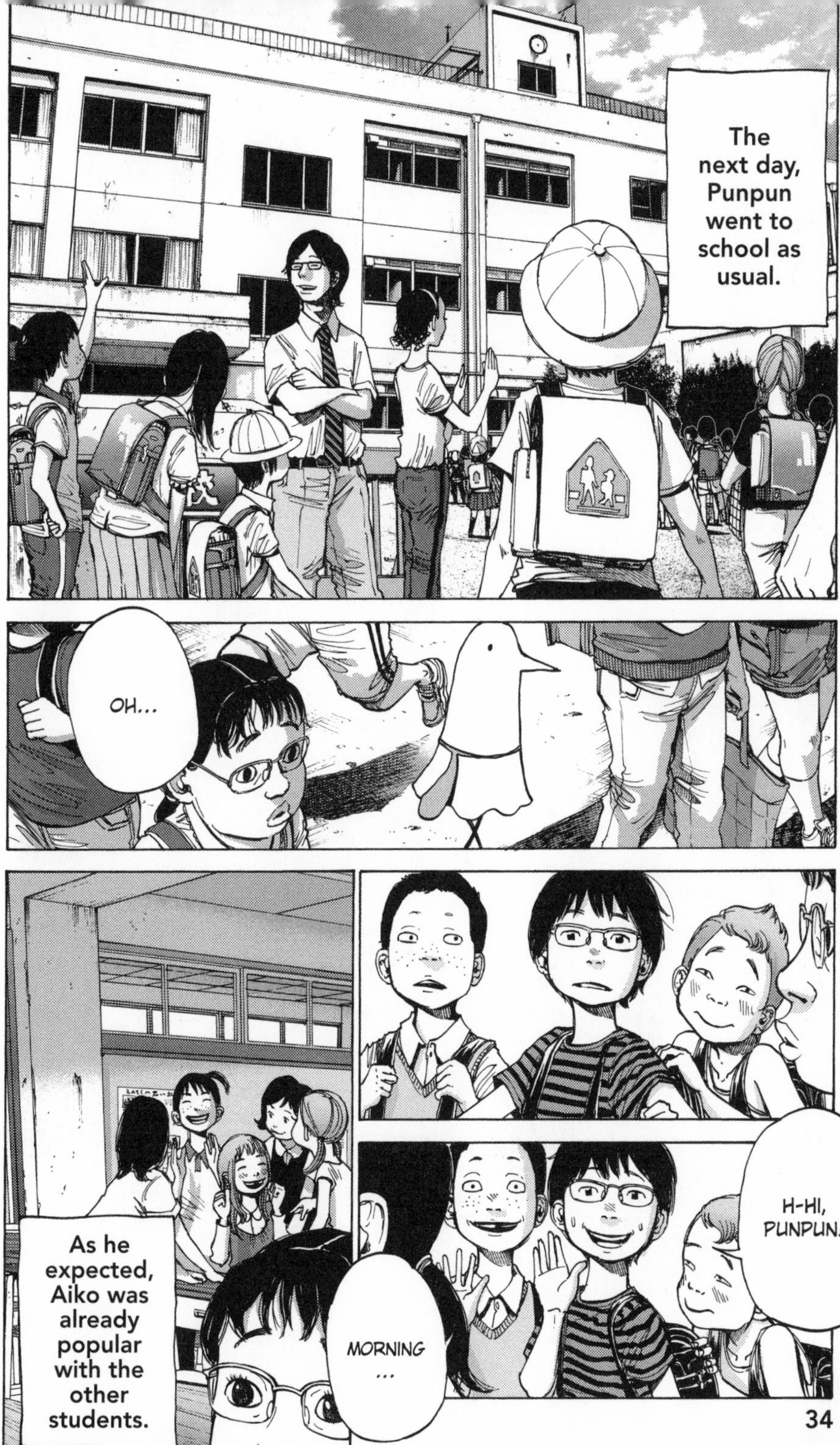

The next day, Punpun went to school as usual.
OH...
H-HI, PUNPUN!
MORNING ...
As he expected, Aiko was already popular with the other students.

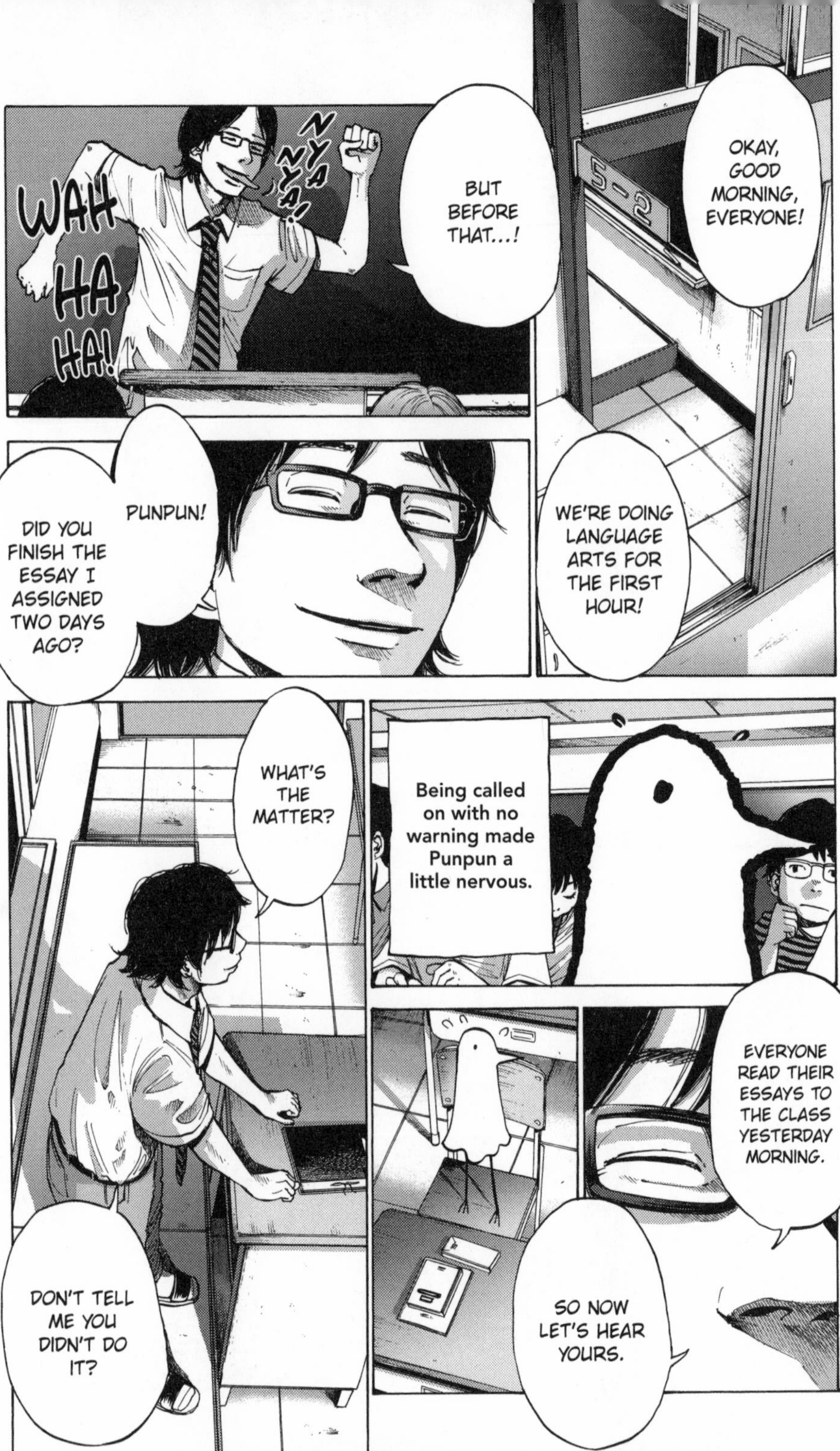
OKAY, GOOD MORNING, EVERYONE!
BUT BEFORE THAT...!
NYA NYA NYA!
WAH HA HA HA!
WE'RE DOING LANGUAGE ARTS FOR THE FIRST HOUR!
PUNPUN!
DID YOU FINISH THE ESSAY I ASSIGNED TWO DAYS AGO?
Being called on with no warning made Punpun a little nervous.
EVERYONE READ THEIR ESSAYS TO THE CLASS YESTERDAY MORNING.
SO NOW LET'S HEAR YOURS.
WHAT'S THE MATTER?
DON'T TELL ME YOU DIDN'T DO IT?

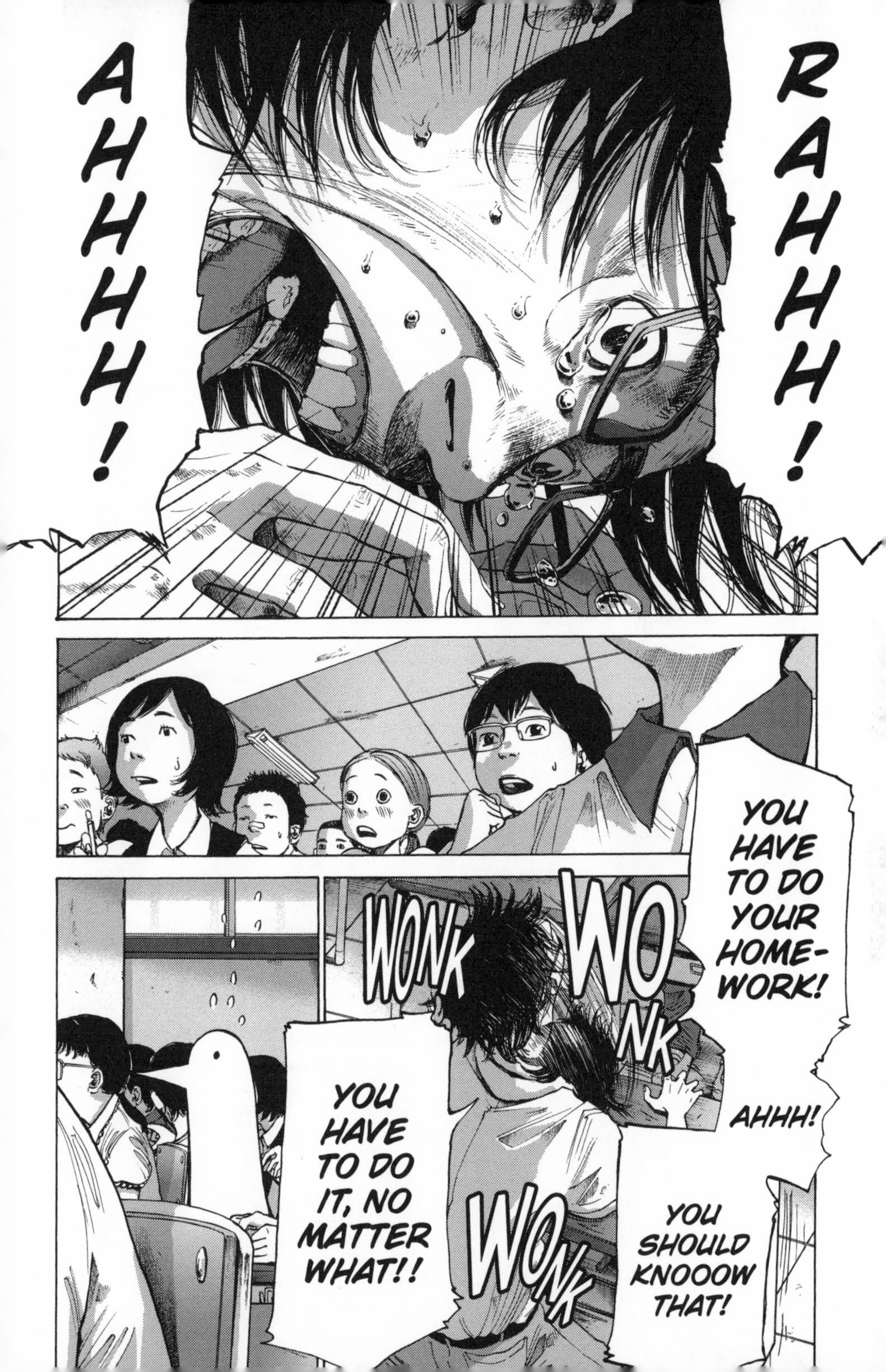

RAHHHH!
AHHHH!
YOU HAVE TO DO YOUR HOME-WORK!
WONK
WONK
AHHH!
YOU SHOULD KNOOOW THAT!
YOU HAVE TO DO IT, NO MATTER WHAT!!
WONK

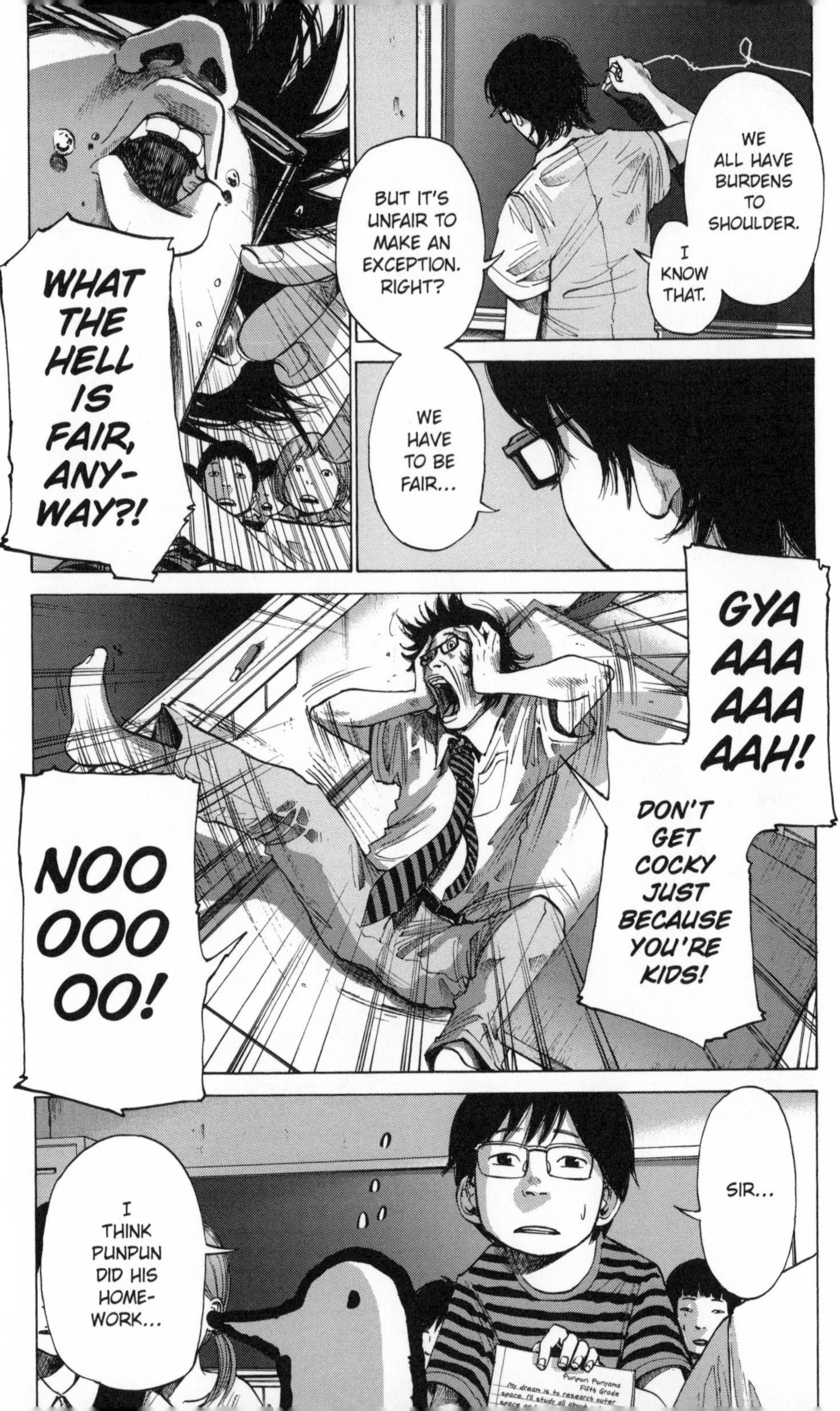
WE ALL HAVE BURDENS TO SHOULDER.
I KNOW THAT.
BUT IT'S UNFAIR TO MAKE AN EXCEPTION. RIGHT?
WE HAVE TO BE FAIR...
WHAT THE HELL IS FAIR, ANY-WAY?!
GYA AAA AAA AAH!
DON'T GET COCKY JUST BECAUSE YOU'RE KIDS!
NOO OOO OO!
SIR...
I THINK PUNPUN DID HIS HOME-WORK...
Punpun Punyama
Fifth Grade
My dream is to research outer
space. I'll study all about

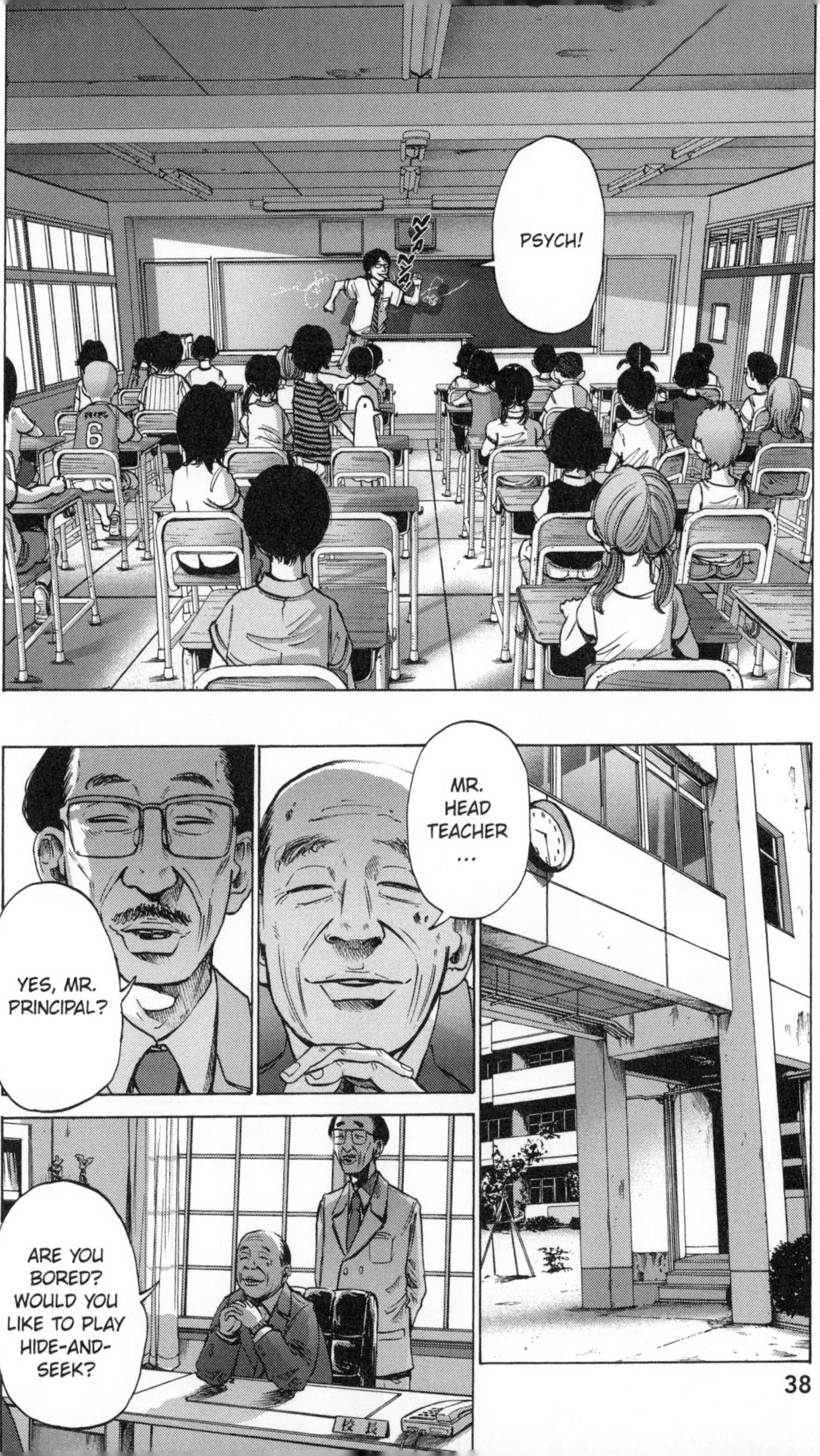
NYANYA!
PSYCH!
MR. HEAD TEACHER ...
YES, MR. PRINCIPAL?
ARE YOU BORED? WOULD YOU LIKE TO PLAY HIDE-AND-SEEK?

E
E
E
E

E
!

YES, I
WOULD.

OKAY,
THEN.
ROCK,
PAPER...

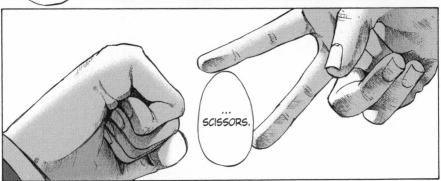

...
SCISSORS.

E
E
!

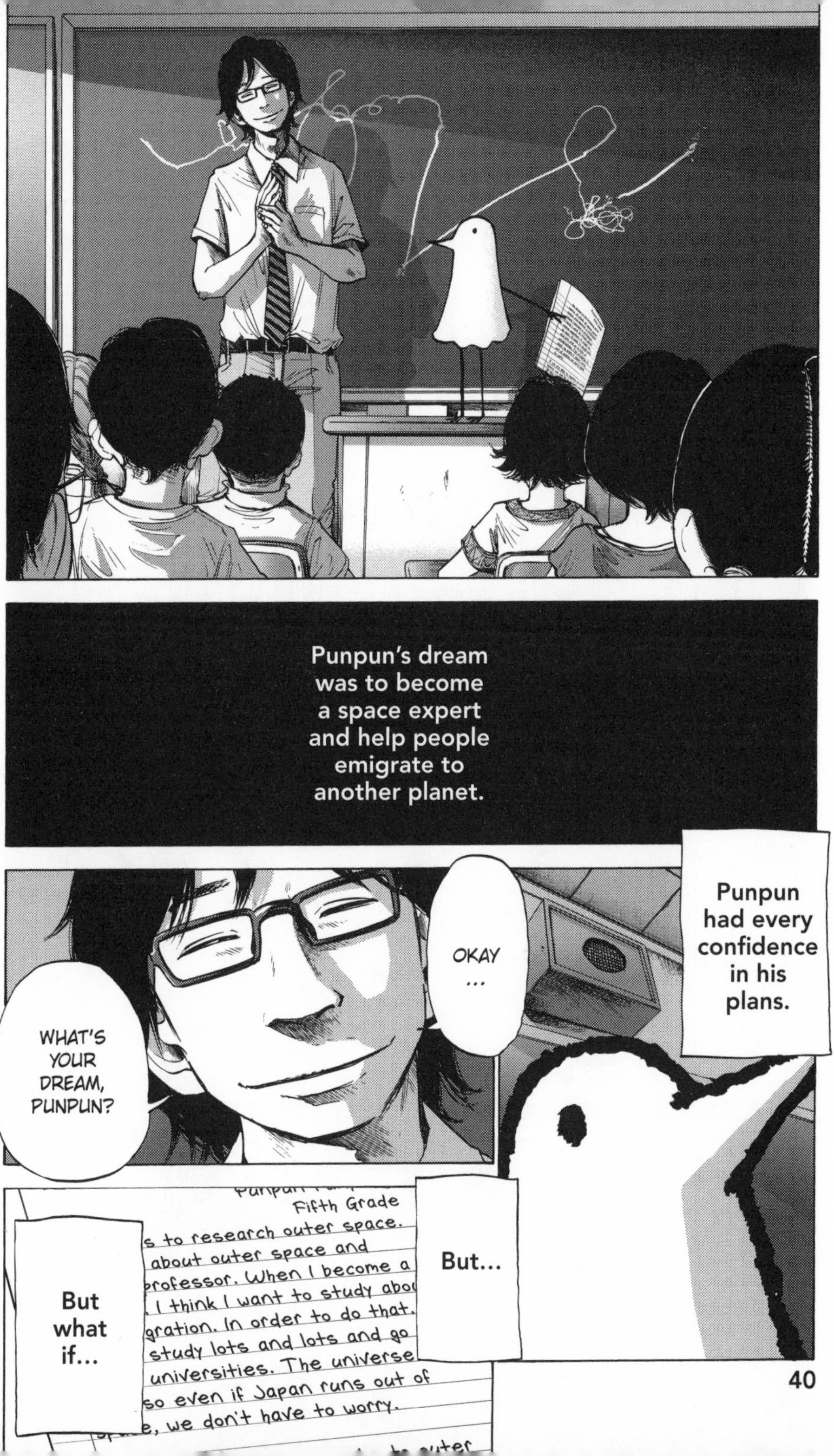

Punpun's dream was to become a space expert and help people emigrate to another planet.
Punpun had every confidence in his plans.
OKAY ...
WHAT'S YOUR DREAM, PUNPUN?
But...
Fifth Grade
s to research outer space.
about outer space and
professor. When I become a
I think I want to study abo
gration. In order to do that,
study lots and lots and go
universities. The universe
so even if Japan runs out of
e, we don't have to worry.
But what if...

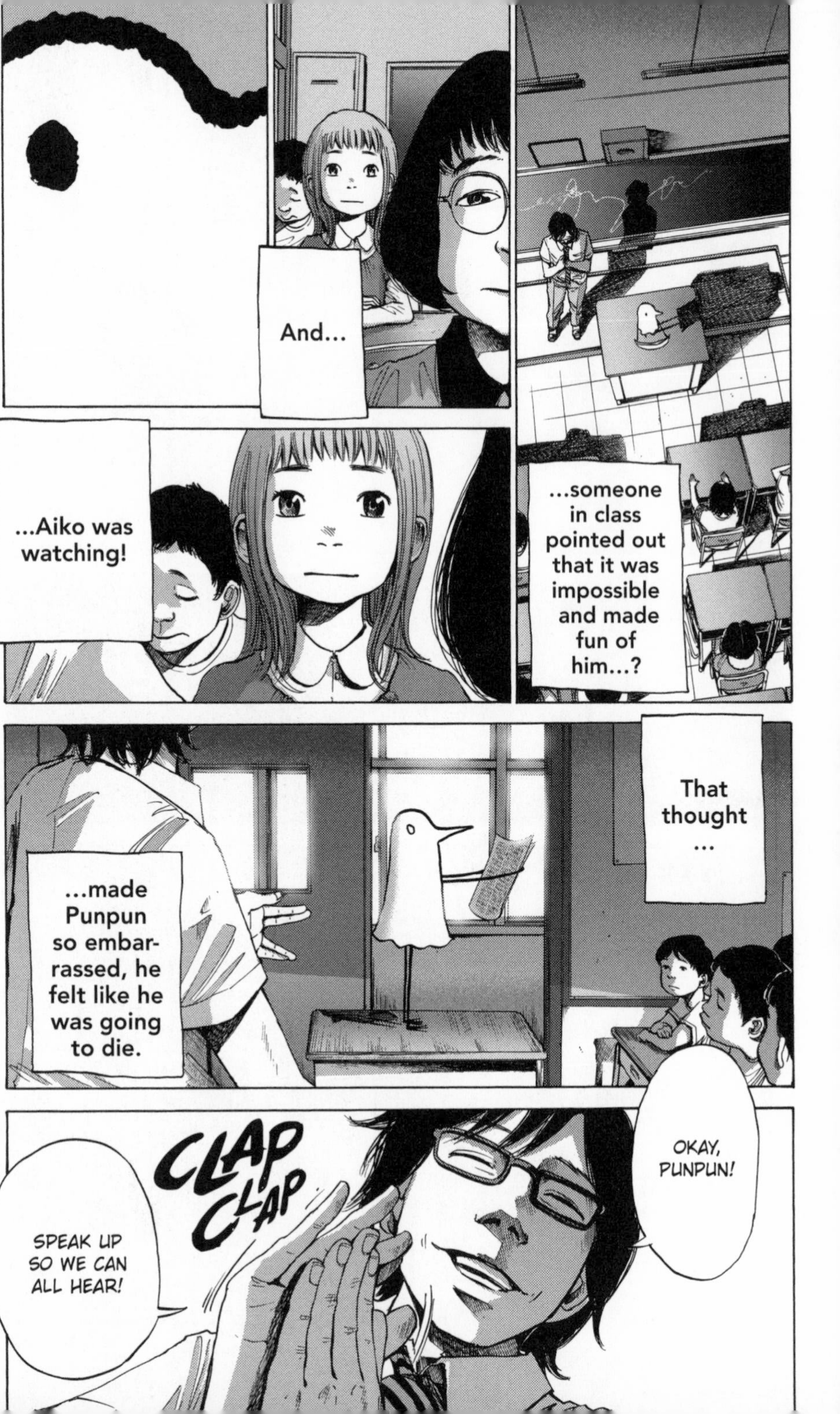
And...
...someone in class pointed out that it was impossible and made fun of him...?
...Aiko was watching!
That thought ...
...made Punpun so embar-rassed, he felt like he was going to die.
OKAY, PUNPUN!
CLAP CLAP
SPEAK UP SO WE CAN ALL HEAR!

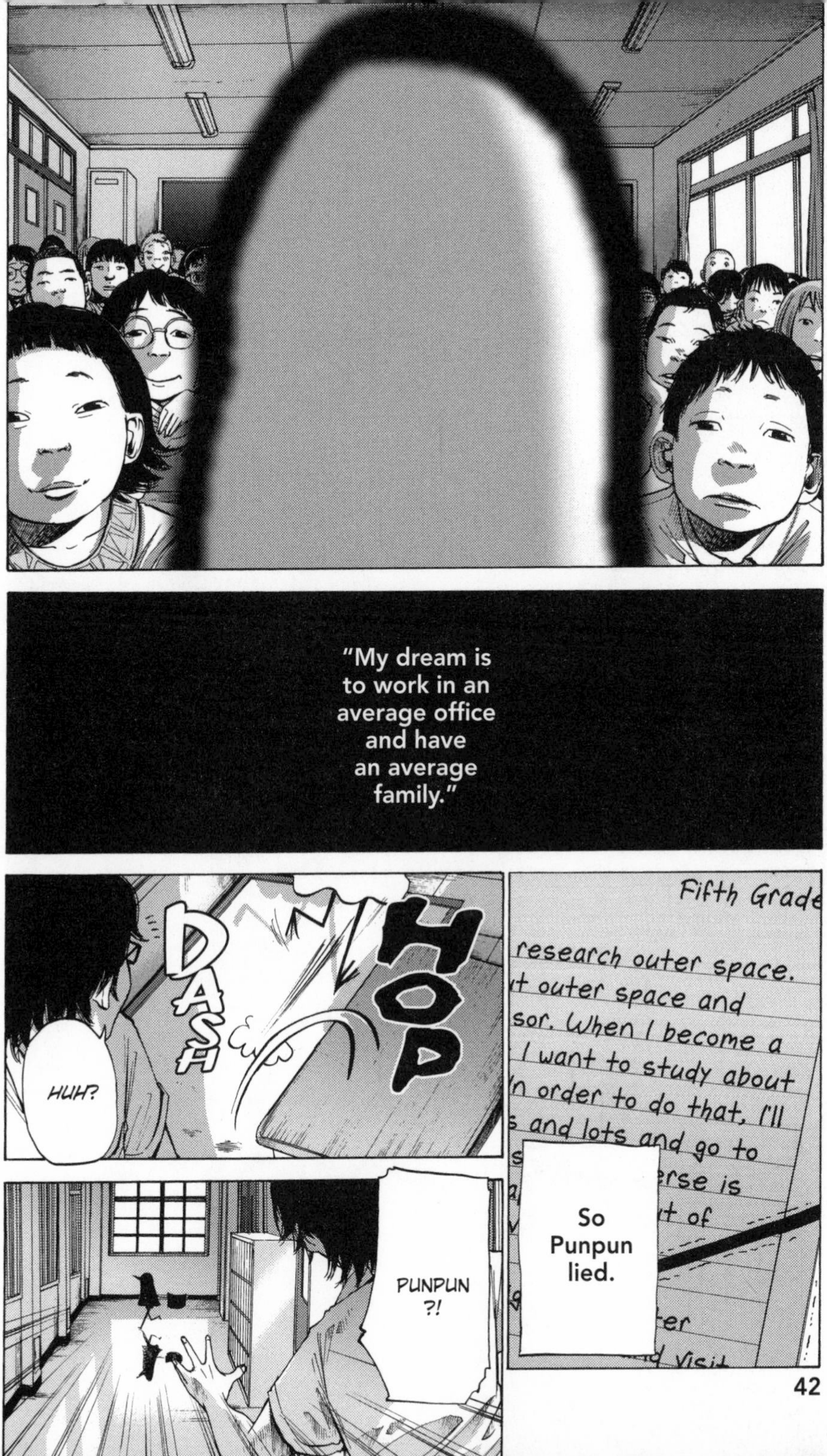

"My dream is to work in an average office and have an average family."
Fifth Grade
research outer space.
ut outer space and
sor. When I become a
I want to study about
In order to do that, I'll
s and lots and go to
erse is
ut of
ter
d visit
So Punpun lied.
HOP
DASH
HUH?
PUNPUN ?!

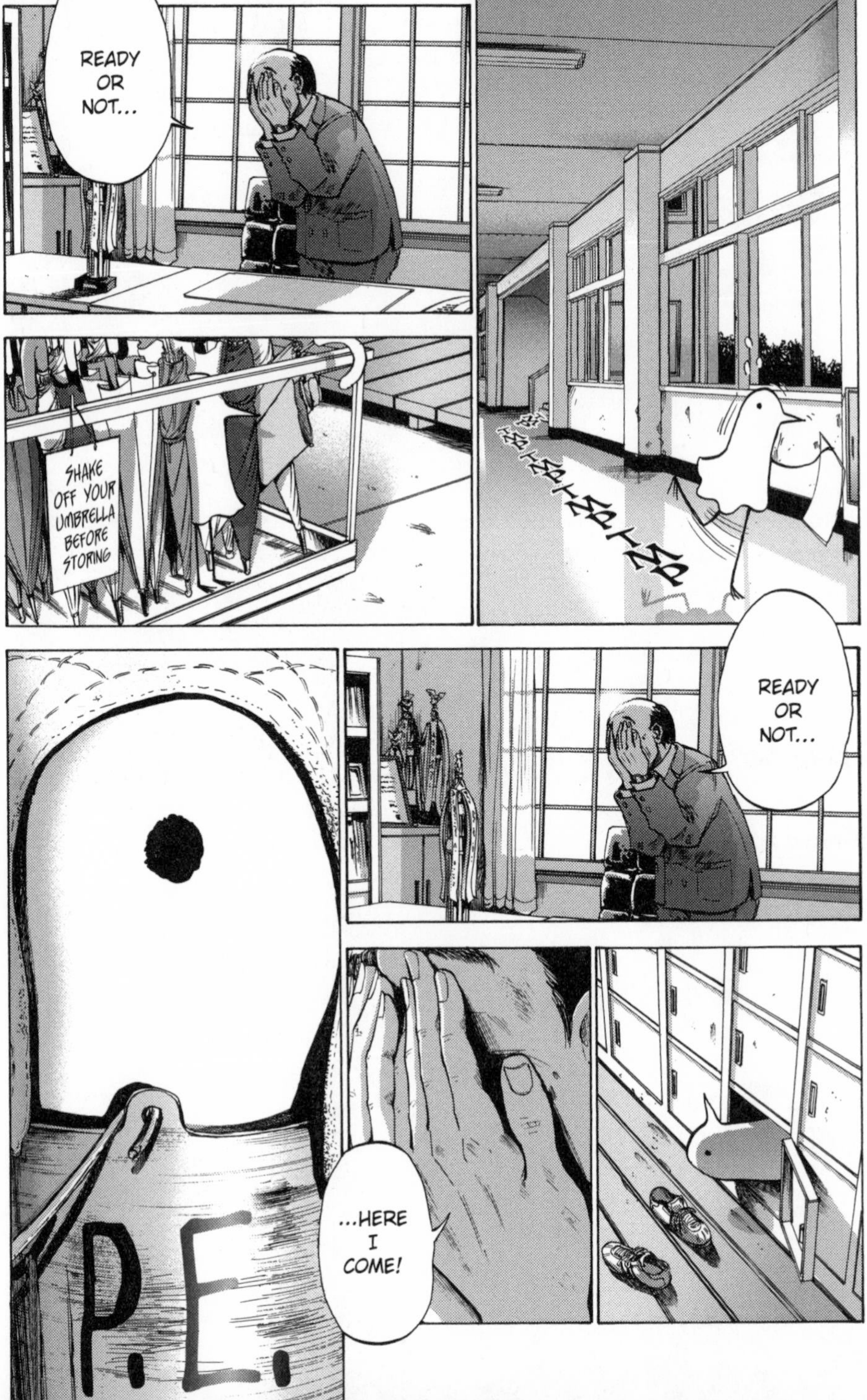
READY OR NOT...
SHAKE OFF YOUR UMBRELLA BEFORE STORING
READY OR NOT...
...HERE I COME!
P.E.

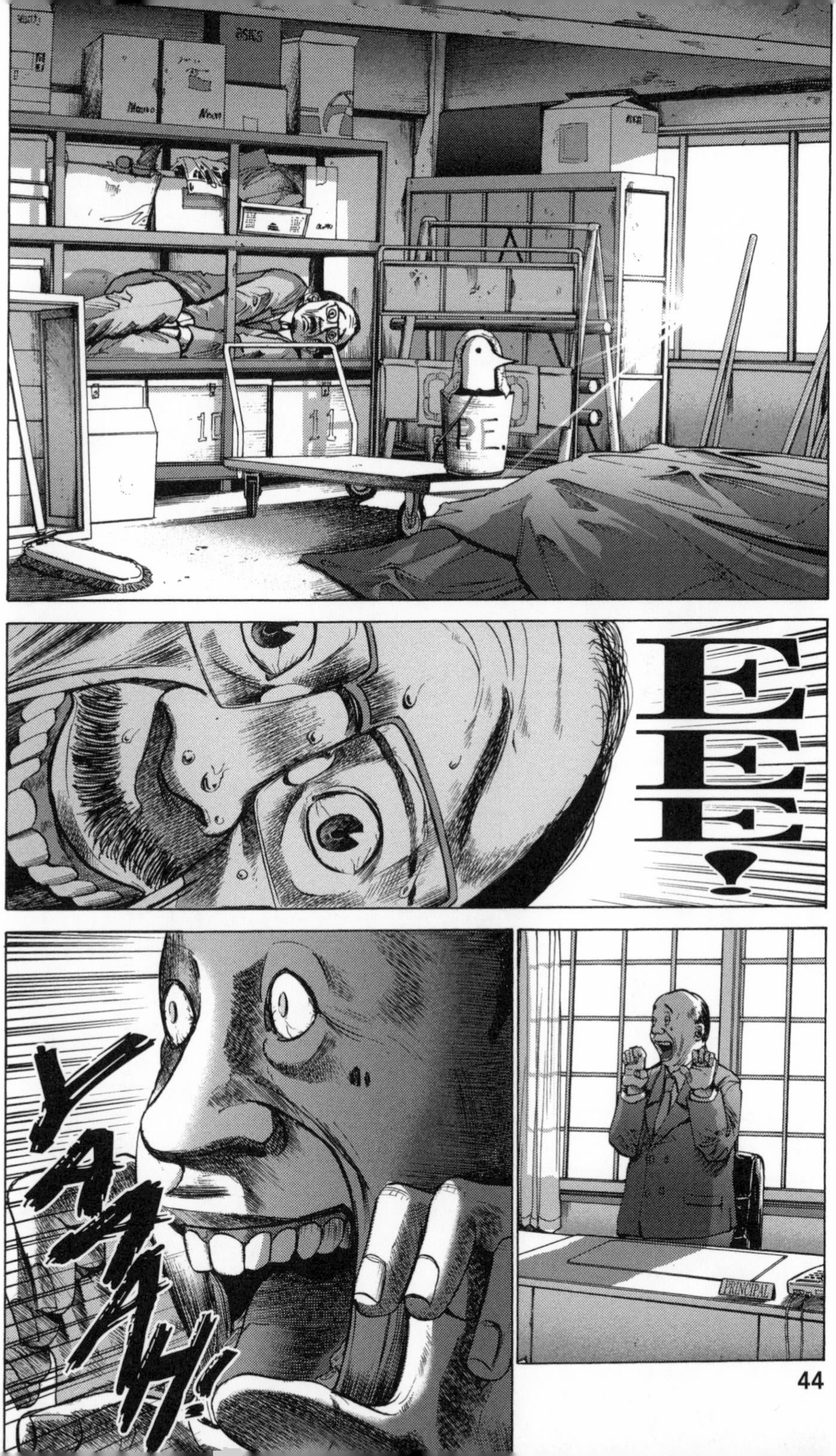
P.E.
EEE!
PRINCIPAL
YAAAH!

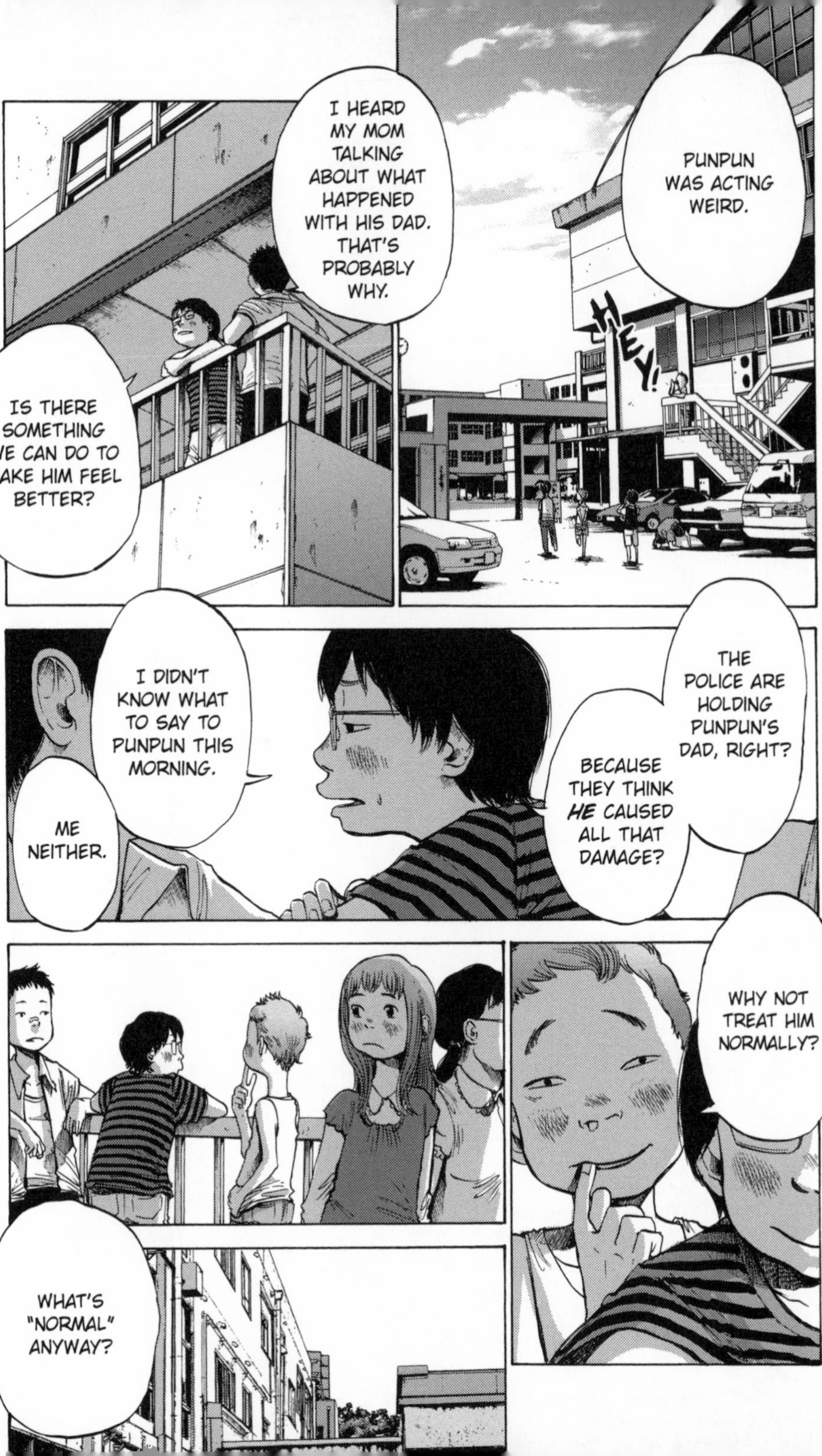
PUNPUN WAS ACTING WEIRD.
HEY!
I HEARD MY MOM TALKING ABOUT WHAT HAPPENED WITH HIS DAD. THAT'S PROBABLY WHY.
IS THERE SOMETHING WE CAN DO TO MAKE HIM FEEL BETTER?
THE POLICE ARE HOLDING PUNPUN'S DAD, RIGHT?
BECAUSE THEY THINK *HE* CAUSED ALL THAT DAMAGE?
I DIDN'T KNOW WHAT TO SAY TO PUNPUN THIS MORNING.
ME NEITHER.
WHY NOT TREAT HIM NORMALLY?
WHAT'S "NORMAL" ANYWAY?

"NORMAL" IS PRETTY HARD...

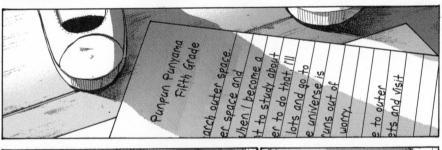

Punpun Punyama
Fifth Grade

...rch outer space...
...er space and
...t to study about
...er to do that I'll
...lots and go to
...e universe is
...runs out of
...worry.
...e to outer
...ets and visit

POING

P.E.

EEE!

46

Caution

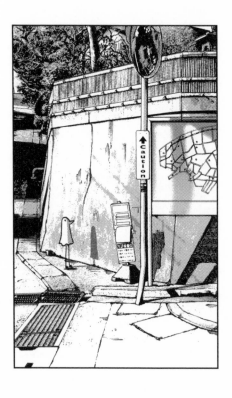

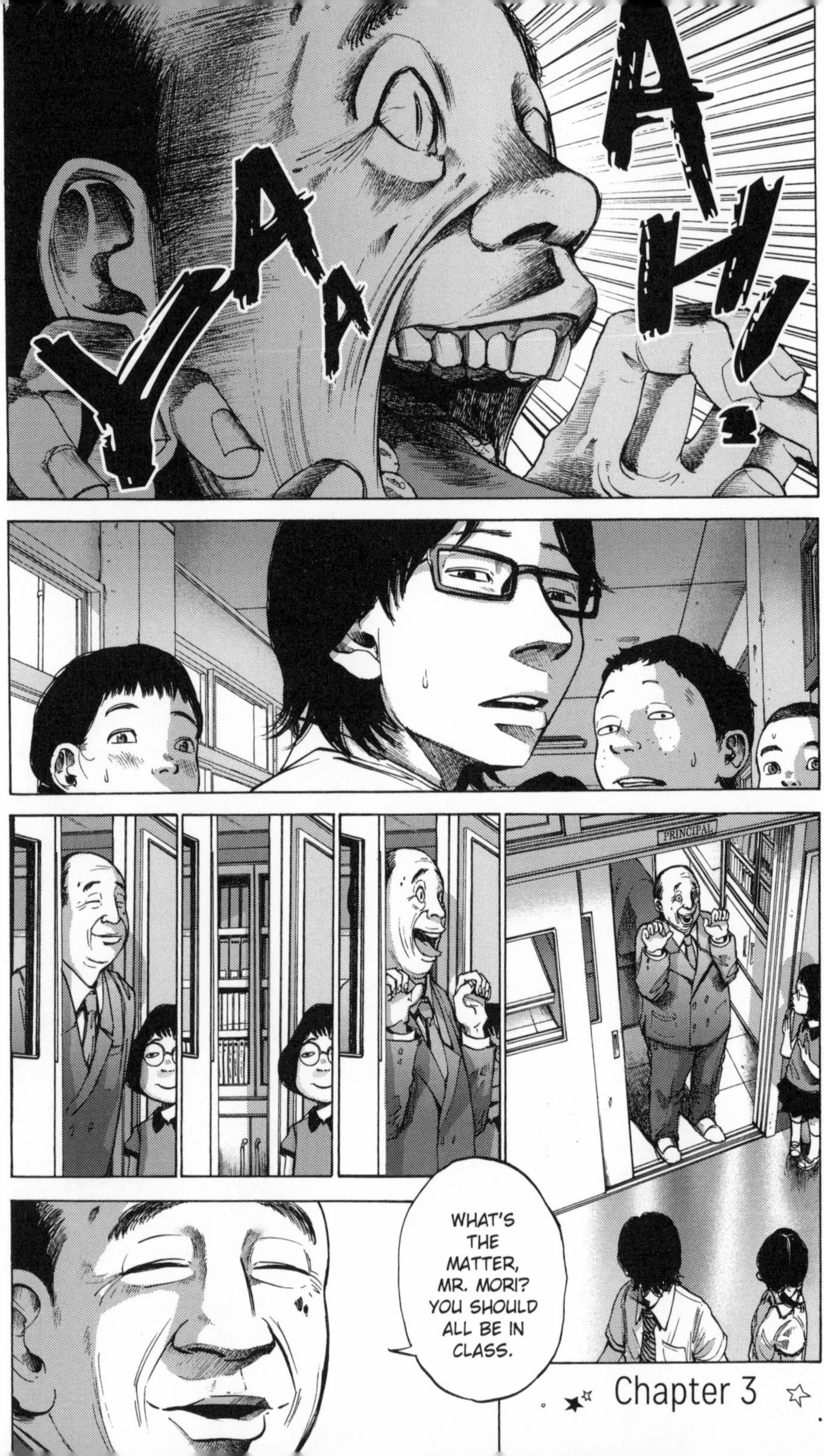
YAAAH!
PRINCIPAL
WHAT'S THE MATTER, MR. MORI? YOU SHOULD ALL BE IN CLASS.

Chapter 3

WELL, UMM...

...ONE OF MY CLASS- MATES RAN OFF.

Punpun was deep in thought.

He wondered if helping mankind emigrate to another planet was an impossible dream for him.

He was so confused...

...he wasn't even sure if he wanted to become a space expert anymore.

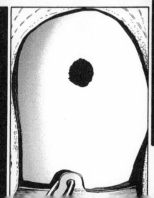

50

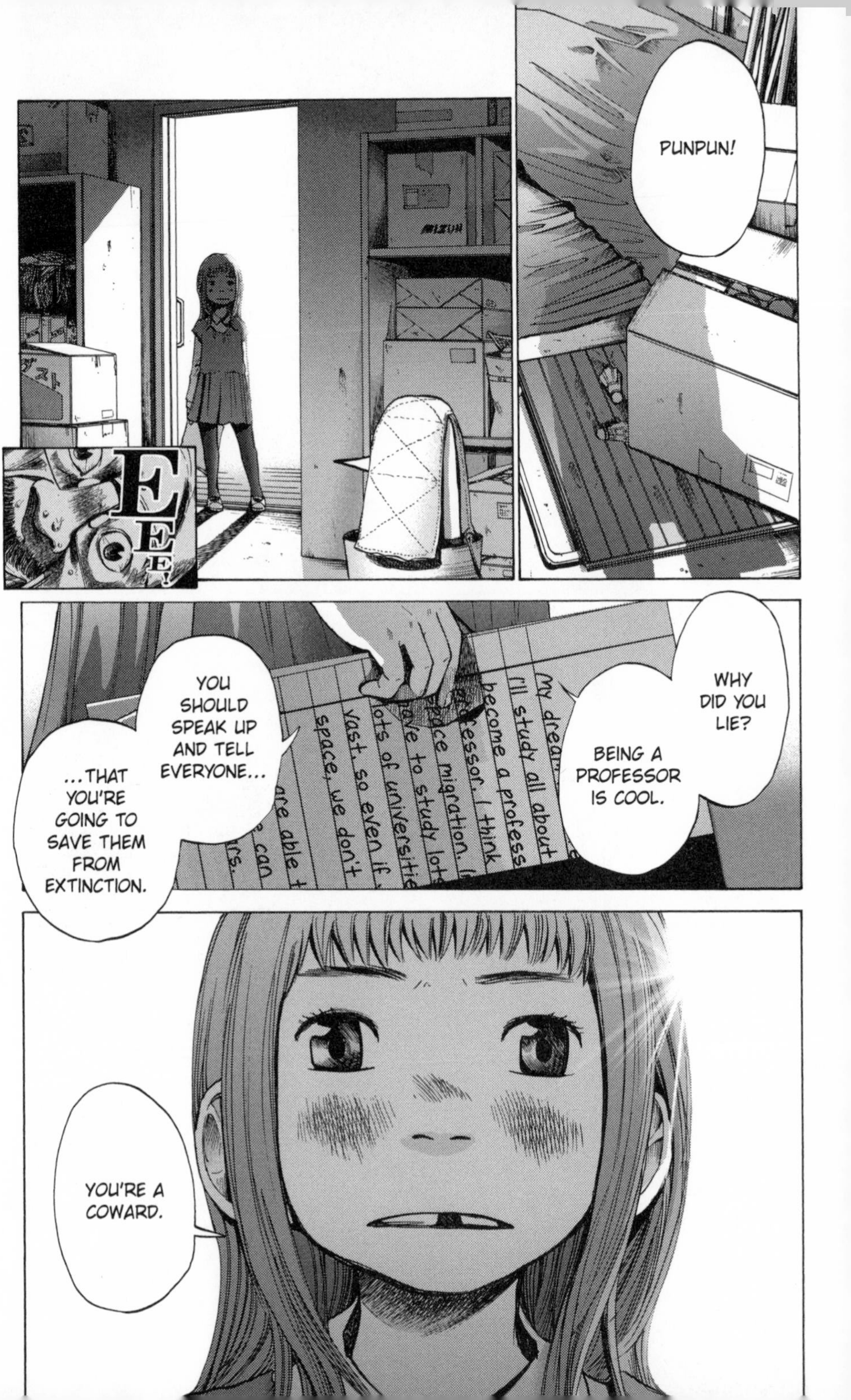
PUNPUN!
EEE!
WHY DID YOU LIE?
BEING A PROFESSOR IS COOL.
YOU SHOULD SPEAK UP AND TELL EVERYONE...
...THAT YOU'RE GOING TO SAVE THEM FROM EXTINCTION.
YOU'RE A COWARD.

YOU WERE SCARED THEY WERE GOING TO LAUGH AT YOU, RIGHT?

SO LET THEM!

PEOPLE WHO DISCOURAGE OTHERS WILL NEVER FIND THEIR OWN HAPPINESS!

WHO CARES WHAT WE DREAM ABOUT?

JUST GETTING THROUGH EACH DAY IS HARD ENOUGH.

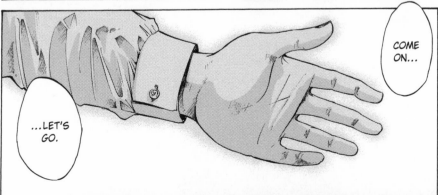

COME ON...

...LET'S GO.

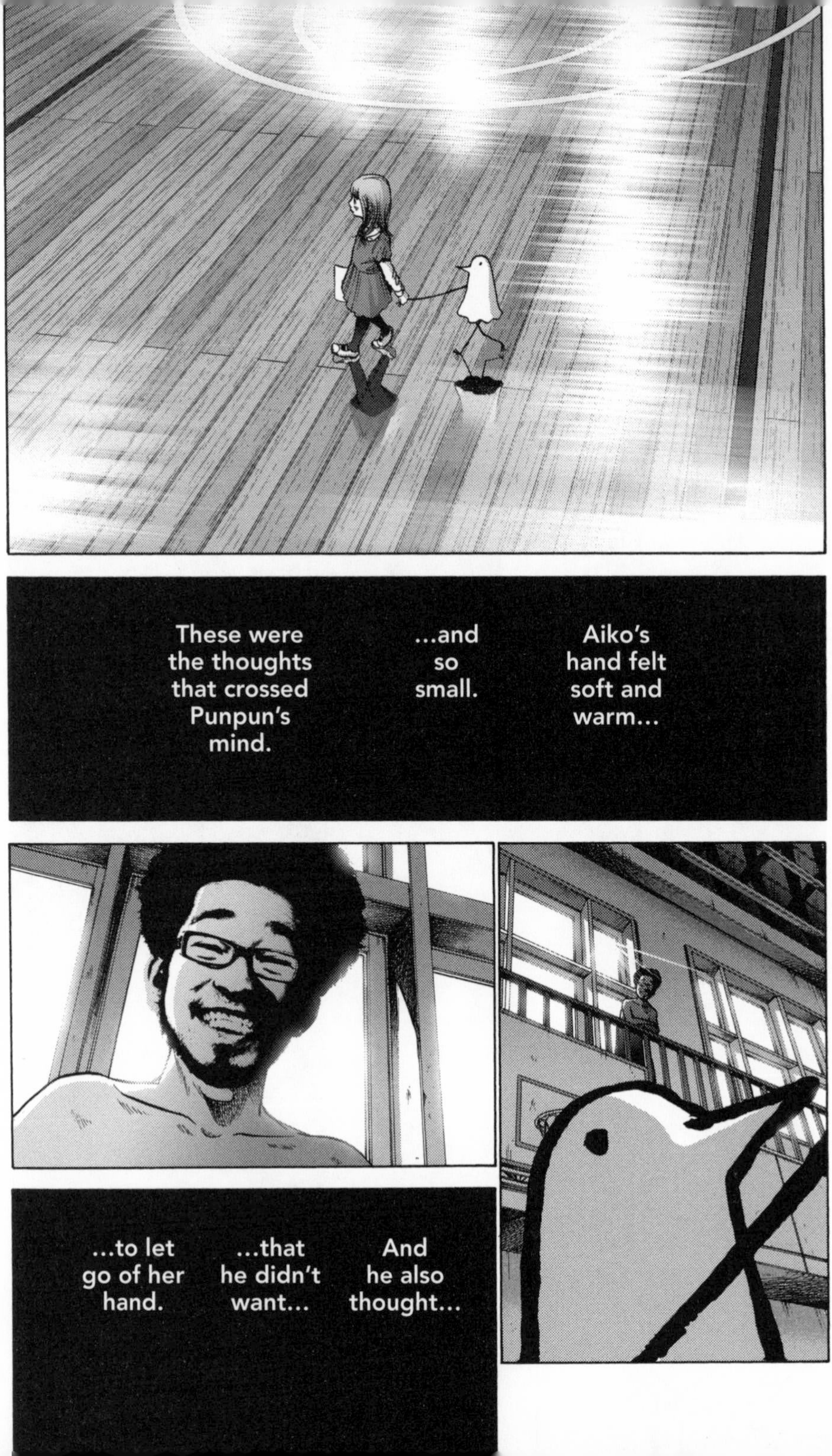
Aiko's hand felt soft and warm...
...and so small.
These were the thoughts that crossed Punpun's mind.
And he also thought...
...that he didn't want...
...to let go of her hand.

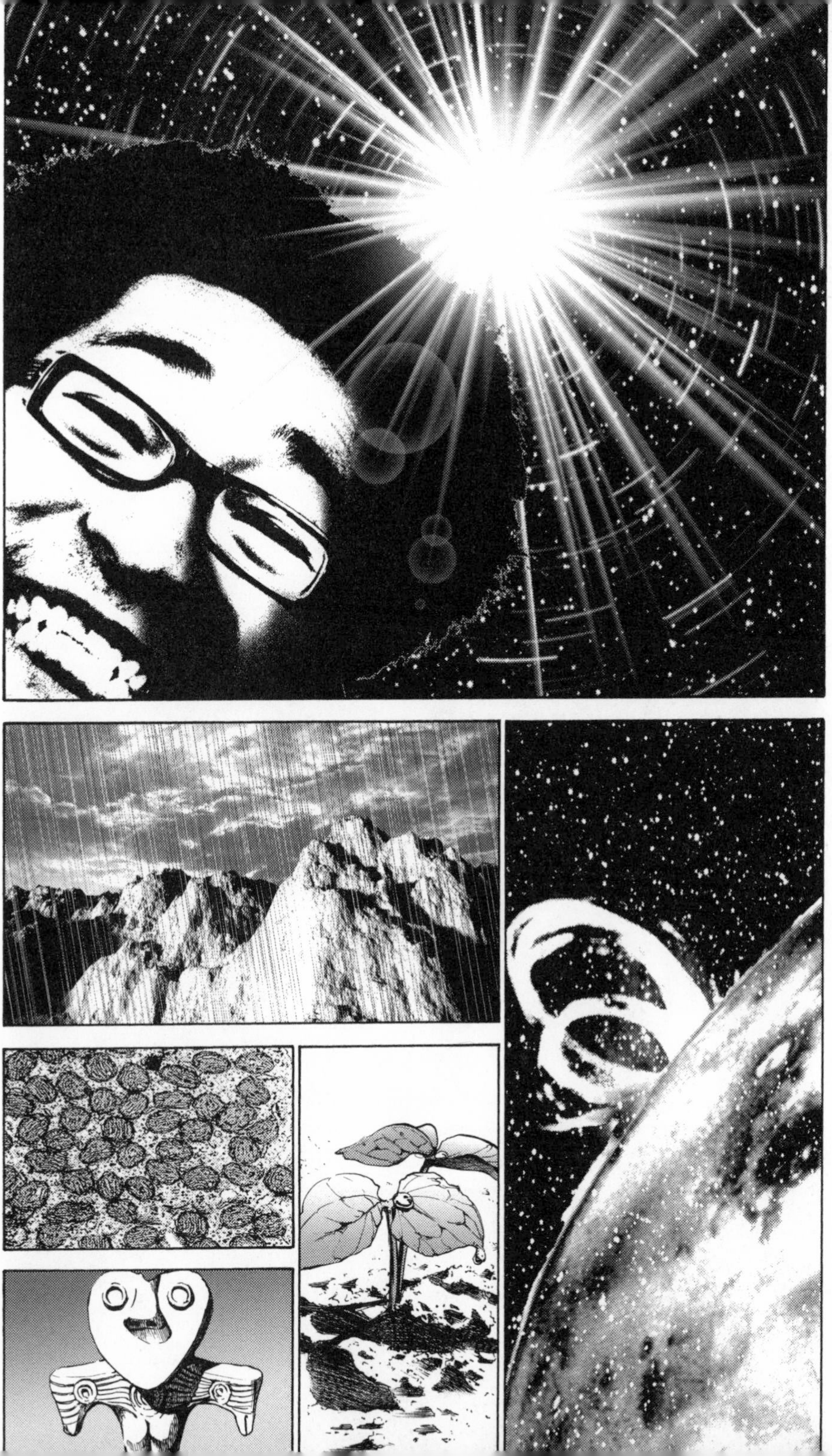

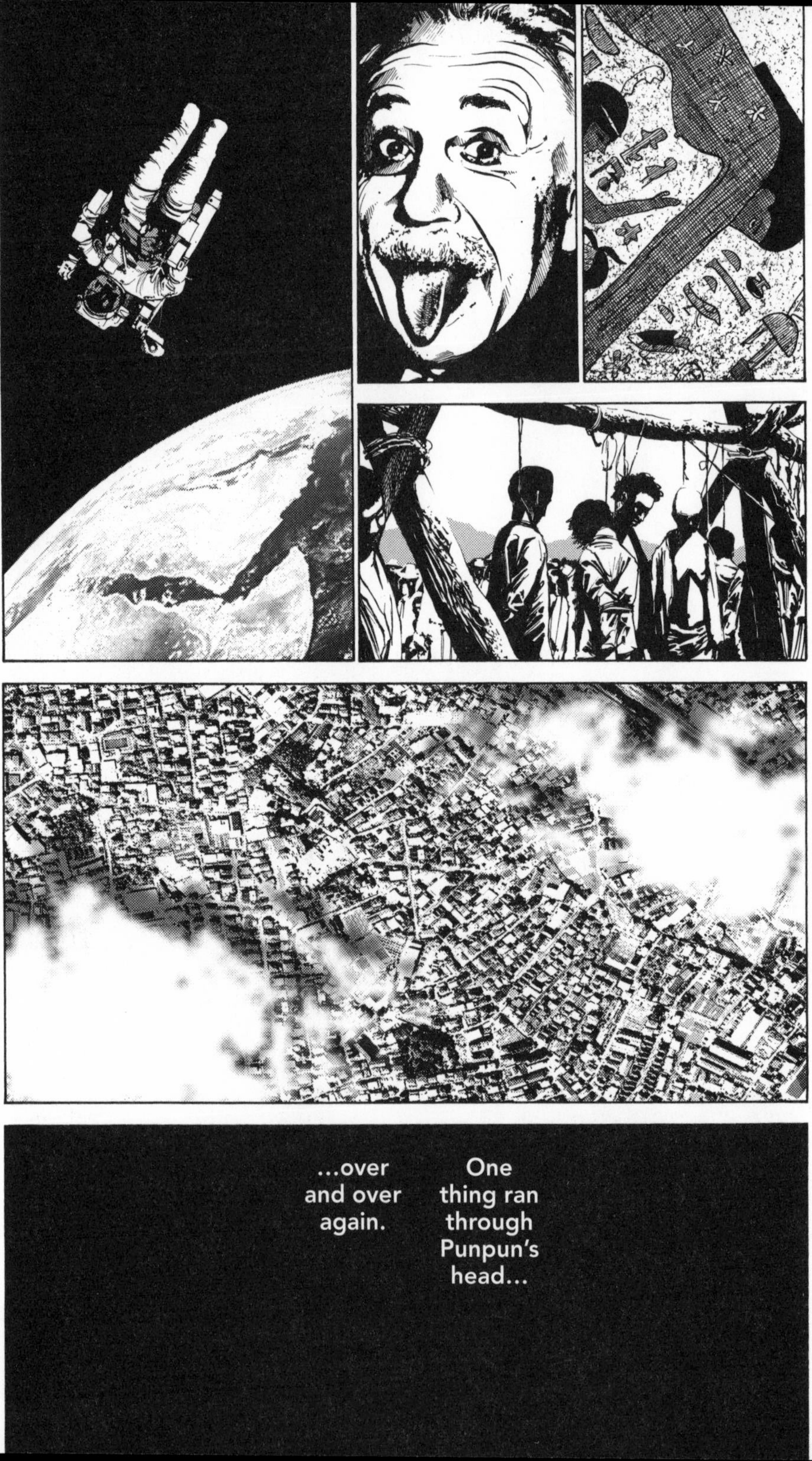
One thing ran through Punpun's head...
...over and over again.

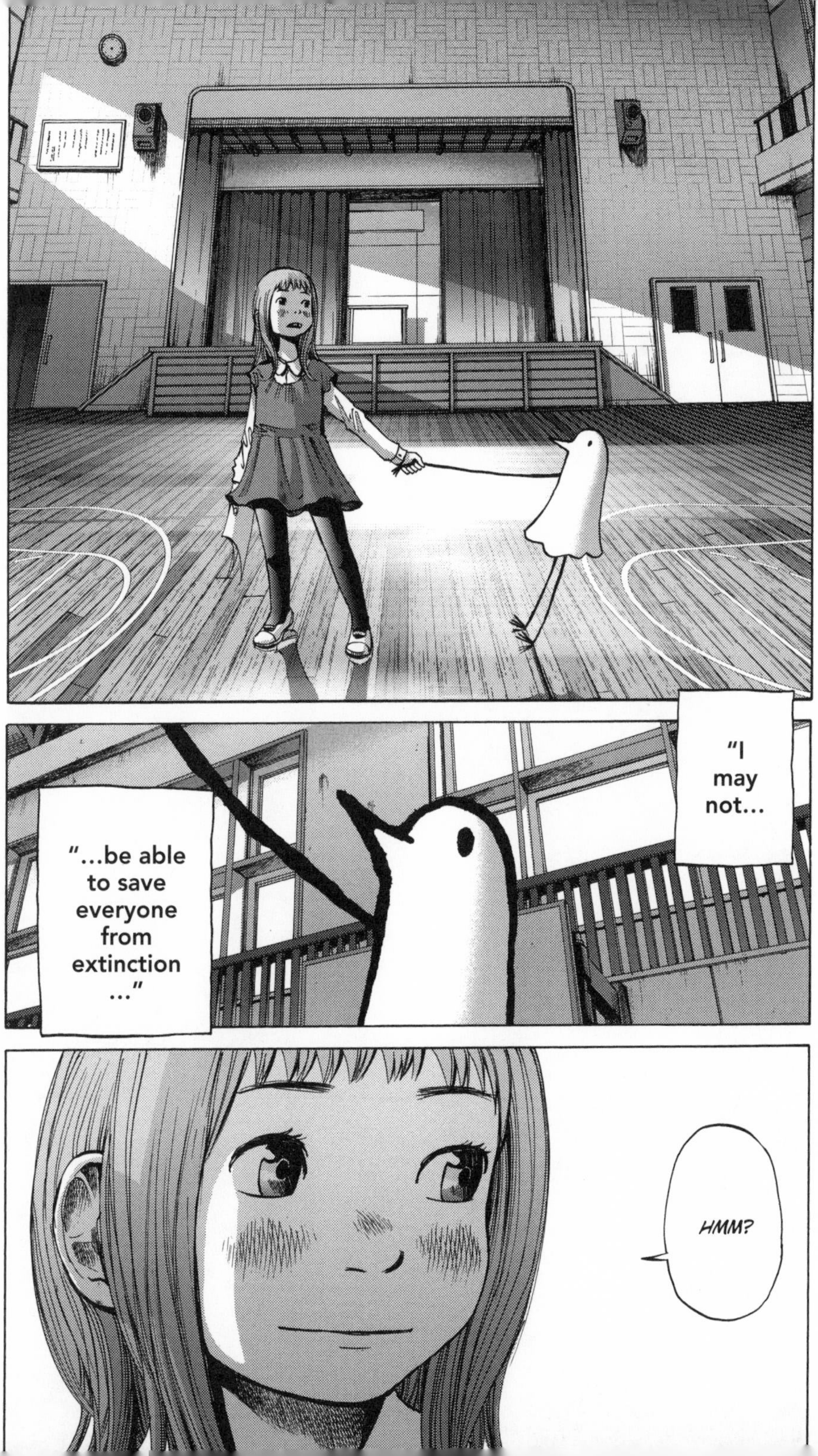
"I may not...
"...be able to save everyone from extinction ..."
HMM?

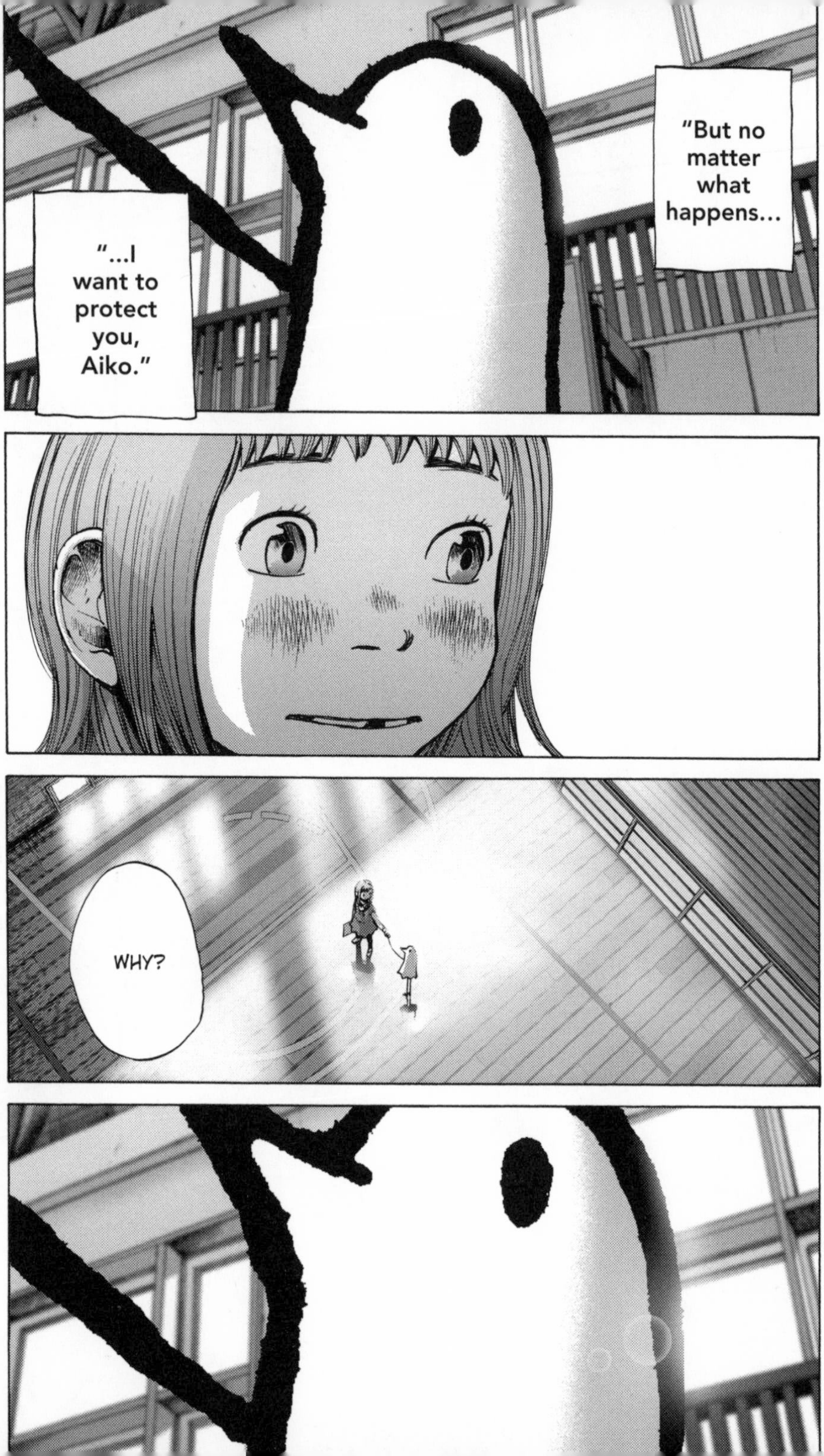
"But no matter what happens...
"...I want to protect you, Aiko."
WHY?

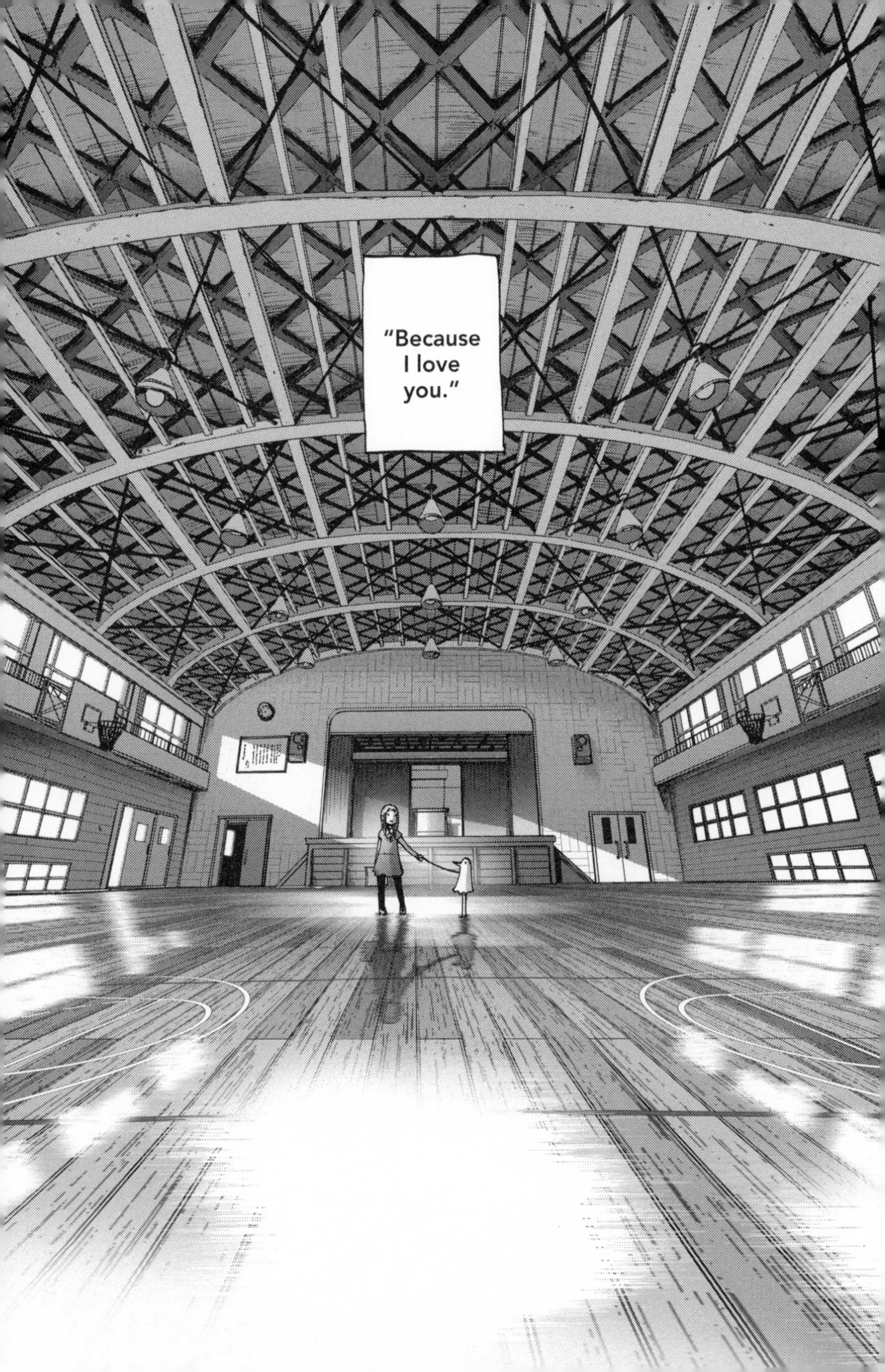
"Because I love you."

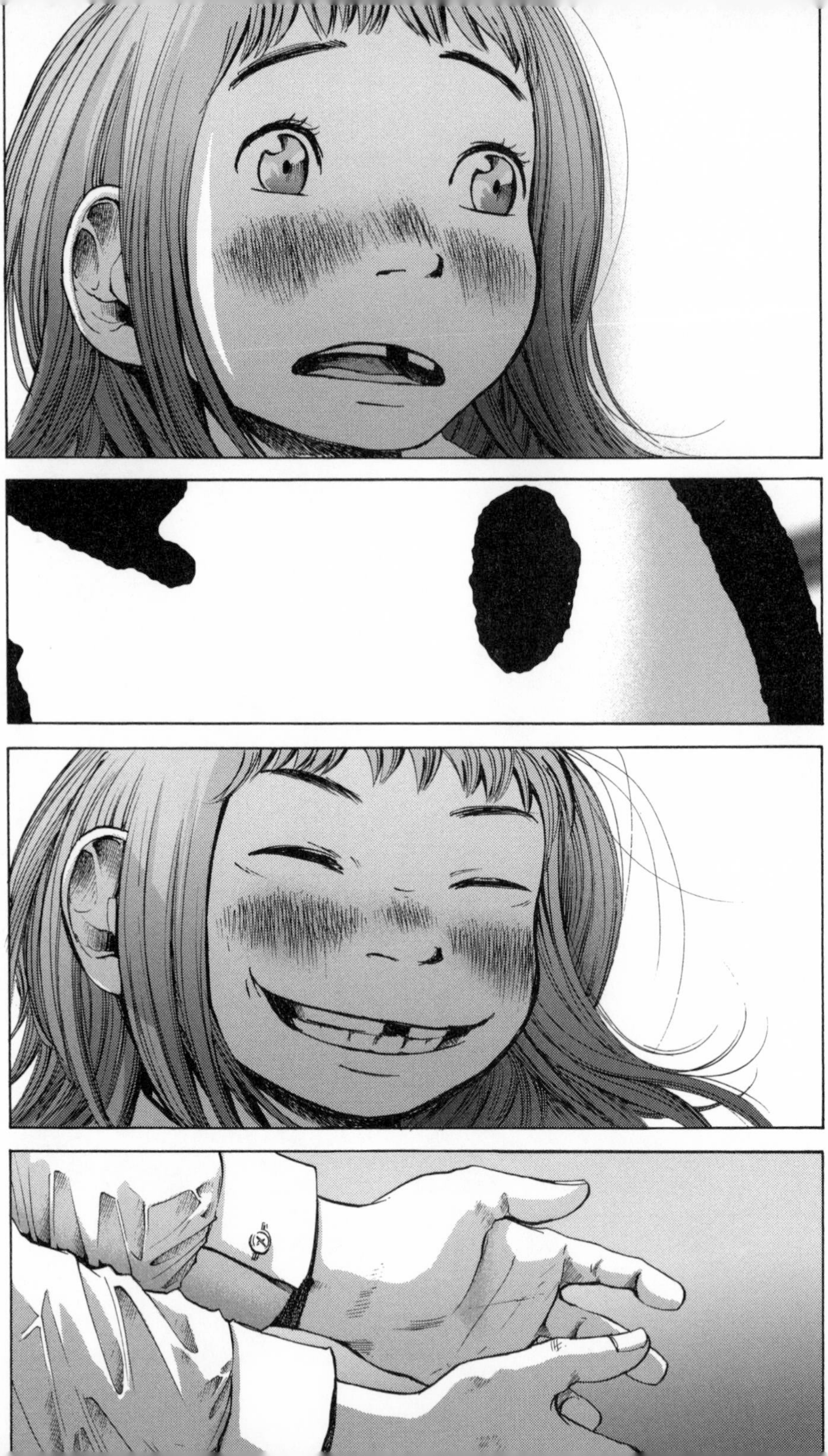

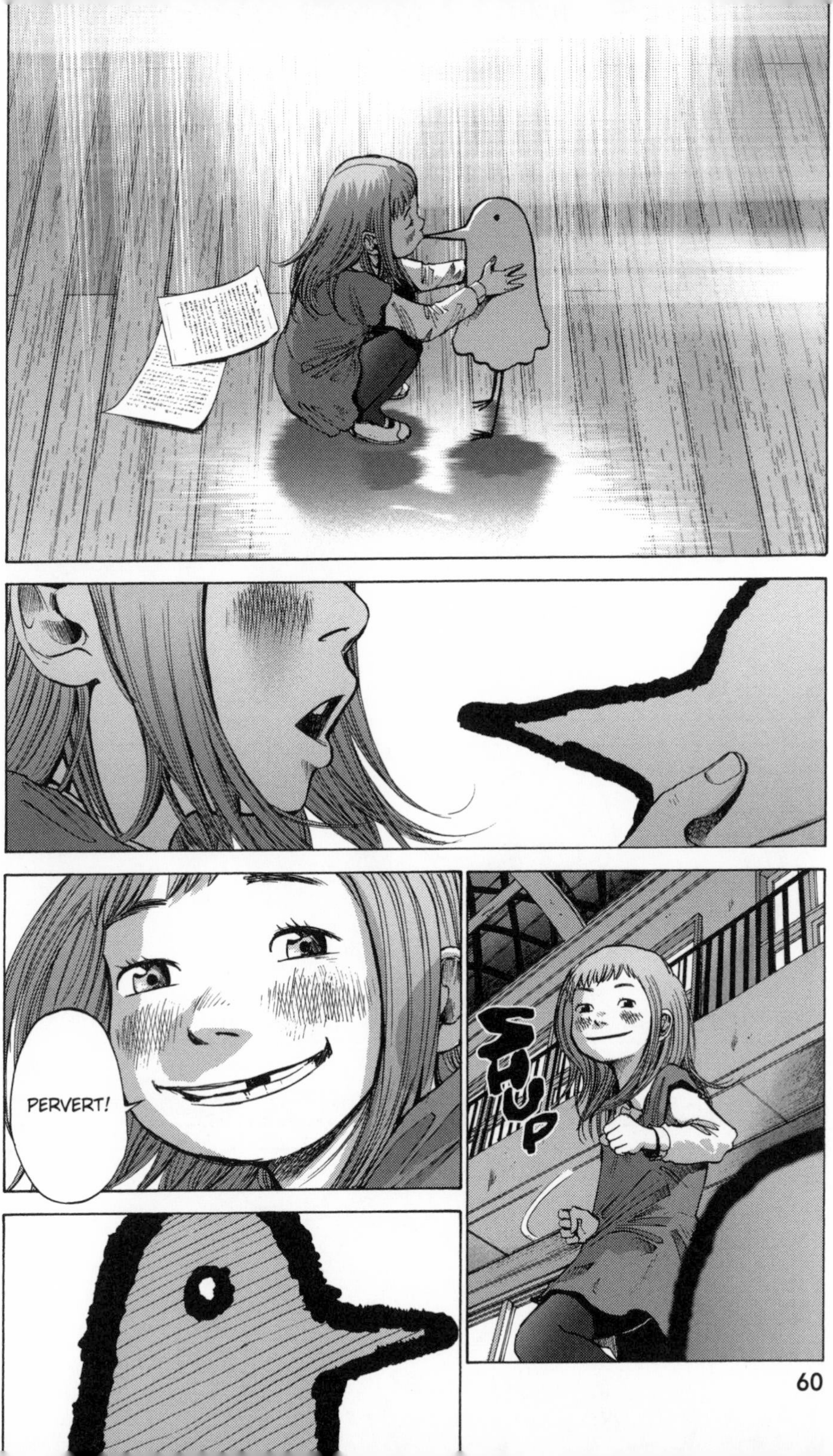
SHUP
PERVERT!

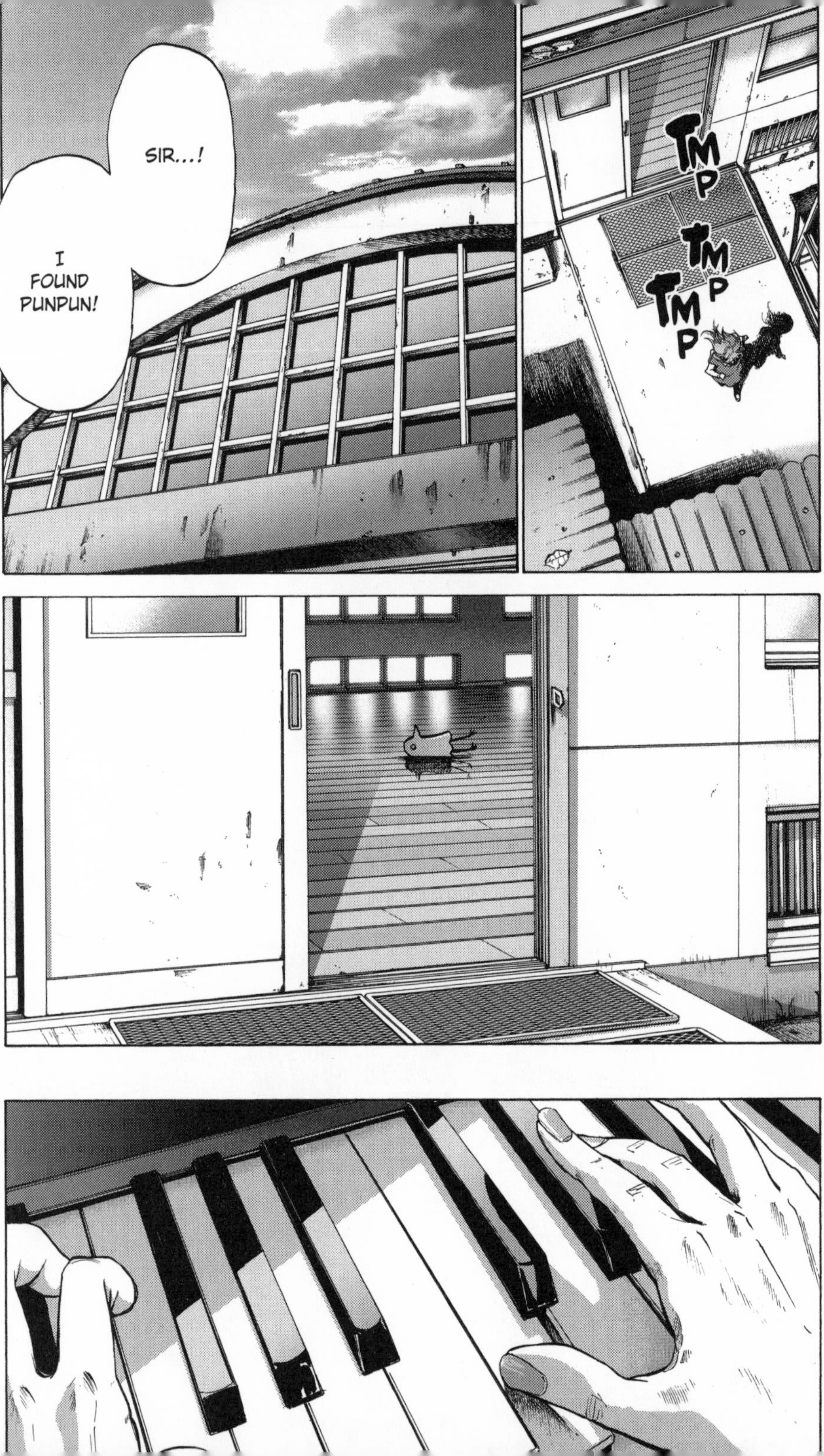
TMP
TMP
TMP
SIR...!
I FOUND PUNPUN!

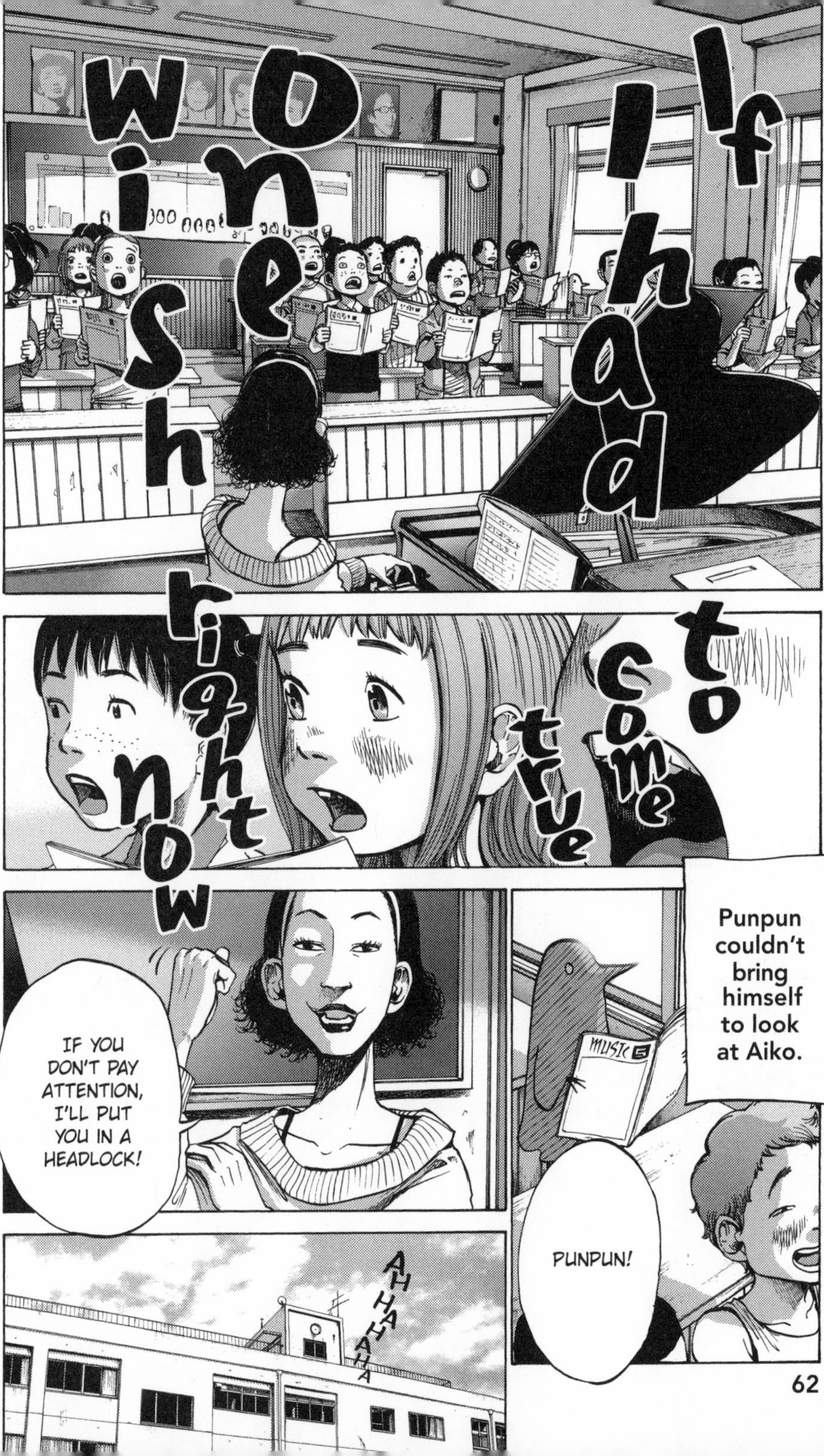
If I had one wish
to come true
right now
Punpun couldn't bring himself to look at Aiko.
PUNPUN!
IF YOU DON'T PAY ATTENTION, I'LL PUT YOU IN A HEADLOCK!
AHHAHAHA

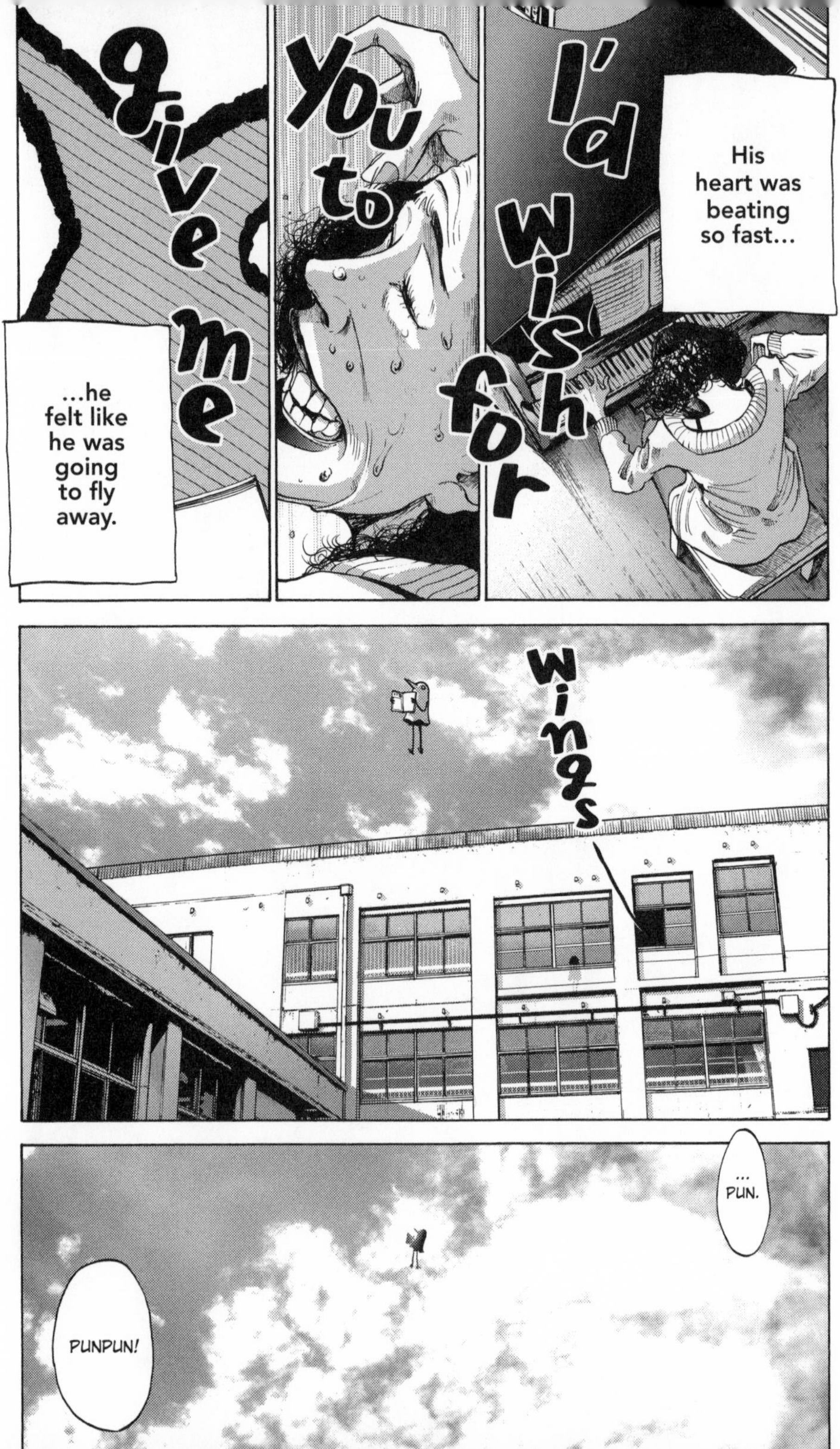
His heart was beating so fast...
I'd wish for
You to
give me
...he felt like he was going to fly away.
wings
...
PUN.
PUNPUN!

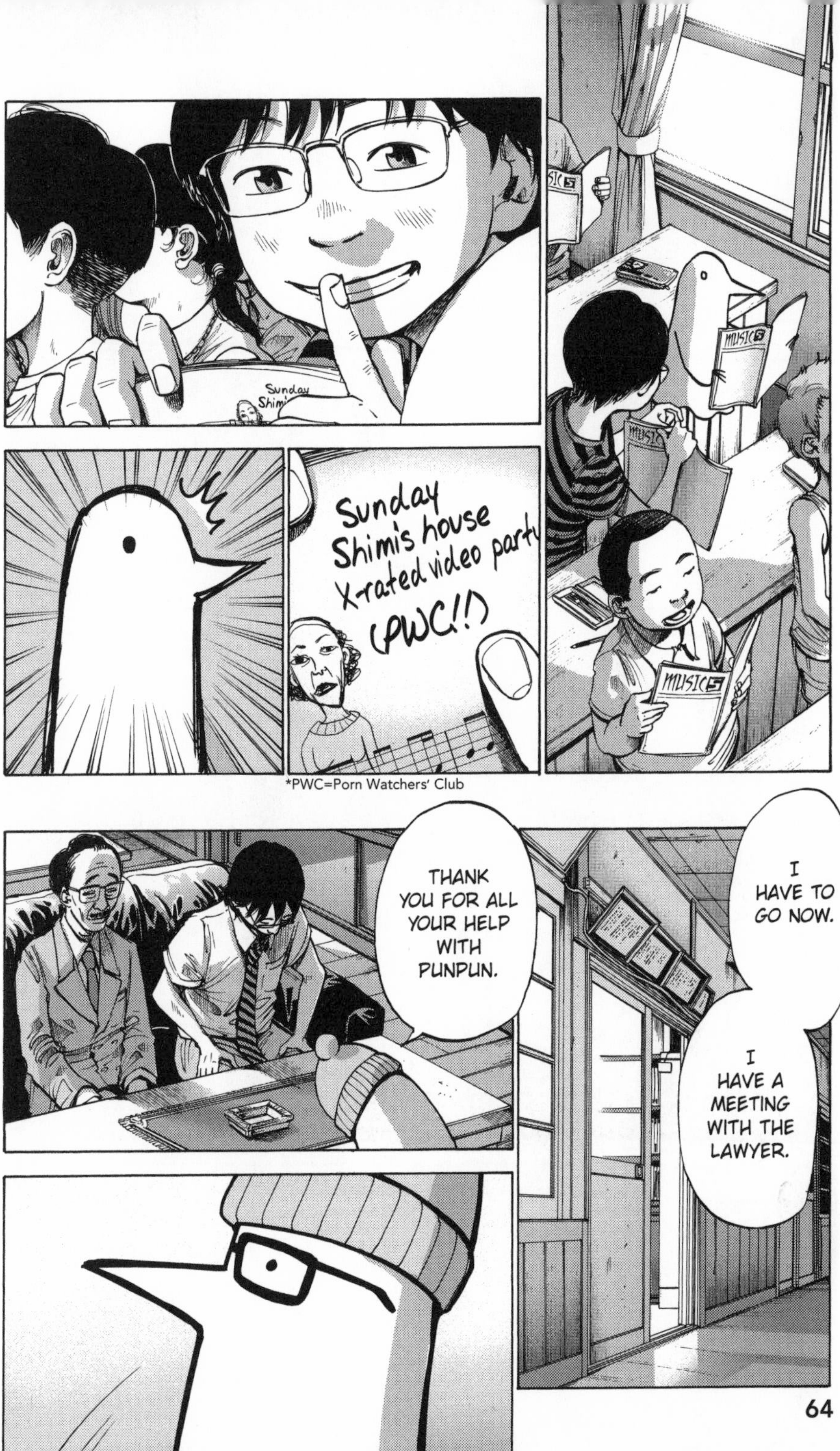
MUSIC
Sunday
Shimi's house
X-rated video party
(PWC!!)
I HAVE TO GO NOW.
I HAVE A MEETING WITH THE LAWYER.
THANK YOU FOR ALL YOUR HELP WITH PUNPUN.
*PWC=Porn Watchers' Club

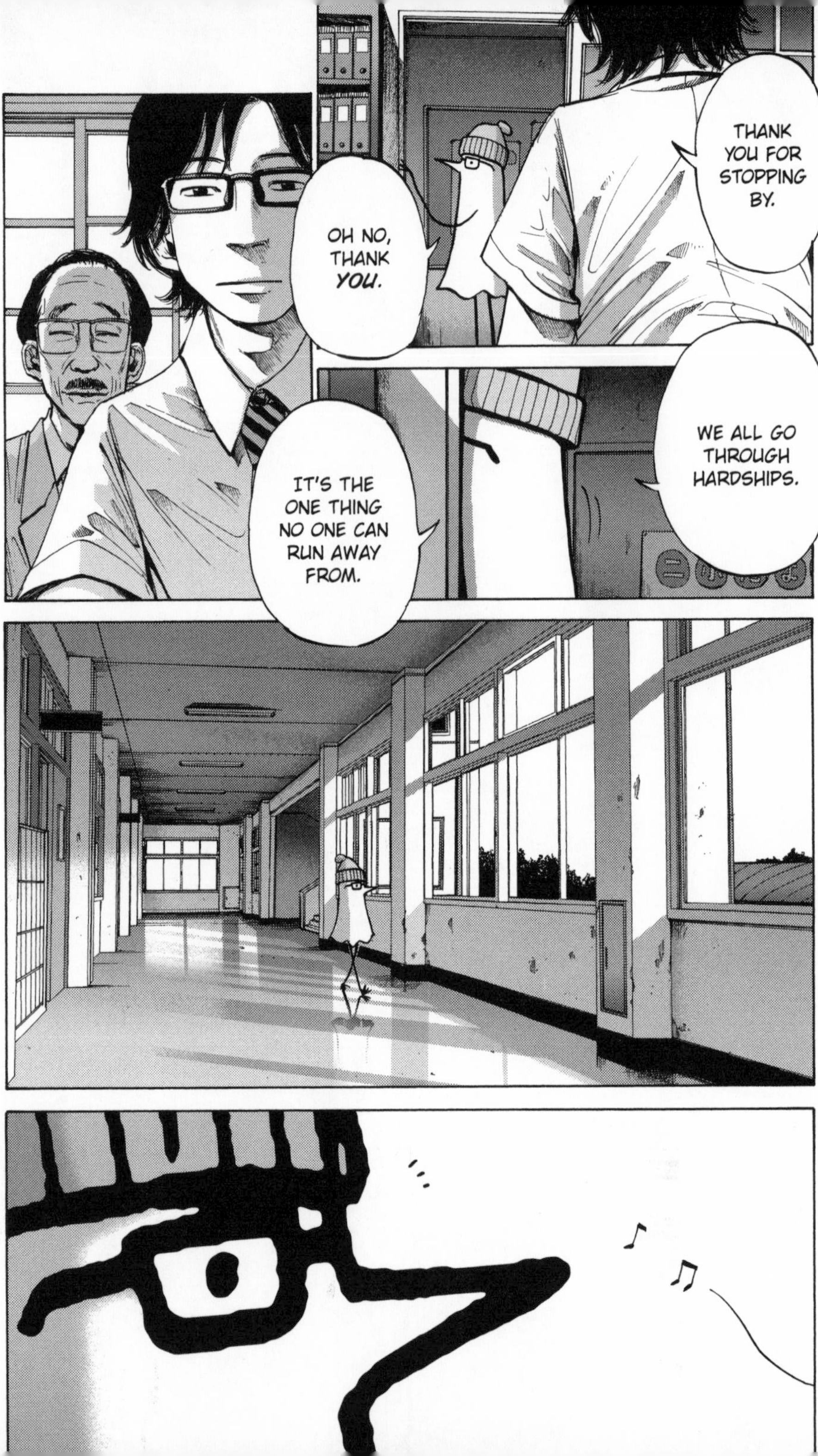
THANK YOU FOR STOPPING BY.
OH NO, THANK *YOU*.
WE ALL GO THROUGH HARDSHIPS.
IT'S THE ONE THING NO ONE CAN RUN AWAY FROM.

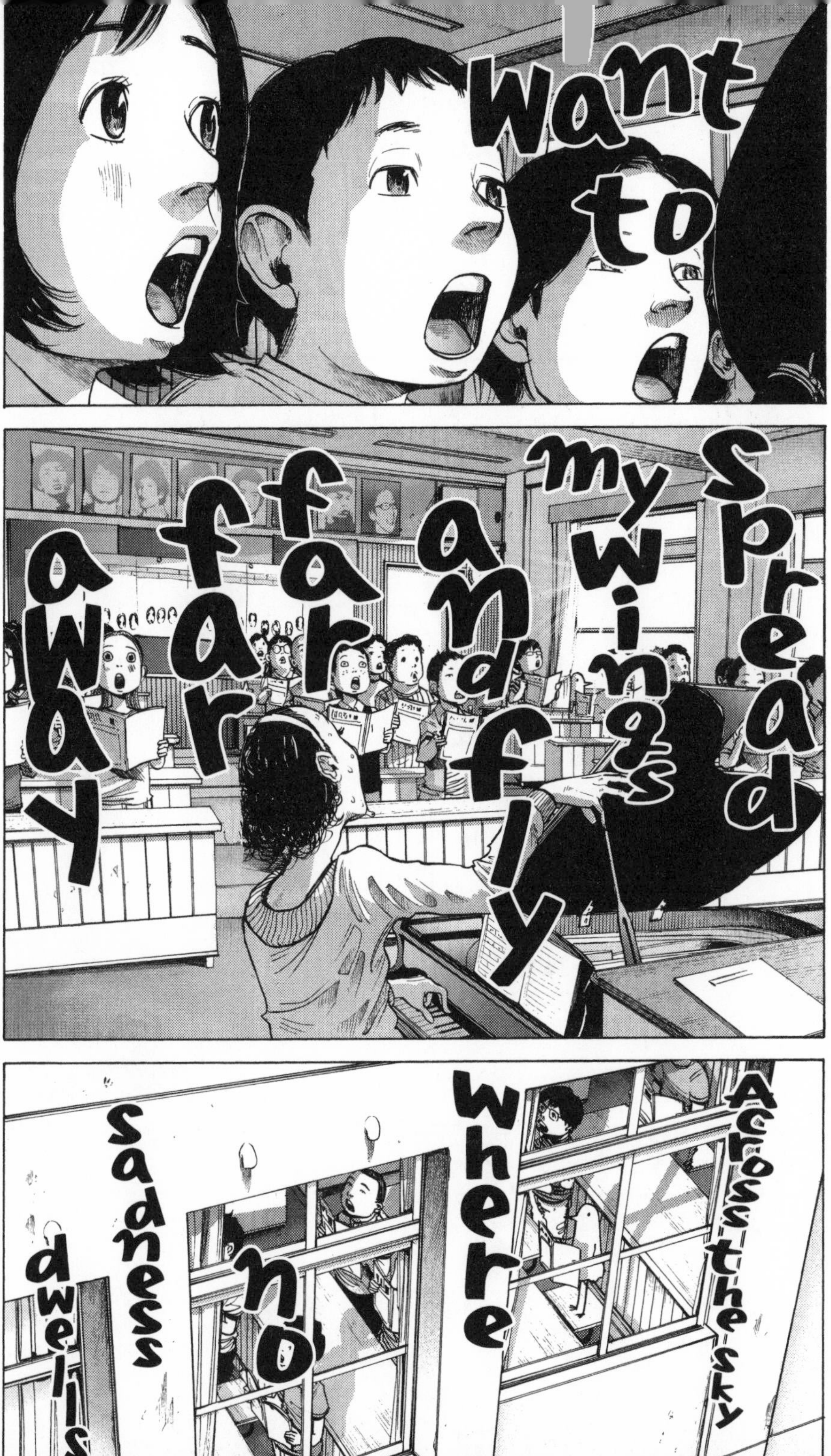

I want to
Spread
my wings
and fly
far
far
away
Across the sky
where
no
sadness
dwells

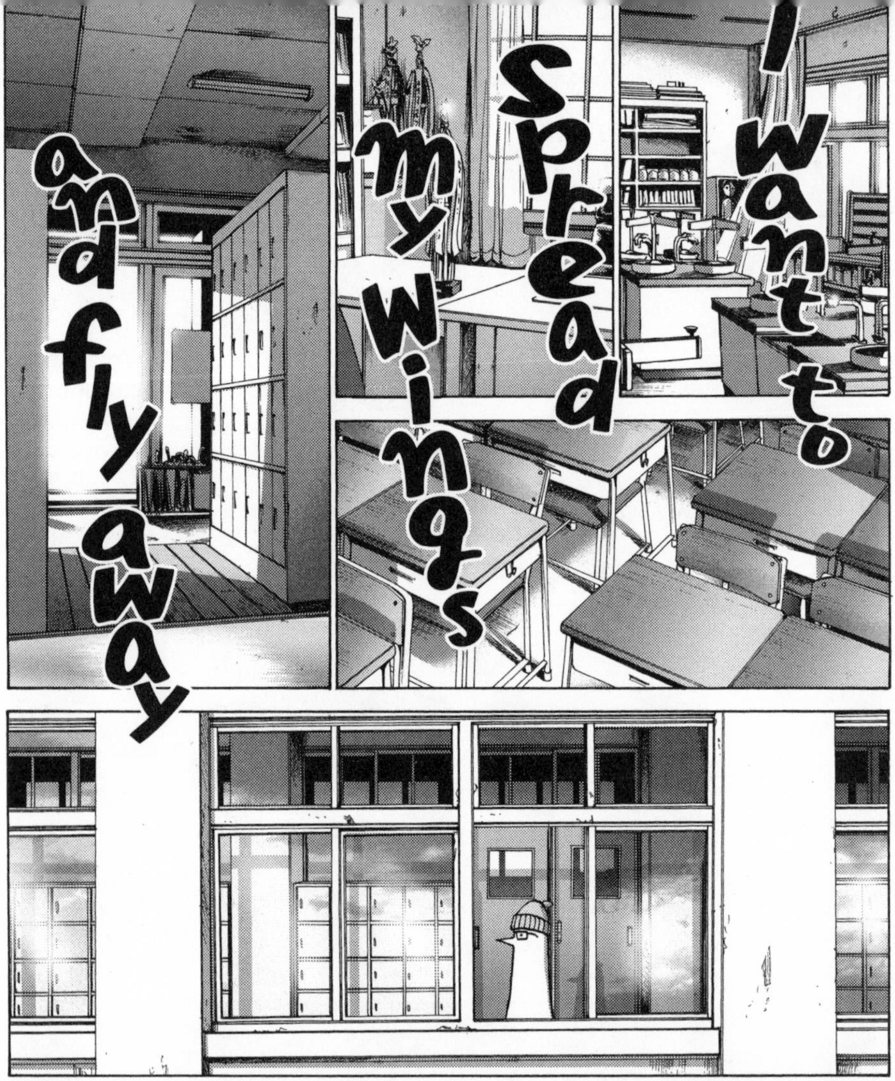
I want to
Spread
my wings
and fly away

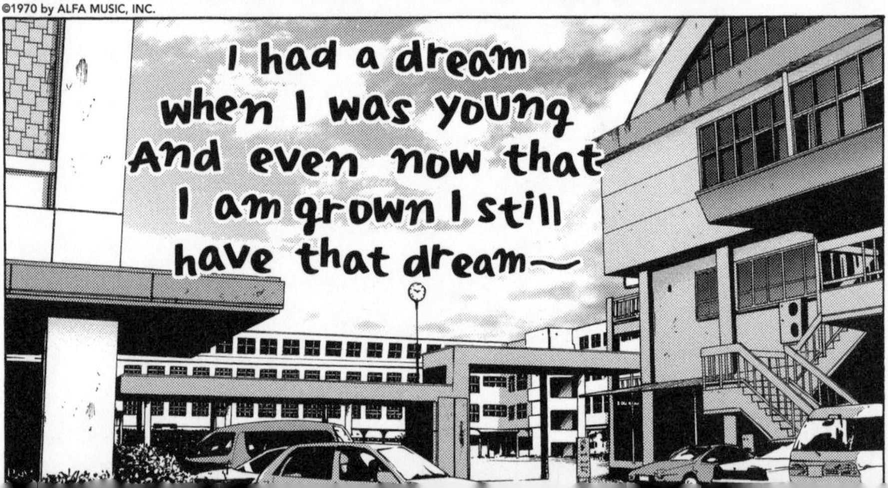
I had a dream
when I was young
And even now that
I am grown I still
have that dream~

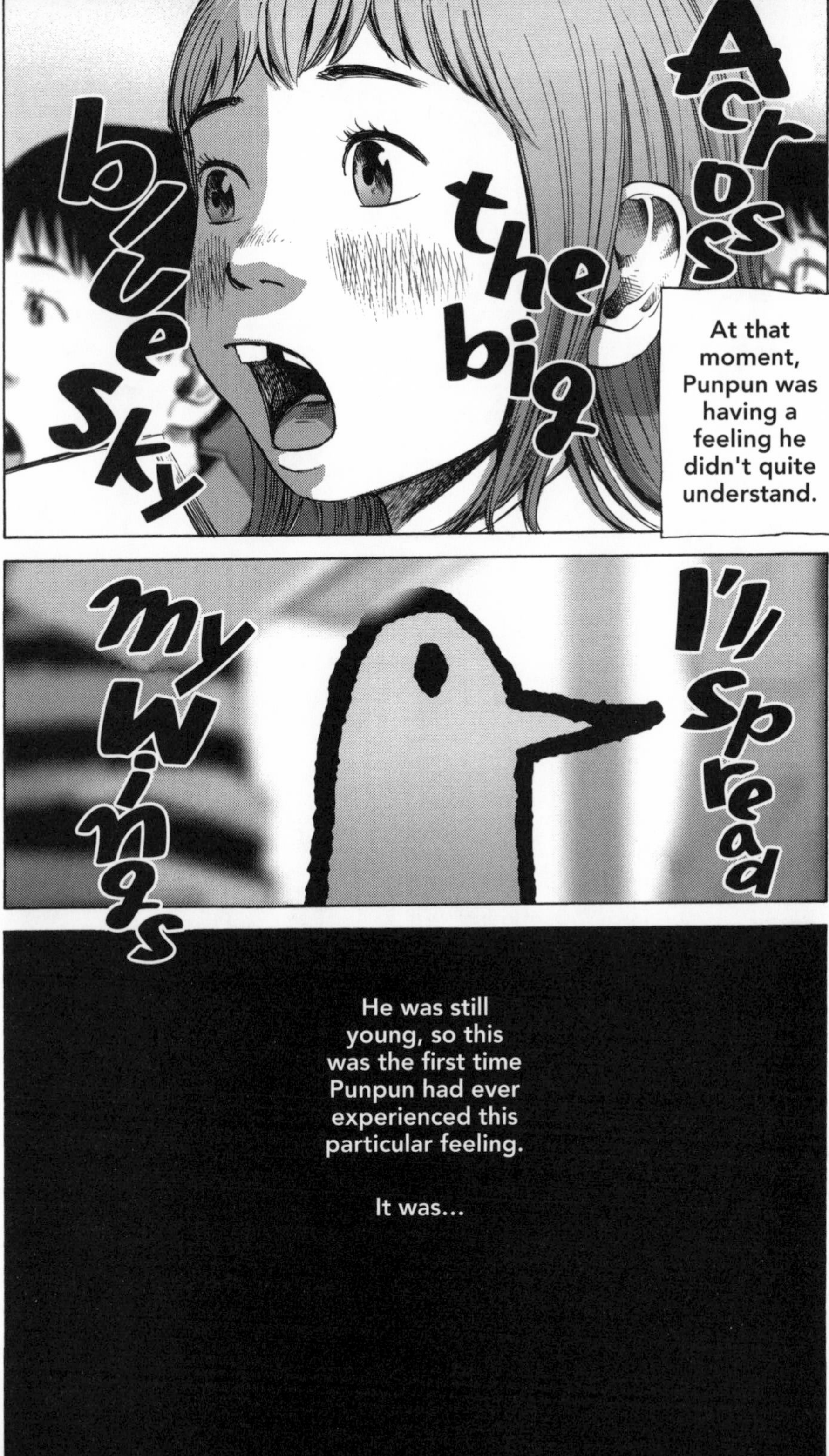
Across the big blue sky
At that moment, Punpun was having a feeling he didn't quite understand.
I'll spread my wings
He was still young, so this was the first time Punpun had ever experienced this particular feeling.
It was...

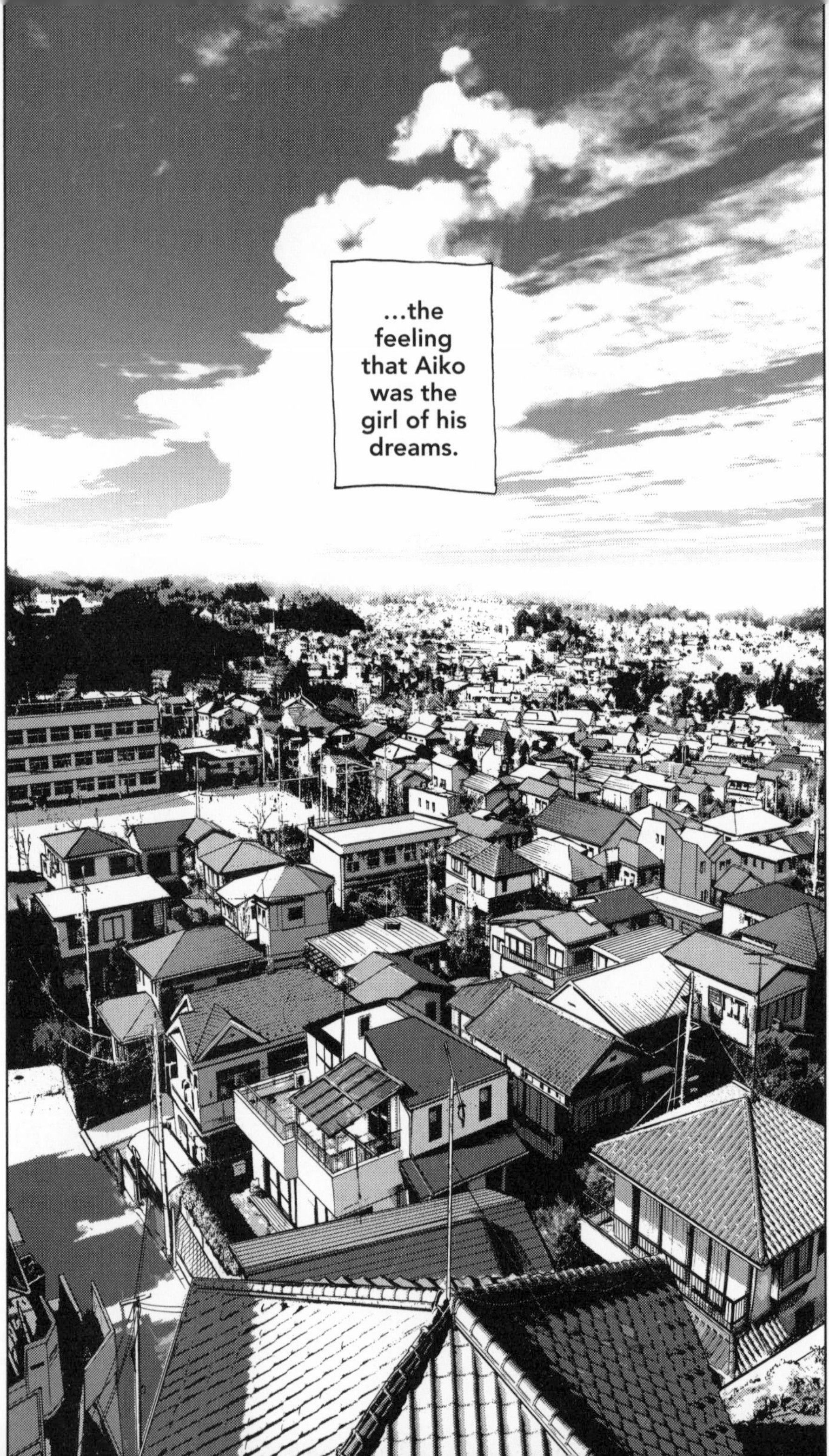
...the feeling that Aiko was the girl of his dreams.

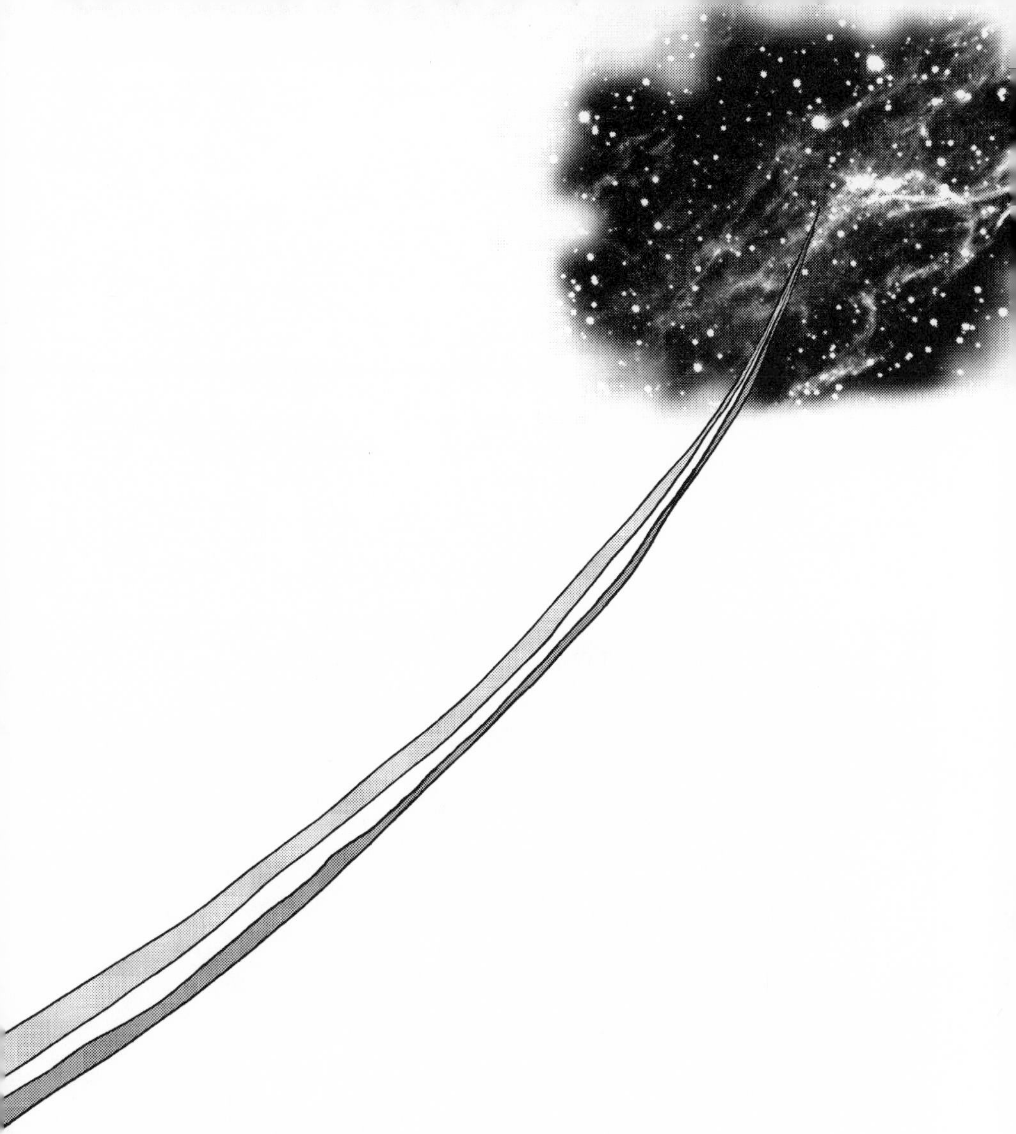

GOODNIGHT PUNPUN

Part One

INIO ASANO

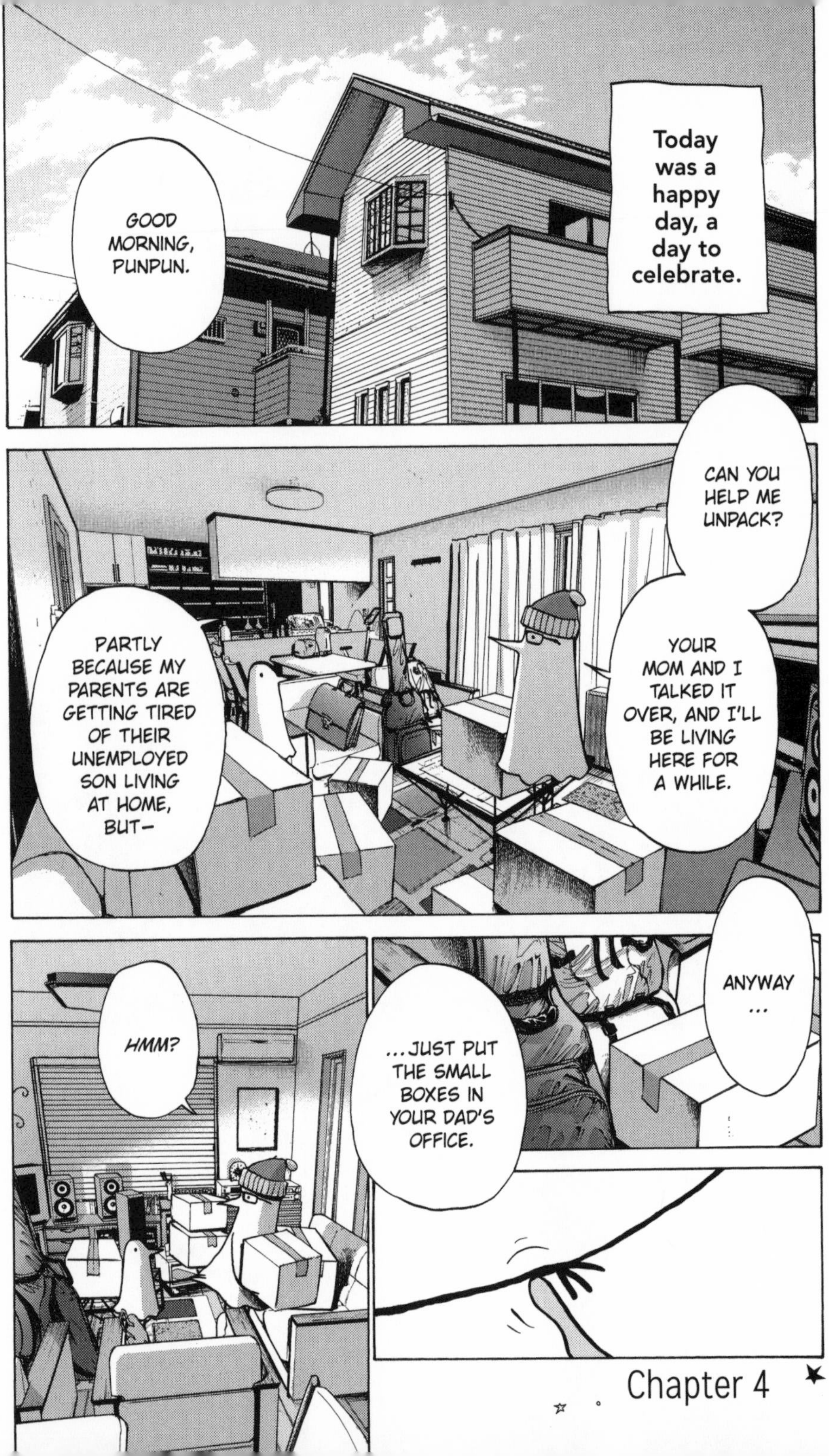
Today was a happy day, a day to celebrate.
GOOD MORNING, PUNPUN.
CAN YOU HELP ME UNPACK?
YOUR MOM AND I TALKED IT OVER, AND I'LL BE LIVING HERE FOR A WHILE.
PARTLY BECAUSE MY PARENTS ARE GETTING TIRED OF THEIR UNEMPLOYED SON LIVING AT HOME, BUT—
ANYWAY ...
...JUST PUT THE SMALL BOXES IN YOUR DAD'S OFFICE.
HMM?

Chapter 4

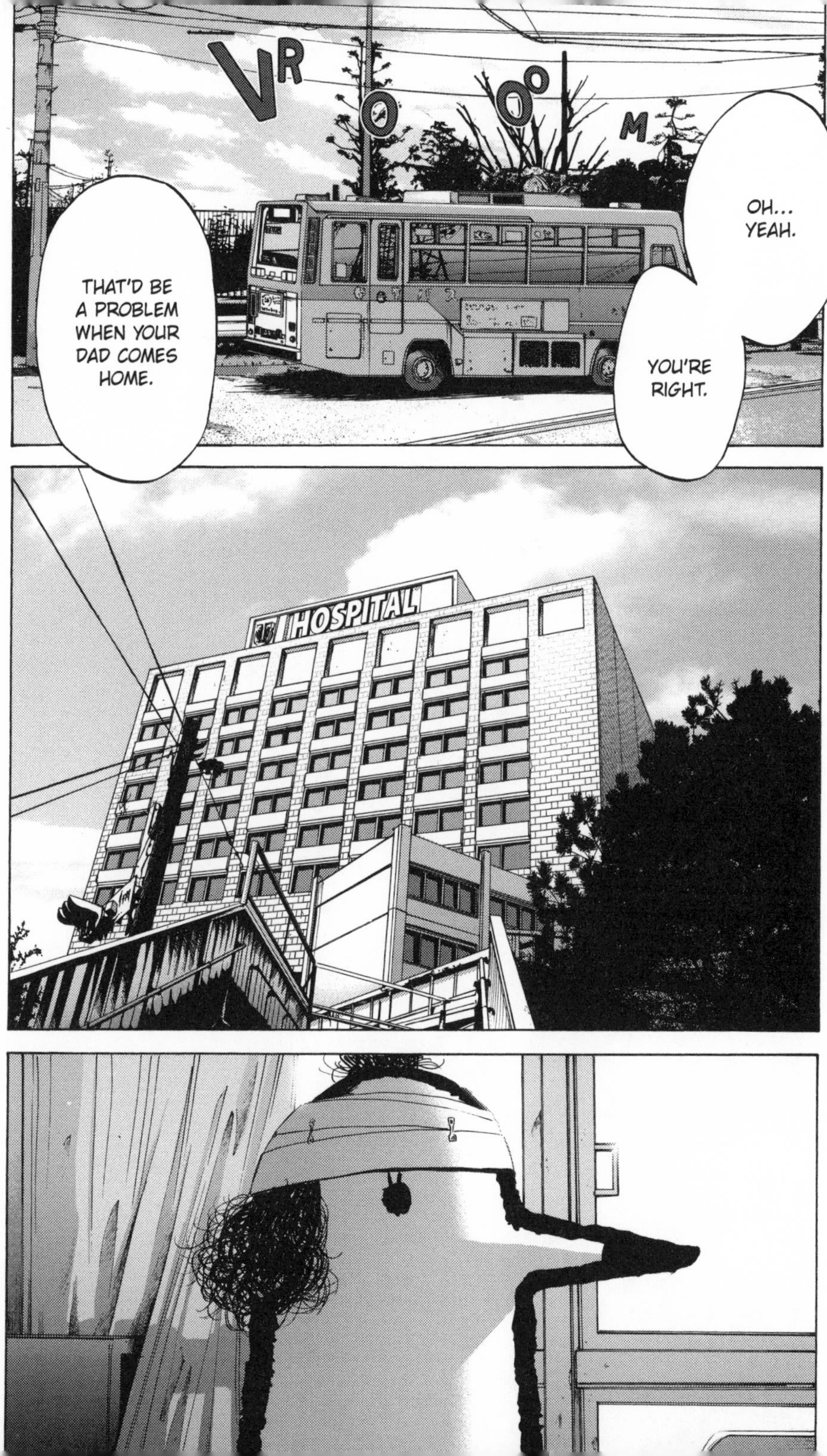
VROOOM
OH... YEAH.
YOU'RE RIGHT.
THAT'D BE A PROBLEM WHEN YOUR DAD COMES HOME.
HOSPITAL

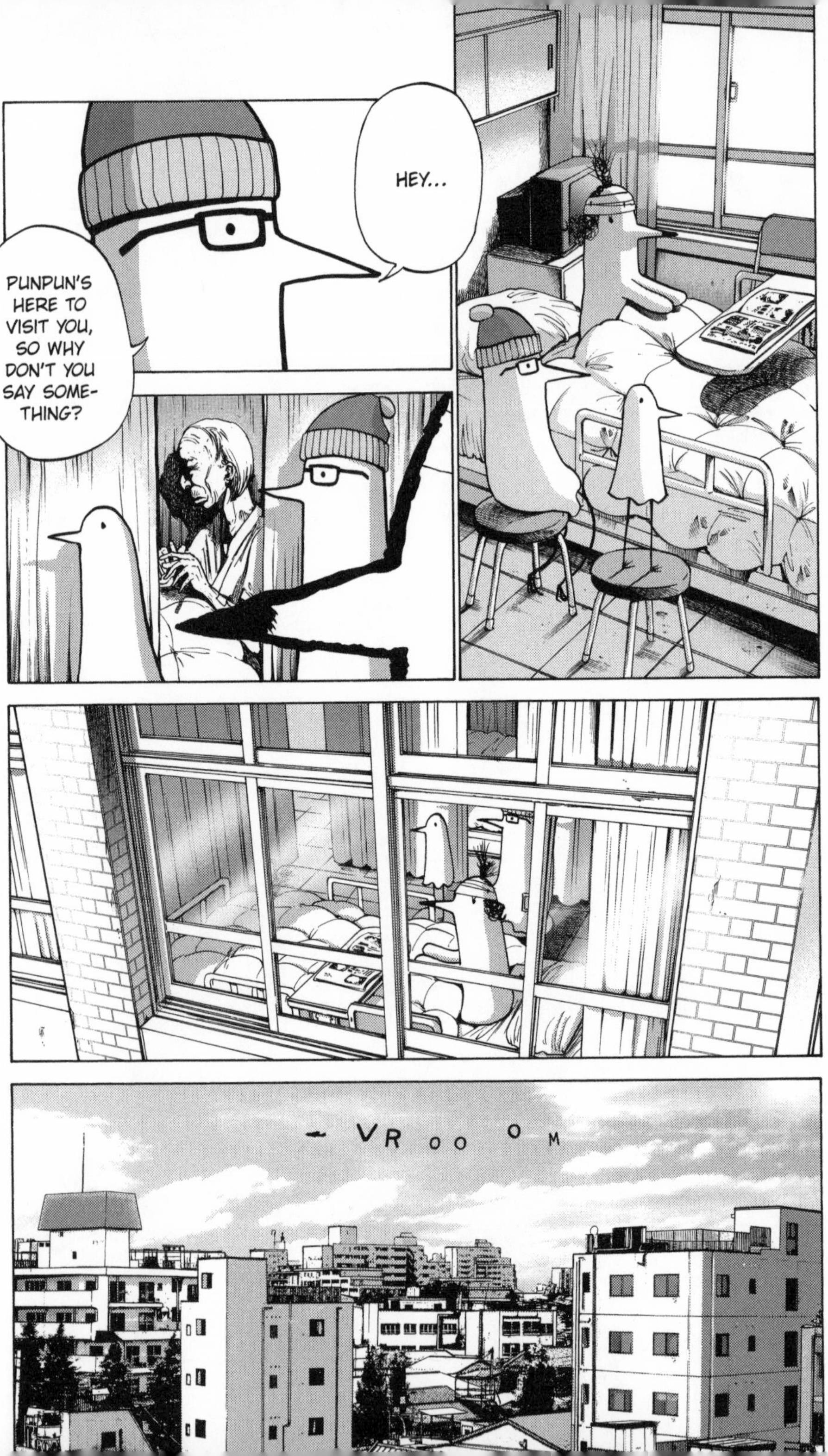
HEY...
PUNPUN'S HERE TO VISIT YOU, SO WHY DON'T YOU SAY SOME-THING?
VR OO O M

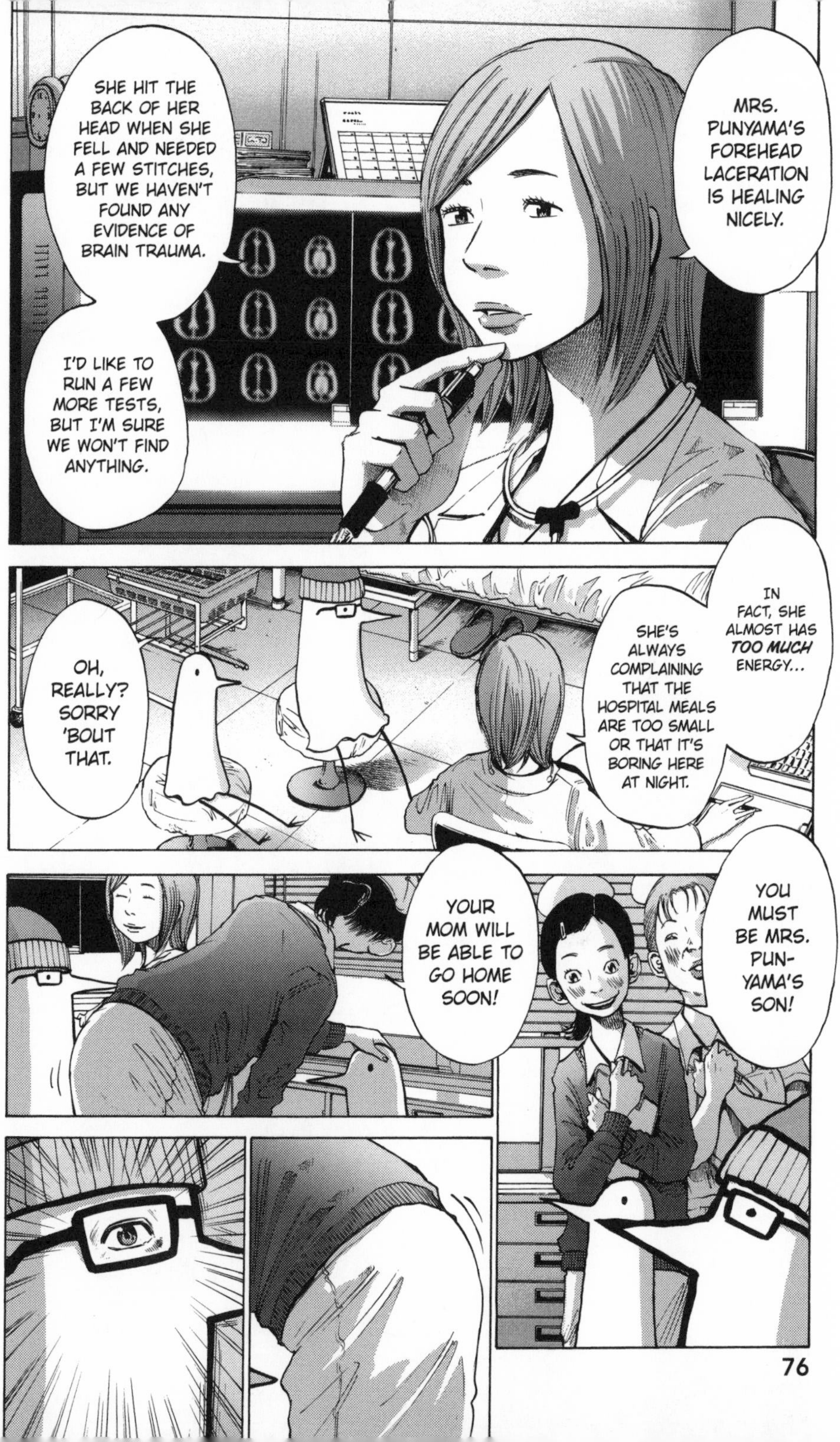
MRS. PUNYAMA'S FOREHEAD LACERATION IS HEALING NICELY.
SHE HIT THE BACK OF HER HEAD WHEN SHE FELL AND NEEDED A FEW STITCHES, BUT WE HAVEN'T FOUND ANY EVIDENCE OF BRAIN TRAUMA.
I'D LIKE TO RUN A FEW MORE TESTS, BUT I'M SURE WE WON'T FIND ANYTHING.
IN FACT, SHE ALMOST HAS TOO MUCH ENERGY...
SHE'S ALWAYS COMPLAINING THAT THE HOSPITAL MEALS ARE TOO SMALL OR THAT IT'S BORING HERE AT NIGHT.
OH, REALLY? SORRY 'BOUT THAT.
YOU MUST BE MRS. PUN-YAMA'S SON!
YOUR MOM WILL BE ABLE TO GO HOME SOON!

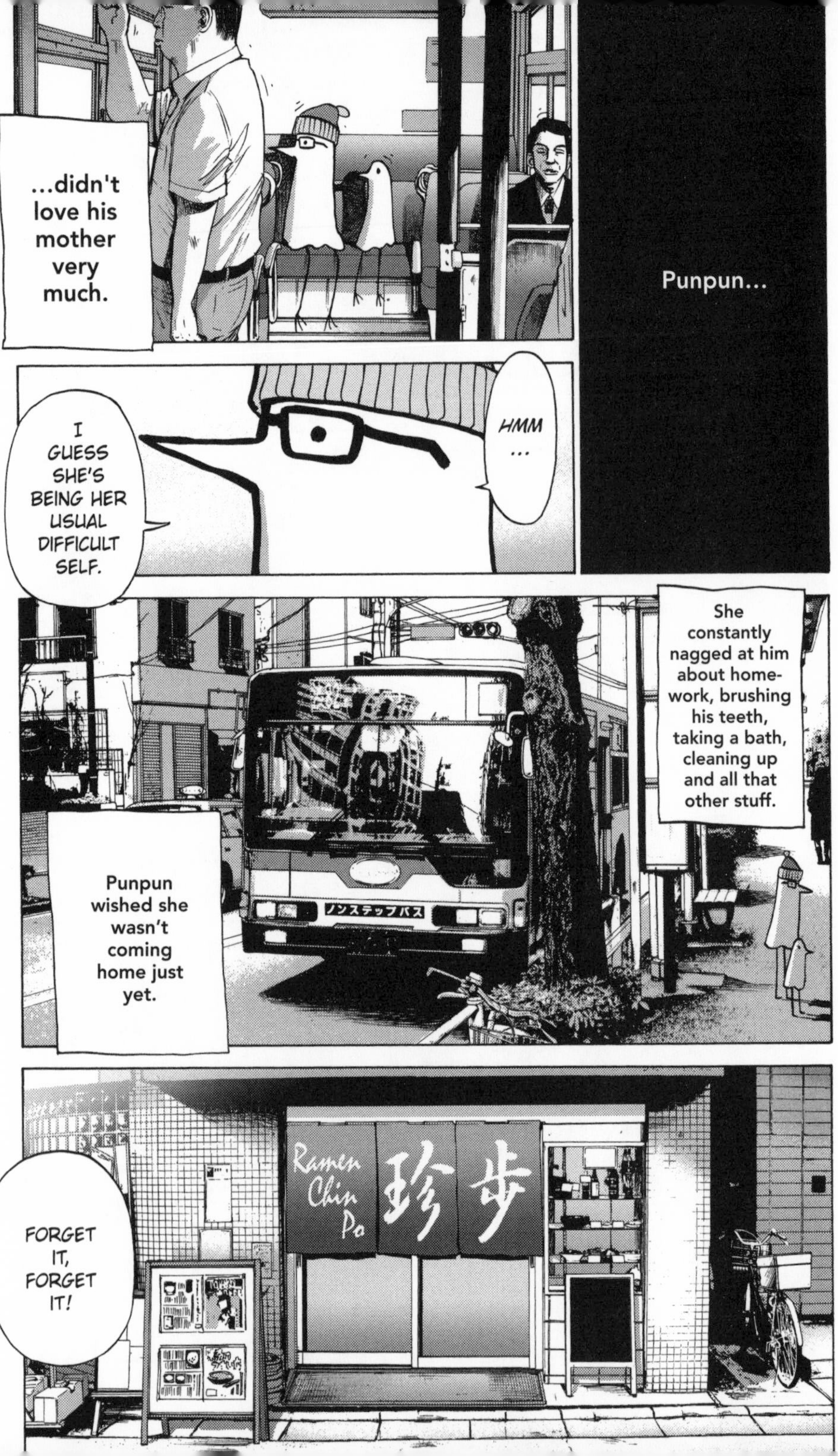
Punpun...
...didn't love his mother very much.
HMM...
I GUESS SHE'S BEING HER USUAL DIFFICULT SELF.
She constantly nagged at him about home-work, brushing his teeth, taking a bath, cleaning up and all that other stuff.
ノンステップバス
Punpun wished she wasn't coming home just yet.
Ramen Chin Po
珍歩
FORGET IT, FORGET IT!

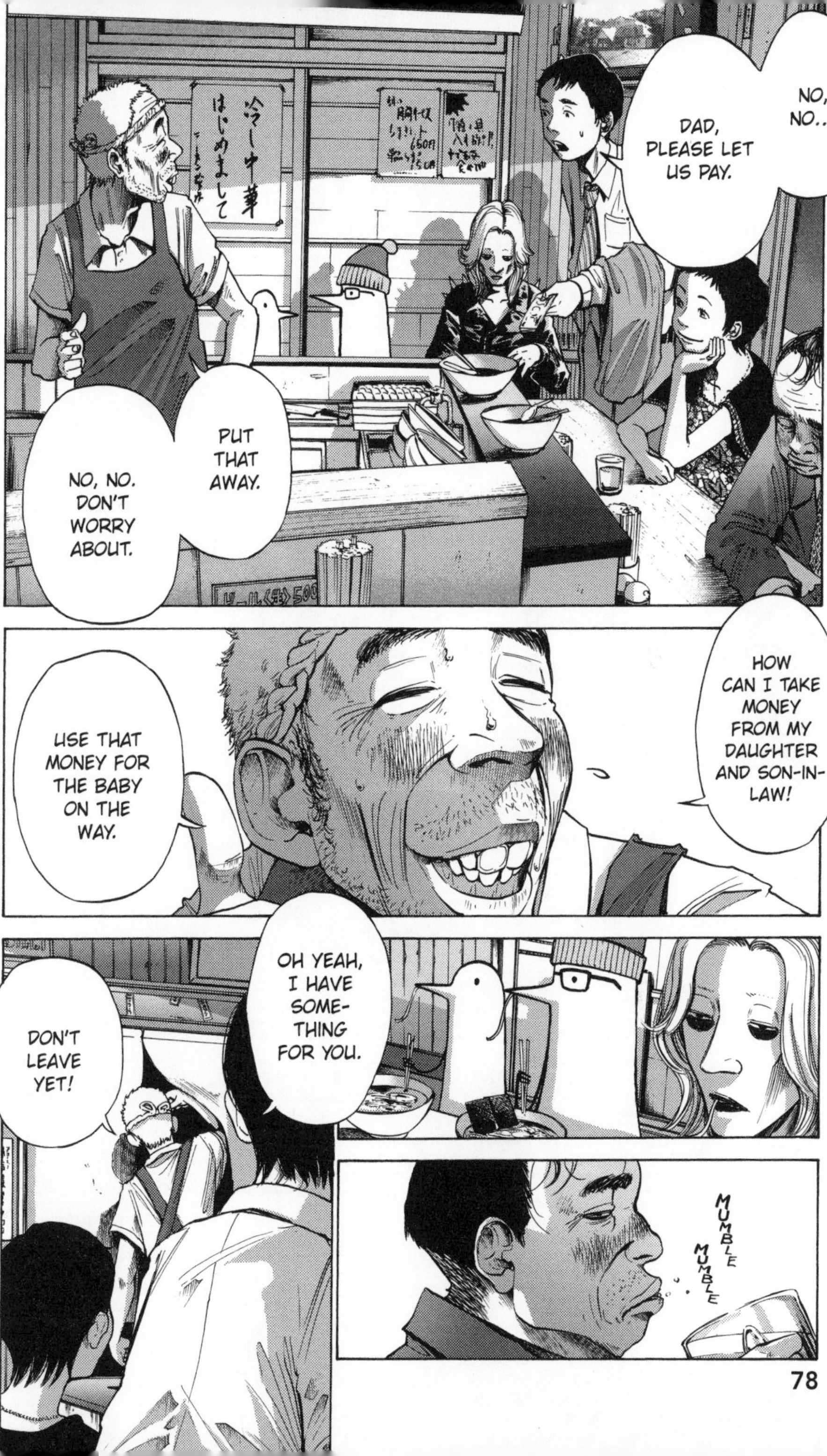
NO, NO...
DAD, PLEASE LET US PAY.
冷し中華
はじめました
PUT THAT AWAY.
NO, NO. DON'T WORRY ABOUT.
HOW CAN I TAKE MONEY FROM MY DAUGHTER AND SON-IN-LAW!
USE THAT MONEY FOR THE BABY ON THE WAY.
MUMBLE
MUMBLE
OH YEAH, I HAVE SOME-THING FOR YOU.
DON'T LEAVE YET!

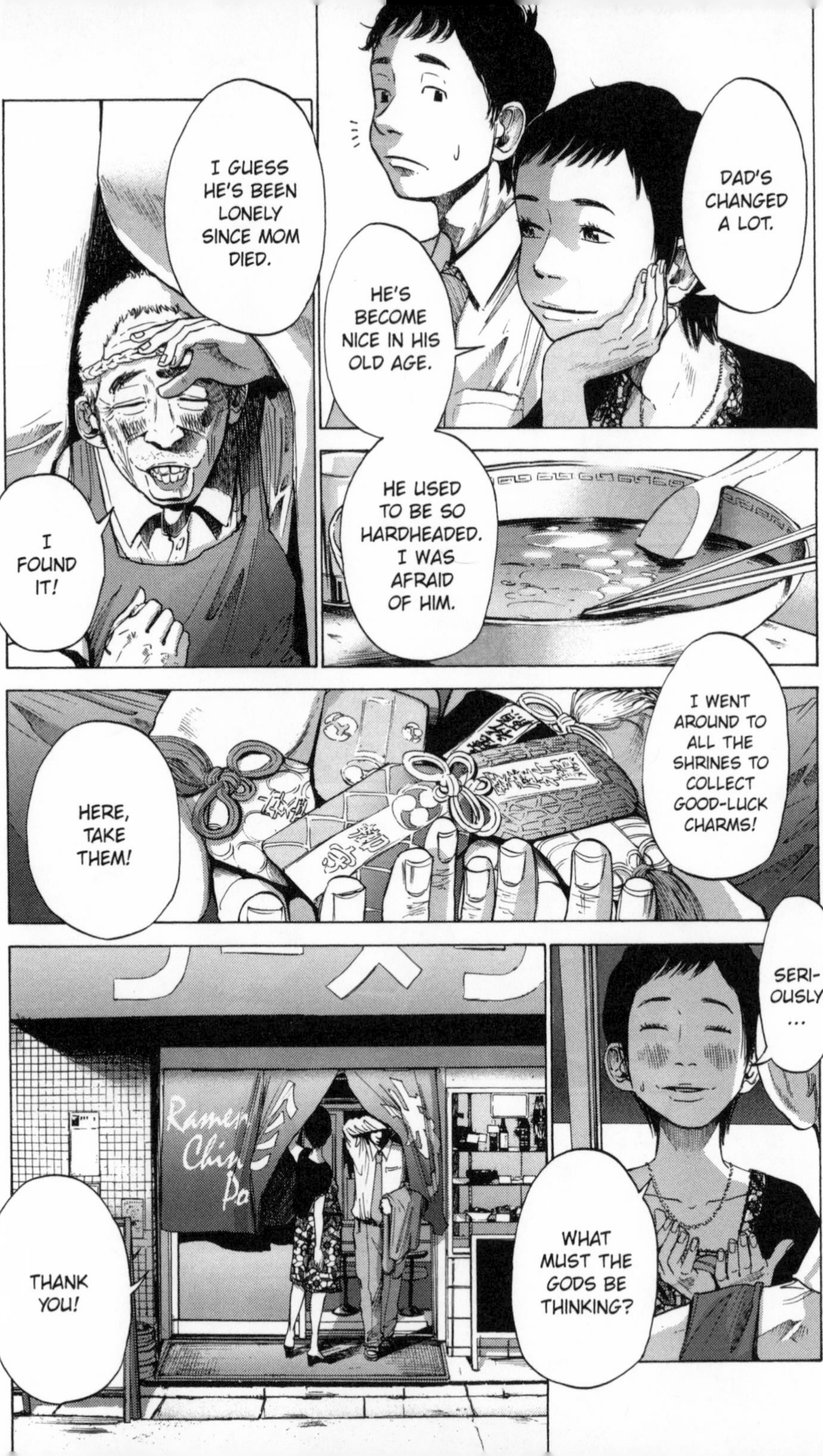
DAD'S CHANGED A LOT.
HE'S BECOME NICE IN HIS OLD AGE.
HE USED TO BE SO HARDHEADED. I WAS AFRAID OF HIM.
I GUESS HE'S BEEN LONELY SINCE MOM DIED.
I FOUND IT!
I WENT AROUND TO ALL THE SHRINES TO COLLECT GOOD-LUCK CHARMS!
HERE, TAKE THEM!
SERI-OUSLY...
WHAT MUST THE GODS BE THINKING?
THANK YOU!
Ramen Chin Po

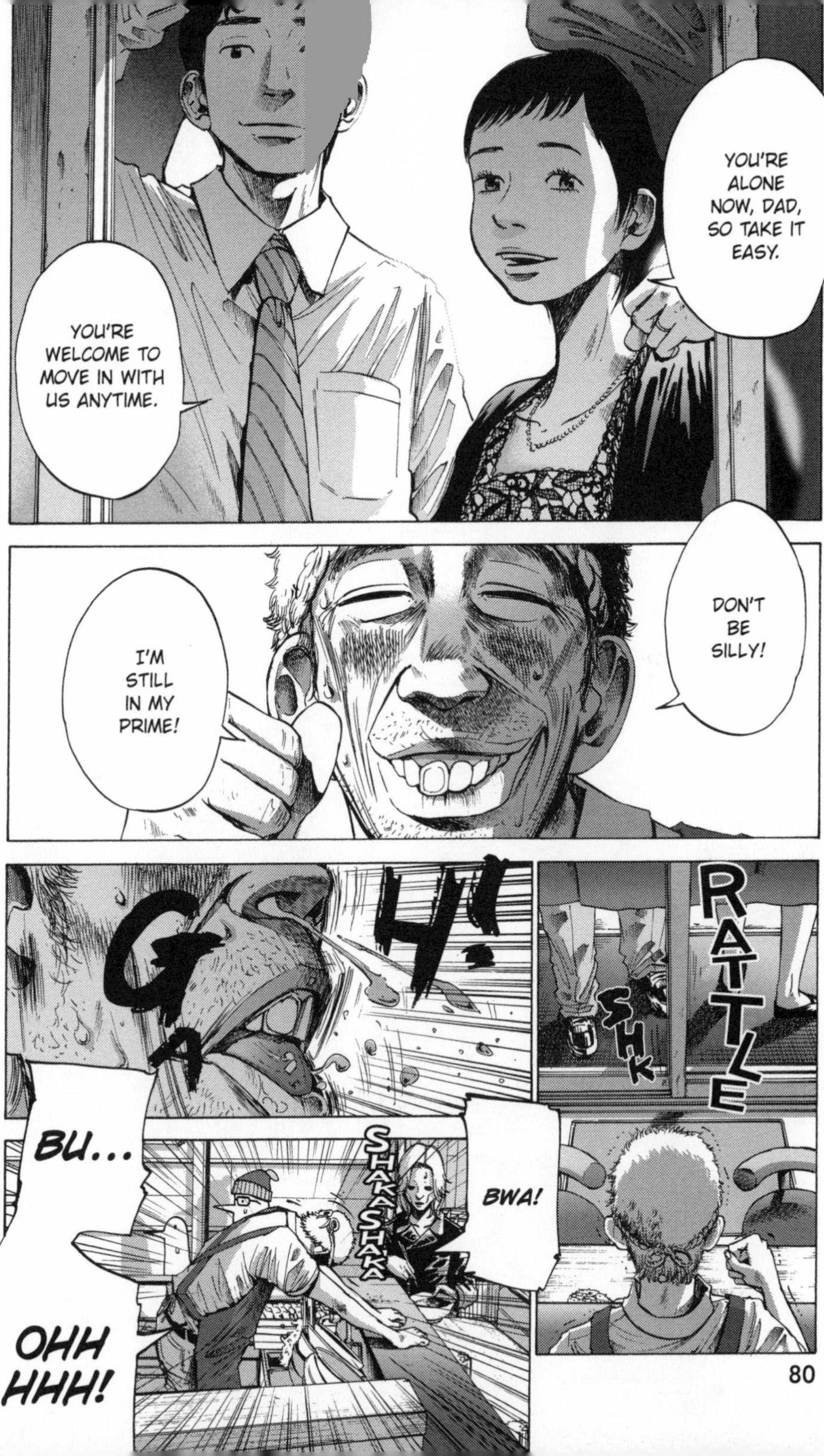
YOU'RE ALONE NOW, DAD, SO TAKE IT EASY.
YOU'RE WELCOME TO MOVE IN WITH US ANYTIME.
DON'T BE SILLY!
I'M STILL IN MY PRIME!
RATTLE
SHK
GAH!
BU...
BWA!
SHAKASHAKA
OHH HHH!

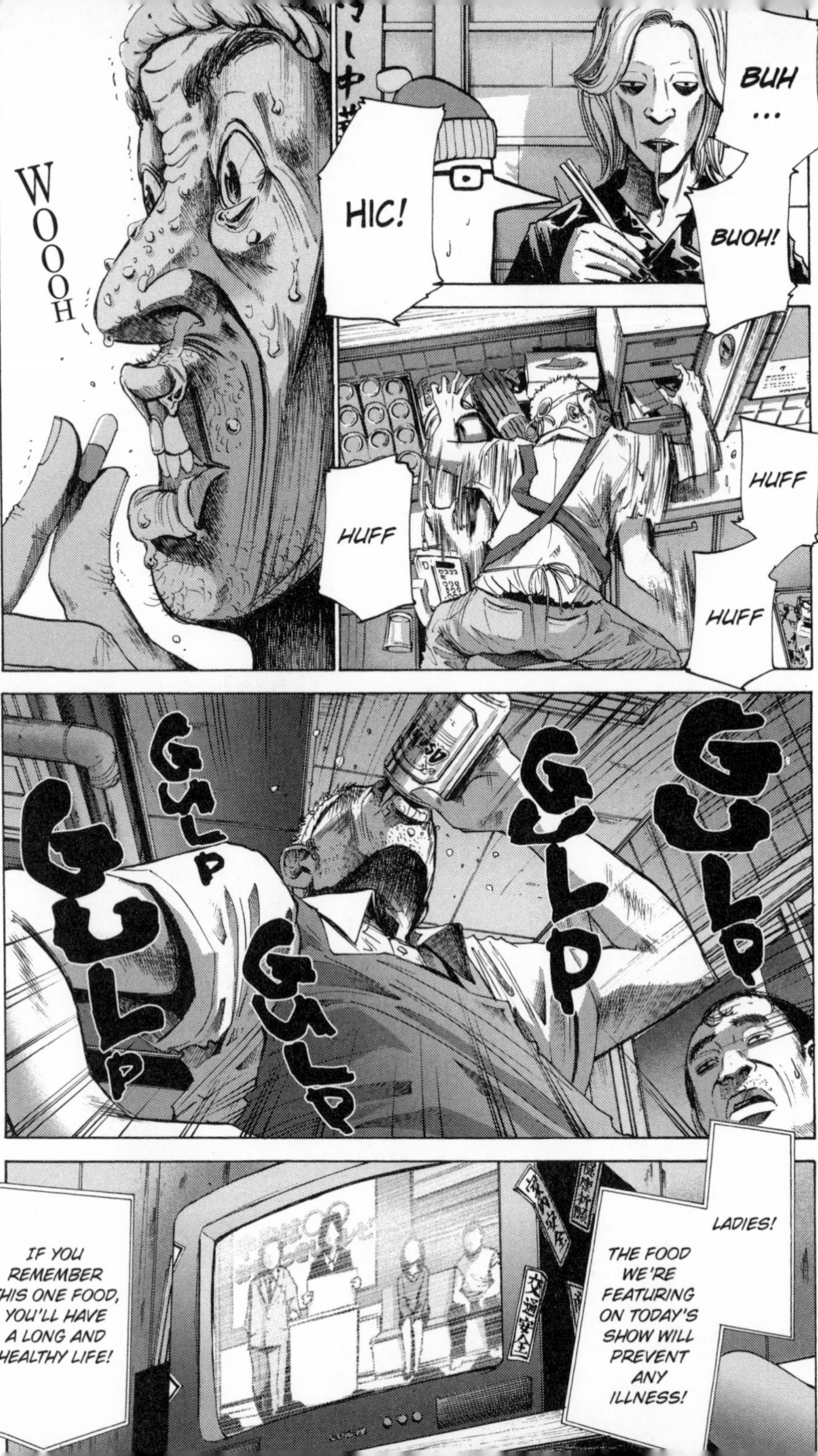
BUH ...
HIC!
BUOH!
HUFF
HUFF
HUFF
WOOOOH
GULP
GULP
GULP
GULP
GULP
LADIES!
THE FOOD WE'RE FEATURING ON TODAY'S SHOW WILL PREVENT ANY ILLNESS!
IF YOU REMEMBER THIS ONE FOOD, YOU'LL HAVE A LONG AND HEALTHY LIFE!

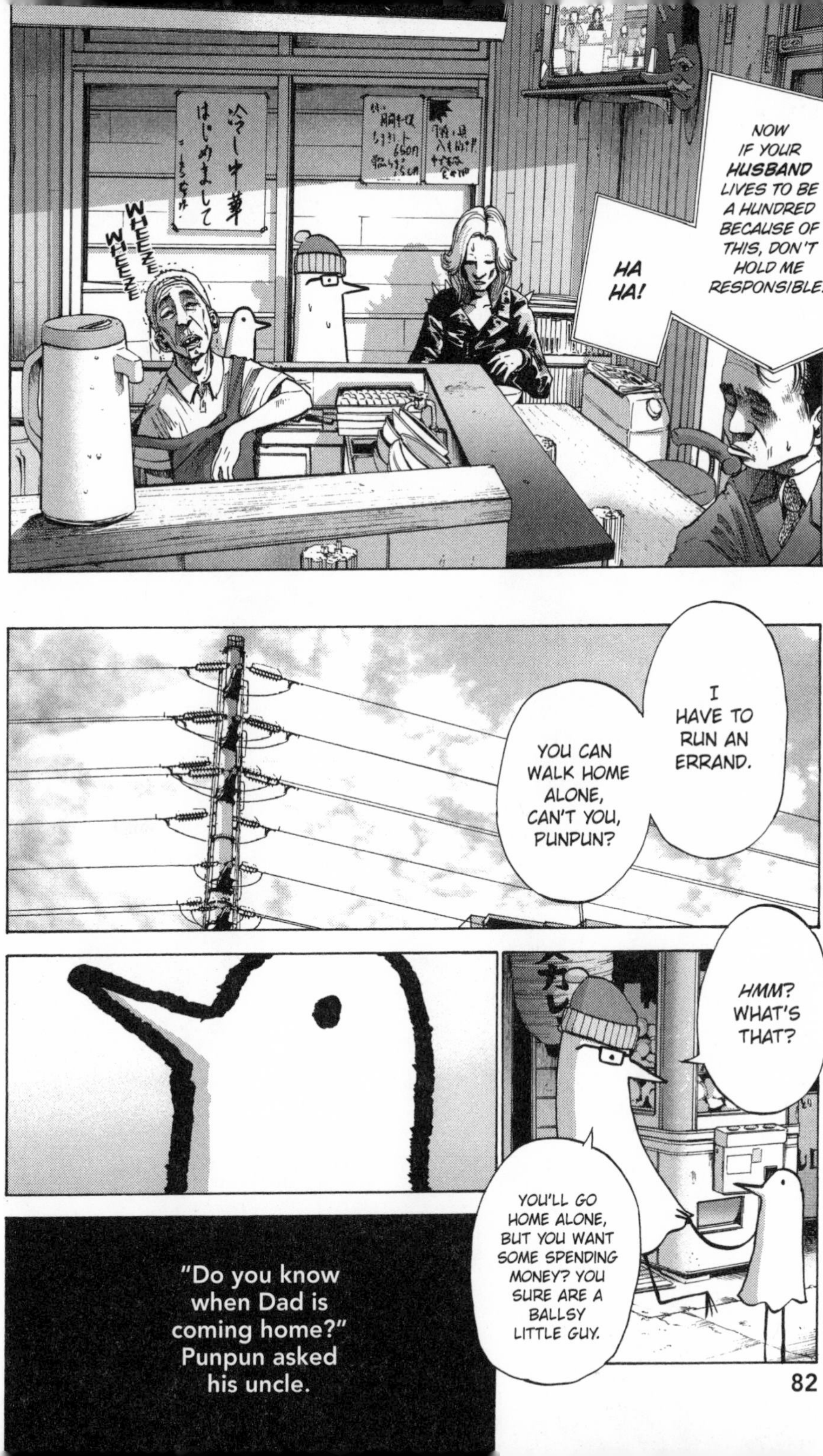
NOW IF YOUR **HUSBAND** LIVES TO BE A HUNDRED BECAUSE OF THIS, DON'T HOLD ME RESPONSIBLE!
HA HA!
冷し中華
はじめました
WHEEZE
WHEEZE
I HAVE TO RUN AN ERRAND.
YOU CAN WALK HOME ALONE, CAN'T YOU, PUNPUN?
HMM? WHAT'S THAT?
YOU'LL GO HOME ALONE, BUT YOU WANT SOME SPENDING MONEY? YOU SURE ARE A BALLSY LITTLE GUY.
"Do you know when Dad is coming home?" Punpun asked his uncle.

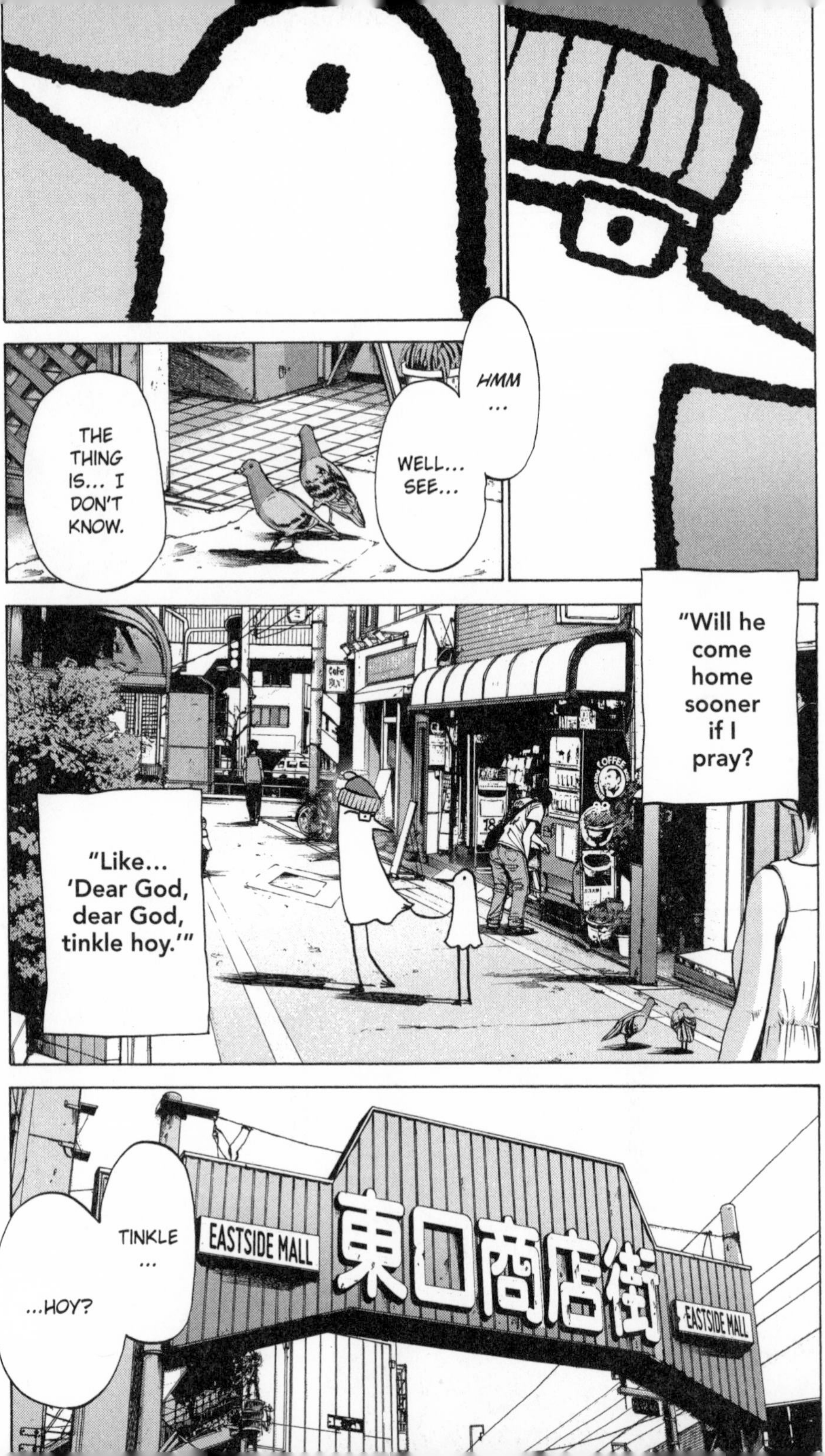
HMM... WELL... SEE...
THE THING IS... I DON'T KNOW.
"Will he come home sooner if I pray?
"Like... 'Dear God, dear God, tinkle hoy.'"
EASTSIDE MALL
東口商店街
EASTSIDE MALL
TINKLE... ...HOY?

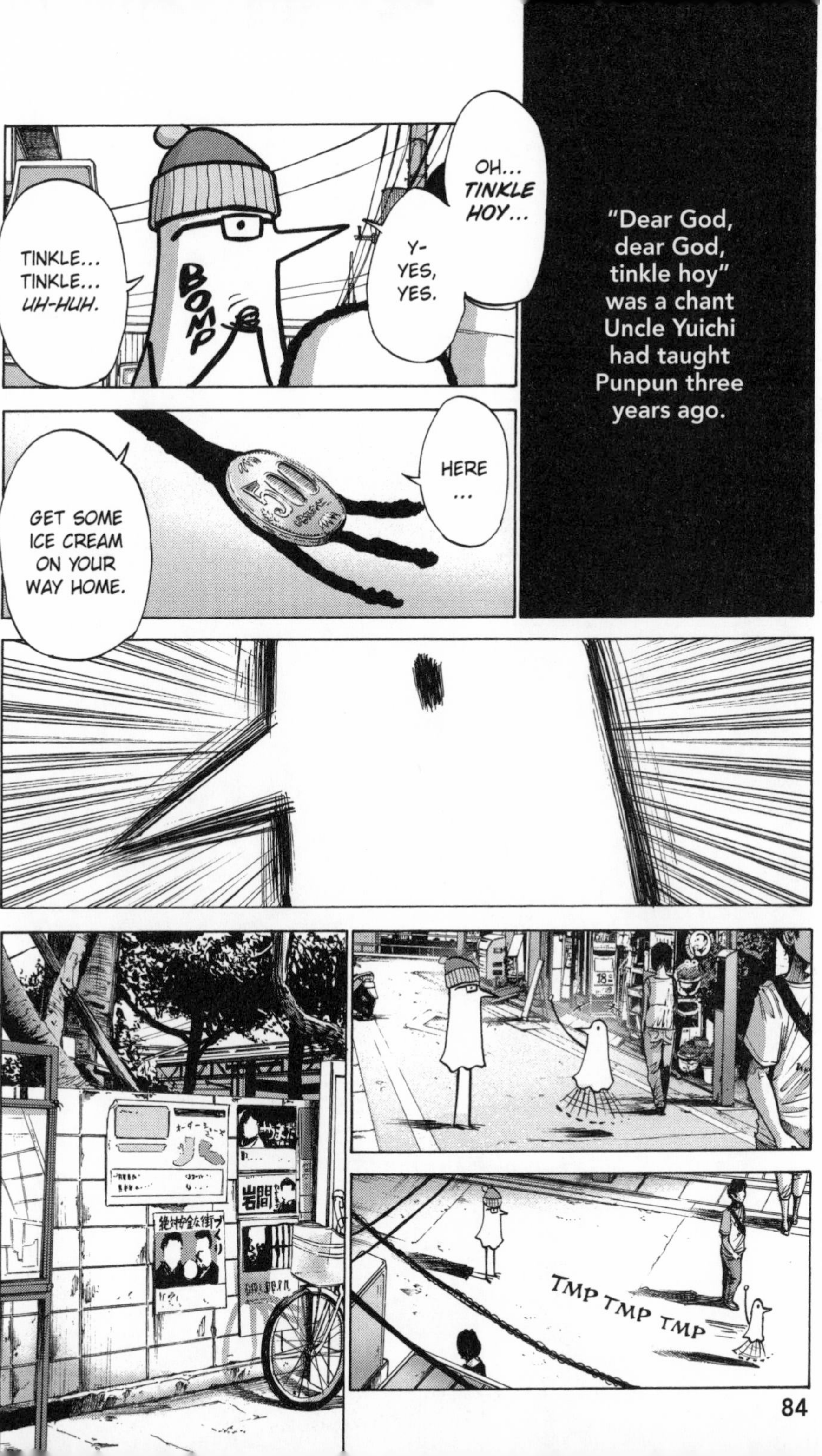
"Dear God, dear God, tinkle hoy" was a chant Uncle Yuichi had taught Punpun three years ago.
OH... TINKLE HOY...
Y-YES, YES.
BOMP
TINKLE... TINKLE... UH-HUH.
HERE...
GET SOME ICE CREAM ON YOUR WAY HOME.
TMP TMP TMP

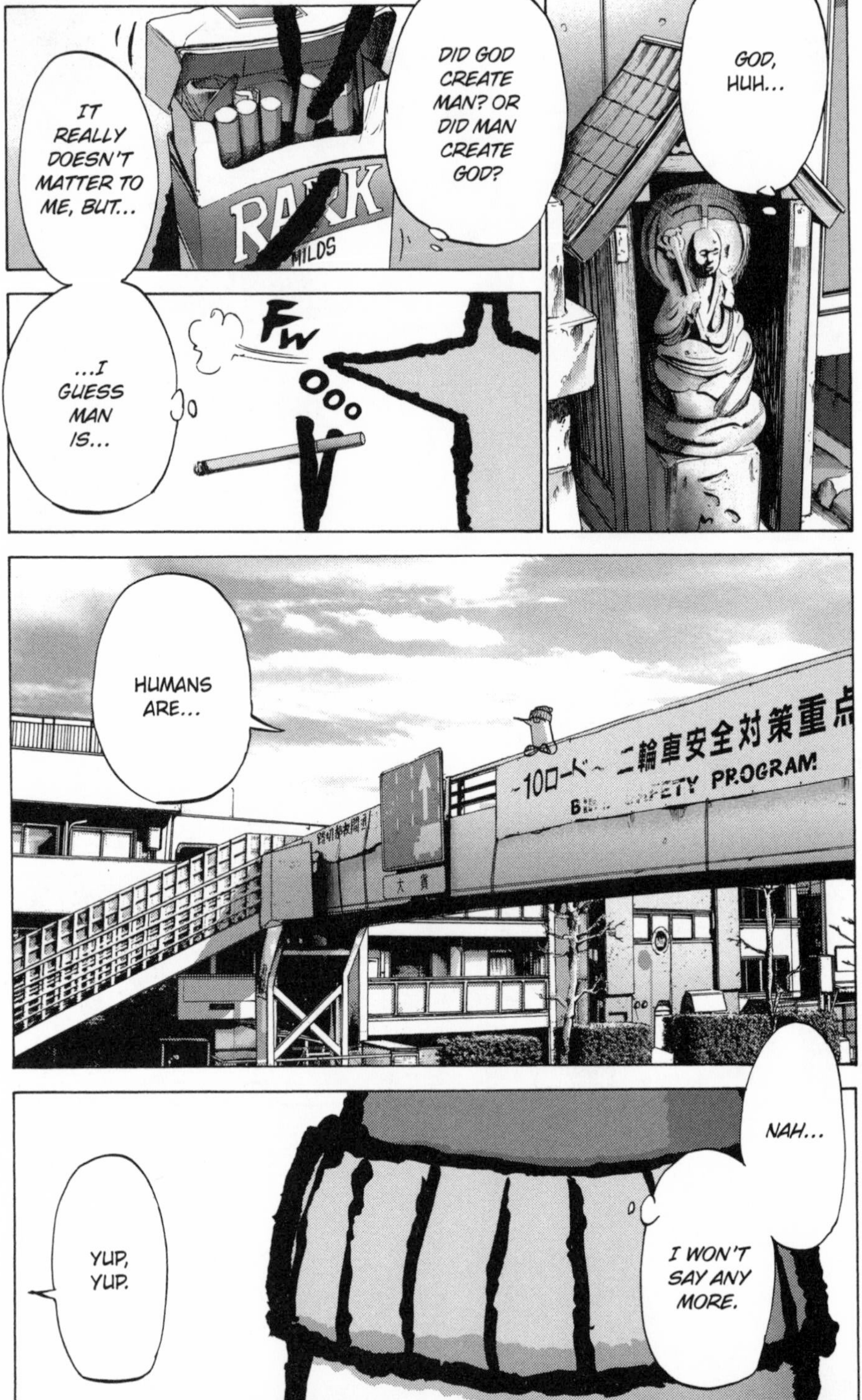
GOD, HUH...
DID GOD CREATE MAN? OR DID MAN CREATE GOD?
IT REALLY DOESN'T MATTER TO ME, BUT...
RARK
MILDS
...I GUESS MAN IS...
FWOOO
HUMANS ARE...
二輪車安全対策重点
PROGRAM
NAH...
I WON'T SAY ANY MORE.
YUP, YUP.

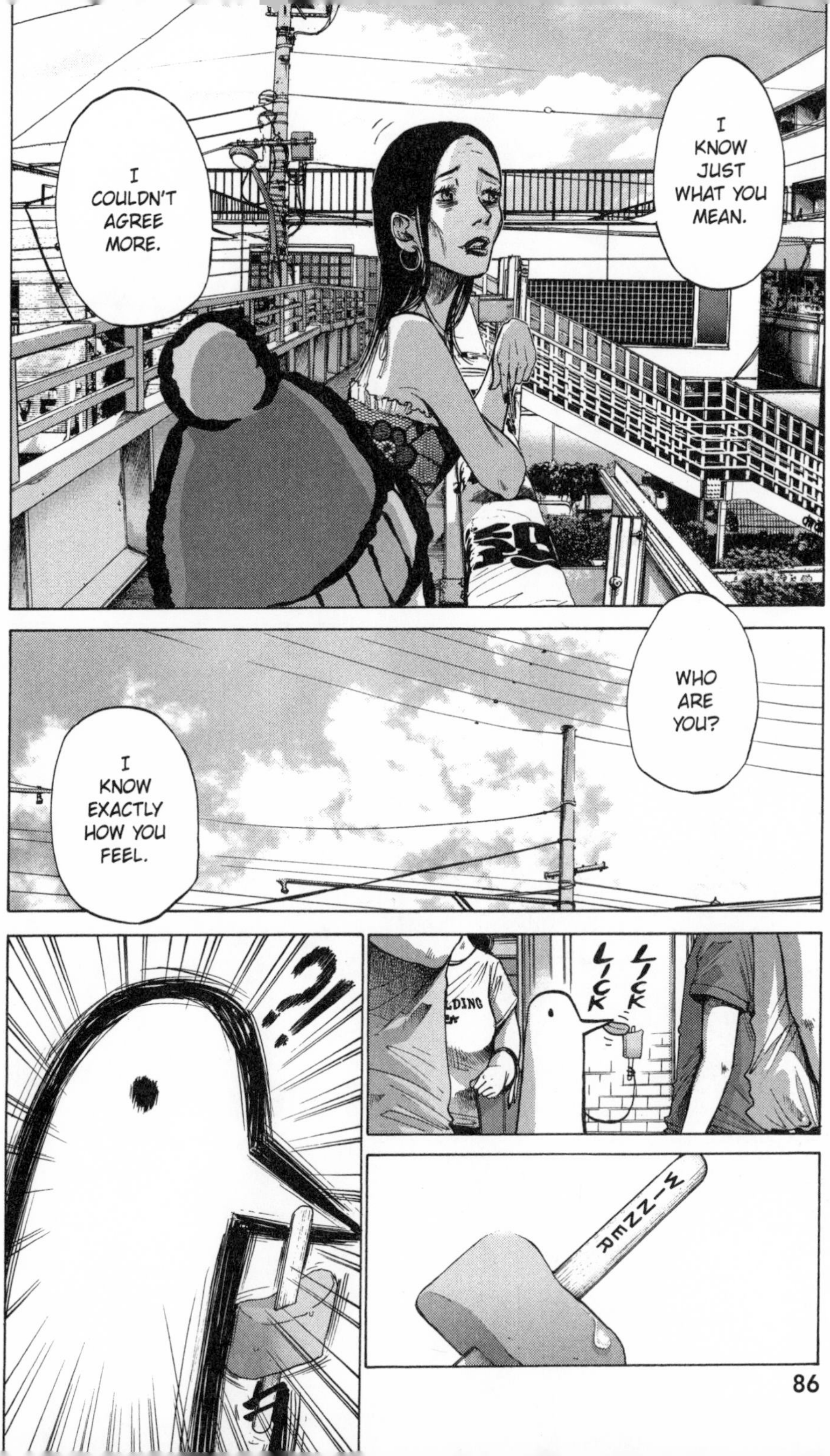
I KNOW JUST WHAT YOU MEAN.
I COULDN'T AGREE MORE.
WHO ARE YOU?
I KNOW EXACTLY HOW YOU FEEL.
LICK LICK
!?

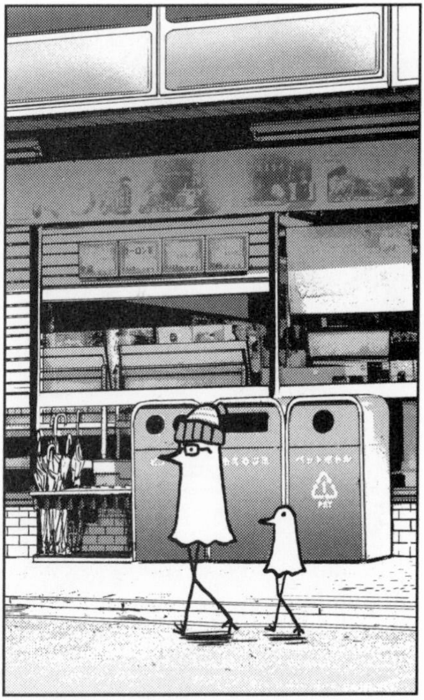
ペットボトル

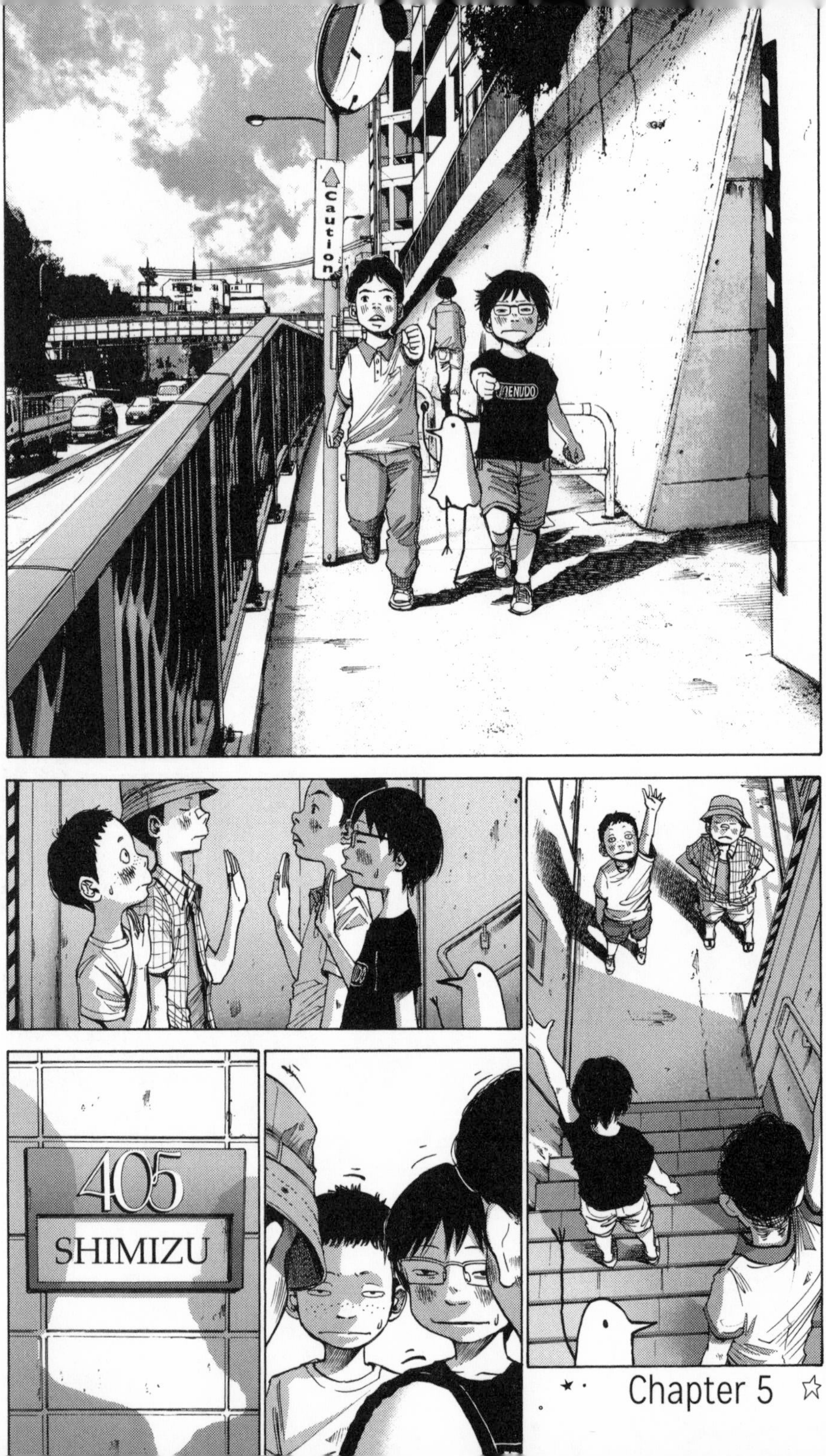
Caution
MENUDO
405
SHIMIZU

Chapter 5

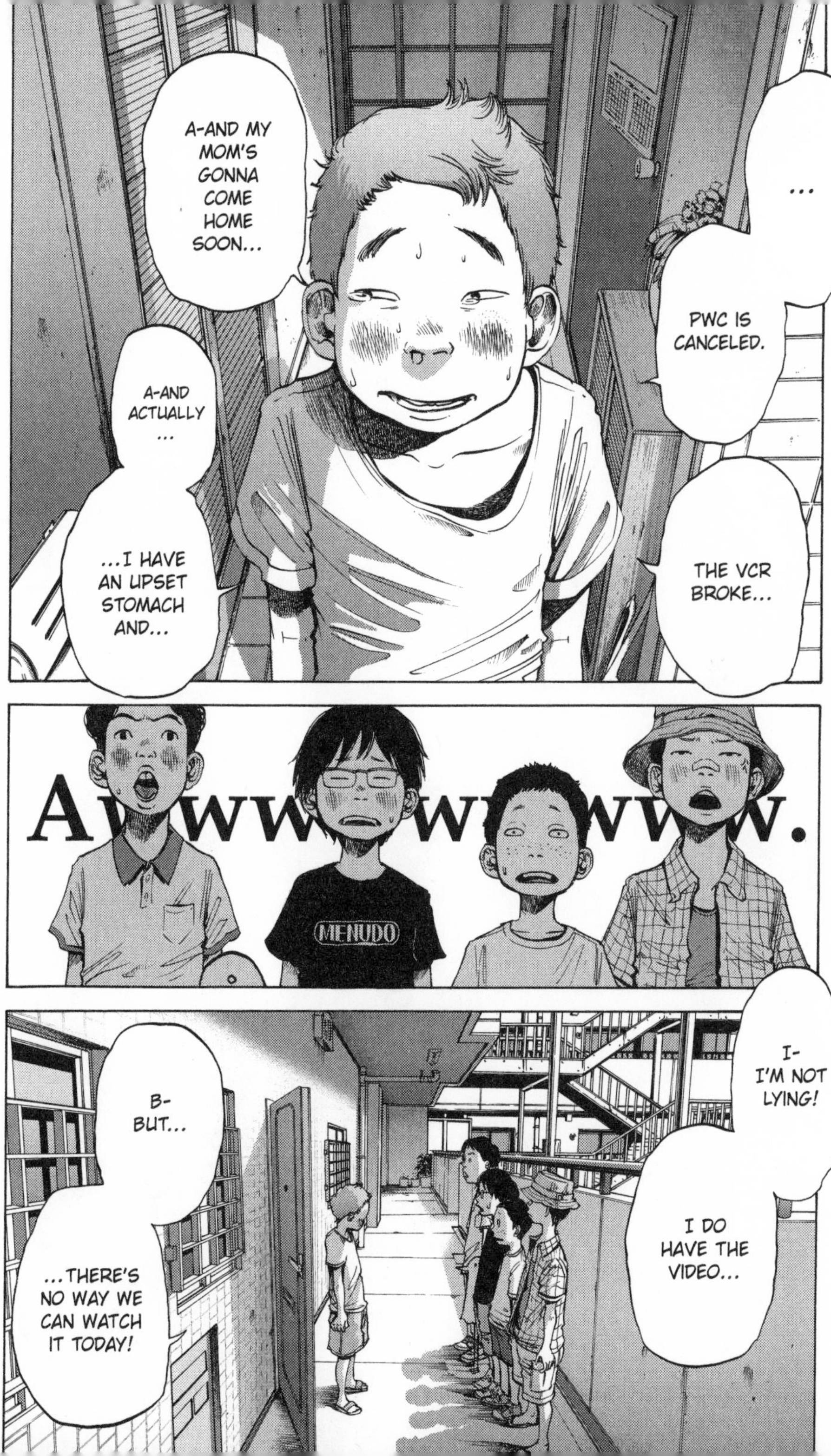
...
PWC IS CANCELED.
THE VCR BROKE...
A-AND MY MOM'S GONNA COME HOME SOON...
A-AND ACTUALLY ...
...I HAVE AN UPSET STOMACH AND...
Awwwwwww.
MENUDO
I- I'M NOT LYING!
I DO HAVE THE VIDEO...
B- BUT...
...THERE'S NO WAY WE CAN WATCH IT TODAY!

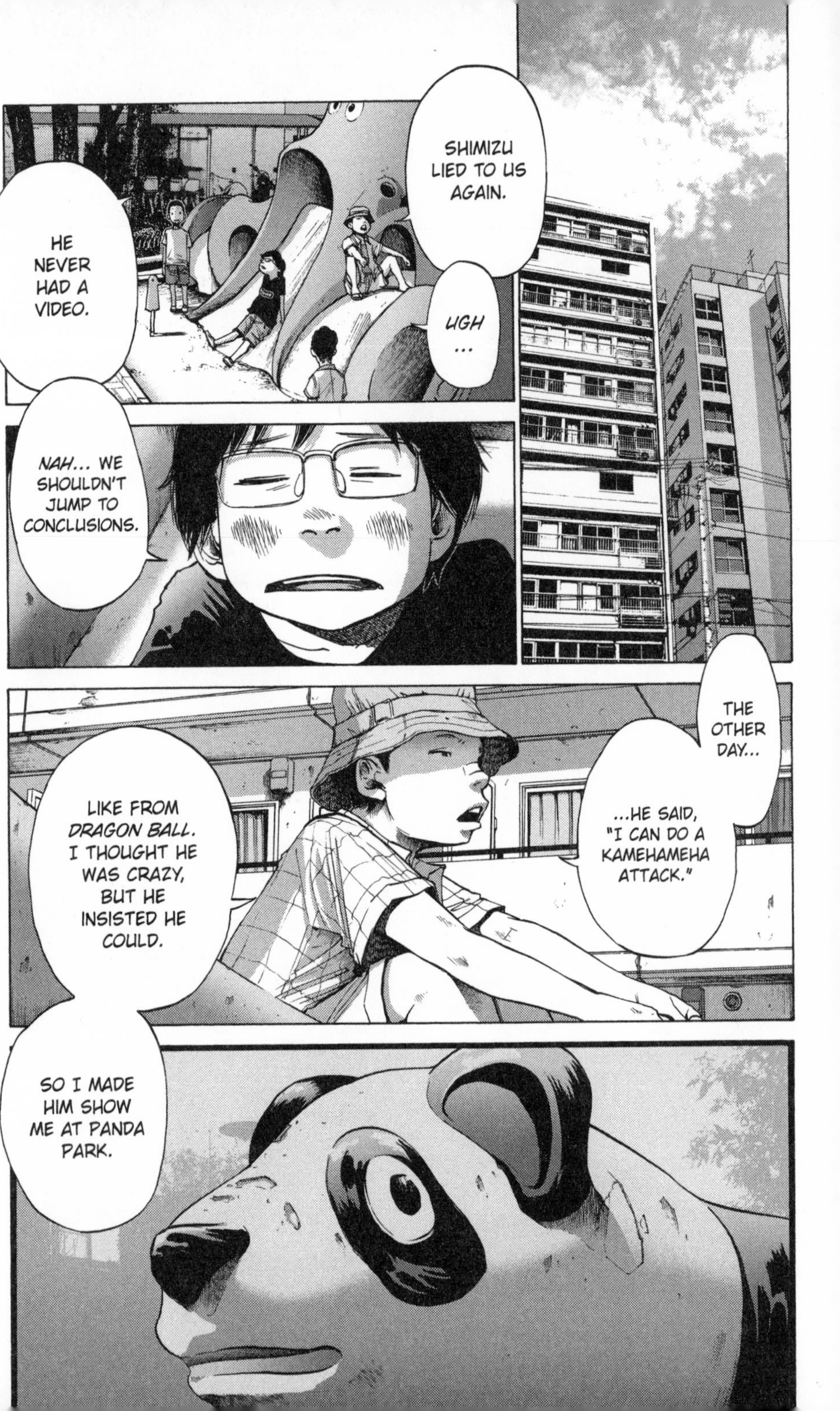
SHIMIZU LIED TO US AGAIN.
HE NEVER HAD A VIDEO.
UGH ...
NAH... WE SHOULDN'T JUMP TO CONCLUSIONS.
THE OTHER DAY...
...HE SAID, "I CAN DO A KAMEHAMEHA ATTACK."
LIKE FROM *DRAGON BALL*. I THOUGHT HE WAS CRAZY, BUT HE INSISTED HE COULD.
SO I MADE HIM SHOW ME AT PANDA PARK.

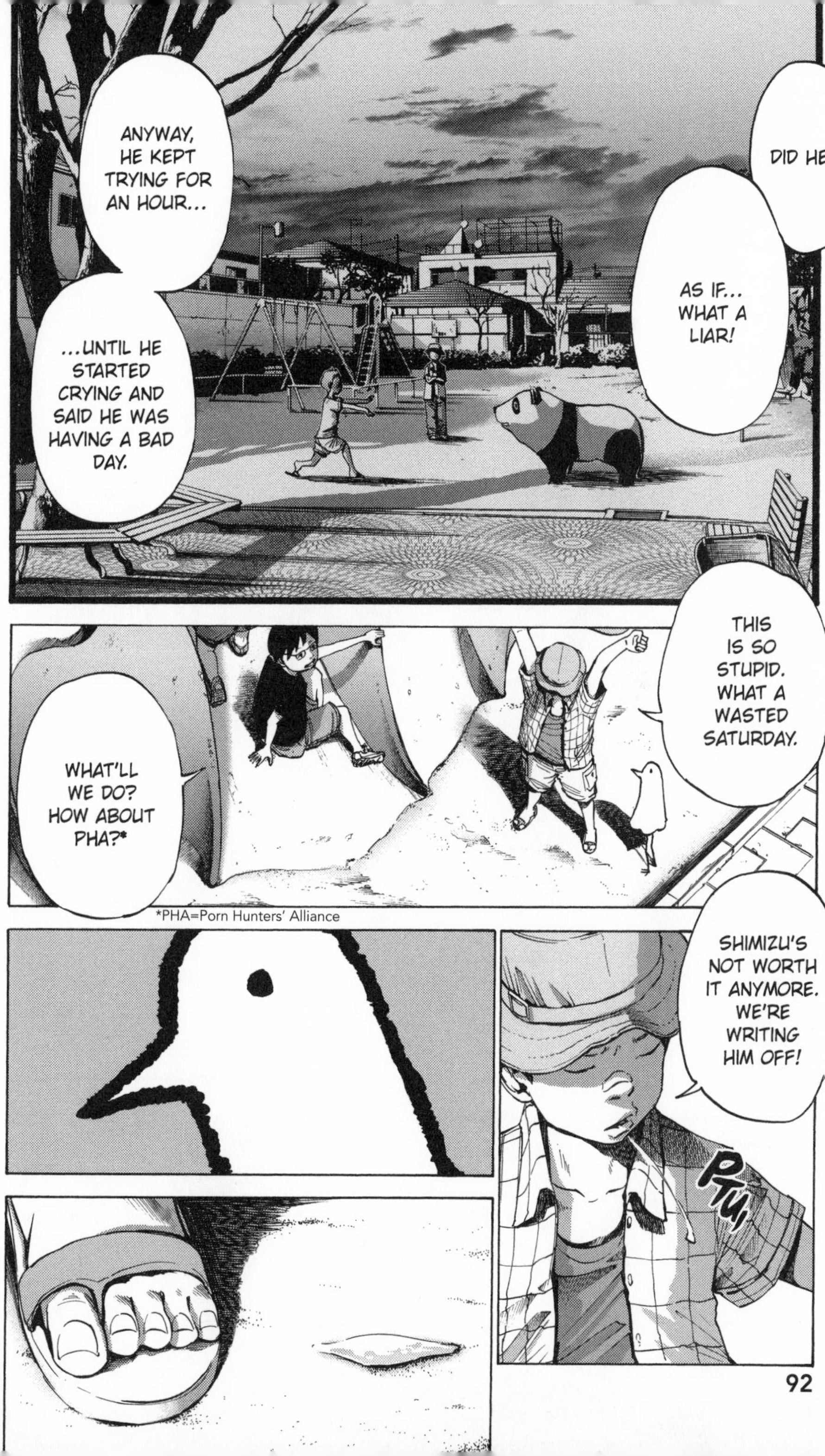
ANYWAY, HE KEPT TRYING FOR AN HOUR...
...UNTIL HE STARTED CRYING AND SAID HE WAS HAVING A BAD DAY.
DID HE?!
AS IF... WHAT A LIAR!
THIS IS SO STUPID. WHAT A WASTED SATURDAY.
WHAT'LL WE DO? HOW ABOUT PHA?*
SHIMIZU'S NOT WORTH IT ANYMORE. WE'RE WRITING HIM OFF!
PTUI

*PHA=Porn Hunters' Alliance

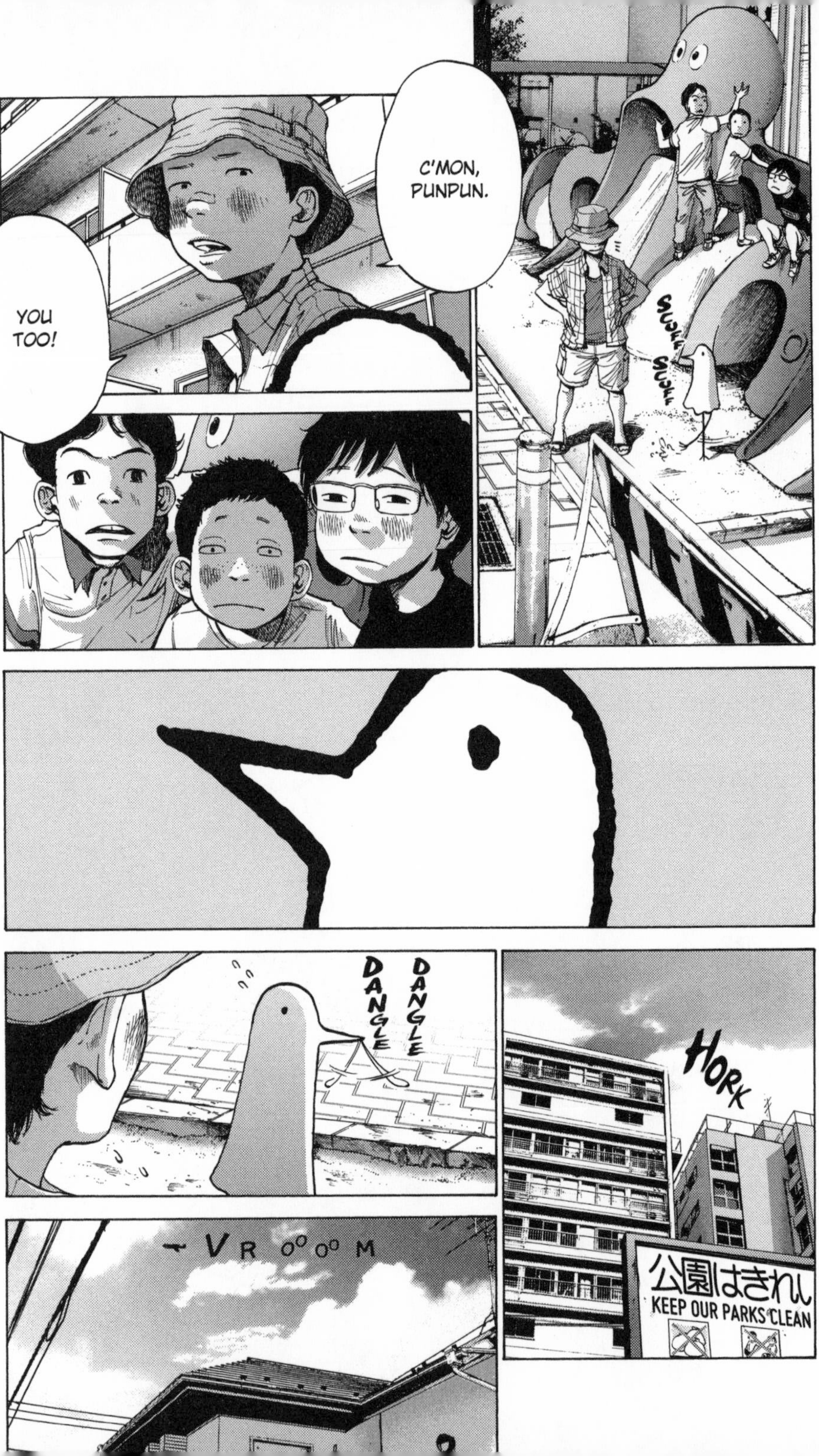

SCUFF SCUFF
C'MON, PUNPUN.
YOU TOO!
HORK
公園はきれい
KEEP OUR PARKS CLEAN
DANGLE DANGLE
VROOOM

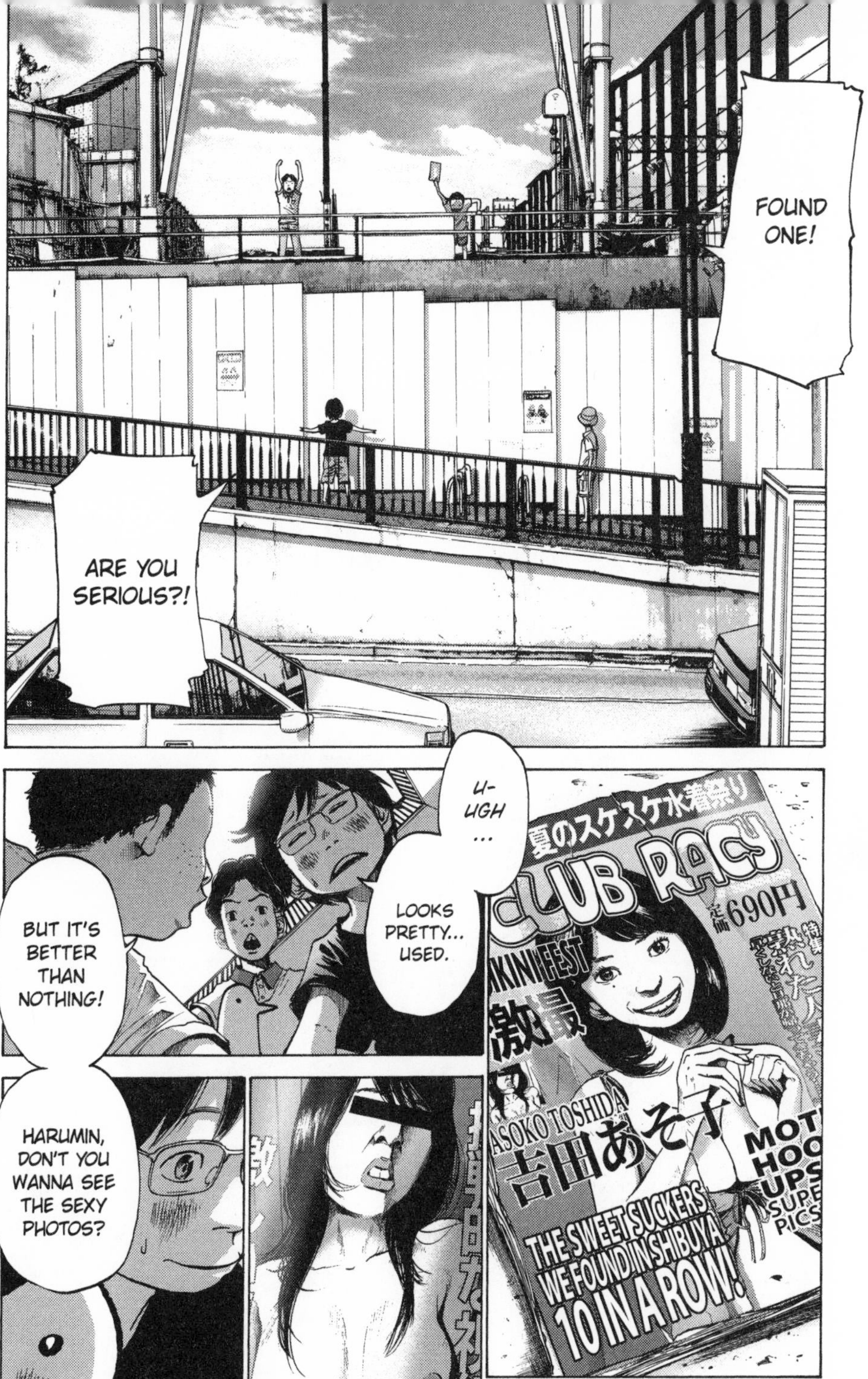
FOUND ONE!
ARE YOU SERIOUS?!
夏のスケスケ水着祭り
CLUB RACY
定価690円
KINI FEST
激撮
ASOKO TOSHIDA
吉田あそ子
THE SWEET SUCKERS WE FOUND IN SHIBUYA 10 IN A ROW!
U-UGH...
LOOKS PRETTY... USED.
BUT IT'S BETTER THAN NOTHING!
HARUMIN, DON'T YOU WANNA SEE THE SEXY PHOTOS?

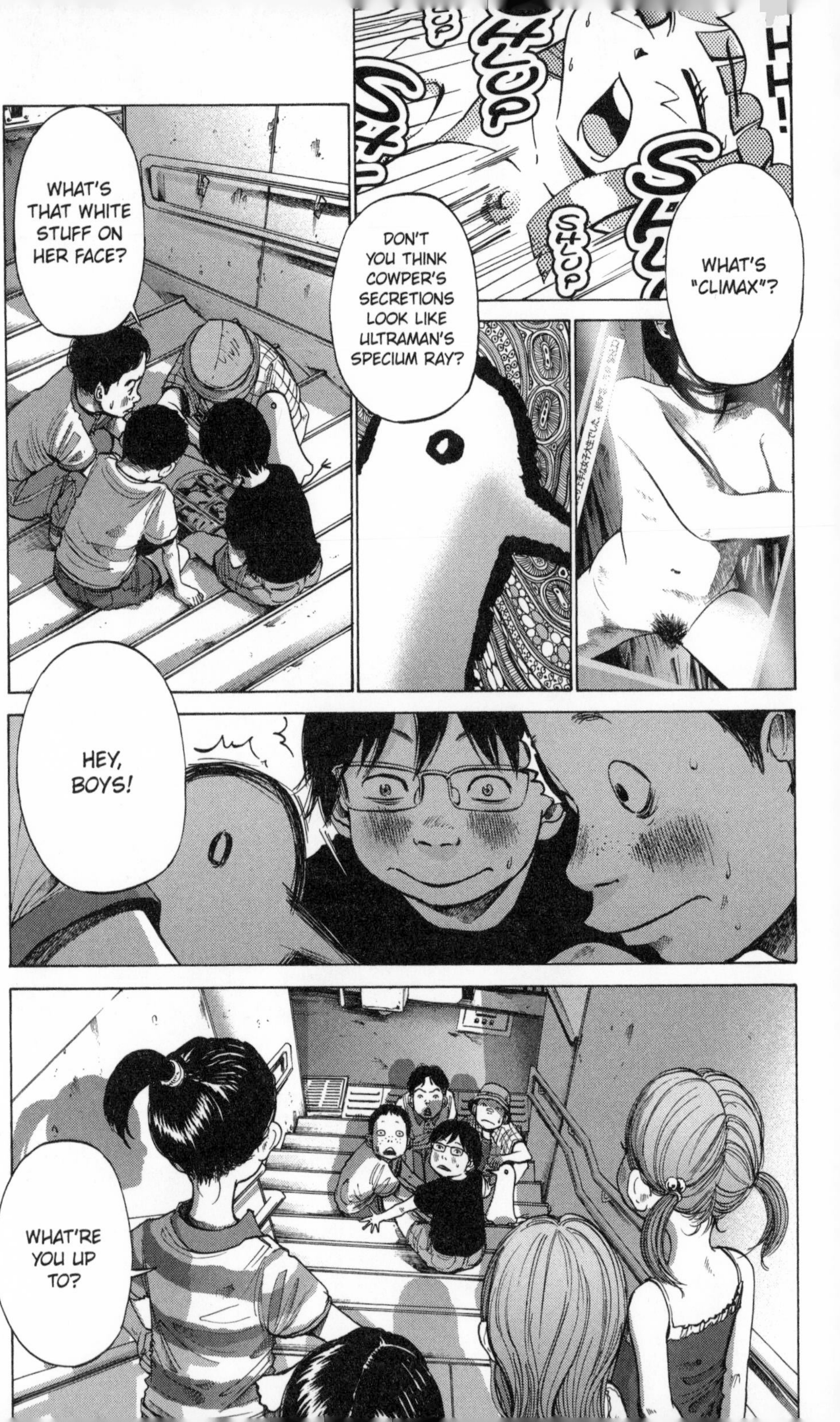

HH!!
SHLUP
SHLUP
SHLUP
WHAT'S "CLIMAX"?
DON'T YOU THINK COWPER'S SECRETIONS LOOK LIKE ULTRAMAN'S SPECIUM RAY?
WHAT'S THAT WHITE STUFF ON HER FACE?
HEY, BOYS!
WHAT'RE YOU UP TO?

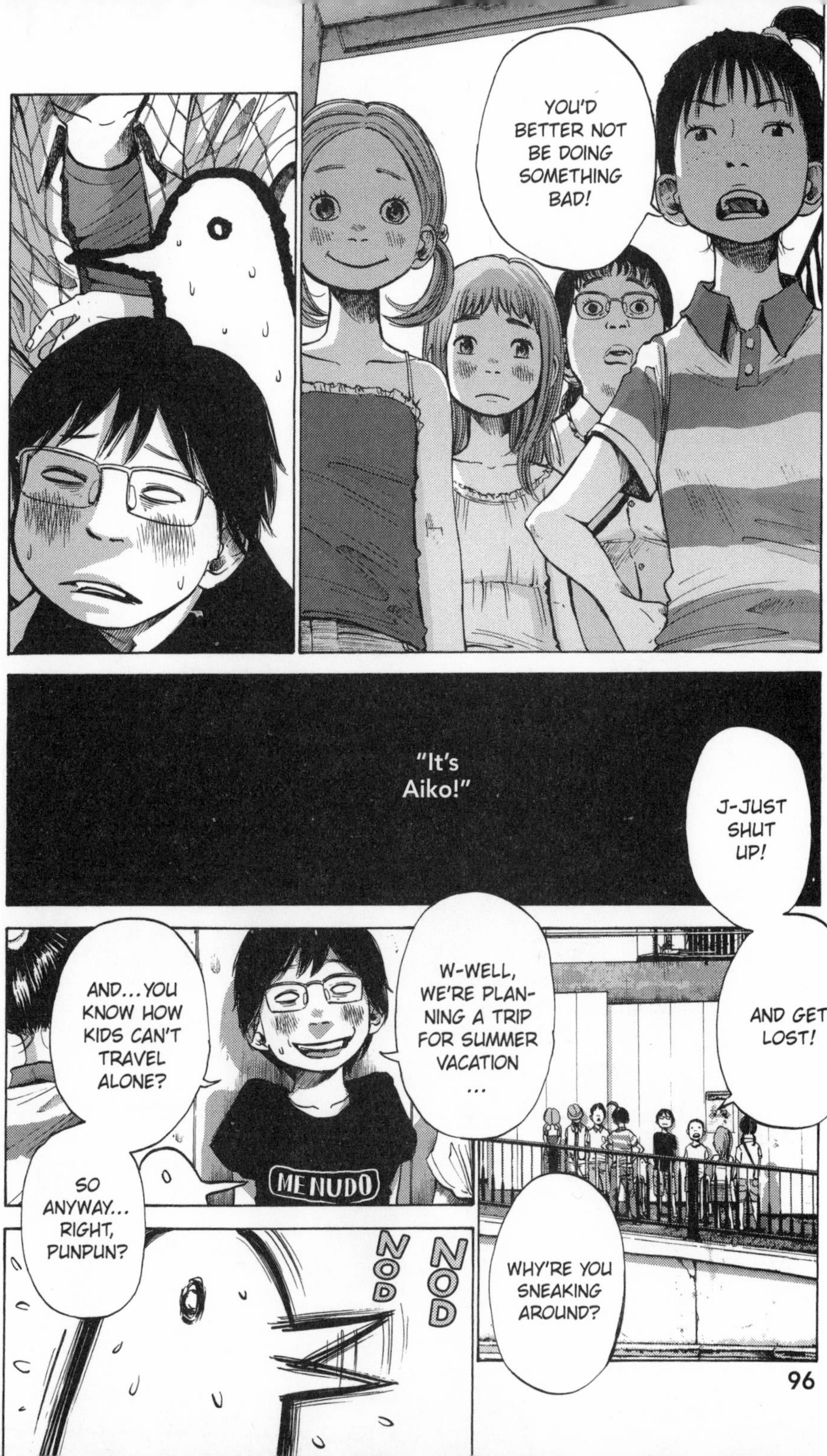
YOU'D BETTER NOT BE DOING SOMETHING BAD!
"It's Aiko!"
J-JUST SHUT UP!
AND GET LOST!
WHY'RE YOU SNEAKING AROUND?
W-WELL, WE'RE PLAN-NING A TRIP FOR SUMMER VACATION ...
AND... YOU KNOW HOW KIDS CAN'T TRAVEL ALONE?
MENUDO
SO ANYWAY... RIGHT, PUNPUN?
NOD NOD

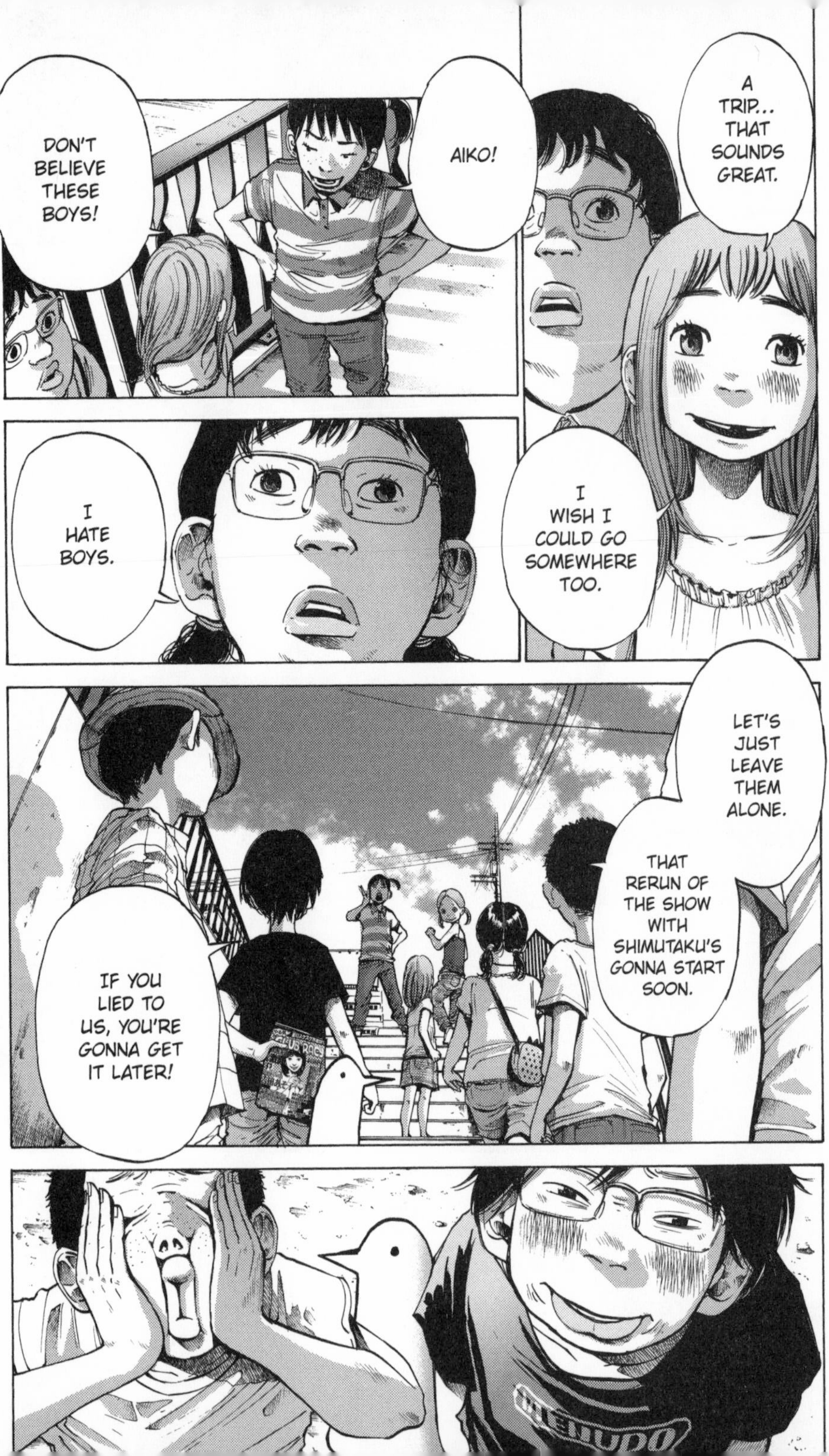
A TRIP... THAT SOUNDS GREAT.
I WISH I COULD GO SOMEWHERE TOO.
AIKO!
DON'T BELIEVE THESE BOYS!
I HATE BOYS.
LET'S JUST LEAVE THEM ALONE.
THAT RERUN OF THE SHOW WITH SHIMUTAKU'S GONNA START SOON.
IF YOU LIED TO US, YOU'RE GONNA GET IT LATER!

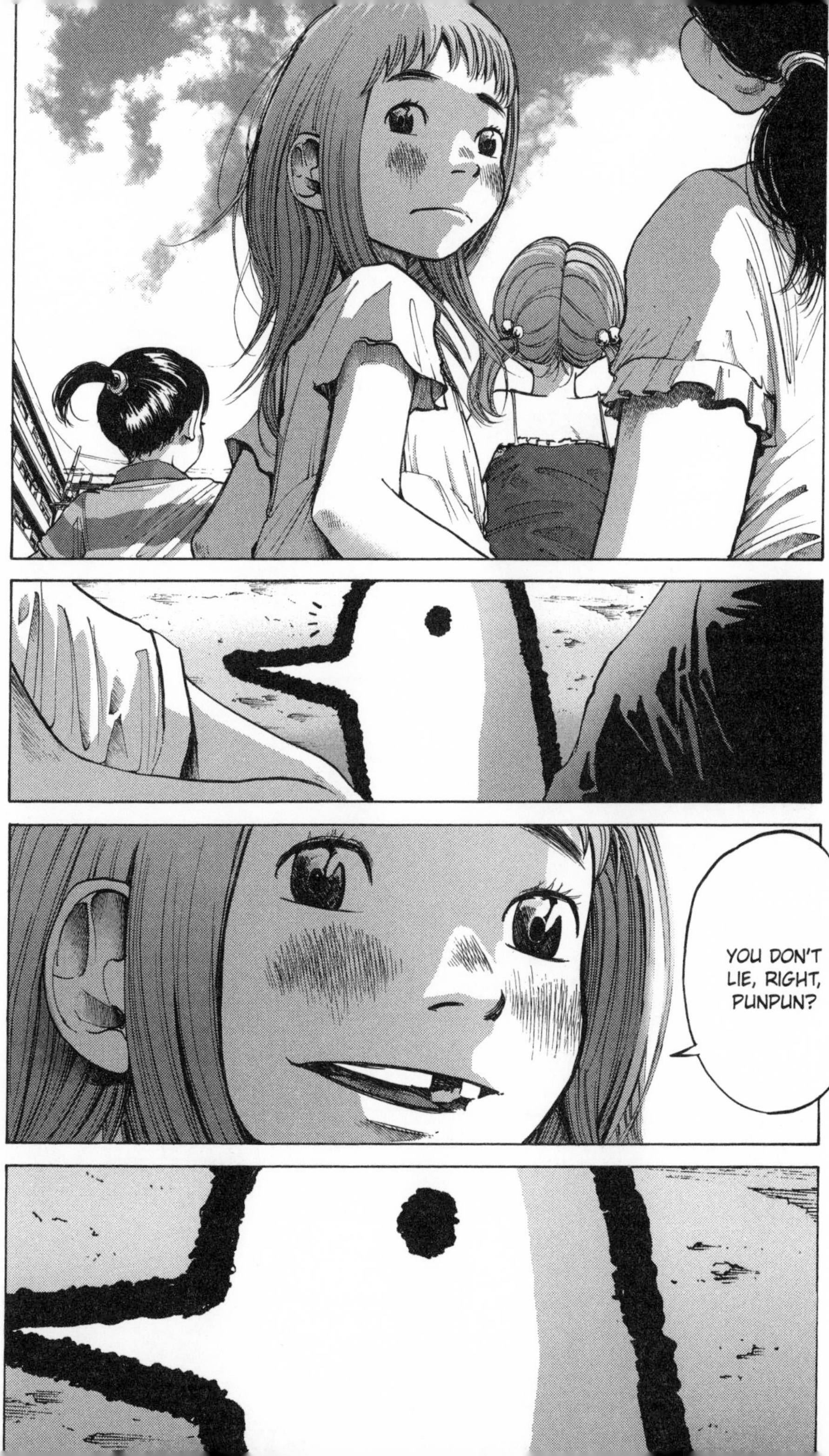
YOU DON'T LIE, RIGHT, PUNPUN?

COWPER'S SECRETIONS!

CLIMAX RAYS!

TMP TMP TMP

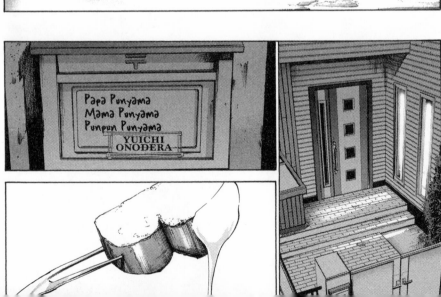

Papa Punyama
Mama Punyama
Punpun Punyama
YUICHI ONODERA

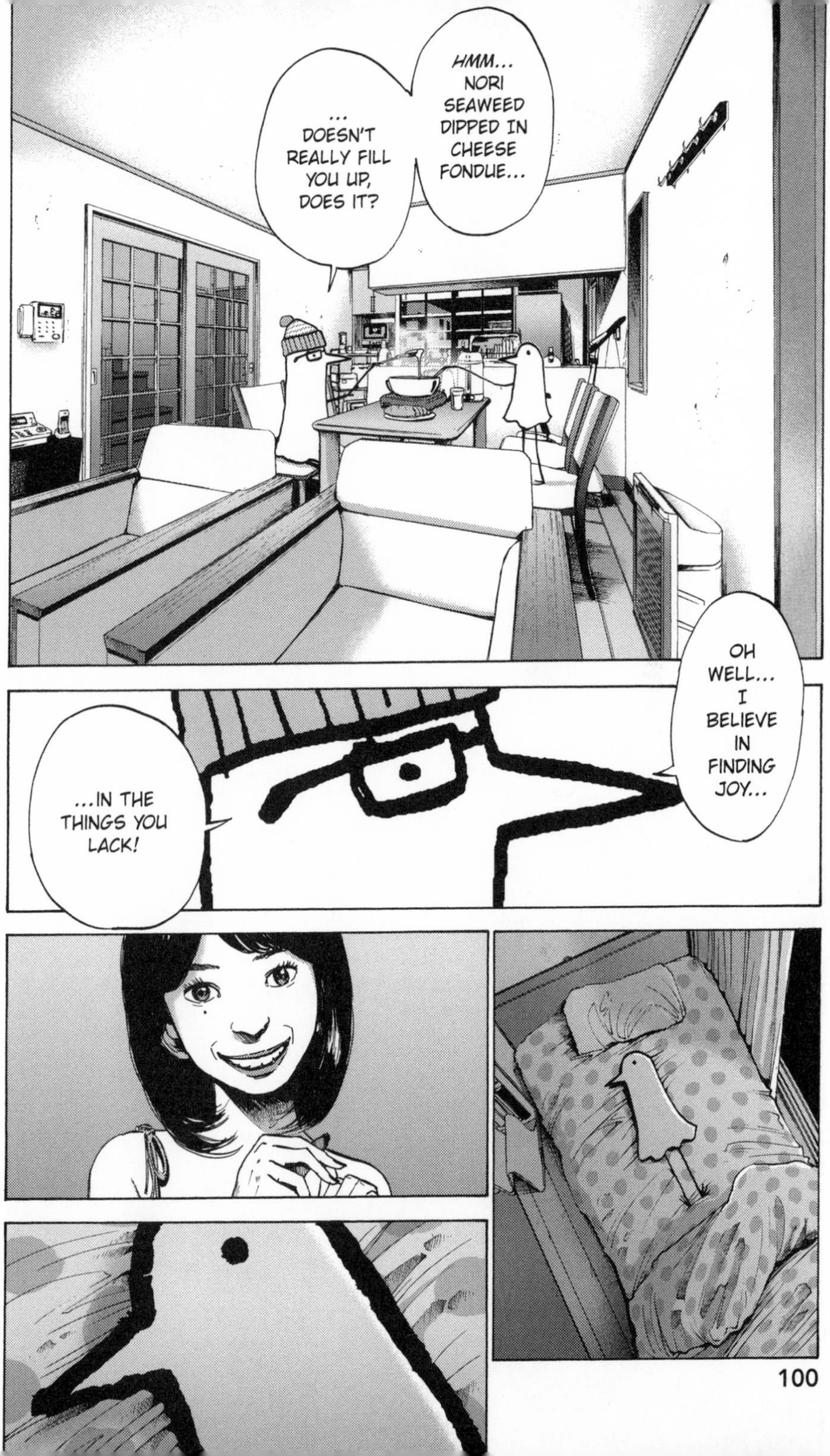
HMM... NORI SEAWEED DIPPED IN CHEESE FONDUE...
...DOESN'T REALLY FILL YOU UP, DOES IT?
OH WELL... I BELIEVE IN FINDING JOY...
...IN THE THINGS YOU LACK!

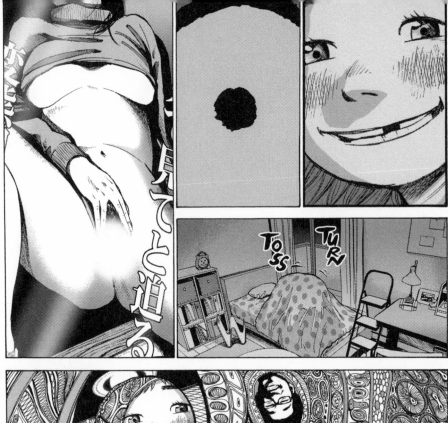

TOSS TURN

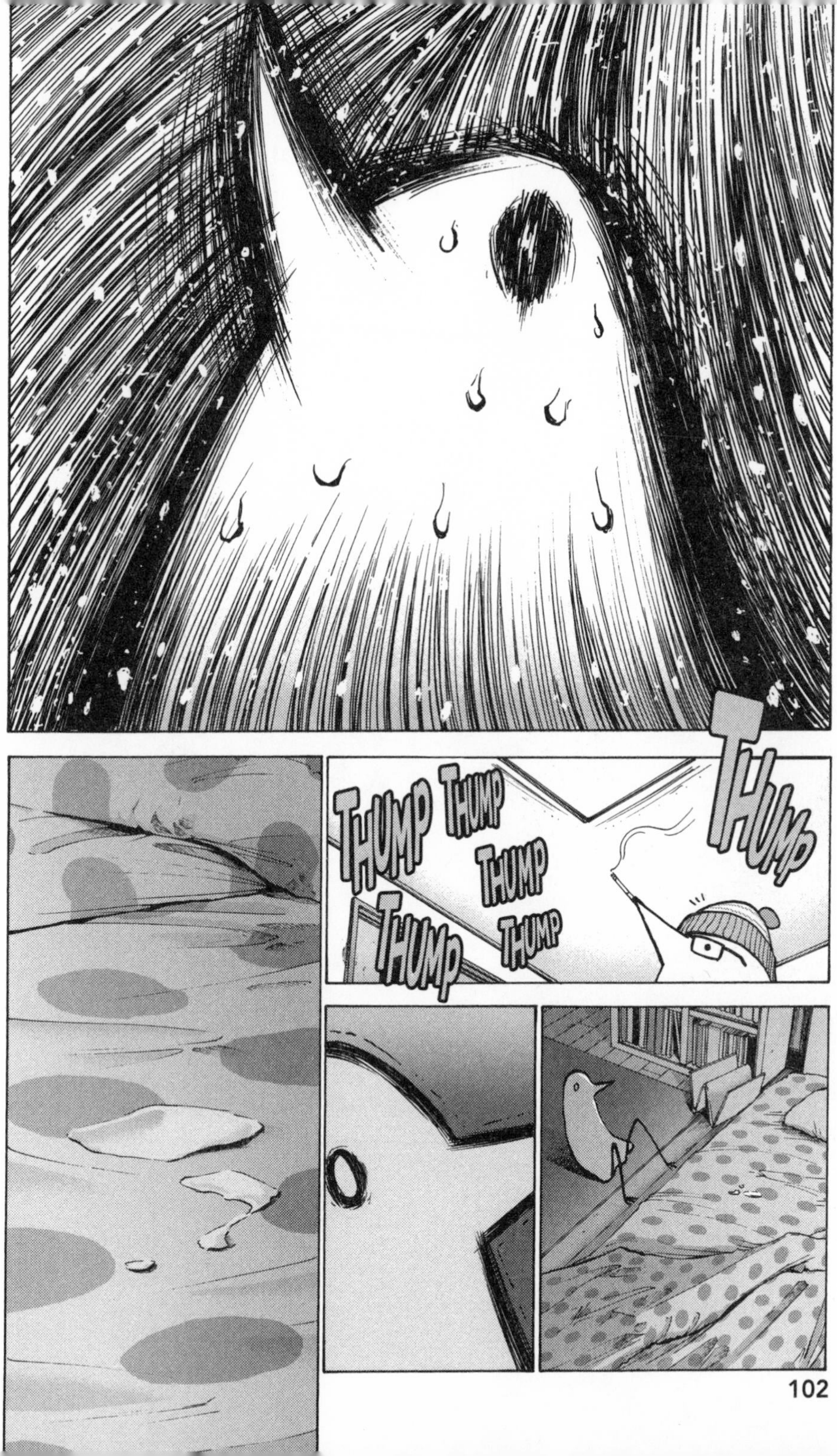
THUMP
THUMP
THUMP
THUMP
THUMP
THUMP

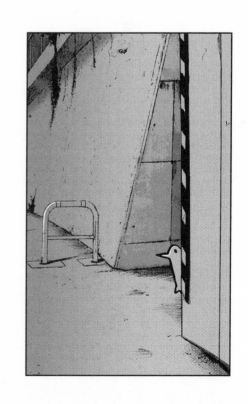

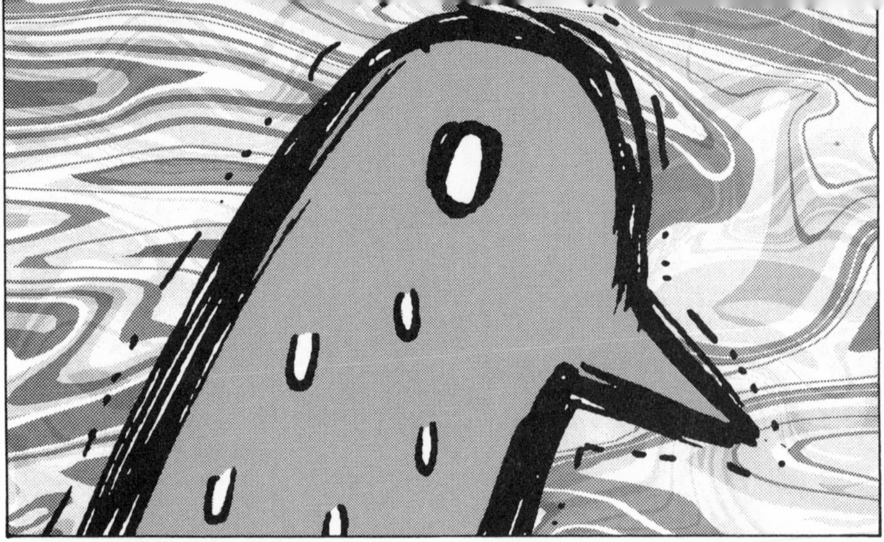

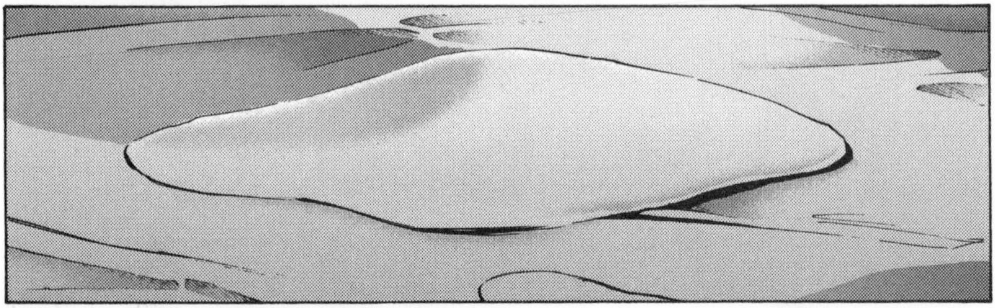

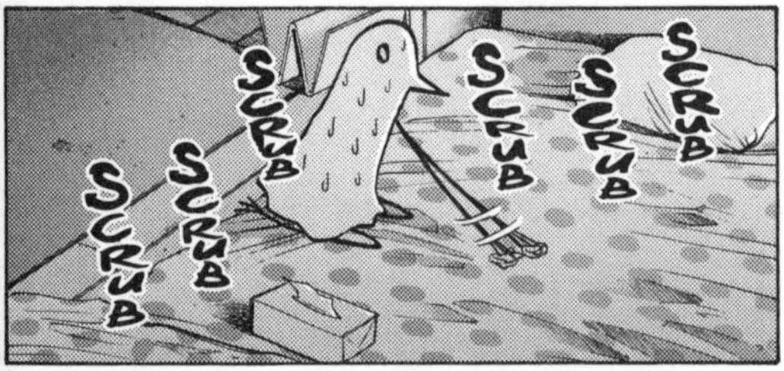
SCRUB
SCRUB
SCRUB
SCRUB
SCRUB
SCRUB

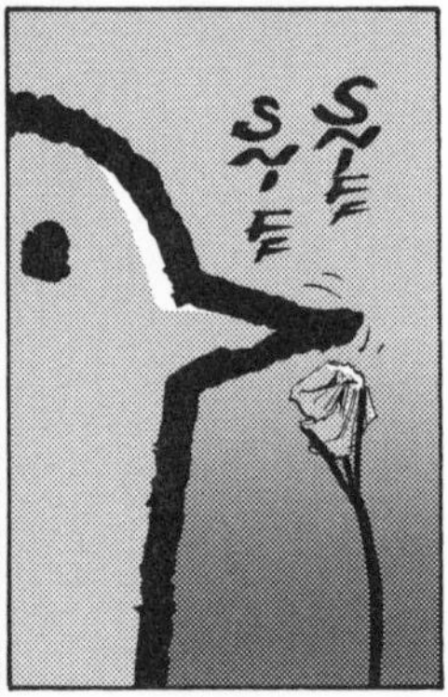
SNIFF
SNIFF

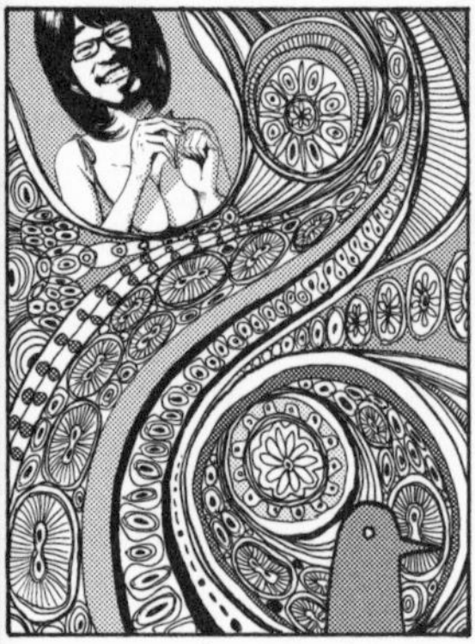

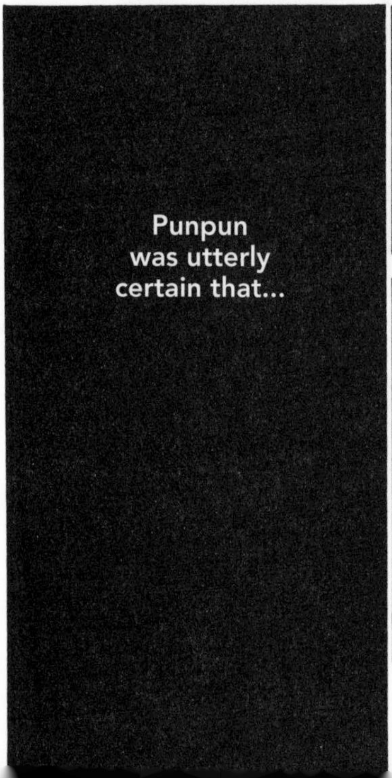
Punpun was utterly certain that...

Chapter 6

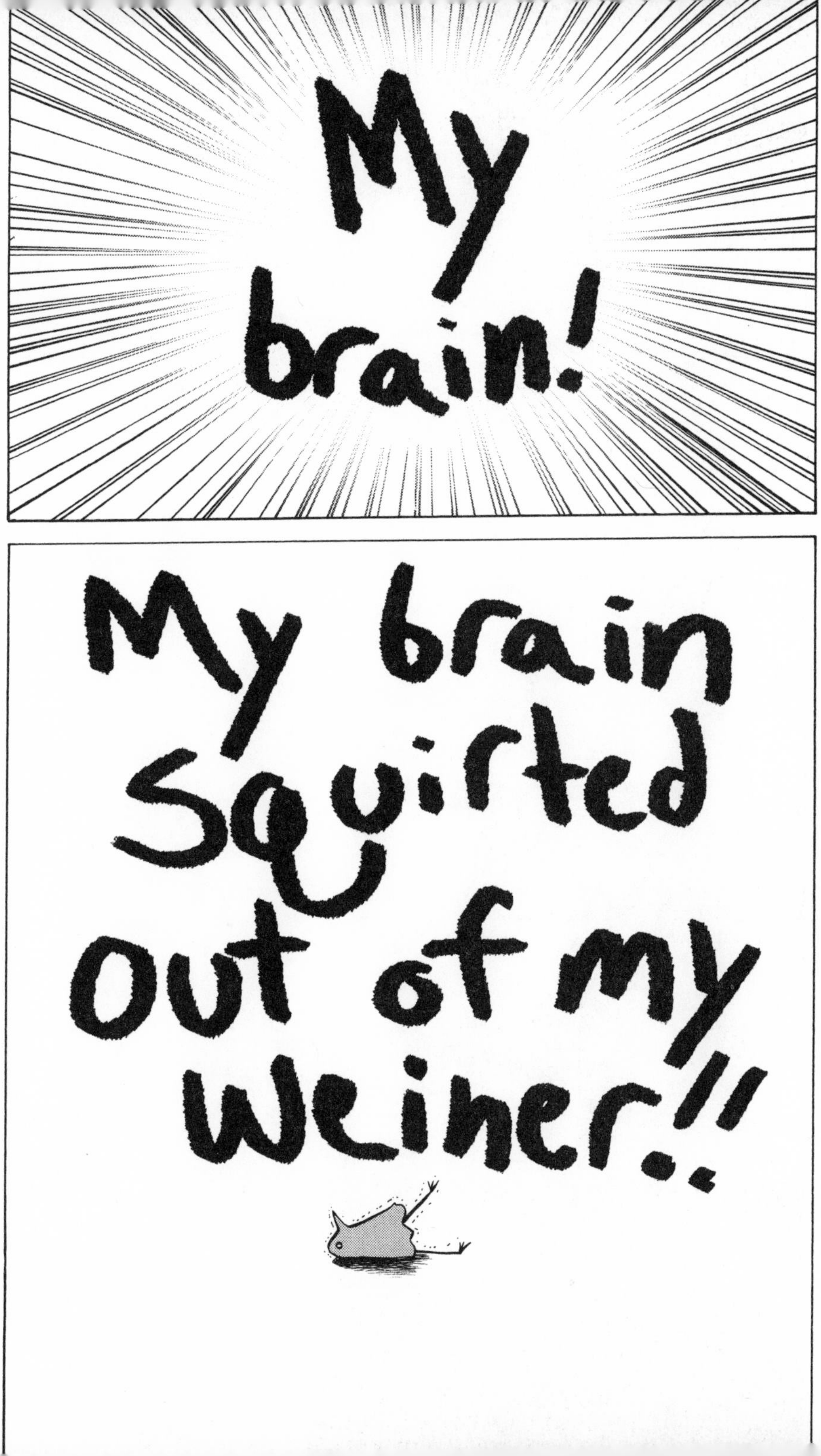
My brain!
My brain squirted out of my weiner!!

A MEDICAL DICTIONARY?

SURE, I HAVE ONE.

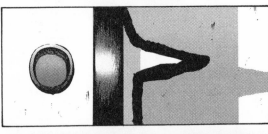

...Punpun asked. "Do you die if your brain melts?"

BUT WHAT FOR?

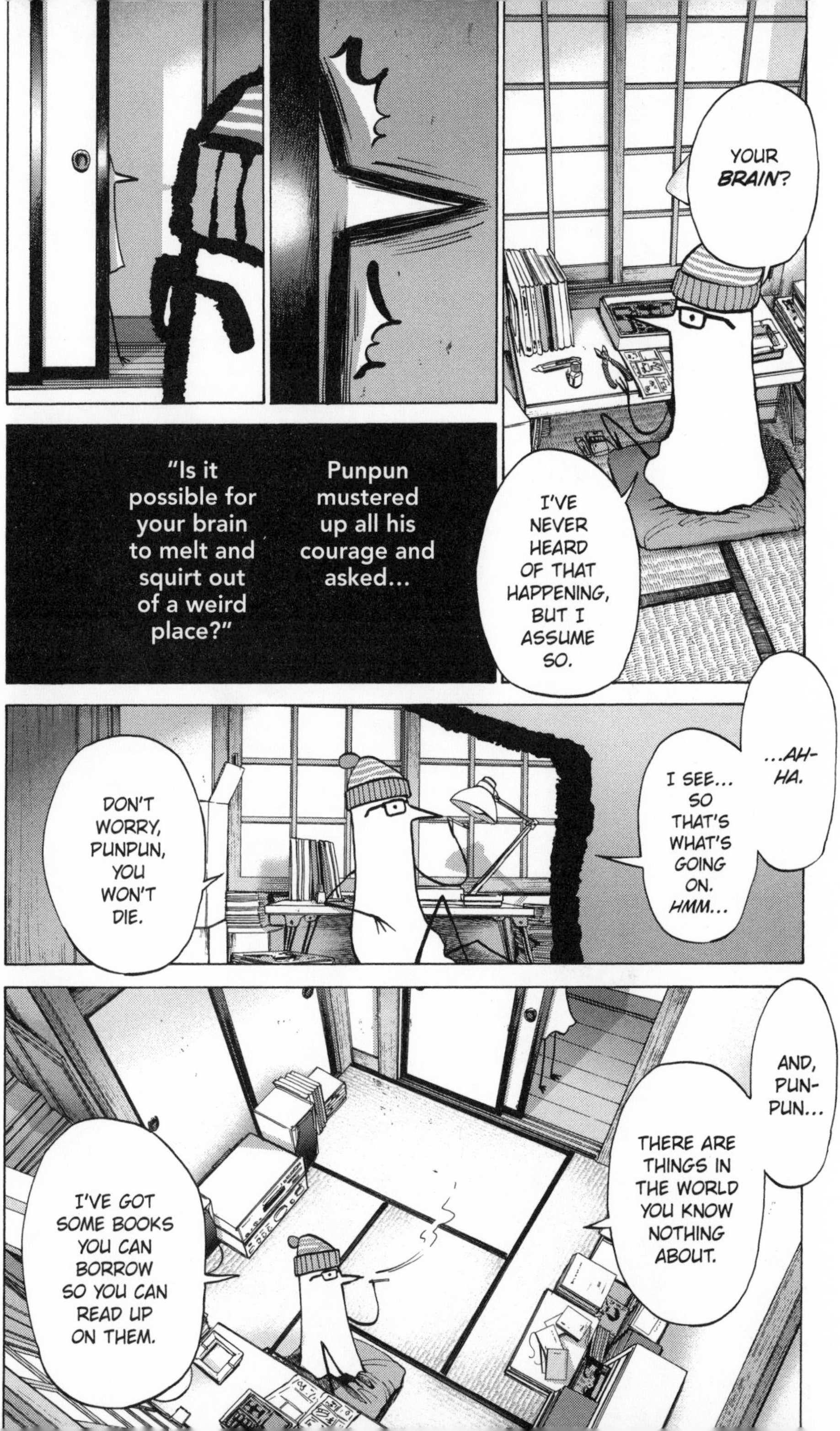
YOUR BRAIN?
I'VE NEVER HEARD OF THAT HAPPENING, BUT I ASSUME SO.
Punpun mustered up all his courage and asked...
"Is it possible for your brain to melt and squirt out of a weird place?"
...AH-HA.
I SEE... SO THAT'S WHAT'S GOING ON. HMM...
DON'T WORRY, PUNPUN, YOU WON'T DIE.
AND, PUN-PUN...
THERE ARE THINGS IN THE WORLD YOU KNOW NOTHING ABOUT.
I'VE GOT SOME BOOKS YOU CAN BORROW SO YOU CAN READ UP ON THEM.

THE UNIVERSE

FAMILY MEDICAL DICTIONARY

THE ILLUSTRATED HISTORY OF **THE SHOWA ERA**

Punpun had a hard time with some of the bigger words, so he pored over the illustrations instead.

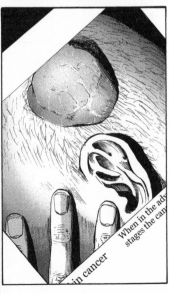

When in the adv stages the can

in cancer

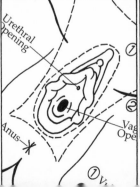

Urethral Opening

Vag Ope

Anus

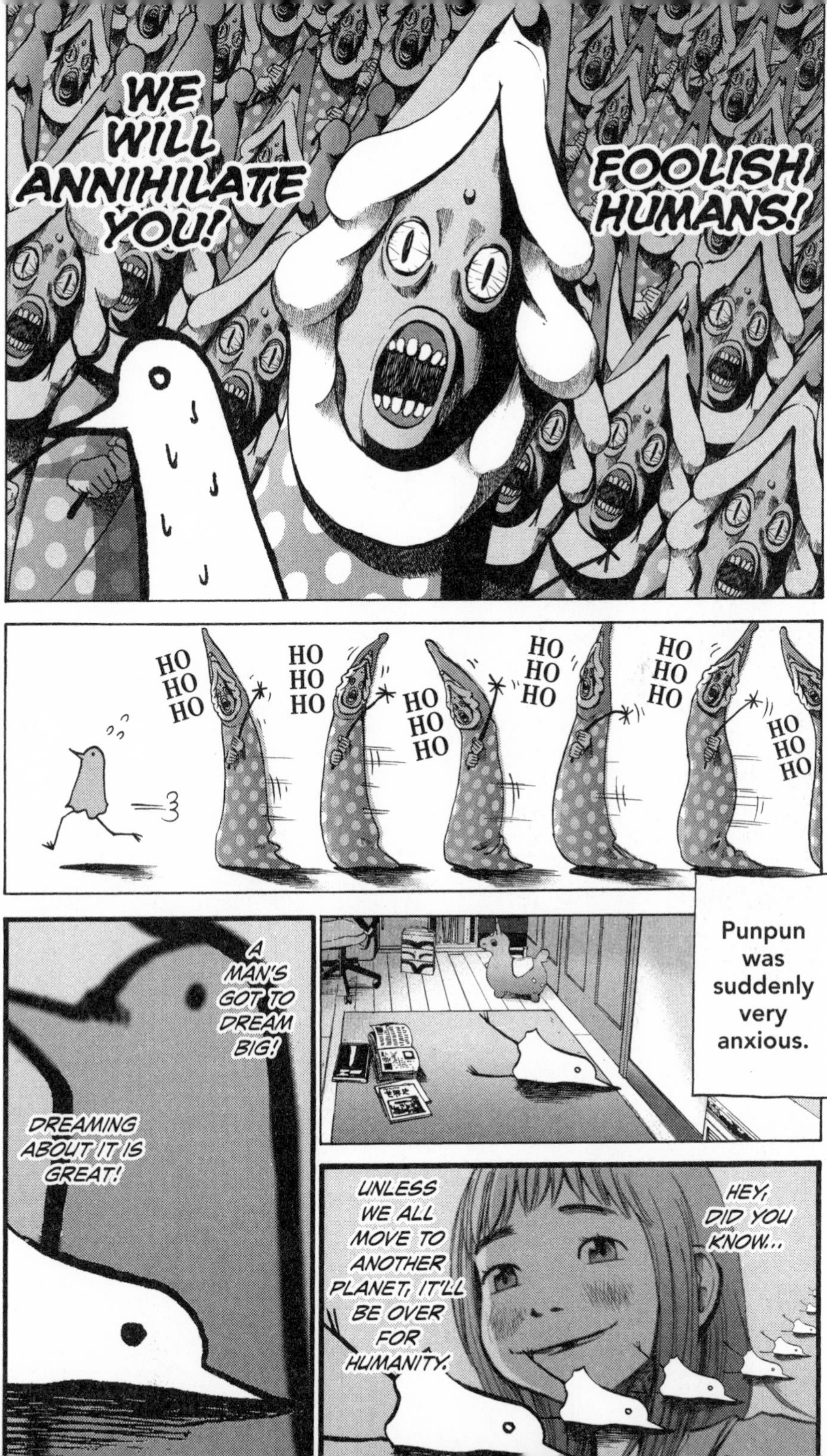
FOOLISH HUMANS!
WE WILL ANNIHILATE YOU!
HO HO HO
HO HO HO
HO HO HO
HO HO HO
HO HO HO
HO HO HO
Punpun was suddenly very anxious.
HEY, DID YOU KNOW...
UNLESS WE ALL MOVE TO ANOTHER PLANET, IT'LL BE OVER FOR HUMANITY.
A MAN'S GOT TO DREAM BIG!
DREAMING ABOUT IT IS GREAT!

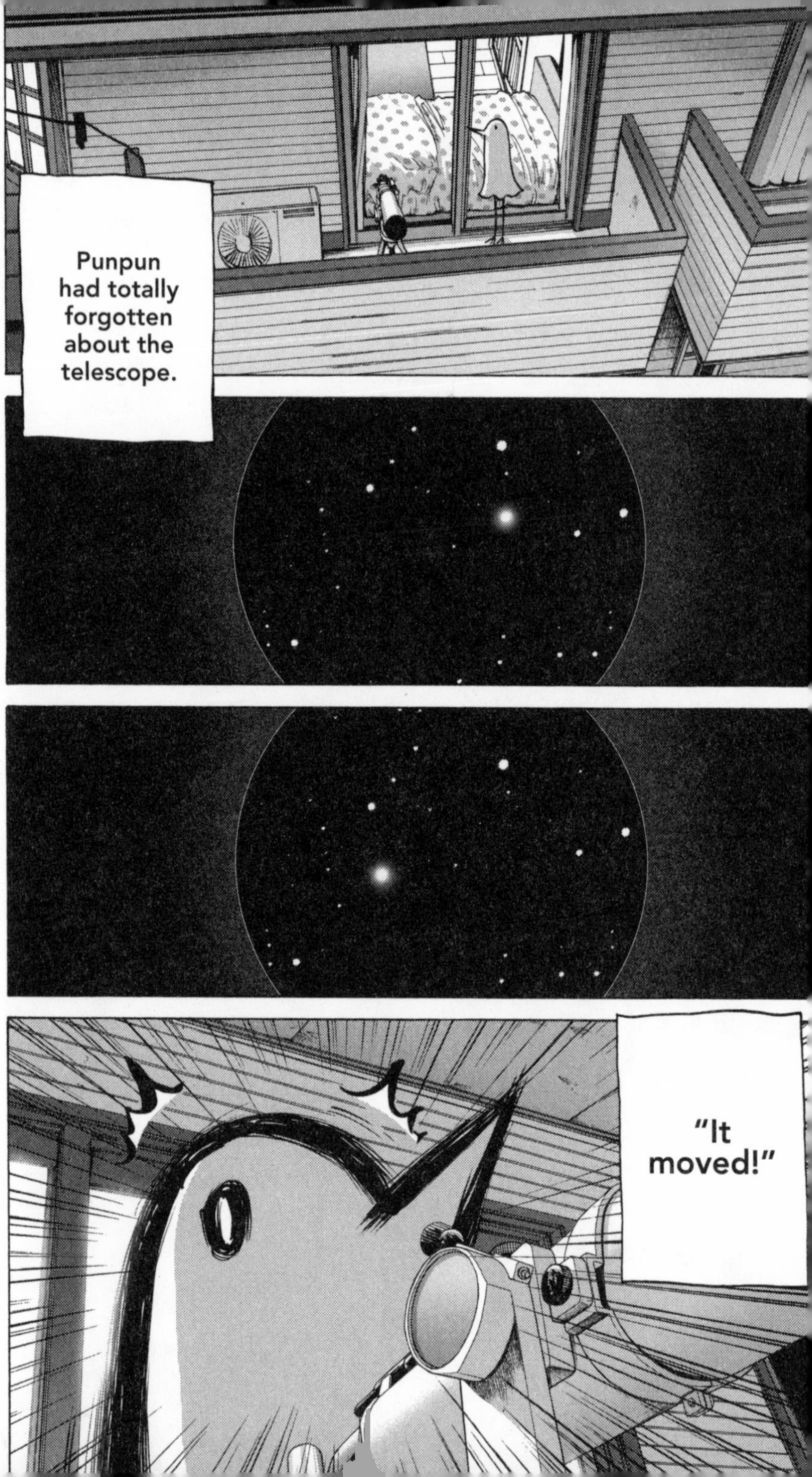
Punpun had totally forgotten about the telescope.
"It moved!"

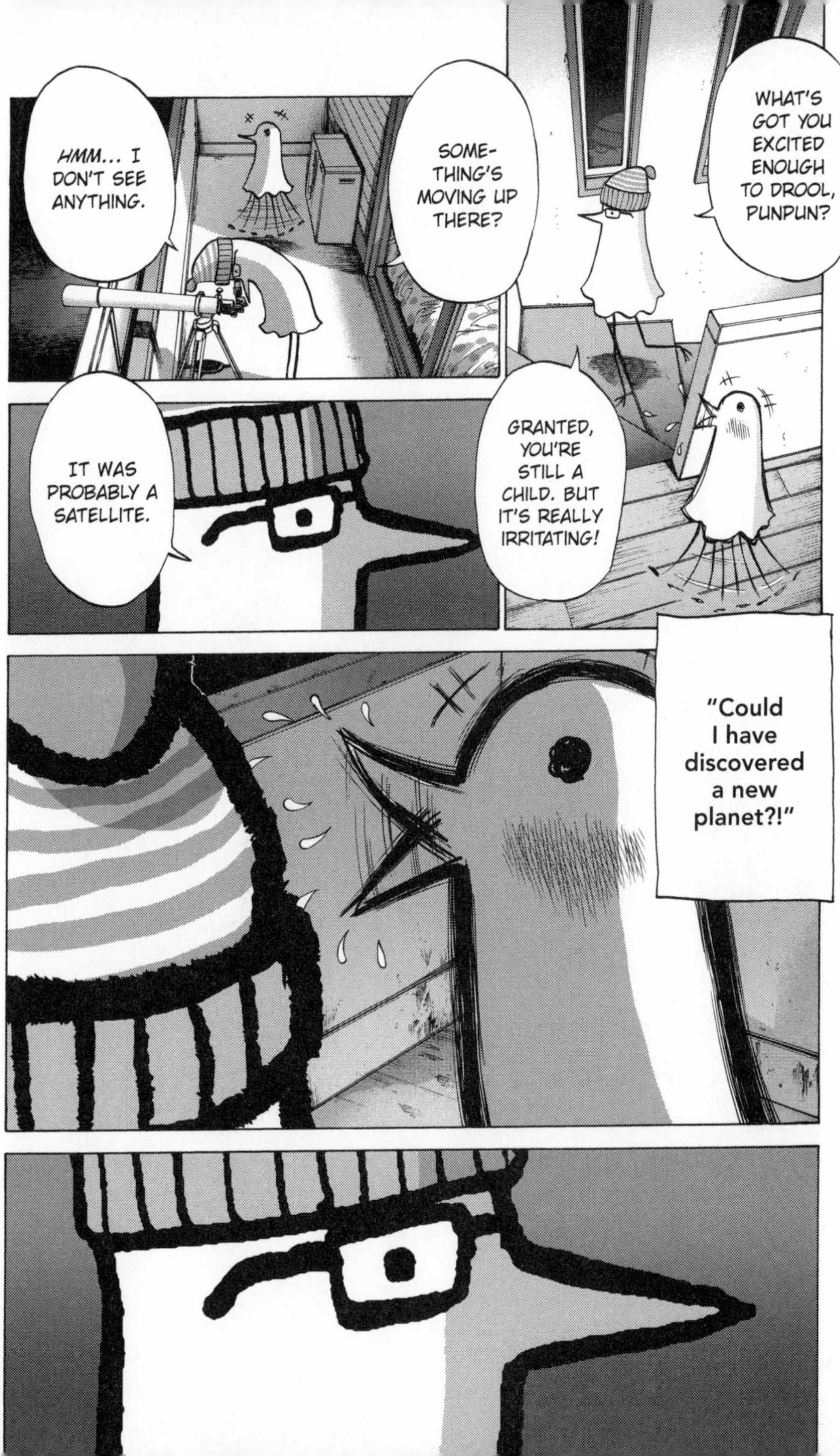
WHAT'S GOT YOU EXCITED ENOUGH TO DROOL, PUNPUN?
SOME-THING'S MOVING UP THERE?
HMM... I DON'T SEE ANYTHING.
IT WAS PROBABLY A SATELLITE.
GRANTED, YOU'RE STILL A CHILD. BUT IT'S REALLY IRRITATING!
"Could I have discovered a new planet?!"

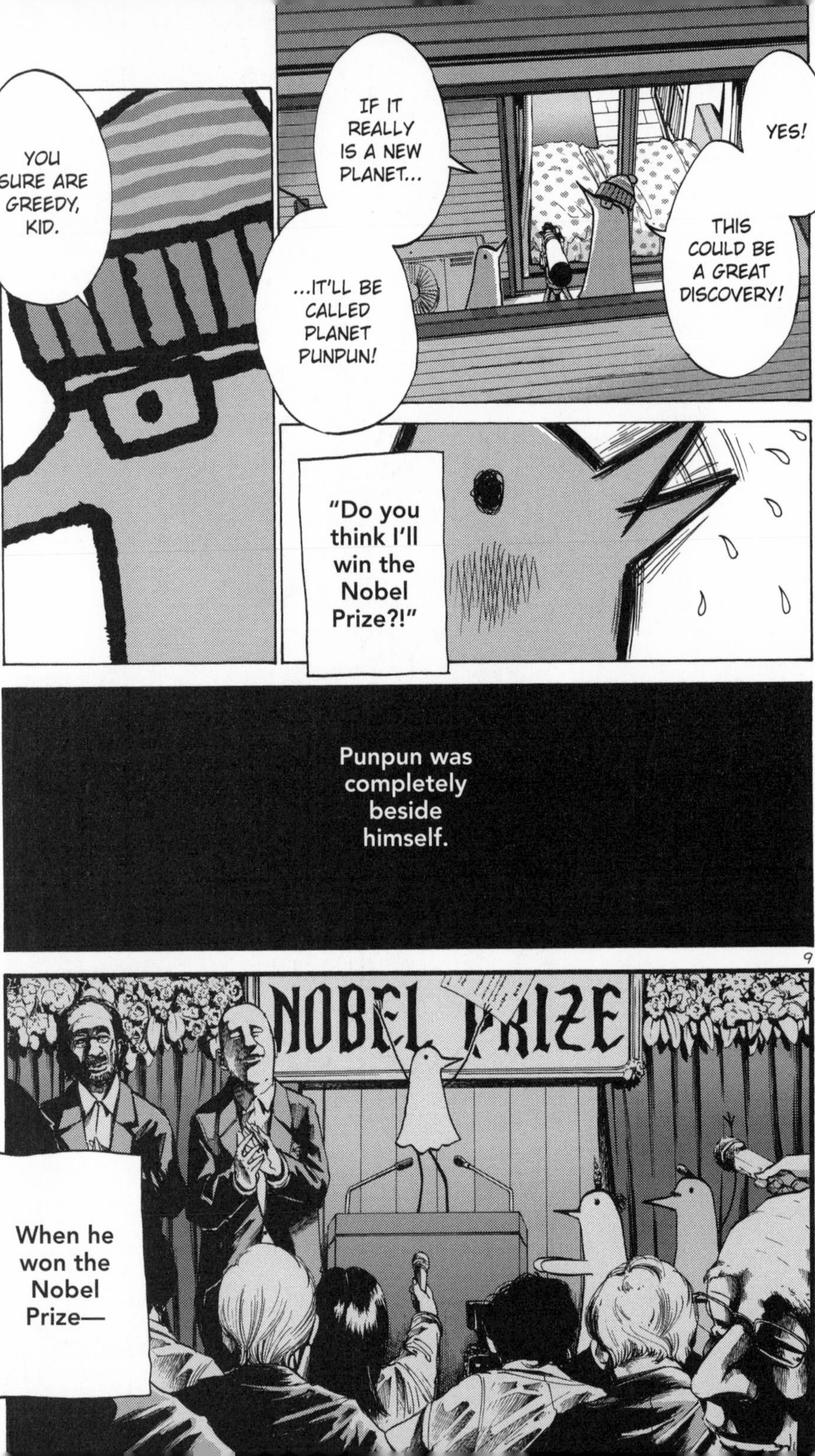
YES!
THIS COULD BE A GREAT DISCOVERY!
IF IT REALLY IS A NEW PLANET...
...IT'LL BE CALLED PLANET PUNPUN!
"Do you think I'll win the Nobel Prize?!"
YOU SURE ARE GREEDY, KID.
Punpun was completely beside himself.
9
NOBEL PRIZE
When he won the Nobel Prize—

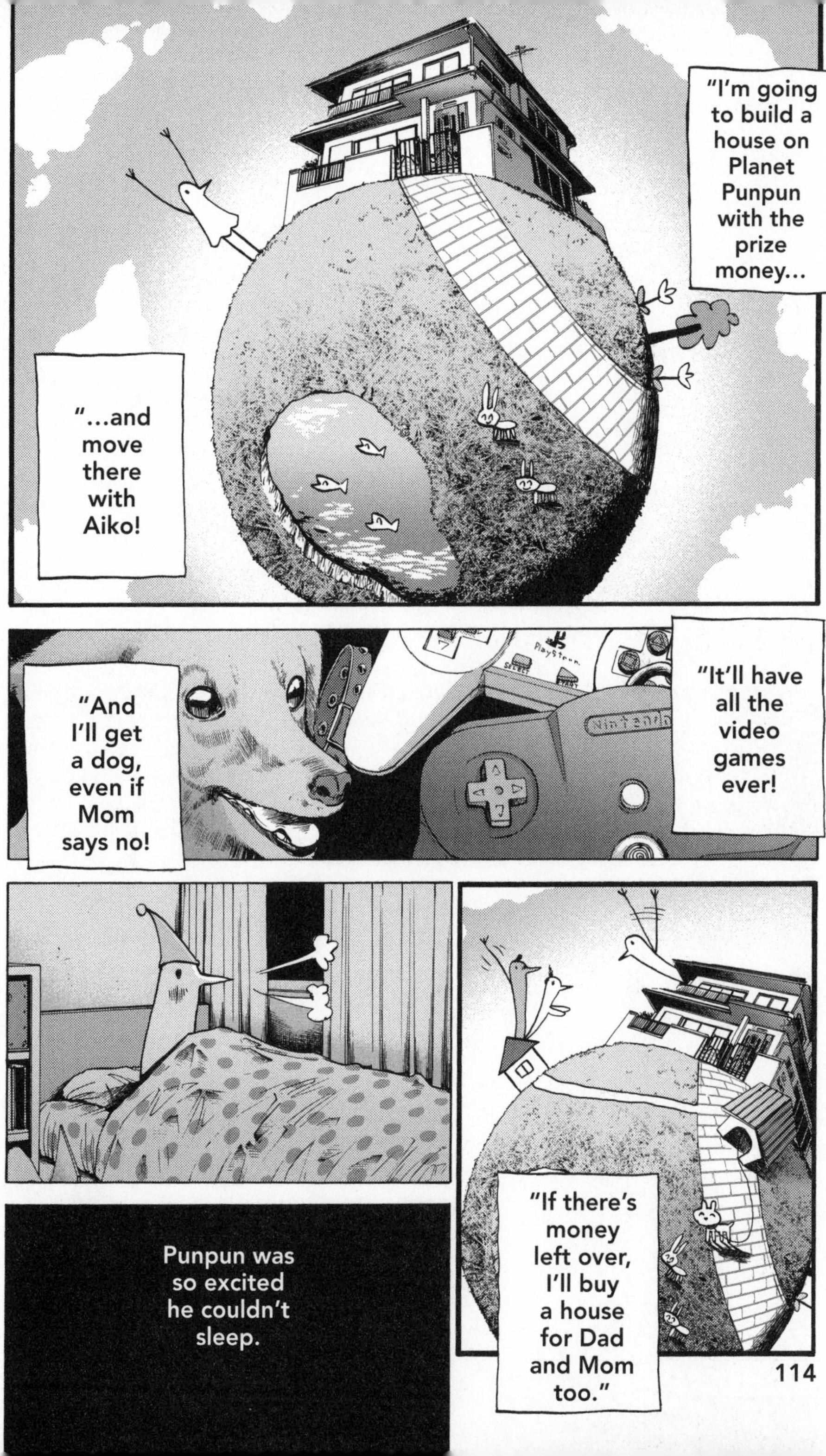
"I'm going to build a house on Planet Punpun with the prize money...
"...and move there with Aiko!
"It'll have all the video games ever!
"And I'll get a dog, even if Mom says no!
"If there's money left over, I'll buy a house for Dad and Mom too."
Punpun was so excited he couldn't sleep.

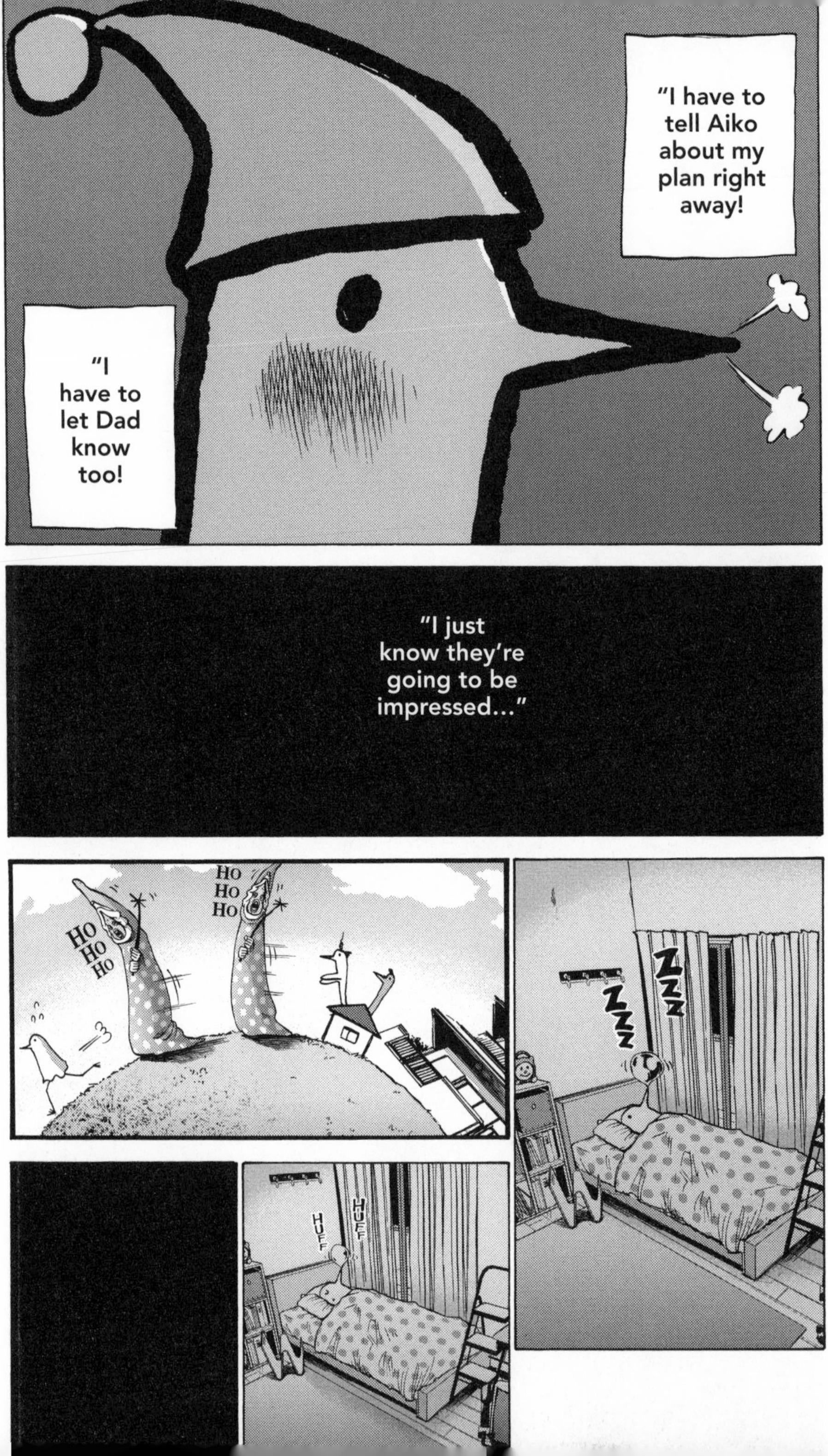
"I have to tell Aiko about my plan right away!
"I have to let Dad know too!
"I just know they're going to be impressed..."
ZZZ
ZZZ
HO HO HO
HO HO HO
HUFF
HUFF

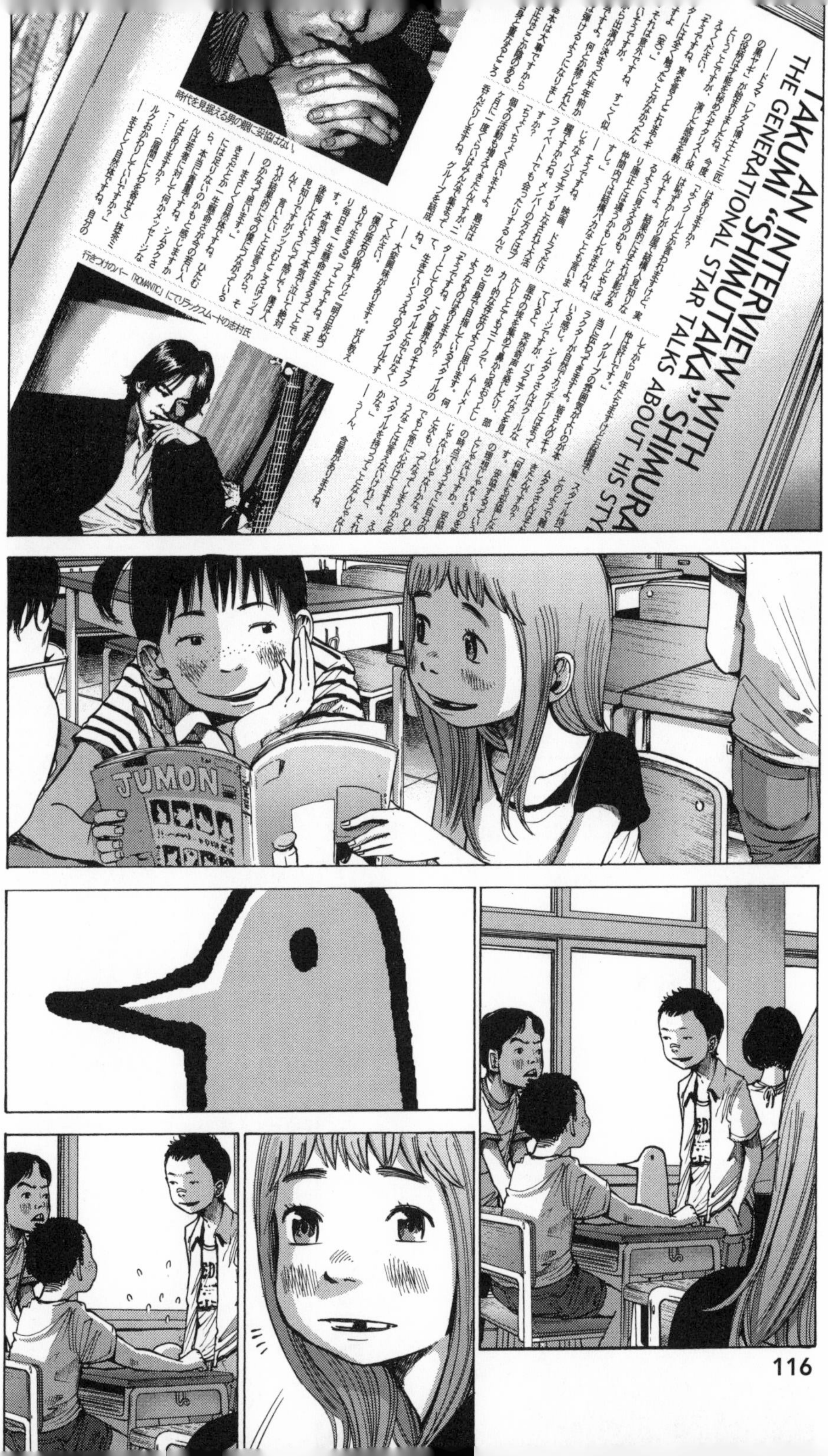
TAKUMI AN INTERVIEW WITH "SHIMUTAKA" SHIMURA
THE GENERATIONAL STAR TALKS ABOUT HIS STY
時代を見据える男の眼に妥協はない
行きつけのバー「ROMANTIC」にてリラックスムードの志村氏
JUMON

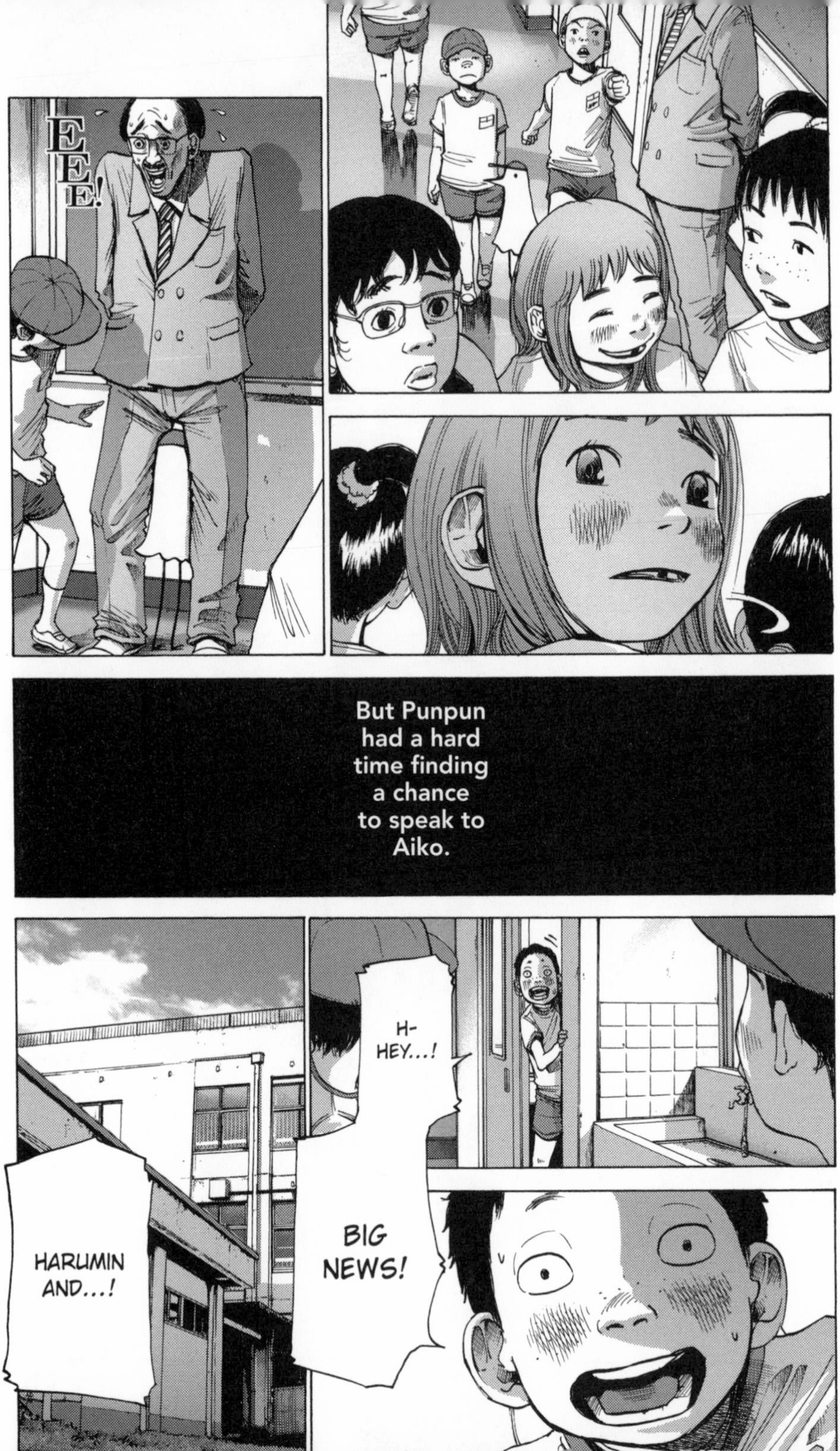
EEE!
But Punpun had a hard time finding a chance to speak to Aiko.
H- HEY...!
BIG NEWS!
HARUMIN AND...!

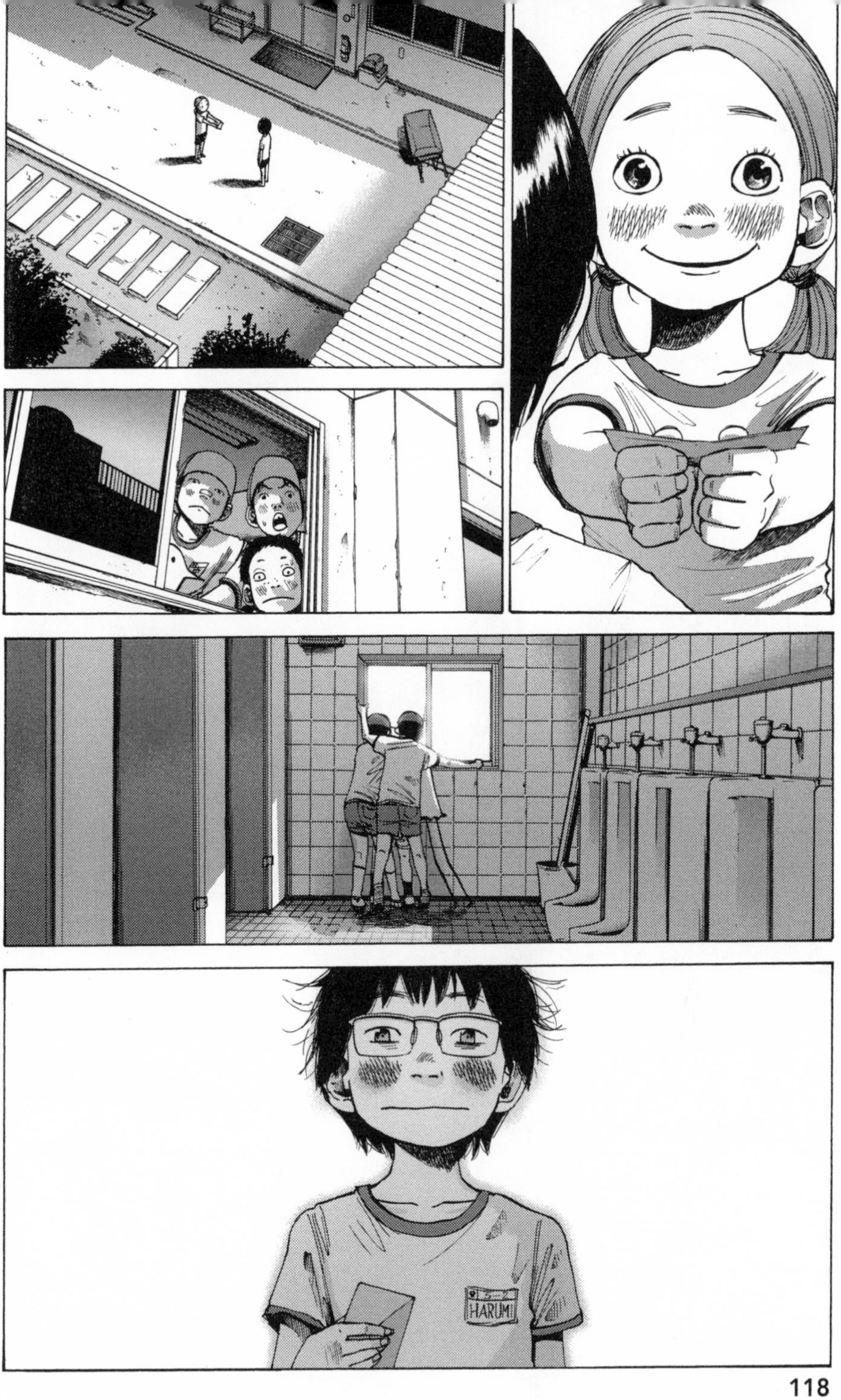
HARUMI

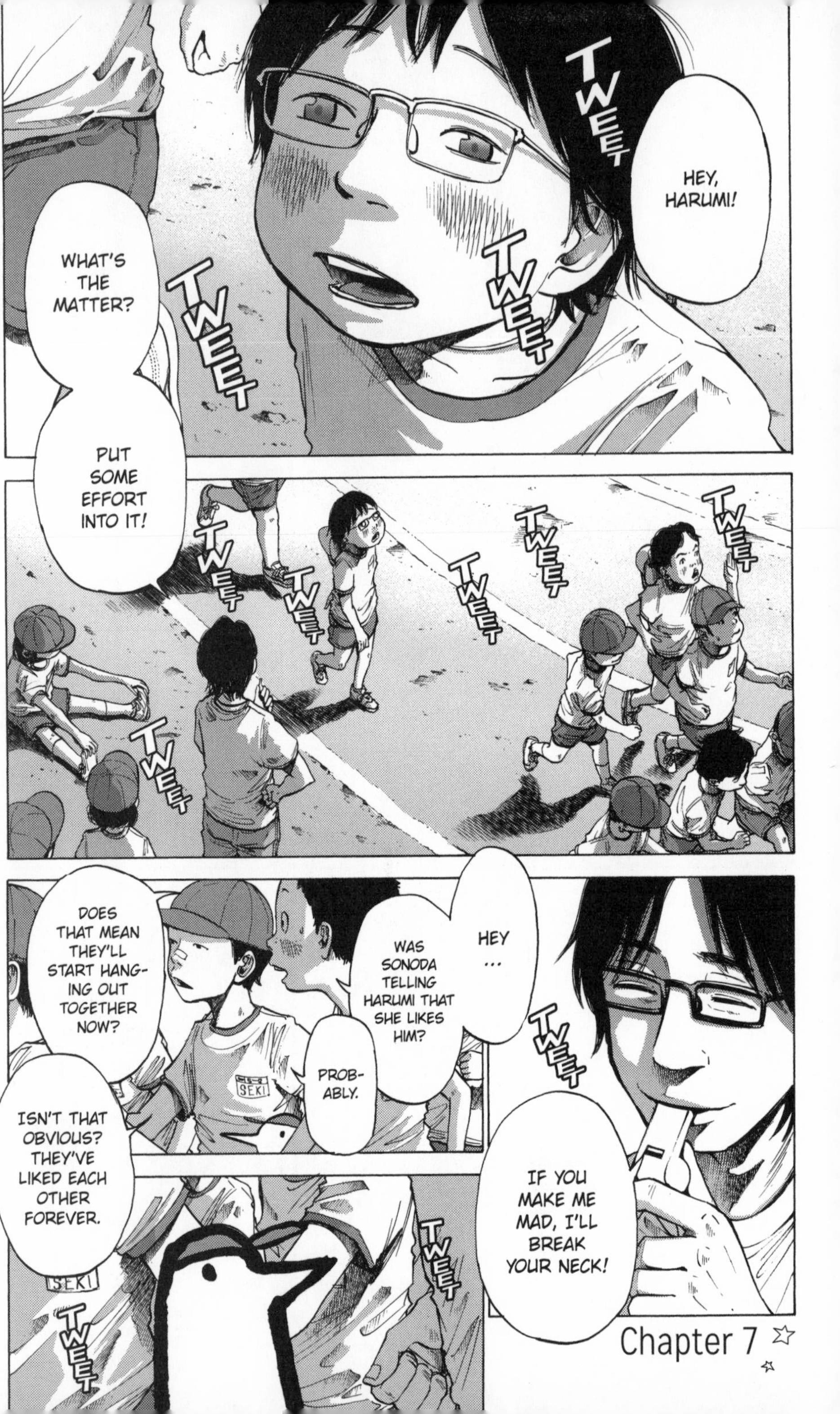
TWEET
HEY, HARUMI!
TWEET
WHAT'S THE MATTER?
TWEET
PUT SOME EFFORT INTO IT!
TWEET
TWEET
TWEET
TWEET
TWEET
TWEET
HEY …
TWEET
IF YOU MAKE ME MAD, I'LL BREAK YOUR NECK!
WAS SONODA TELLING HARUMI THAT SHE LIKES HIM?
PROB-ABLY.
DOES THAT MEAN THEY'LL START HANG-ING OUT TOGETHER NOW?
SEKI
ISN'T THAT OBVIOUS? THEY'VE LIKED EACH OTHER FOREVER.
TWEET
SEKI
TWEET

Chapter 7 ☆

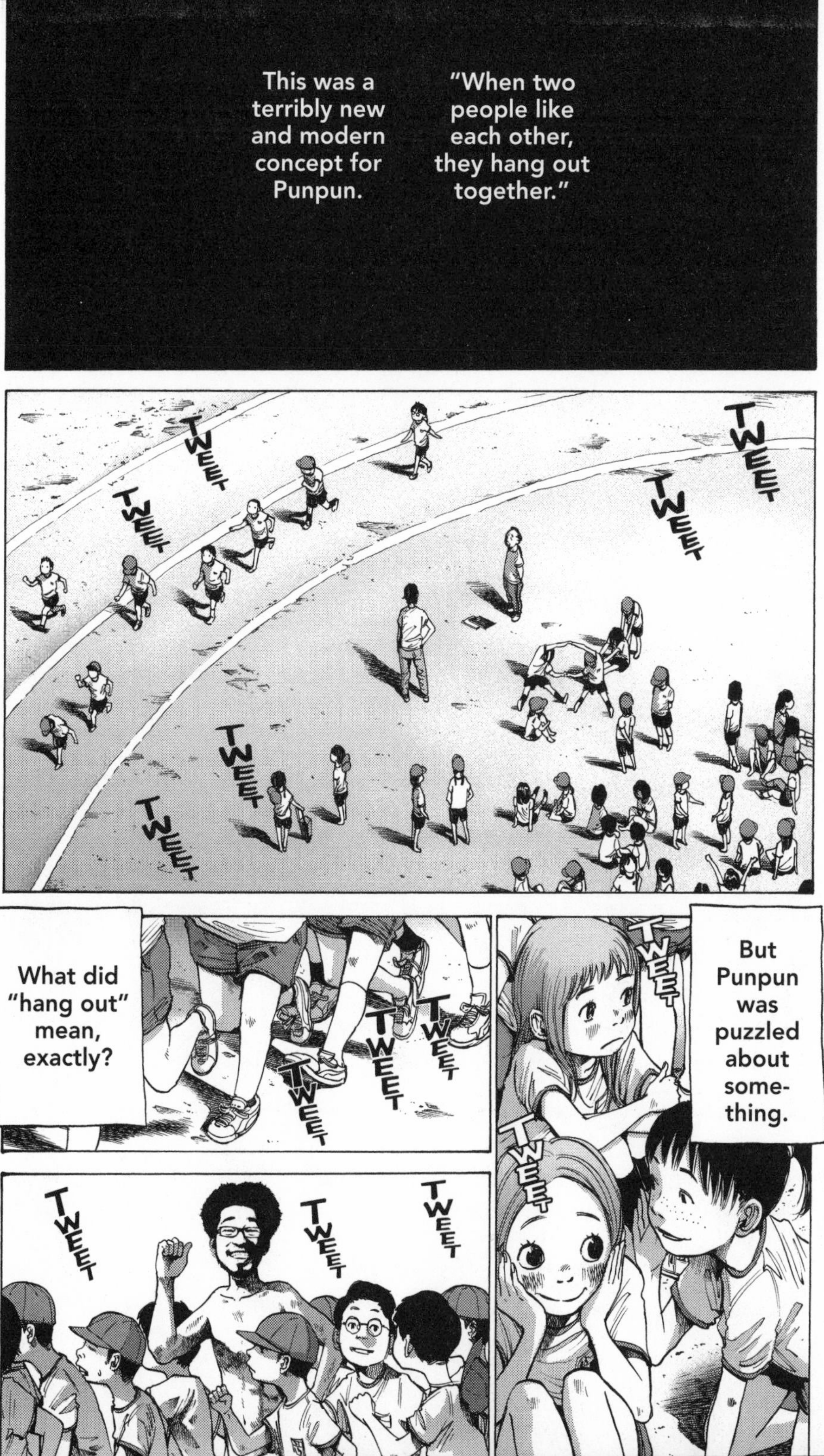
"When two people like each other, they hang out together."
This was a terribly new and modern concept for Punpun.
TWEET
TWEET
TWEET
TWEET
TWEET
TWEET
TWEET
TWEET
But Punpun was puzzled about some-thing.
TWEET
What did "hang out" mean, exactly?
TWEET
TWEET
TWEET
TWEET
TWEET
TWEET

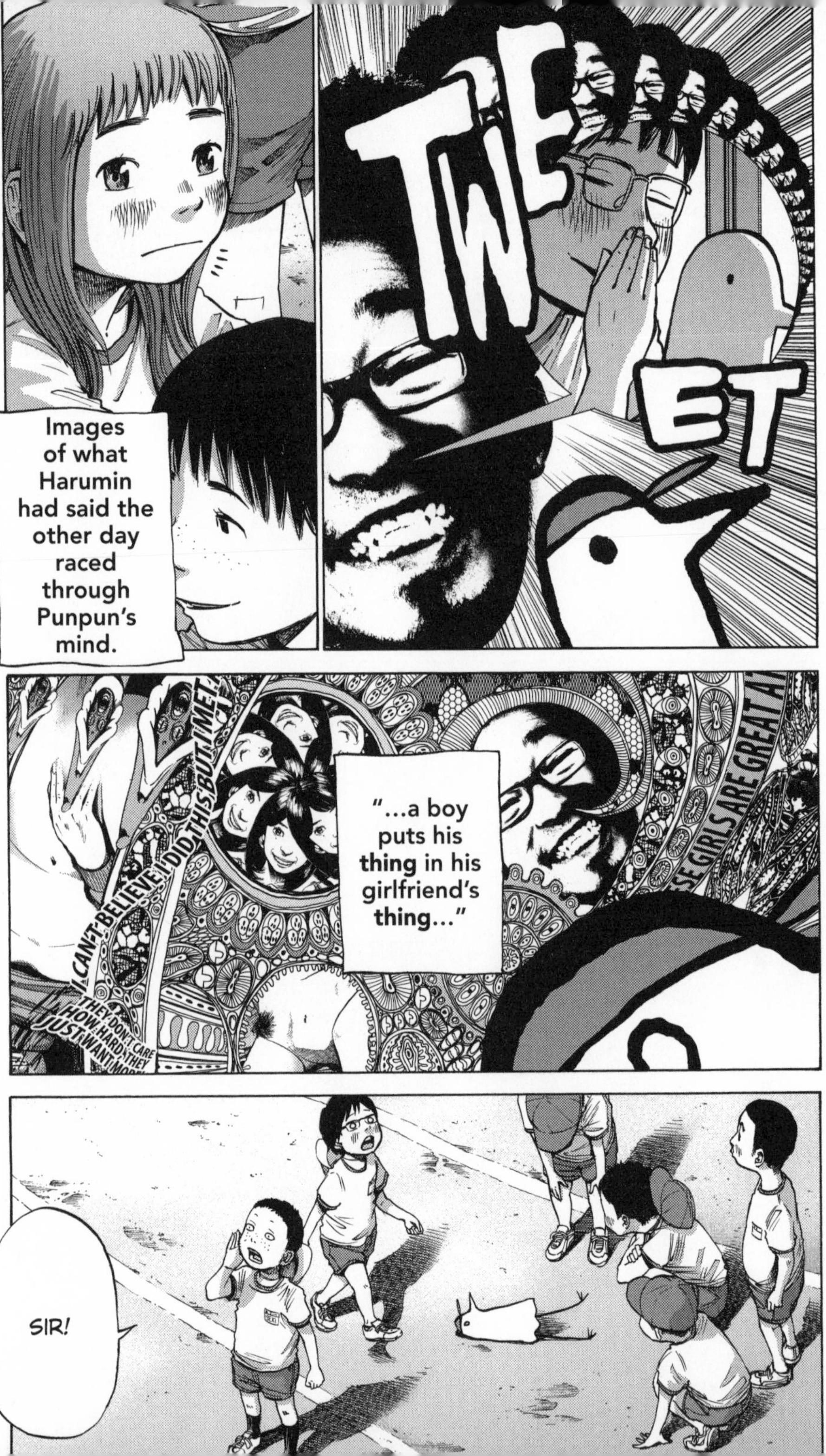
TWEET
Images of what Harumin had said the other day raced through Punpun's mind.
I CAN'T BELIEVE I DID THIS BUT I MET
THEY DON'T CARE HOW HARD THEY
"...a boy puts his thing in his girlfriend's thing..."
SIR!

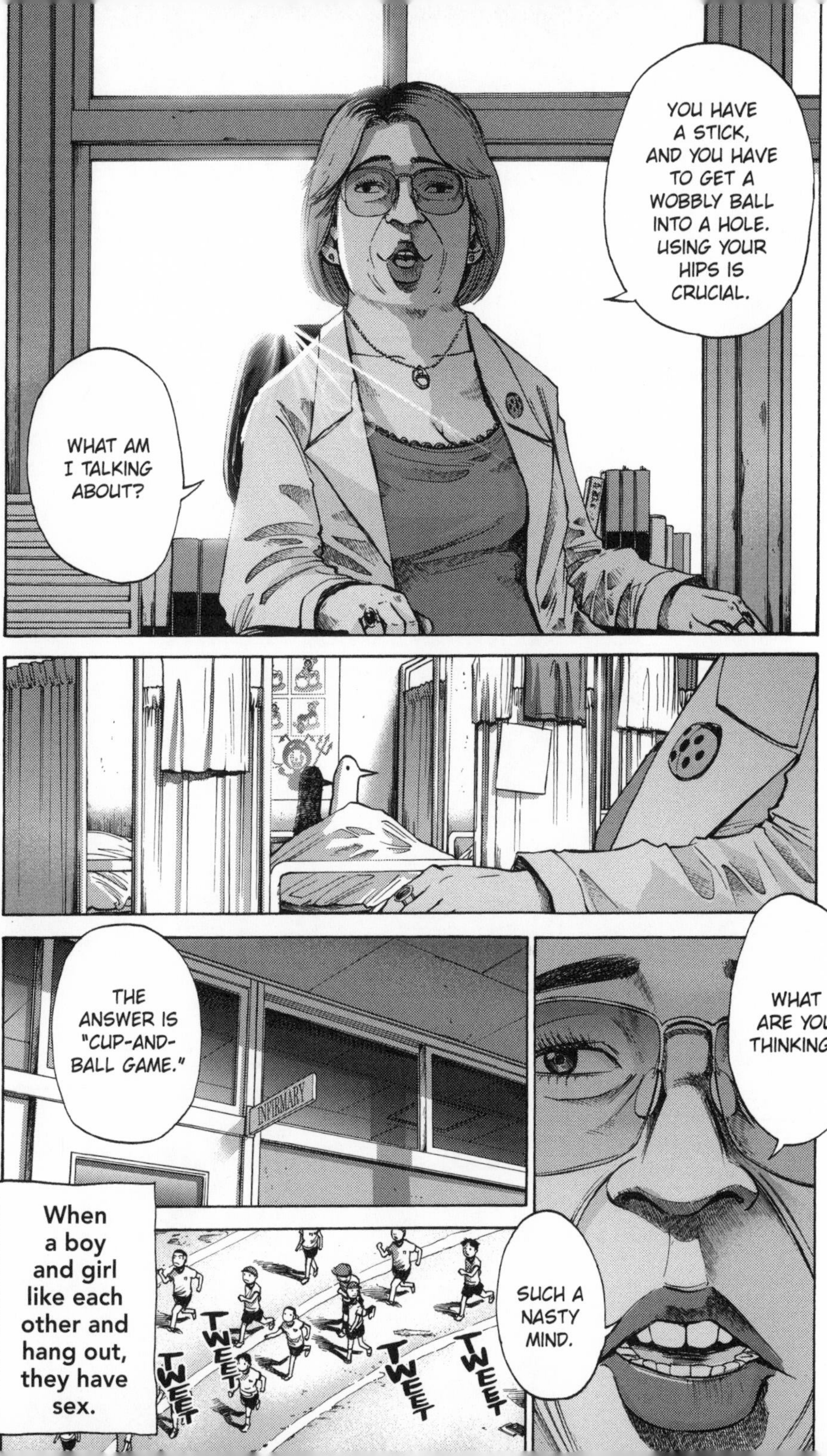
YOU HAVE A STICK, AND YOU HAVE TO GET A WOBBLY BALL INTO A HOLE. USING YOUR HIPS IS CRUCIAL.
WHAT AM I TALKING ABOUT?
WHAT ARE YOU THINKING?
SUCH A NASTY MIND.
THE ANSWER IS "CUP-AND-BALL GAME."
INFIRMARY
When a boy and girl like each other and hang out, they have sex.
TWEET
TWEET
TWEET
TWEET

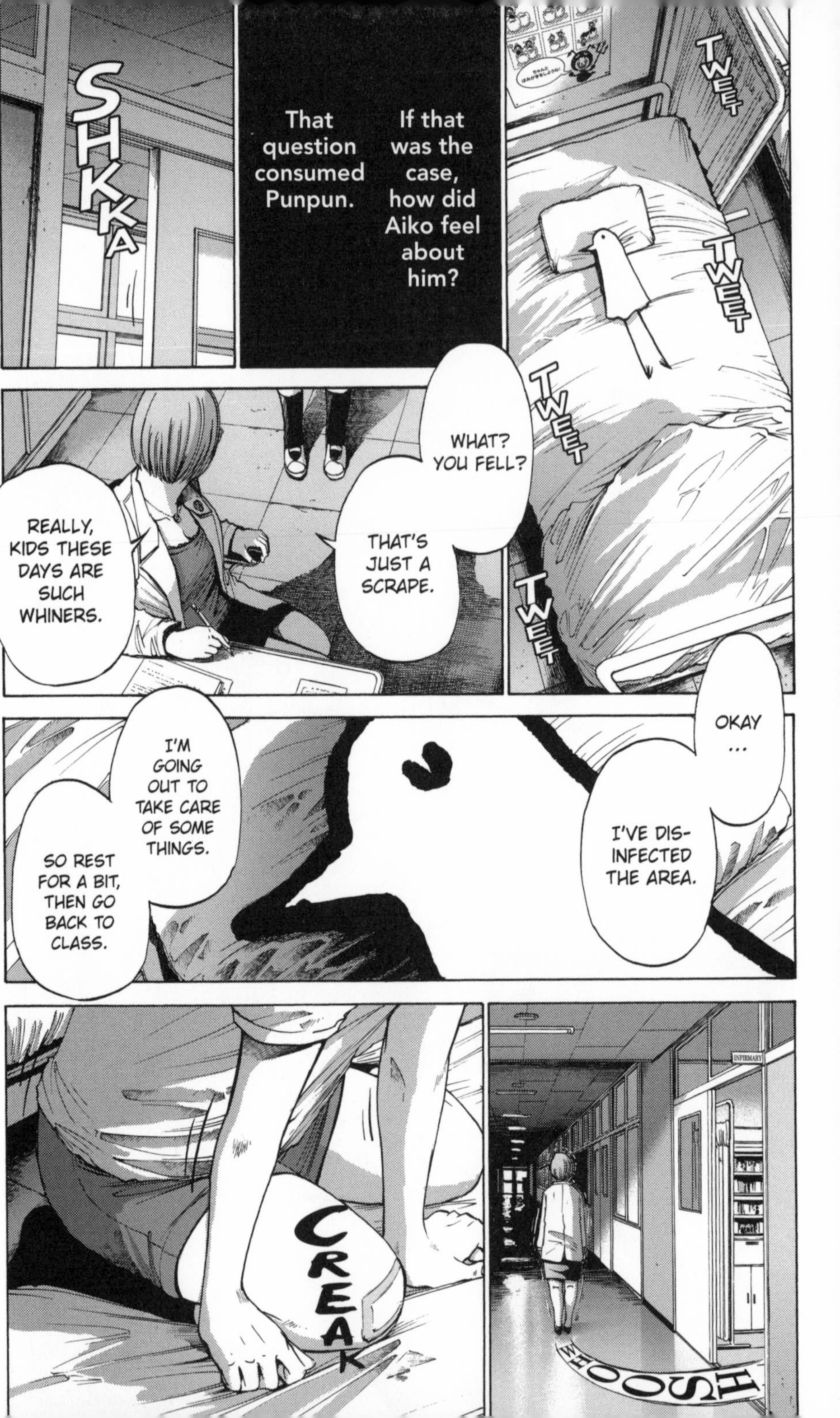
TWEET
TWEET
TWEET
TWEET
If that was the case, how did Aiko feel about him?
That question consumed Punpun.
SHKKA
WHAT? YOU FELL?
THAT'S JUST A SCRAPE.
REALLY, KIDS THESE DAYS ARE SUCH WHINERS.
OKAY ...
I'VE DIS-INFECTED THE AREA.
I'M GOING OUT TO TAKE CARE OF SOME THINGS.
SO REST FOR A BIT, THEN GO BACK TO CLASS.
INFIRMARY
WHOOSH
CREAK

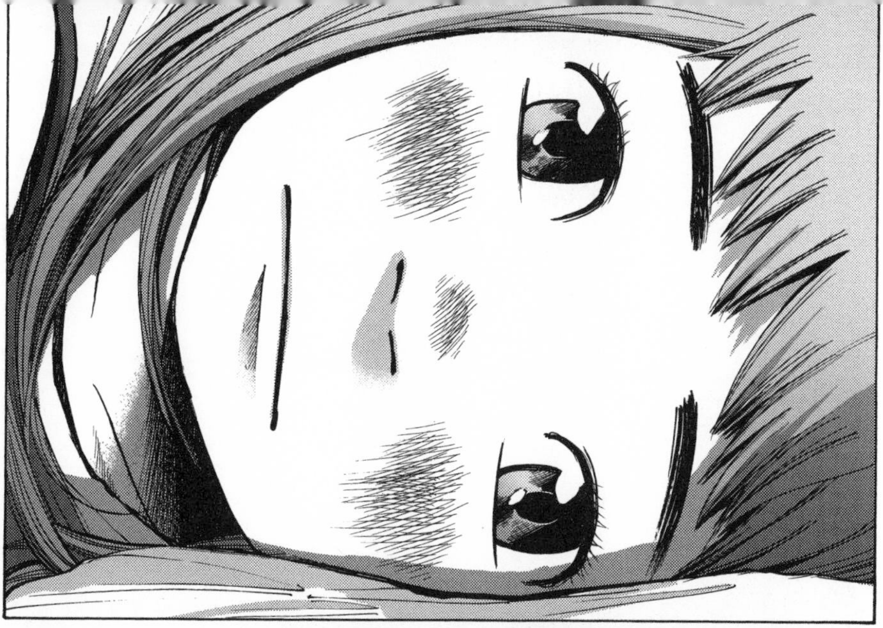
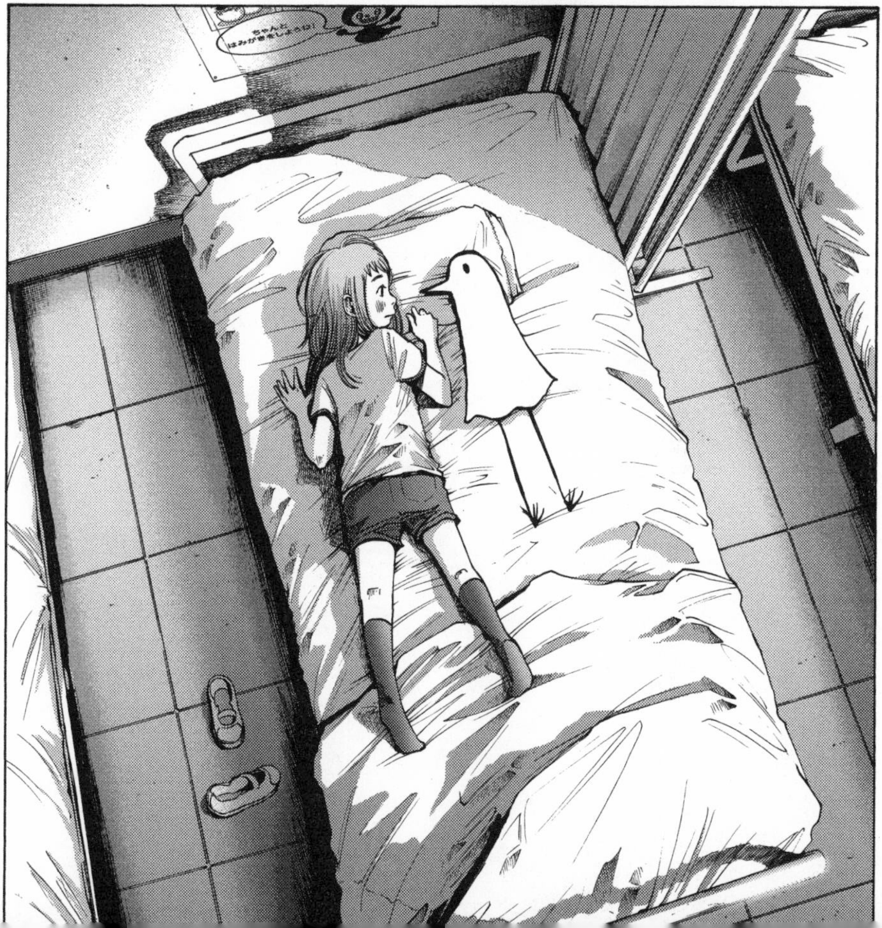
ちゃんと
はみがきしようね!

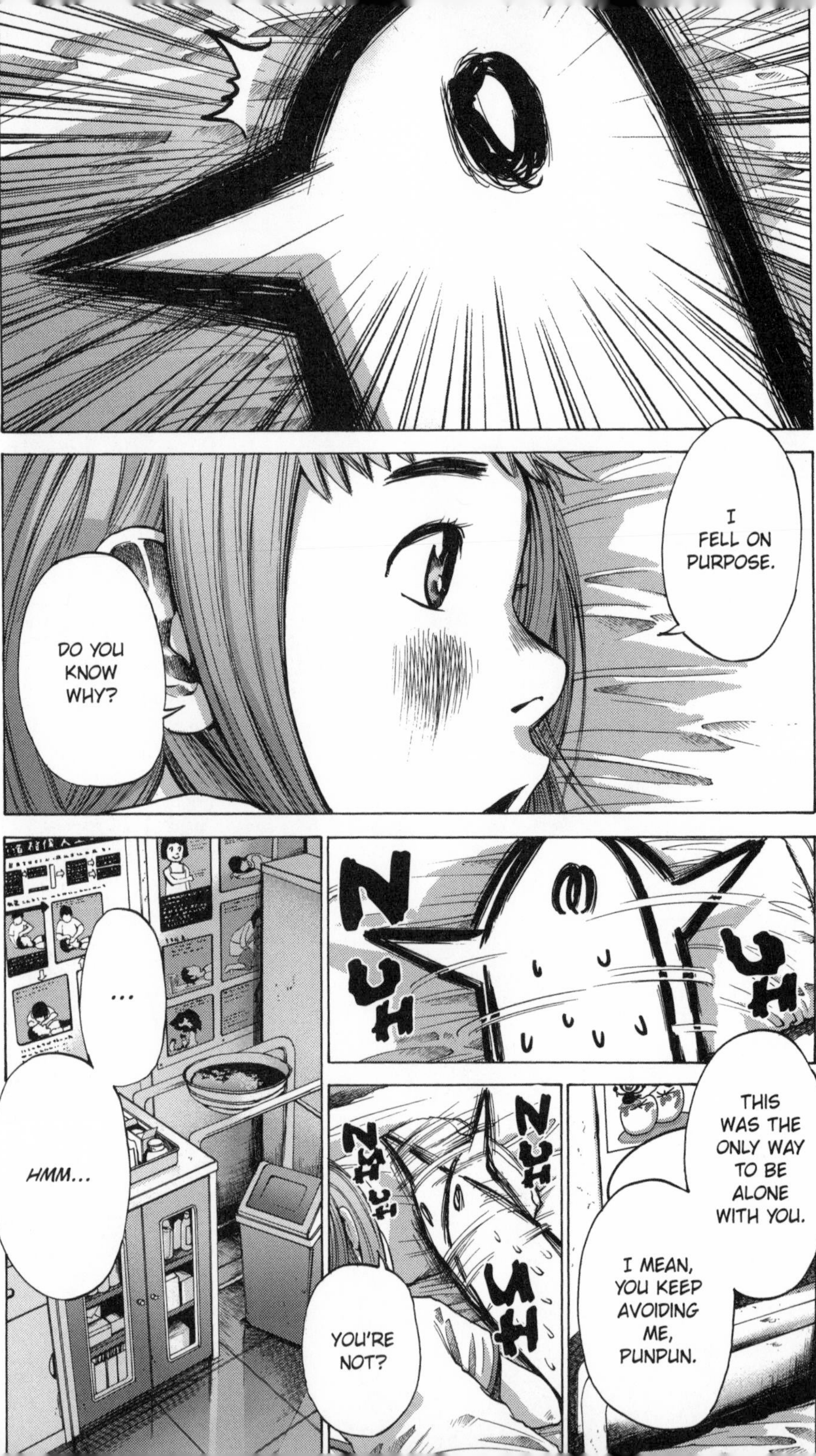
I FELL ON PURPOSE.
DO YOU KNOW WHY?
THIS WAS THE ONLY WAY TO BE ALONE WITH YOU.
I MEAN, YOU KEEP AVOIDING ME, PUNPUN.
YOU'RE NOT?
...
HMM...

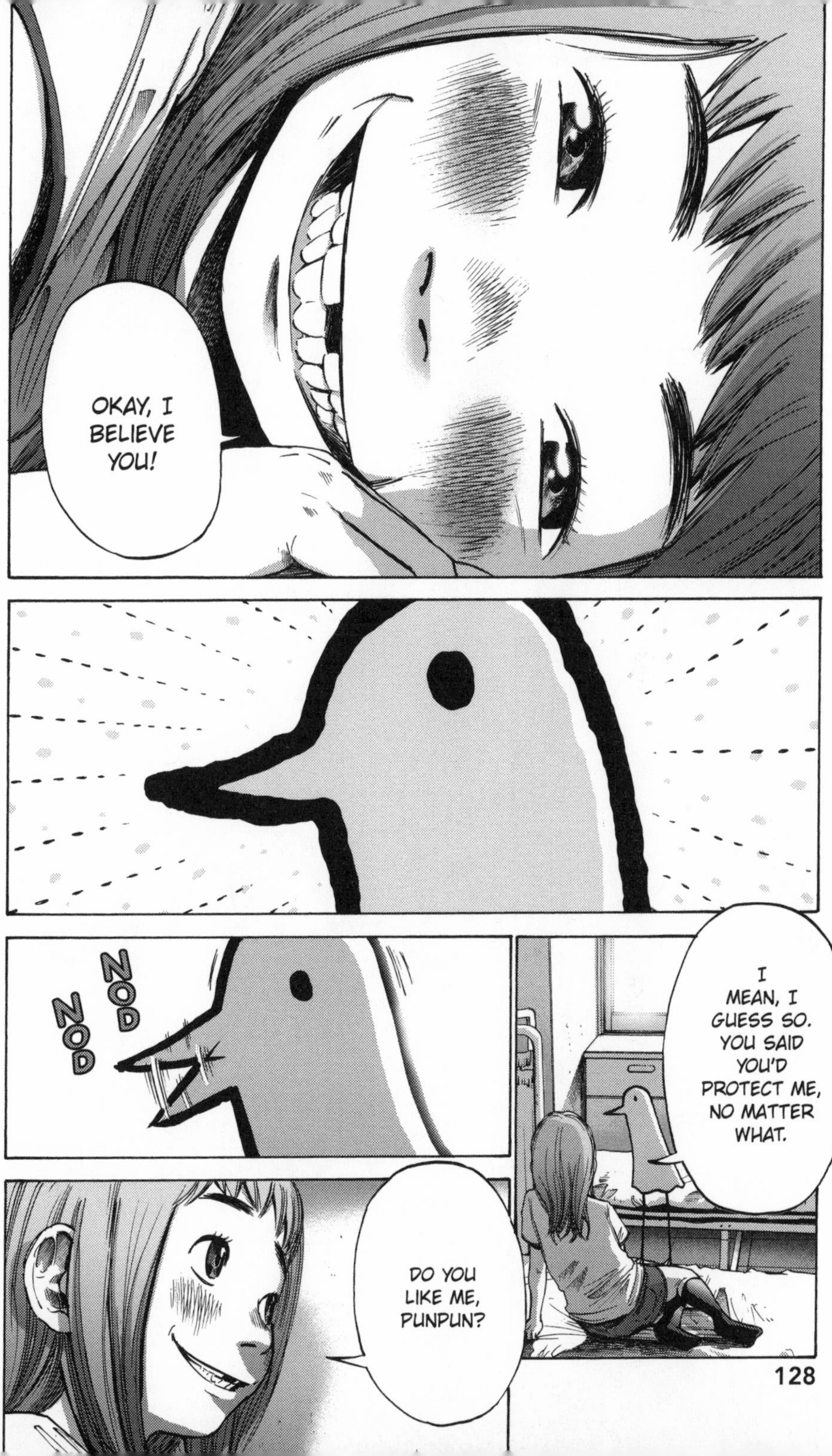
OKAY, I BELIEVE YOU!
I MEAN, I GUESS SO. YOU SAID YOU'D PROTECT ME, NO MATTER WHAT.
NOD
NOD
DO YOU LIKE ME, PUNPUN?

NOD NOD

THEN...

...I LIKE YOU TOO, PUNPUN!

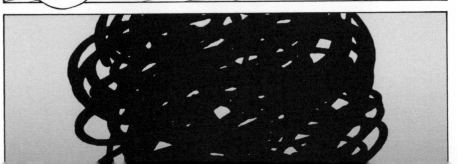

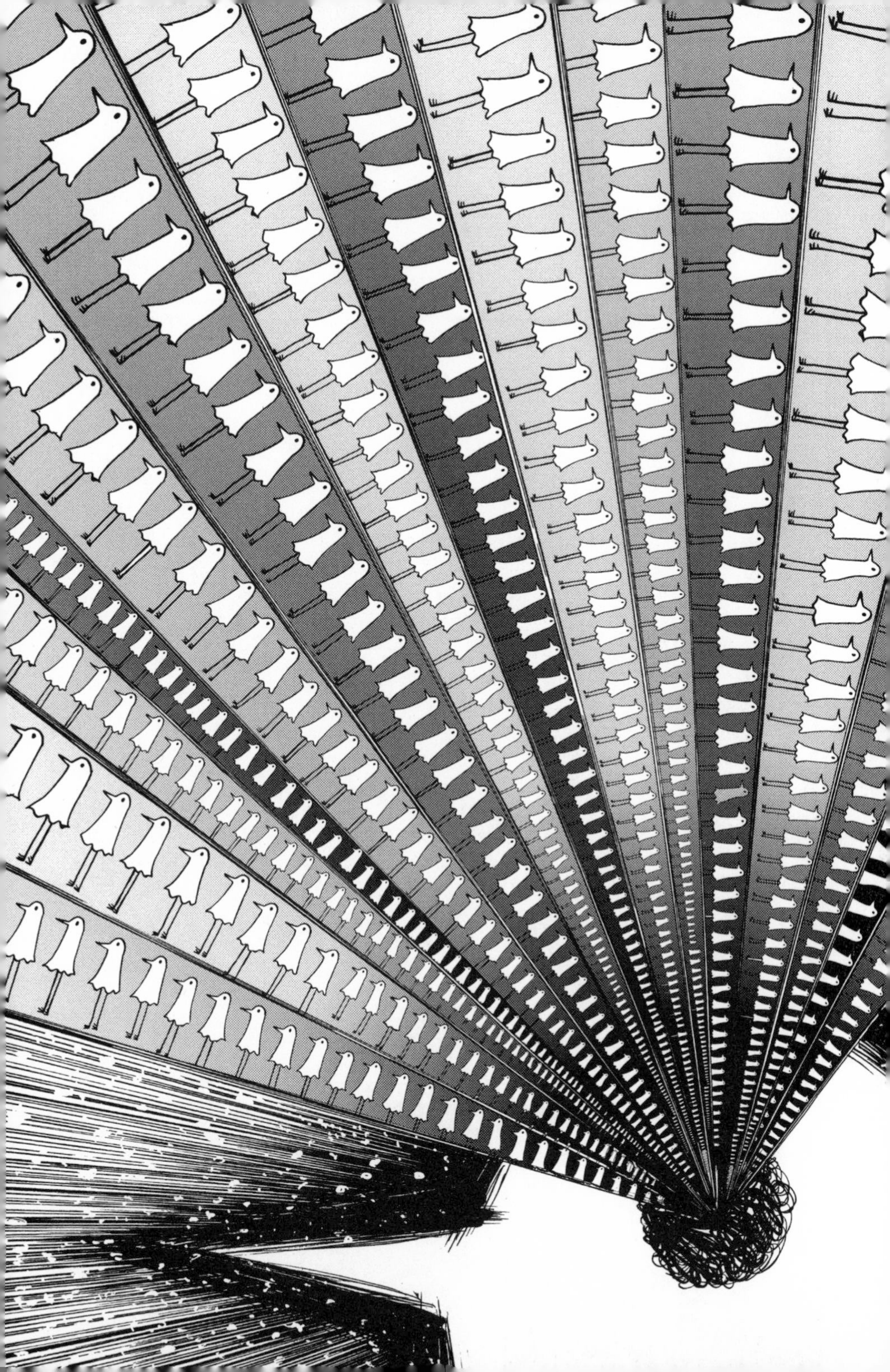

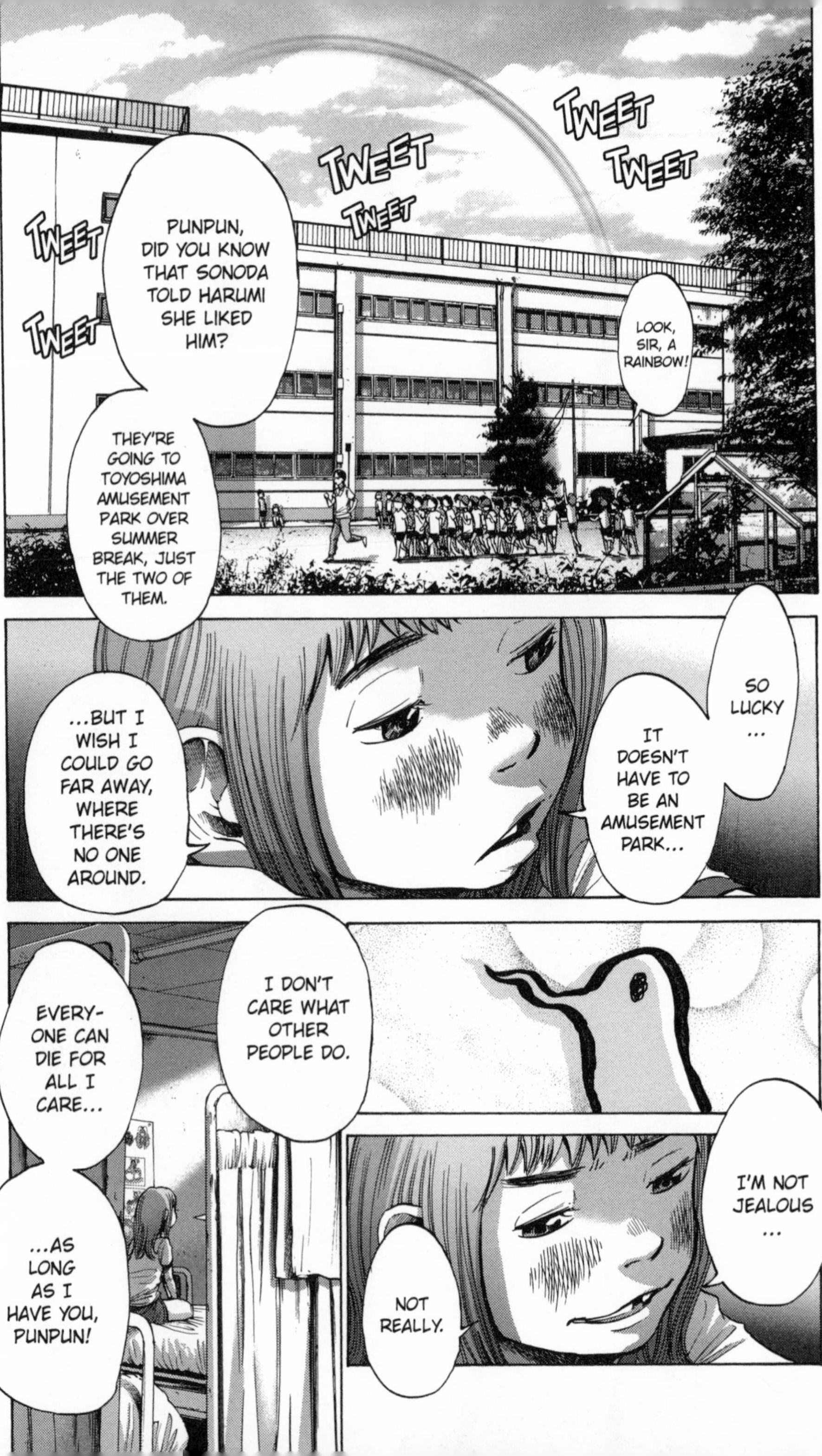
LOOK, SIR, A RAINBOW!
TWEET
TWEET
TWEET
TWEET
PUNPUN, DID YOU KNOW THAT SONODA TOLD HARUMI SHE LIKED HIM?
THEY'RE GOING TO TOYOSHIMA AMUSEMENT PARK OVER SUMMER BREAK, JUST THE TWO OF THEM.
TWEET
TWEET
SO LUCKY ...
IT DOESN'T HAVE TO BE AN AMUSEMENT PARK...
...BUT I WISH I COULD GO FAR AWAY, WHERE THERE'S NO ONE AROUND.
I'M NOT JEALOUS ...
NOT REALLY.
I DON'T CARE WHAT OTHER PEOPLE DO.
EVERY-ONE CAN DIE FOR ALL I CARE...
...AS LONG AS I HAVE YOU, PUNPUN!

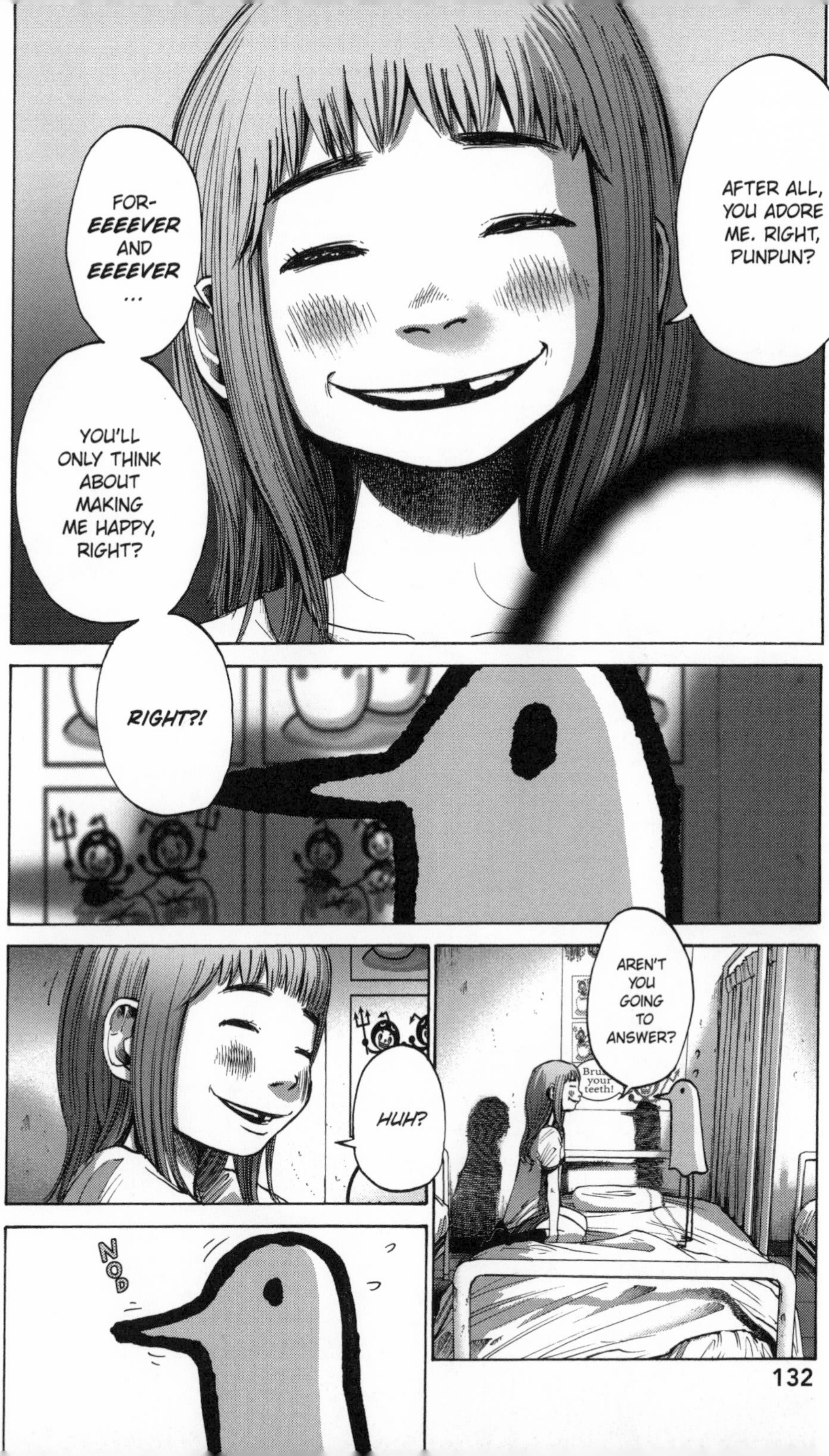
AFTER ALL, YOU ADORE ME. RIGHT, PUNPUN?
FOR-EEEEVER AND EEEEVER...
YOU'LL ONLY THINK ABOUT MAKING ME HAPPY, RIGHT?
RIGHT?!
AREN'T YOU GOING TO ANSWER?
Bru your teeth!
HUH?
NOD

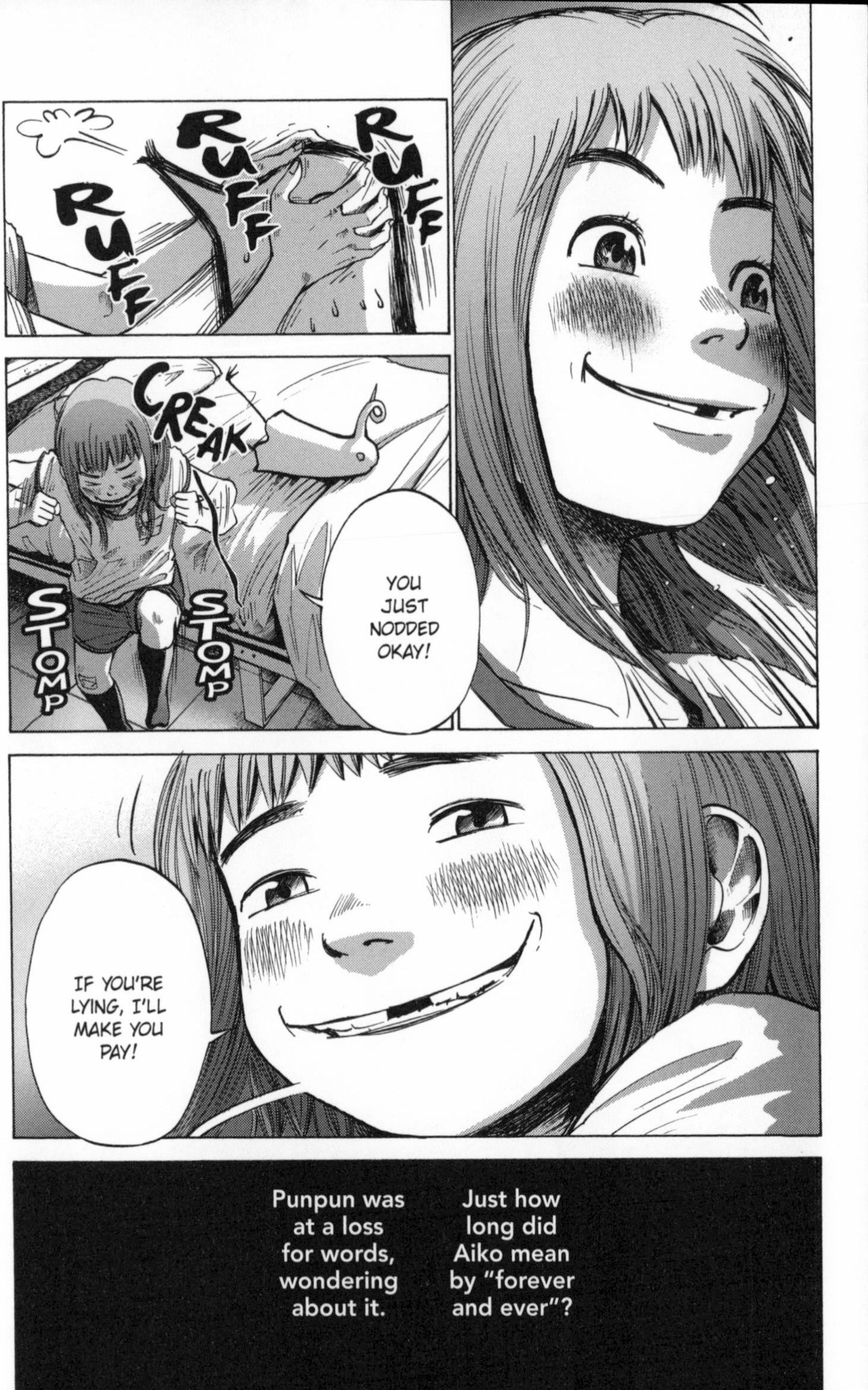
YOU JUST NODDED OKAY!
RUFF RUFF RUFF
CREAK
STOMP STOMP
IF YOU'RE LYING, I'LL MAKE YOU PAY!
Just how long did Aiko mean by "forever and ever"?
Punpun was at a loss for words, wondering about it.

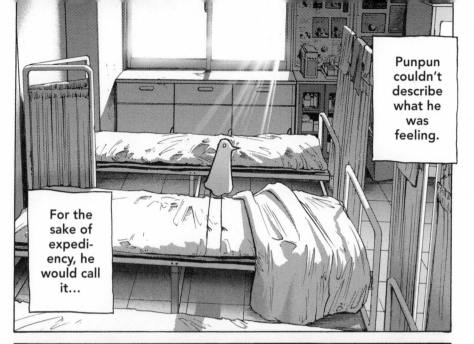

Punpun couldn't describe what he was feeling.

For the sake of expediency, he would call it...

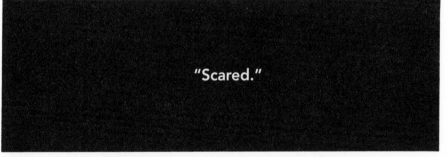

"Scared."

HARUMIN!

HARUMIN!

HEY, DID YOU GUYS ALREADY KISS?!

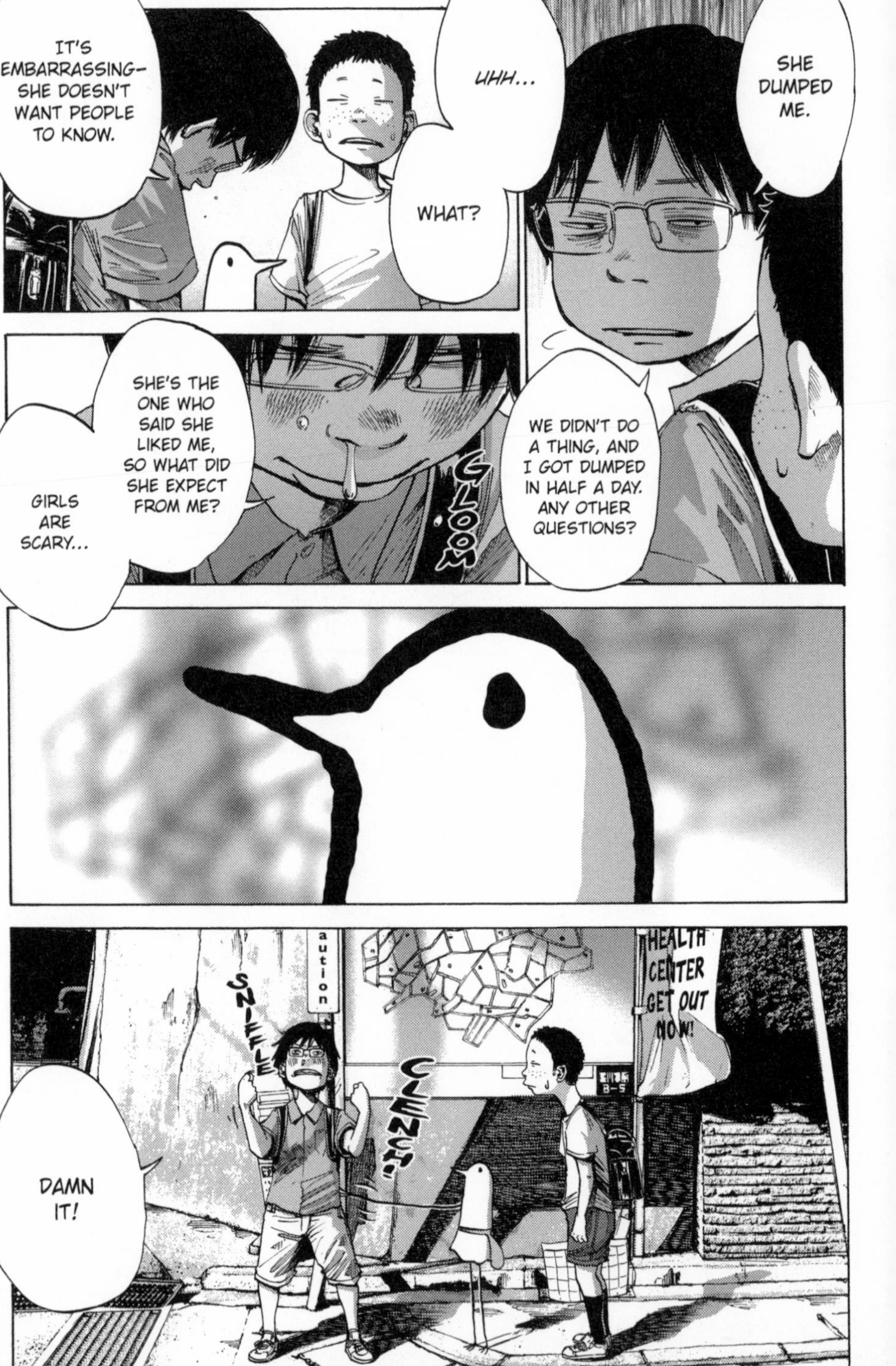

SHE DUMPED ME.
WE DIDN'T DO A THING, AND I GOT DUMPED IN HALF A DAY. ANY OTHER QUESTIONS?
WHAT?
UHH...
IT'S EMBARRASSING- SHE DOESN'T WANT PEOPLE TO KNOW.
SHE'S THE ONE WHO SAID SHE LIKED ME, SO WHAT DID SHE EXPECT FROM ME?
GLOOM
GIRLS ARE SCARY...
HEALTH CENTER GET OUT NOW!
aution
SNIFFLE
CLENCH!
DAMN IT!

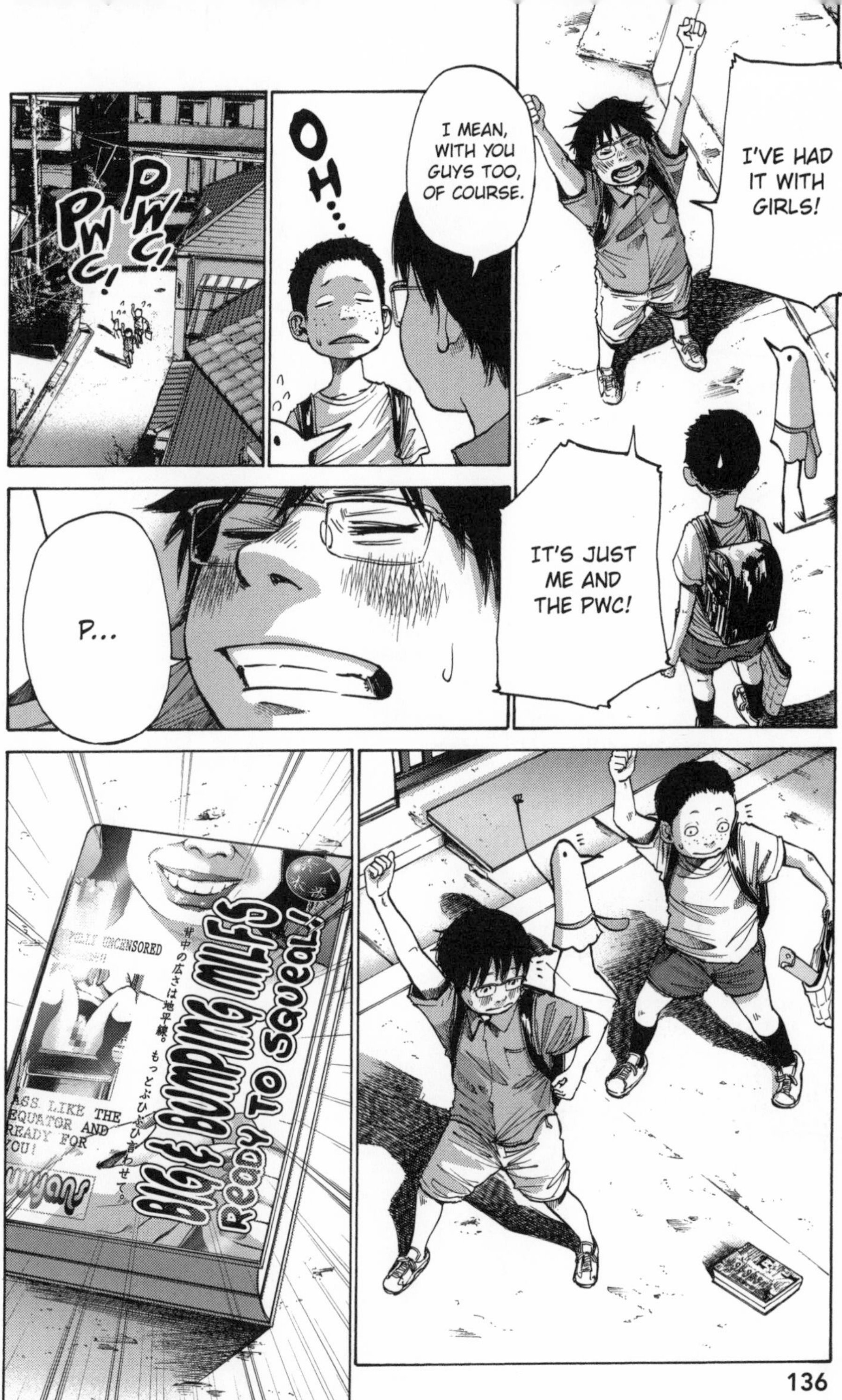
I'VE HAD IT WITH GIRLS!
IT'S JUST ME AND THE PWC!
OH...
I MEAN, WITH YOU GUYS TOO, OF COURSE.
PWC! PWC!
P...
BIG & BOUNCING MILFS
READY TO SQUEAL!
FULLY UNCENSORED
背中の広さは地平線。もっとぶひぶひ言わせて。
ASS. LIKE THE EQUATOR AND READY FOR YOU!

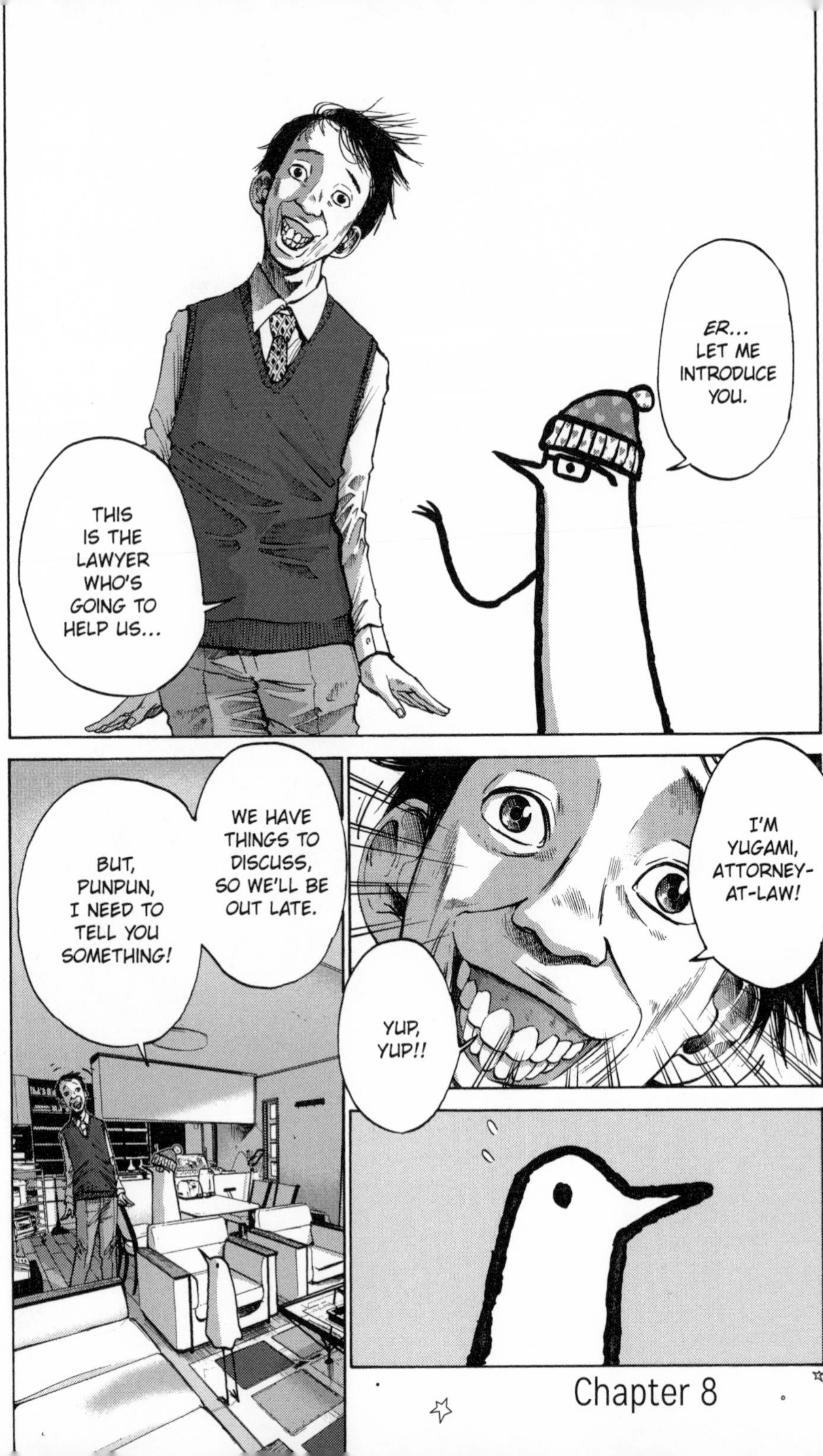
ER... LET ME INTRODUCE YOU.
THIS IS THE LAWYER WHO'S GOING TO HELP US...
I'M YUGAMI, ATTORNEY-AT-LAW!
YUP, YUP!!
WE HAVE THINGS TO DISCUSS, SO WE'LL BE OUT LATE.
BUT, PUNPUN, I NEED TO TELL YOU SOMETHING!

Chapter 8

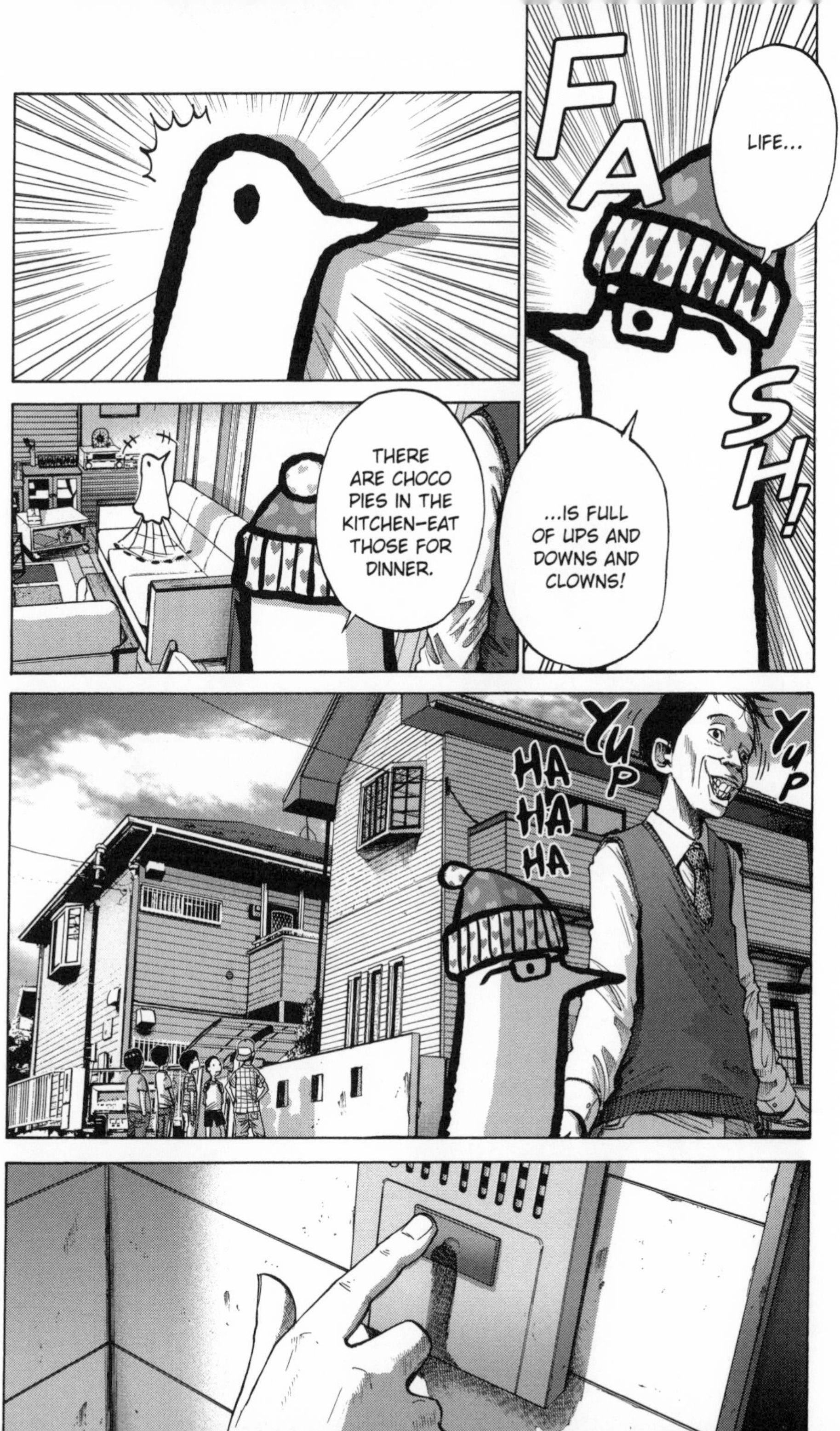
FASHI!
LIFE...
...IS FULL OF UPS AND DOWNS AND CLOWNS!
THERE ARE CHOCO PIES IN THE KITCHEN—EAT THOSE FOR DINNER.
YUP
YUP
HA HA HA

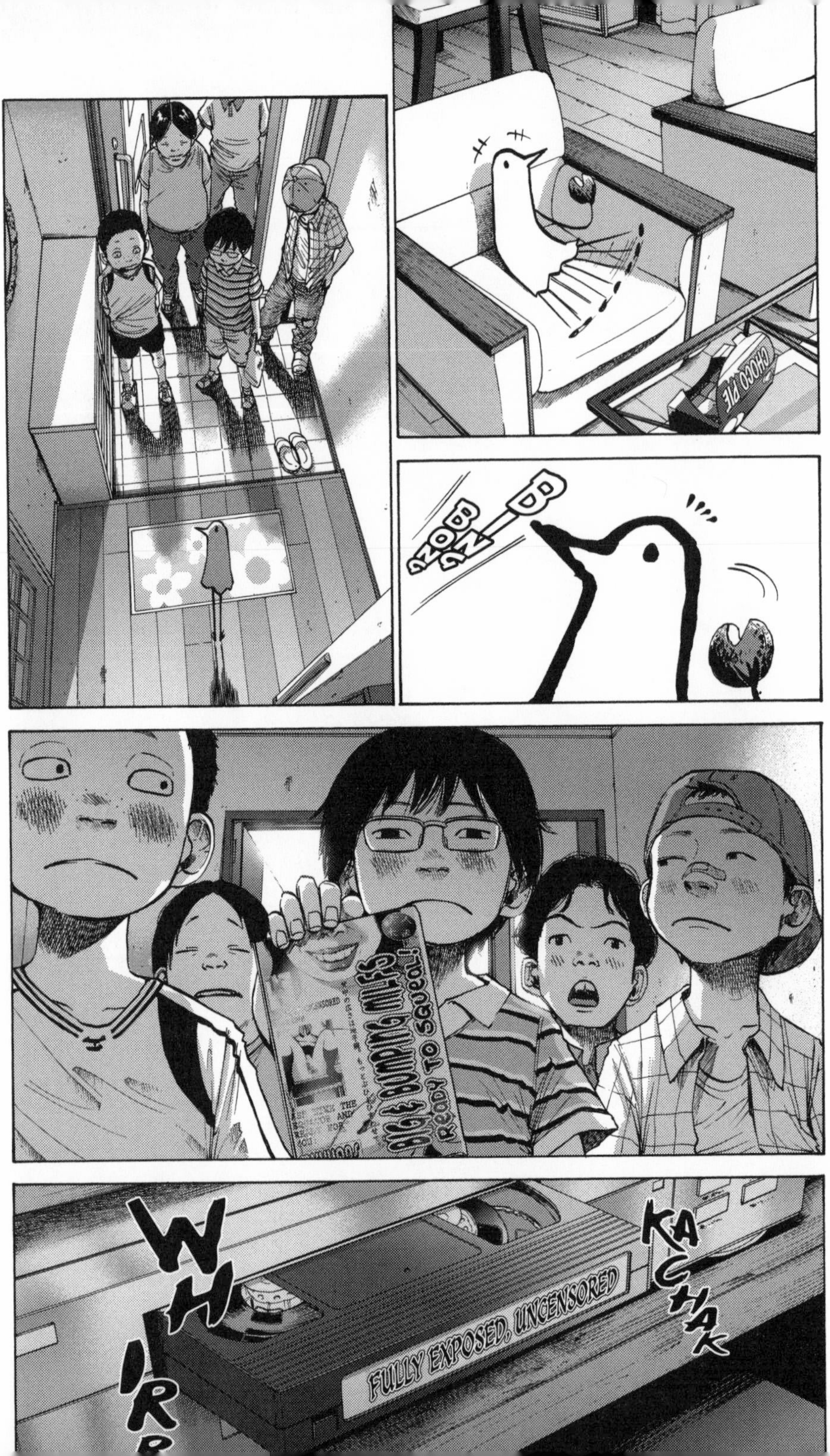
CHOCO PIE
BIG & BUMPING MILFS
READY TO SQUEAL!
UNCENSORED
KACHAK
FULLY EXPOSED, UNCENSORED
WHIR

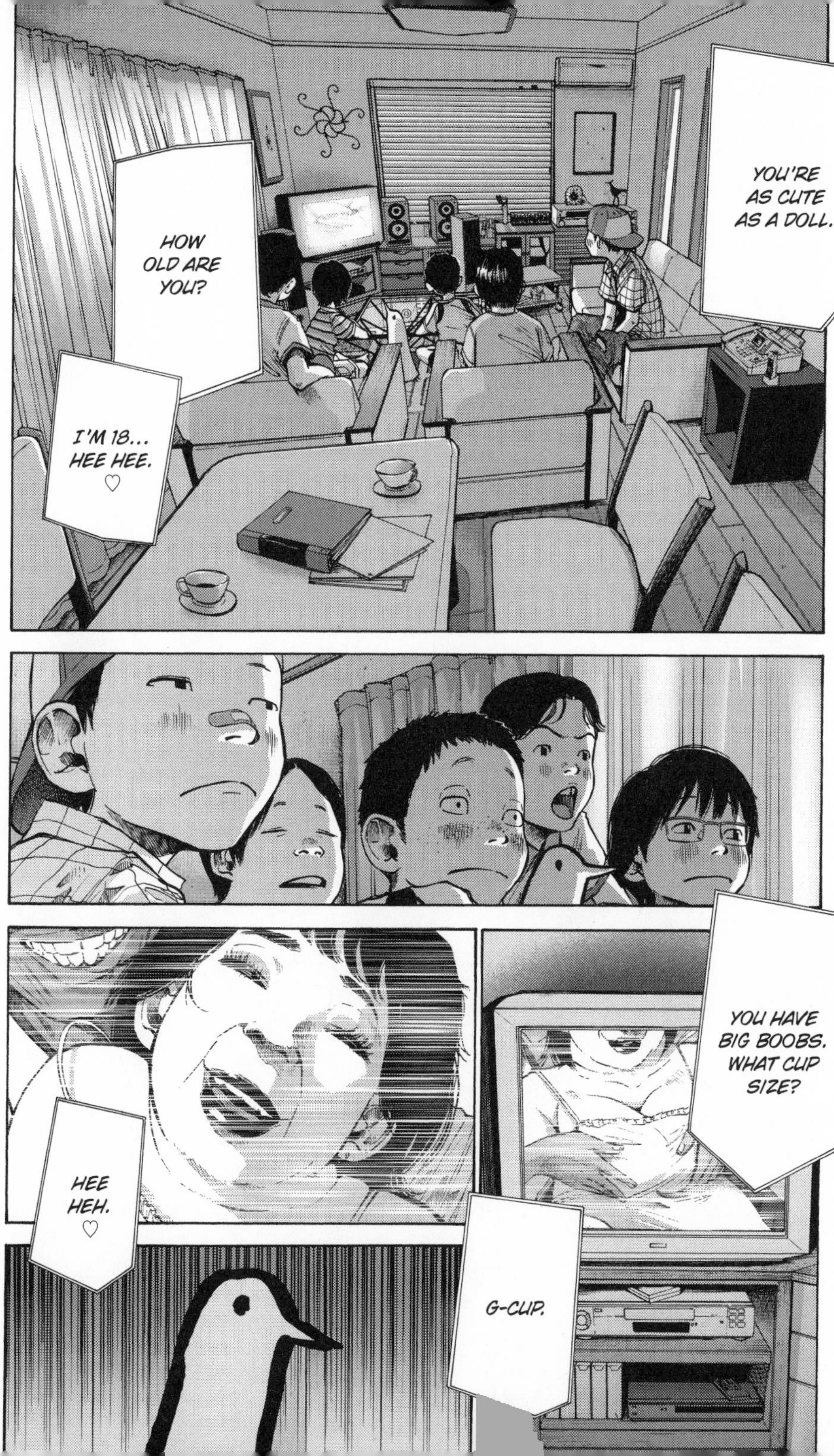
YOU'RE AS CUTE AS A DOLL.
HOW OLD ARE YOU?
I'M 18... HEE HEE. ♡
YOU HAVE BIG BOOBS. WHAT CUP SIZE?
HEE HEH. ♡
G-CUP.

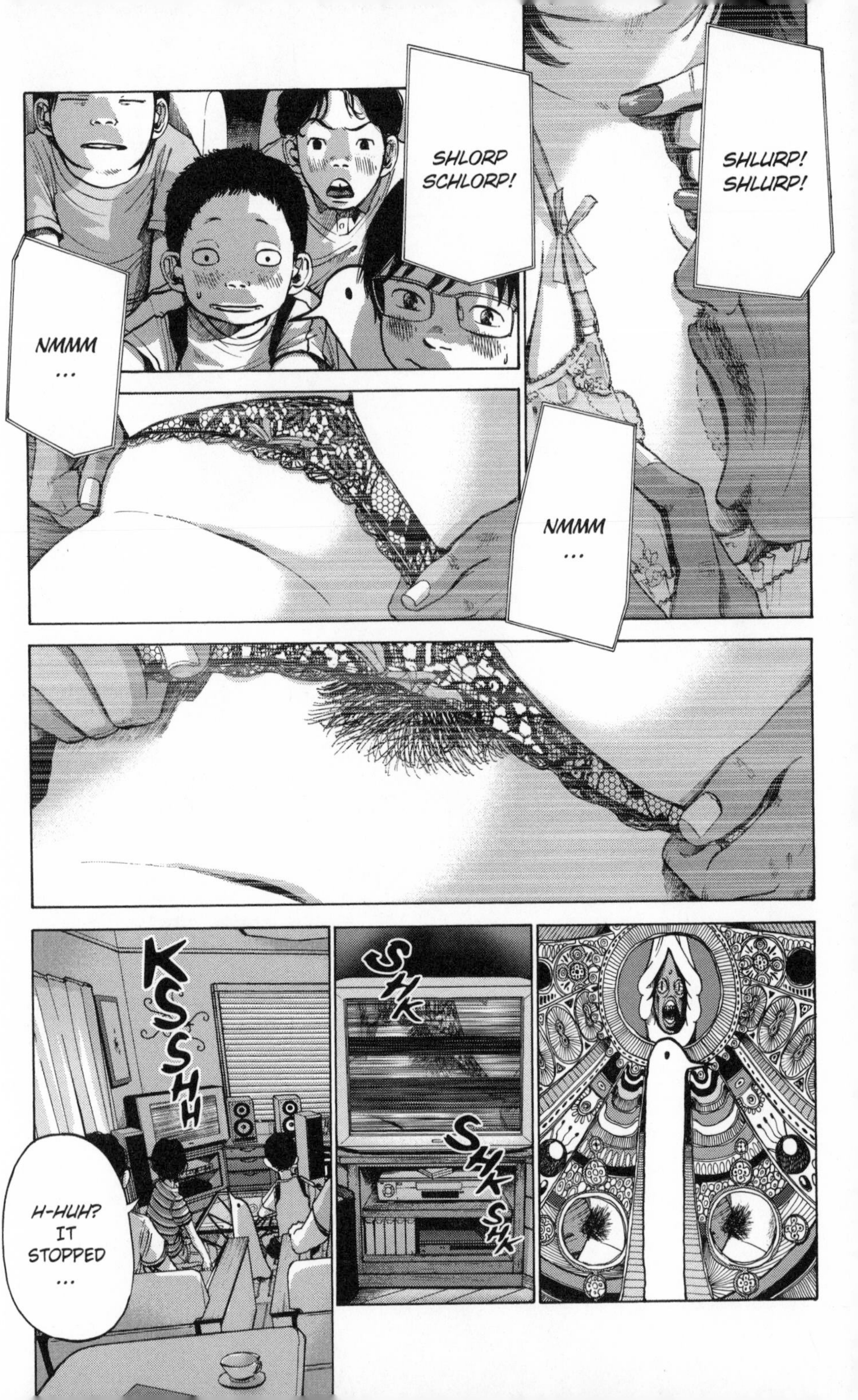
SHLURP! SHLURP!
NMMM ...
SHLORP SCHLORP!
NMMM ...
SHK SHK SHK
KSSHH
H-HUH? IT STOPPED ...

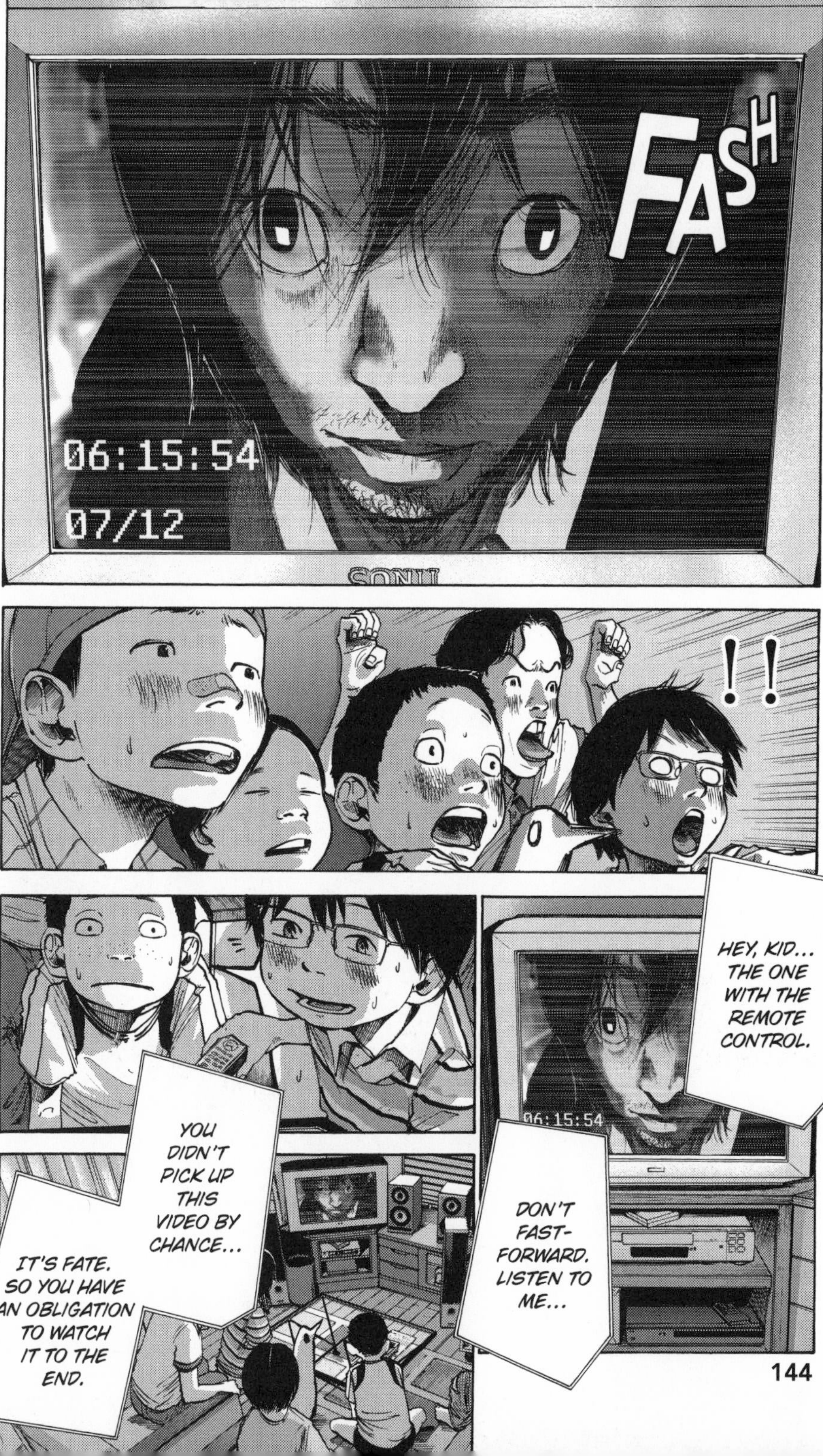
FASH
06:15:54
07/12
!!
HEY, KID... THE ONE WITH THE REMOTE CONTROL.
06:15:54
DON'T FAST-FORWARD. LISTEN TO ME...
YOU DIDN'T PICK UP THIS VIDEO BY CHANCE...
IT'S FATE. SO YOU HAVE AN OBLIGATION TO WATCH IT TO THE END.

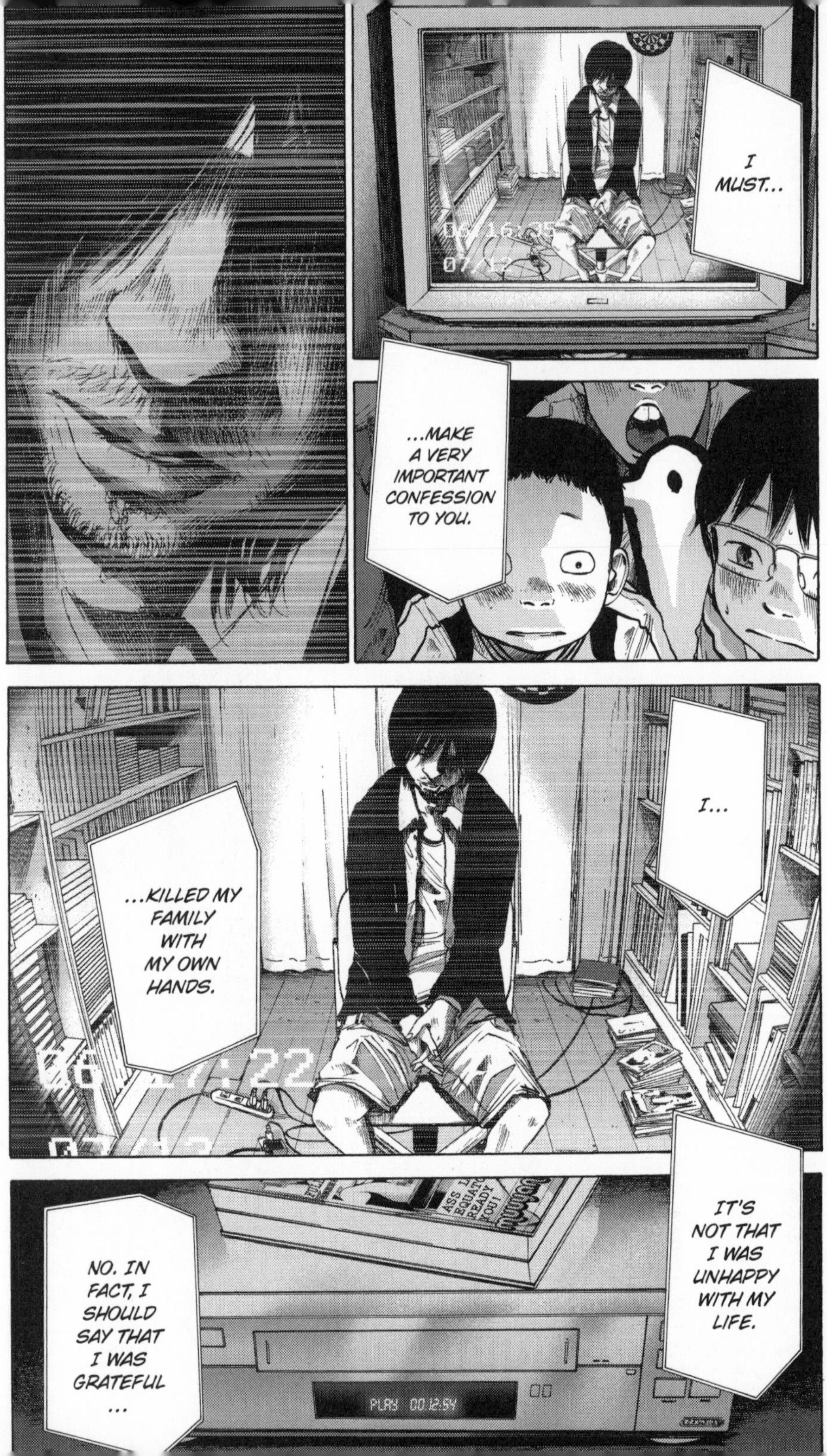
I MUST...
...MAKE A VERY IMPORTANT CONFESSION TO YOU.
I...
...KILLED MY FAMILY WITH MY OWN HANDS.
IT'S NOT THAT I WAS UNHAPPY WITH MY LIFE.
NO. IN FACT, I SHOULD SAY THAT I WAS GRATEFUL ...
PLAY 00:12:54

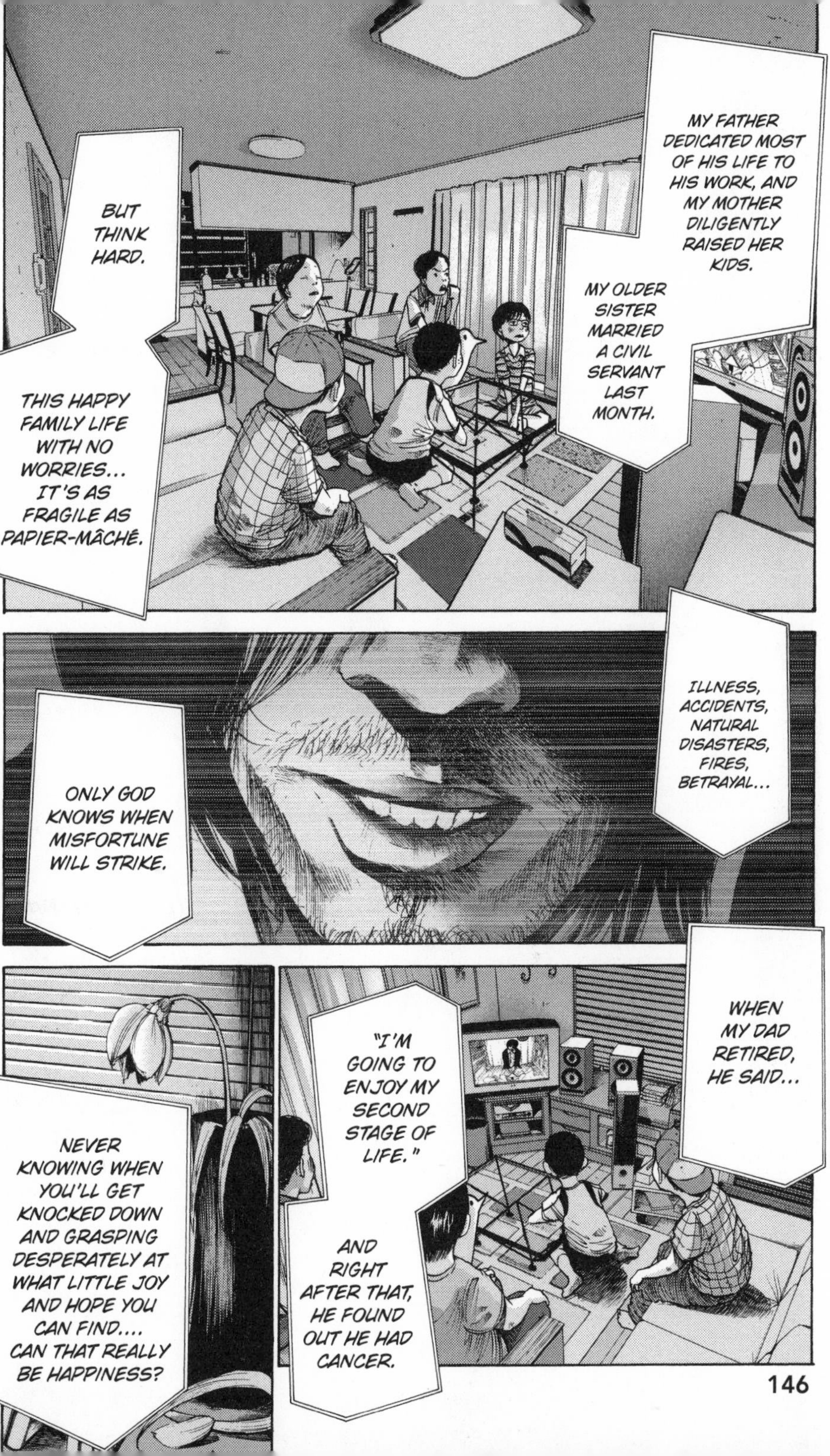
MY FATHER DEDICATED MOST OF HIS LIFE TO HIS WORK, AND MY MOTHER DILIGENTLY RAISED HER KIDS.
MY OLDER SISTER MARRIED A CIVIL SERVANT LAST MONTH.
BUT THINK HARD.
THIS HAPPY FAMILY LIFE WITH NO WORRIES... IT'S AS FRAGILE AS PAPIER-MÂCHÉ.
ILLNESS, ACCIDENTS, NATURAL DISASTERS, FIRES, BETRAYAL...
ONLY GOD KNOWS WHEN MISFORTUNE WILL STRIKE.
WHEN MY DAD RETIRED, HE SAID...
"I'M GOING TO ENJOY MY SECOND STAGE OF LIFE."
AND RIGHT AFTER THAT, HE FOUND OUT HE HAD CANCER.
NEVER KNOWING WHEN YOU'LL GET KNOCKED DOWN AND GRASPING DESPERATELY AT WHAT LITTLE JOY AND HOPE YOU CAN FIND.... CAN THAT REALLY BE HAPPINESS?

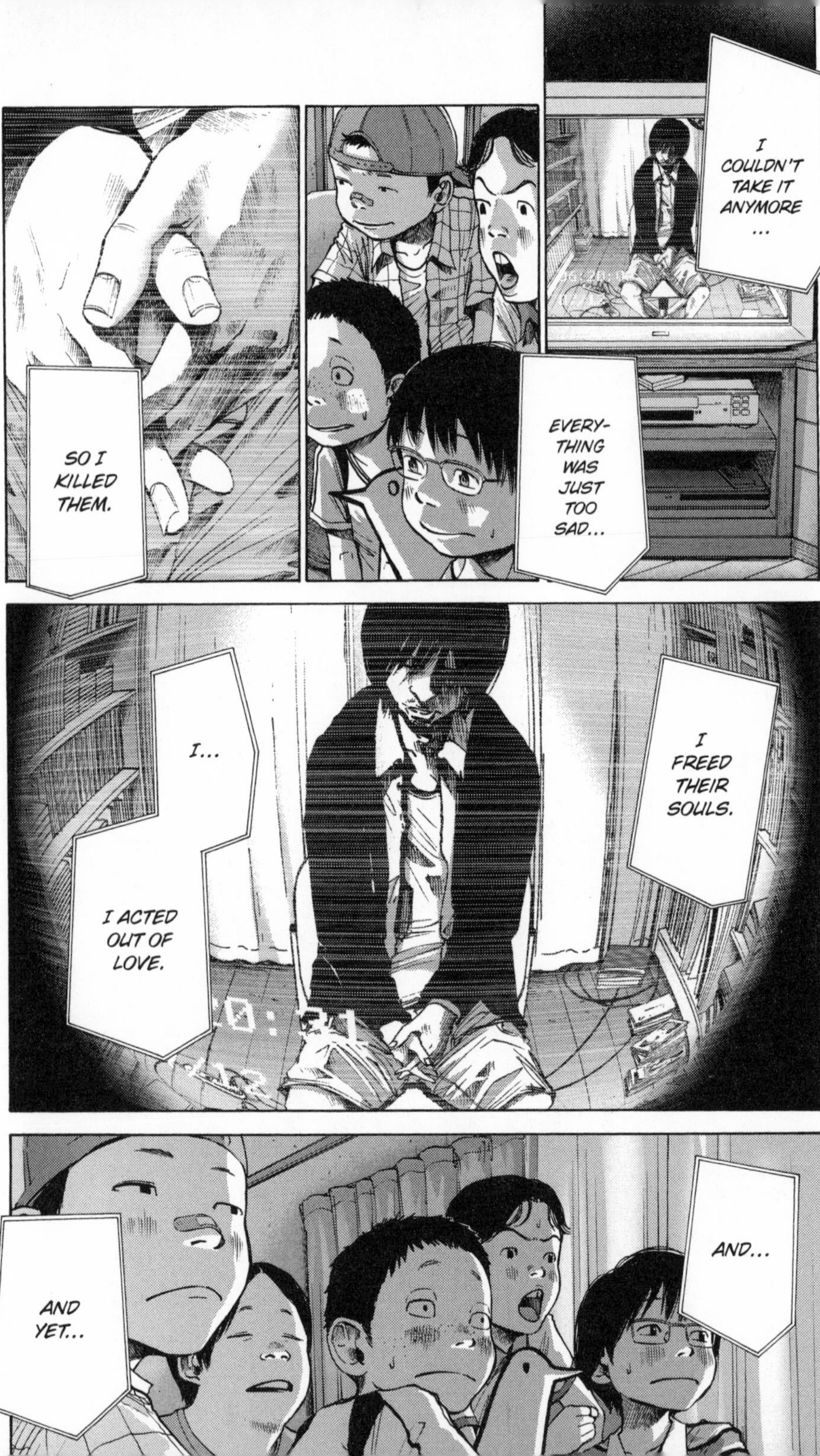
I COULDN'T TAKE IT ANYMORE...
EVERY-THING WAS JUST TOO SAD...
SO I KILLED THEM.
I FREED THEIR SOULS.
I...
I ACTED OUT OF LOVE.
AND...
AND YET...

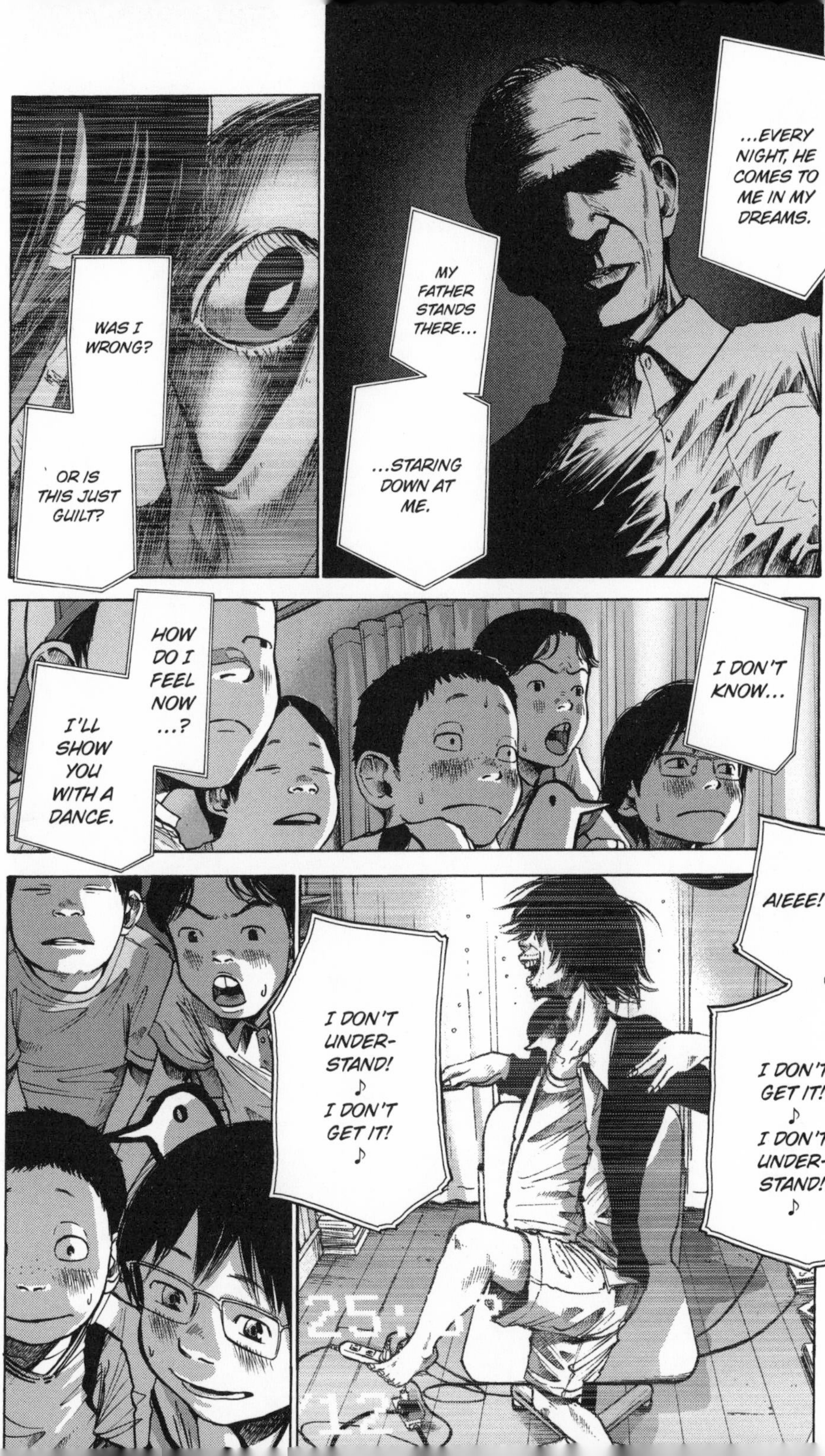
...EVERY NIGHT, HE COMES TO ME IN MY DREAMS.
MY FATHER STANDS THERE...
...STARING DOWN AT ME.
WAS I WRONG?
OR IS THIS JUST GUILT?
I DON'T KNOW...
HOW DO I FEEL NOW ...?
I'LL SHOW YOU WITH A DANCE.
AIEEE!
I DON'T GET IT! ♪ I DON'T UNDER-STAND! ♪
I DON'T UNDER-STAND! ♪ I DON'T GET IT! ♪

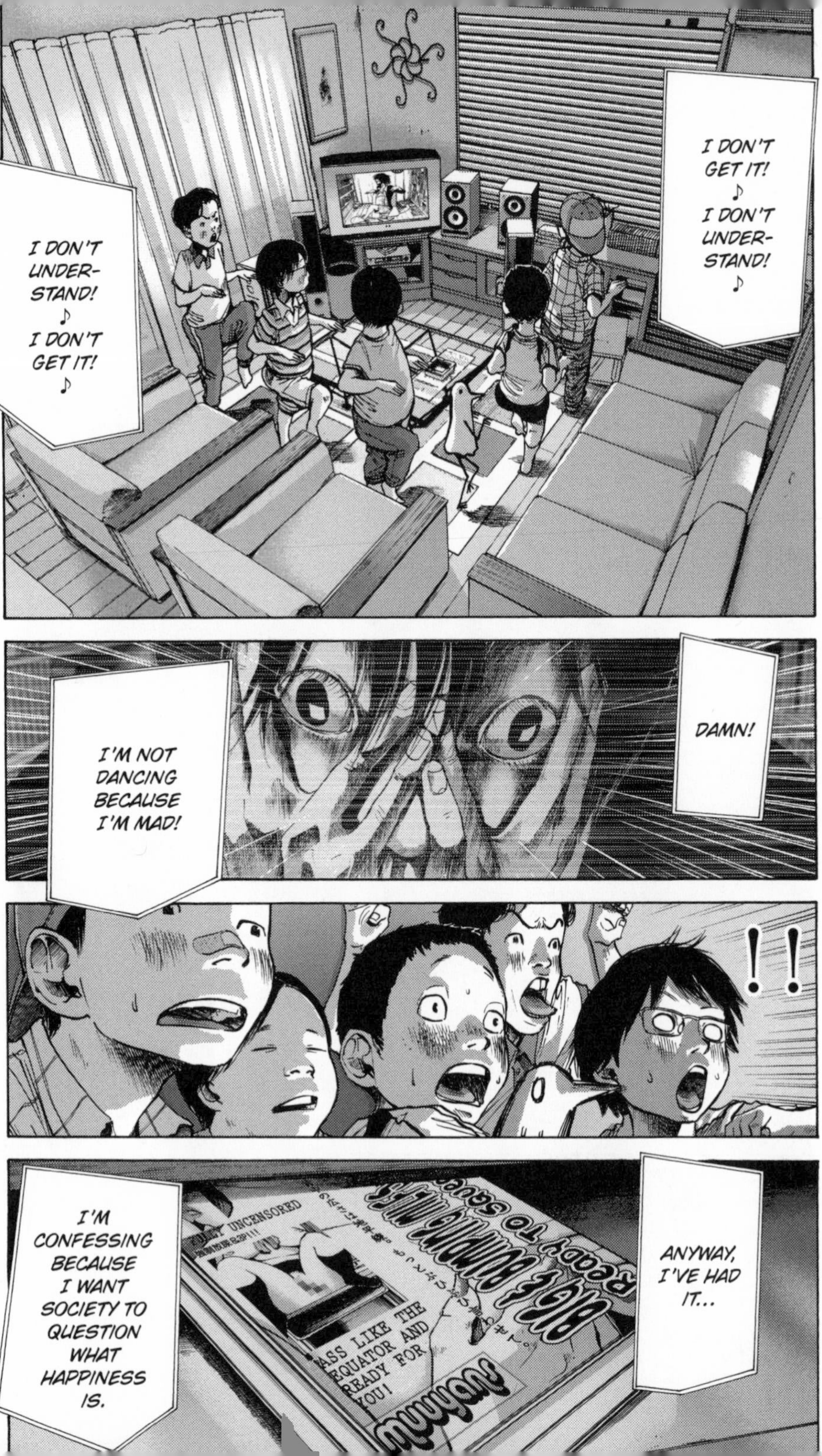
I DON'T GET IT! ♪ I DON'T UNDERSTAND! ♪
I DON'T UNDERSTAND! ♪ I DON'T GET IT! ♪
DAMN!
I'M NOT DANCING BECAUSE I'M MAD!
!!
ANYWAY, I'VE HAD IT...
UNCENSORED
ASS LIKE THE EQUATOR AND READY FOR YOU!
I'M CONFESSING BECAUSE I WANT SOCIETY TO QUESTION WHAT HAPPINESS IS.

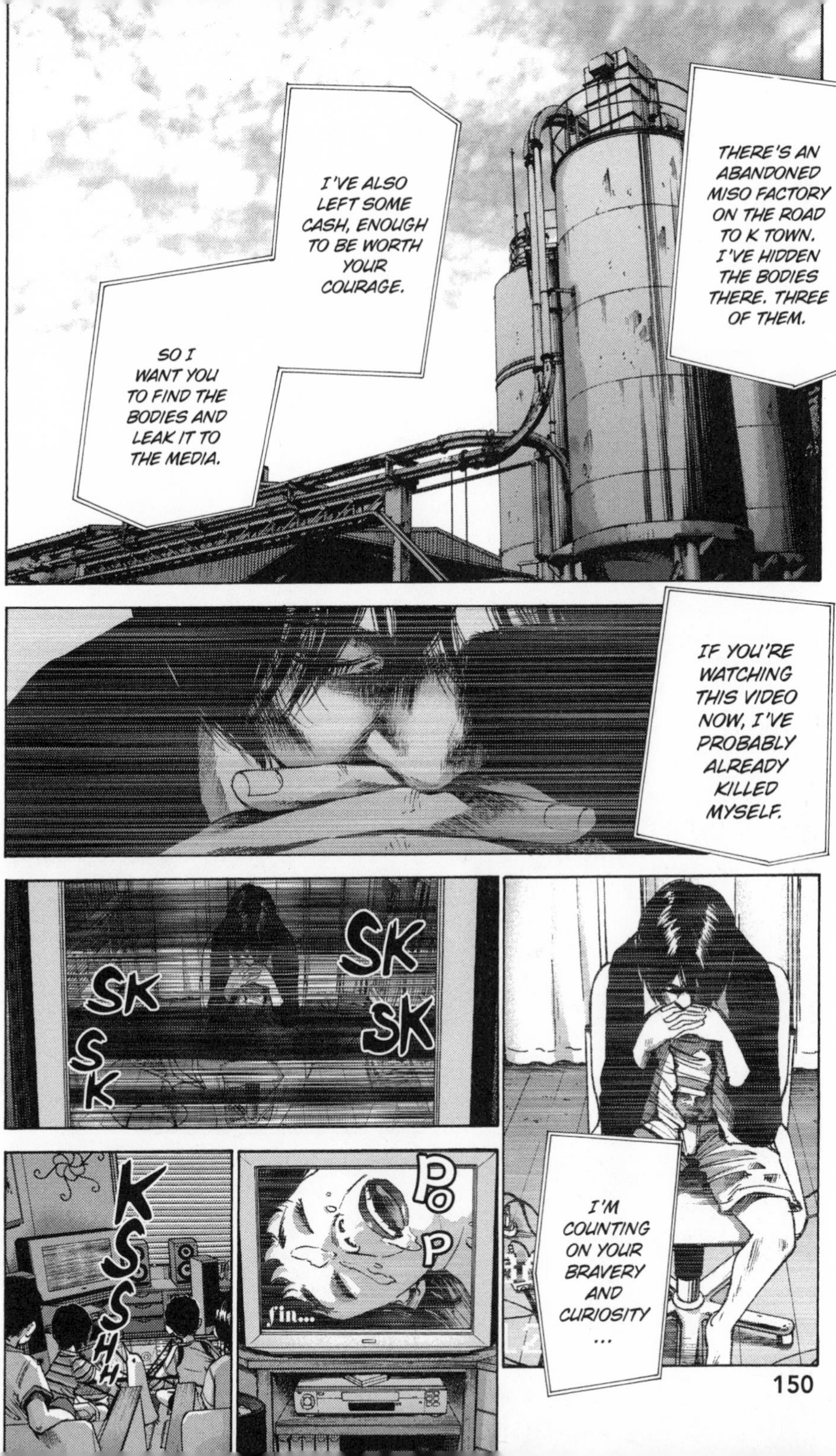
THERE'S AN ABANDONED MISO FACTORY ON THE ROAD TO K TOWN. I'VE HIDDEN THE BODIES THERE. THREE OF THEM.
I'VE ALSO LEFT SOME CASH, ENOUGH TO BE WORTH YOUR COURAGE.
SO I WANT YOU TO FIND THE BODIES AND LEAK IT TO THE MEDIA.
IF YOU'RE WATCHING THIS VIDEO NOW, I'VE PROBABLY ALREADY KILLED MYSELF.
I'M COUNTING ON YOUR BRAVERY AND CURIOSITY ...
SK
SK
SK
SK
POP
fin...
KSSHH

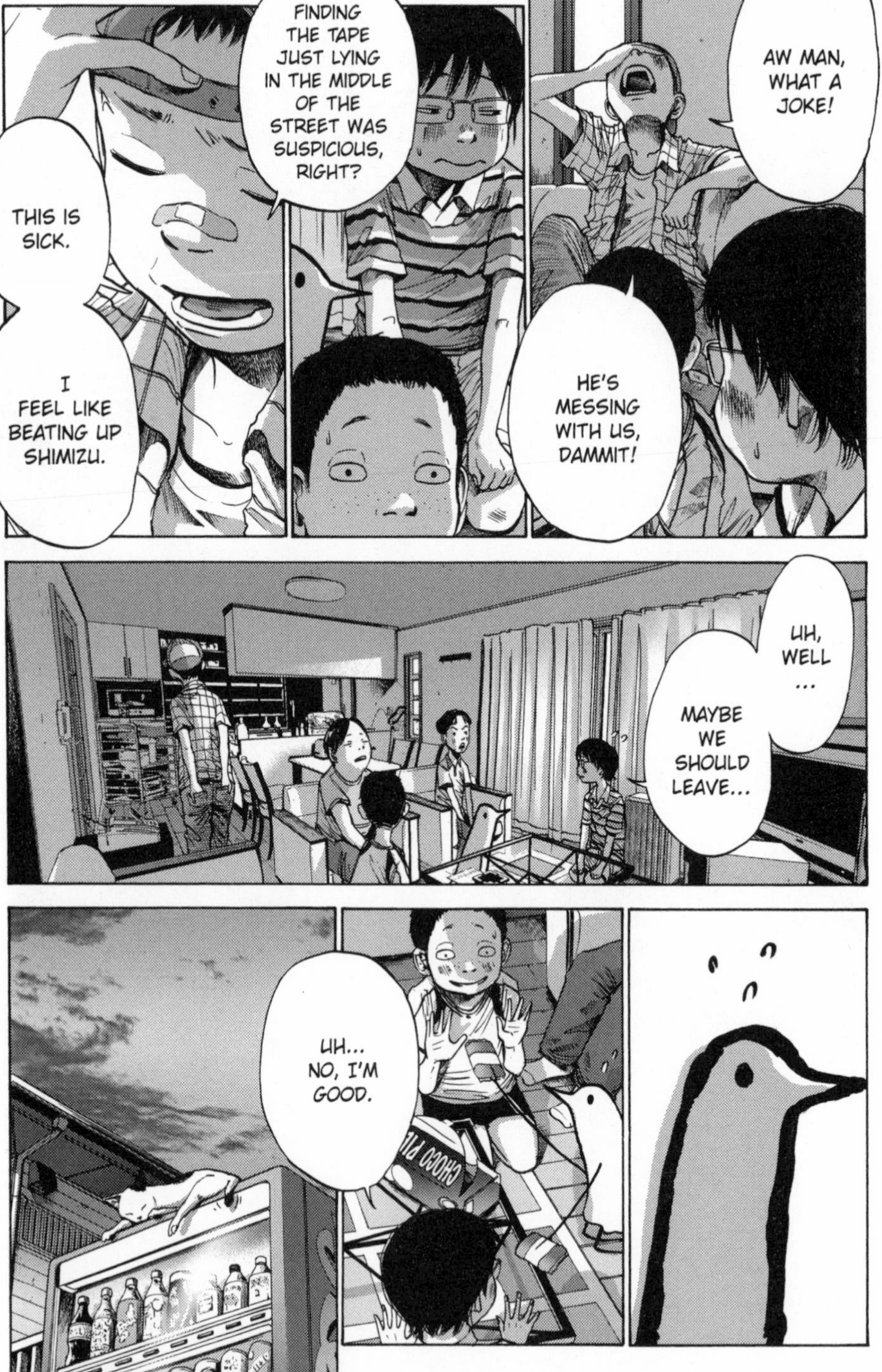
AW MAN, WHAT A JOKE!
HE'S MESSING WITH US, DAMMIT!
FINDING THE TAPE JUST LYING IN THE MIDDLE OF THE STREET WAS SUSPICIOUS, RIGHT?
THIS IS SICK.
I FEEL LIKE BEATING UP SHIMIZU.
UH, WELL ...
MAYBE WE SHOULD LEAVE...
UH... NO, I'M GOOD.

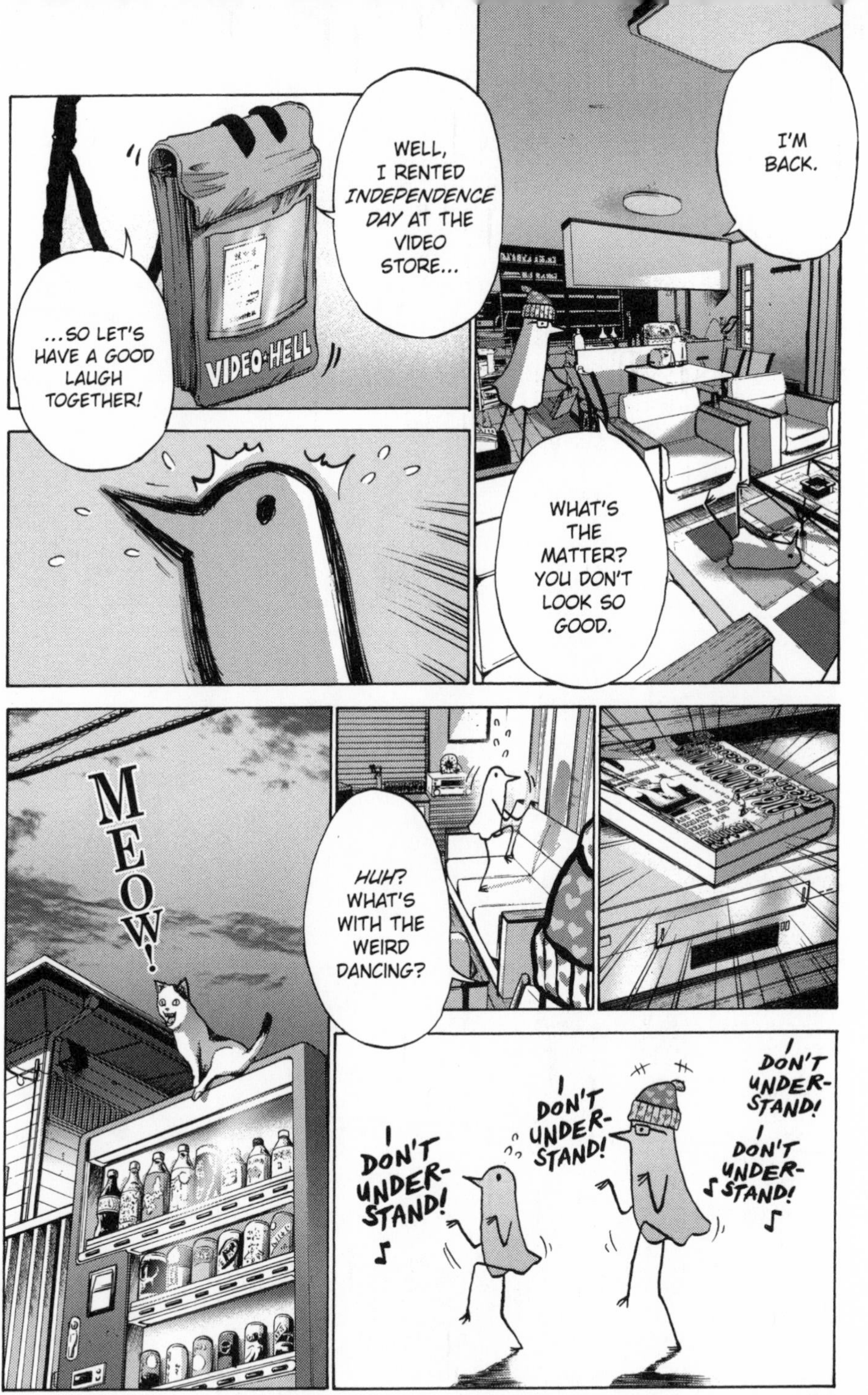
I'M BACK.
WHAT'S THE MATTER? YOU DON'T LOOK SO GOOD.
WELL, I RENTED *INDEPENDENCE DAY* AT THE VIDEO STORE...
VIDEO-HELL
...SO LET'S HAVE A GOOD LAUGH TOGETHER!
HUH? WHAT'S WITH THE WEIRD DANCING?
I DON'T UNDERSTAND!
I DON'T UNDERSTAND!
I DON'T UNDERSTAND!
I DON'T UNDERSTAND!
MEOW!

Chapter 9

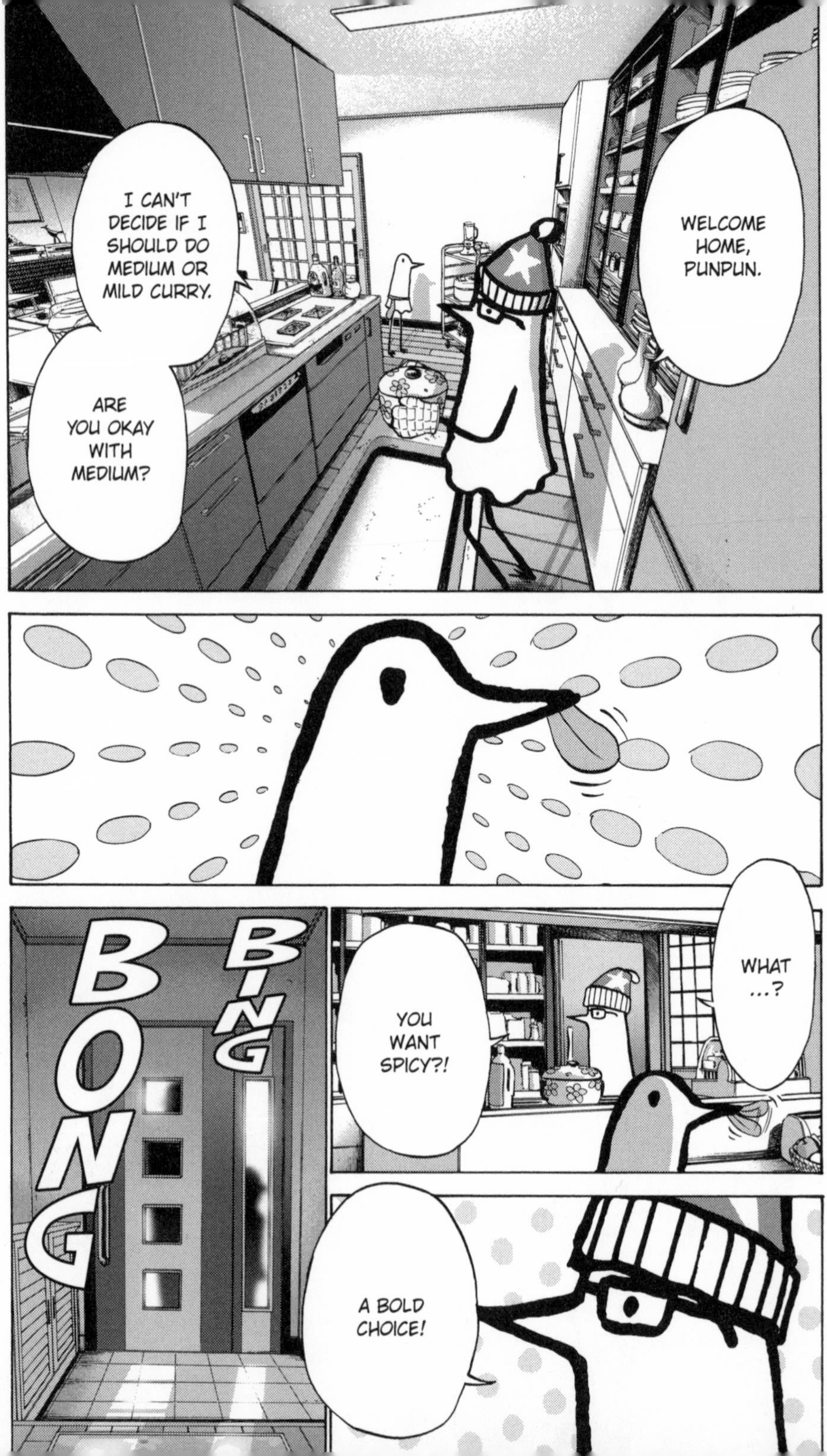
WELCOME HOME, PUNPUN.
I CAN'T DECIDE IF I SHOULD DO MEDIUM OR MILD CURRY.
ARE YOU OKAY WITH MEDIUM?
WHAT ...?
YOU WANT SPICY?!
A BOLD CHOICE!
BING
BONG

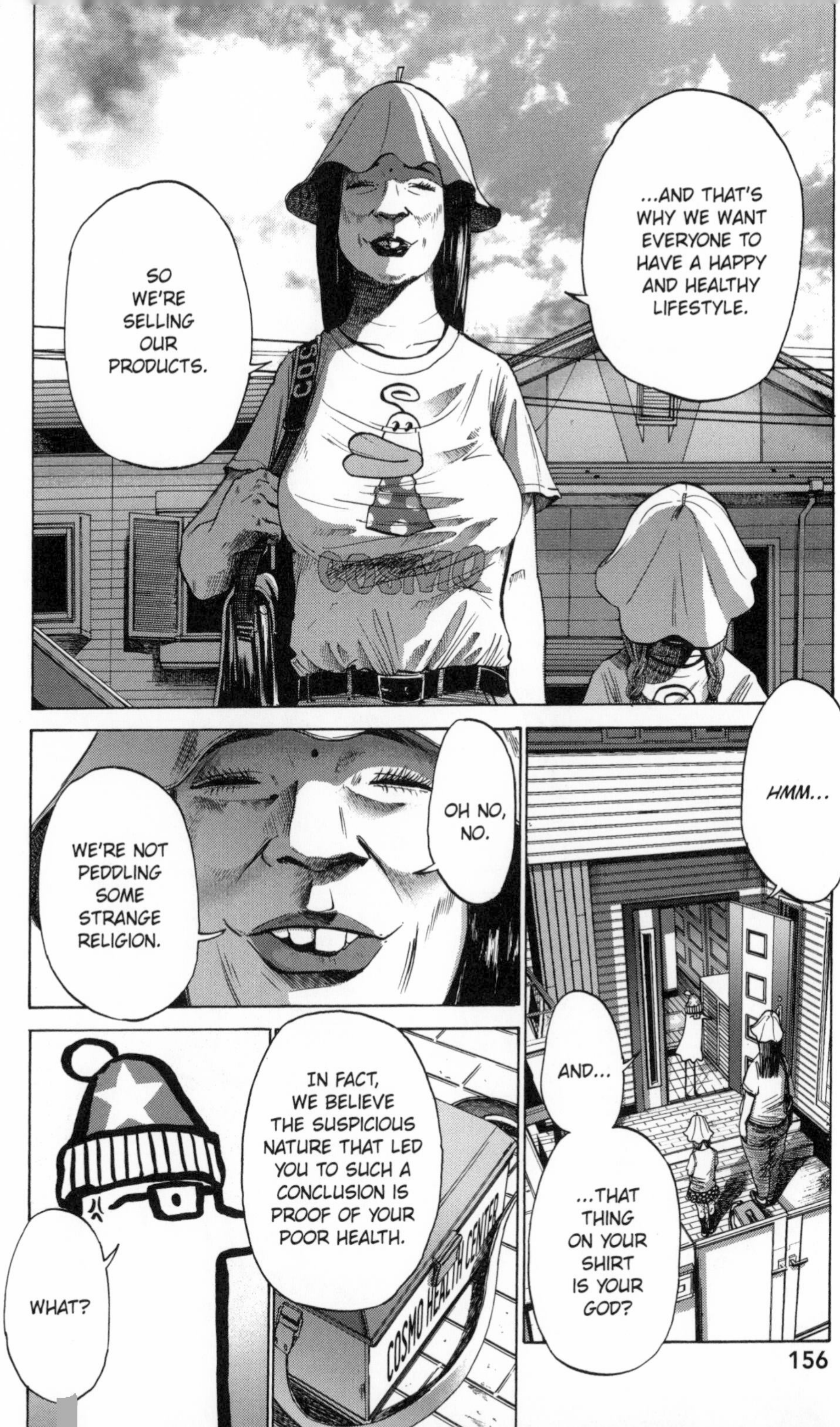
...AND THAT'S WHY WE WANT EVERYONE TO HAVE A HAPPY AND HEALTHY LIFESTYLE.
SO WE'RE SELLING OUR PRODUCTS.
HMM...
AND...
...THAT THING ON YOUR SHIRT IS YOUR GOD?
OH NO, NO.
WE'RE NOT PEDDLING SOME STRANGE RELIGION.
IN FACT, WE BELIEVE THE SUSPICIOUS NATURE THAT LED YOU TO SUCH A CONCLUSION IS PROOF OF YOUR POOR HEALTH.
COSMO HEALTH CENTER
WHAT?

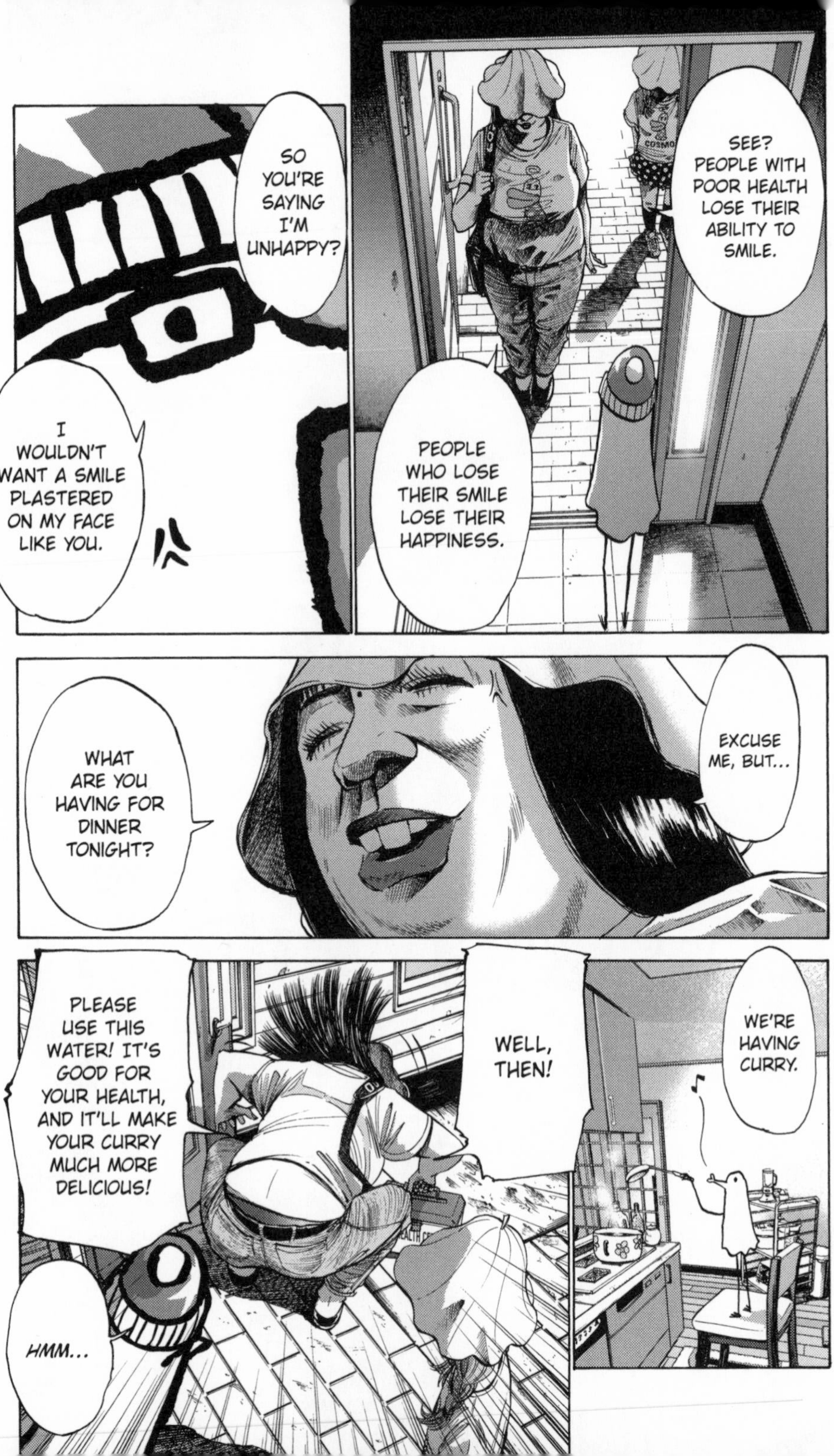
SEE? PEOPLE WITH POOR HEALTH LOSE THEIR ABILITY TO SMILE.
PEOPLE WHO LOSE THEIR SMILE LOSE THEIR HAPPINESS.
SO YOU'RE SAYING I'M UNHAPPY?
I WOULDN'T WANT A SMILE PLASTERED ON MY FACE LIKE YOU.
EXCUSE ME, BUT...
WHAT ARE YOU HAVING FOR DINNER TONIGHT?
WE'RE HAVING CURRY.
WELL, THEN!
PLEASE USE THIS WATER! IT'S GOOD FOR YOUR HEALTH, AND IT'LL MAKE YOUR CURRY MUCH MORE DELICIOUS!
HMM...

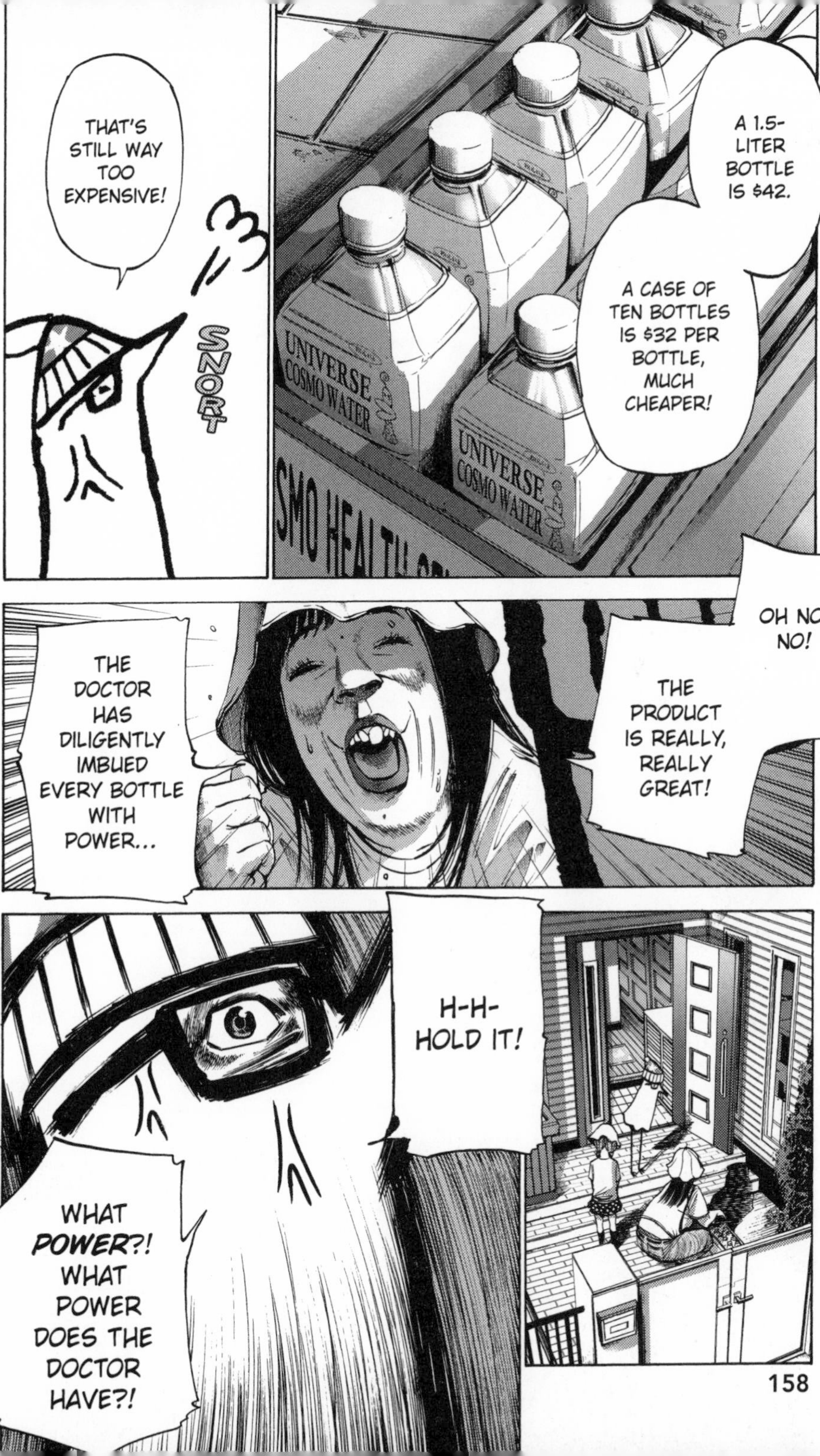
A 1.5-LITER BOTTLE IS $42.
A CASE OF TEN BOTTLES IS $32 PER BOTTLE, MUCH CHEAPER!
UNIVERSE COSMO WATER
UNIVERSE COSMO WATER
THAT'S STILL WAY TOO EXPENSIVE!
SNORT
OH NO, NO!
THE PRODUCT IS REALLY, REALLY GREAT!
THE DOCTOR HAS DILIGENTLY IMBUED EVERY BOTTLE WITH POWER...
H-H-HOLD IT!
WHAT **POWER**?! WHAT POWER DOES THE DOCTOR HAVE?!

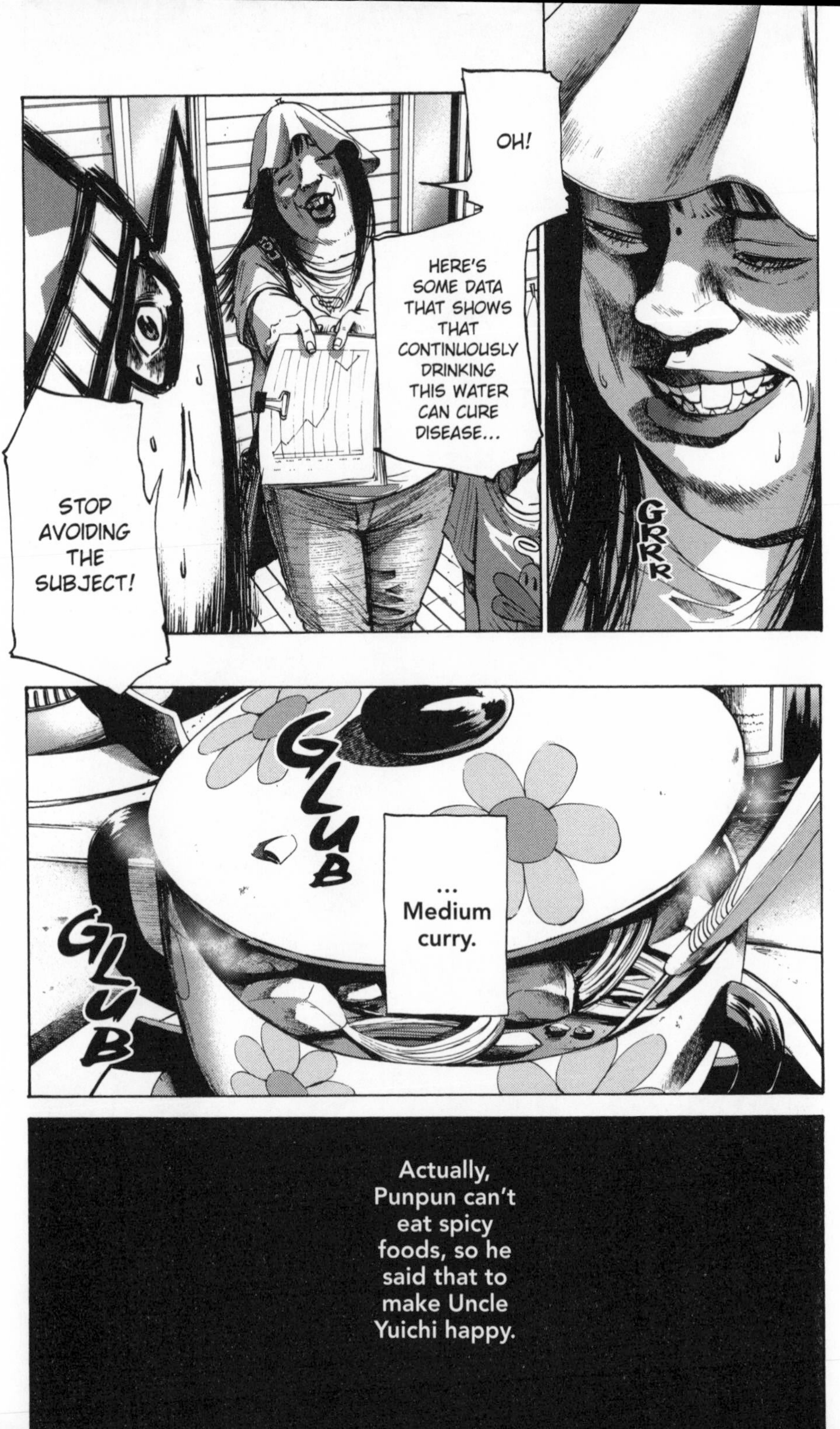
OH!
HERE'S SOME DATA THAT SHOWS THAT CONTINUOUSLY DRINKING THIS WATER CAN CURE DISEASE...
GRRR
STOP AVOIDING THE SUBJECT!
GLUB
... Medium curry.
GLUB
Actually, Punpun can't eat spicy foods, so he said that to make Uncle Yuichi happy.

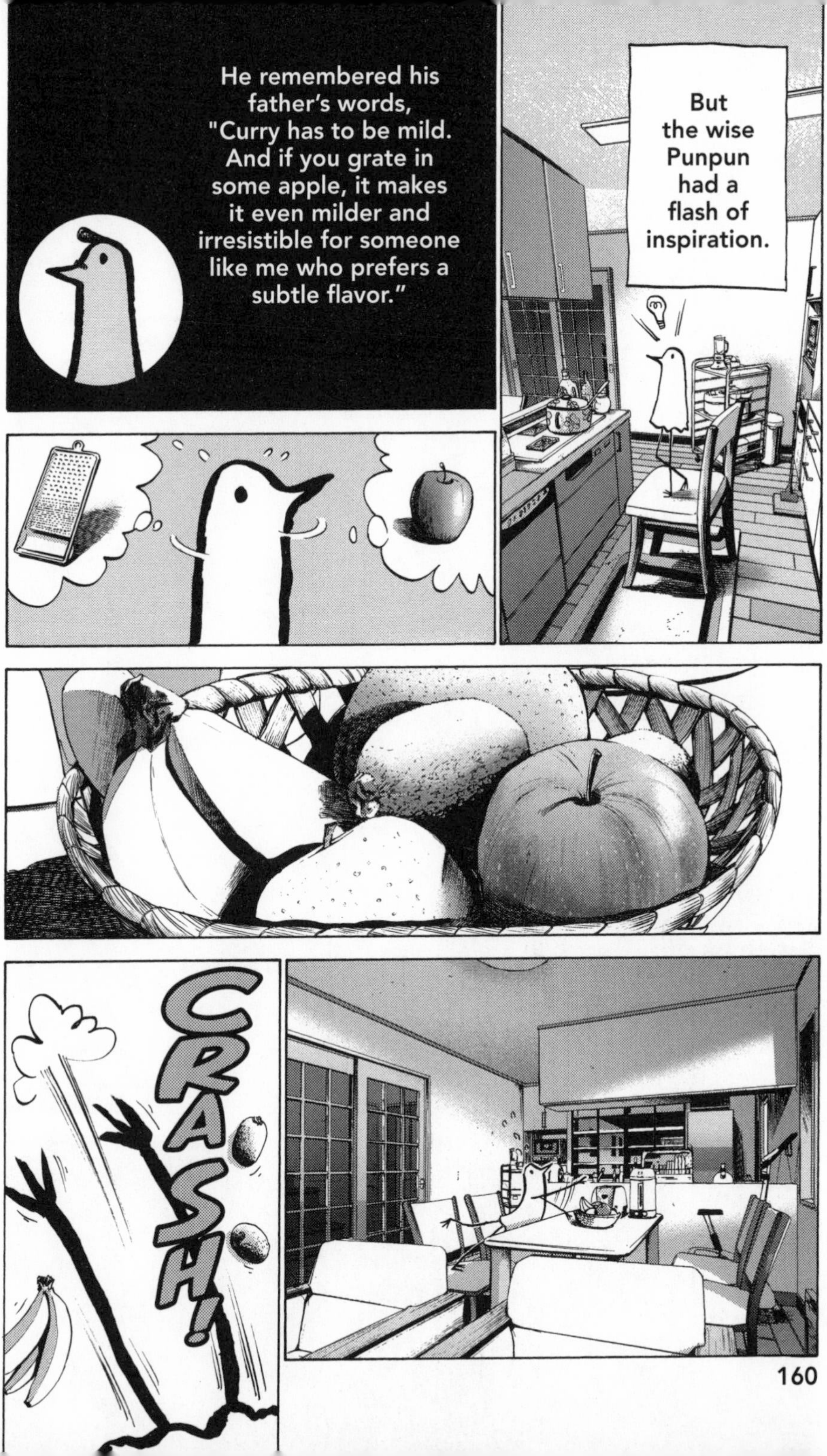

But the wise Punpun had a flash of inspiration.
He remembered his father's words, "Curry has to be mild. And if you grate in some apple, it makes it even milder and irresistible for someone like me who prefers a subtle flavor."
CRASH!

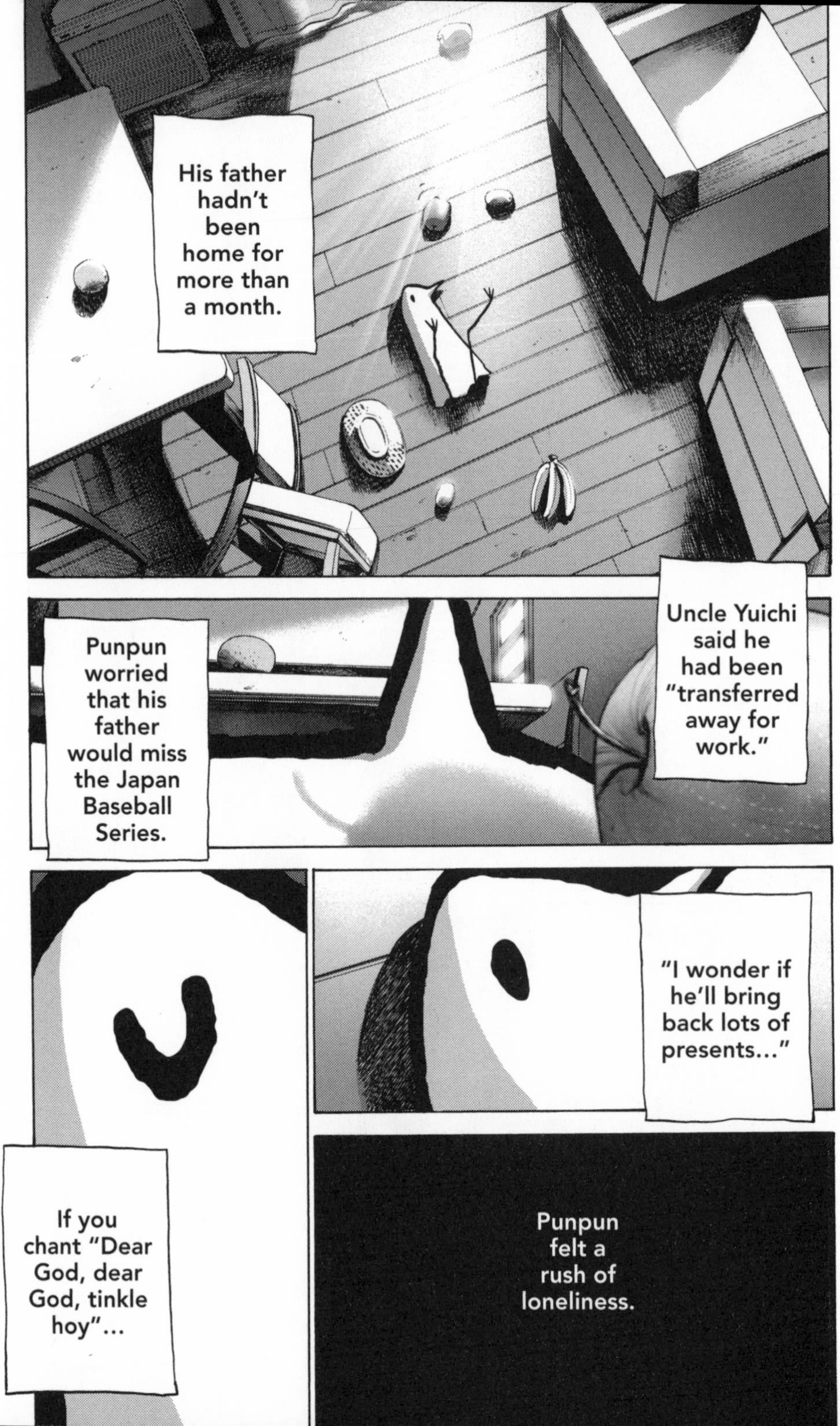
His father hadn't been home for more than a month.
Uncle Yuichi said he had been "transferred away for work."
Punpun worried that his father would miss the Japan Baseball Series.
"I wonder if he'll bring back lots of presents..."
Punpun felt a rush of loneliness.
If you chant "Dear God, dear God, tinkle hoy"...

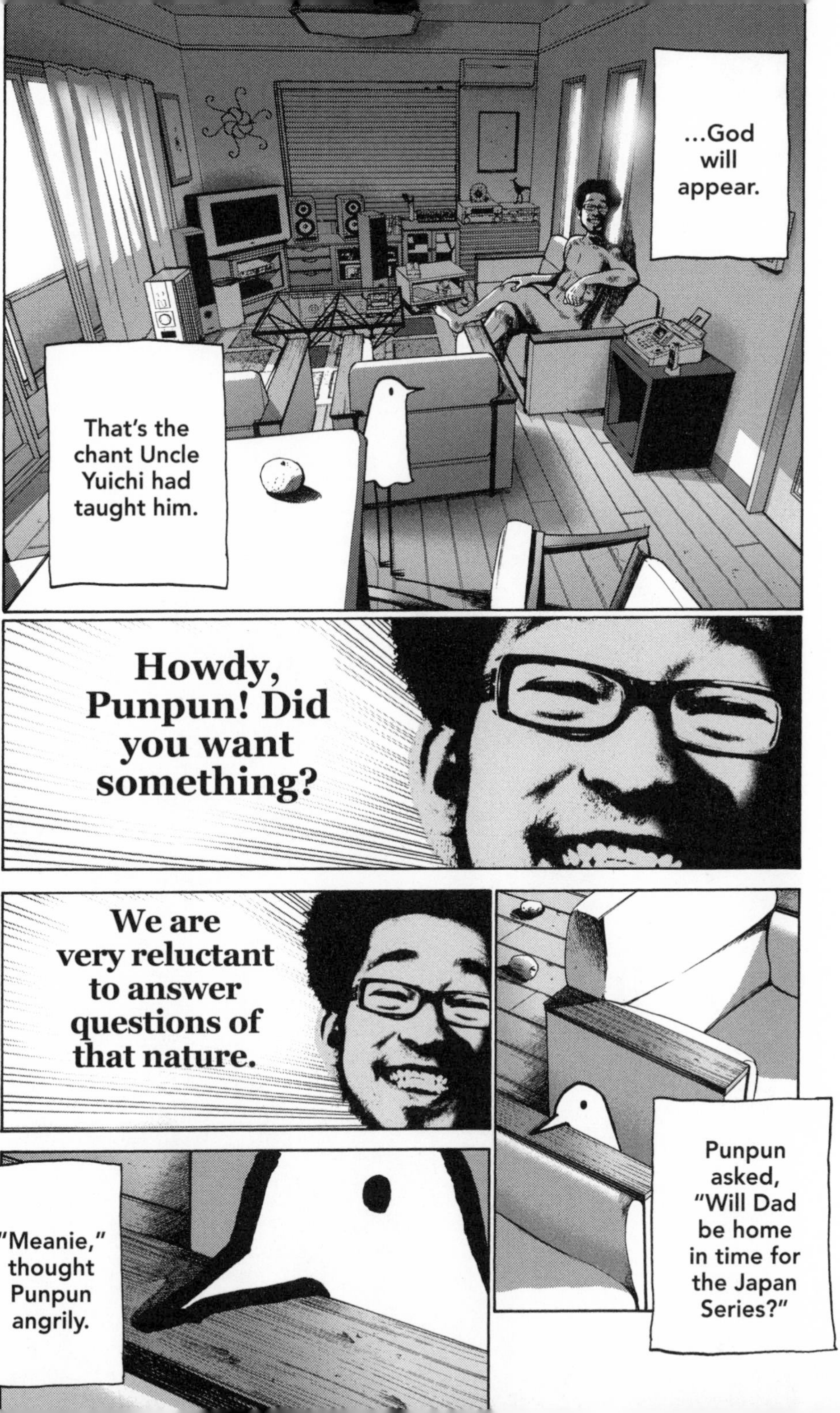
...God will appear.
That's the chant Uncle Yuichi had taught him.
Howdy, Punpun! Did you want something?
Punpun asked, "Will Dad be home in time for the Japan Series?"
We are very reluctant to answer questions of that nature.
"Meanie," thought Punpun angrily.

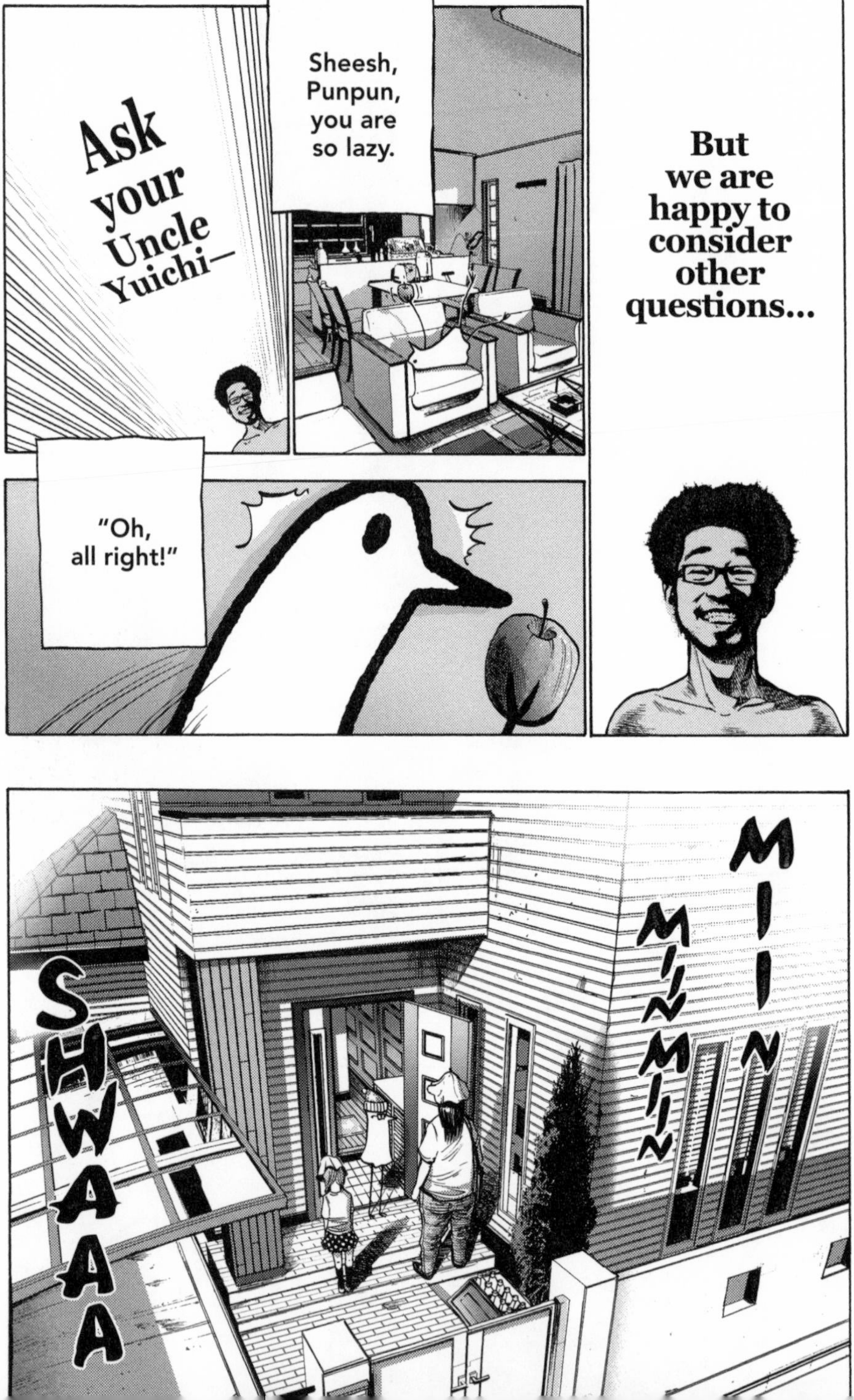
But we are happy to consider other questions...
Sheesh, Punpun, you are so lazy.
Ask your Uncle Yuichi—
"Oh, all right!"
MIIN
MINMIN
SHWAAA

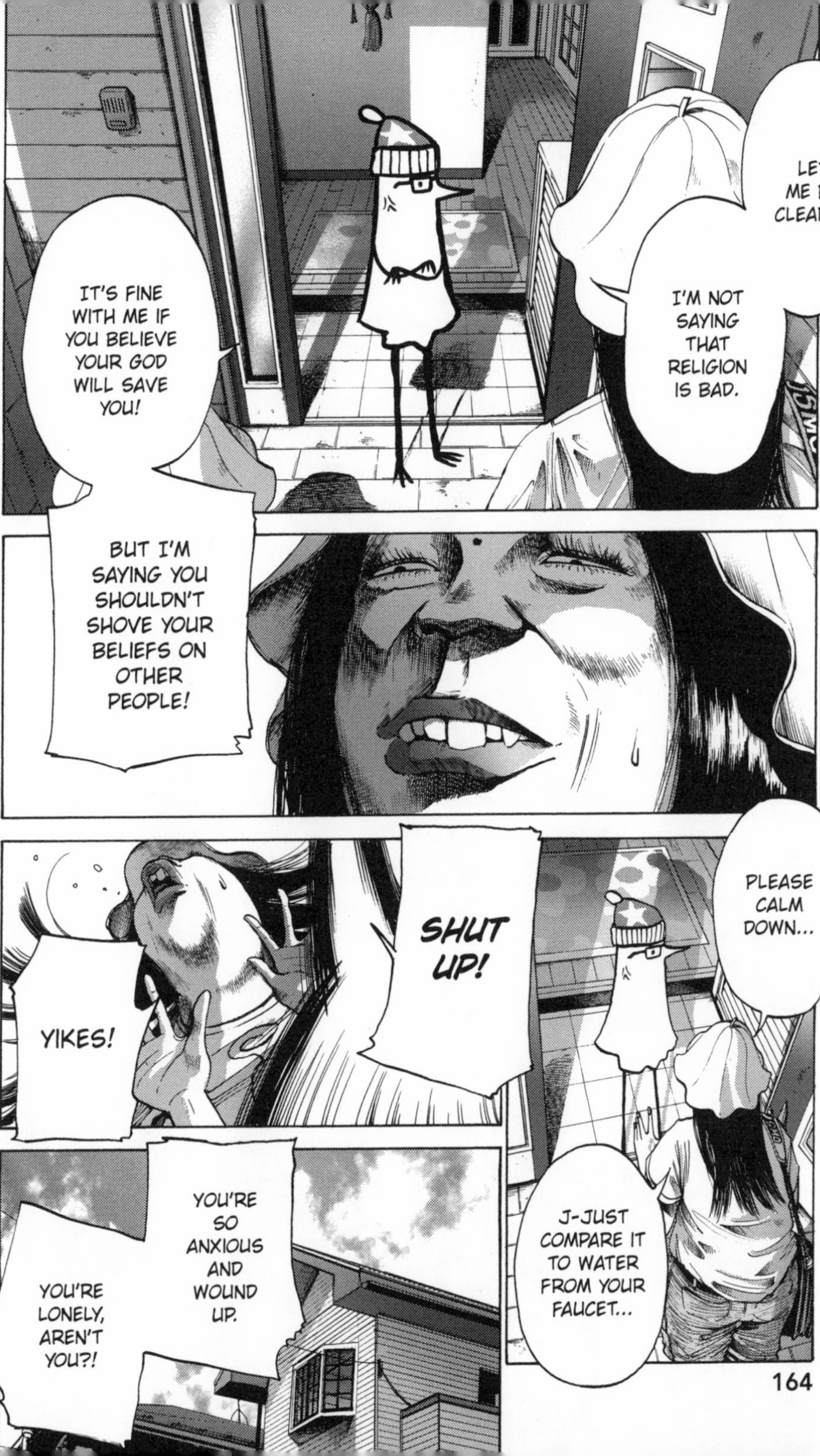
LET ME BE CLEAR...
I'M NOT SAYING THAT RELIGION IS BAD.
IT'S FINE WITH ME IF YOU BELIEVE YOUR GOD WILL SAVE YOU!
BUT I'M SAYING YOU SHOULDN'T SHOVE YOUR BELIEFS ON OTHER PEOPLE!
PLEASE CALM DOWN...
J-JUST COMPARE IT TO WATER FROM YOUR FAUCET...
SHUT UP!
YIKES!
YOU'RE SO ANXIOUS AND WOUND UP.
YOU'RE LONELY, AREN'T YOU?!

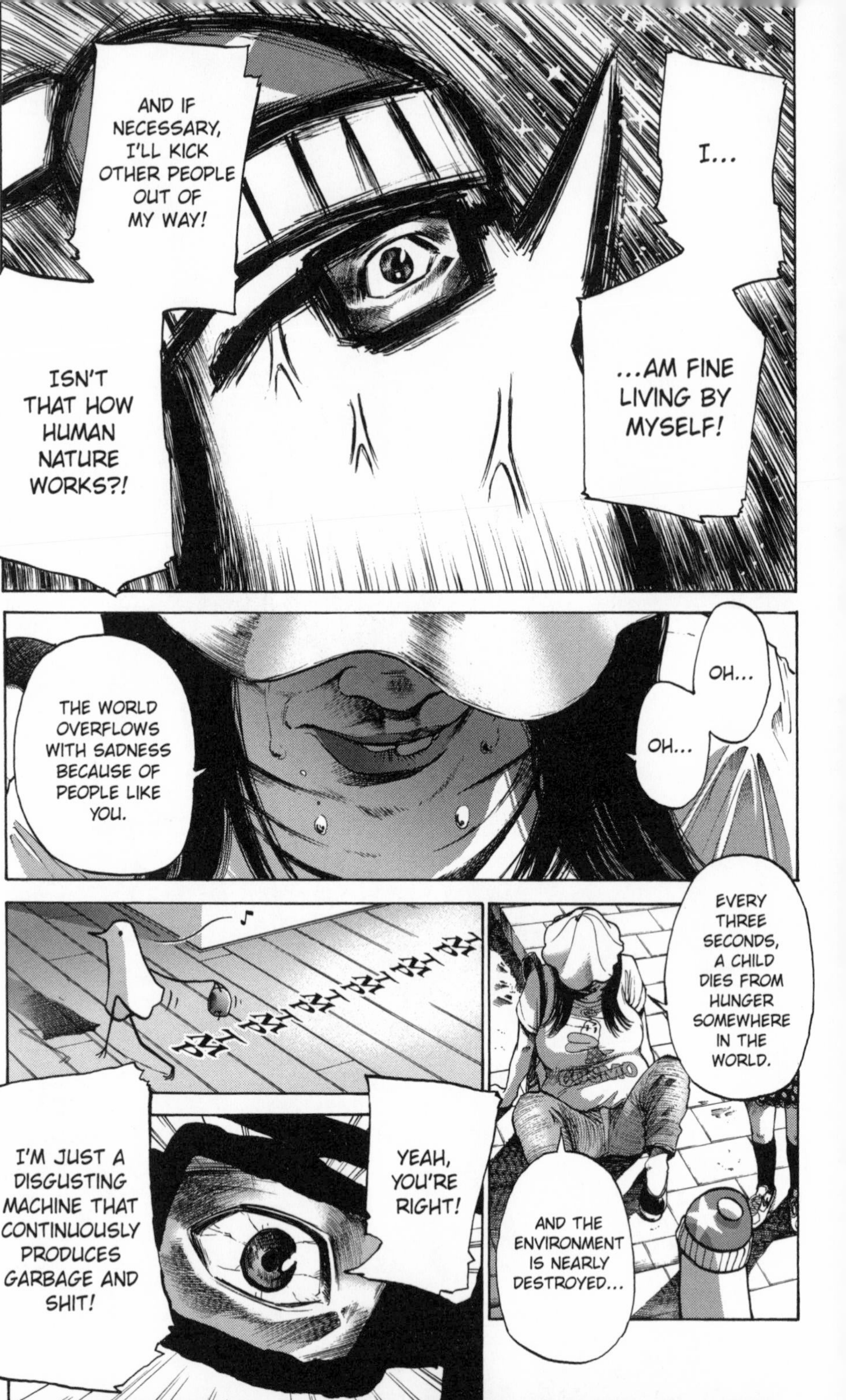
I...
...AM FINE LIVING BY MYSELF!
AND IF NECESSARY, I'LL KICK OTHER PEOPLE OUT OF MY WAY!
ISN'T THAT HOW HUMAN NATURE WORKS?!
OH...
OH...
THE WORLD OVERFLOWS WITH SADNESS BECAUSE OF PEOPLE LIKE YOU.
EVERY THREE SECONDS, A CHILD DIES FROM HUNGER SOMEWHERE IN THE WORLD.
AND THE ENVIRONMENT IS NEARLY DESTROYED...
YEAH, YOU'RE RIGHT!
I'M JUST A DISGUSTING MACHINE THAT CONTINUOUSLY PRODUCES GARBAGE AND SHIT!

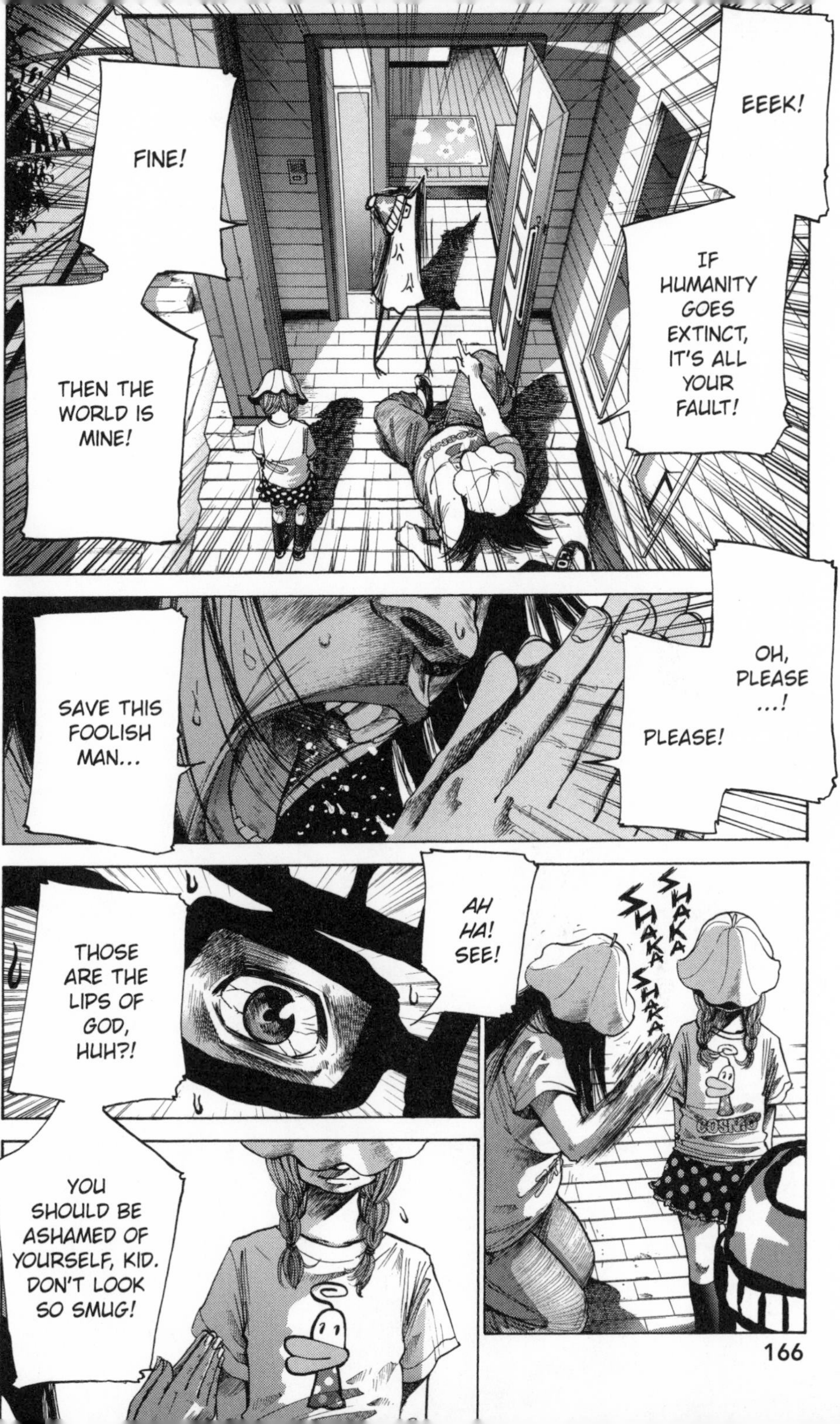
EEEK!
IF HUMANITY GOES EXTINCT, IT'S ALL YOUR FAULT!
FINE!
THEN THE WORLD IS MINE!
OH, PLEASE ...!
PLEASE!
SAVE THIS FOOLISH MAN...
SHAKA SHAKA
SHAKA SHAKA
AH HA! SEE!
THOSE ARE THE LIPS OF GOD, HUH?!
YOU SHOULD BE ASHAMED OF YOURSELF, KID. DON'T LOOK SO SMUG!

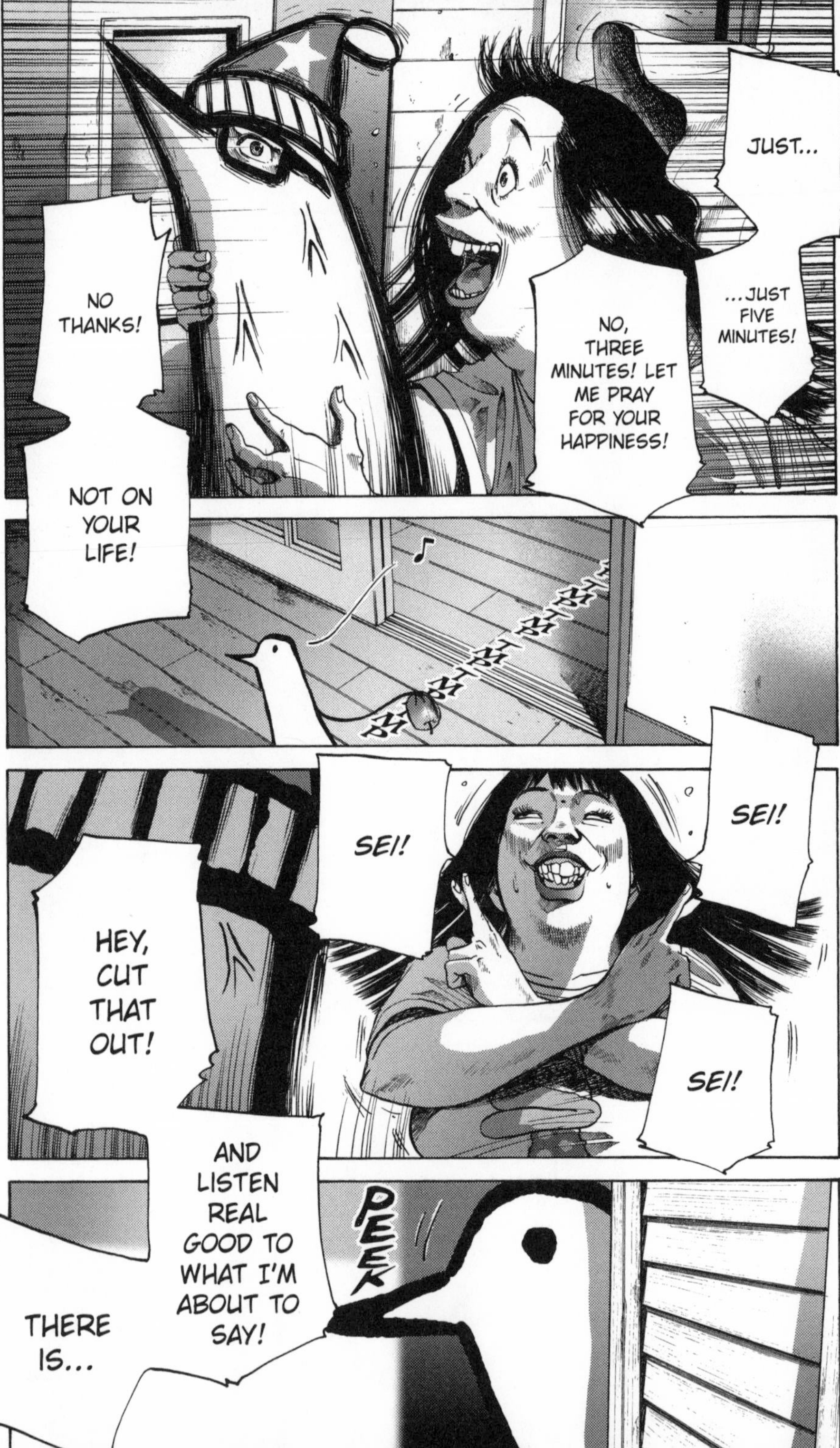
JUST...
...JUST FIVE MINUTES!
NO, THREE MINUTES! LET ME PRAY FOR YOUR HAPPINESS!
NO THANKS!
NOT ON YOUR LIFE!
SEI!
SEI!
SEI!
HEY, CUT THAT OUT!
PEEK
AND LISTEN REAL GOOD TO WHAT I'M ABOUT TO SAY!
THERE IS...

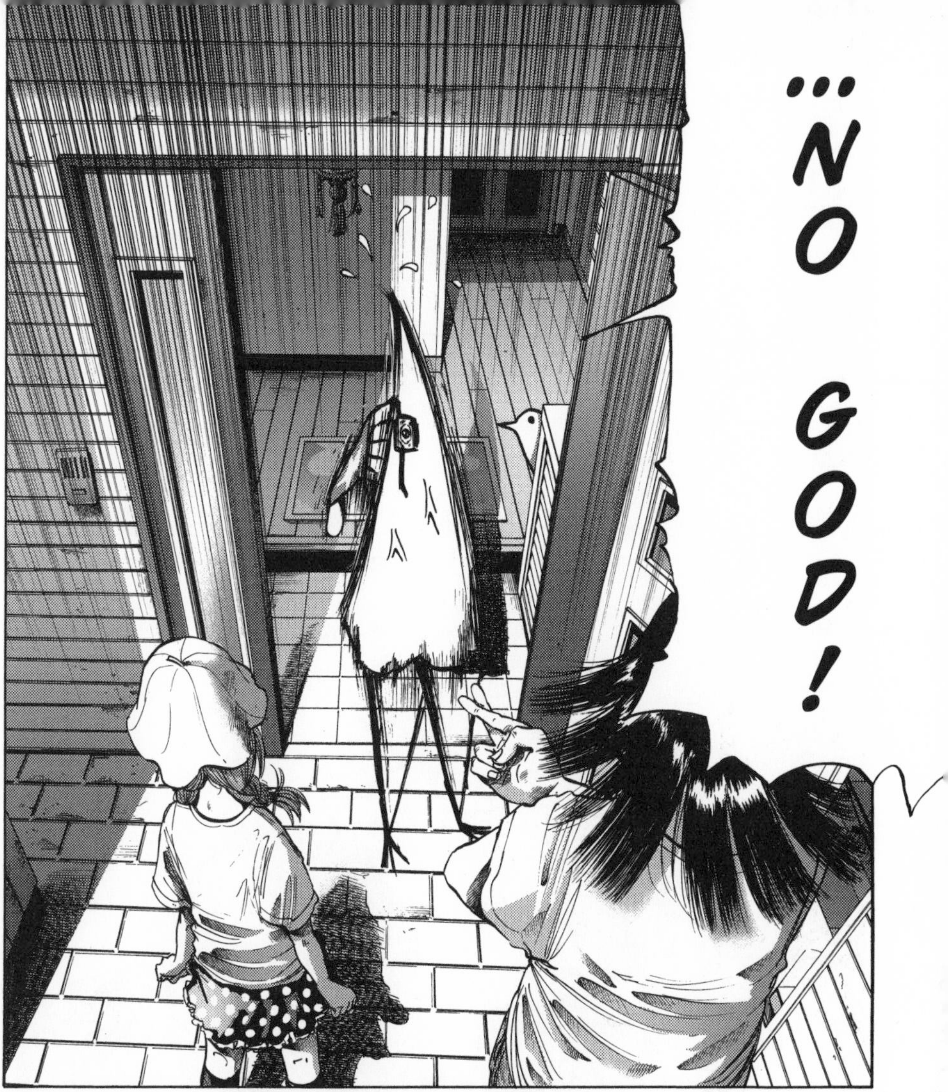
...NO GOD!

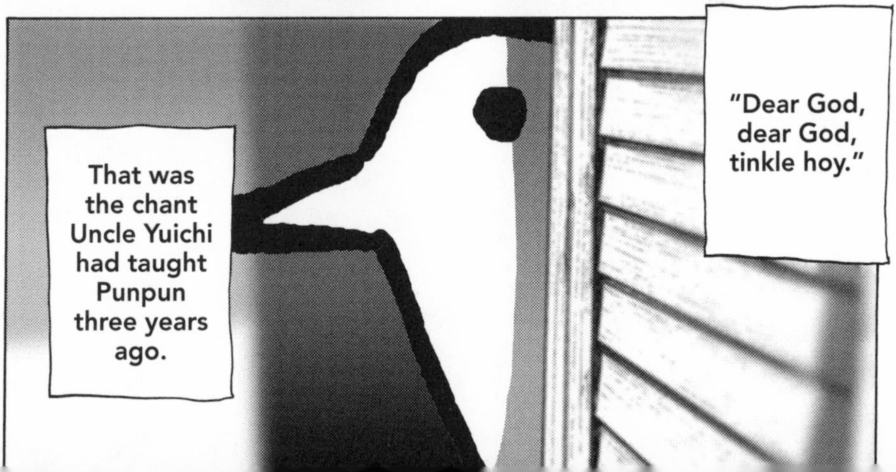
"Dear God, dear God, tinkle hoy."
That was the chant Uncle Yuichi had taught Punpun three years ago.

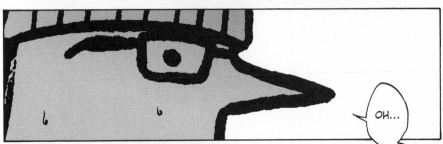

OH...

PU...

PUNPUN...

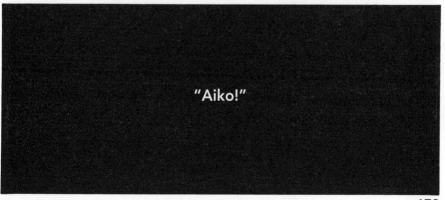

"Aiko!"

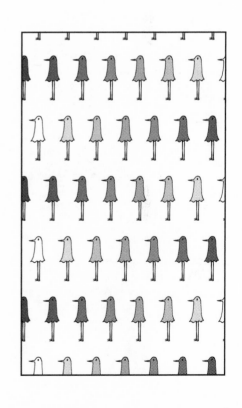

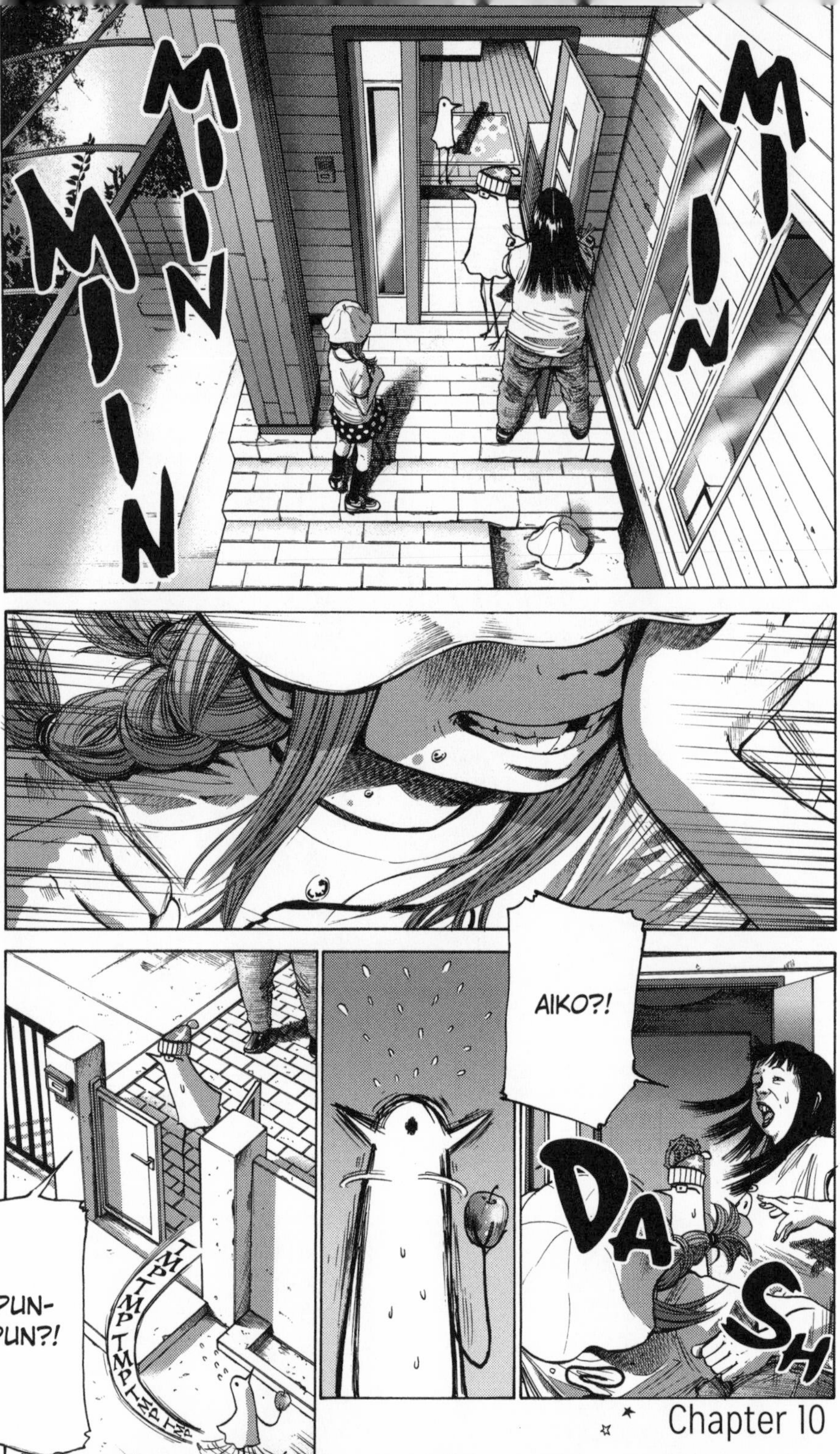
MIIN
MIIN
MIIIN
AIKO?!
DASH
PUN-PUN?!

Chapter 10

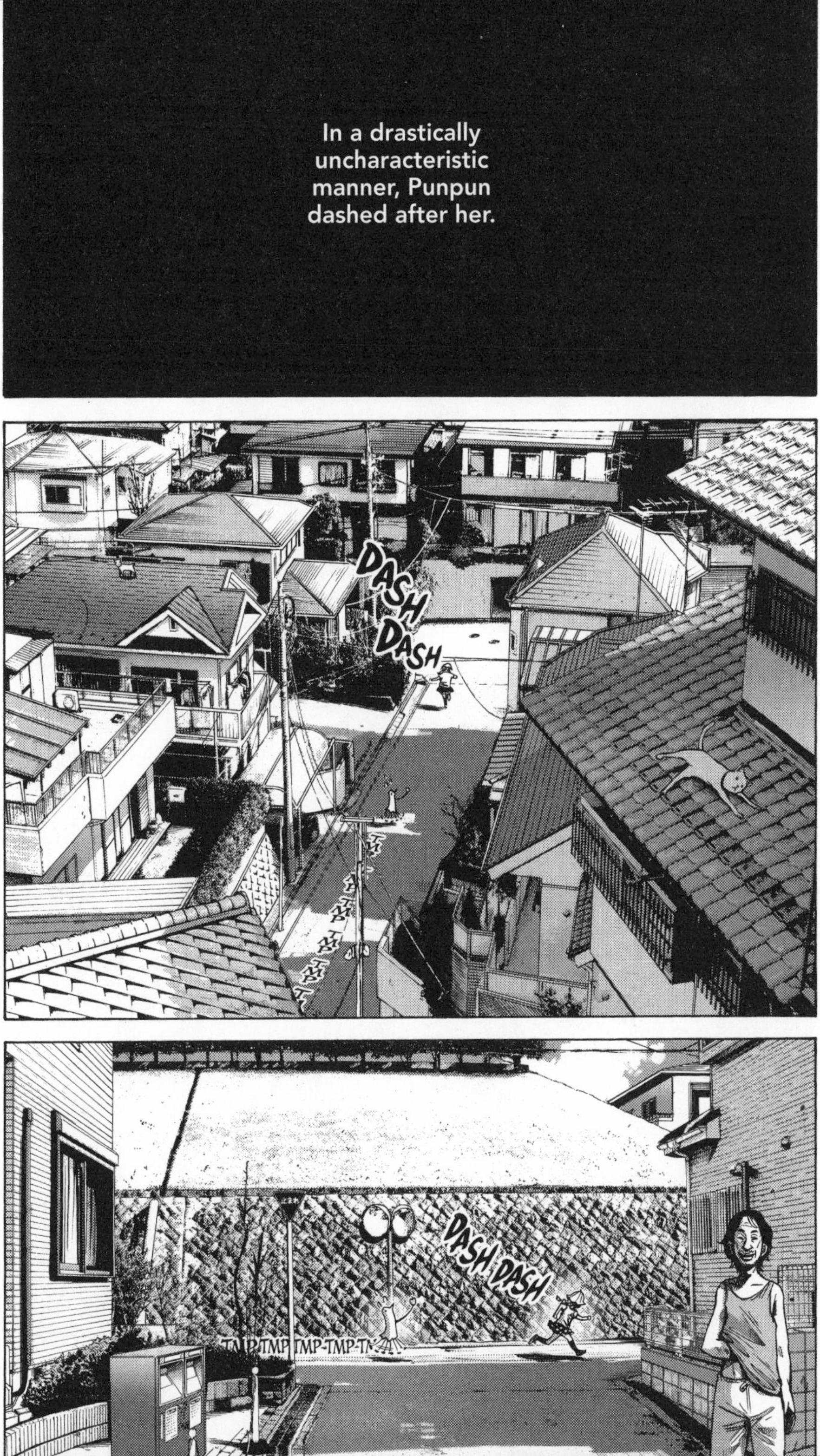
In a drastically uncharacteristic manner, Punpun dashed after her.
DASH DASH
DASH DASH

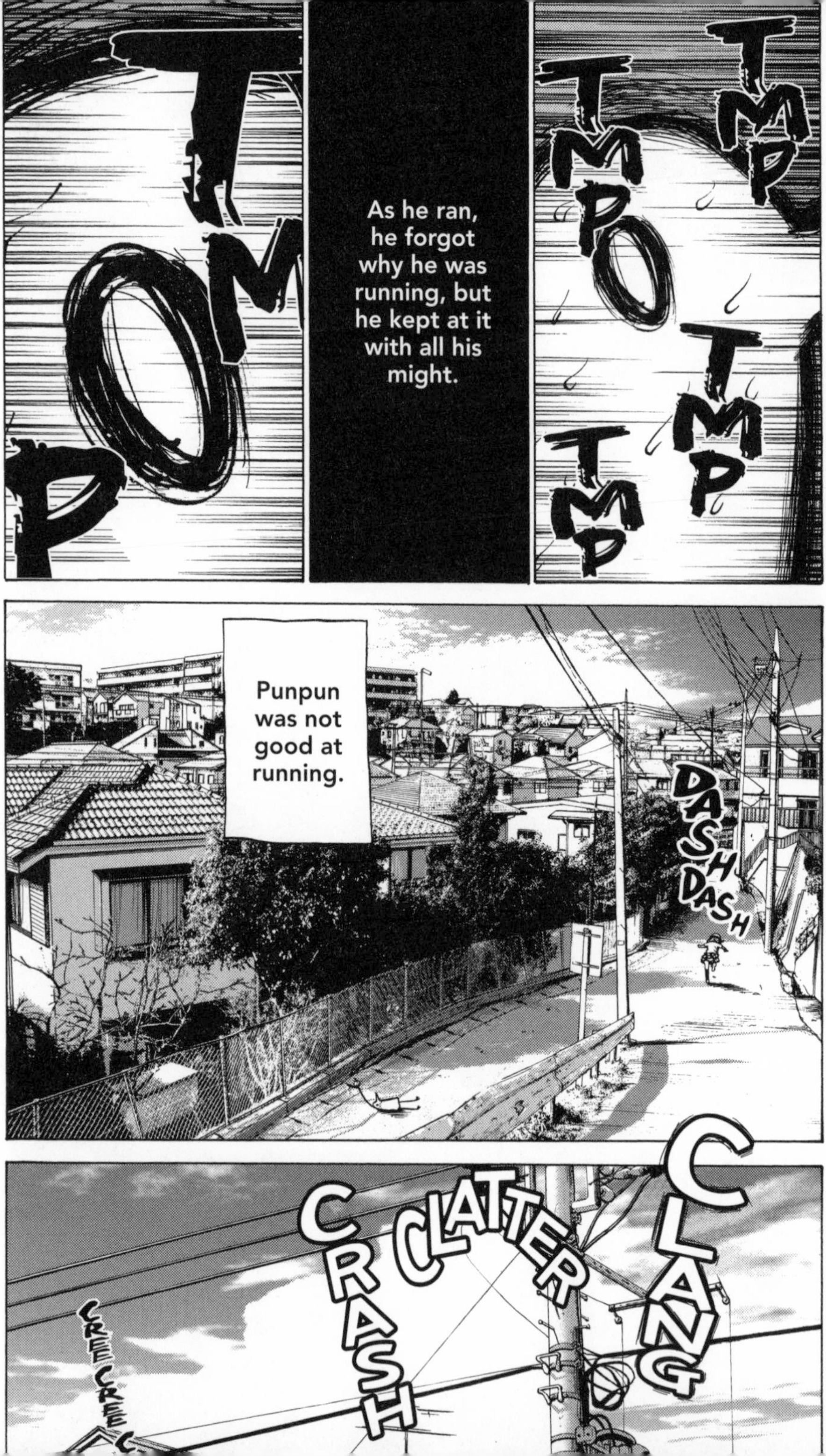
TMP
TMPO
TMP
TMP
As he ran, he forgot why he was running, but he kept at it with all his might.
TOMP
Punpun was not good at running.
DASH DASH
CLANG
CLATTER
CRASH
CREE CREE

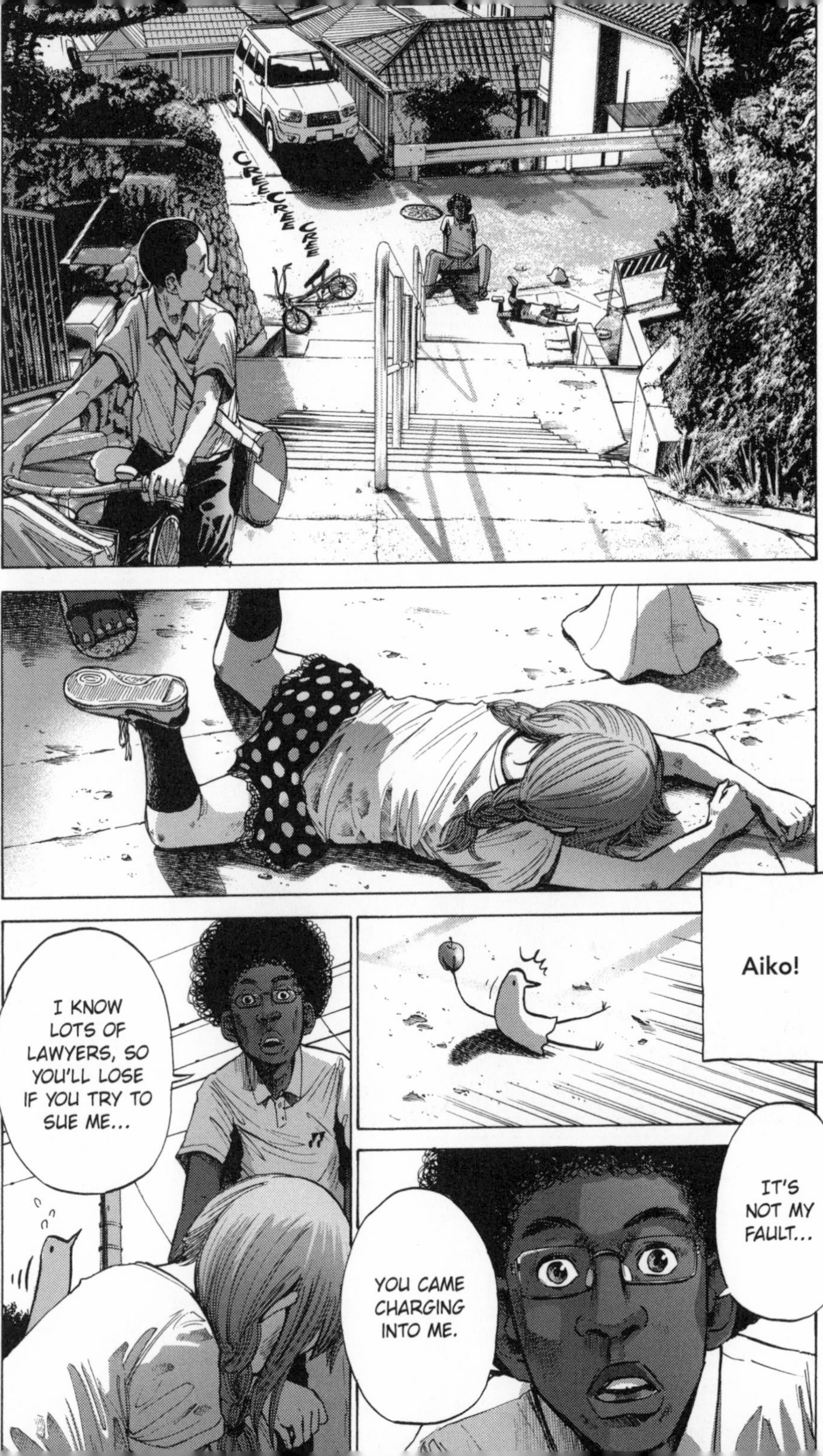
CREE CREE CREE
Aiko!
IT'S NOT MY FAULT...
YOU CAME CHARGING INTO ME.
I KNOW LOTS OF LAWYERS, SO YOU'LL LOSE IF YOU TRY TO SUE ME...

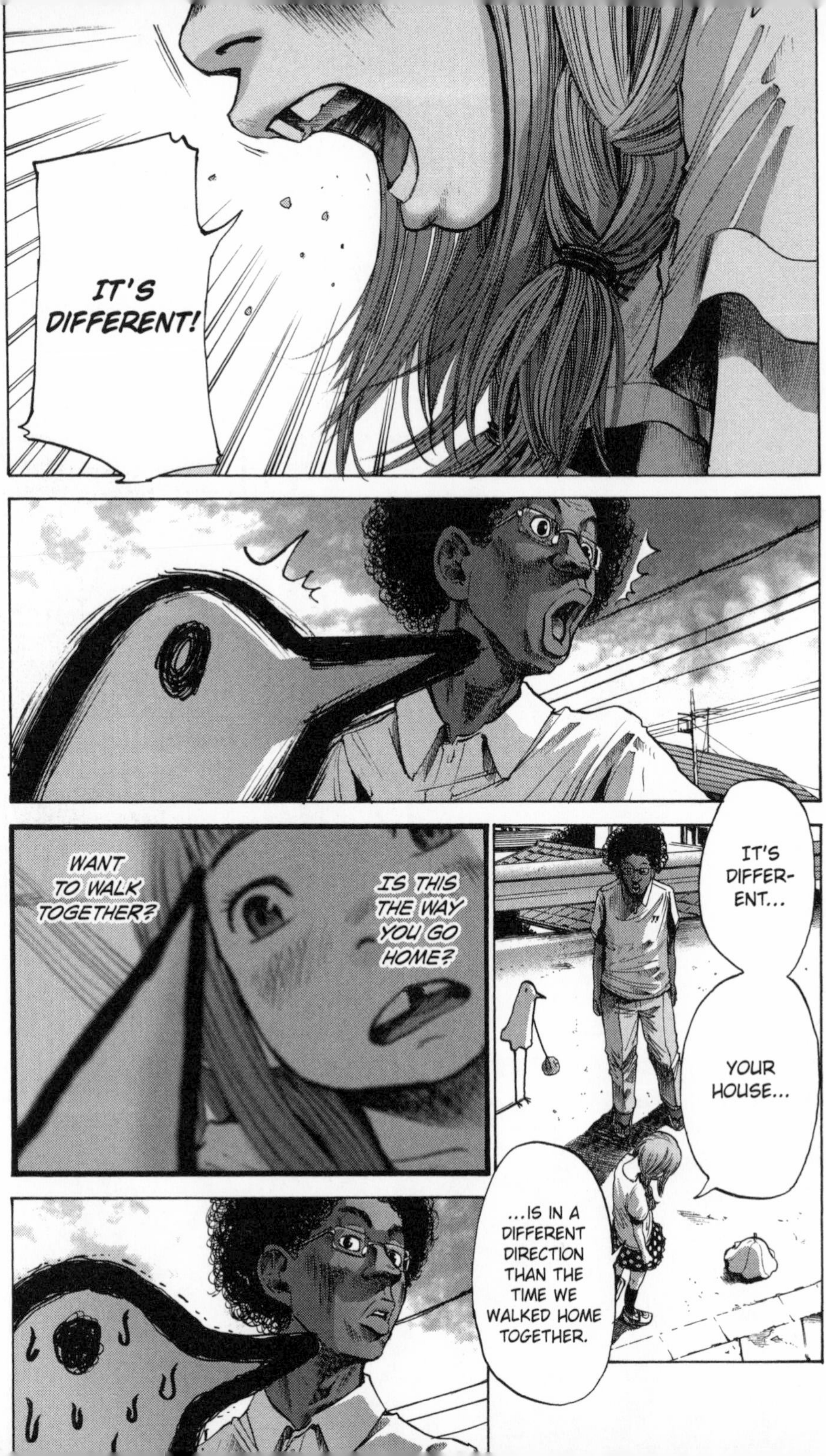
IT'S DIFFERENT!
IT'S DIFFER-ENT...
YOUR HOUSE...
...IS IN A DIFFERENT DIRECTION THAN THE TIME WE WALKED HOME TOGETHER.
IS THIS THE WAY YOU GO HOME?
WANT TO WALK TOGETHER?

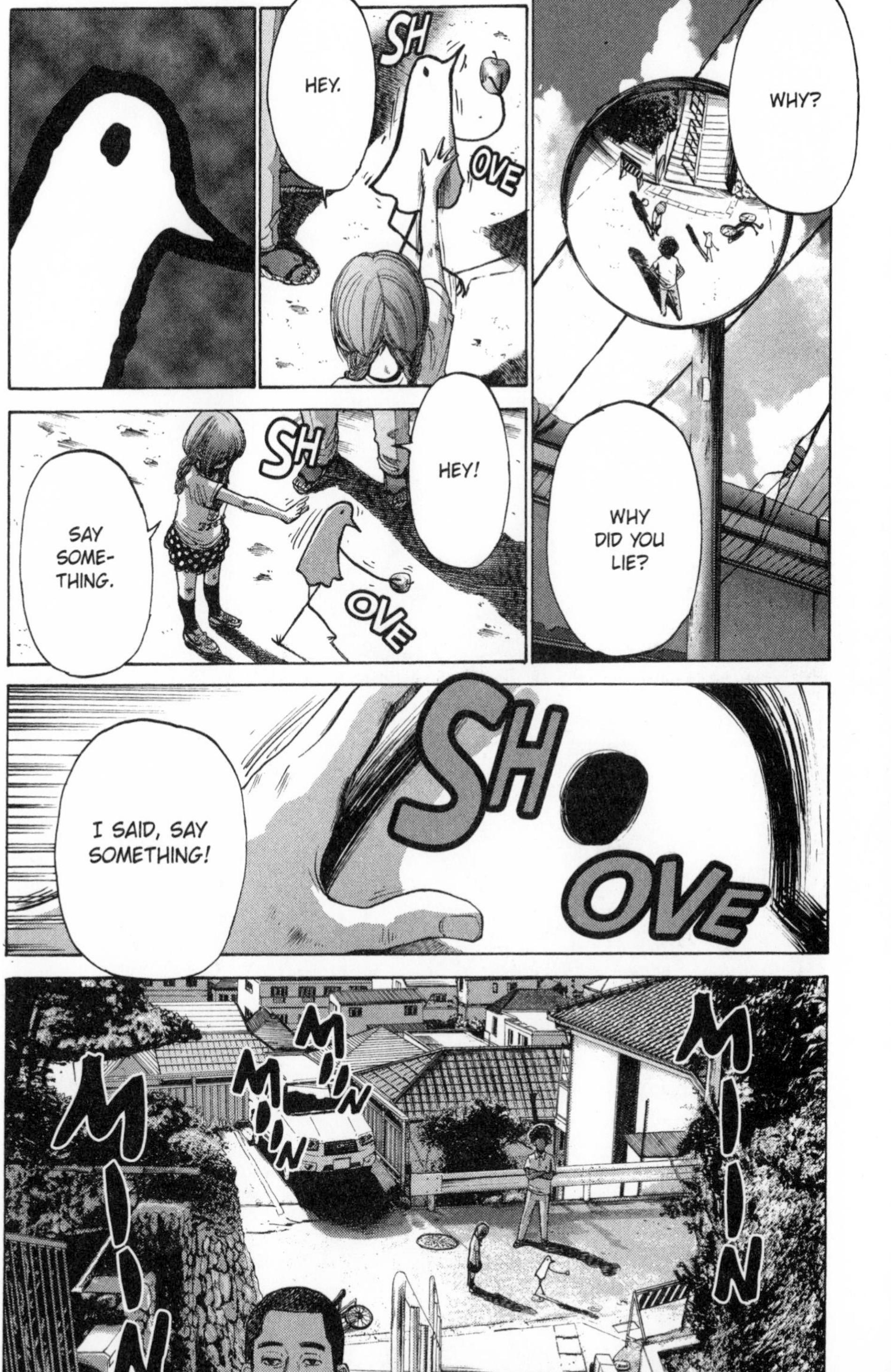
WHY?
WHY DID YOU LIE?
HEY.
SHOVE
HEY!
SHOVE
SAY SOMETHING.
SHOVE
I SAID, SAY SOMETHING!
MIIN
MIN MIN
MIIN

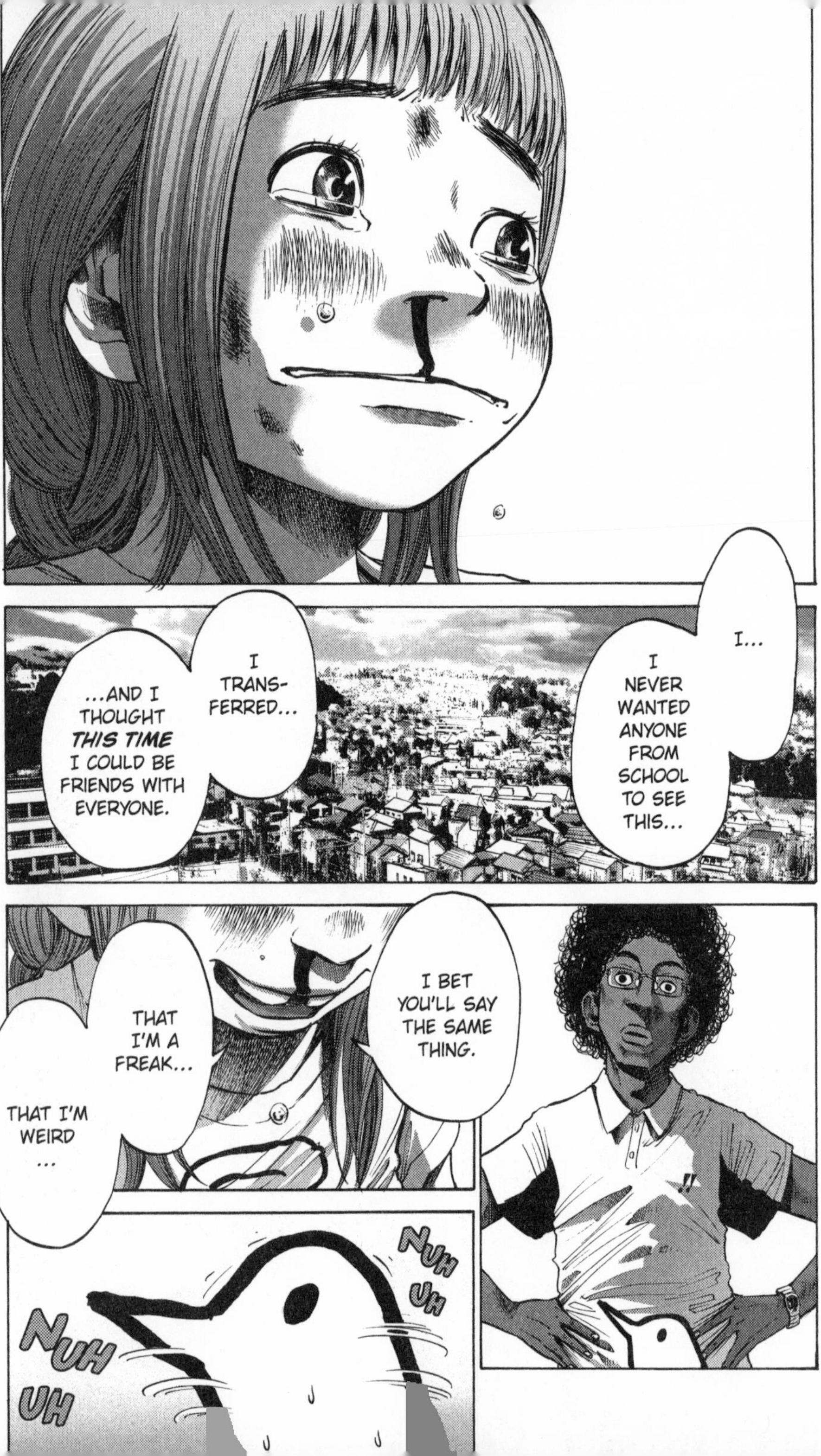
I...
I NEVER WANTED ANYONE FROM SCHOOL TO SEE THIS...
I TRANS-FERRED...
...AND I THOUGHT *THIS TIME* I COULD BE FRIENDS WITH EVERYONE.
I BET YOU'LL SAY THE SAME THING.
THAT I'M A FREAK...
THAT I'M WEIRD ...
NUH UH
NUH UH

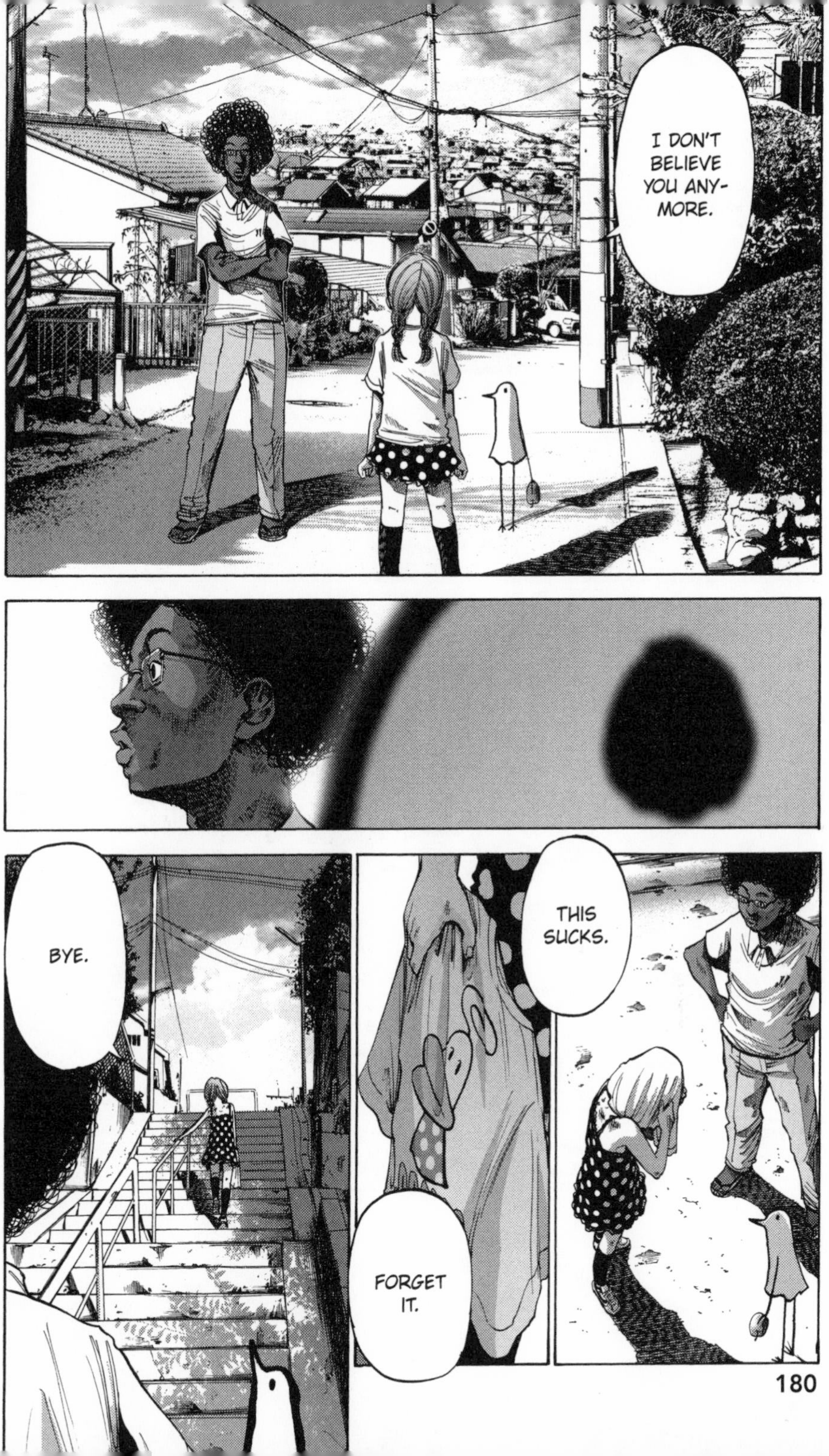
I DON'T BELIEVE YOU ANY-MORE.
THIS SUCKS.
FORGET IT.
BYE.

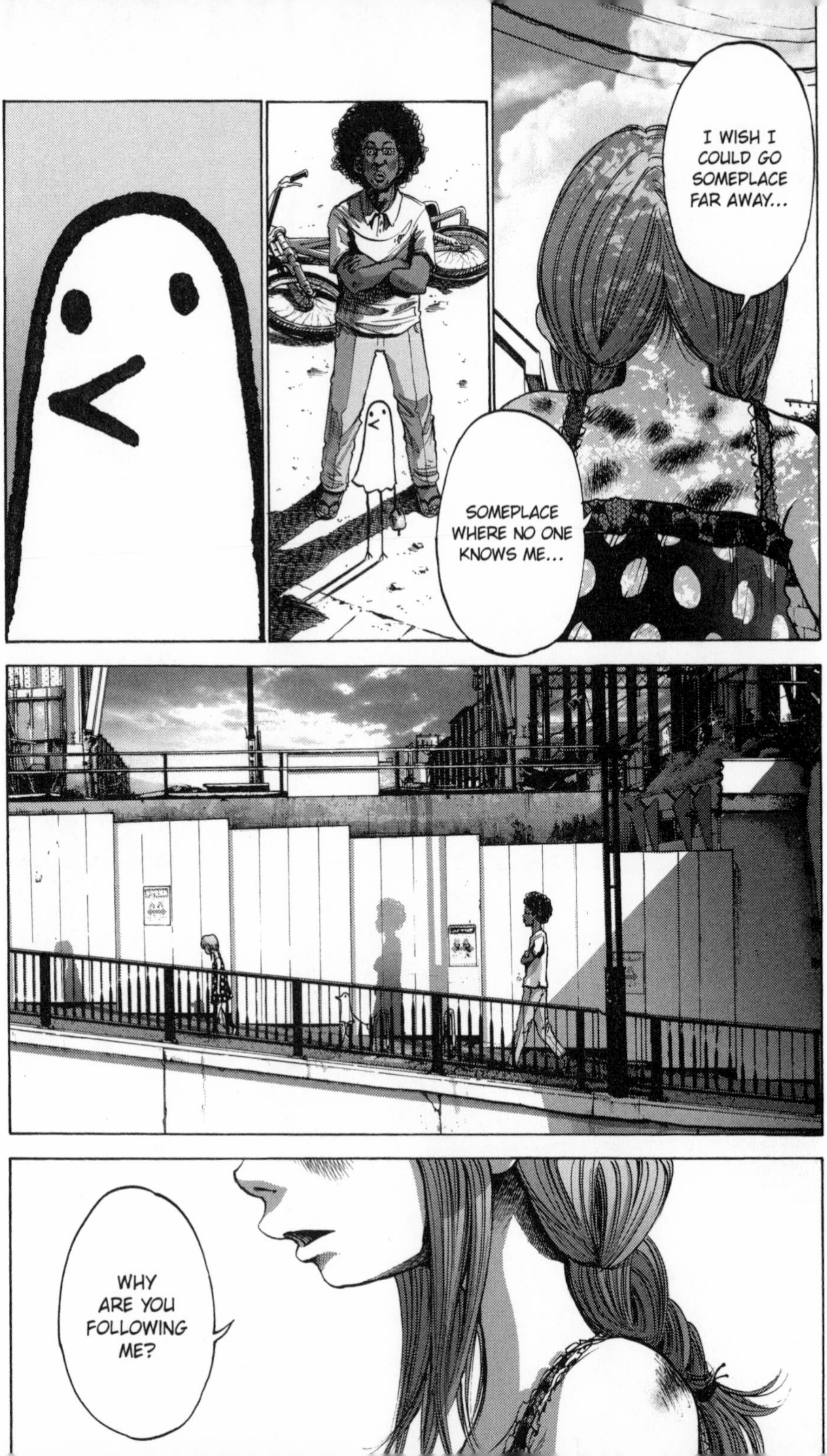
I WISH I COULD GO SOMEPLACE FAR AWAY...
SOMEPLACE WHERE NO ONE KNOWS ME...
WHY ARE YOU FOLLOWING ME?

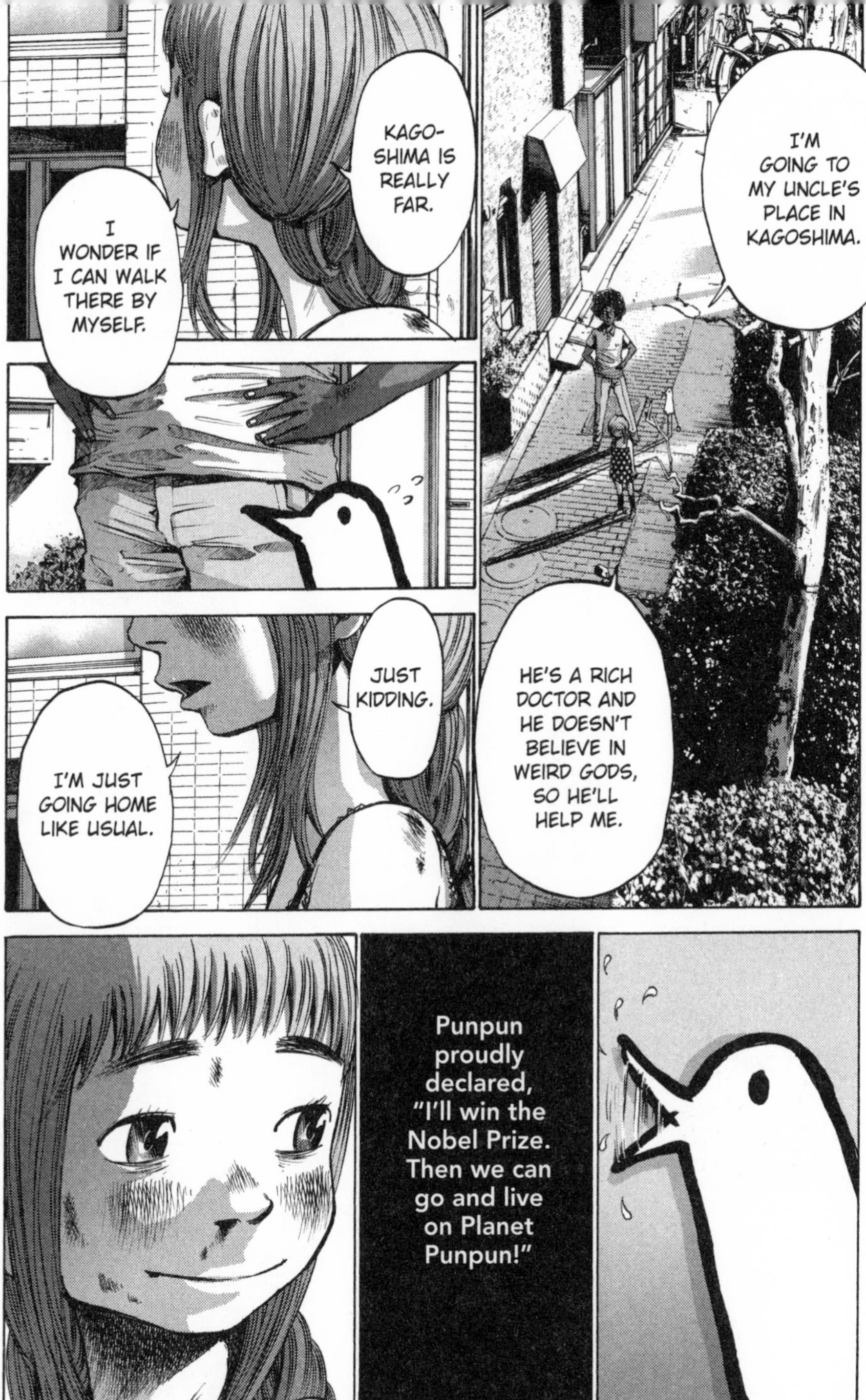
I'M GOING TO MY UNCLE'S PLACE IN KAGOSHIMA.
HE'S A RICH DOCTOR AND HE DOESN'T BELIEVE IN WEIRD GODS, SO HE'LL HELP ME.
KAGO-SHIMA IS REALLY FAR.
I WONDER IF I CAN WALK THERE BY MYSELF.
JUST KIDDING.
I'M JUST GOING HOME LIKE USUAL.
Punpun proudly declared, "I'll win the Nobel Prize. Then we can go and live on Planet Punpun!"

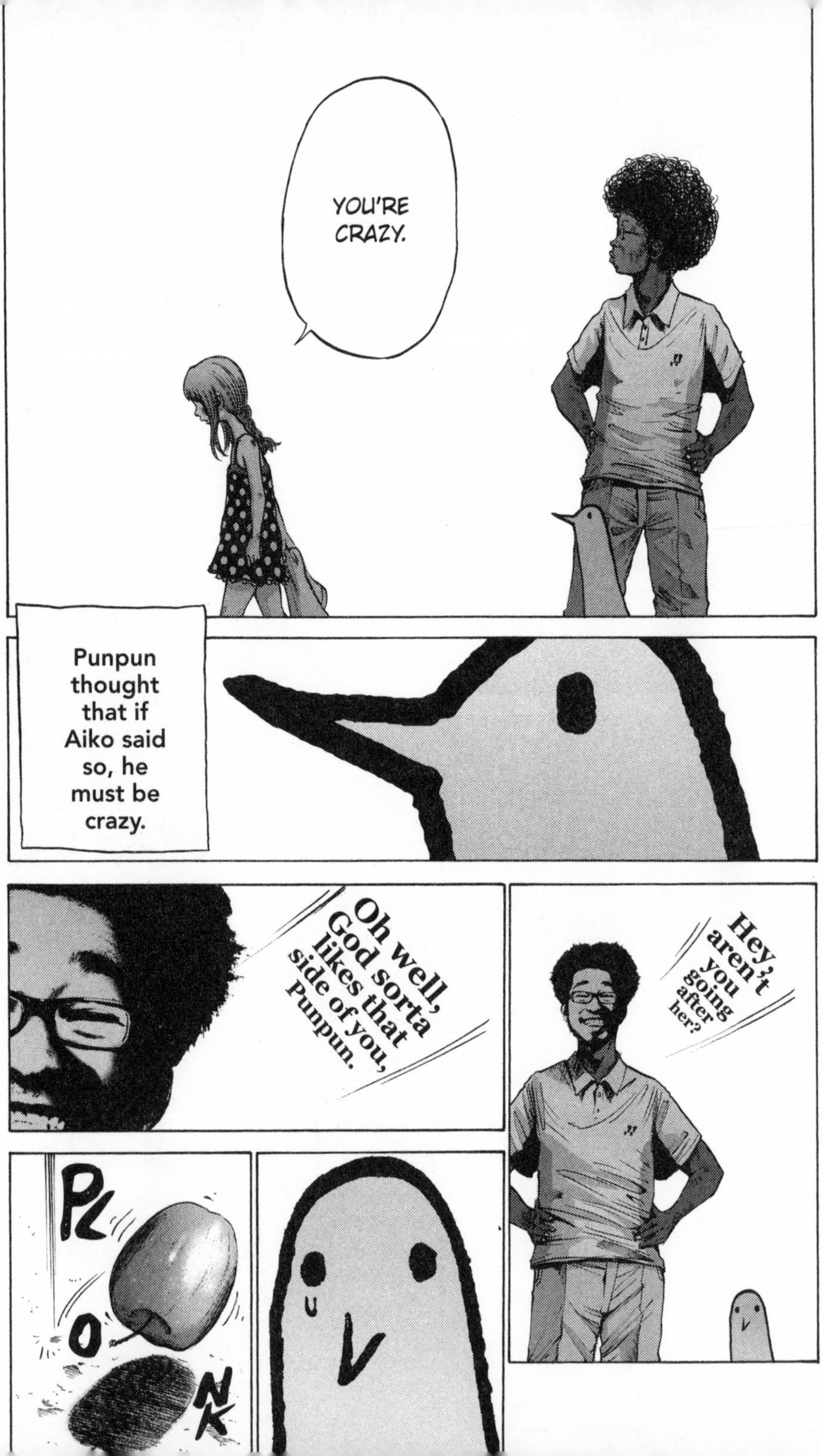
YOU'RE CRAZY.
Punpun thought that if Aiko said so, he must be crazy.
Hey, aren't you going after her?
Oh well, God sorta likes that side of you, Punpun.
PLONK

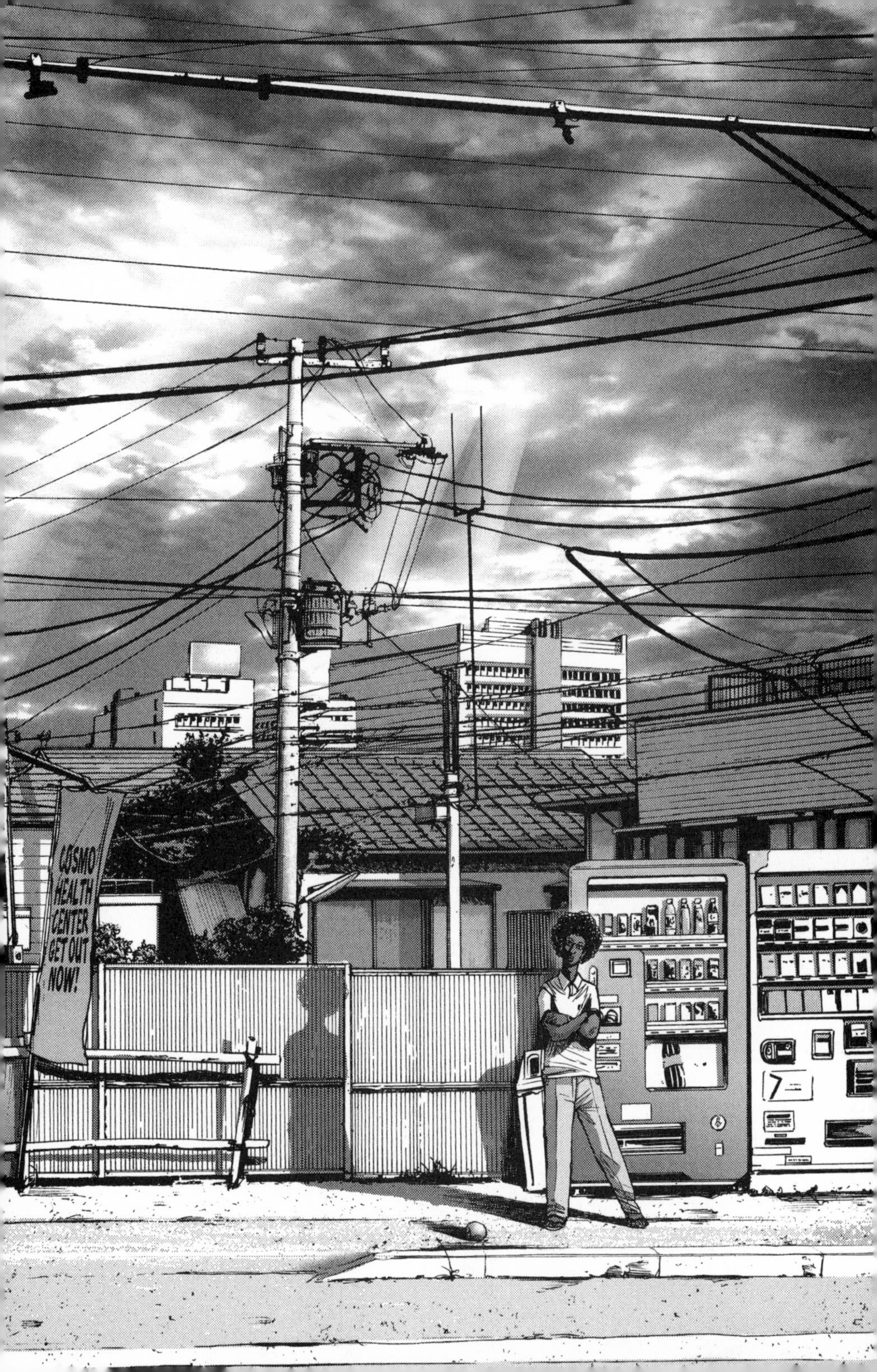
COSMO HEALTH CENTER GET OUT NOW!

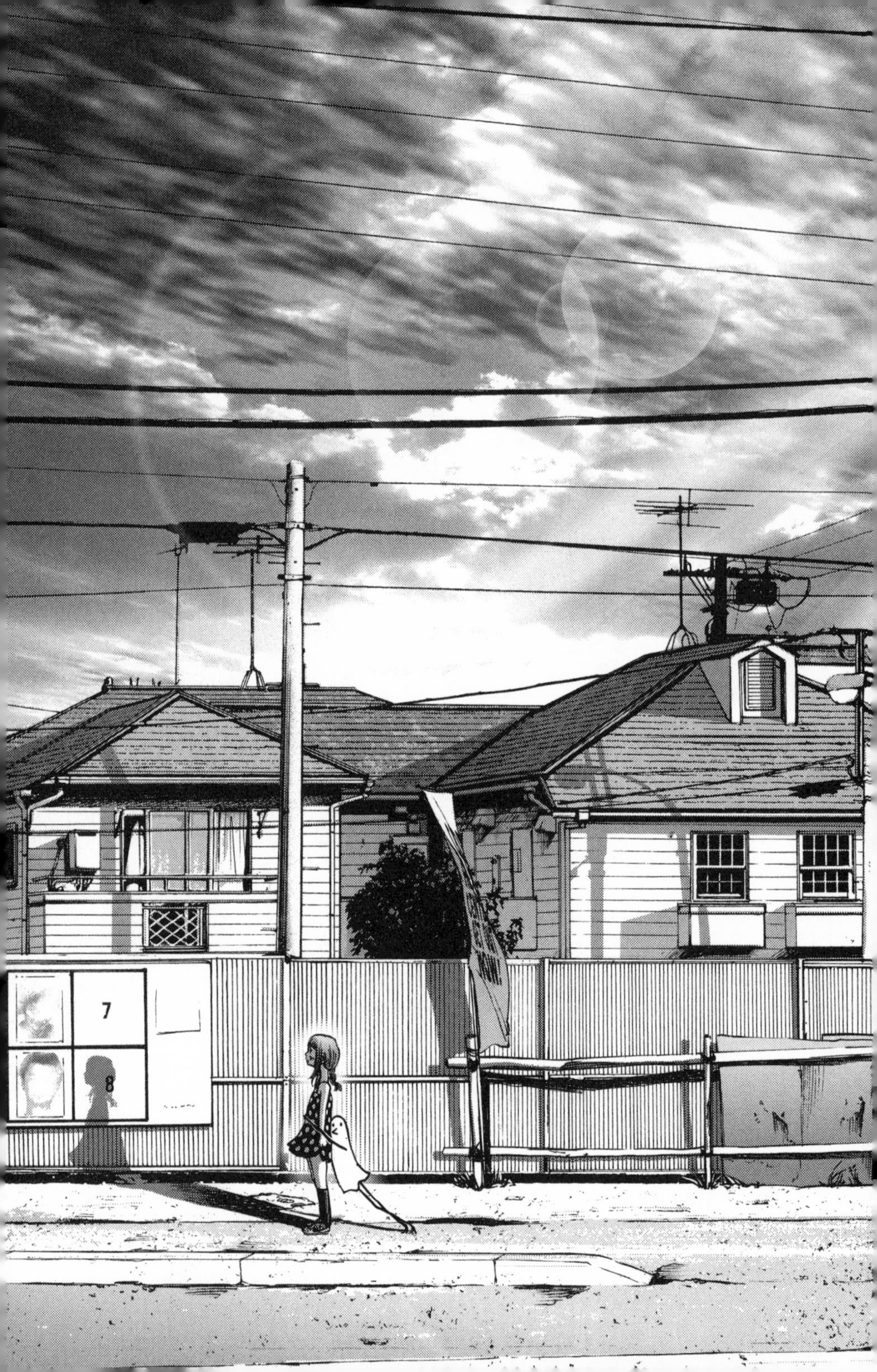
7
8

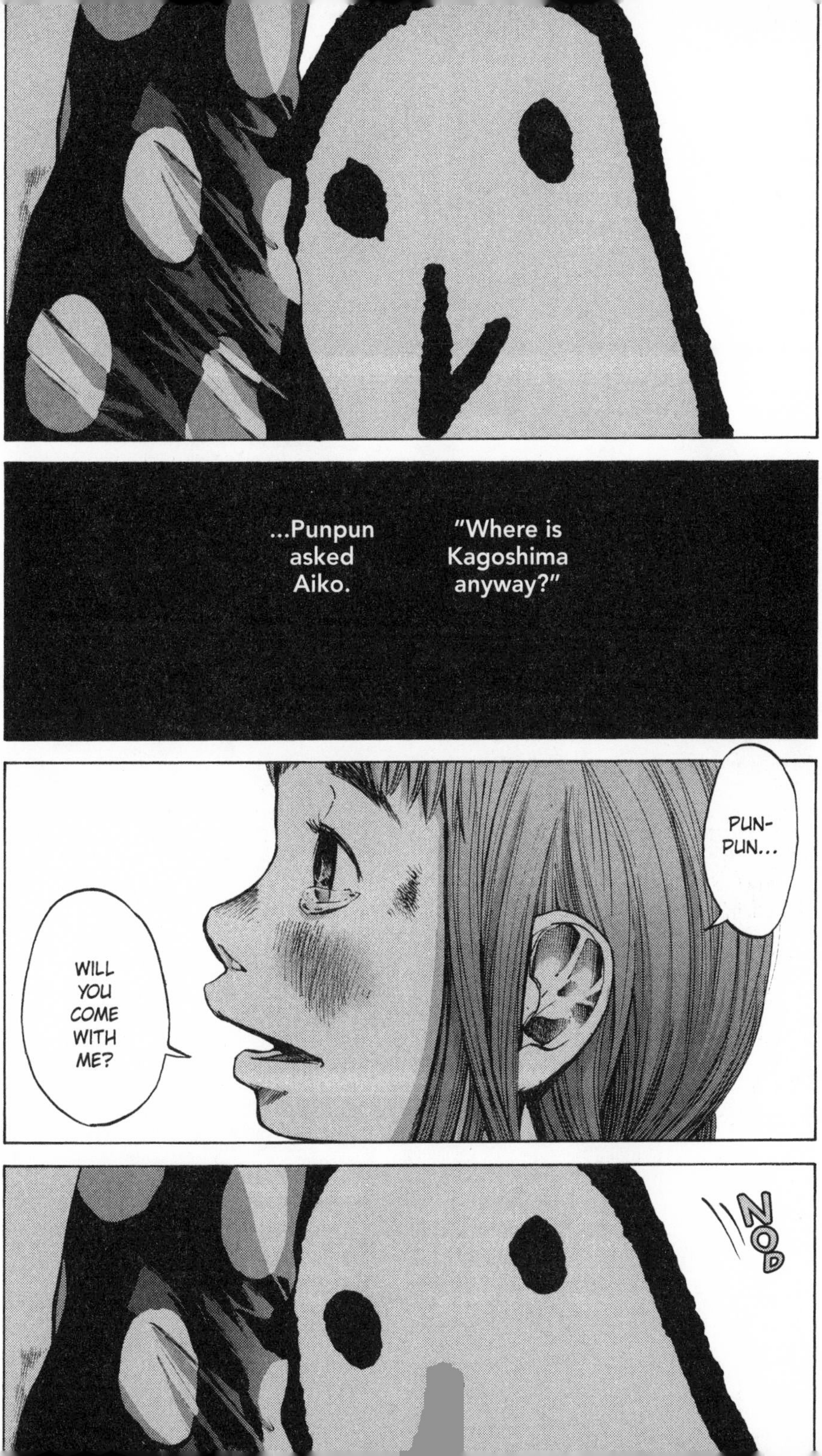
"Where is Kagoshima anyway?"
...Punpun asked Aiko.
PUN-PUN...
WILL YOU COME WITH ME?
NOD

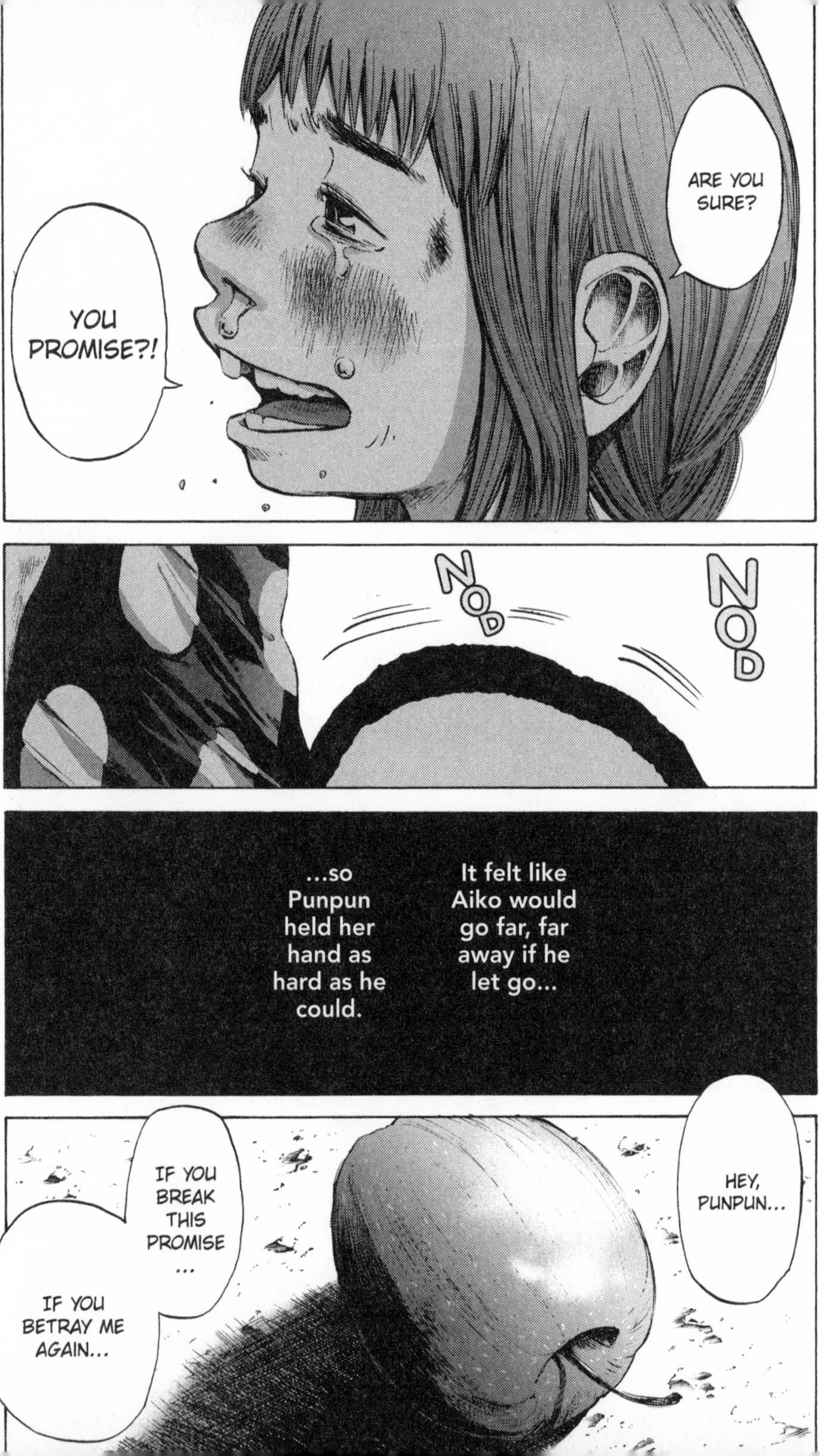
ARE YOU SURE?
YOU PROMISE?!
NOD
NOD
It felt like Aiko would go far, far away if he let go...
...so Punpun held her hand as hard as he could.
HEY, PUNPUN...
IF YOU BREAK THIS PROMISE ...
IF YOU BETRAY ME AGAIN...

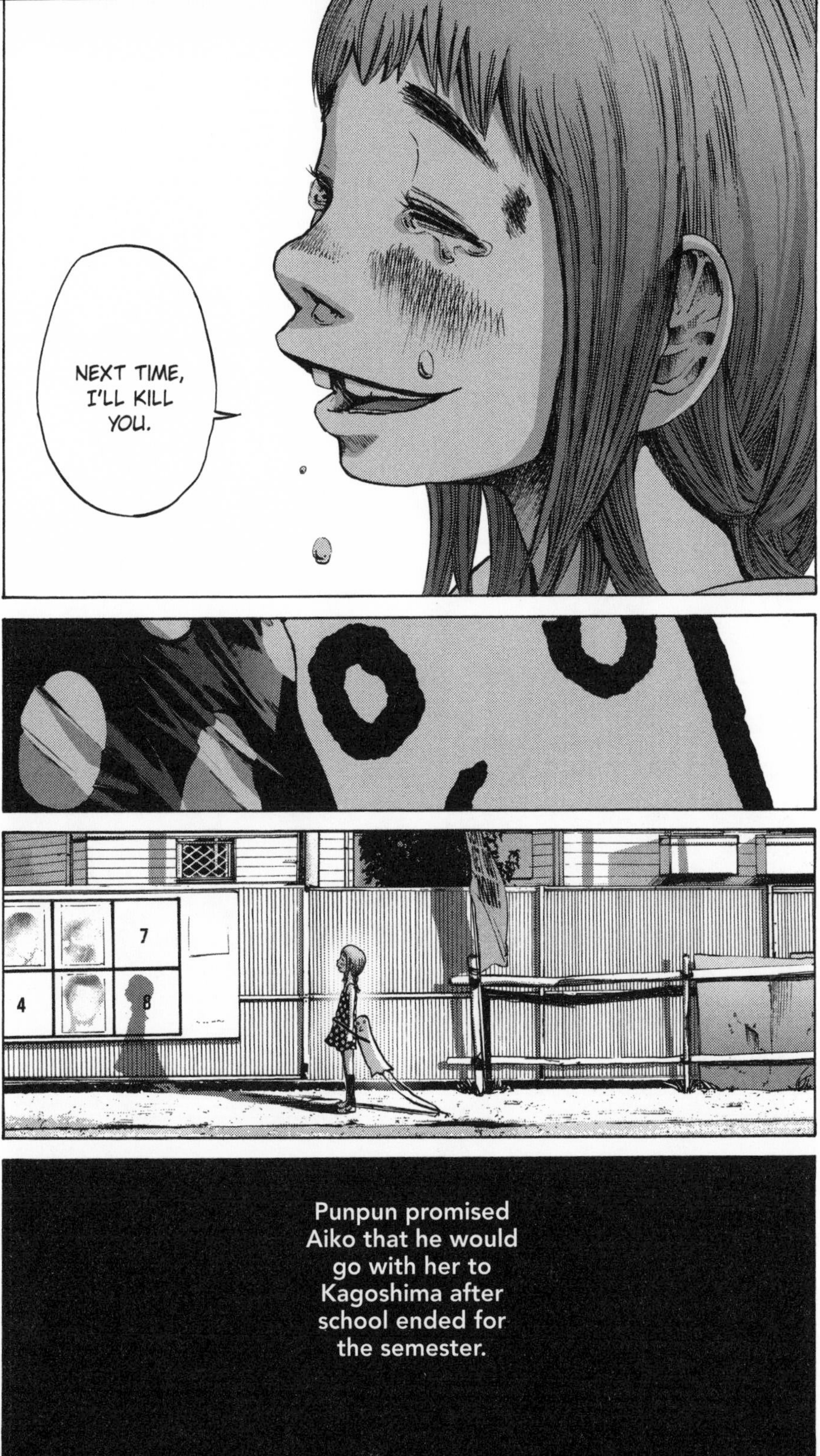
NEXT TIME, I'LL KILL YOU.
Punpun promised Aiko that he would go with her to Kagoshima after school ended for the semester.

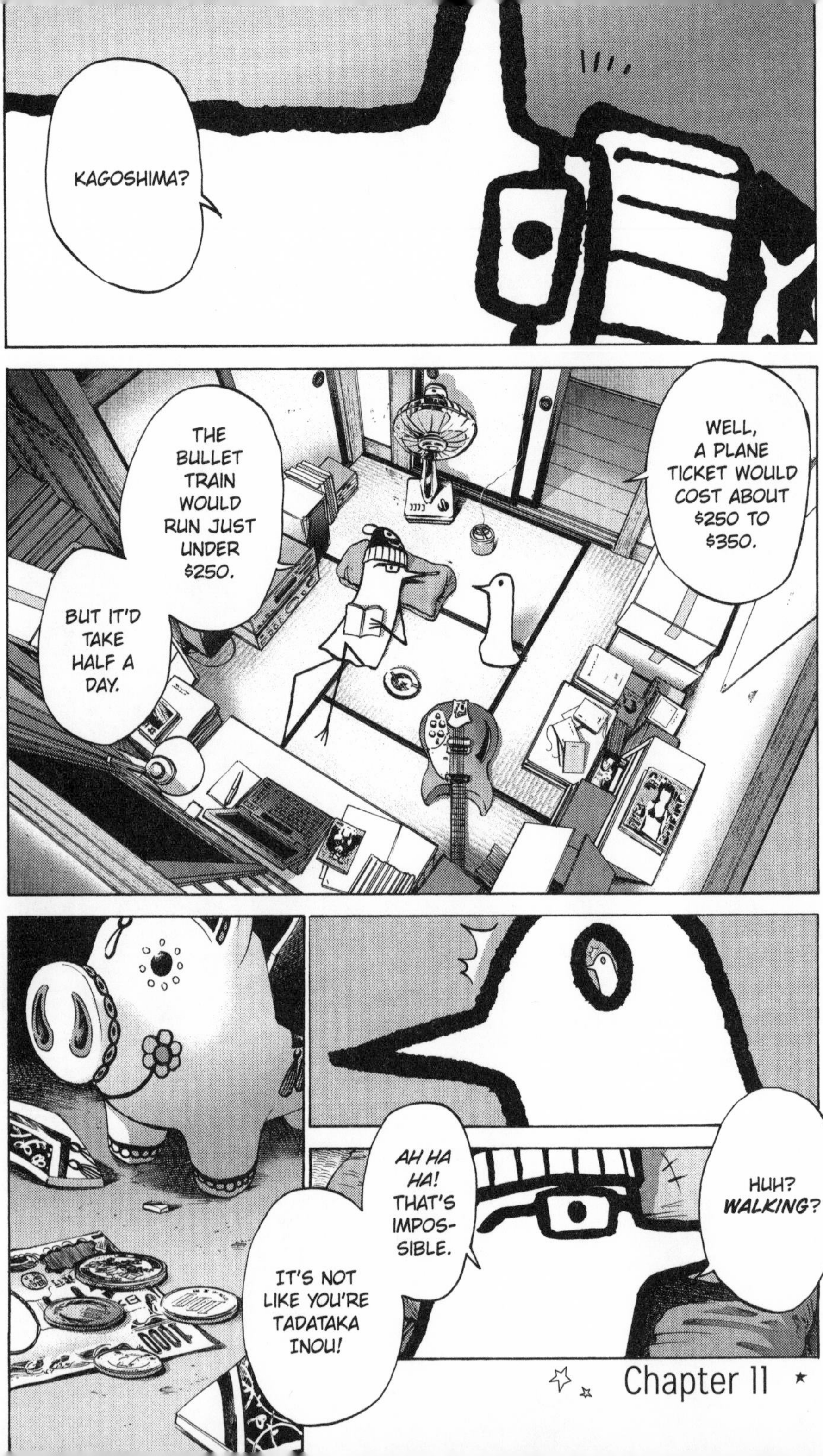
KAGOSHIMA?
WELL, A PLANE TICKET WOULD COST ABOUT $250 TO $350.
THE BULLET TRAIN WOULD RUN JUST UNDER $250.
BUT IT'D TAKE HALF A DAY.
HUH? *WALKING*?
AH HA HA! THAT'S IMPOSSIBLE.
IT'S NOT LIKE YOU'RE TADATAKA INOU!
Chapter 11

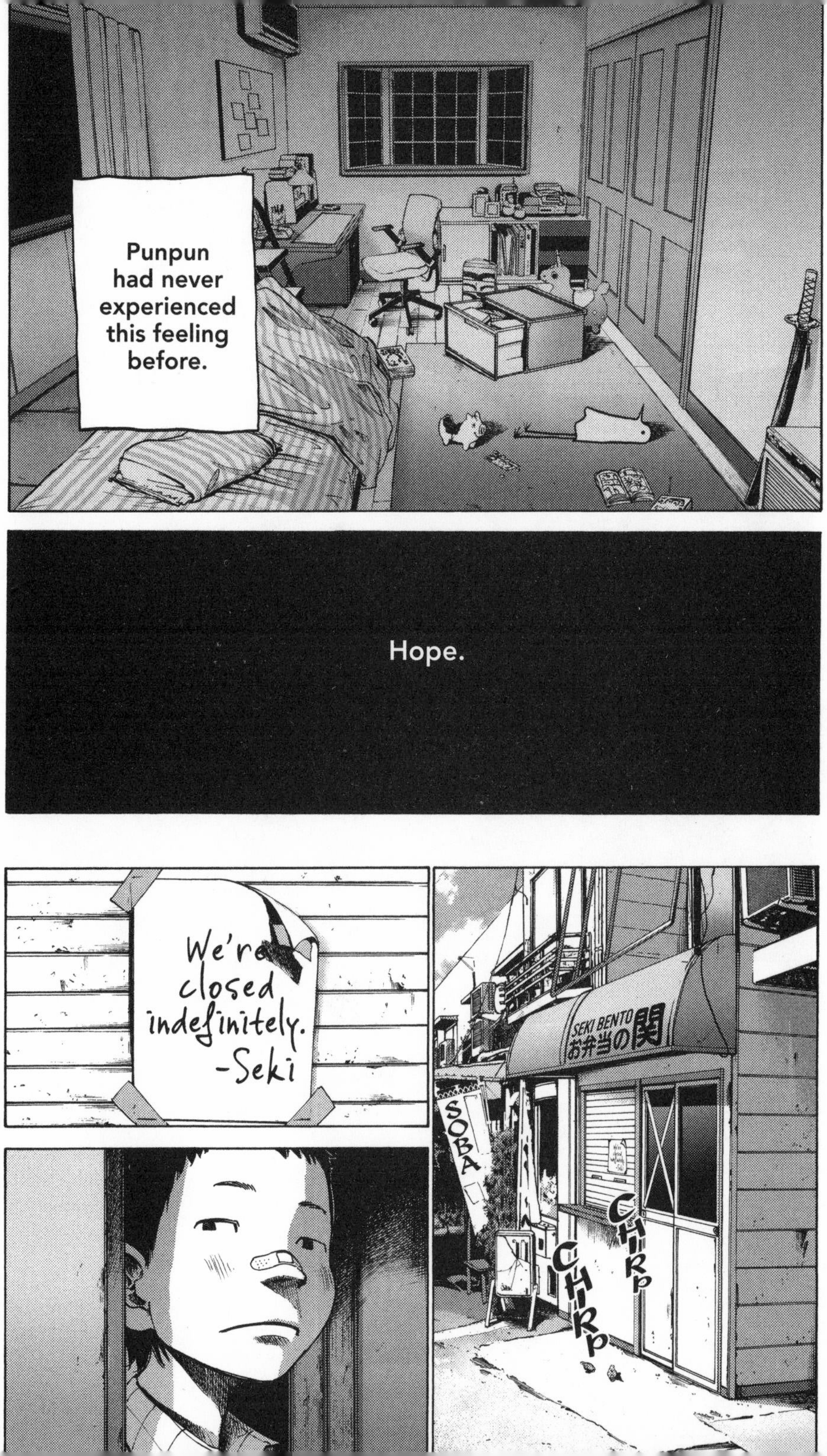

Punpun had never experienced this feeling before.
Hope.
SEKI BENTO
お弁当の関
SOBA
CHIRP
CHIRP
We're closed indefinitely. -Seki

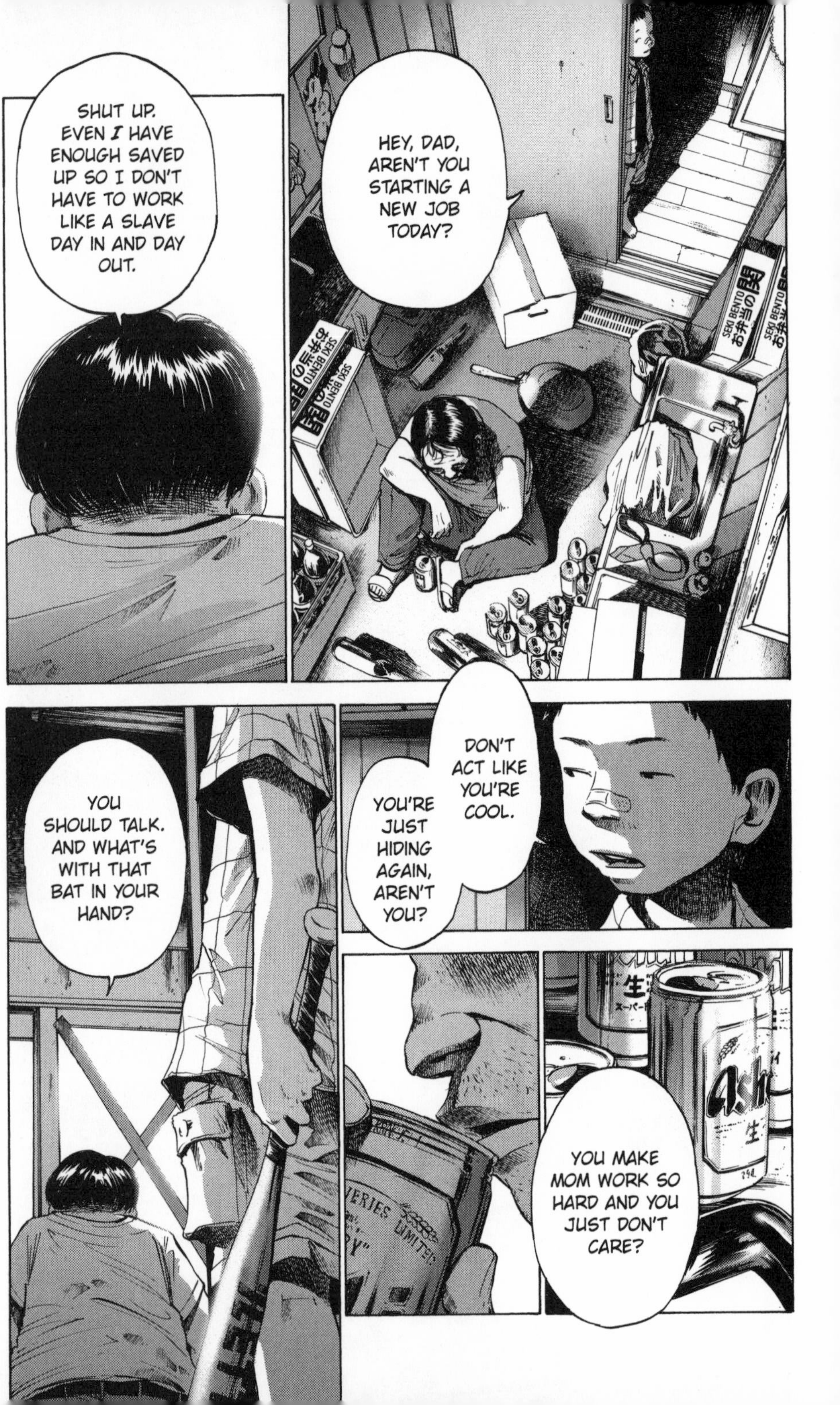
HEY, DAD, AREN'T YOU STARTING A NEW JOB TODAY?
SHUT UP. EVEN *I* HAVE ENOUGH SAVED UP SO I DON'T HAVE TO WORK LIKE A SLAVE DAY IN AND DAY OUT.
DON'T ACT LIKE YOU'RE COOL.
YOU'RE JUST HIDING AGAIN, AREN'T YOU?
YOU MAKE MOM WORK SO HARD AND YOU JUST DON'T CARE?
YOU SHOULD TALK. AND WHAT'S WITH THAT BAT IN YOUR HAND?

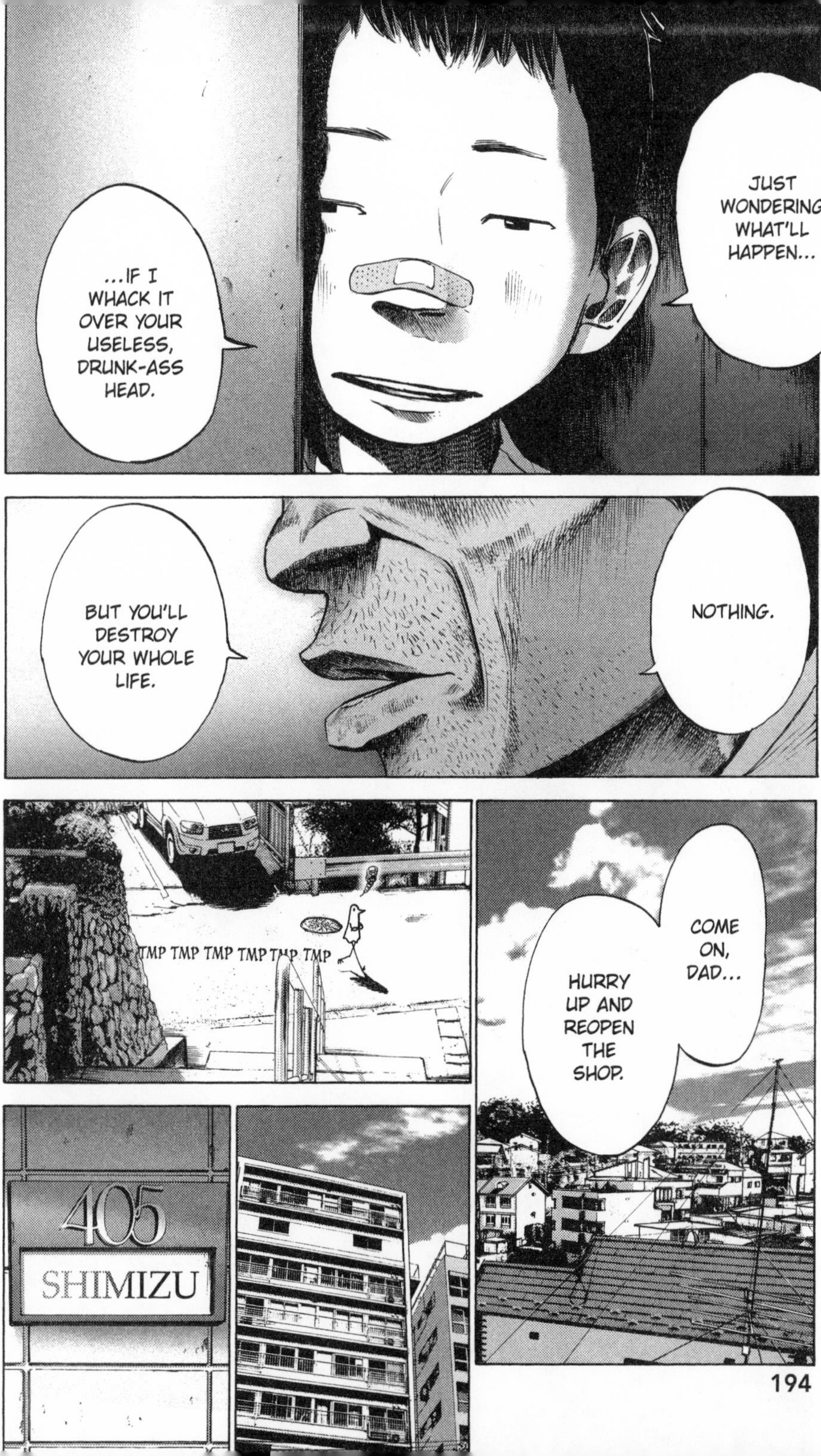
JUST WONDERING WHAT'LL HAPPEN...
...IF I WHACK IT OVER YOUR USELESS, DRUNK-ASS HEAD.
NOTHING.
BUT YOU'LL DESTROY YOUR WHOLE LIFE.
COME ON, DAD...
HURRY UP AND REOPEN THE SHOP.
TMP TMP TMP TMP TMP TMP
405
SHIMIZU

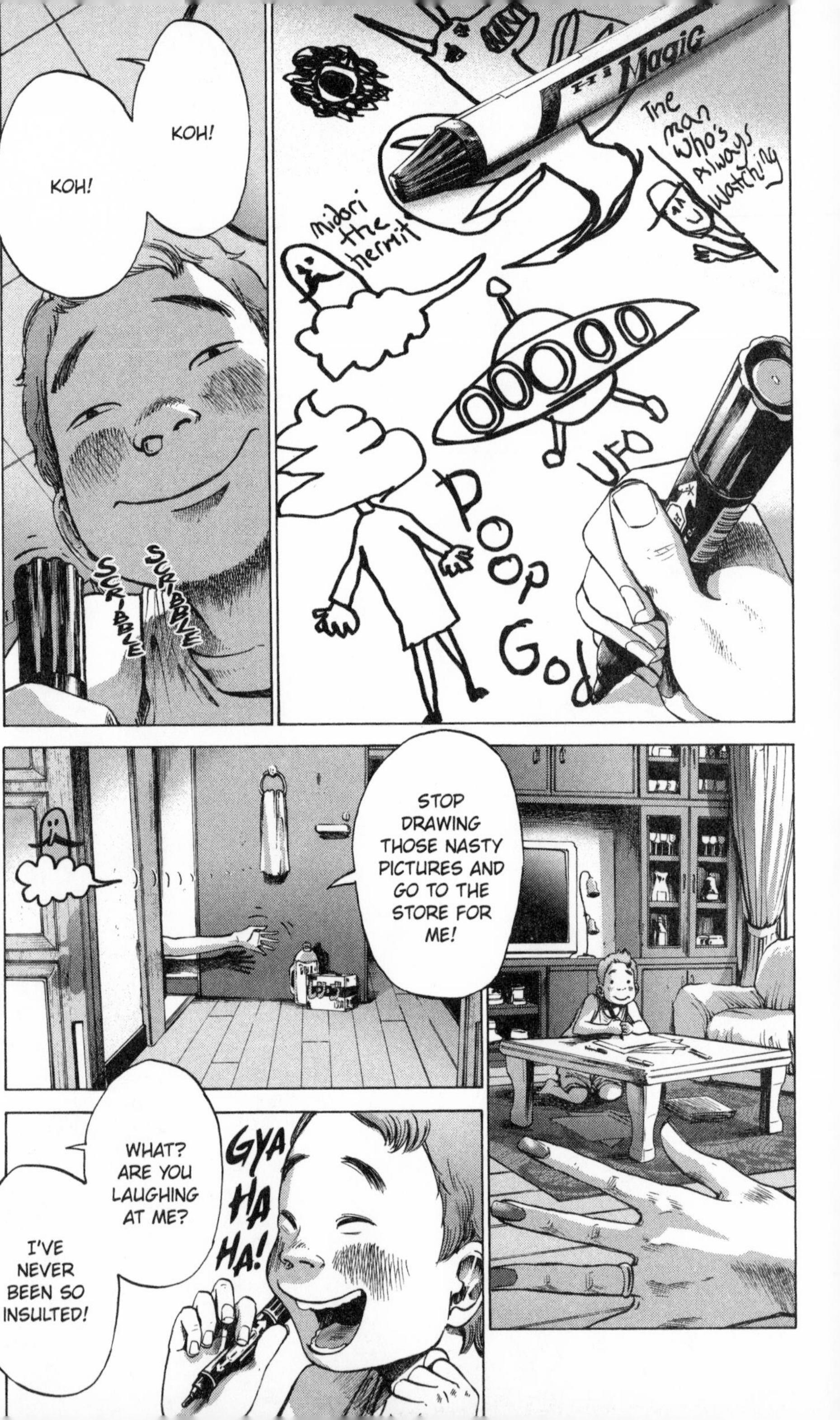
Magic
The man who's always watching
midori the hermit
UFO
POOP God
KOH!
KOH!
SCRIBBLE
SCRIBBLE
STOP DRAWING THOSE NASTY PICTURES AND GO TO THE STORE FOR ME!
GYA HA HA HA!
WHAT? ARE YOU LAUGHING AT ME?
I'VE NEVER BEEN SO INSULTED!

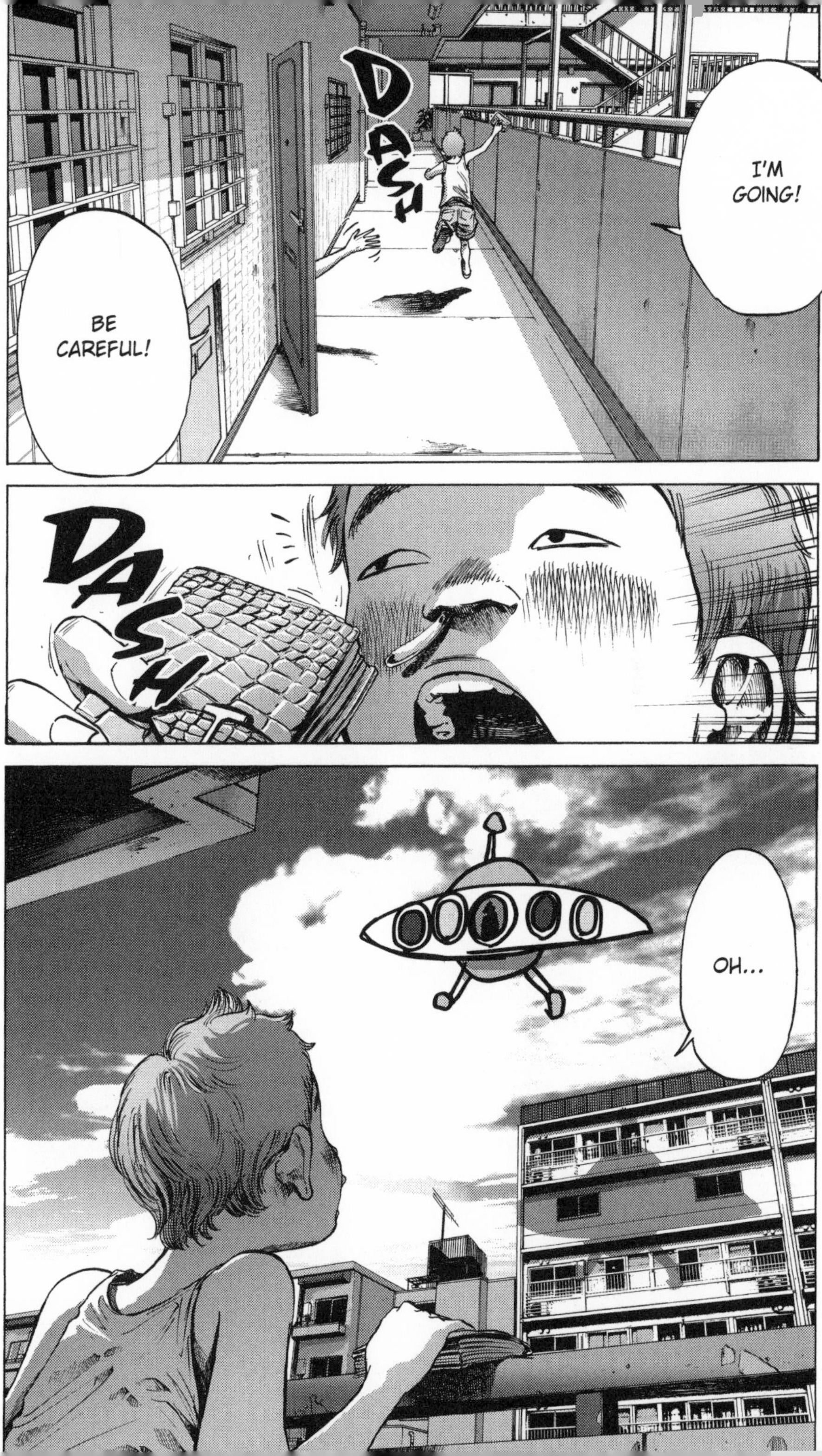
I'M GOING!
DASH
BE CAREFUL!
DASH
OH...

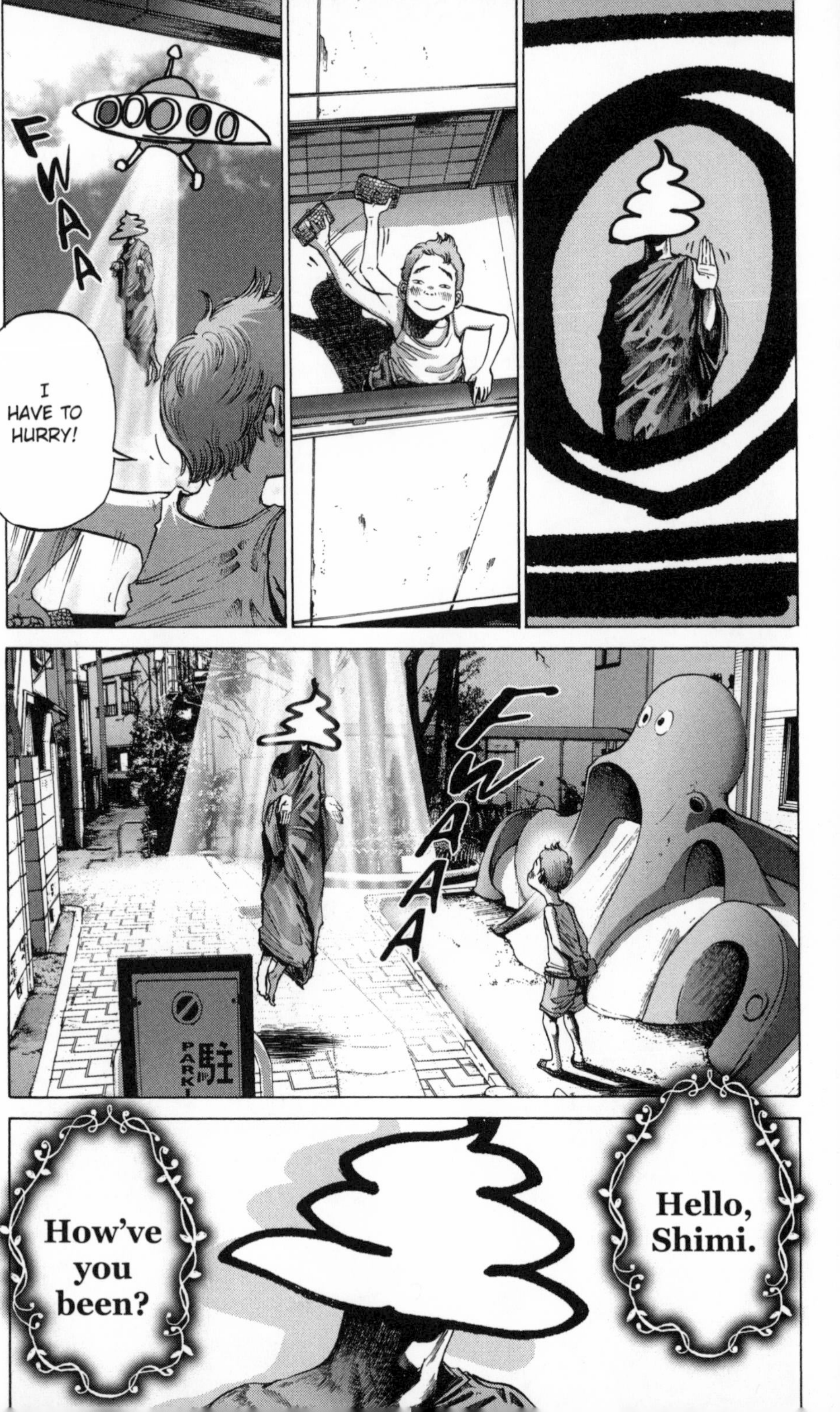
FWAA
I HAVE TO HURRY!
FWAAAA
Hello, Shimi.
How've you been?

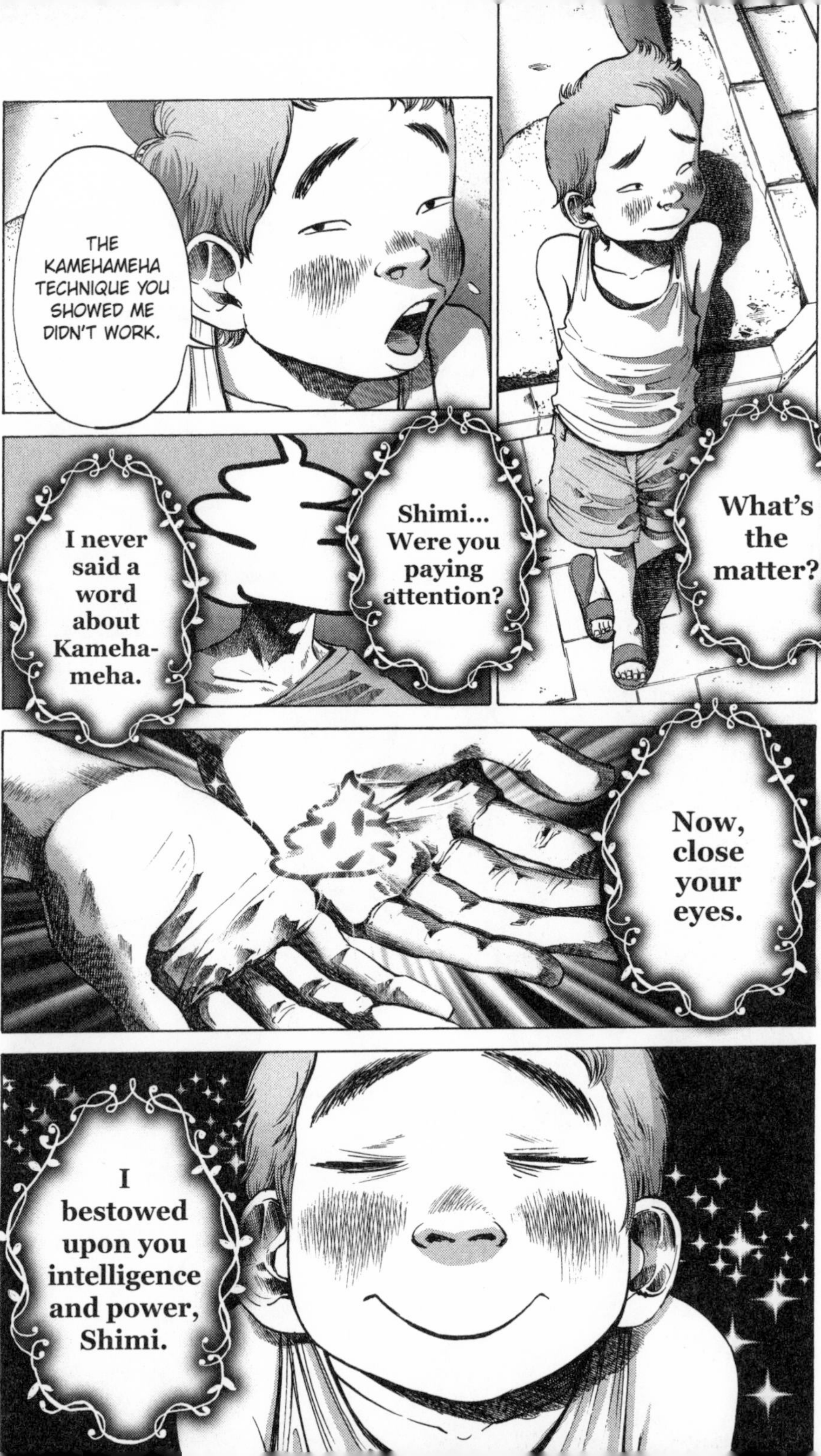
What's the matter?
THE KAMEHAMEHA TECHNIQUE YOU SHOWED ME DIDN'T WORK.
Shimi... Were you paying attention?
I never said a word about Kameha-meha.
Now, close your eyes.
I bestowed upon you intelligence and power, Shimi.

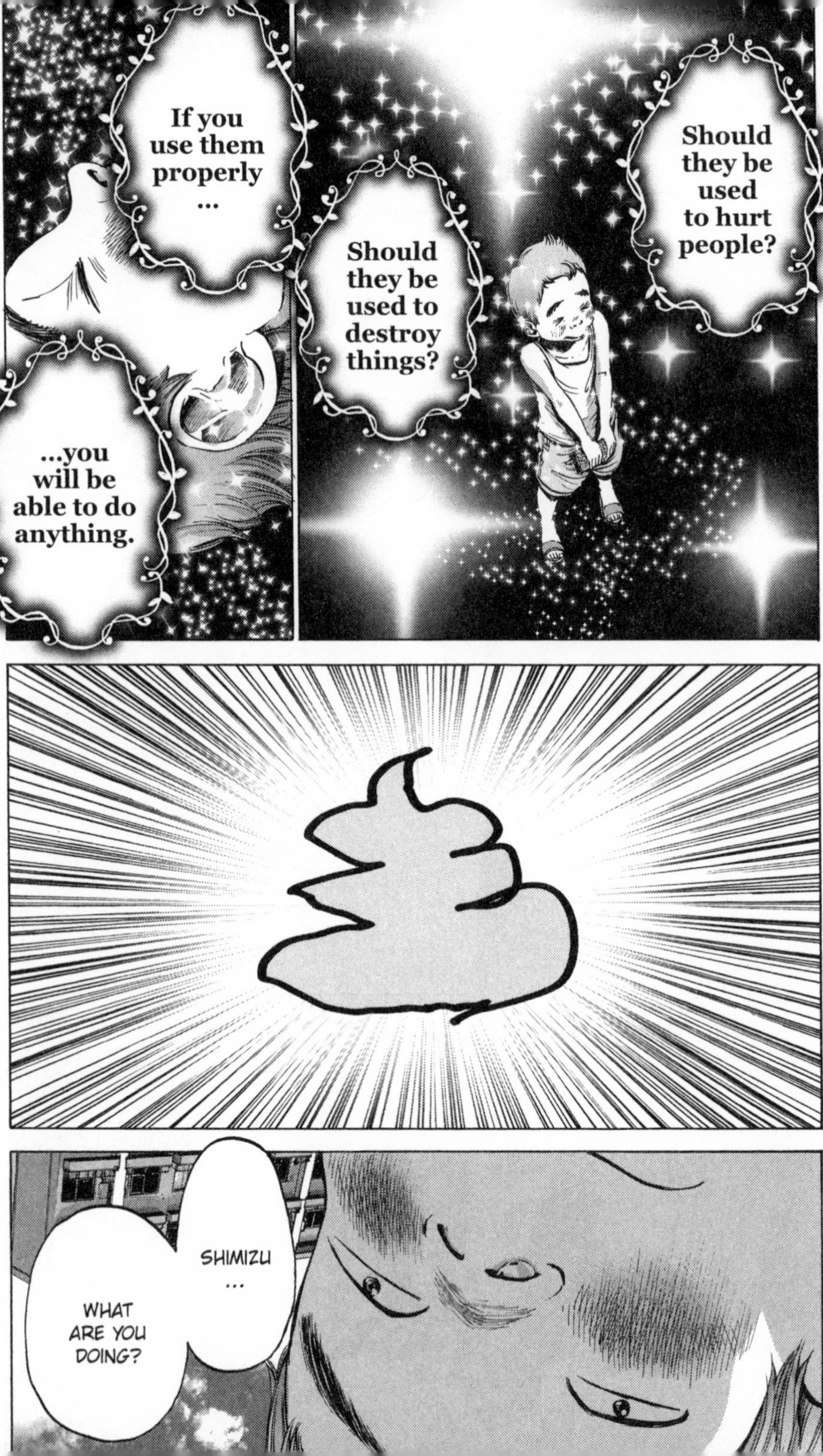
Should they be used to hurt people?
Should they be used to destroy things?
If you use them properly ...
...you will be able to do anything.
SHIMIZU ...
WHAT ARE YOU DOING?

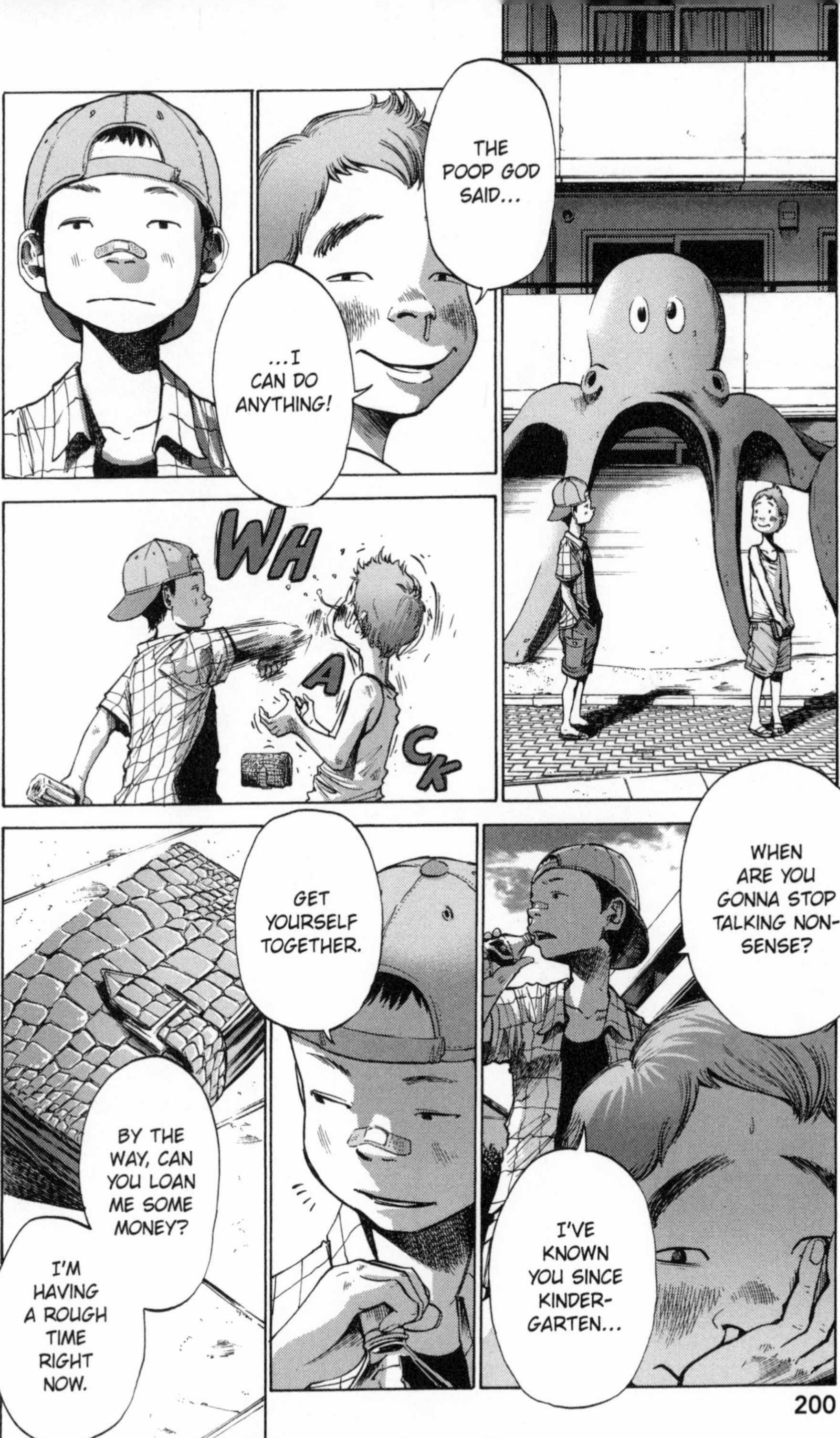
THE POOP GOD SAID...
...I CAN DO ANYTHING!
WHACK
WHEN ARE YOU GONNA STOP TALKING NON-SENSE?
I'VE KNOWN YOU SINCE KINDER-GARTEN...
GET YOURSELF TOGETHER.
BY THE WAY, CAN YOU LOAN ME SOME MONEY?
I'M HAVING A ROUGH TIME RIGHT NOW.

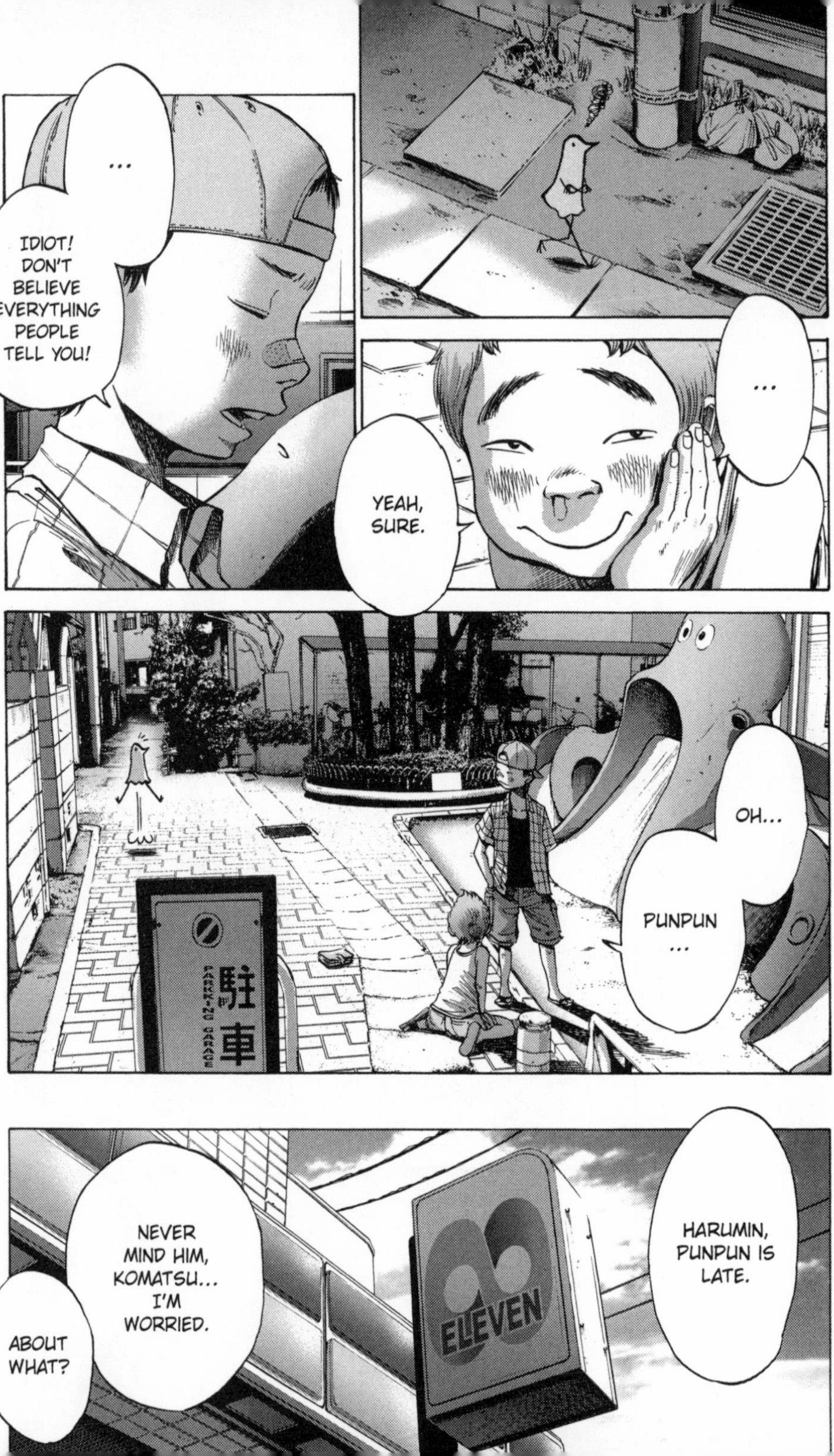
...
YEAH, SURE.
...
IDIOT! DON'T BELIEVE EVERYTHING PEOPLE TELL YOU!
OH...
PUNPUN ...
駐車
PARKING GARAGE
HARUMIN, PUNPUN IS LATE.
ELEVEN
NEVER MIND HIM, KOMATSU... I'M WORRIED.
ABOUT WHAT?

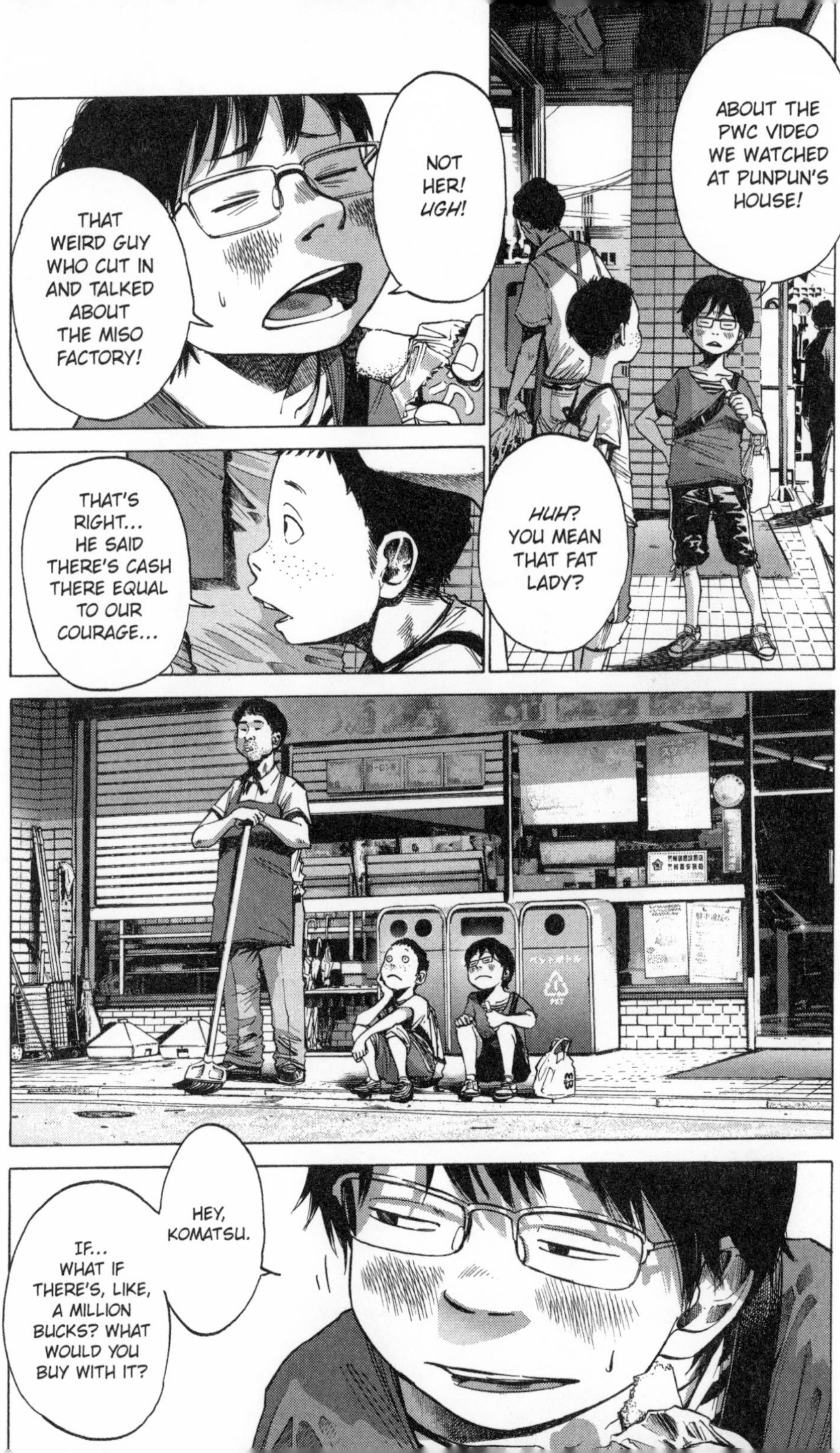
ABOUT THE PWC VIDEO WE WATCHED AT PUNPUN'S HOUSE!
HUH? YOU MEAN THAT FAT LADY?
NOT HER! UGH!
THAT WEIRD GUY WHO CUT IN AND TALKED ABOUT THE MISO FACTORY!
THAT'S RIGHT... HE SAID THERE'S CASH THERE EQUAL TO OUR COURAGE...
HEY, KOMATSU.
IF... WHAT IF THERE'S, LIKE, A MILLION BUCKS? WHAT WOULD YOU BUY WITH IT?

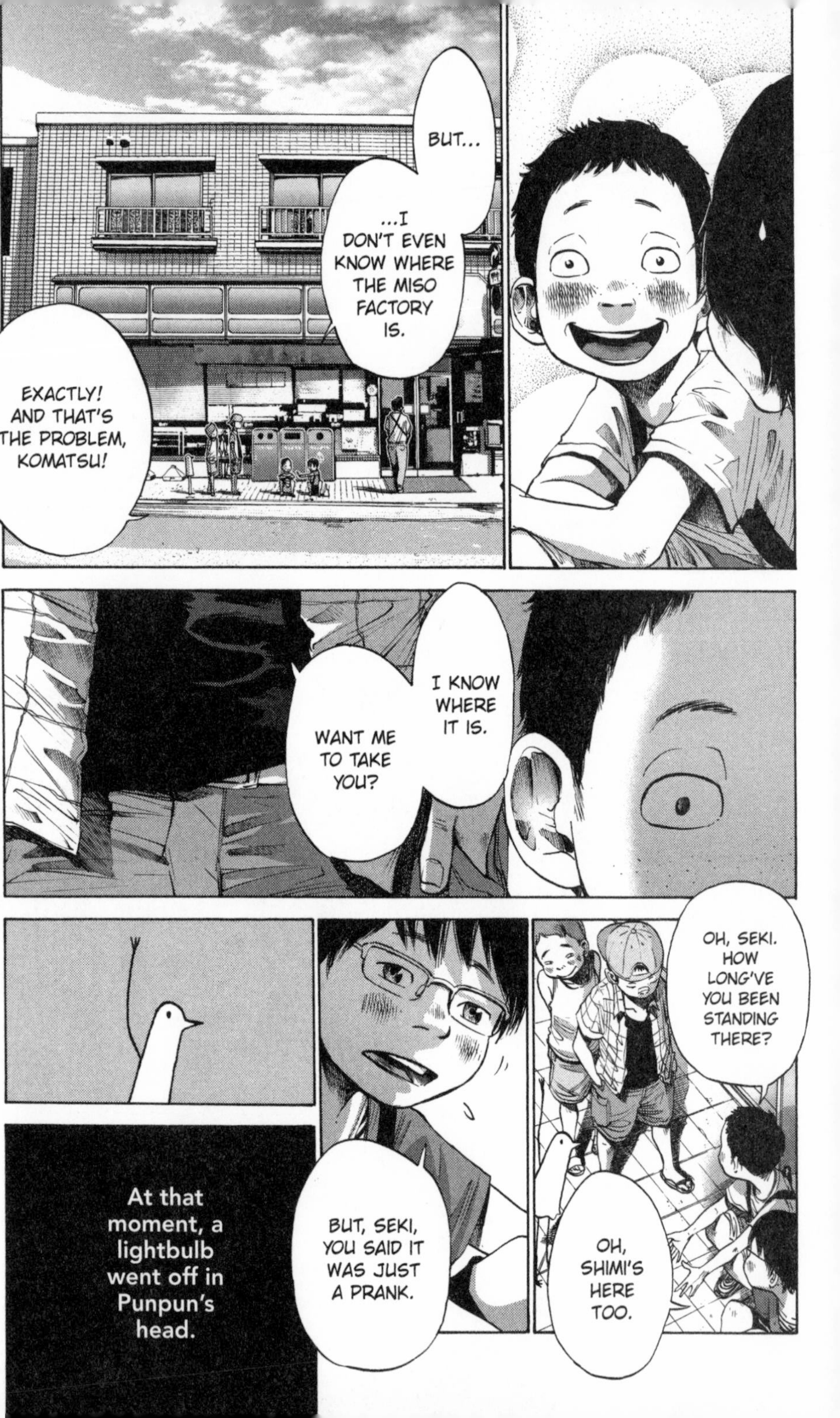
BUT...
...I DON'T EVEN KNOW WHERE THE MISO FACTORY IS.
EXACTLY! AND THAT'S THE PROBLEM, KOMATSU!
I KNOW WHERE IT IS.
WANT ME TO TAKE YOU?
OH, SEKI. HOW LONG'VE YOU BEEN STANDING THERE?
OH, SHIMI'S HERE TOO.
BUT, SEKI, YOU SAID IT WAS JUST A PRANK.
At that moment, a lightbulb went off in Punpun's head.

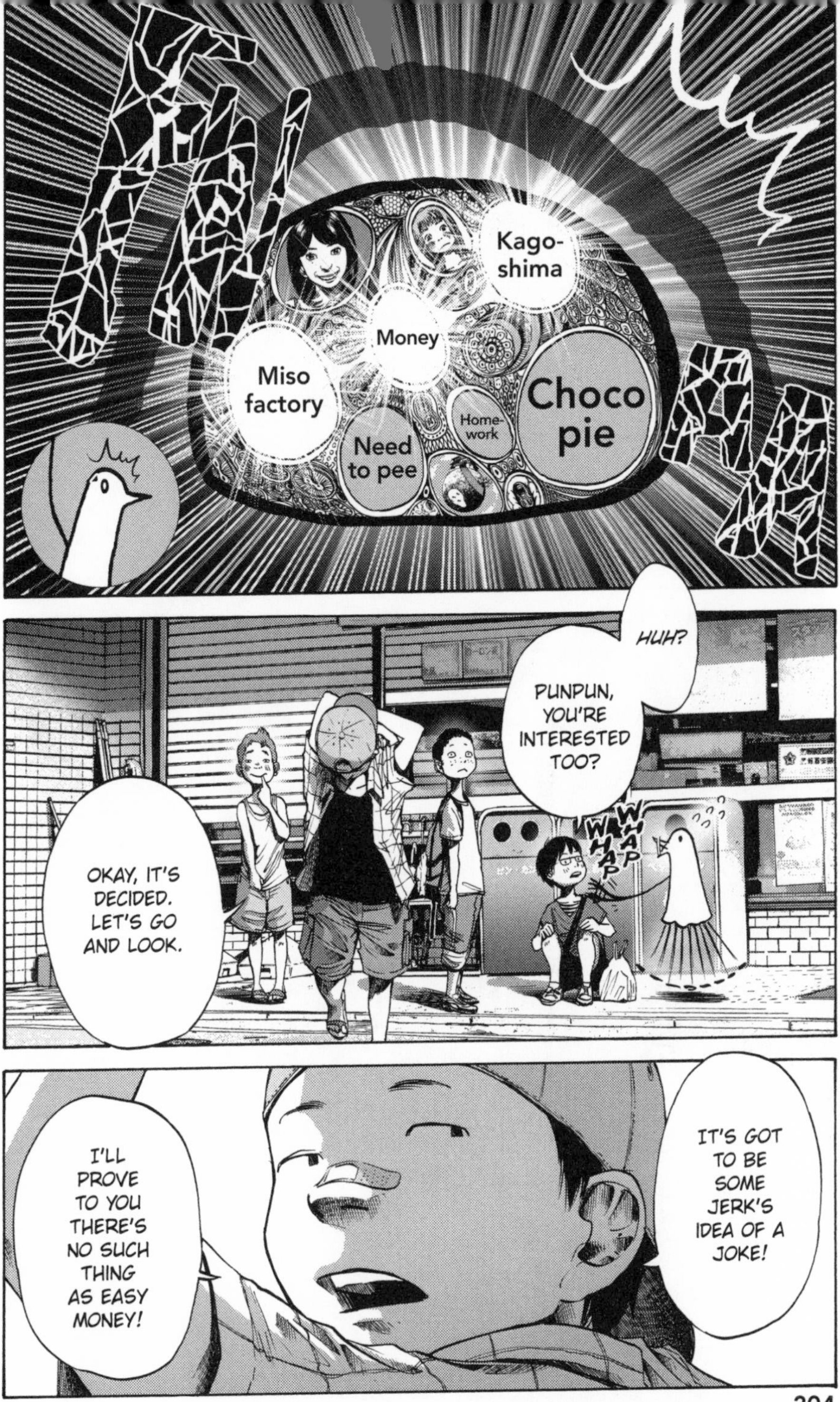
Kago-shima
Money
Choco pie
Miso factory
Home-work
Need to pee
HUH?
PUNPUN, YOU'RE INTERESTED TOO?
WHAP WHAP
OKAY, IT'S DECIDED. LET'S GO AND LOOK.
IT'S GOT TO BE SOME JERK'S IDEA OF A JOKE!
I'LL PROVE TO YOU THERE'S NO SUCH THING AS EASY MONEY!

Chapter 12

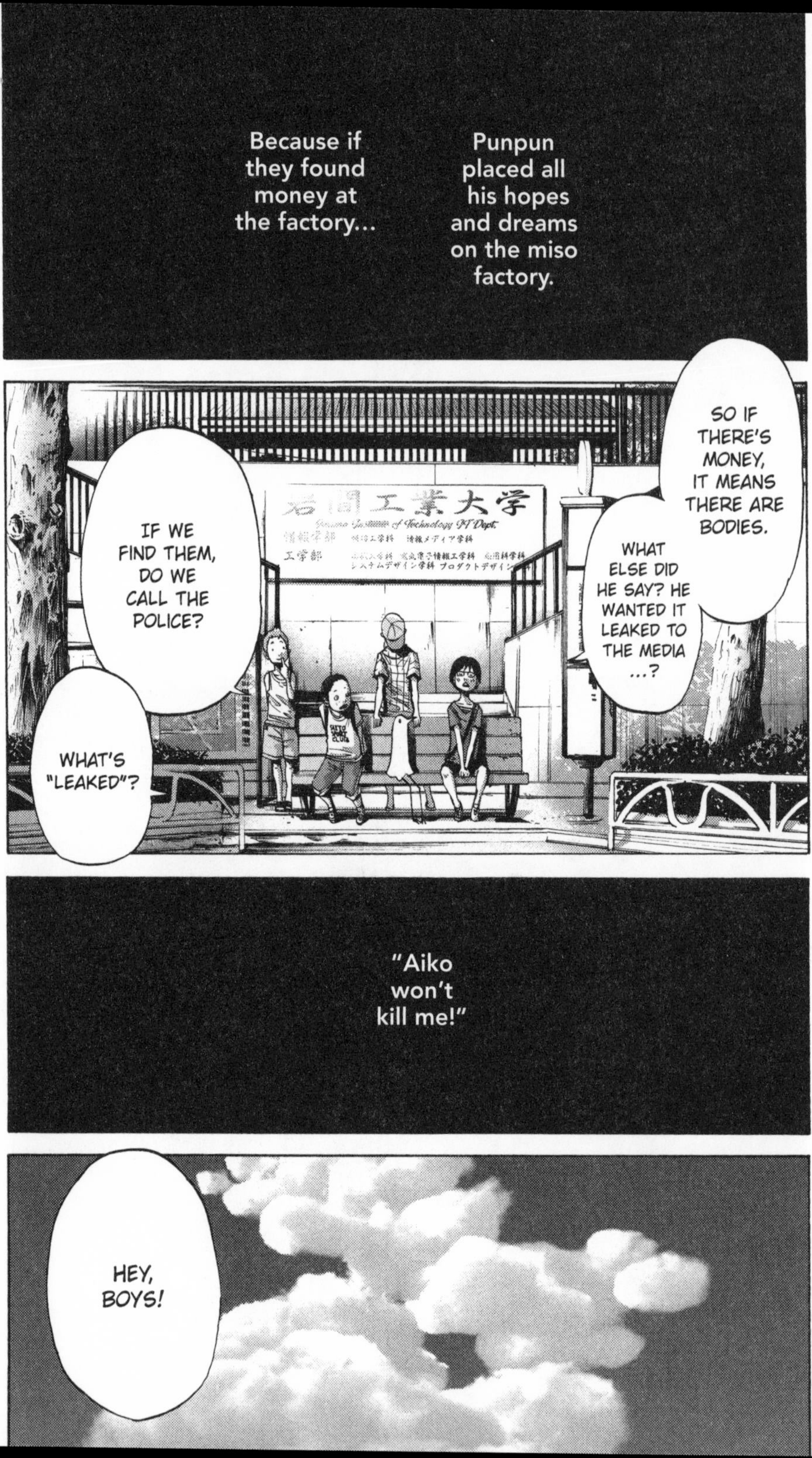
Punpun placed all his hopes and dreams on the miso factory.
Because if they found money at the factory...
SO IF THERE'S MONEY, IT MEANS THERE ARE BODIES.
WHAT ELSE DID HE SAY? HE WANTED IT LEAKED TO THE MEDIA ...?
岩間工業大学
IF WE FIND THEM, DO WE CALL THE POLICE?
WHAT'S "LEAKED"?
"Aiko won't kill me!"
HEY, BOYS!

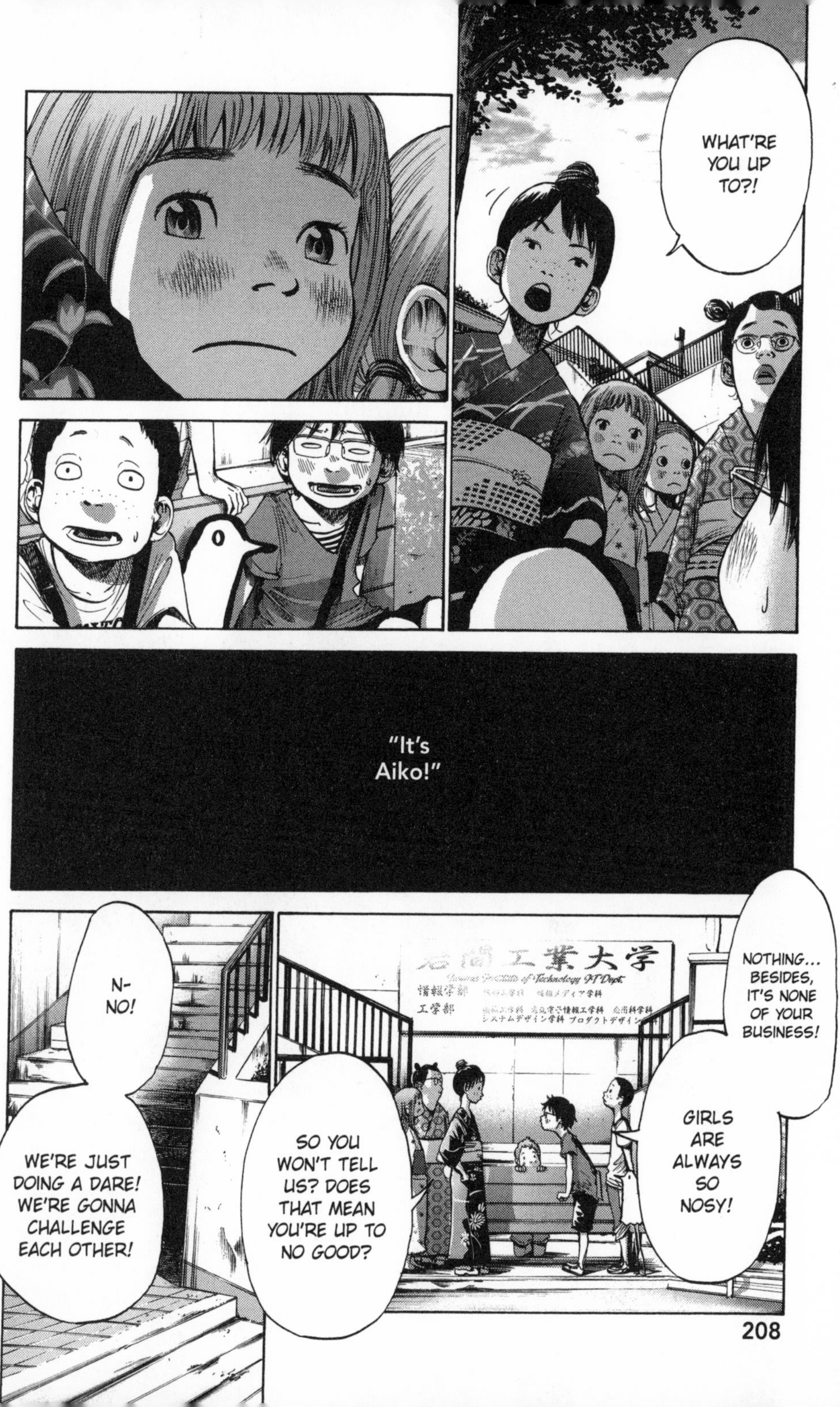
WHAT'RE YOU UP TO?!
"It's Aiko!"
NOTHING... BESIDES, IT'S NONE OF YOUR BUSINESS!
GIRLS ARE ALWAYS SO NOSY!
SO YOU WON'T TELL US? DOES THAT MEAN YOU'RE UP TO NO GOOD?
N- NO!
WE'RE JUST DOING A DARE! WE'RE GONNA CHALLENGE EACH OTHER!

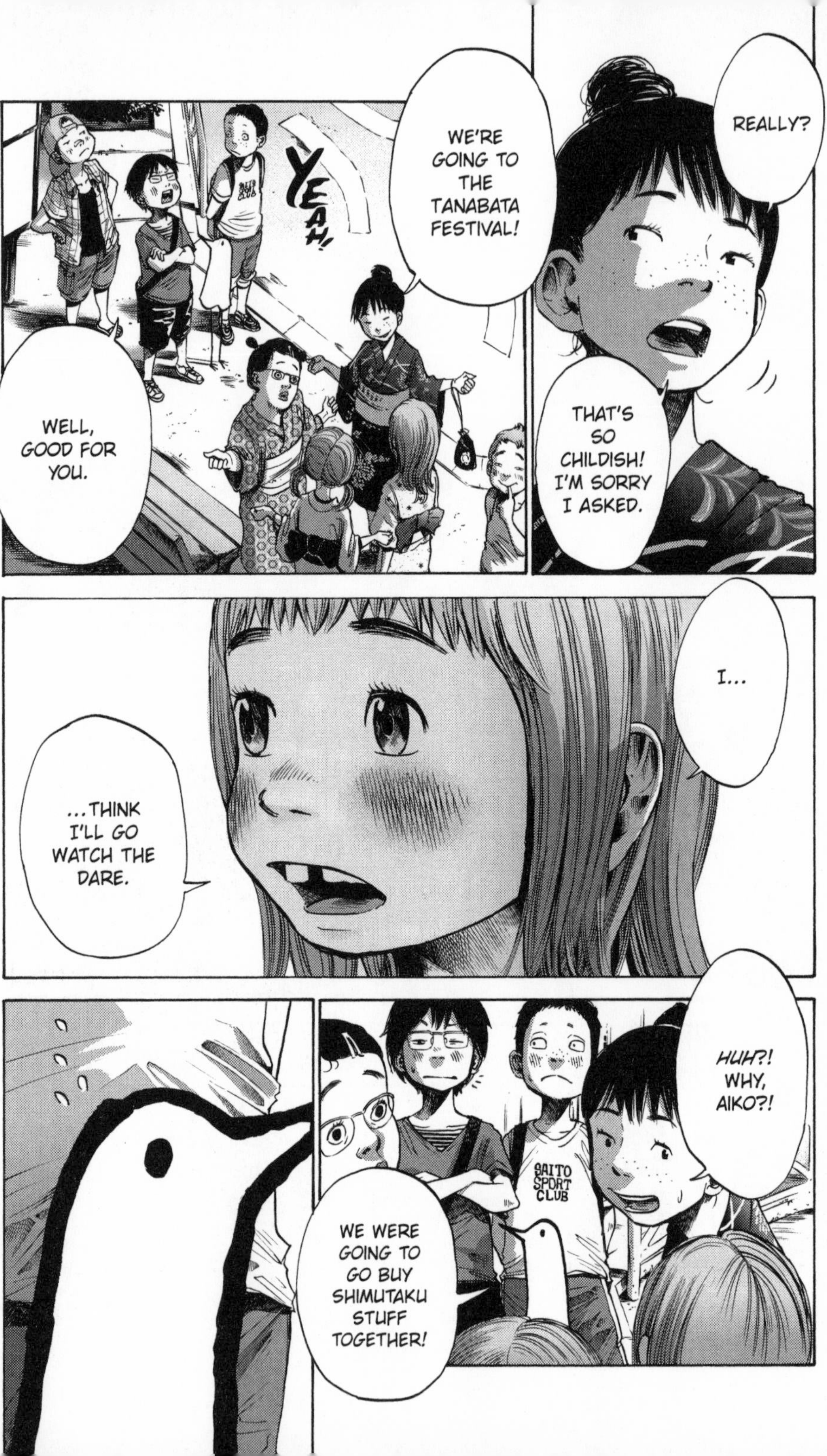
REALLY?
THAT'S SO CHILDISH! I'M SORRY I ASKED.
WE'RE GOING TO THE TANABATA FESTIVAL!
YEAH!
WELL, GOOD FOR YOU.
I...
...THINK I'LL GO WATCH THE DARE.
HUH?! WHY, AIKO?!
SAITO SPORT CLUB
WE WERE GOING TO GO BUY SHIMUTAKU STUFF TOGETHER!

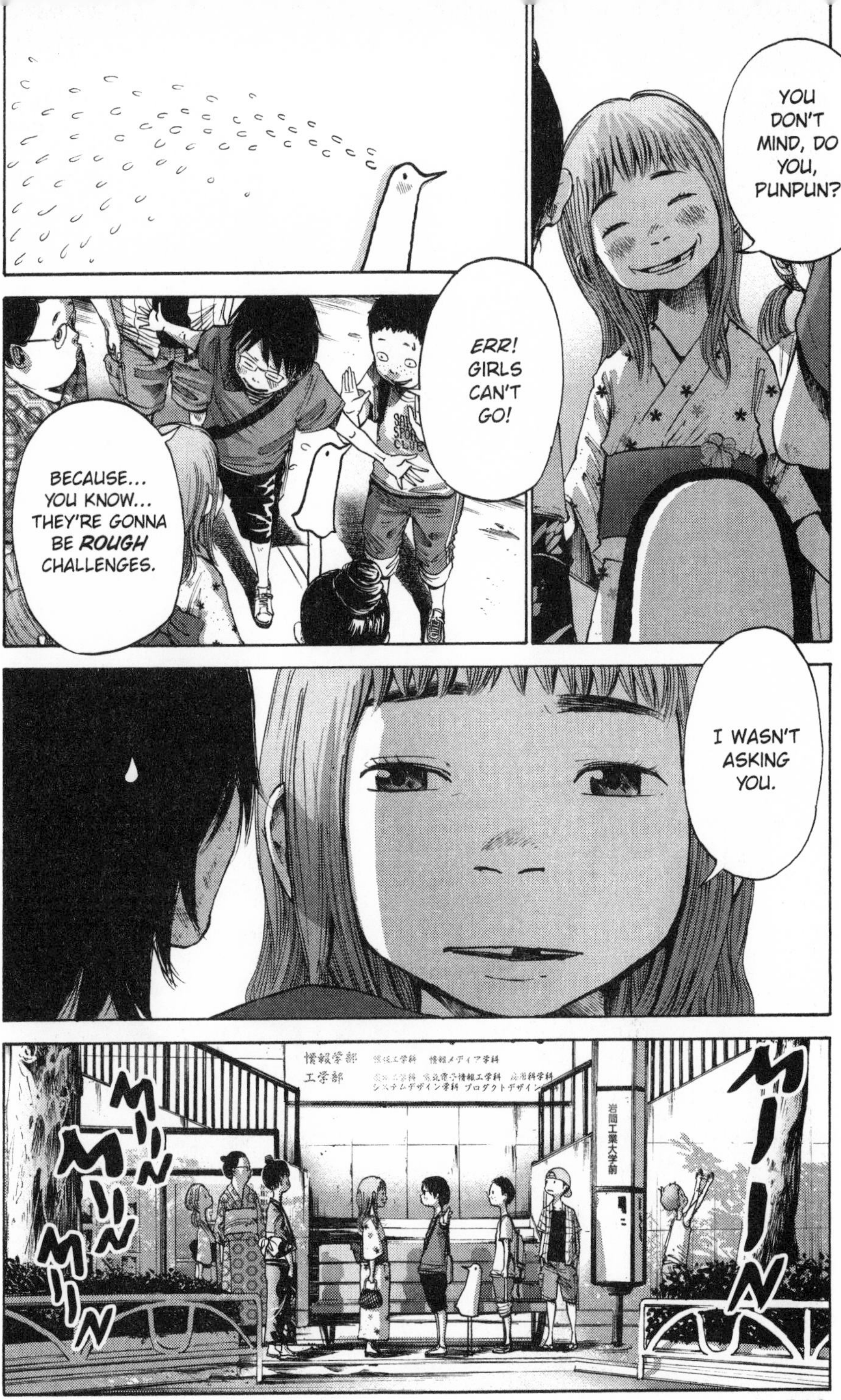
YOU DON'T MIND, DO YOU, PUNPUN?
ERR! GIRLS CAN'T GO!
BECAUSE... YOU KNOW... THEY'RE GONNA BE ROUGH CHALLENGES.
I WASN'T ASKING YOU.
情報学部
情報メディア学科
工学部
システムデザイン学科
岩間工業大学前

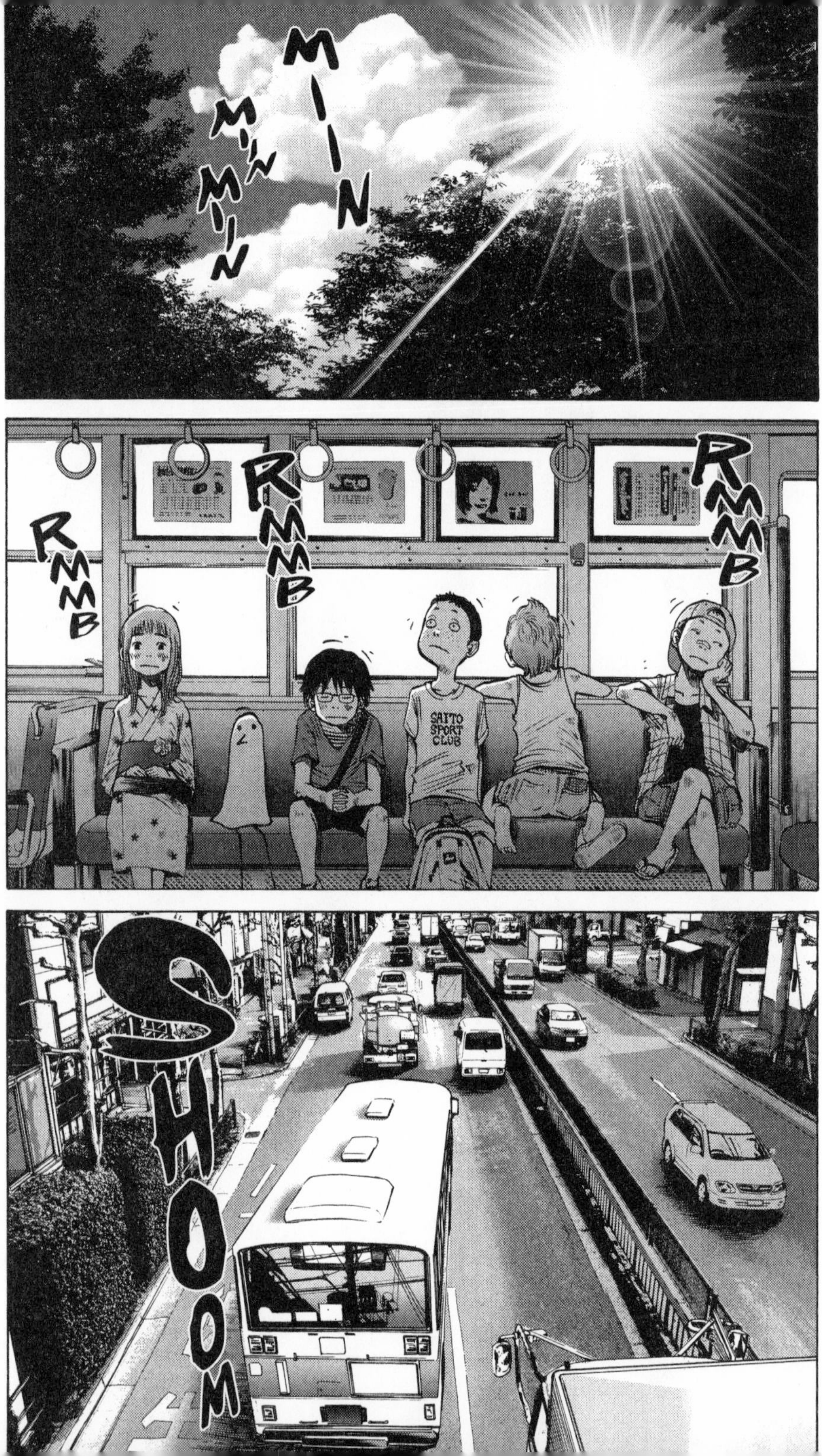
MIIN
MIN
MIN
RMMB
RMMB
SAITO SPORT CLUB
RMMB
SHOOM

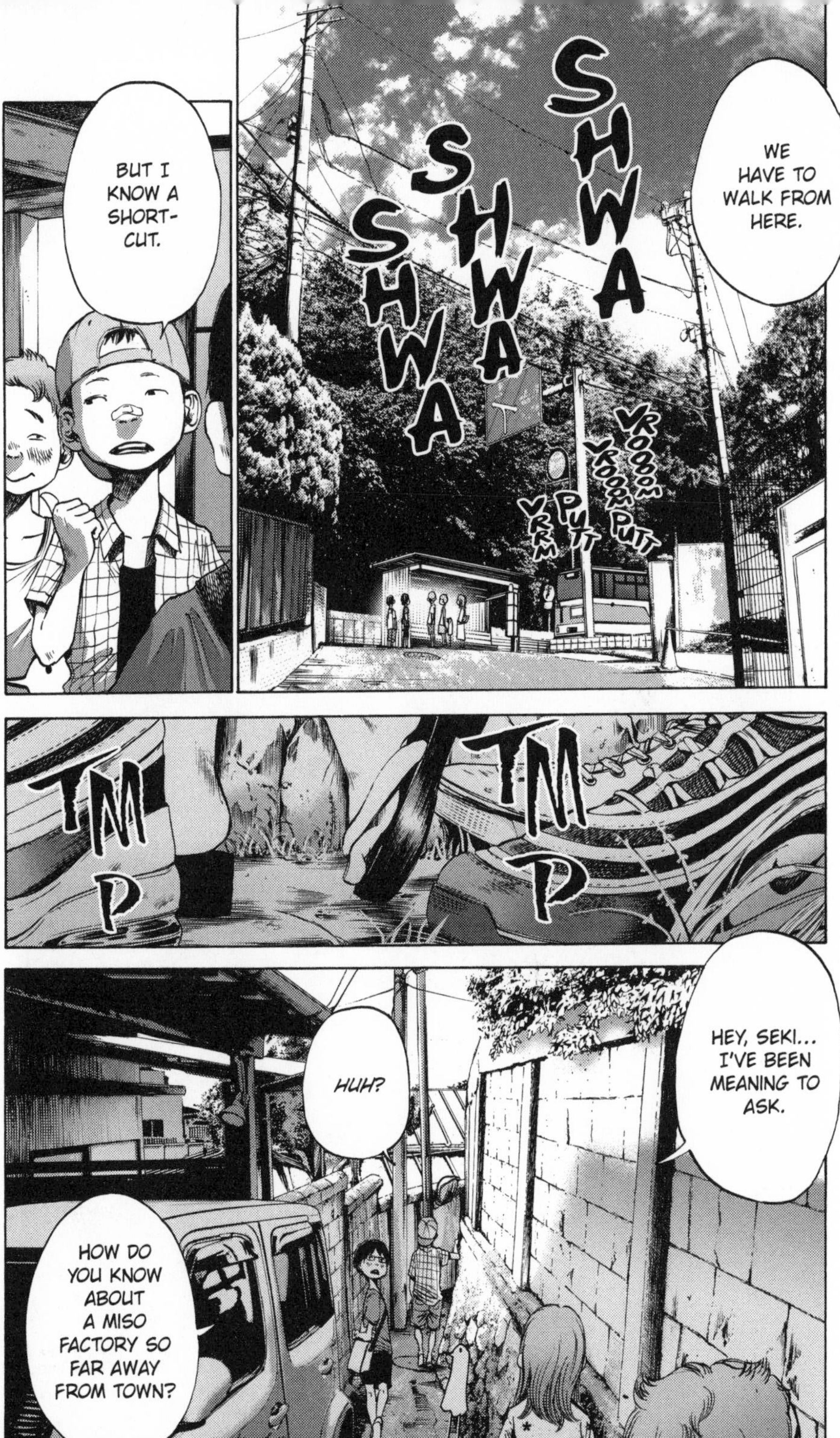
WE HAVE TO WALK FROM HERE.
SHWA
SHWA
SHWA
VROOOOM
VROOM PUTT
PUTT
VRRM
BUT I KNOW A SHORT-CUT.
TMP
TMP
HEY, SEKI... I'VE BEEN MEANING TO ASK.
HUH?
HOW DO YOU KNOW ABOUT A MISO FACTORY SO FAR AWAY FROM TOWN?

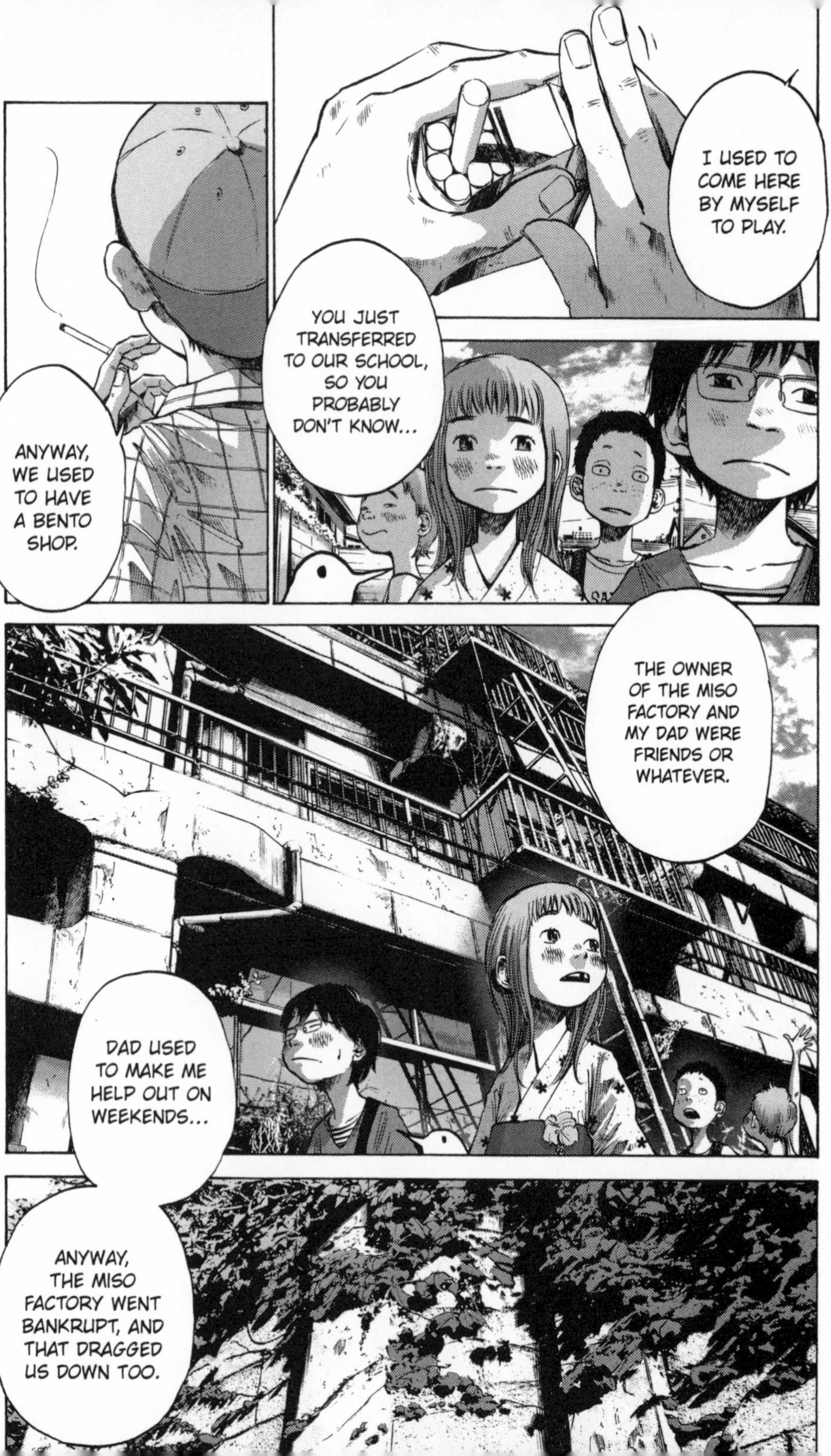
I USED TO COME HERE BY MYSELF TO PLAY.
YOU JUST TRANSFERRED TO OUR SCHOOL, SO YOU PROBABLY DON'T KNOW...
ANYWAY, WE USED TO HAVE A BENTO SHOP.
THE OWNER OF THE MISO FACTORY AND MY DAD WERE FRIENDS OR WHATEVER.
DAD USED TO MAKE ME HELP OUT ON WEEKENDS...
ANYWAY, THE MISO FACTORY WENT BANKRUPT, AND THAT DRAGGED US DOWN TOO.

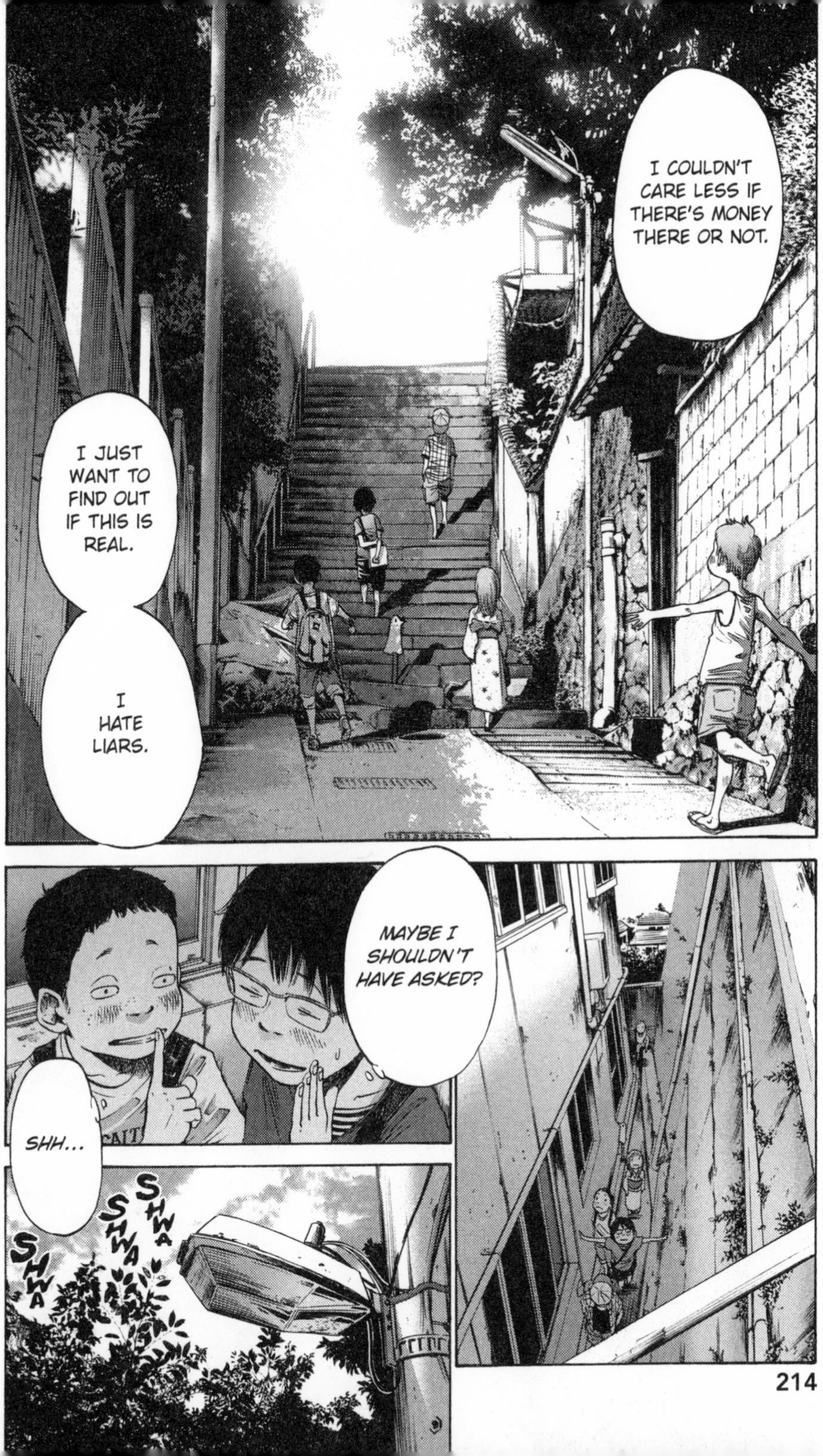
I COULDN'T CARE LESS IF THERE'S MONEY THERE OR NOT.
I JUST WANT TO FIND OUT IF THIS IS REAL.
I HATE LIARS.
MAYBE I SHOULDN'T HAVE ASKED?
SHH...
SHWA SHWA SHWA SHWA

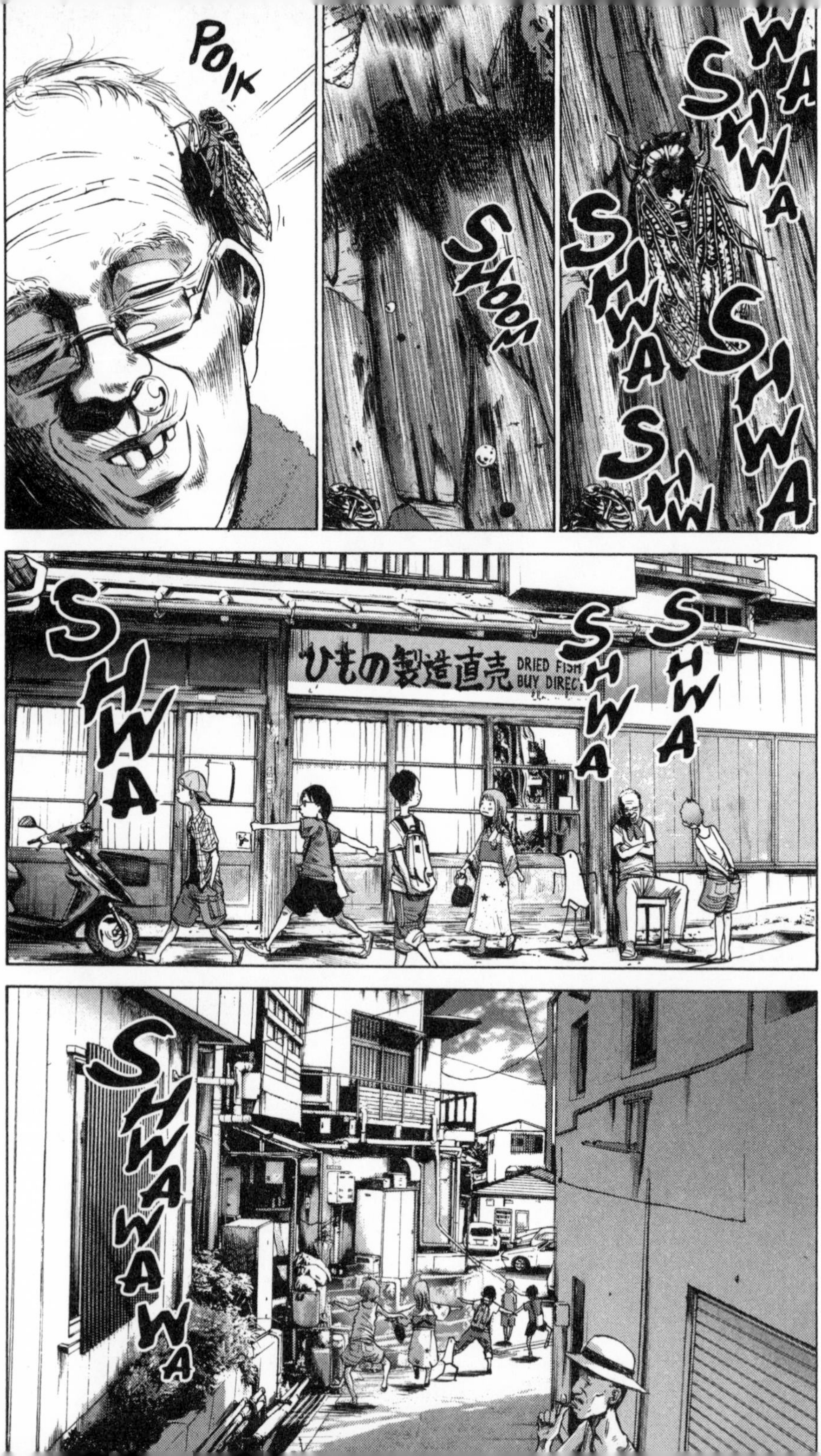
WA
SHWA
SHWA
SHWA
SHWA
SHW
SHOOM
POIK
SHWA
SHWA
ひもの製造直売
DRIED FISH
BUY DIREC
SHWA
SHWAWAWAWA

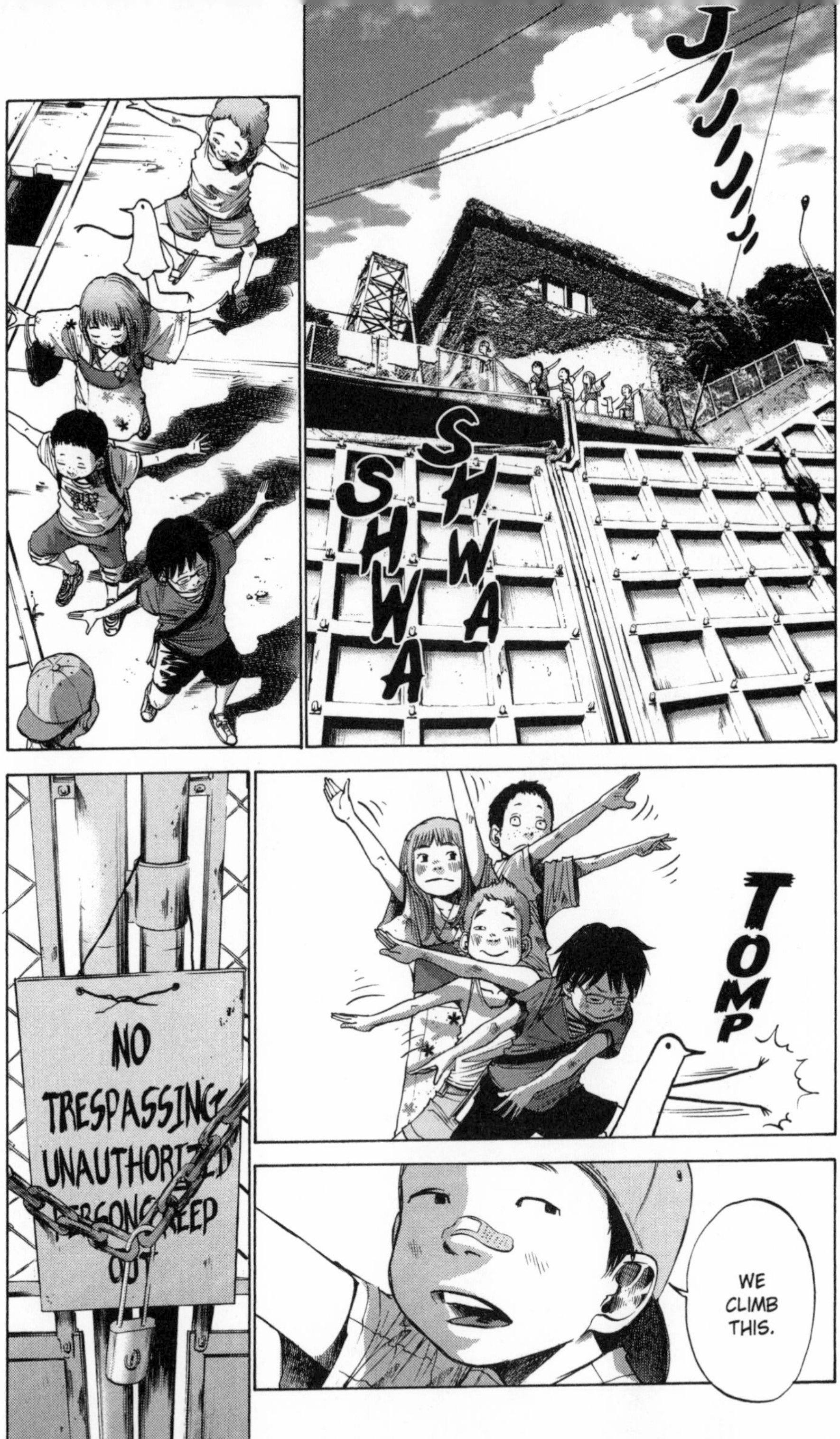
JJJJJJJJ
SHWA
SHWA
TOMP
WE CLIMB THIS.
NO
TRESPASSING
UNAUTHORIZED
KEEP
OUT

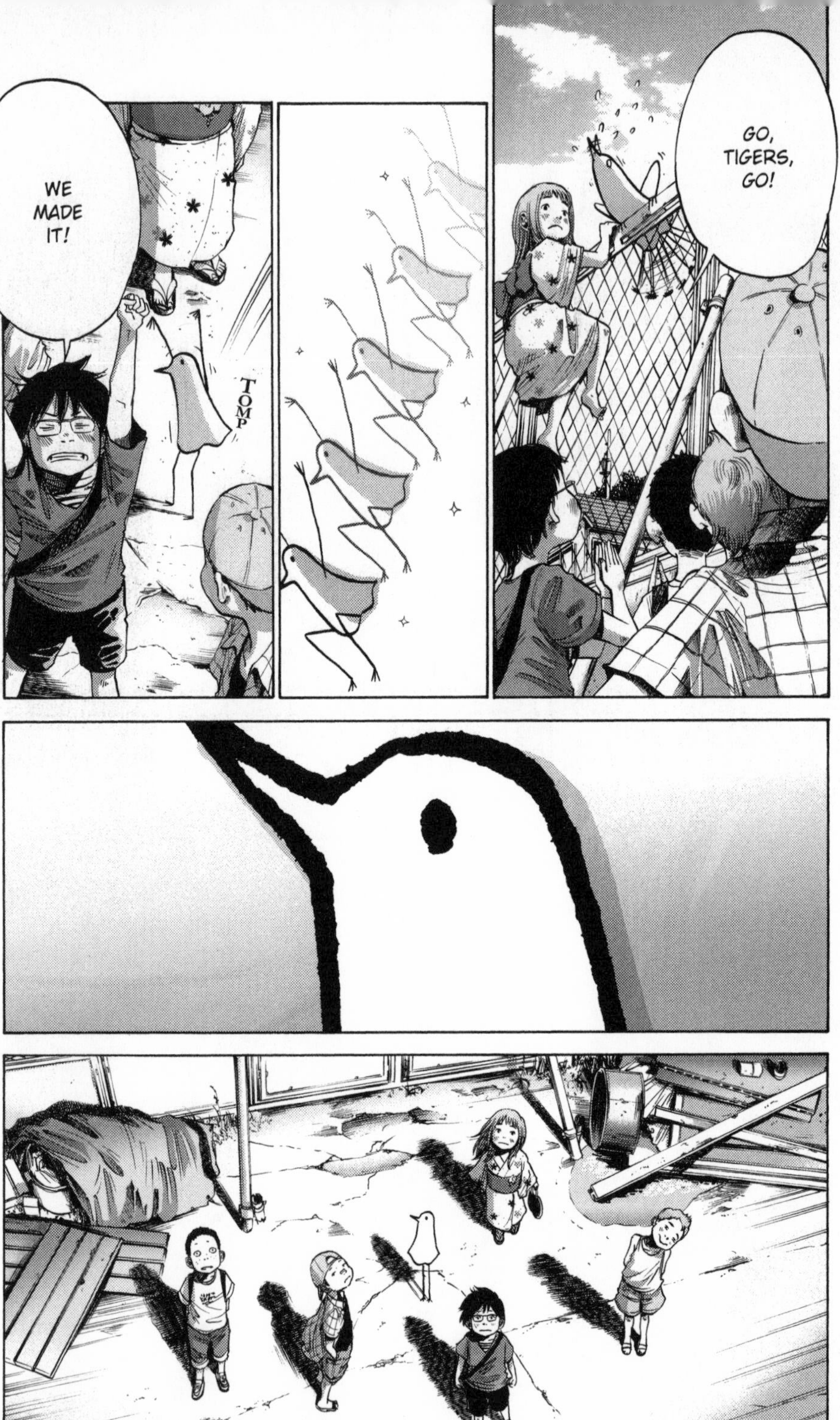
GO, TIGERS, GO!
WE MADE IT!
TOMP

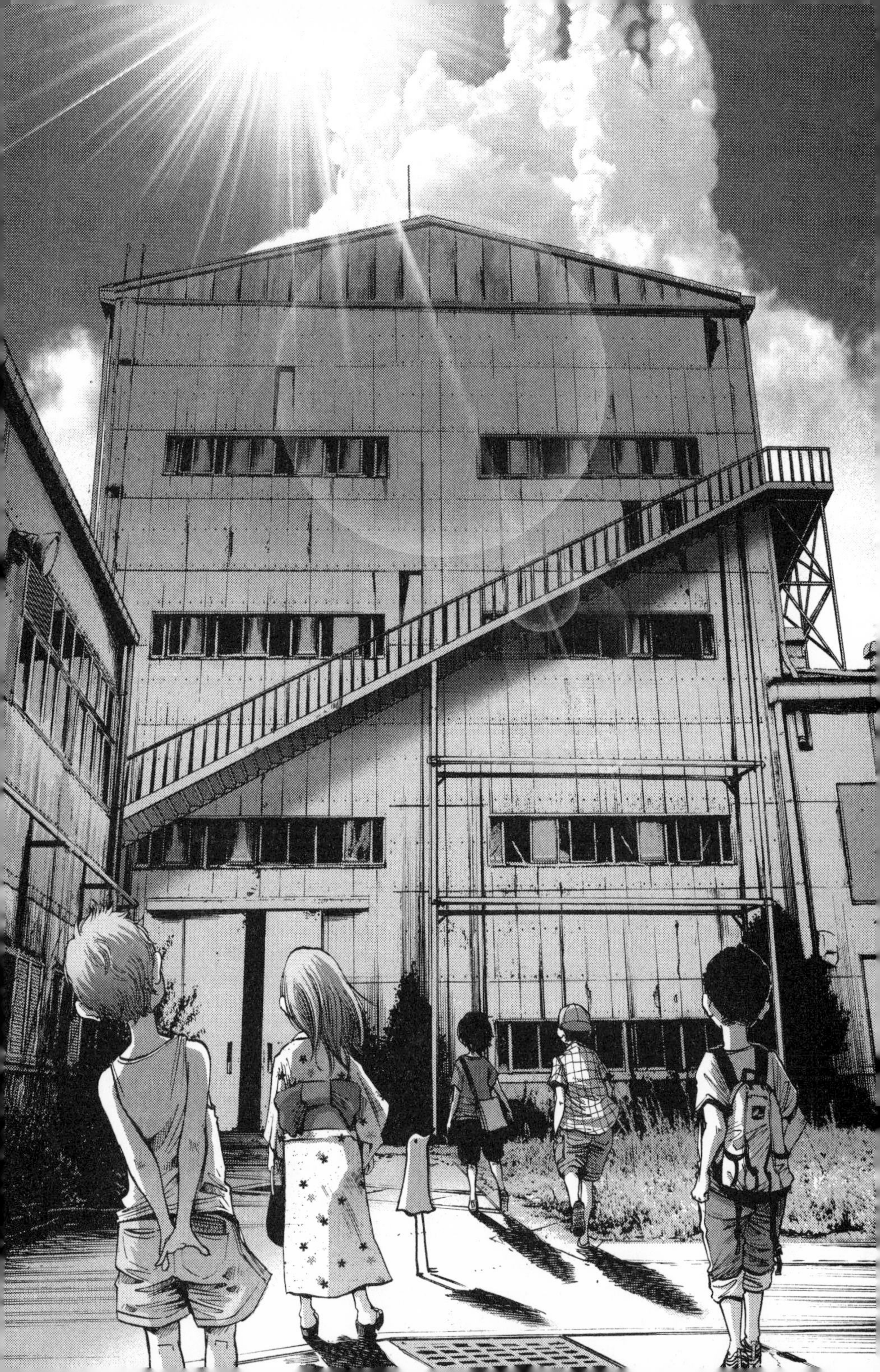

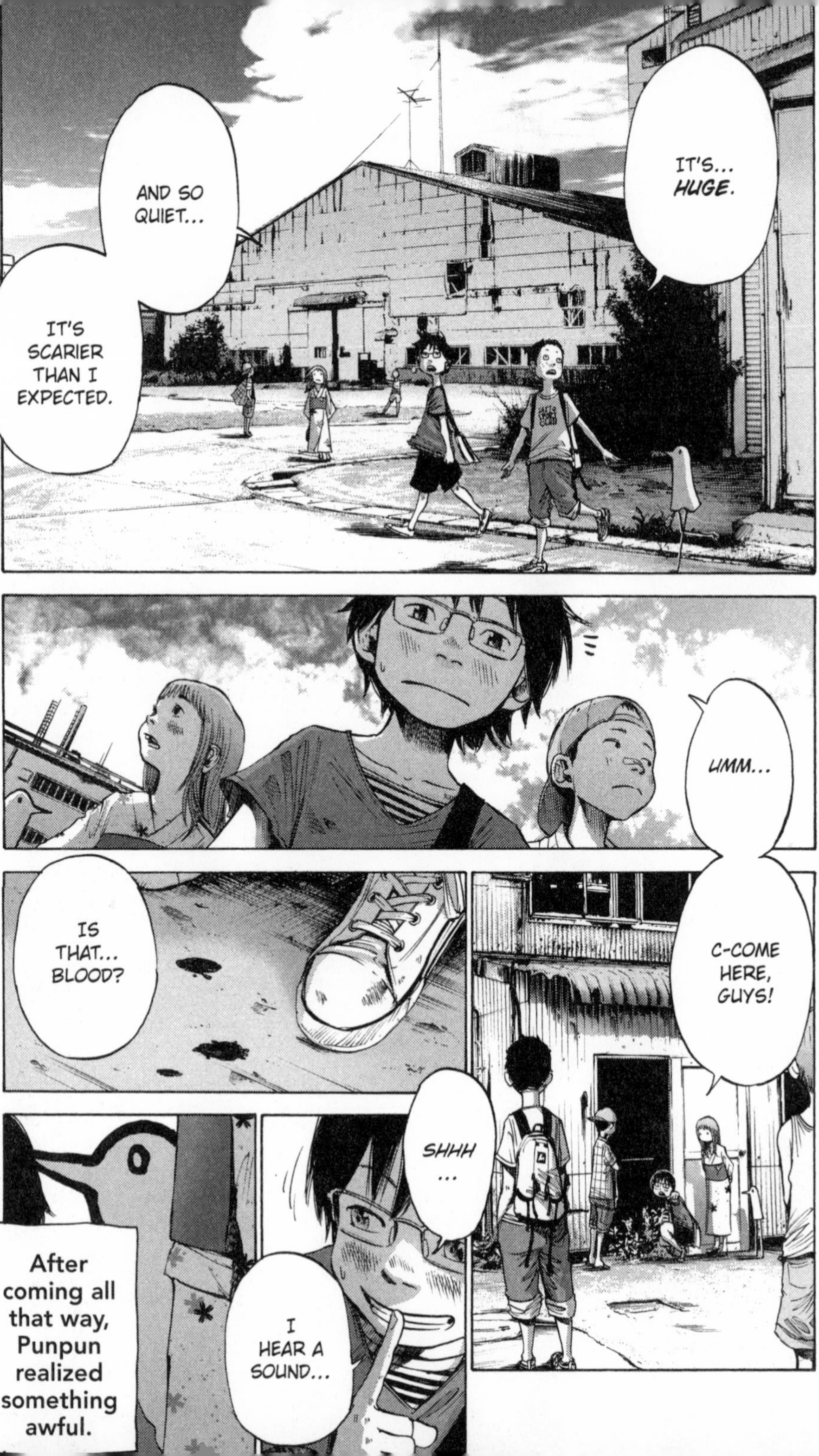
IT'S... HUGE.
AND SO QUIET...
IT'S SCARIER THAN I EXPECTED.
UMM...
C-COME HERE, GUYS!
IS THAT... BLOOD?
SHHH...
I HEAR A SOUND...
After coming all that way, Punpun realized something awful.

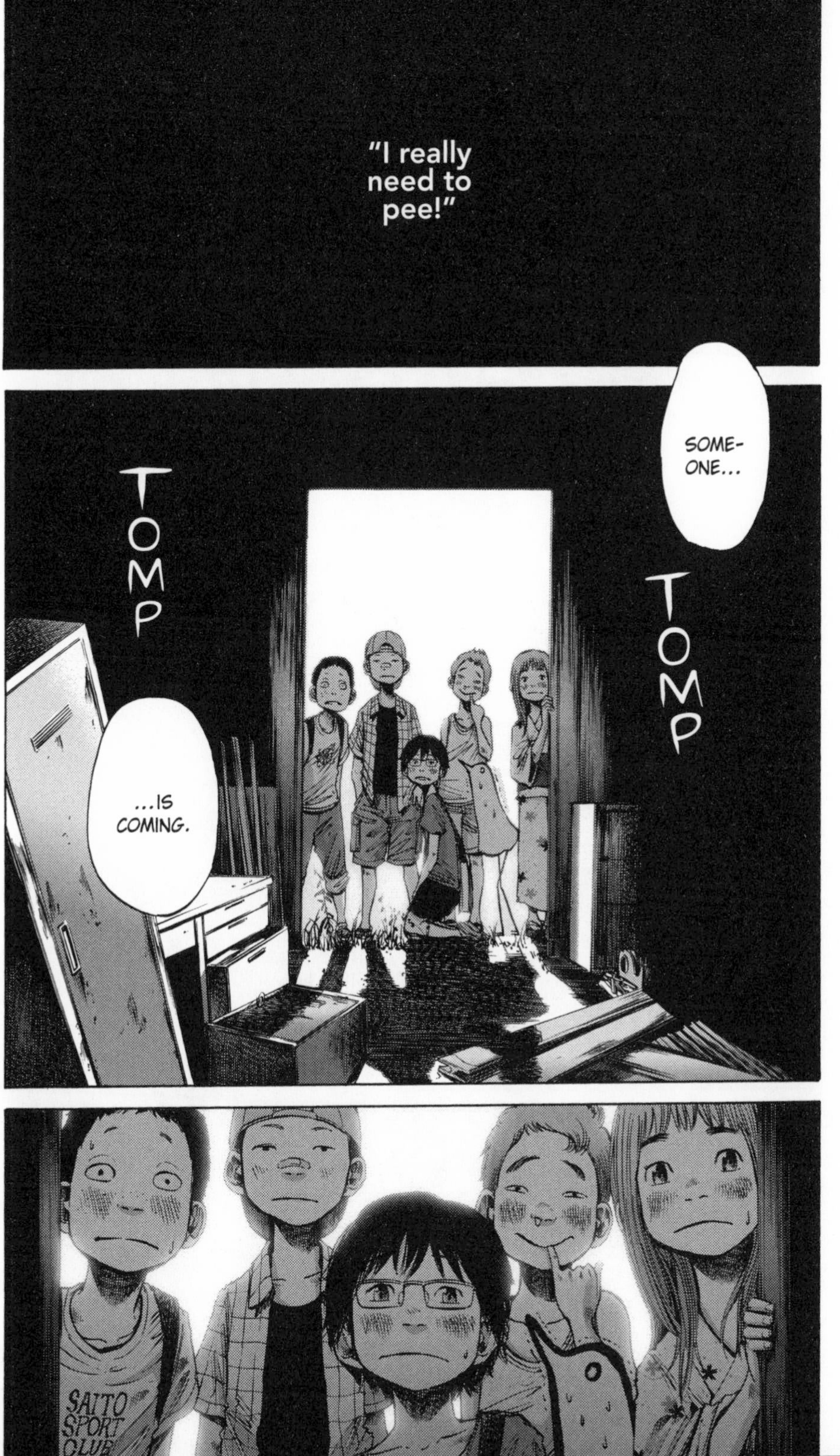
"I really need to pee!"
SOME-ONE...
TOMP
TOMP
...IS COMING.
SAITO SPORT

GOODNIGHT PUNPUN INIO ASANO
Part One

BACKGROUND ASSISTANTS: Yuki Toribuchi
                       Satsuki Sato
        CG ASSISTANT: Hisashi Saito
        COOPERATION: Kumatsuto
                     Yasumasa Iwama

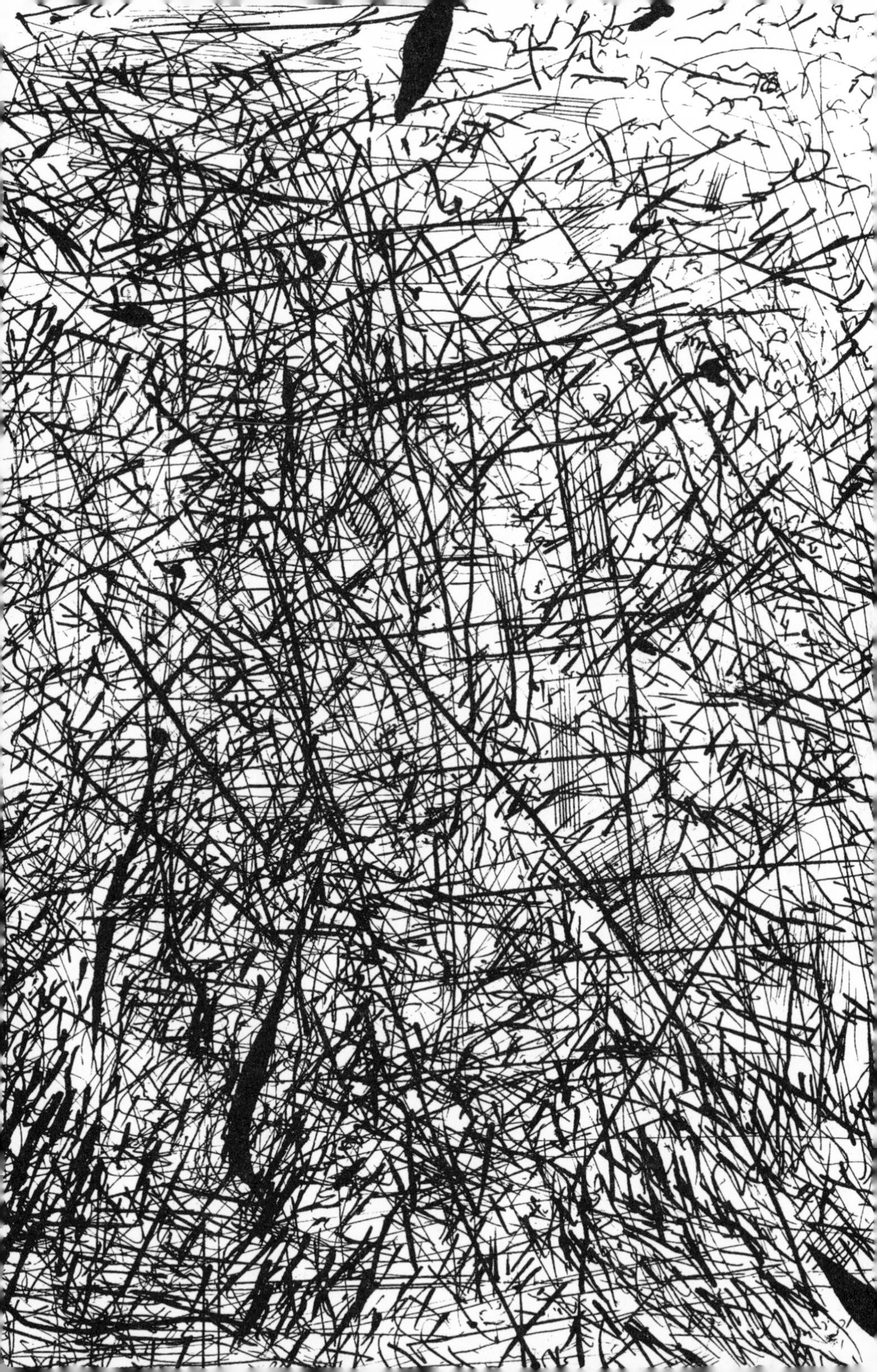

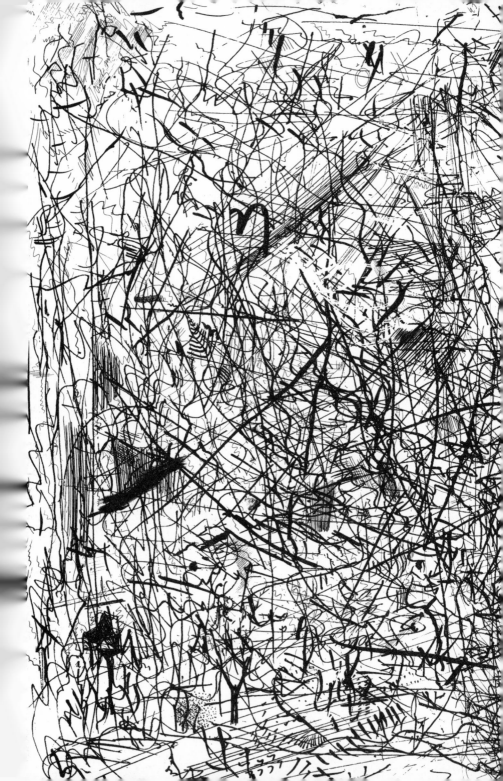

GOODNIGHT PUNPUN

Part Two

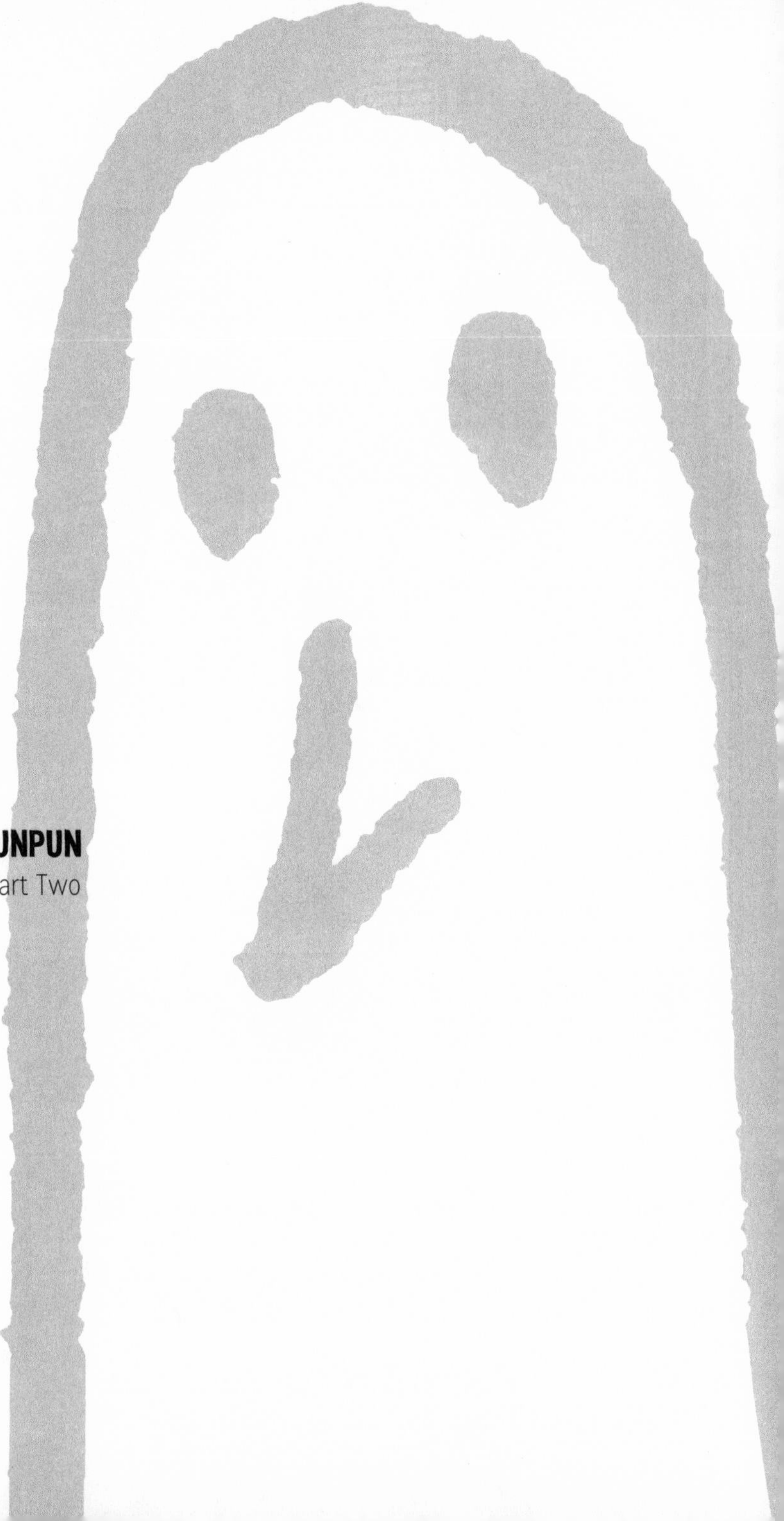

CONTENTS

★ Chapter 13 ☆

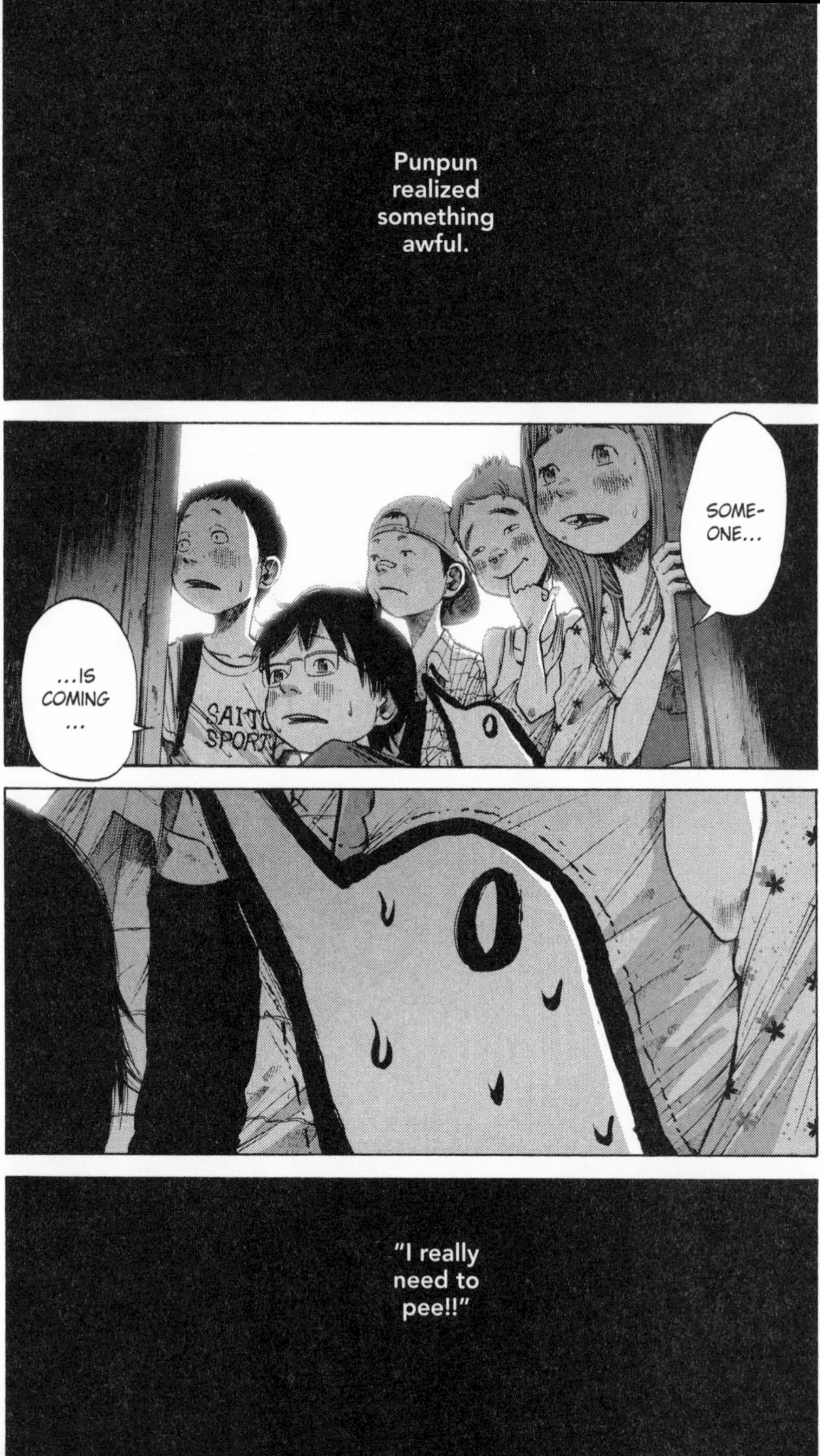
Punpun realized something awful.
SOME-ONE...
...IS COMING ...
"I really need to pee!!"

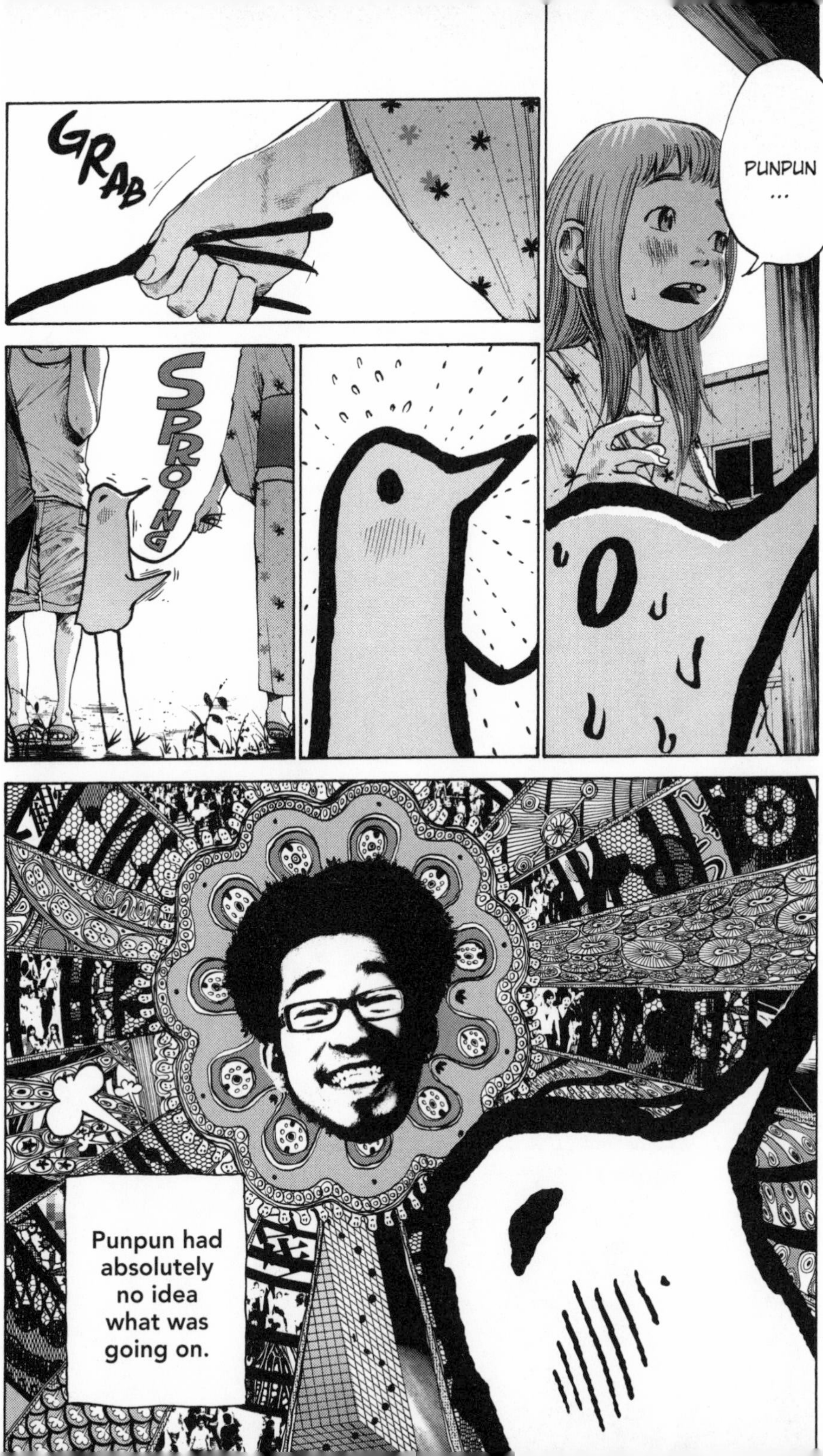
PUNPUN ...
GRAB
SPROING
Punpun had absolutely no idea what was going on.

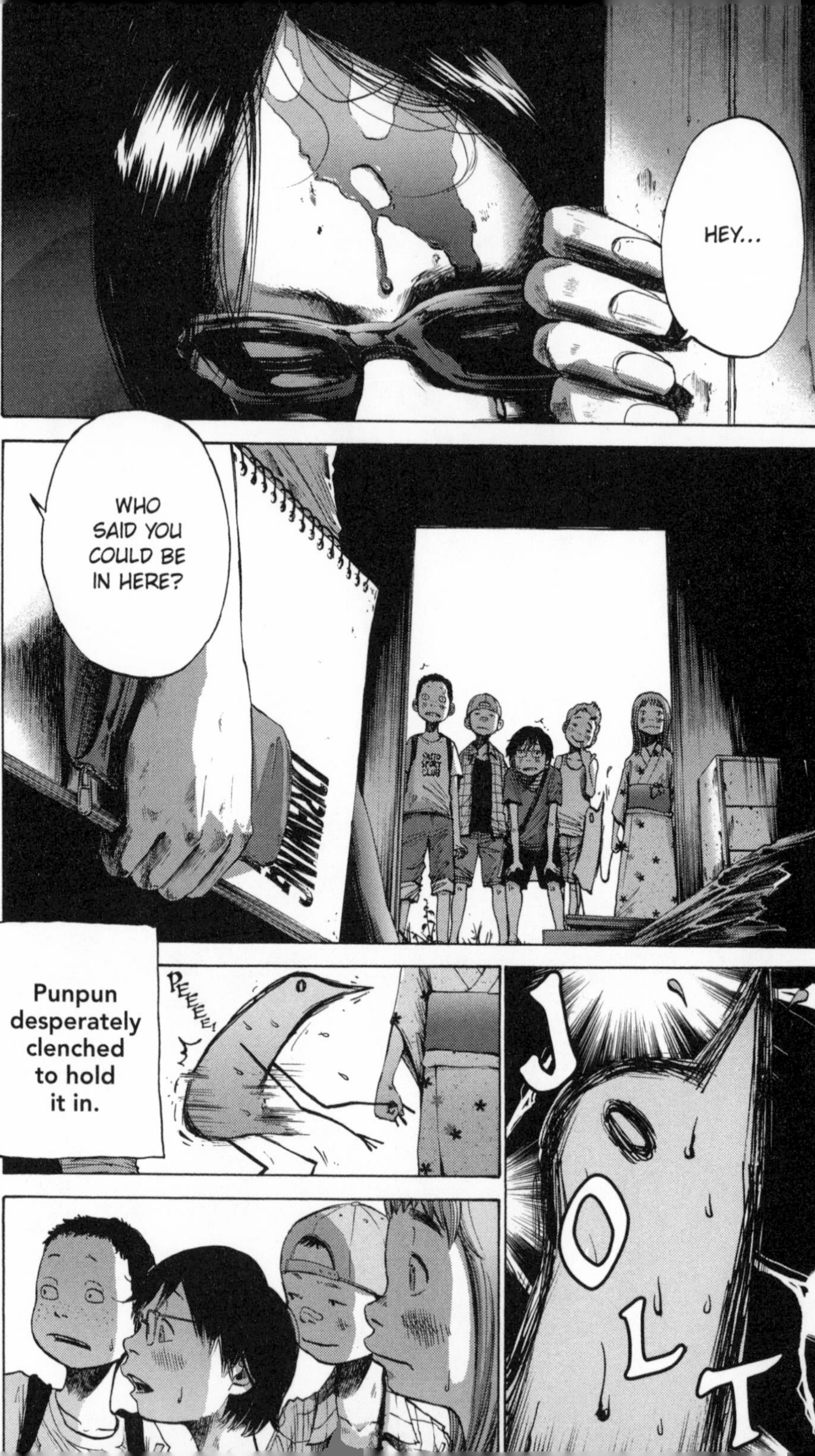
HEY...
WHO SAID YOU COULD BE IN HERE?
DRAWING
JOLT
PEEEE!
Punpun desperately clenched to hold it in.

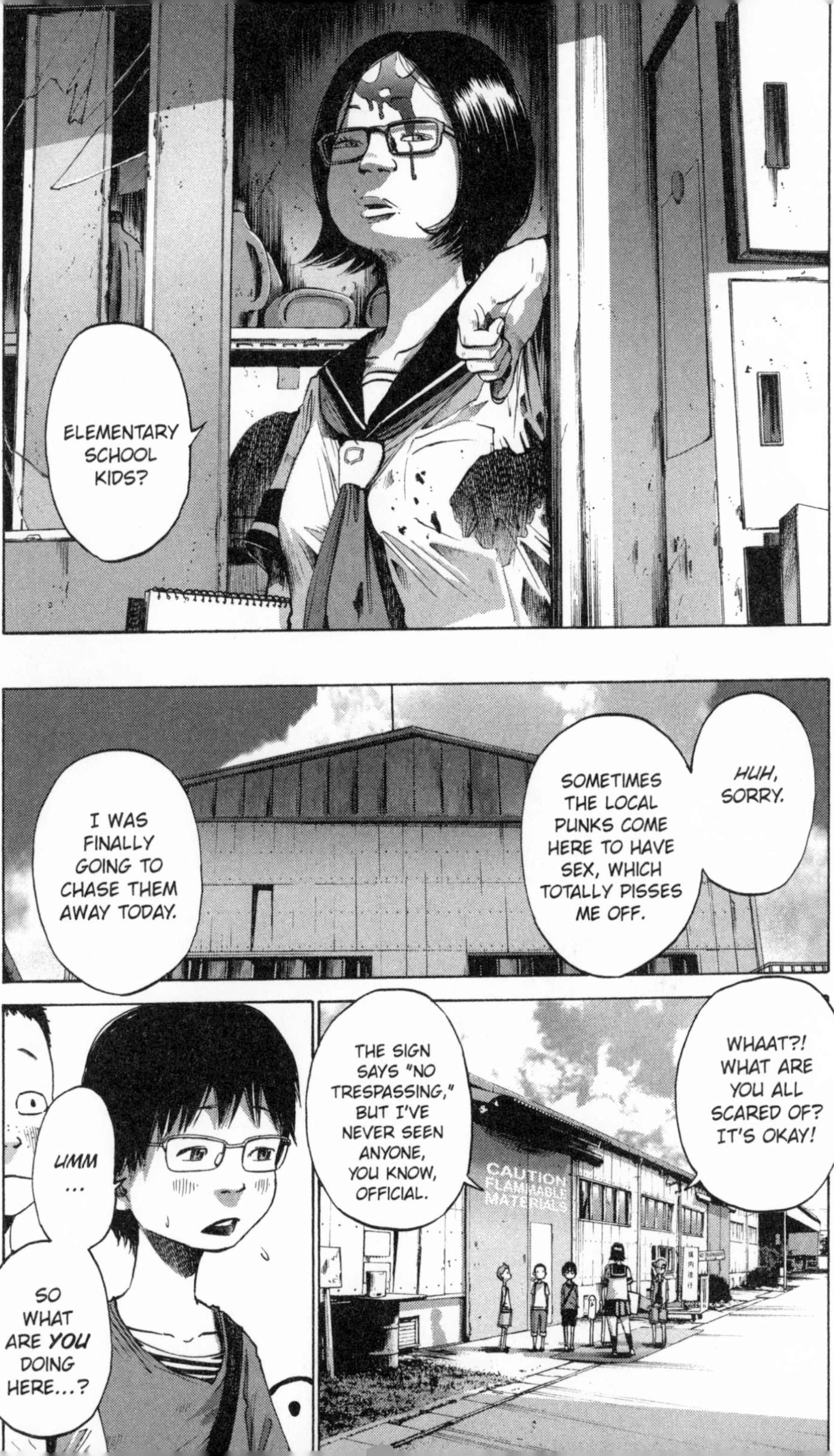
ELEMENTARY SCHOOL KIDS?
HUH, SORRY.
SOMETIMES THE LOCAL PUNKS COME HERE TO HAVE SEX, WHICH TOTALLY PISSES ME OFF.
I WAS FINALLY GOING TO CHASE THEM AWAY TODAY.
WHAAT?! WHAT ARE YOU ALL SCARED OF? IT'S OKAY!
THE SIGN SAYS "NO TRESPASSING," BUT I'VE NEVER SEEN ANYONE, YOU KNOW, OFFICIAL.
CAUTION FLAMMABLE MATERIALS
UMM ...
SO WHAT ARE *YOU* DOING HERE...?

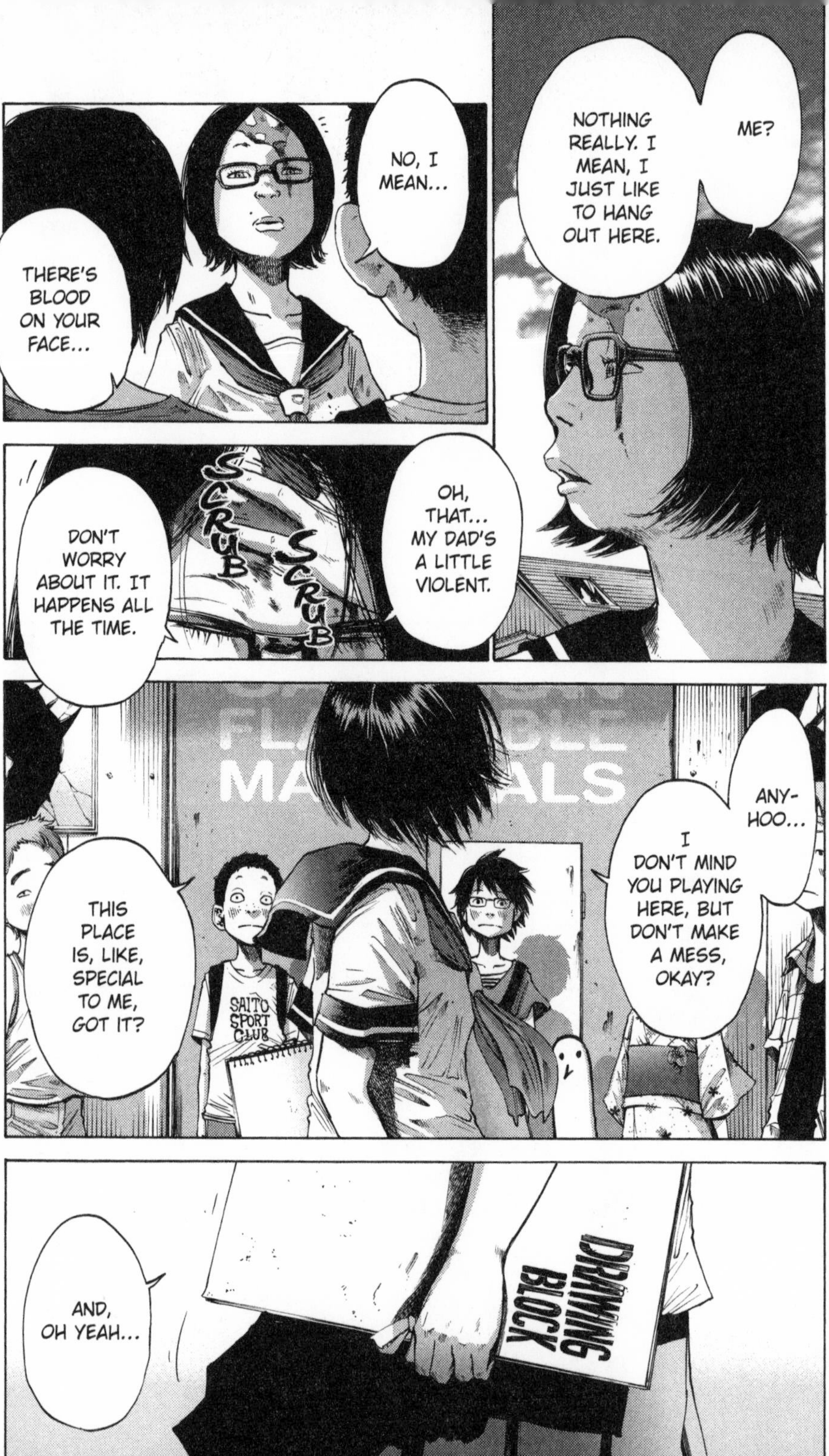
ME?
NOTHING REALLY. I MEAN, I JUST LIKE TO HANG OUT HERE.
NO, I MEAN...
THERE'S BLOOD ON YOUR FACE...
OH, THAT... MY DAD'S A LITTLE VIOLENT.
SCRUB SCRUB
DON'T WORRY ABOUT IT. IT HAPPENS ALL THE TIME.
ANY-HOO...
I DON'T MIND YOU PLAYING HERE, BUT DON'T MAKE A MESS, OKAY?
THIS PLACE IS, LIKE, SPECIAL TO ME, GOT IT?
SAITO SPORT CLUB
DRAWING BLOCK
AND, OH YEAH...

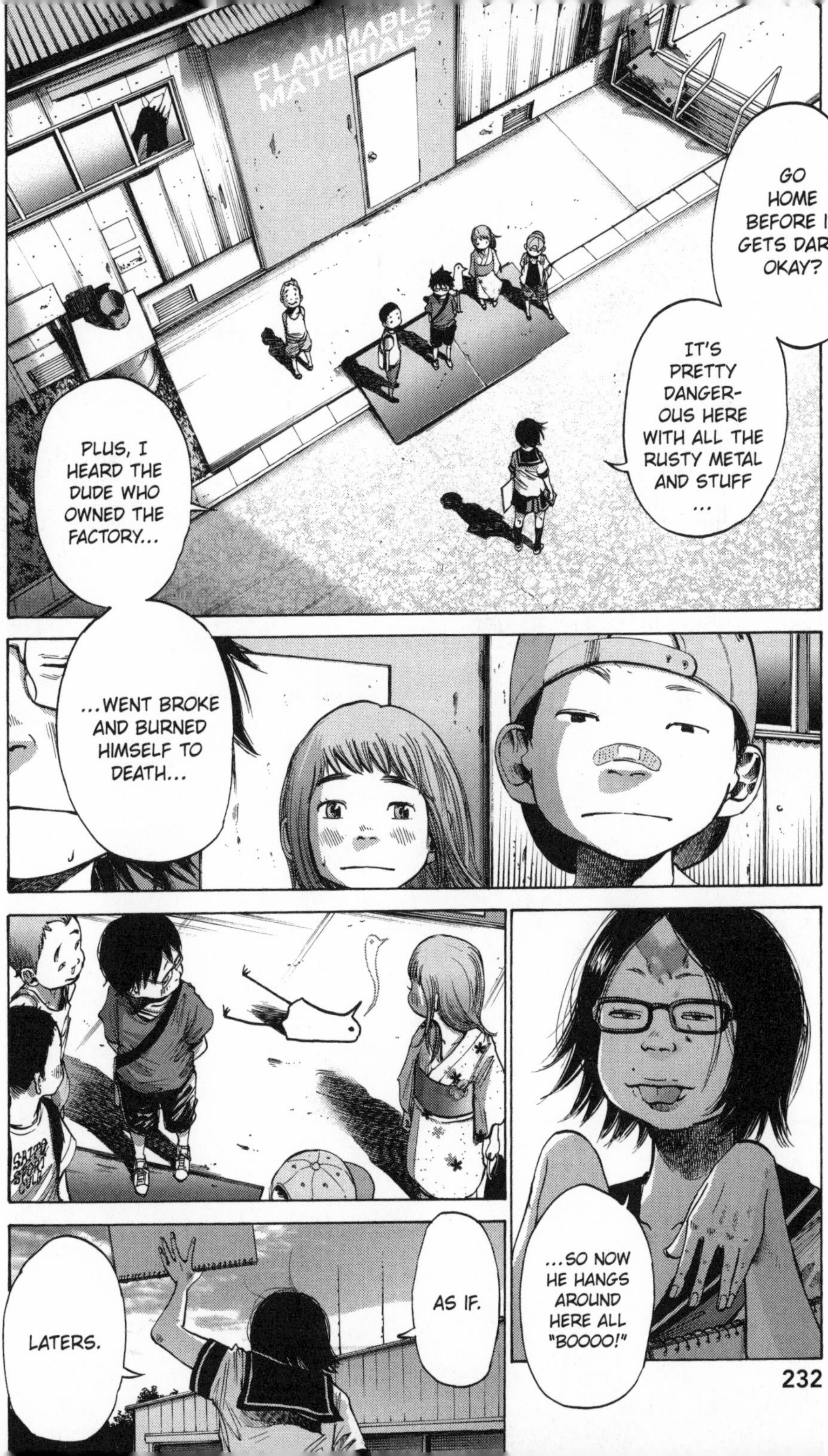
FLAMMABLE MATERIALS
GO HOME BEFORE IT GETS DARK, OKAY?
IT'S PRETTY DANGER-OUS HERE WITH ALL THE RUSTY METAL AND STUFF ...
PLUS, I HEARD THE DUDE WHO OWNED THE FACTORY...
...WENT BROKE AND BURNED HIMSELF TO DEATH...
...SO NOW HE HANGS AROUND HERE ALL "BOOOO!"
AS IF.
LATERS.

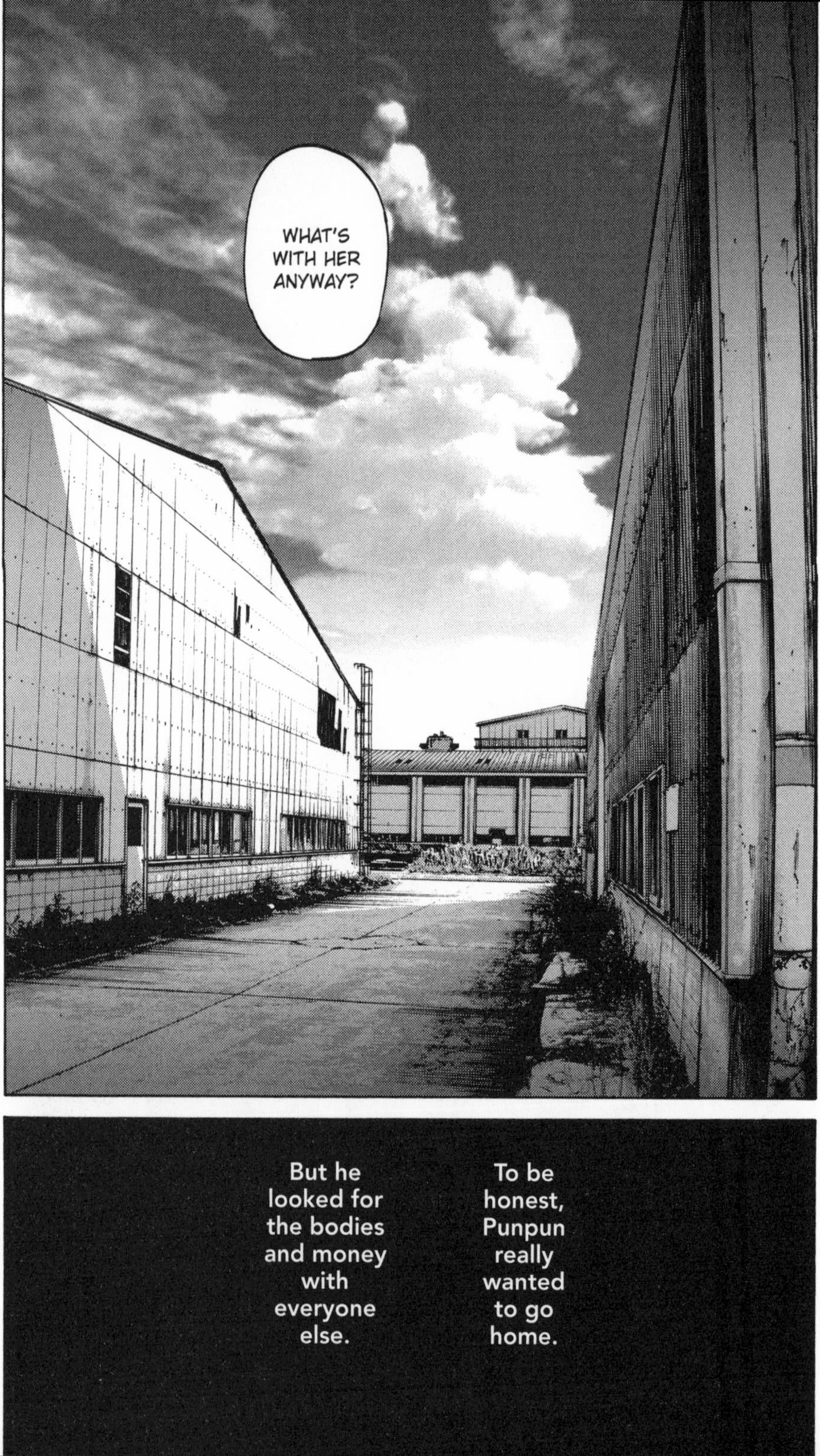
WHAT'S WITH HER ANYWAY?
To be honest, Punpun really wanted to go home.
But he looked for the bodies and money with everyone else.

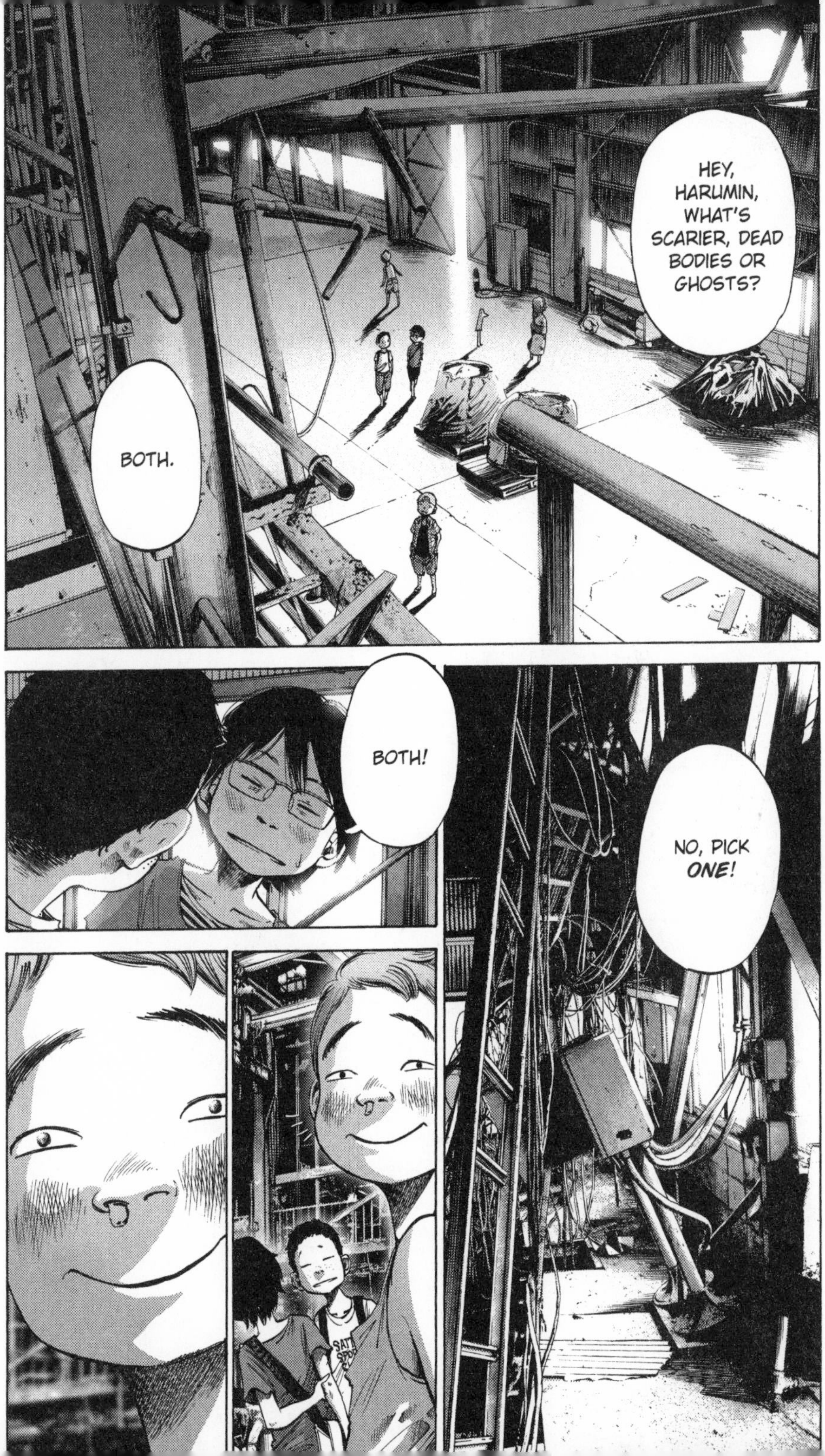
HEY, HARUMIN, WHAT'S SCARIER, DEAD BODIES OR GHOSTS?
BOTH.
NO, PICK ONE!
BOTH!

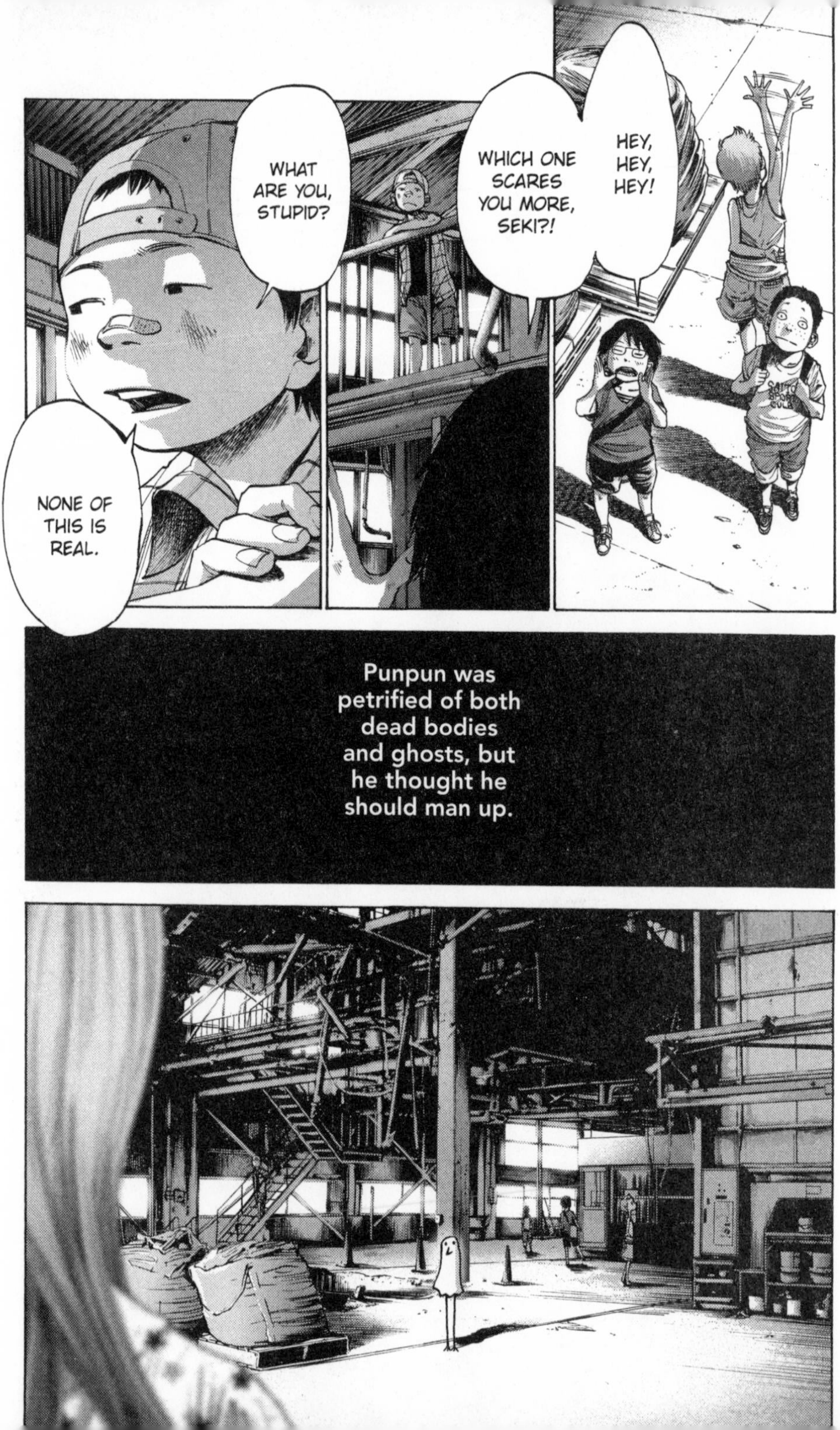
HEY, HEY, HEY!
WHICH ONE SCARES YOU MORE, SEKI?!
WHAT ARE YOU, STUPID?
NONE OF THIS IS REAL.
Punpun was petrified of both dead bodies and ghosts, but he thought he should man up.

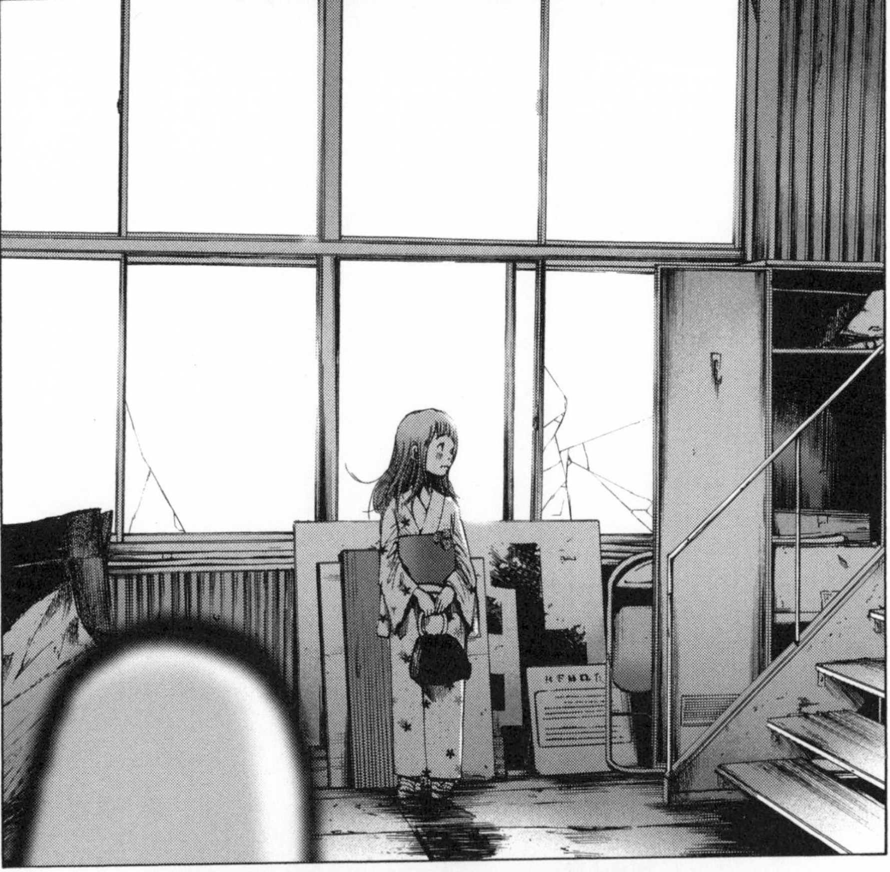

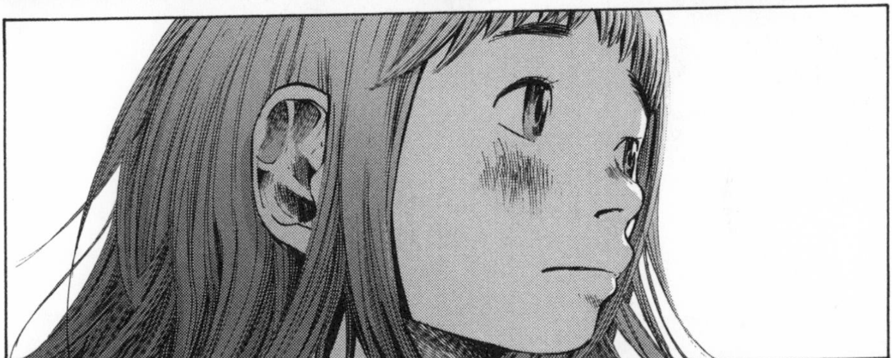

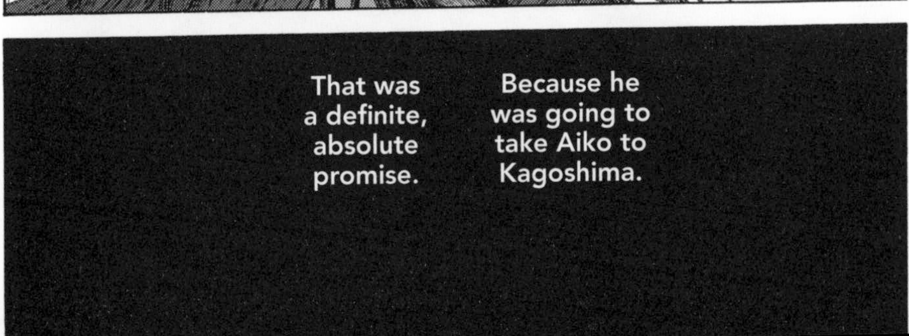
Because he was going to take Aiko to Kagoshima.
That was a definite, absolute promise.

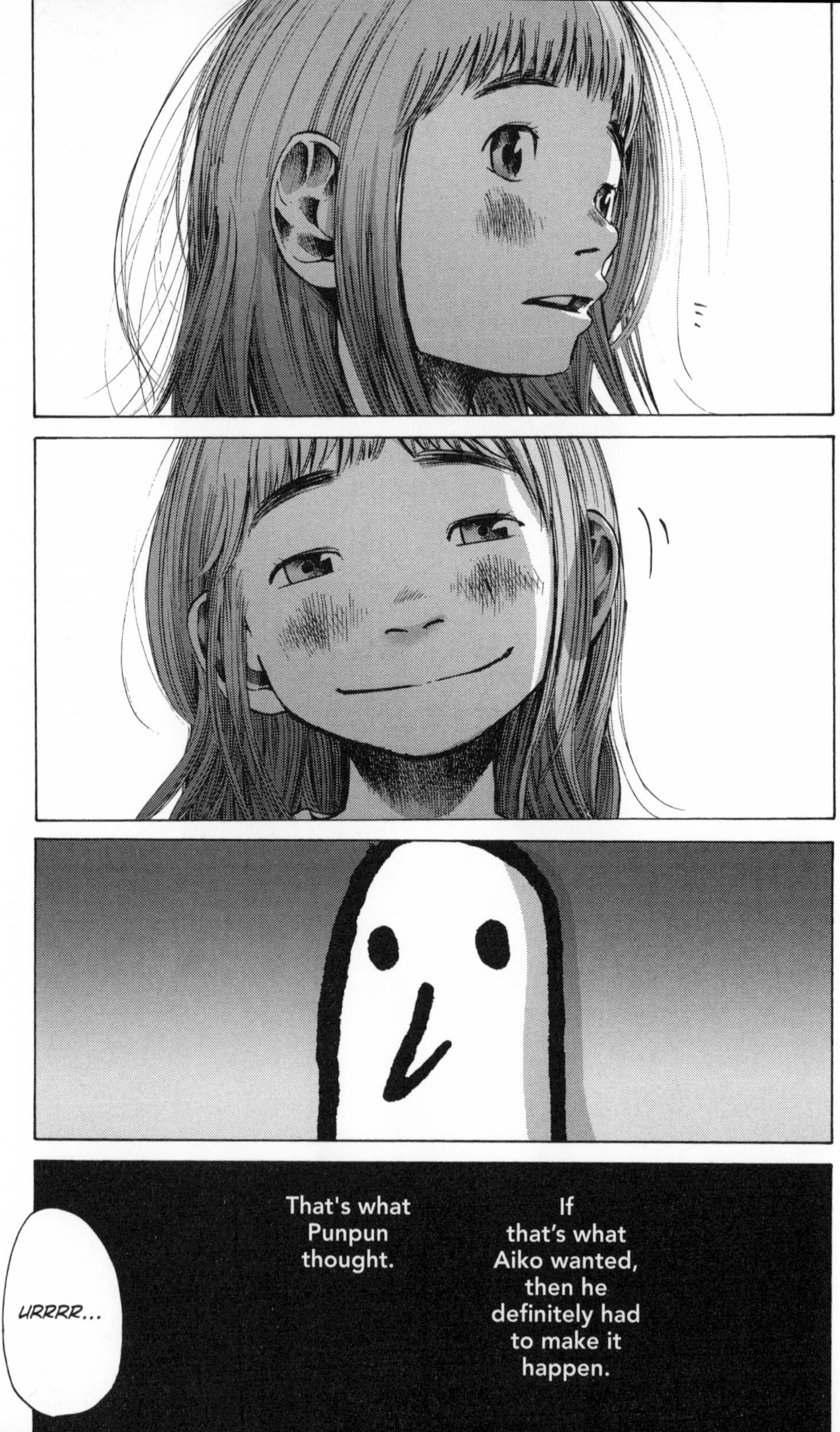
If that's what Aiko wanted, then he definitely had to make it happen.
That's what Punpun thought.
URRRR...

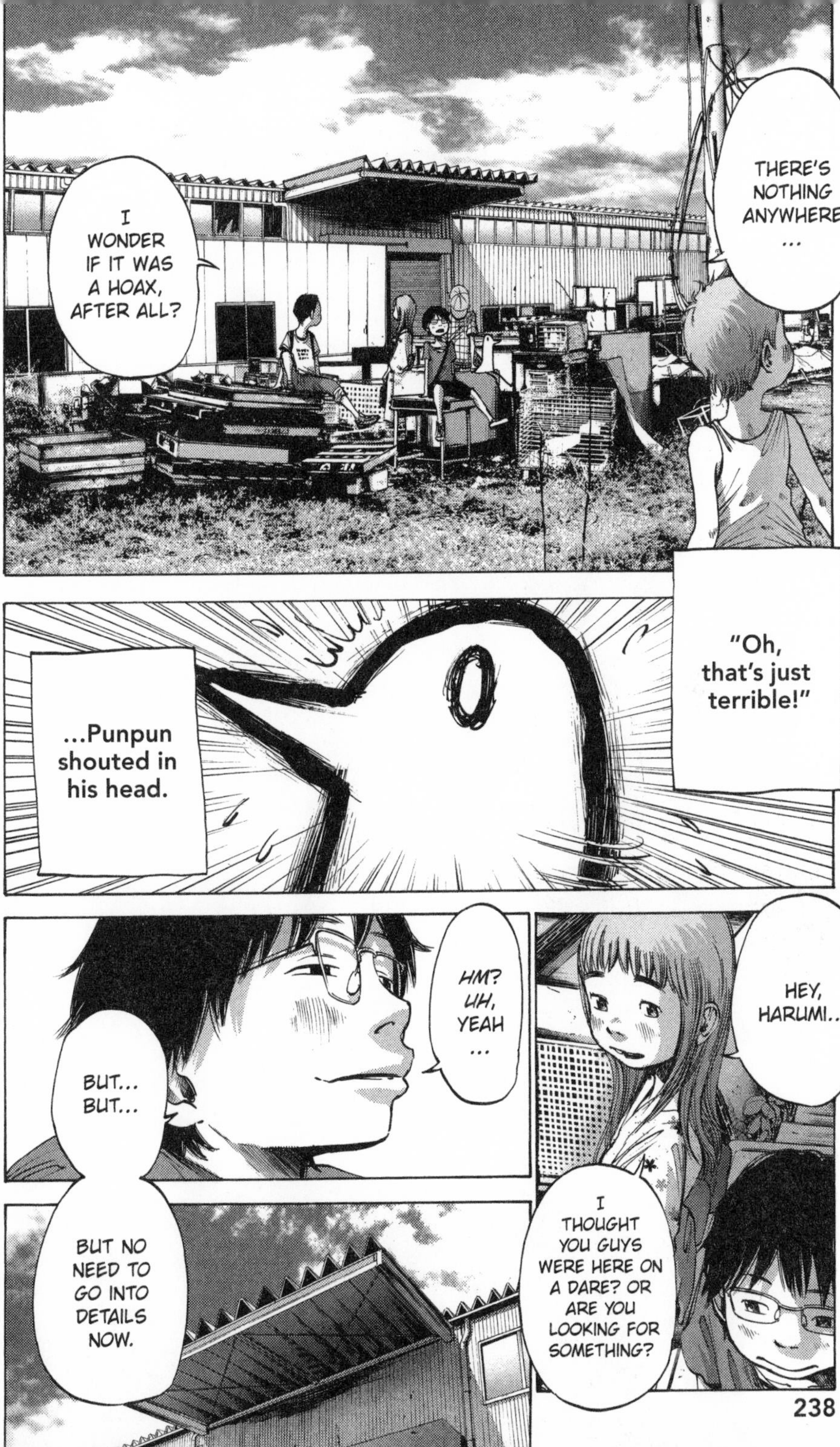

THERE'S NOTHING ANYWHERE ...
I WONDER IF IT WAS A HOAX, AFTER ALL?
"Oh, that's just terrible!"
...Punpun shouted in his head.
HEY, HARUMI...
I THOUGHT YOU GUYS WERE HERE ON A DARE? OR ARE YOU LOOKING FOR SOMETHING?
HM? UH, YEAH ...
BUT... BUT...
BUT NO NEED TO GO INTO DETAILS NOW.

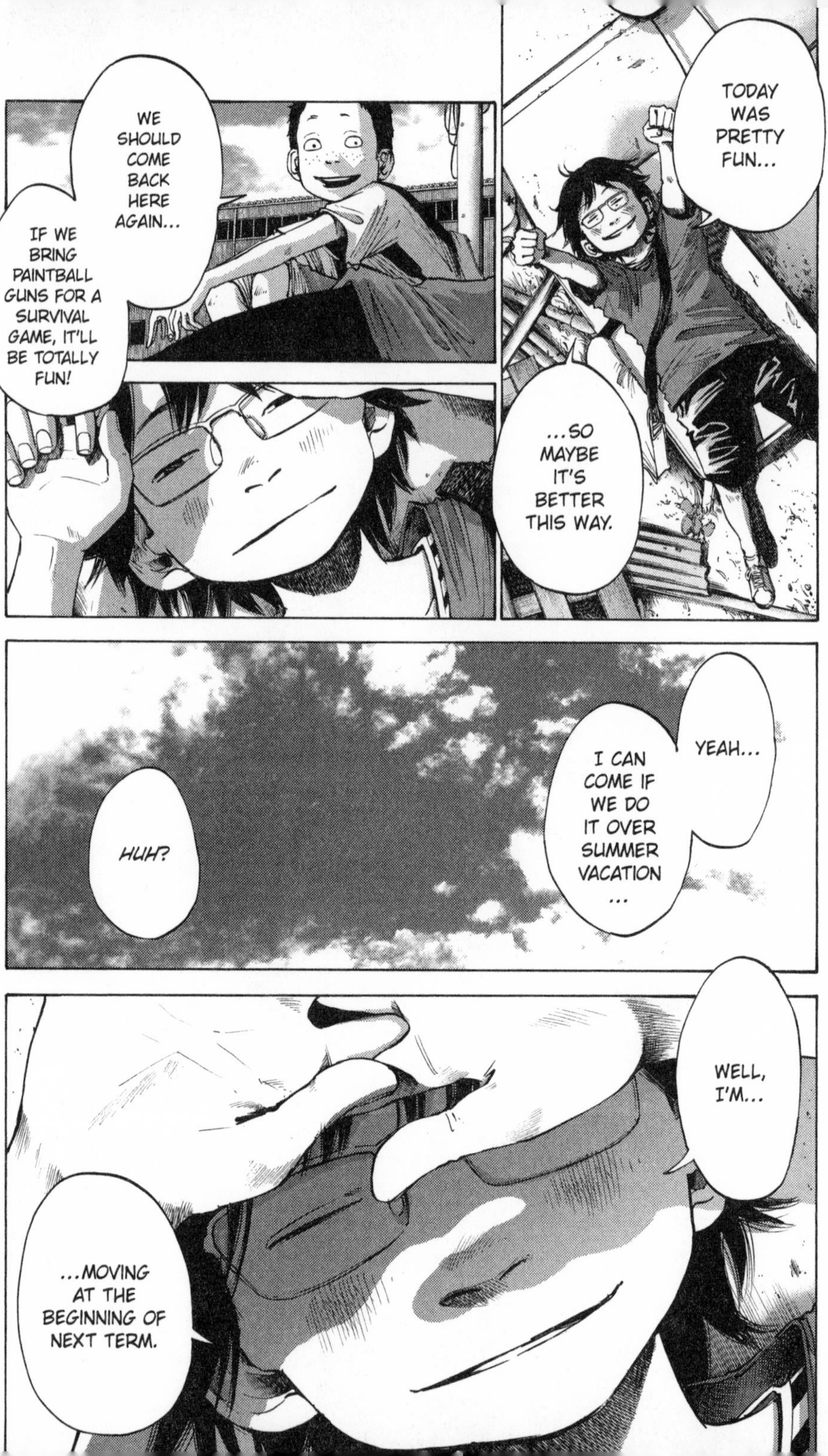
TODAY WAS PRETTY FUN...
...SO MAYBE IT'S BETTER THIS WAY.
WE SHOULD COME BACK HERE AGAIN...
IF WE BRING PAINTBALL GUNS FOR A SURVIVAL GAME, IT'LL BE TOTALLY FUN!
YEAH...
I CAN COME IF WE DO IT OVER SUMMER VACATION...
HUH?
WELL, I'M...
...MOVING AT THE BEGINNING OF NEXT TERM.

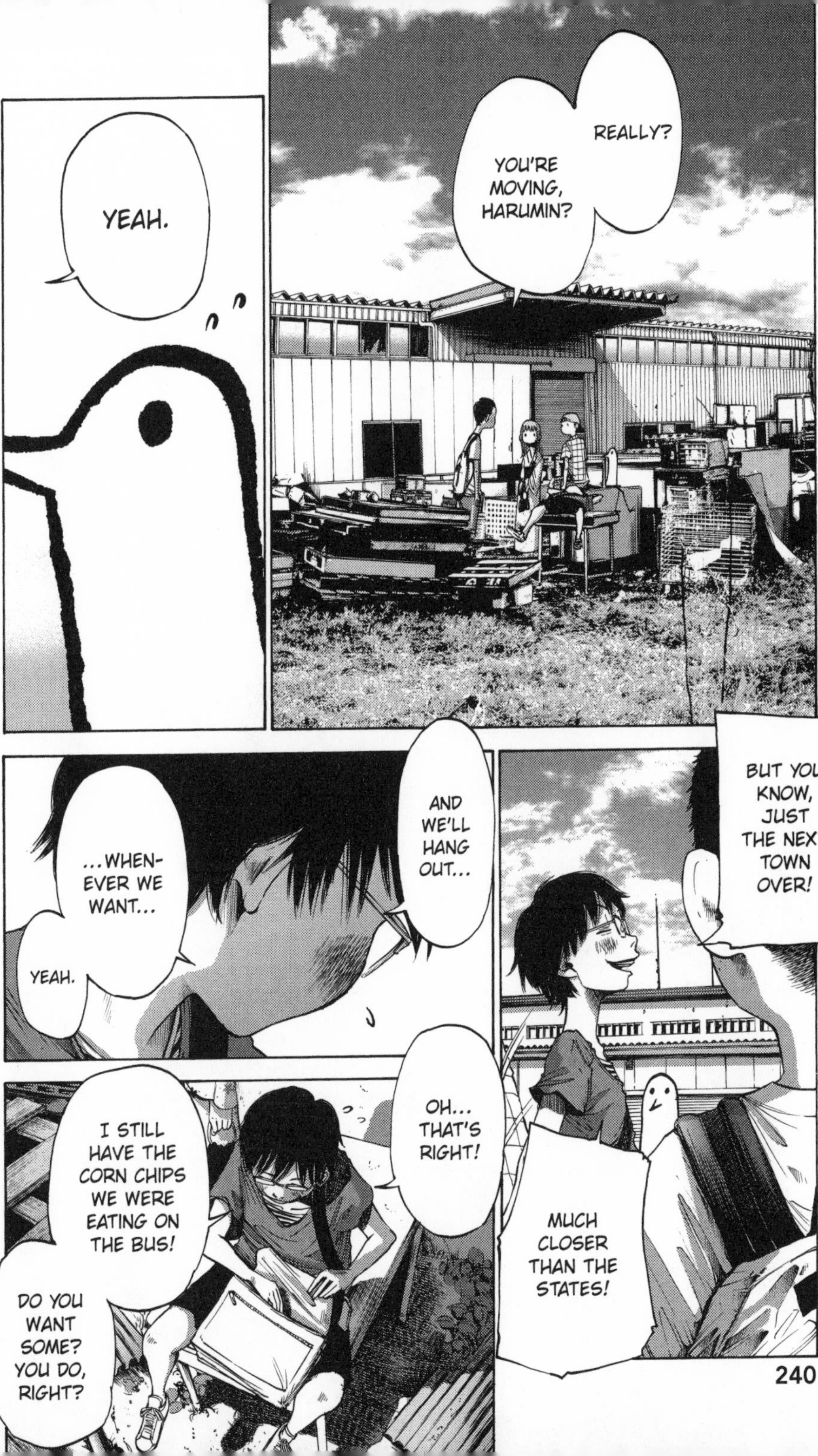
REALLY?
YOU'RE MOVING, HARUMIN?
YEAH.
BUT YOU KNOW, JUST THE NEXT TOWN OVER!
MUCH CLOSER THAN THE STATES!
AND WE'LL HANG OUT...
...WHENEVER WE WANT...
YEAH.
OH... THAT'S RIGHT!
I STILL HAVE THE CORN CHIPS WE WERE EATING ON THE BUS!
DO YOU WANT SOME? YOU DO, RIGHT?

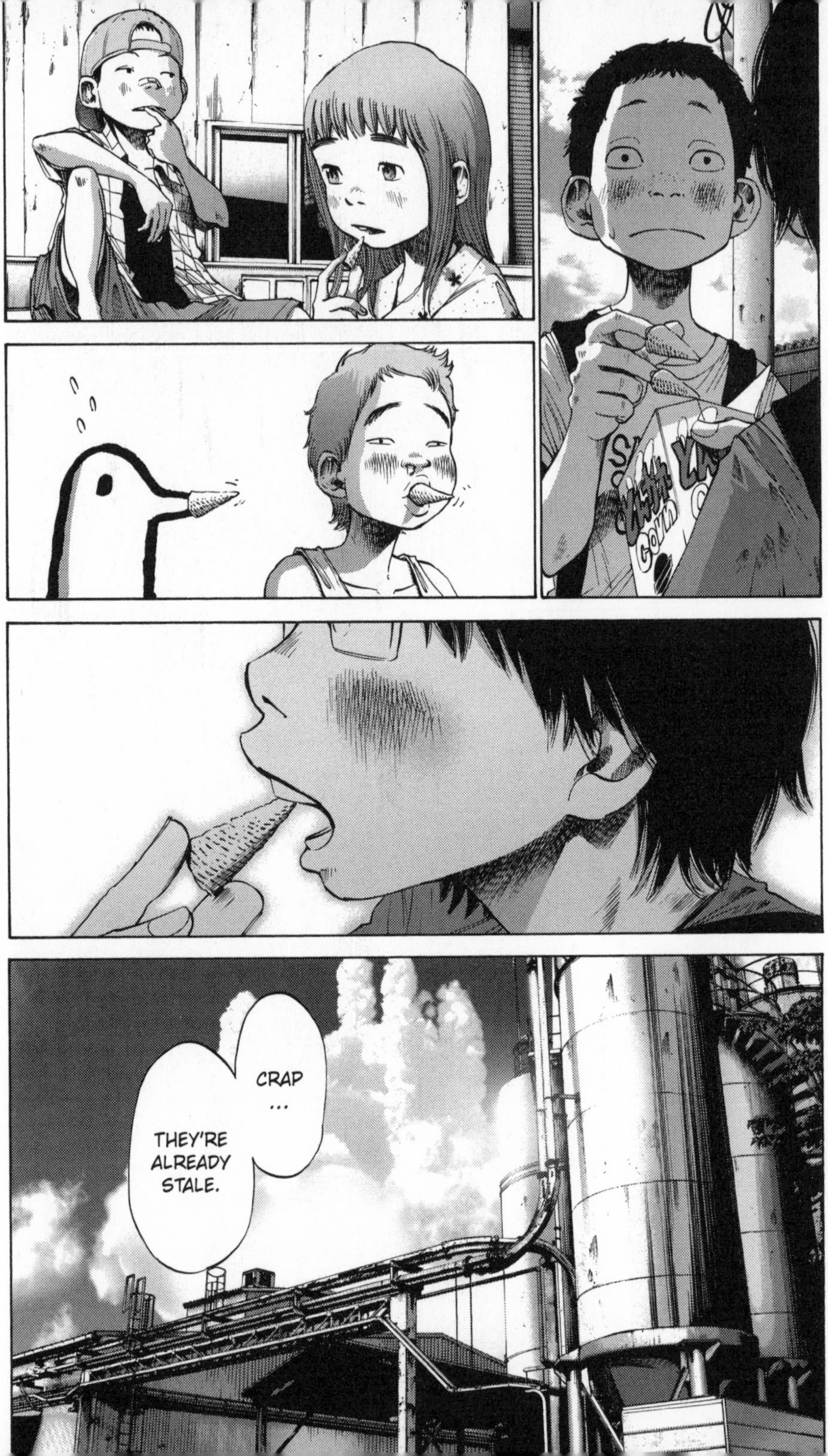
CRAP ... THEY'RE ALREADY STALE.

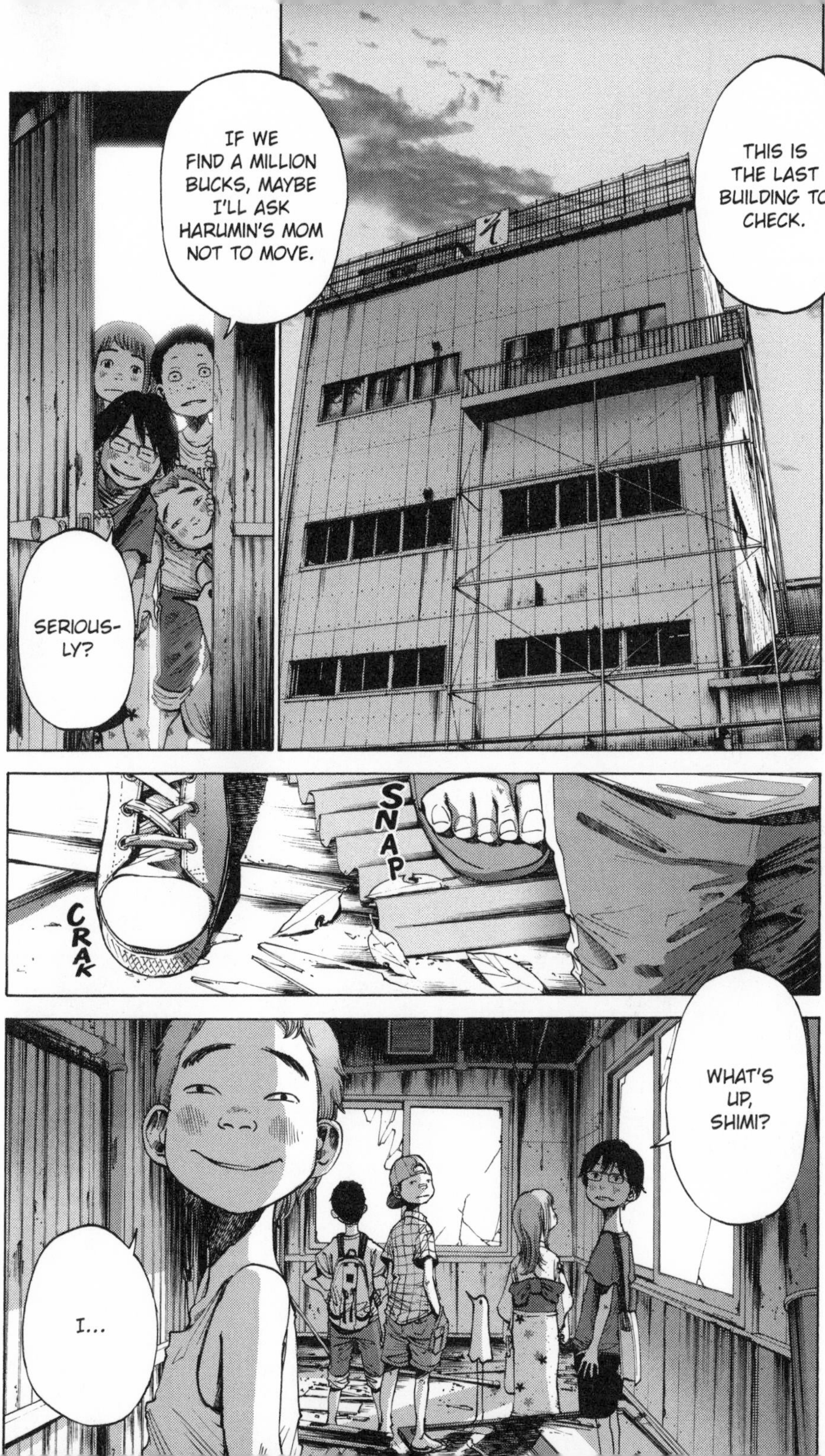
THIS IS THE LAST BUILDING TO CHECK.
IF WE FIND A MILLION BUCKS, MAYBE I'LL ASK HARUMIN'S MOM NOT TO MOVE.
SERIOUS-LY?
SNAP
CRAK
WHAT'S UP, SHIMI?
I...

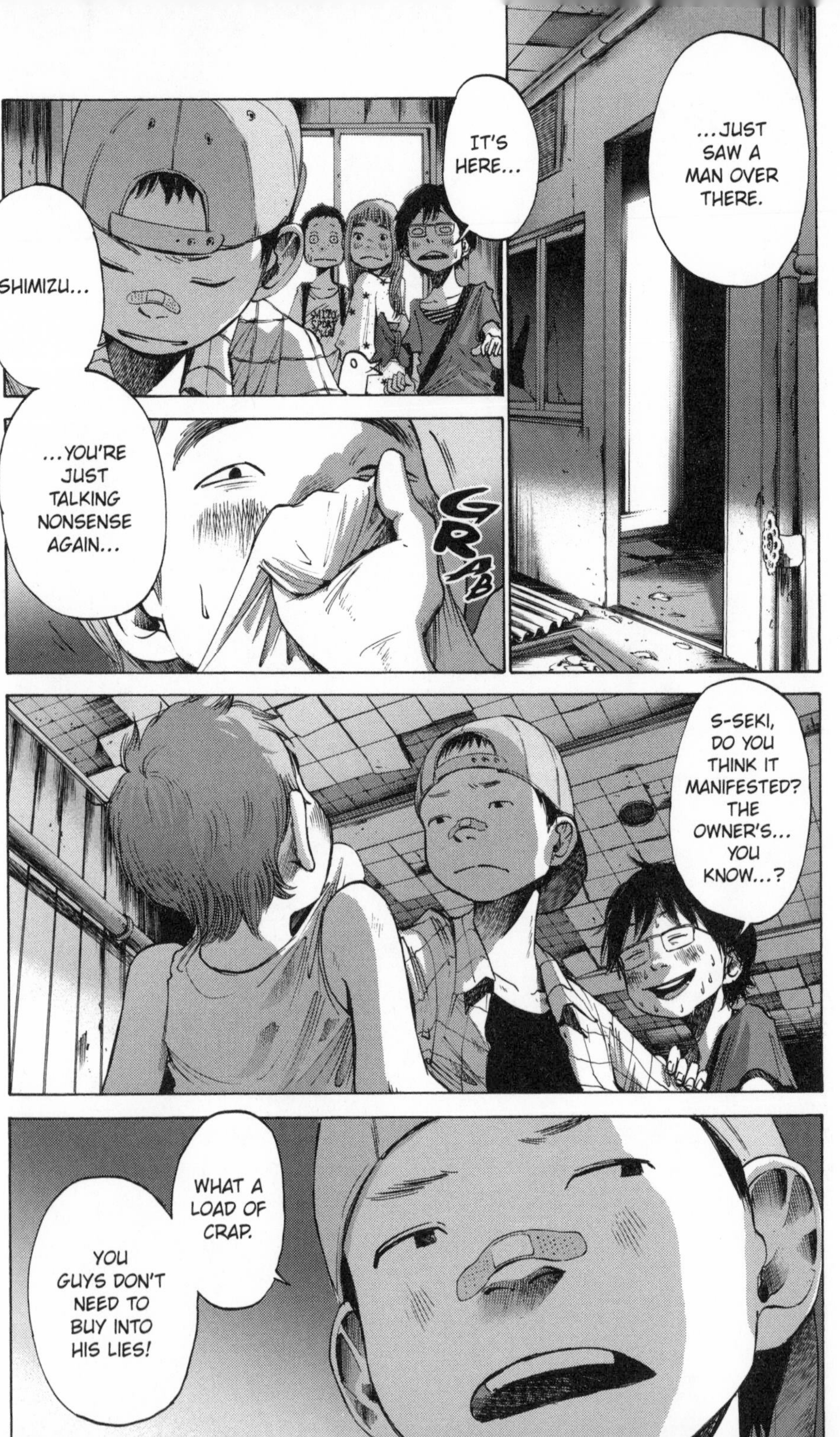
IT'S HERE...
...JUST SAW A MAN OVER THERE.
SHIMIZU...
...YOU'RE JUST TALKING NONSENSE AGAIN...
GRAB
S-SEKI, DO YOU THINK IT MANIFESTED? THE OWNER'S... YOU KNOW...?
WHAT A LOAD OF CRAP.
YOU GUYS DON'T NEED TO BUY INTO HIS LIES!

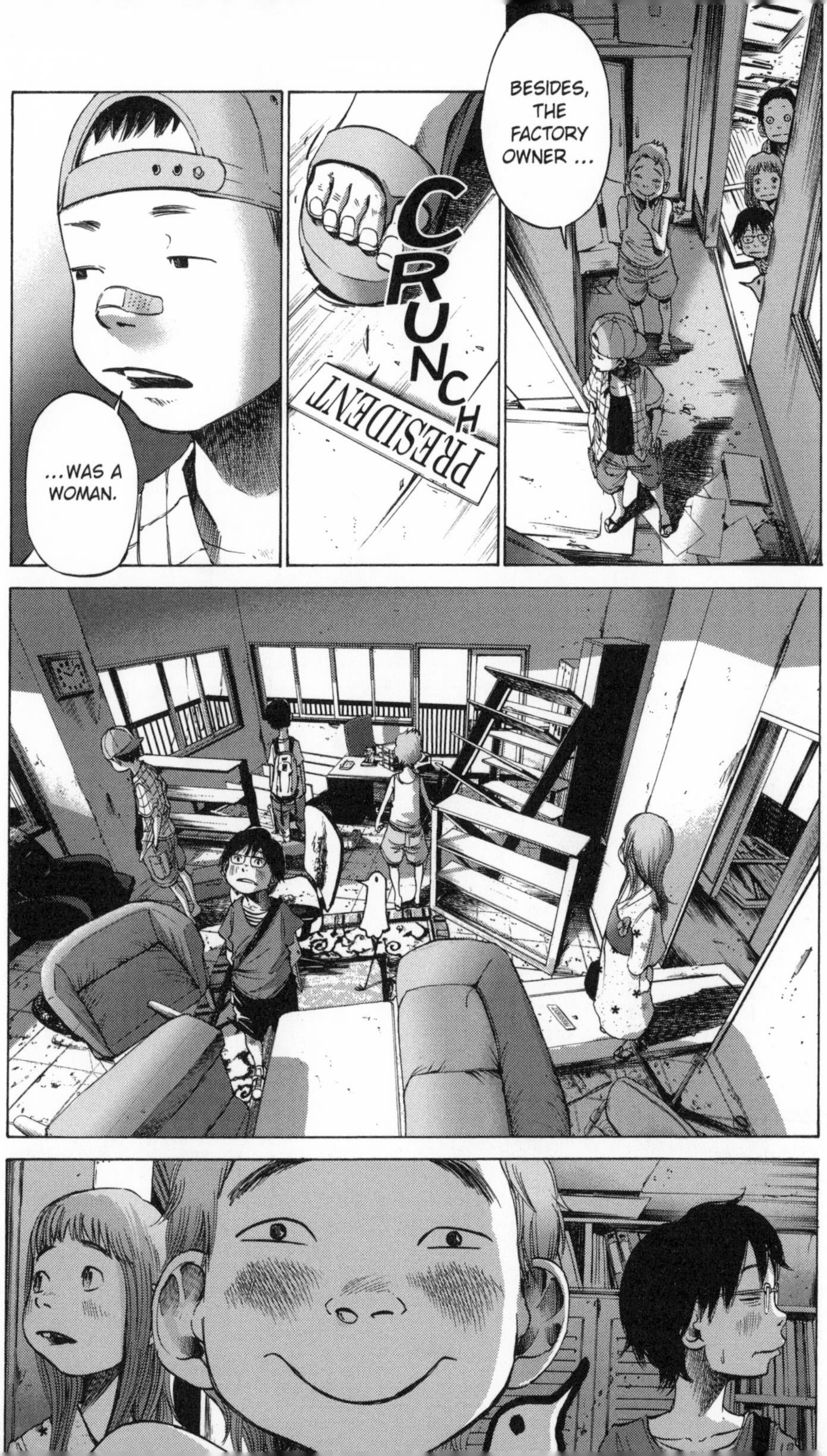
BESIDES, THE FACTORY OWNER ...
CRUNCH
PRESIDENT
...WAS A WOMAN.

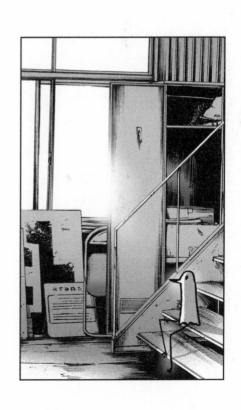

Chapter 14

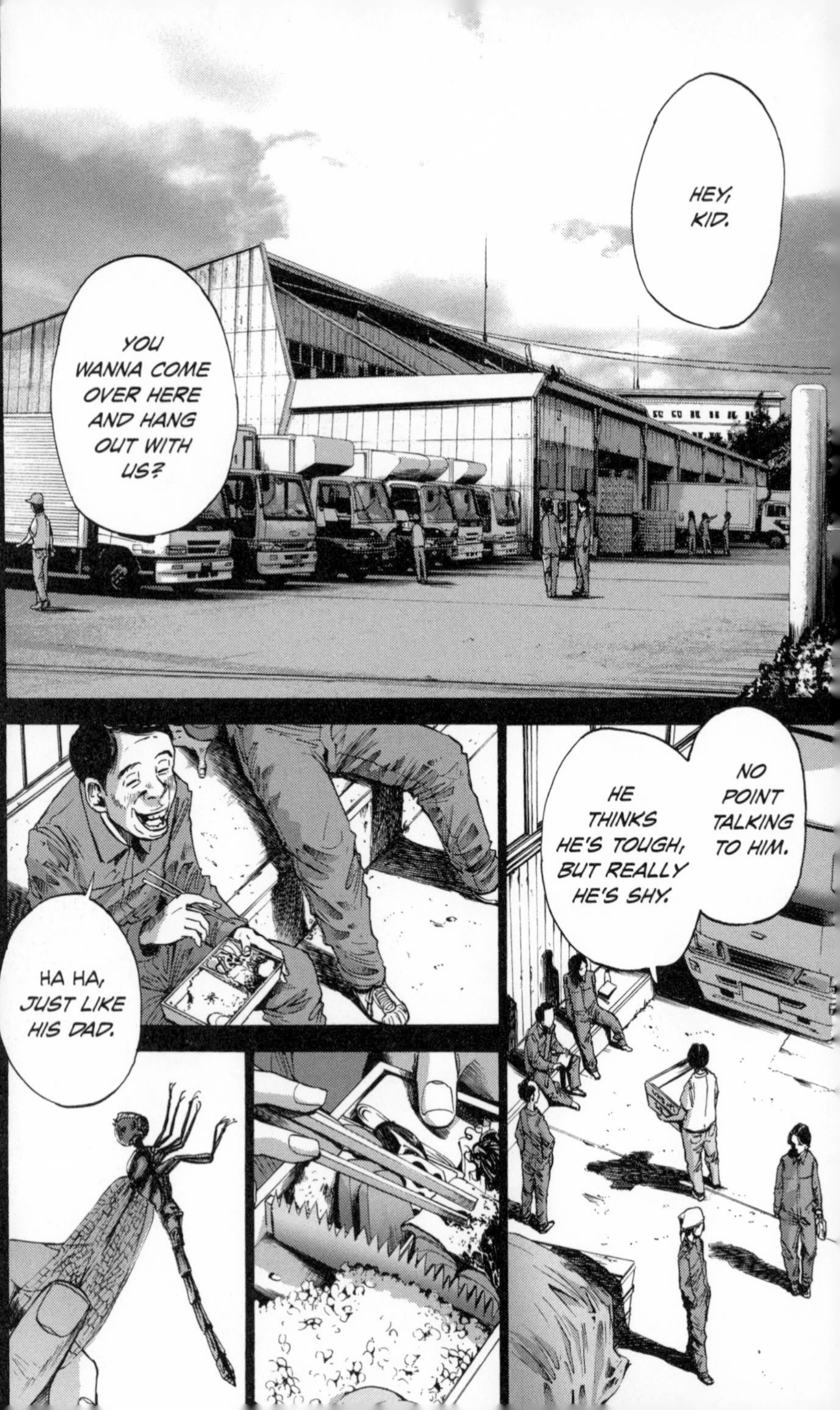
HEY, KID.
YOU WANNA COME OVER HERE AND HANG OUT WITH US?
NO POINT TALKING TO HIM.
HE THINKS HE'S TOUGH, BUT REALLY HE'S SHY.
HA HA, JUST LIKE HIS DAD.

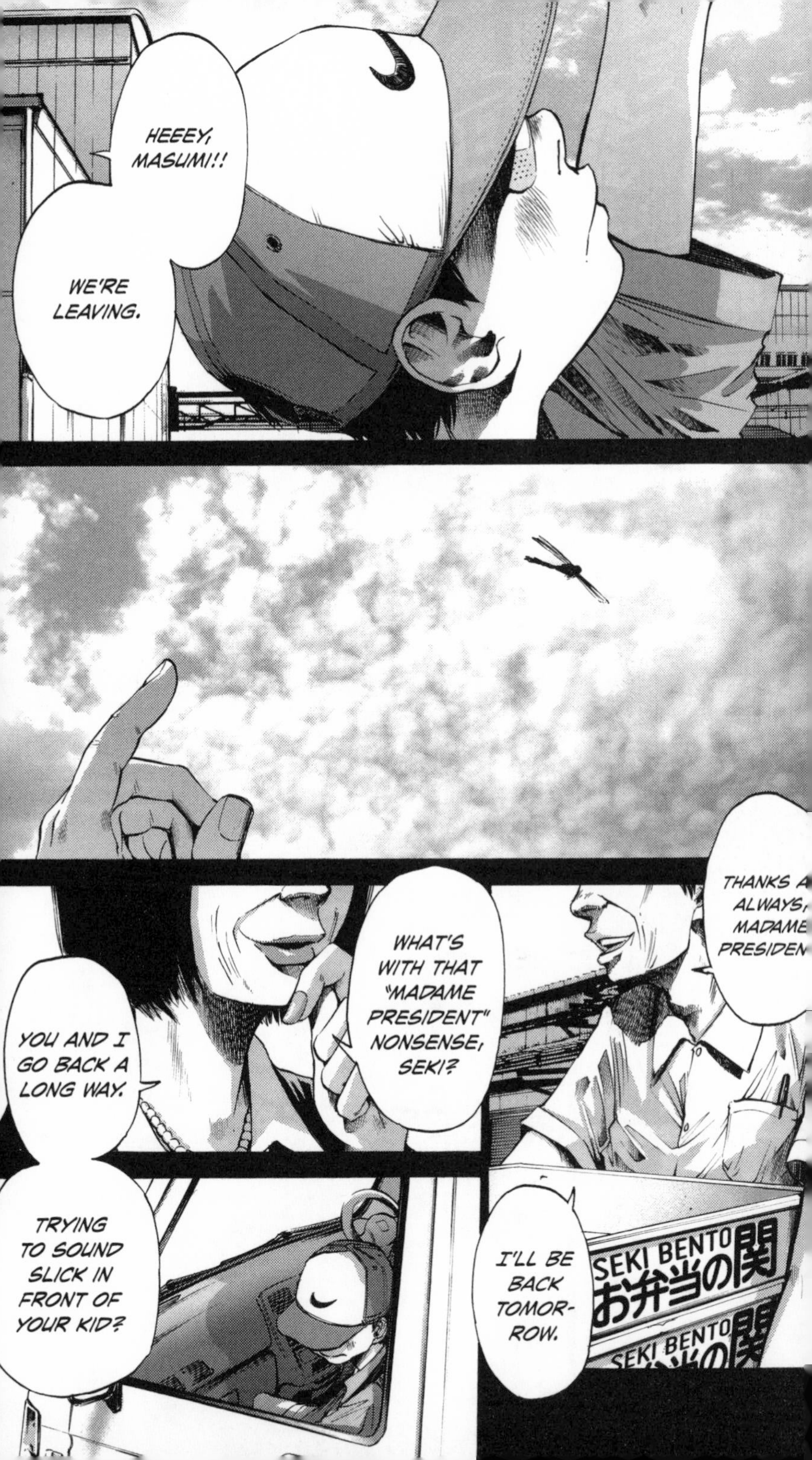
HEEEY, MASUMI!!
WE'RE LEAVING.
THANKS A ALWAYS, MADAME PRESIDEN
WHAT'S WITH THAT "MADAME PRESIDENT" NONSENSE, SEKI?
YOU AND I GO BACK A LONG WAY.
SEKI BENTO
お弁当の関
I'LL BE BACK TOMOR-ROW.
TRYING TO SOUND SLICK IN FRONT OF YOUR KID?

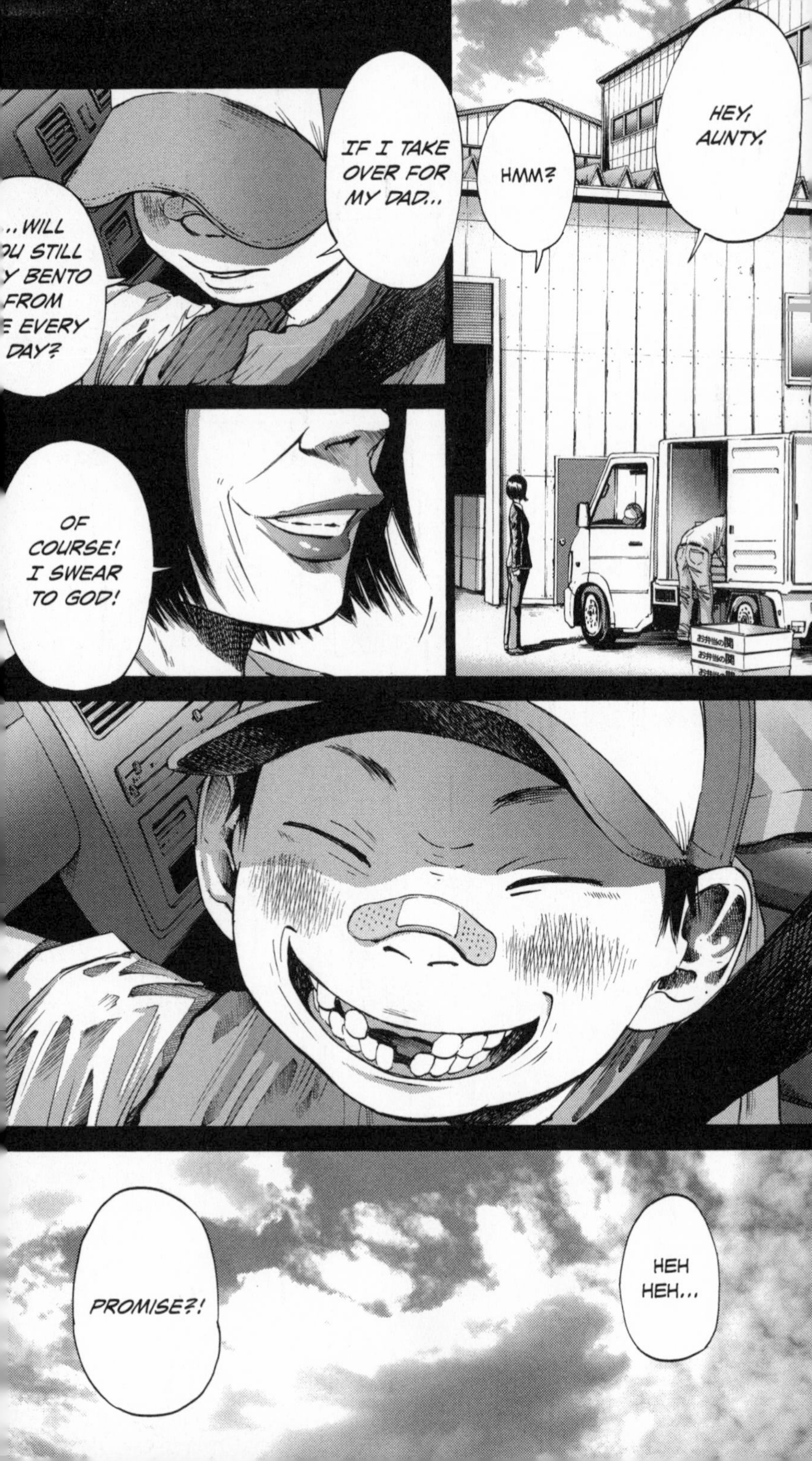
HEY, AUNTY.
HMM?
IF I TAKE OVER FOR MY DAD...
...WILL OU STILL Y BENTO FROM E EVERY DAY?
OF COURSE! I SWEAR TO GOD!
HEH HEH...
PROMISE?!

THERE'S NOTHING HERE EITHER...

MMM... MAYBE IT'S TIME TO GIVE UP?

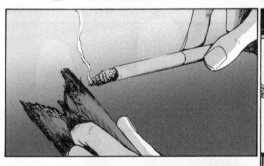

YOU CAN GET ON THE ROOF FROM OUT HERE.

HEY, SEKI... ARE YOU COMING...?

SERIOUSLY ?!

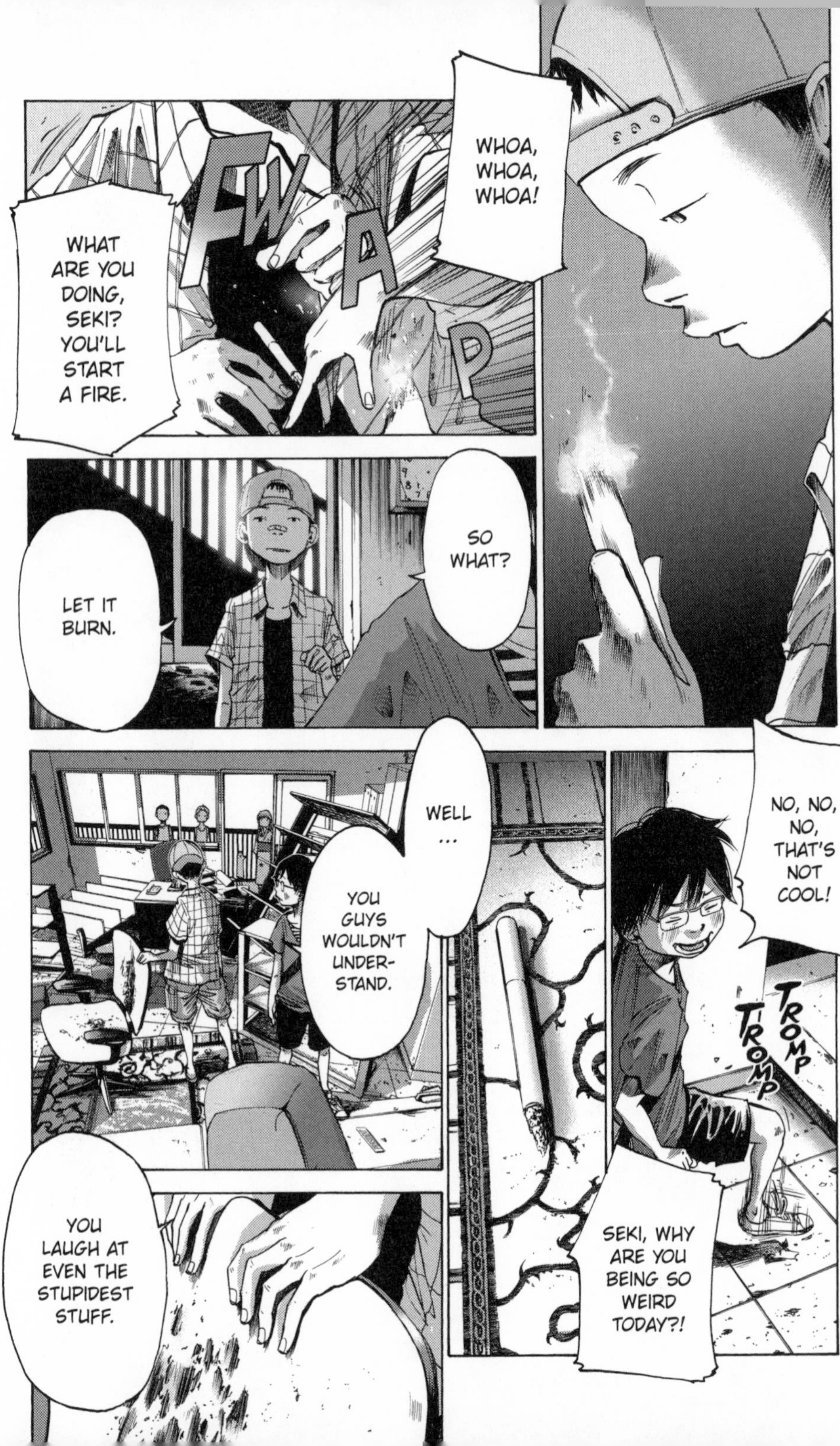
WHOA, WHOA, WHOA!
FWAP
WHAT ARE YOU DOING, SEKI? YOU'LL START A FIRE.
SO WHAT?
LET IT BURN.
NO, NO, NO, THAT'S NOT COOL!
TROMP TROMP
SEKI, WHY ARE YOU BEING SO WEIRD TODAY?!
WELL ...
YOU GUYS WOULDN'T UNDER-STAND.
YOU LAUGH AT EVEN THE STUPIDEST STUFF.

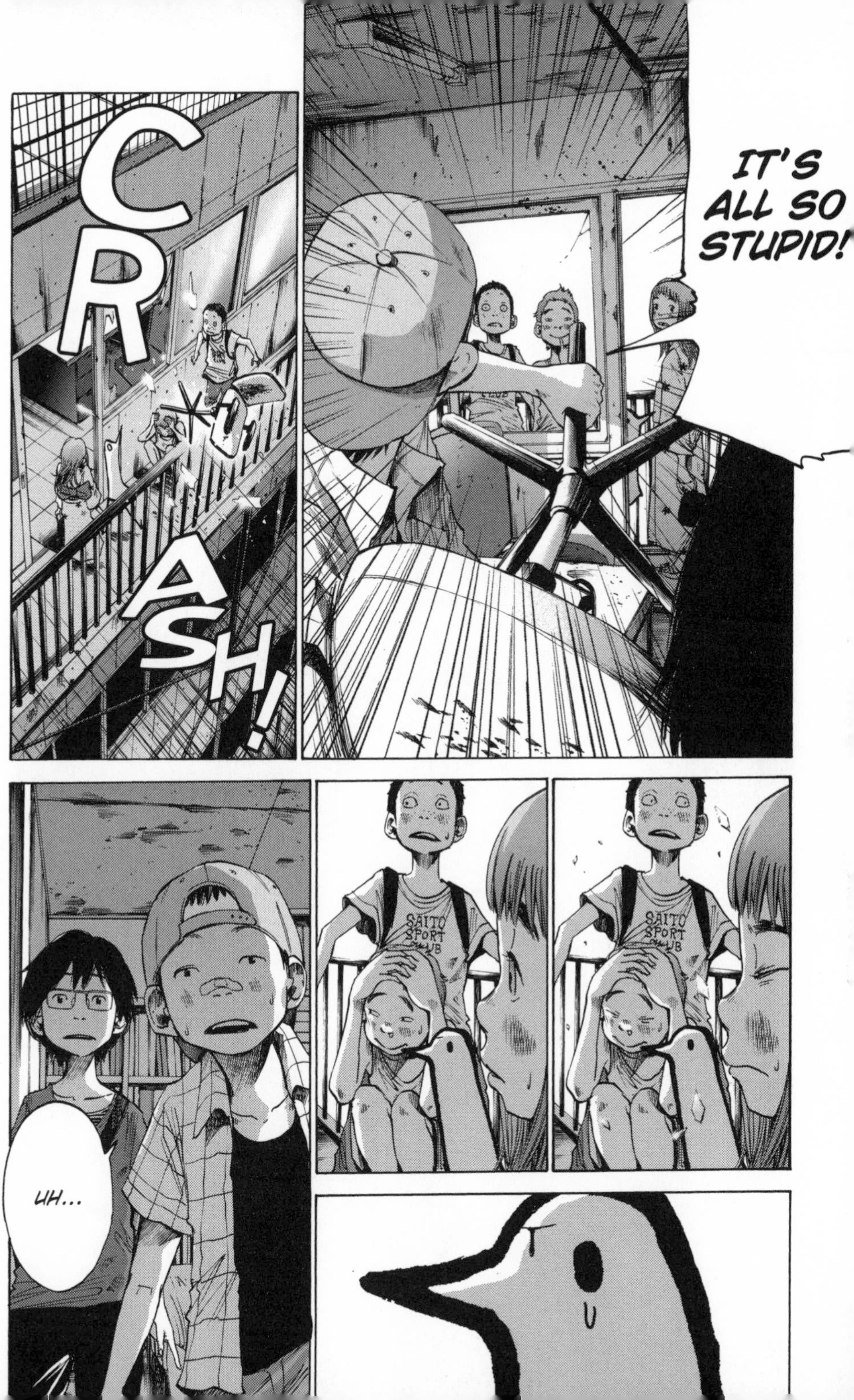
IT'S ALL SO STUPID!
CRASH!
UH...

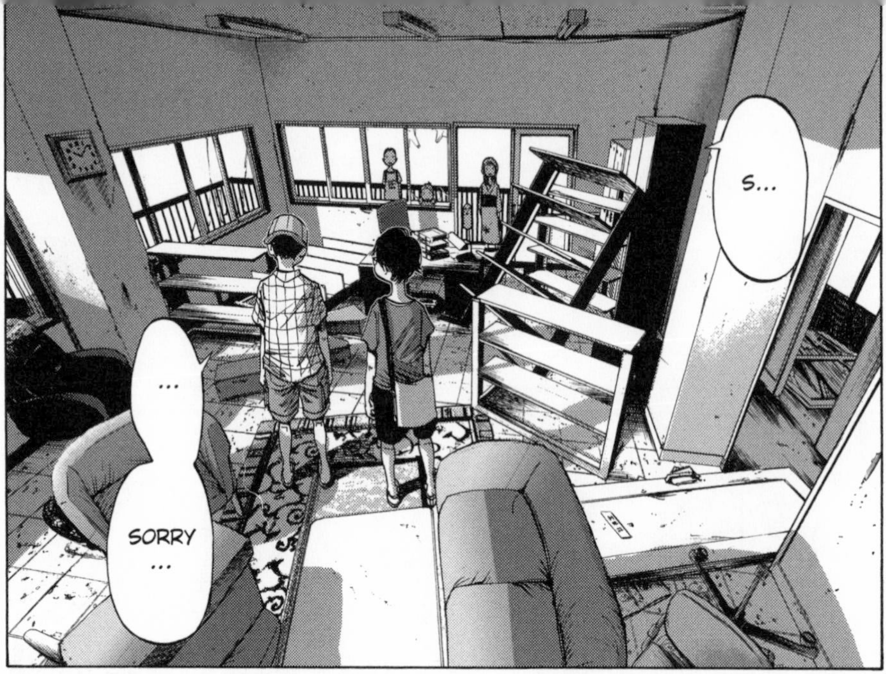
S...
...
SORRY ...

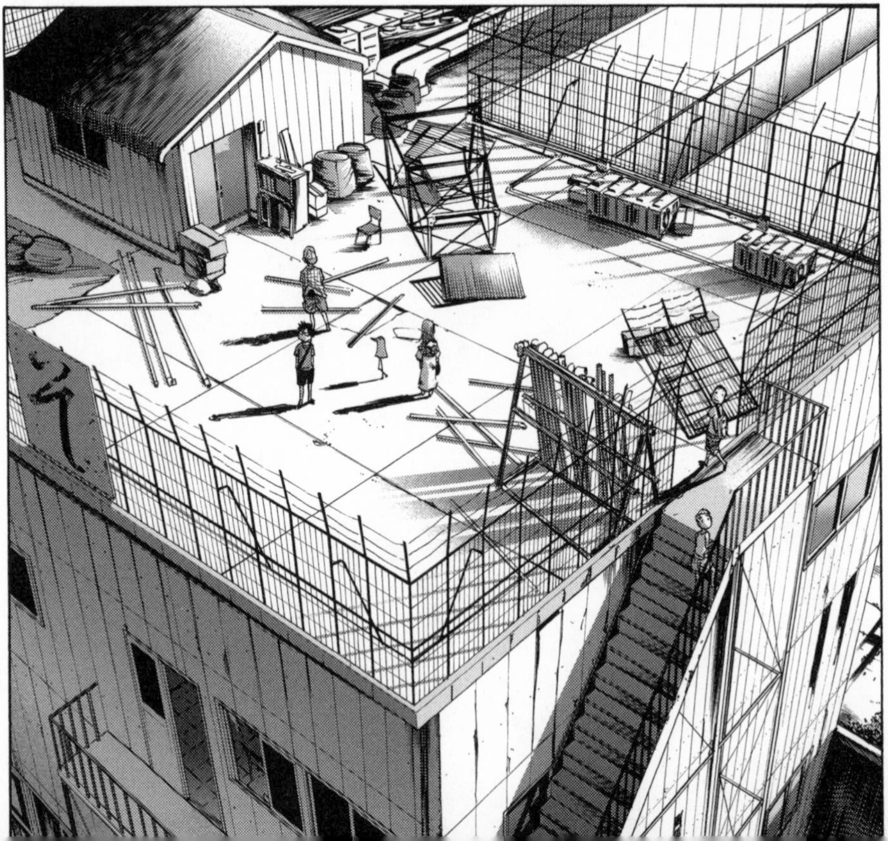

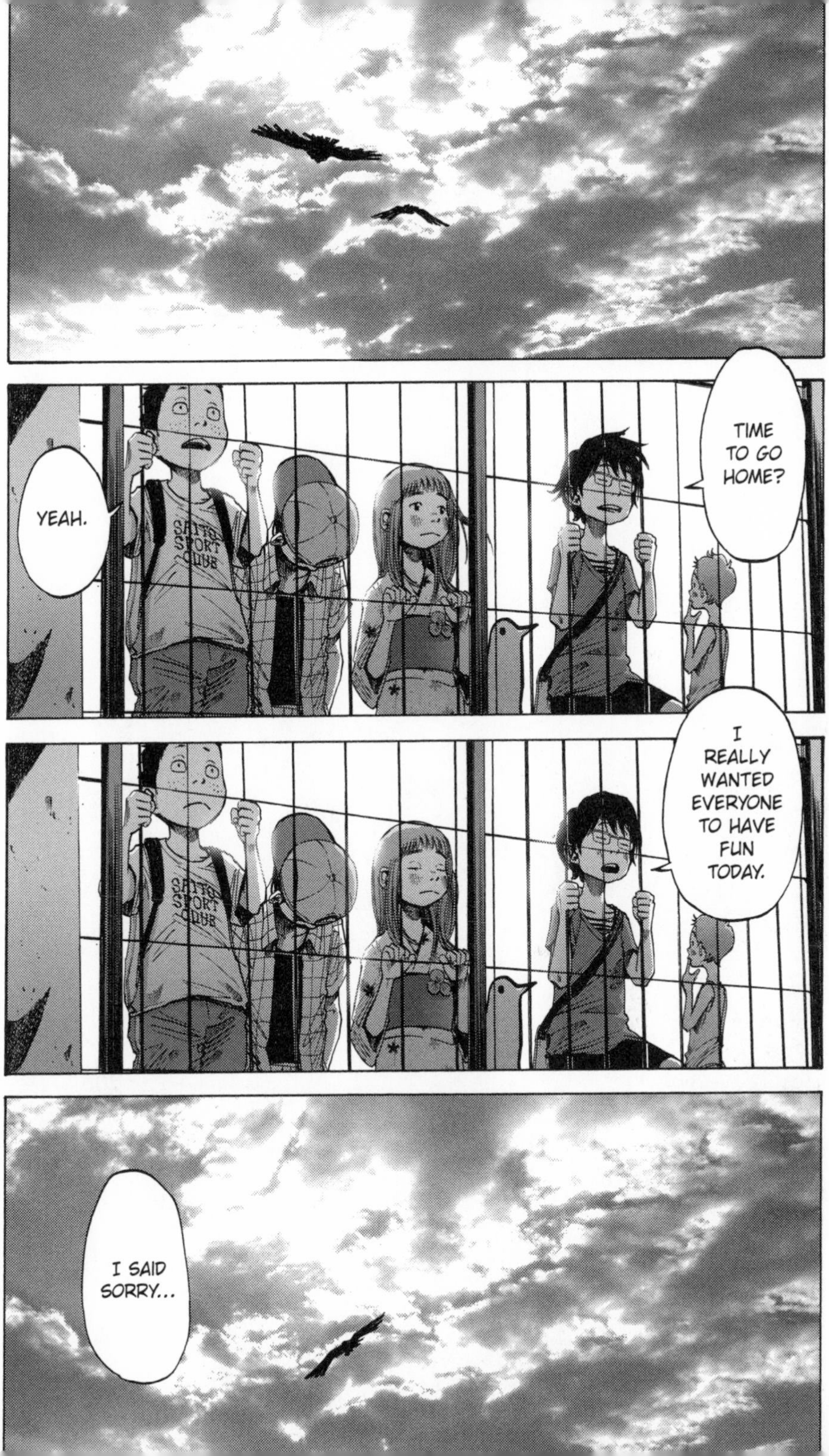
TIME TO GO HOME?
YEAH.
I REALLY WANTED EVERYONE TO HAVE FUN TODAY.
I SAID SORRY...

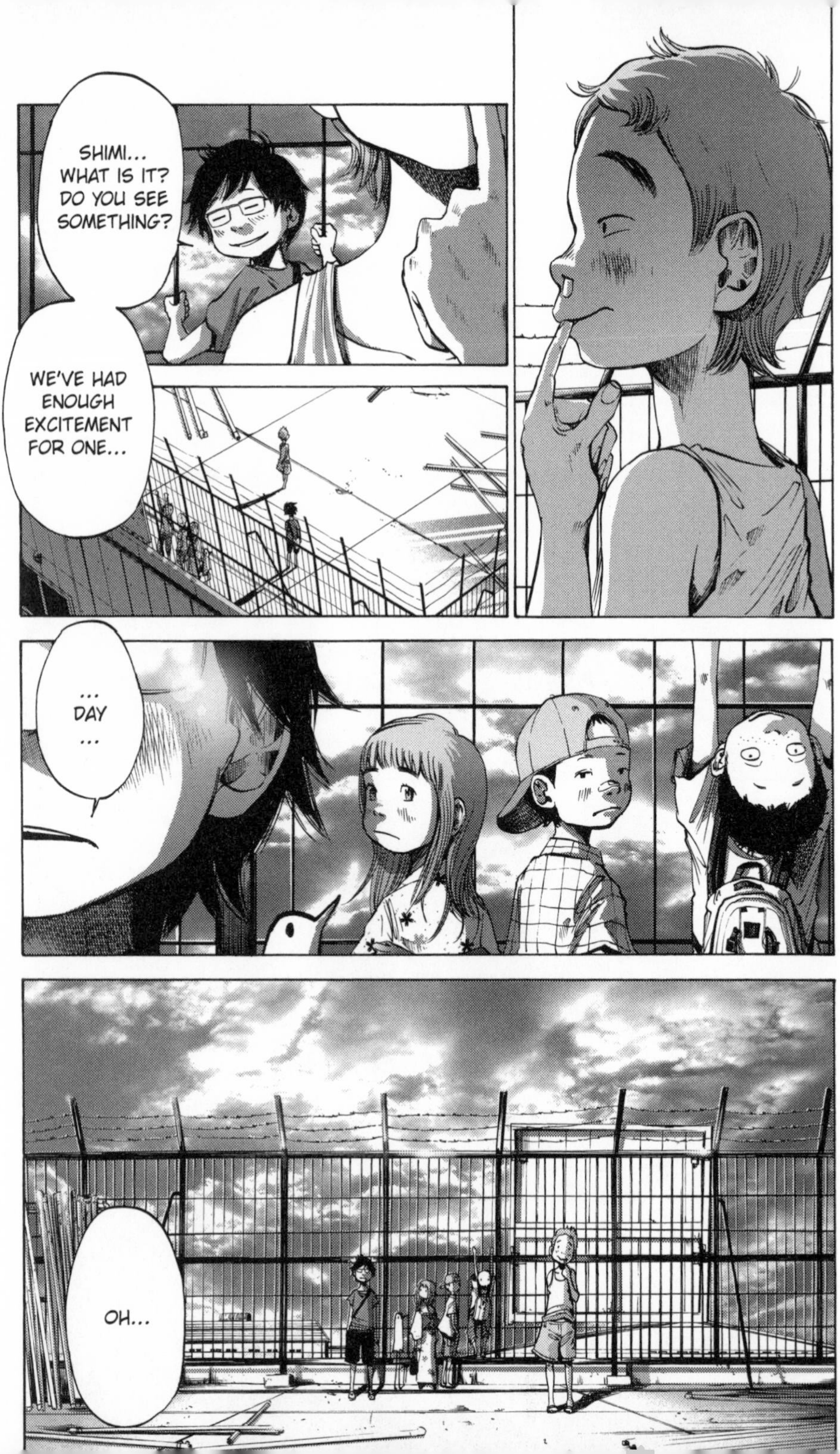
SHIMI... WHAT IS IT? DO YOU SEE SOMETHING?
WE'VE HAD ENOUGH EXCITEMENT FOR ONE...
... DAY ...
OH...

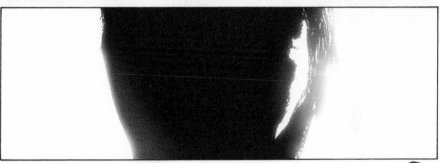

HA...

HA
HA
HA
HA!

HA...

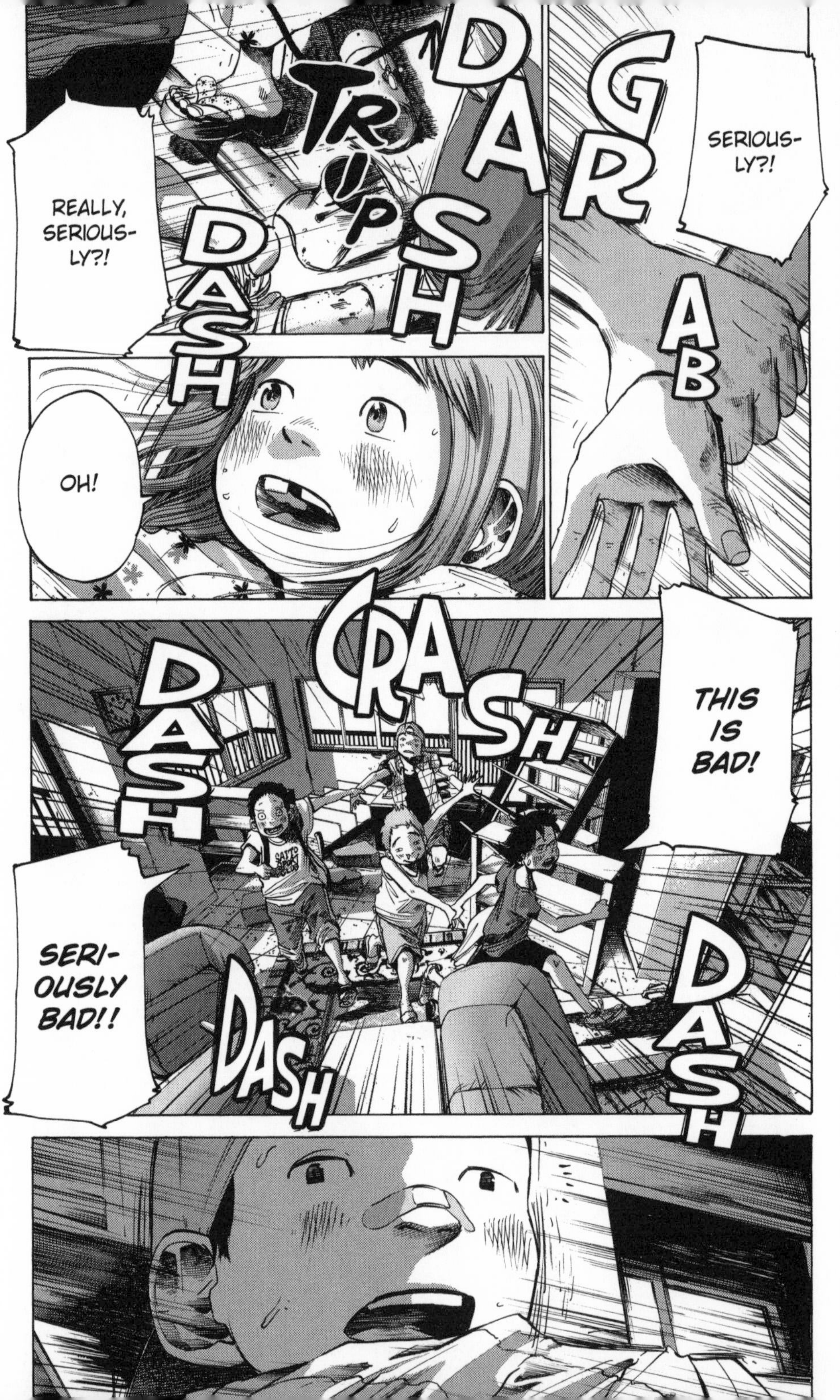
SERIOUS-
LY?!
GRAB
TRIP
DASH
DASH
REALLY, SERIOUS-
LY?!
OH!
CRASH
THIS IS BAD!
DASH
DASH
DASH
SERI-
OUSLY BAD!!

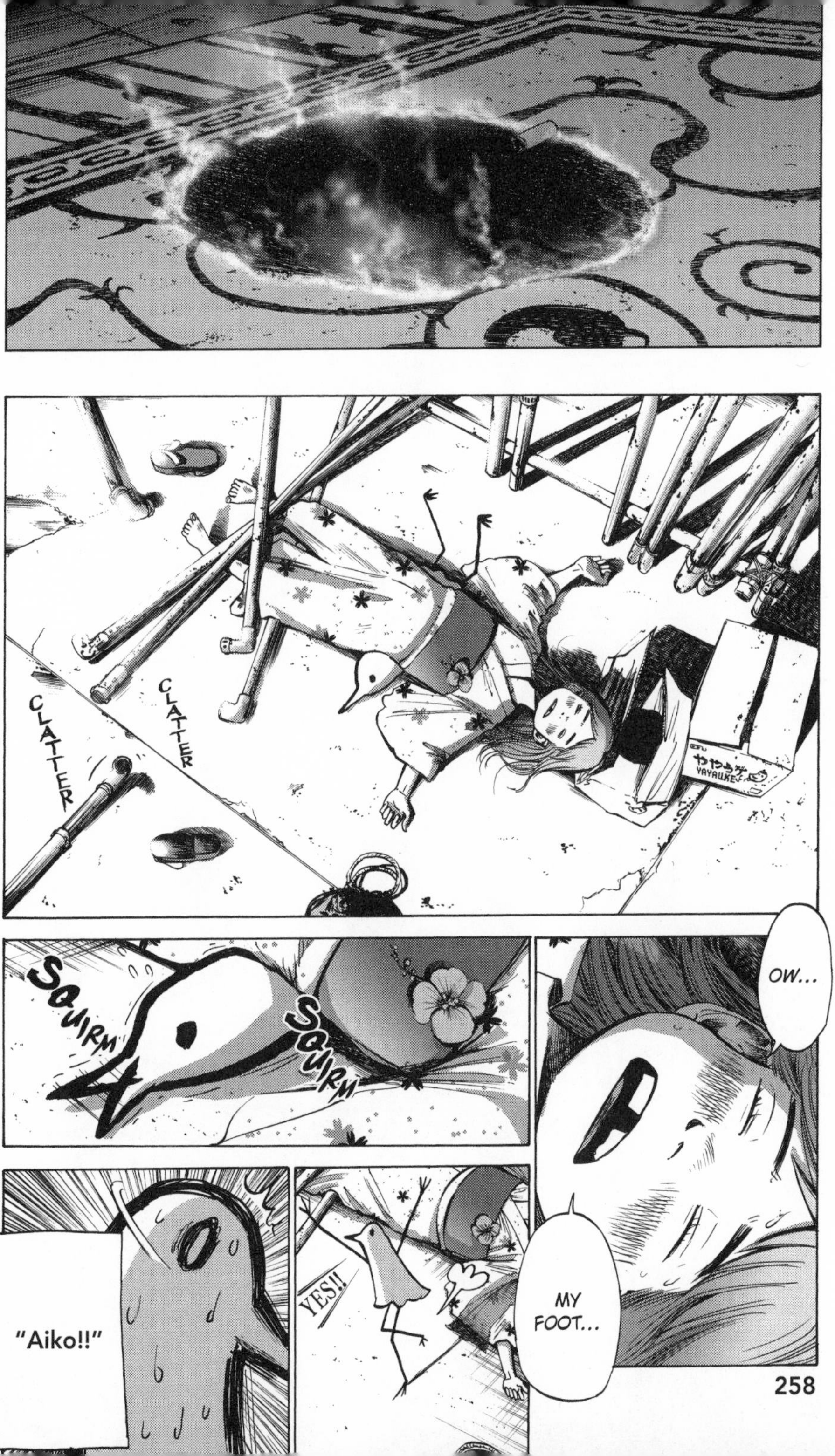
CLATTER
CLATTER
YAYAUKE
OW...
MY FOOT...
SQUIRM
SQUIRM
YES!!
"Aiko!!"

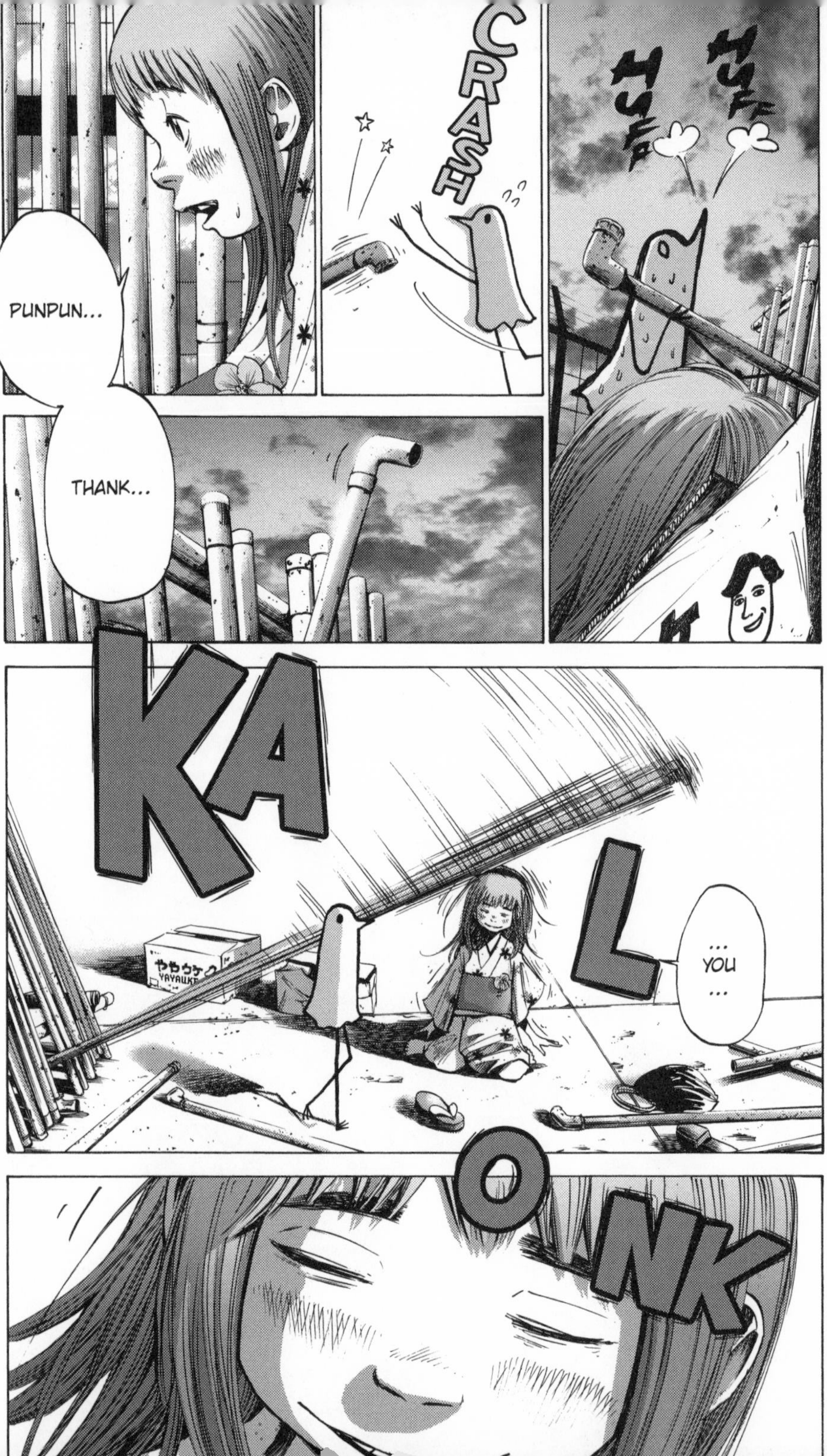
HUFF
HUFF
CRASH
PUNPUN...
THANK...
KA
L
ONK
... YOU ...

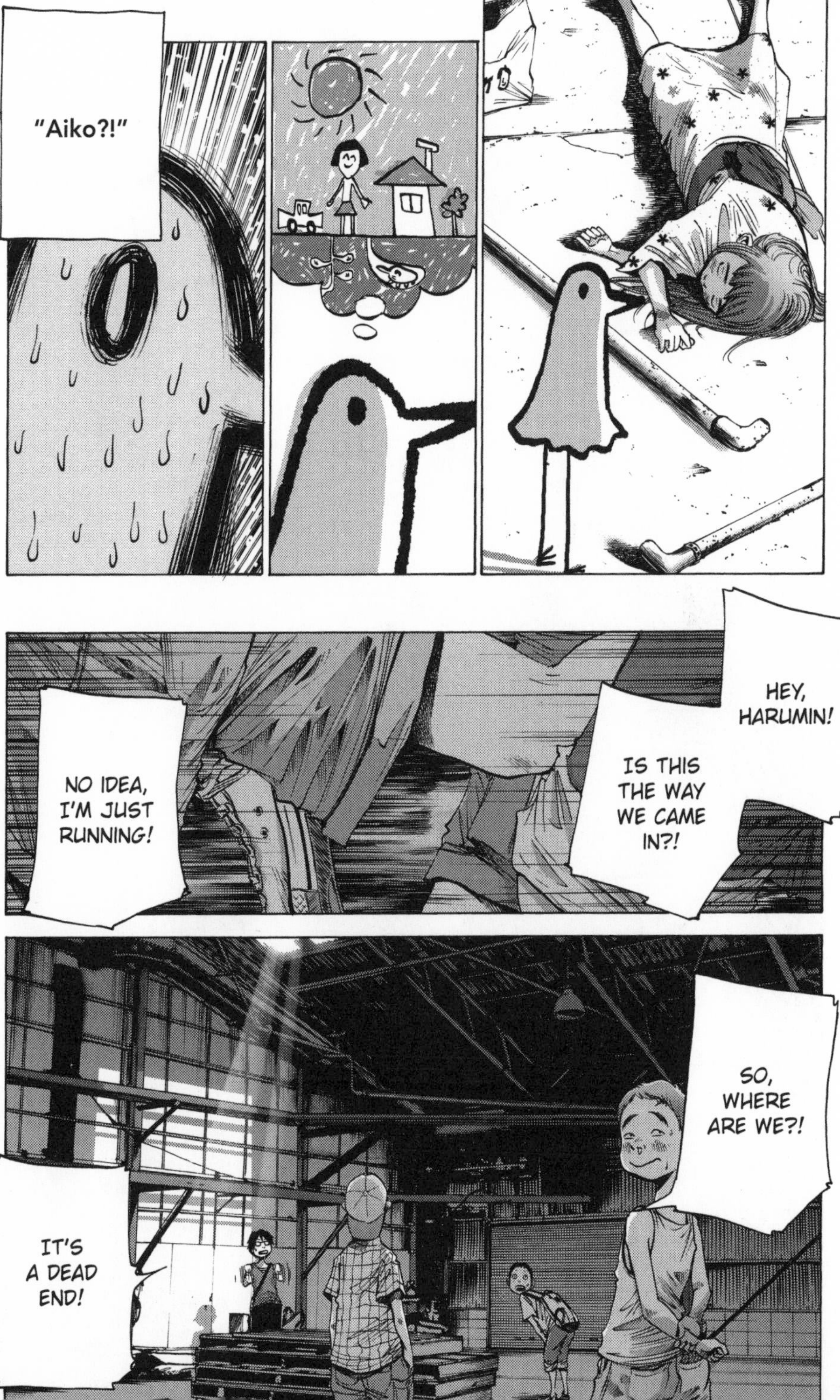
"Aiko?!"
HEY, HARUMIN!
IS THIS THE WAY WE CAME IN?!
NO IDEA, I'M JUST RUNNING!
SO, WHERE ARE WE?!
IT'S A DEAD END!

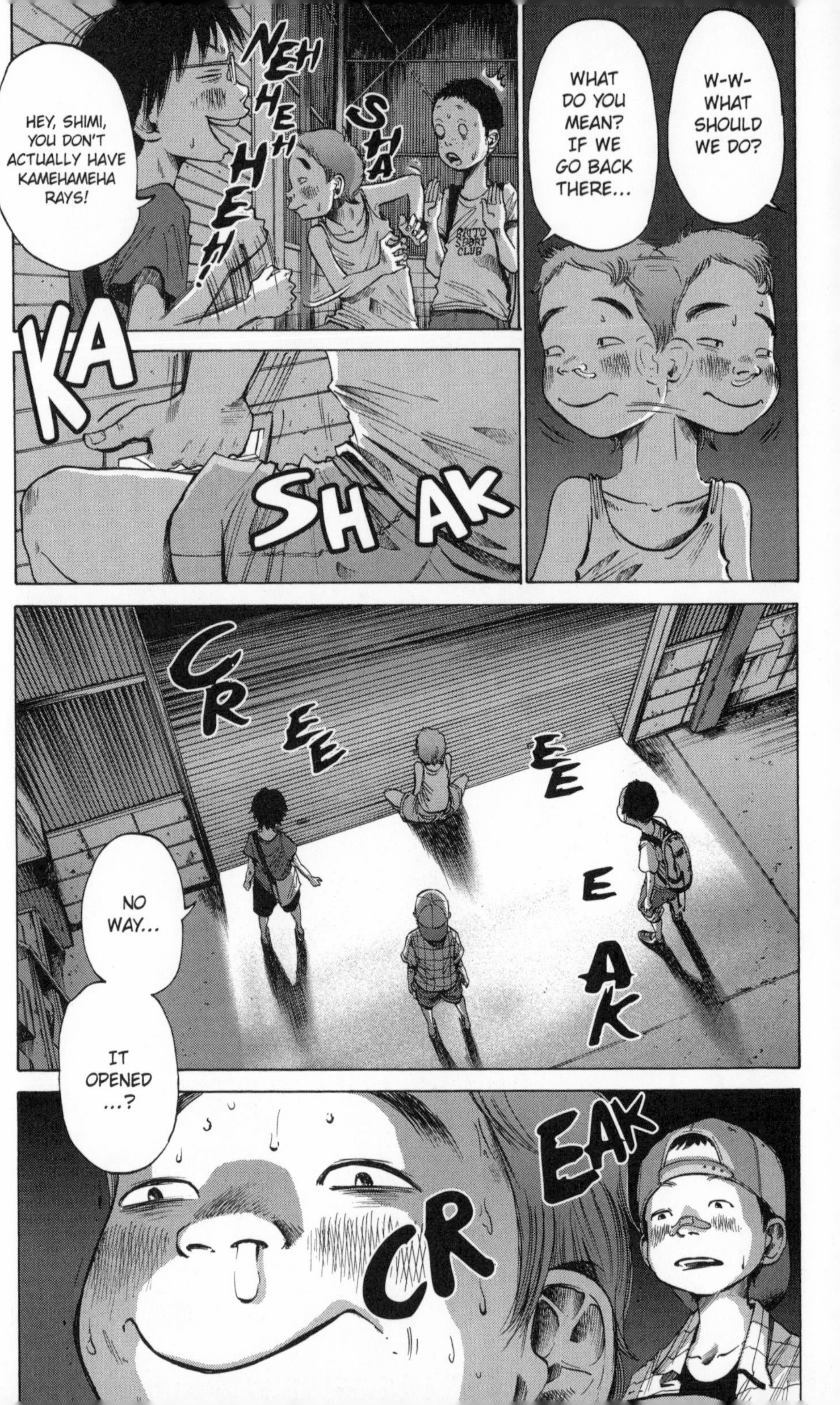
W-W-WHAT SHOULD WE DO?
WHAT DO YOU MEAN? IF WE GO BACK THERE...
SHA
NEH HEH HEH HEH!
HEY, SHIMI, YOU DON'T ACTUALLY HAVE KAMEHAMEHA RAYS!
KA
SHAK
CREEEEAK
NO WAY...
IT OPENED...?
CREAK

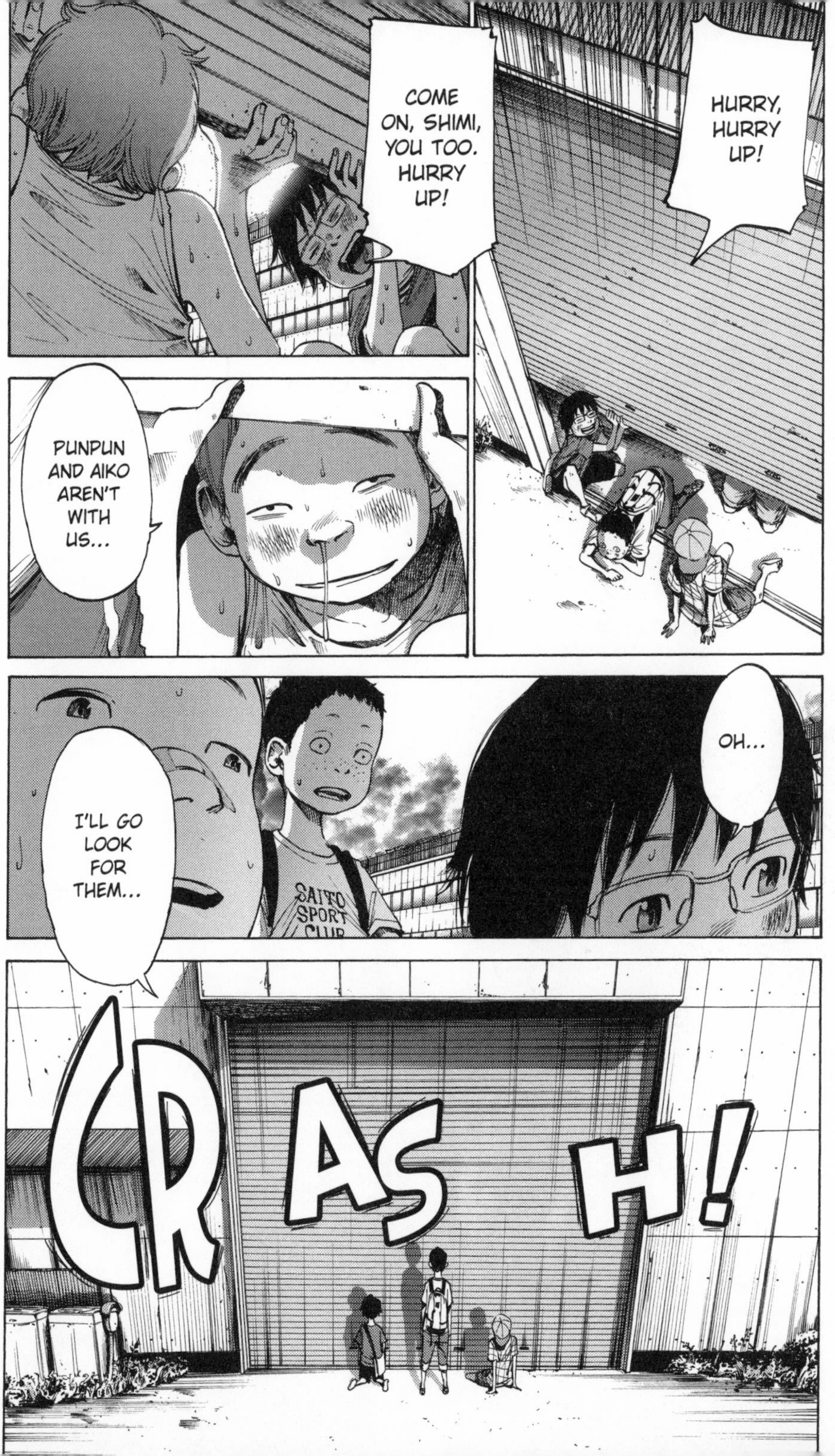
HURRY, HURRY UP!
COME ON, SHIMI, YOU TOO. HURRY UP!
PUNPUN AND AIKO AREN'T WITH US...
OH...
SAITO SPORT CLUB
I'LL GO LOOK FOR THEM...
CRASH!

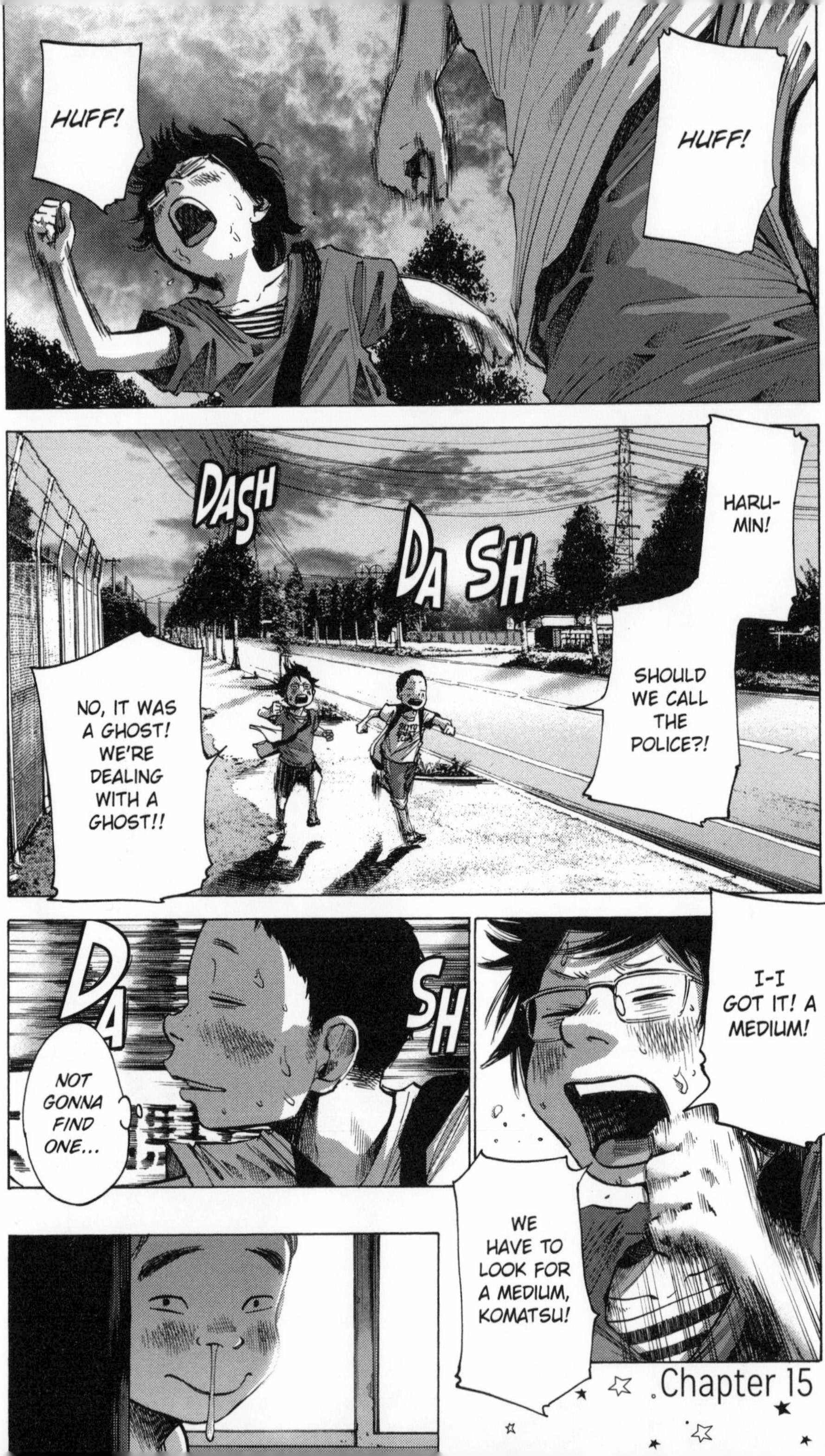
HUFF!
HUFF!
HARU-MIN!
SHOULD WE CALL THE POLICE?!
DASH
DASH
NO, IT WAS A GHOST! WE'RE DEALING WITH A GHOST!!
I-I GOT IT! A MEDIUM!
WE HAVE TO LOOK FOR A MEDIUM, KOMATSU!
DASH
NOT GONNA FIND ONE...
Chapter 15

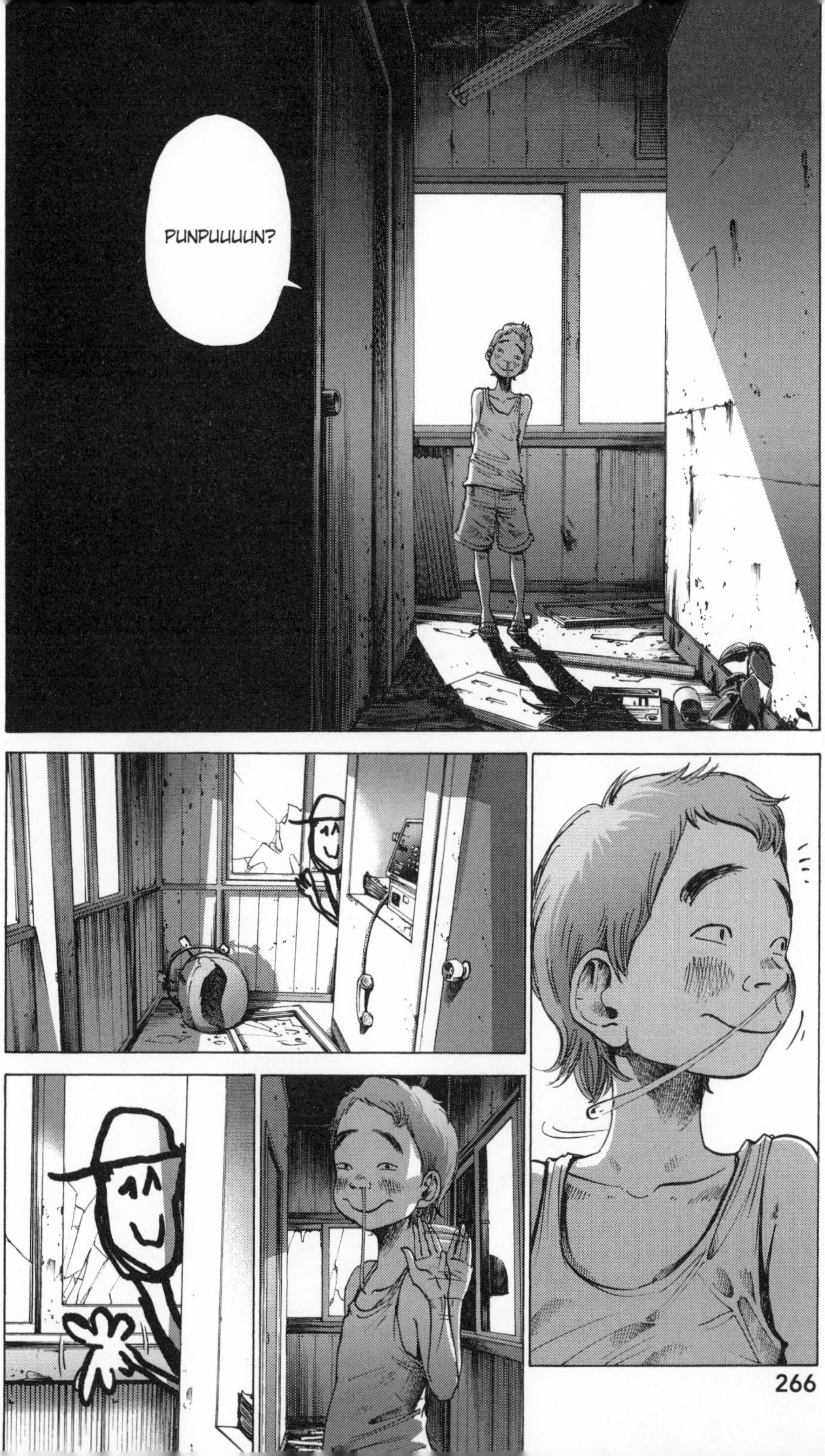
PUNPUUUUN?

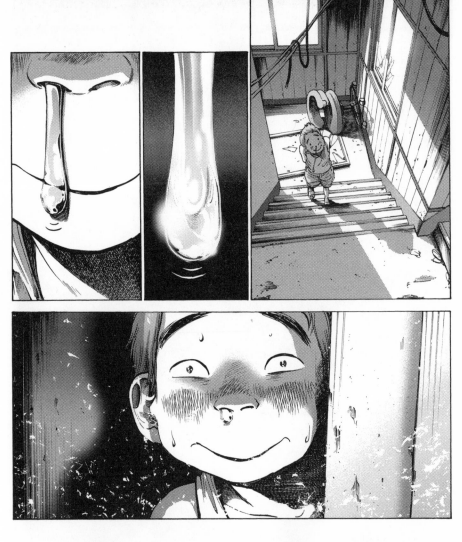

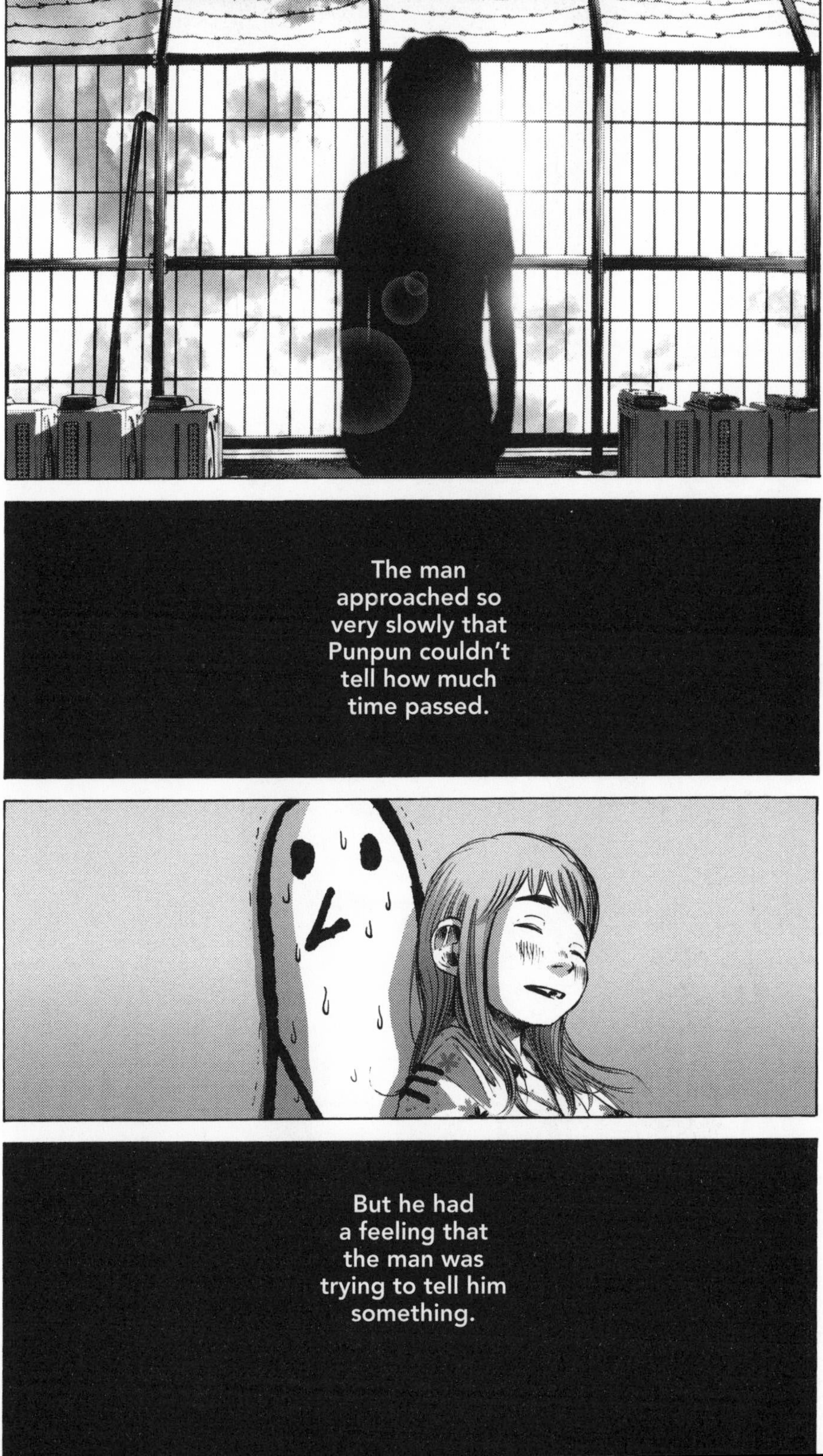
The man approached so very slowly that Punpun couldn't tell how much time passed.
But he had a feeling that the man was trying to tell him something.

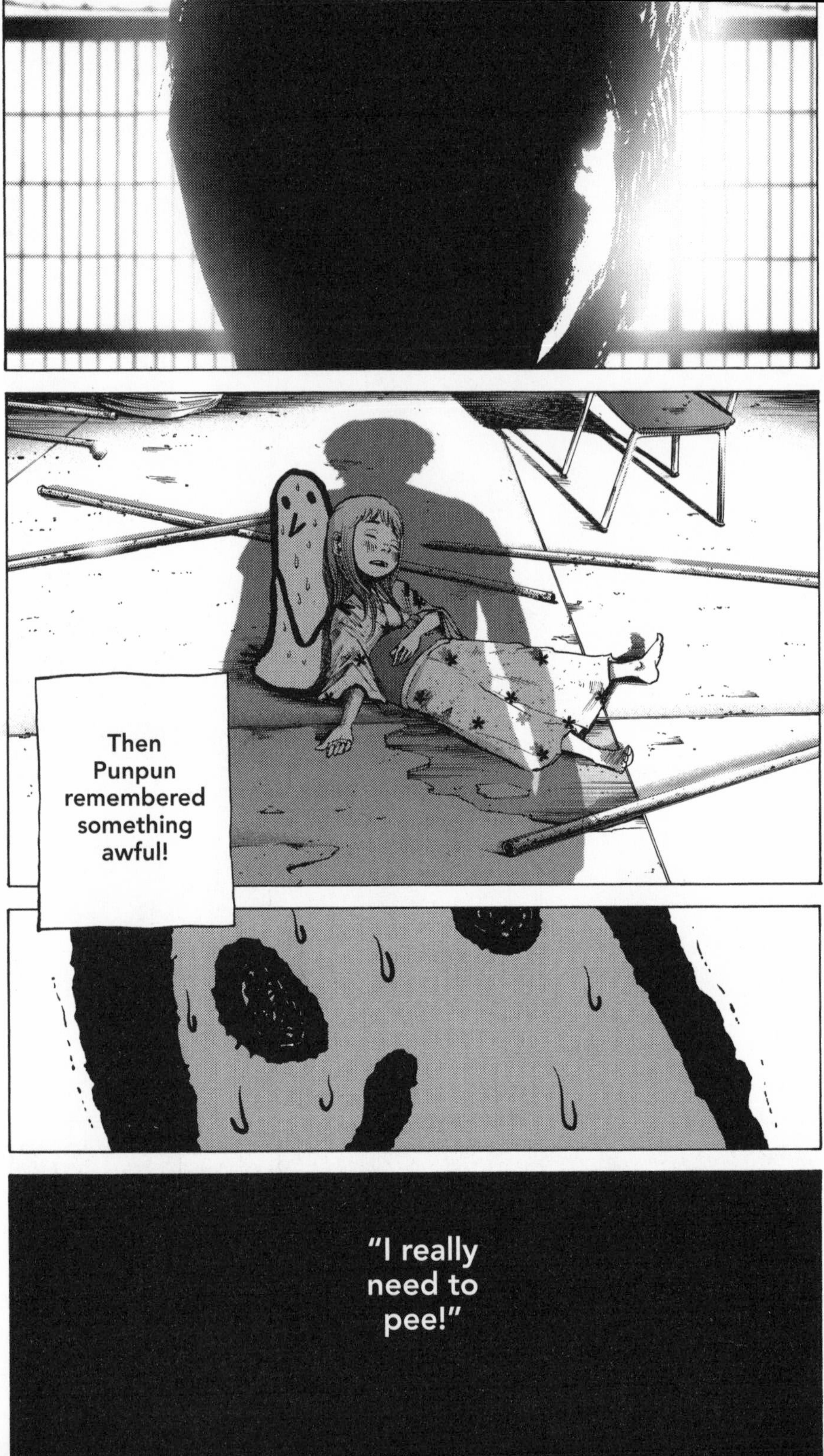
Then Punpun remembered something awful!
"I really need to pee!"

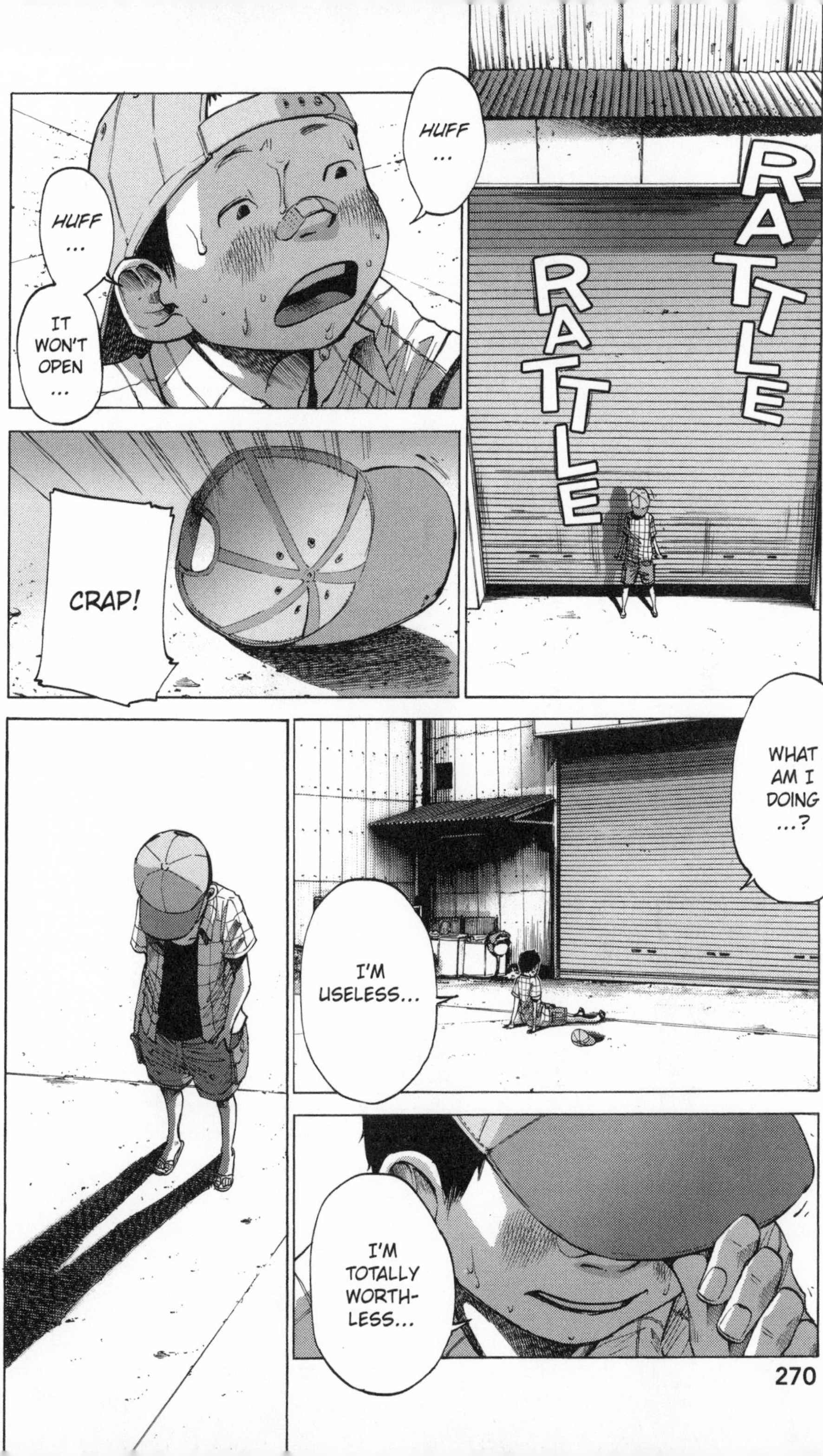
RATTLE
RATTLE
HUFF ...
HUFF ...
IT WON'T OPEN ...
CRAP!
WHAT AM I DOING ...?
I'M USELESS...
I'M TOTALLY WORTH-LESS...

SEKI!

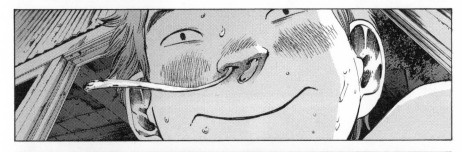

THERE'S
A FIRE!

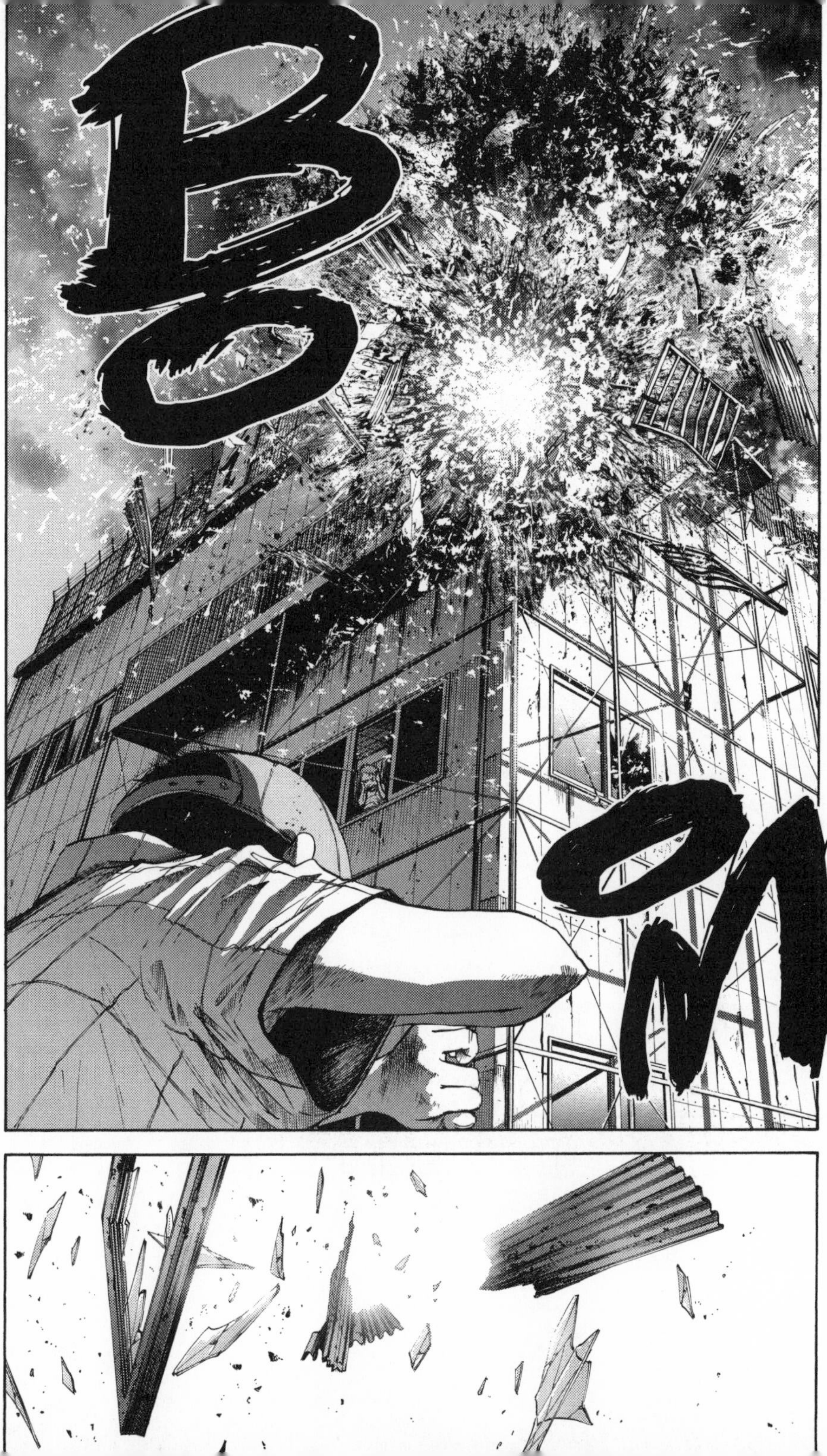
BOOM

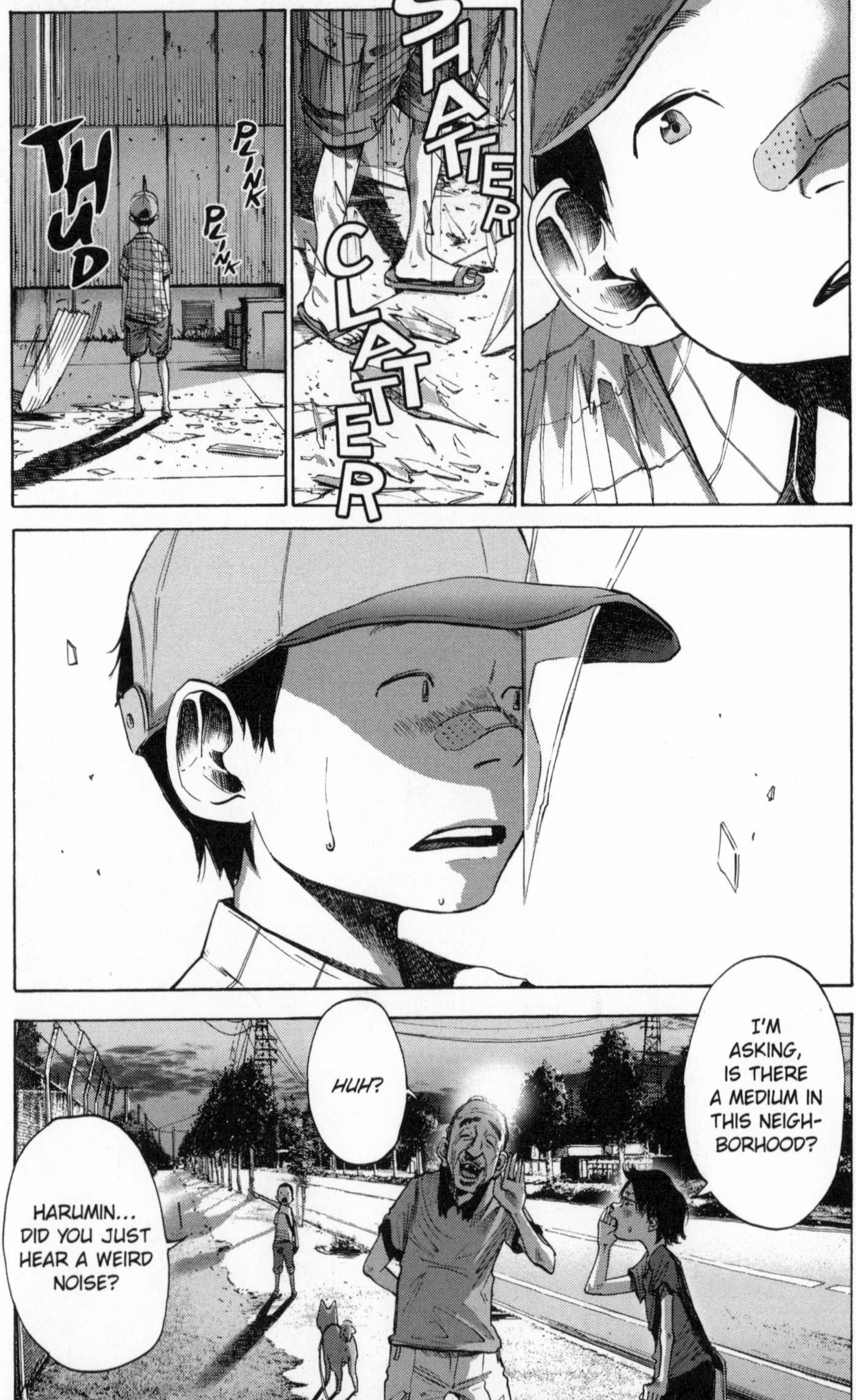
SHATTER
CLATTER
THUD
PLINK
PLINK
I'M ASKING, IS THERE A MEDIUM IN THIS NEIGH-BORHOOD?
HUH?
HARUMIN... DID YOU JUST HEAR A WEIRD NOISE?

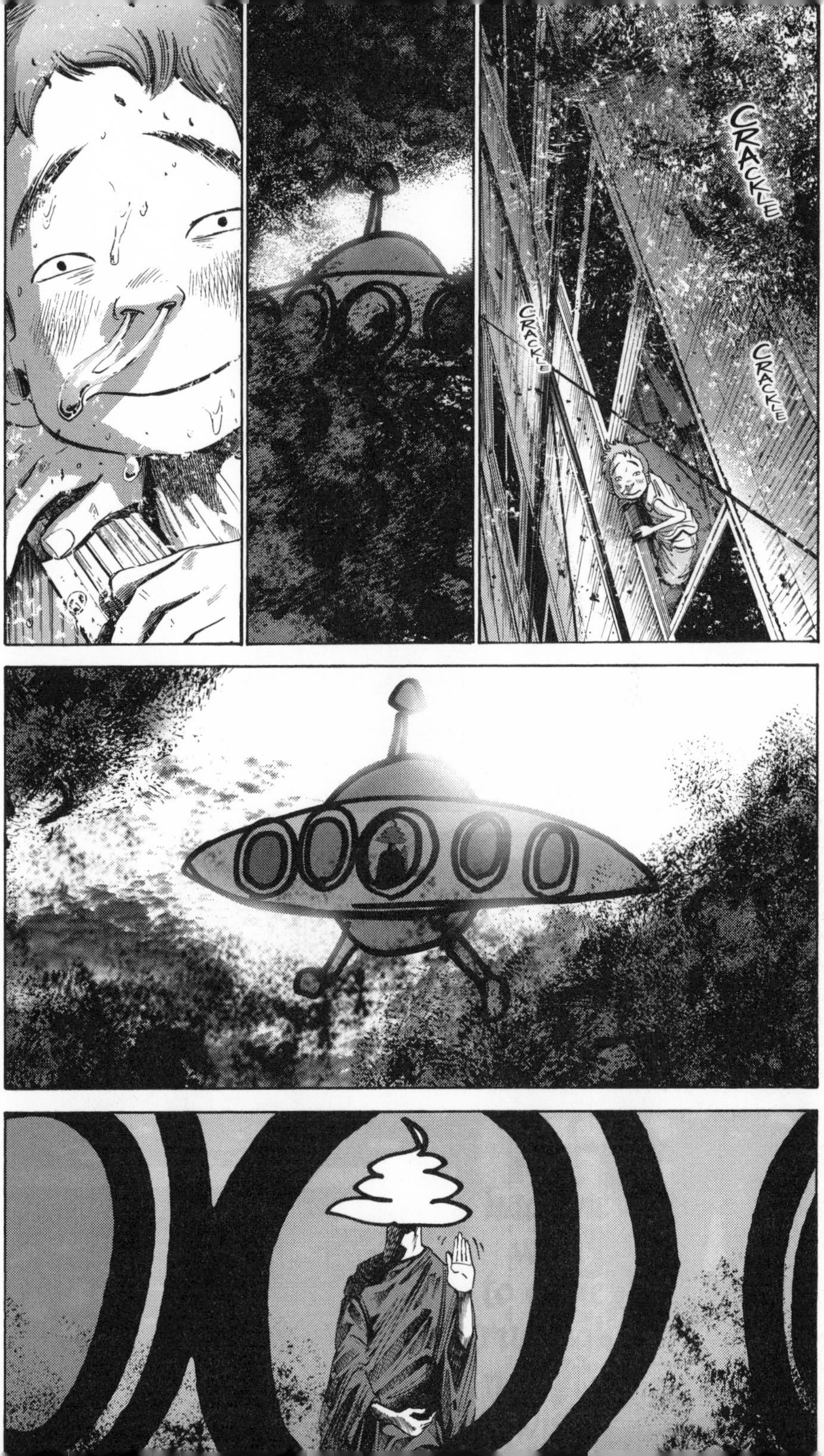
CRACKLE
CRACKLE
CRACKLE

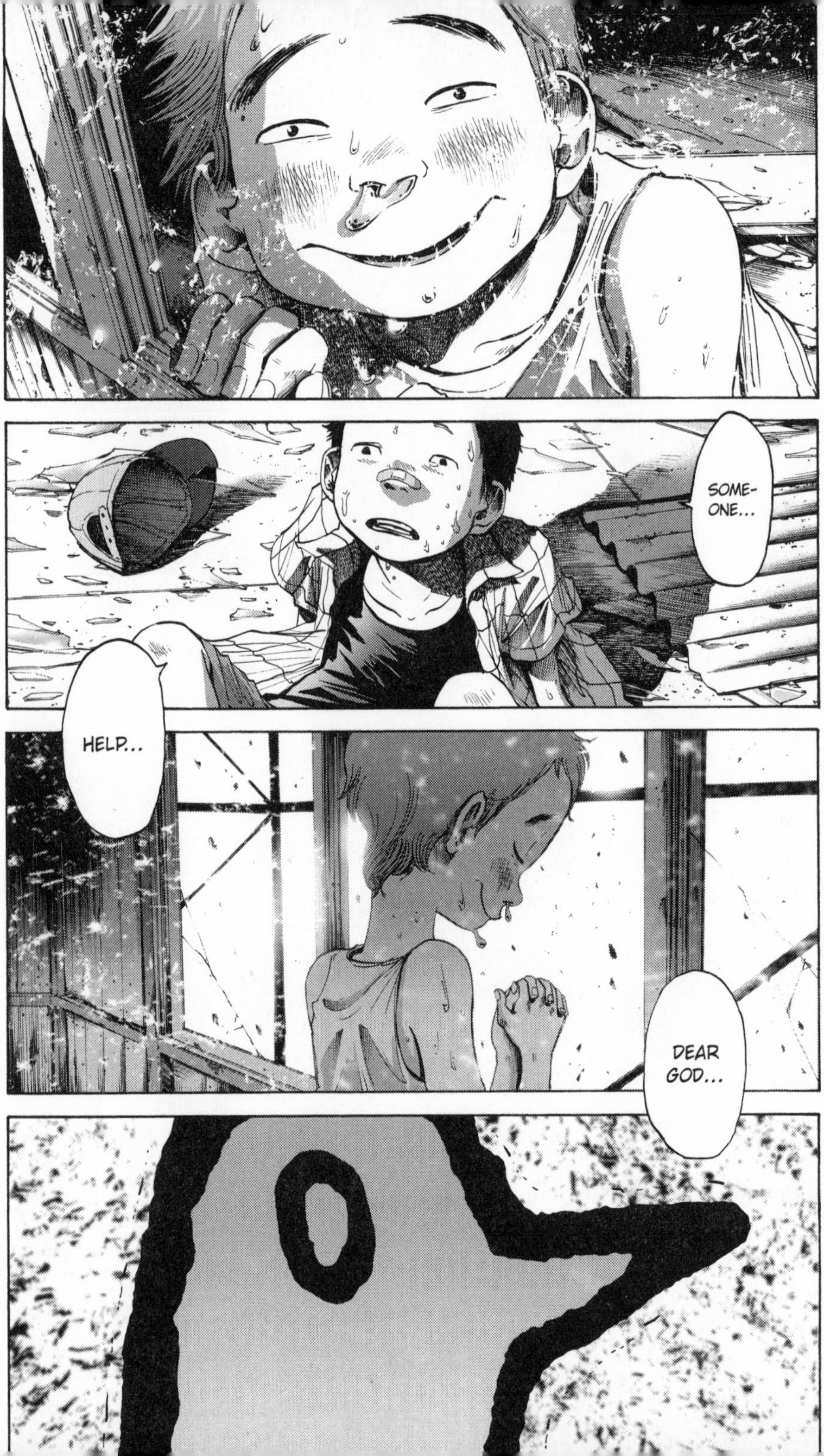
SOME-ONE...
HELP...
DEAR GOD...

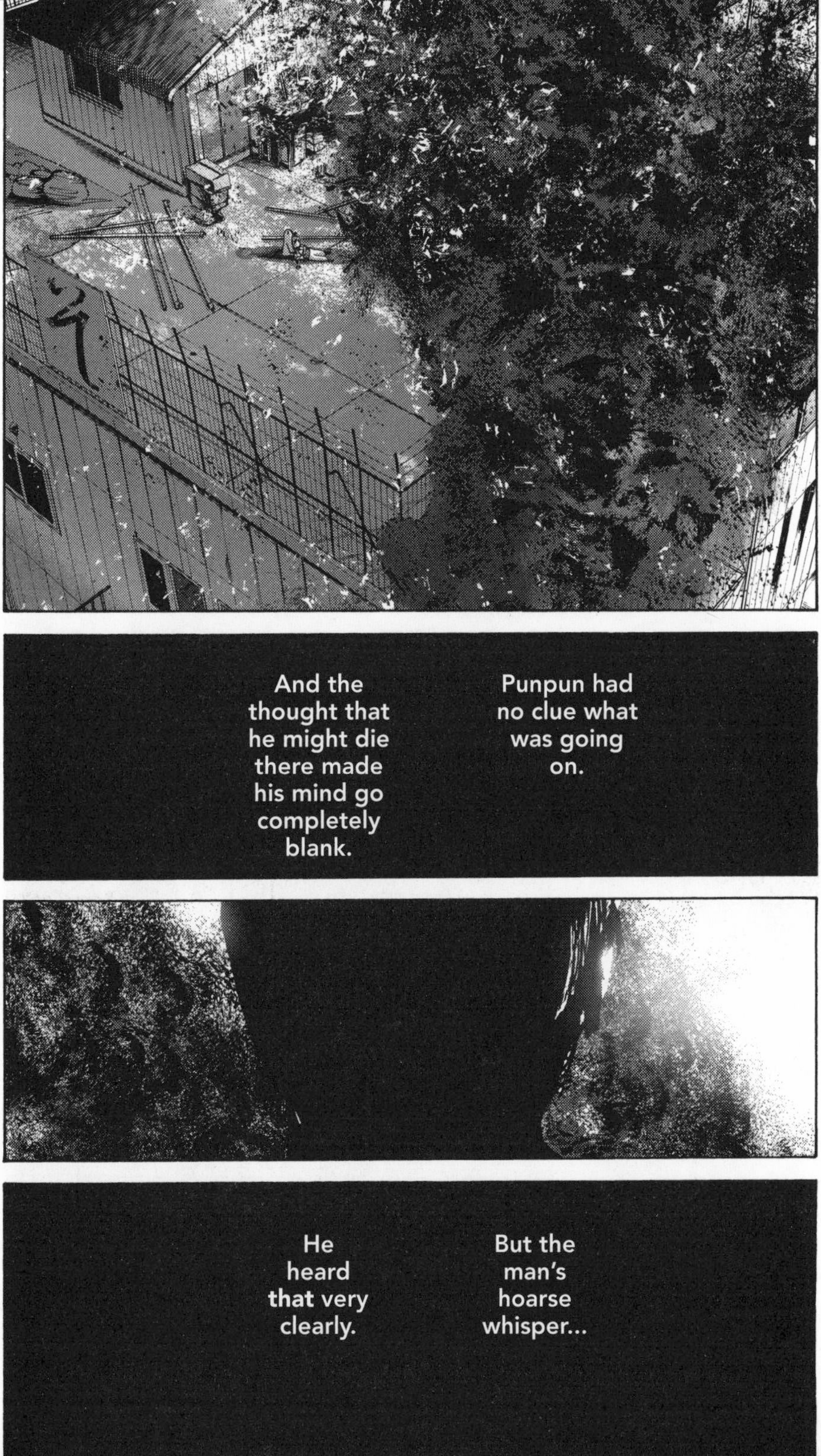
Punpun had no clue what was going on.
And the thought that he might die there made his mind go completely blank.
But the man's hoarse whisper...
He heard **that** very clearly.

"I..."

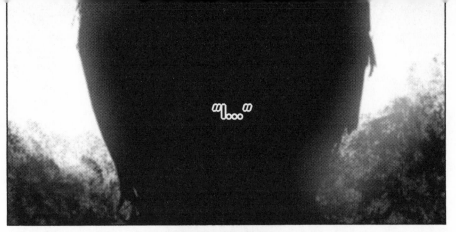

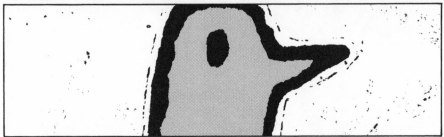

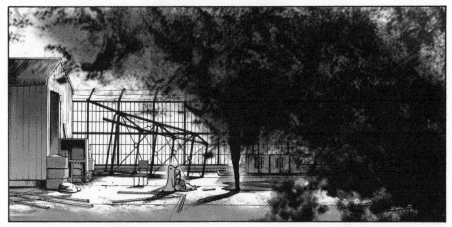

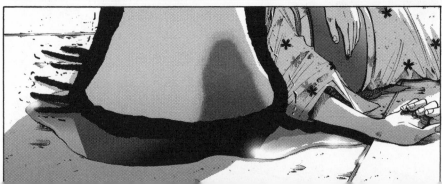

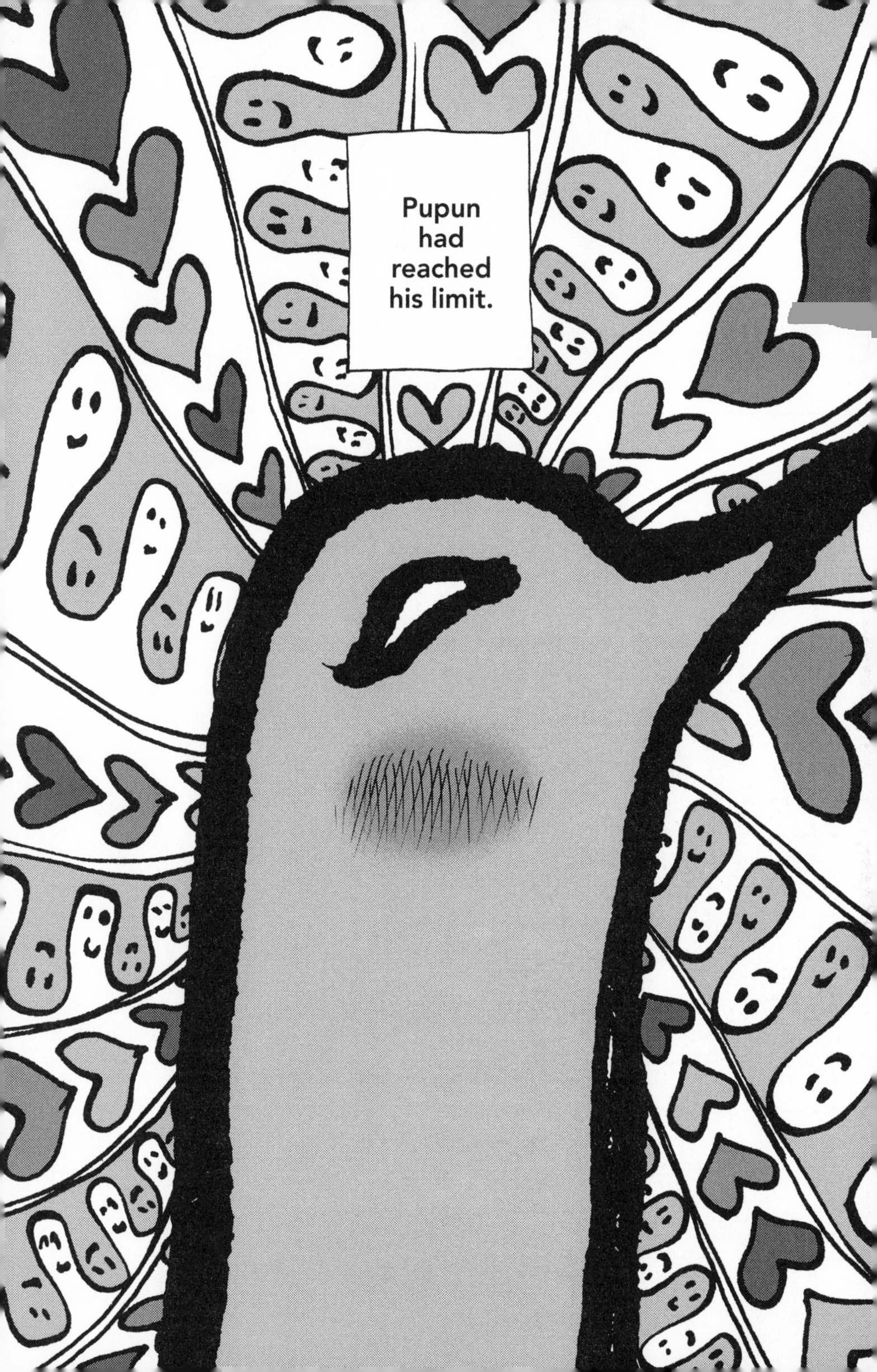
Pupun had reached his limit.

Chapter 16

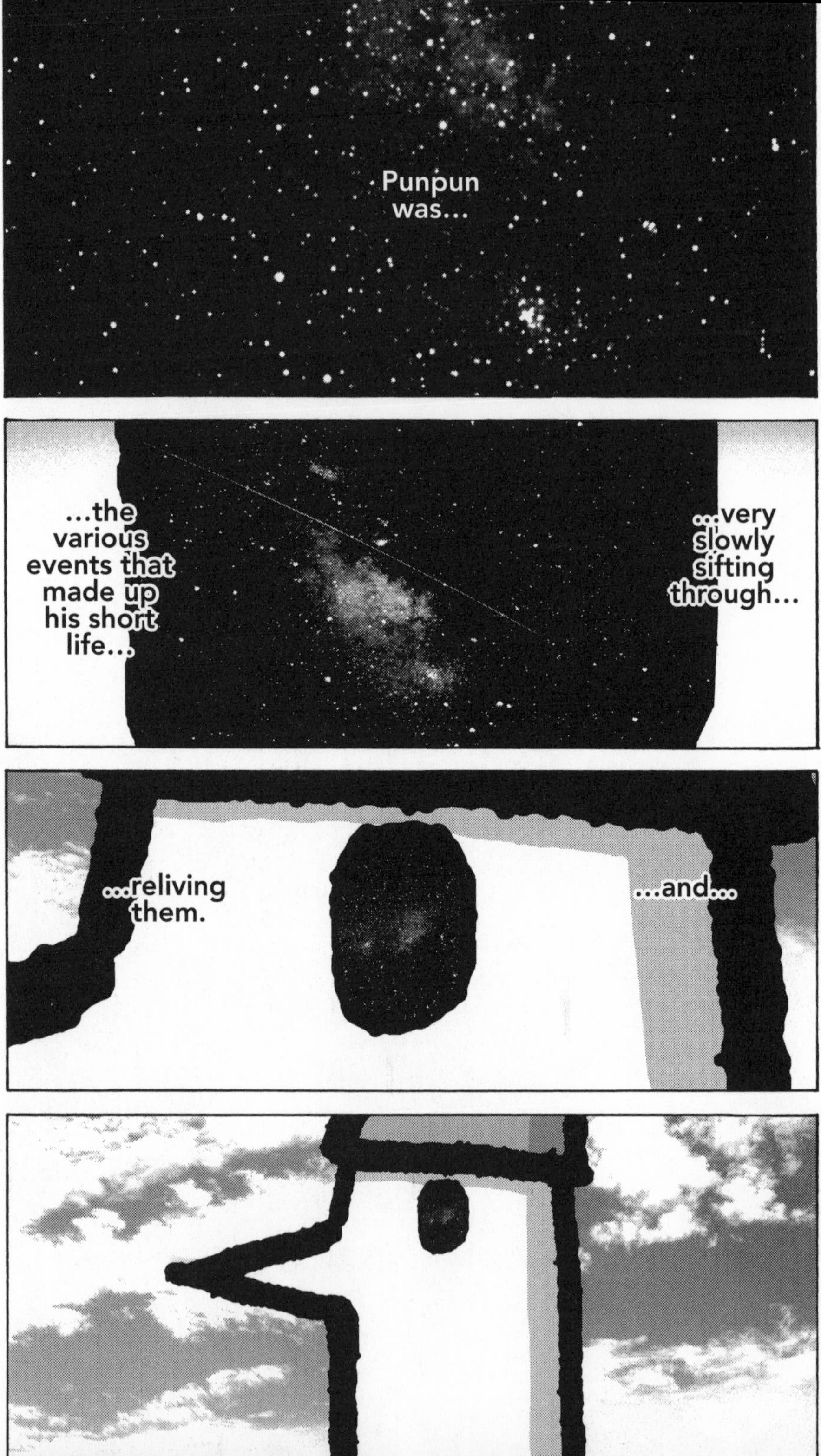
Punpun was...
...very slowly sifting through...
...the various events that made up his short life...
...and...
...reliving them.

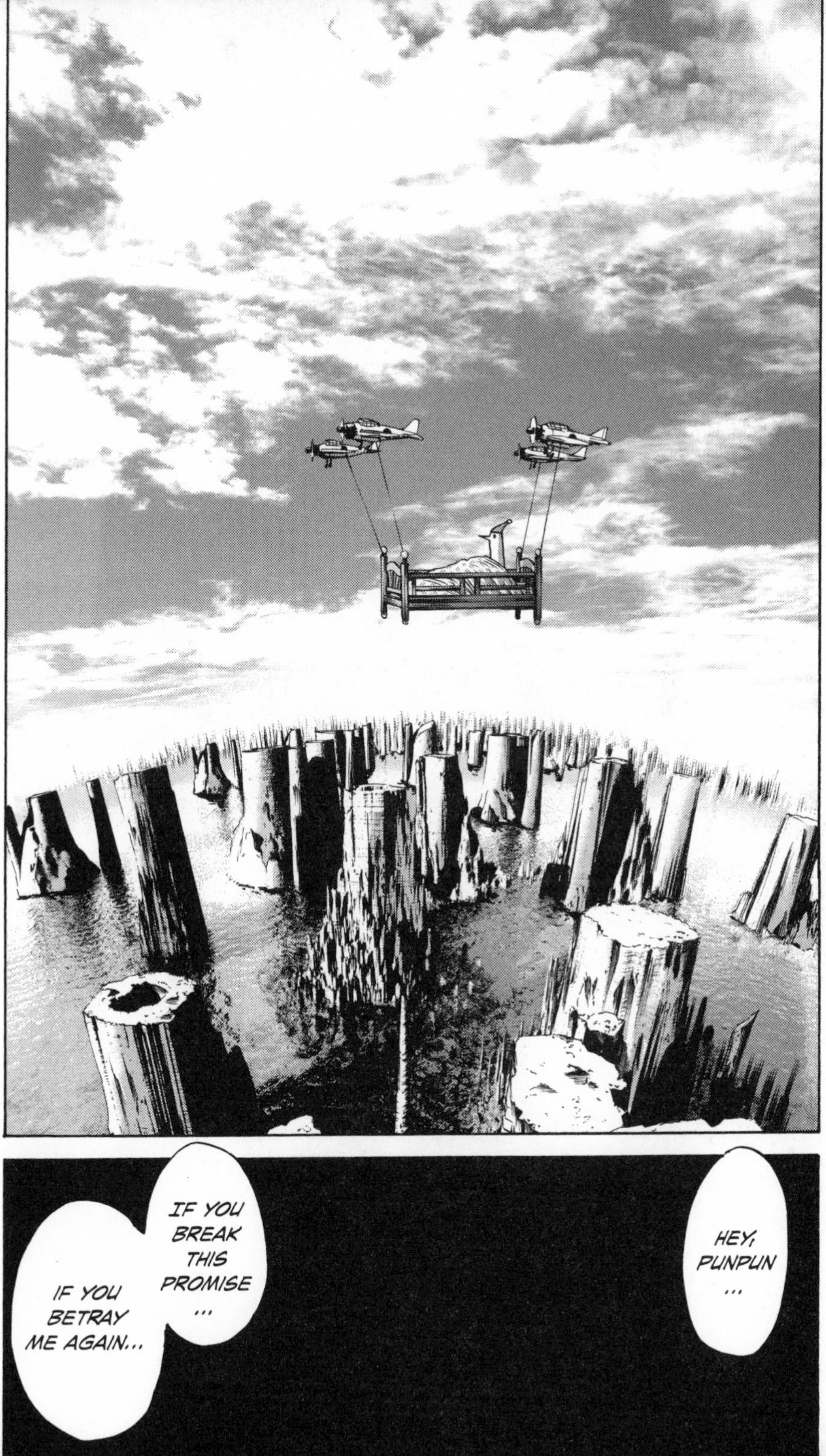
HEY, PUNPUN ...
IF YOU BREAK THIS PROMISE ...
IF YOU BETRAY ME AGAIN...

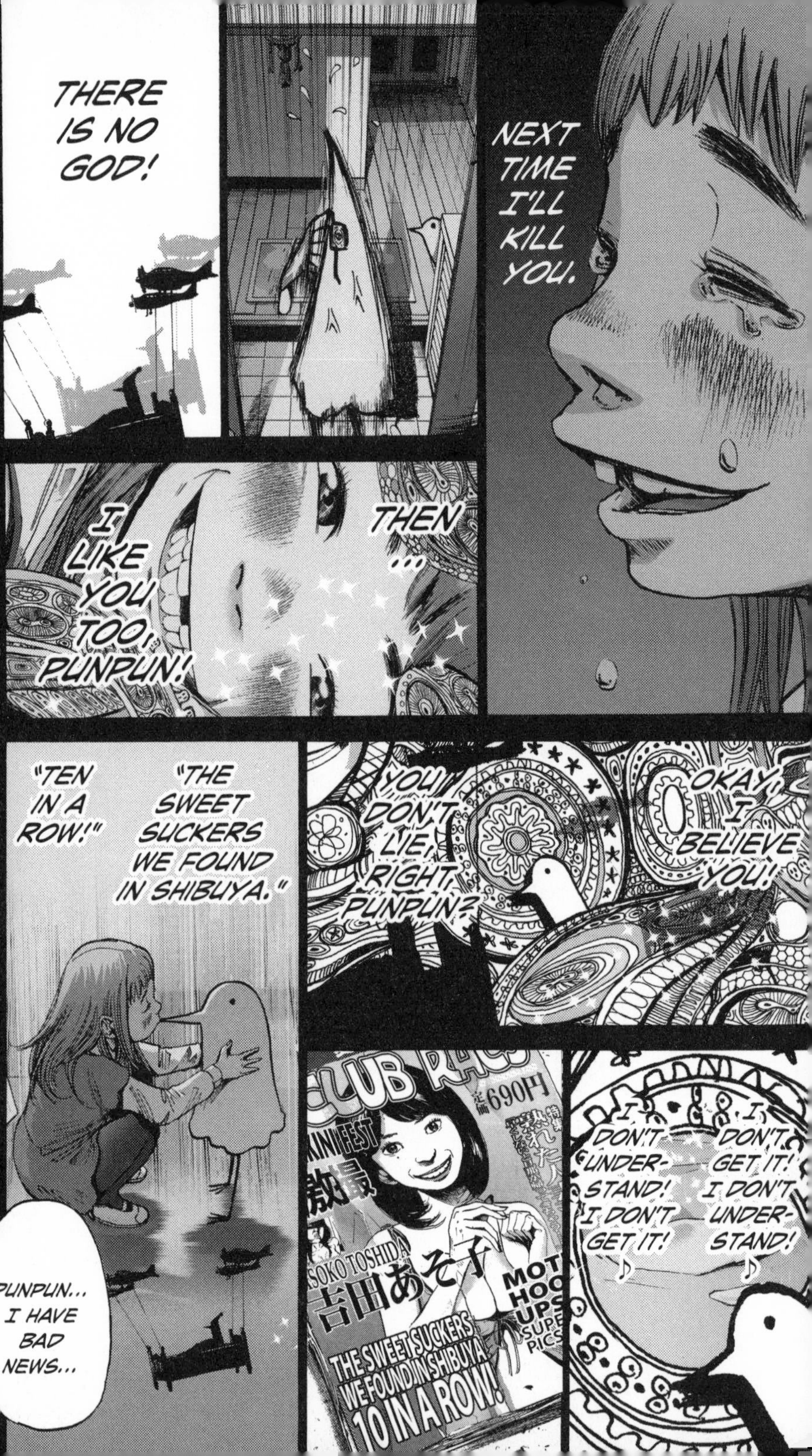
NEXT TIME I'LL KILL YOU.
THERE IS NO GOD!
THEN...
I LIKE YOU TOO, PUNPUN!
OKAY, I BELIEVE YOU!
YOU DON'T LIE, RIGHT, PUNPUN?
I DON'T GET IT! I DON'T UNDERSTAND! ♪
I DON'T UNDERSTAND! I DON'T GET IT! ♪
定価690円
吉田あそ子
THE SWEET SUCKERS WE FOUND IN SHIBUYA 10 IN A ROW!
"THE SWEET SUCKERS WE FOUND IN SHIBUYA."
"TEN IN A ROW!"
PUNPUN... I HAVE BAD NEWS...

WAS A BURGLAR.
PUNPUN ...
IT'S TRUE.
SOMEONE REALLY BROKE INTO OUR HOUSE.
YOU BELIEVE ME, DON'T YOU, PUNPUN?!

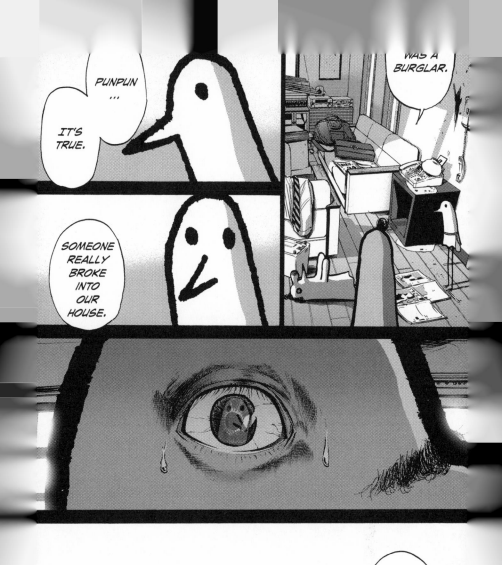

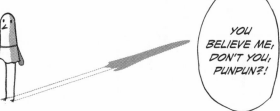

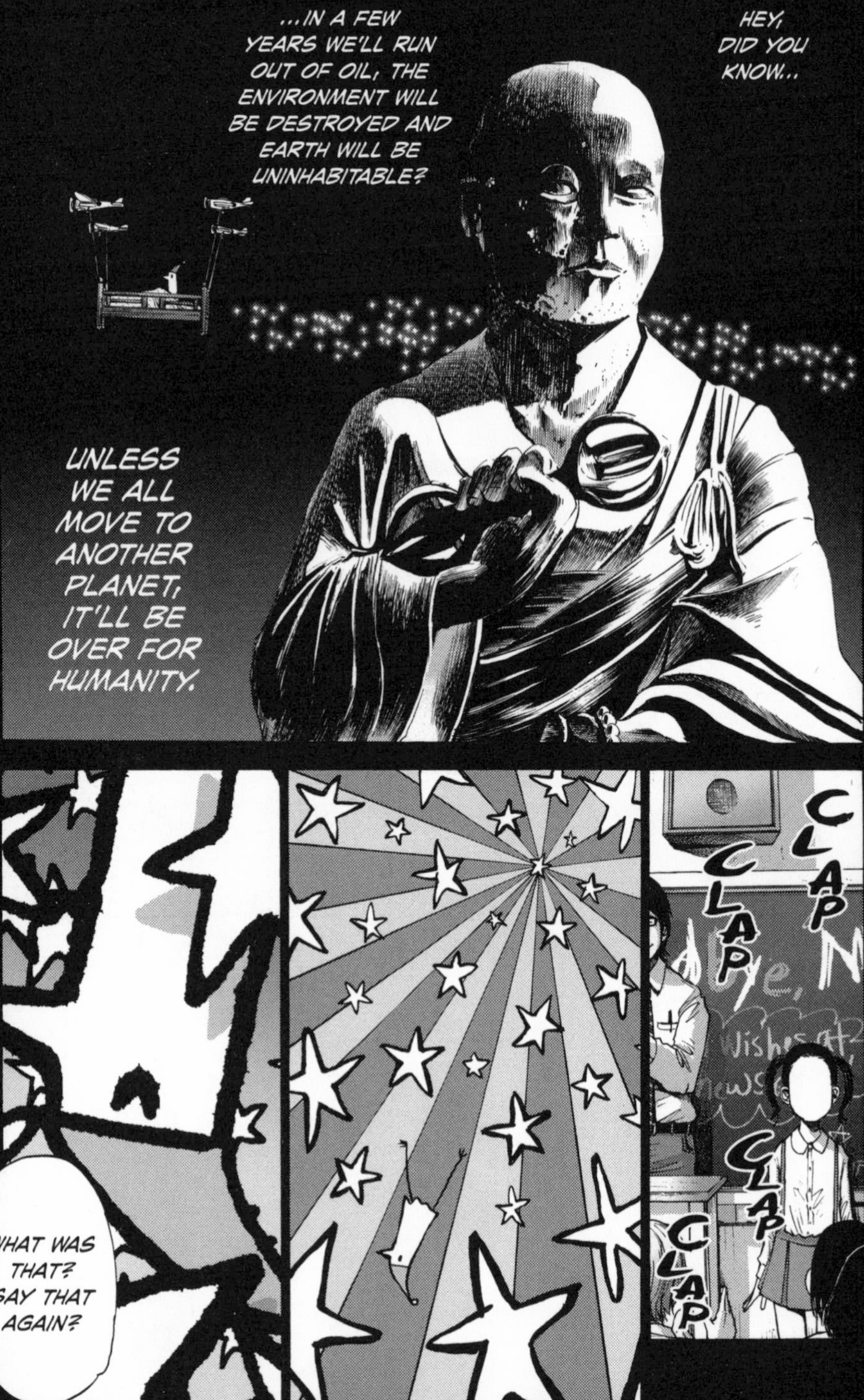
HEY, DID YOU KNOW...
...IN A FEW YEARS WE'LL RUN OUT OF OIL, THE ENVIRONMENT WILL BE DESTROYED AND EARTH WILL BE UNINHABITABLE?
UNLESS WE ALL MOVE TO ANOTHER PLANET, IT'LL BE OVER FOR HUMANITY.
CLAP
CLAP
CLAP
CLAP
WHAT WAS THAT? SAY THAT AGAIN?

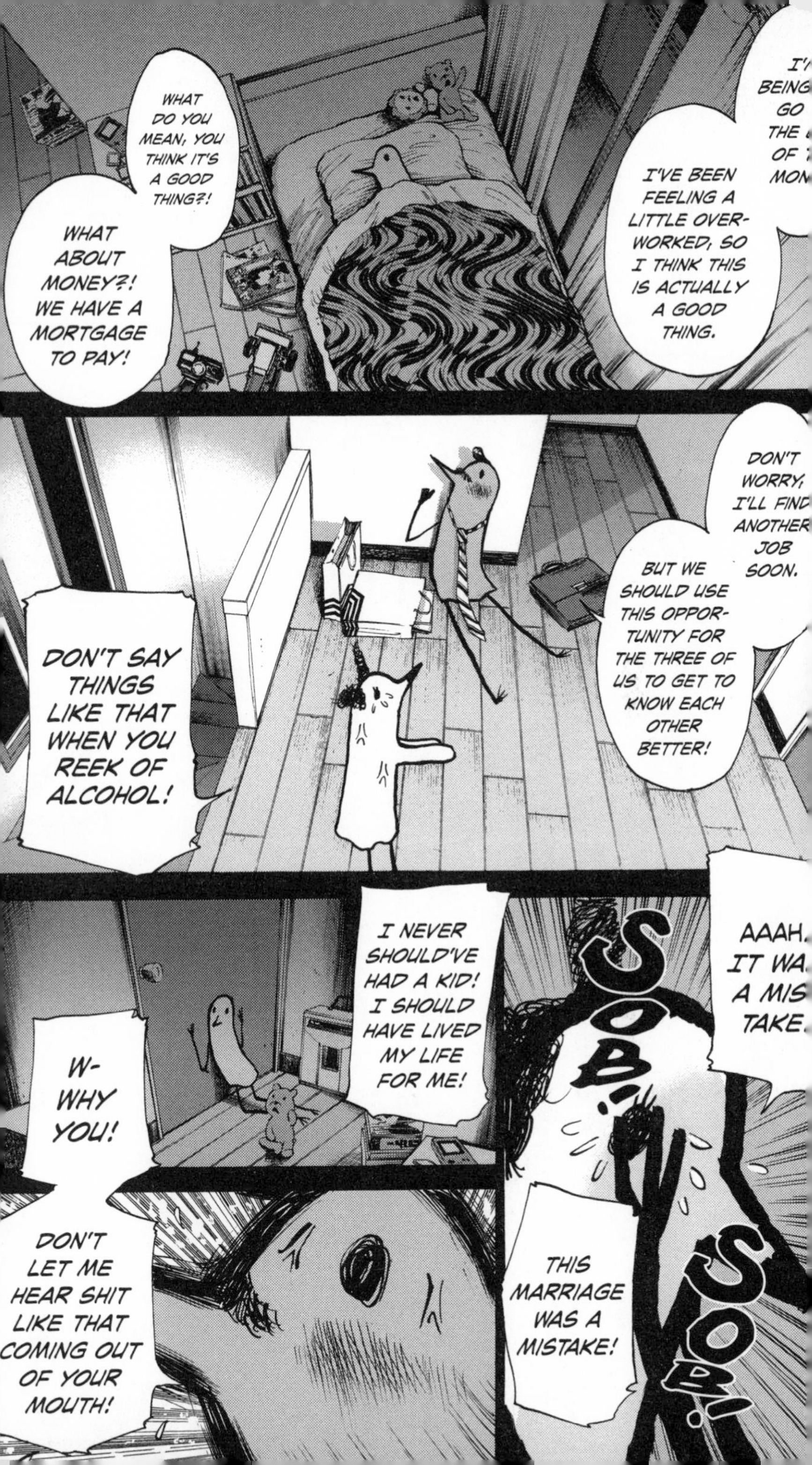
I'VE BEEN FEELING A LITTLE OVER-WORKED; SO I THINK THIS IS ACTUALLY A GOOD THING.
WHAT DO YOU MEAN, YOU THINK IT'S A GOOD THING?!
WHAT ABOUT MONEY?! WE HAVE A MORTGAGE TO PAY!
DON'T WORRY; I'LL FIND ANOTHER JOB SOON.
BUT WE SHOULD USE THIS OPPORTUNITY FOR THE THREE OF US TO GET TO KNOW EACH OTHER BETTER!
DON'T SAY THINGS LIKE THAT WHEN YOU REEK OF ALCOHOL!
SOB!!
SOB!
THIS MARRIAGE WAS A MISTAKE!
I NEVER SHOULD'VE HAD A KID! I SHOULD HAVE LIVED MY LIFE FOR ME!
W-WHY YOU!
DON'T LET ME HEAR SHIT LIKE THAT COMING OUT OF YOUR MOUTH!

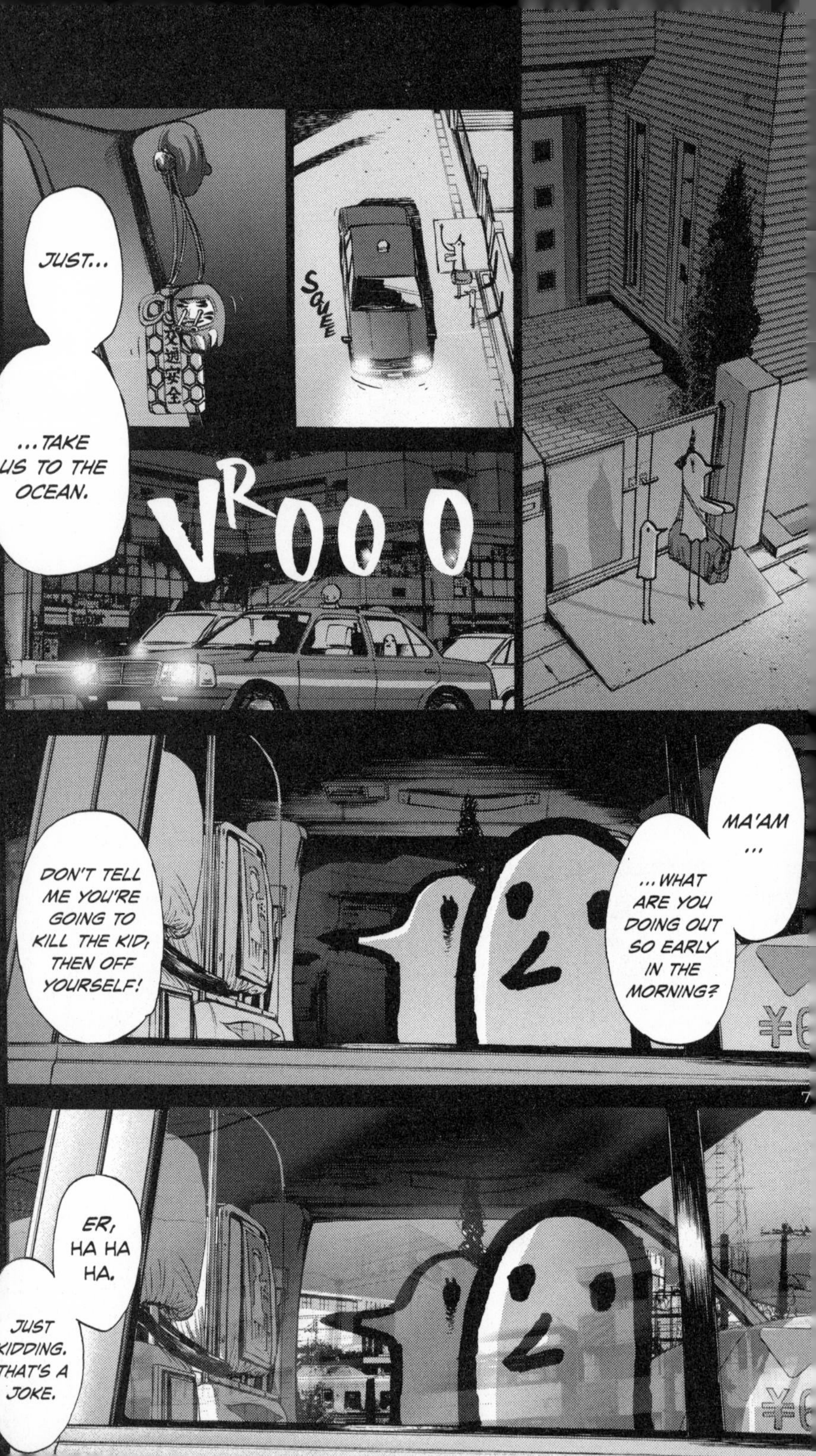
SQUEE
JUST...
...TAKE US TO THE OCEAN.
VROOO
MA'AM...
...WHAT ARE YOU DOING OUT SO EARLY IN THE MORNING?
DON'T TELL ME YOU'RE GOING TO KILL THE KID, THEN OFF YOURSELF!
ER, HA HA HA.
JUST KIDDING. THAT'S A JOKE.

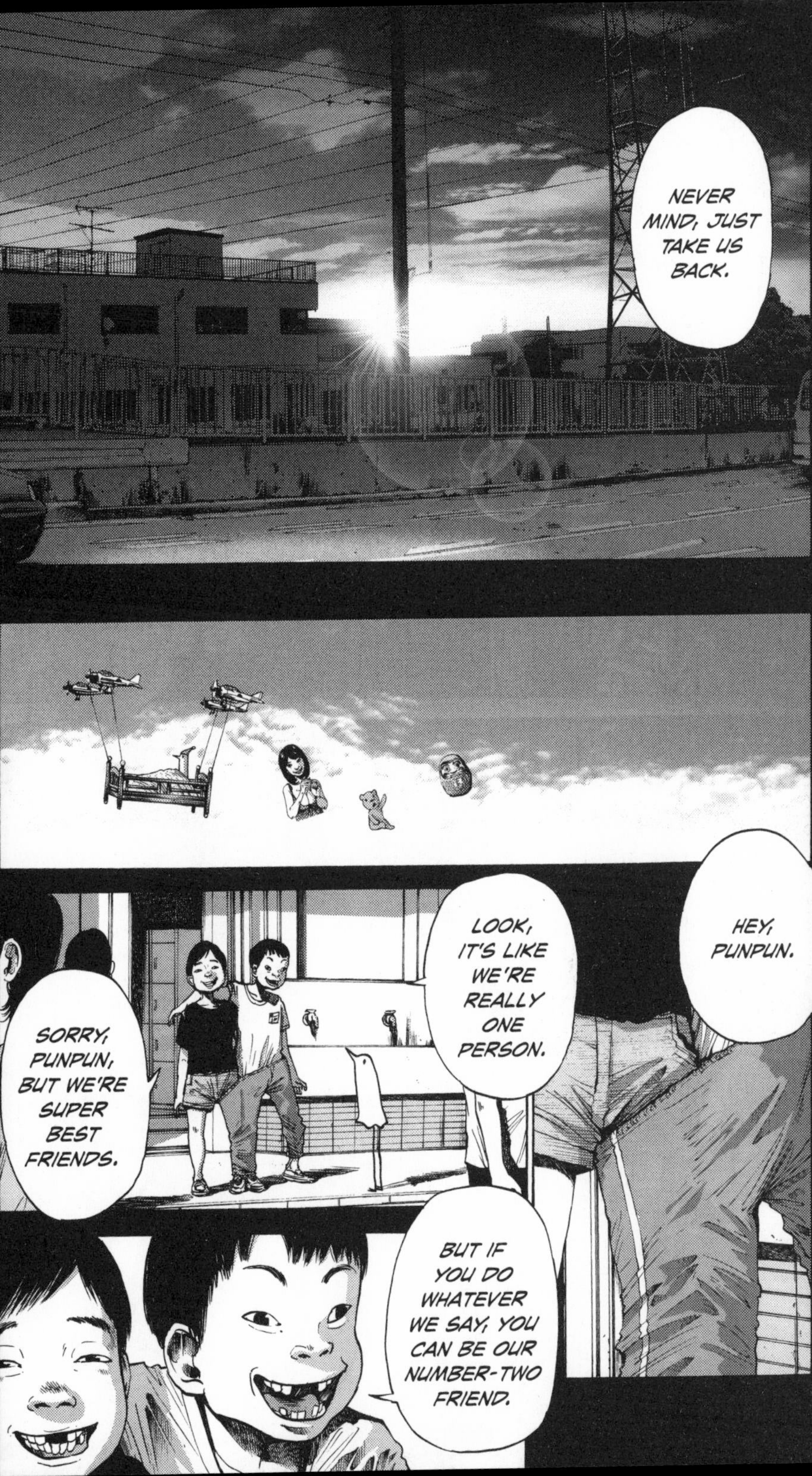
NEVER MIND, JUST TAKE US BACK.
HEY, PUNPUN.
LOOK, IT'S LIKE WE'RE REALLY ONE PERSON.
SORRY, PUNPUN, BUT WE'RE SUPER BEST FRIENDS.
BUT IF YOU DO WHATEVER WE SAY, YOU CAN BE OUR NUMBER-TWO FRIEND.

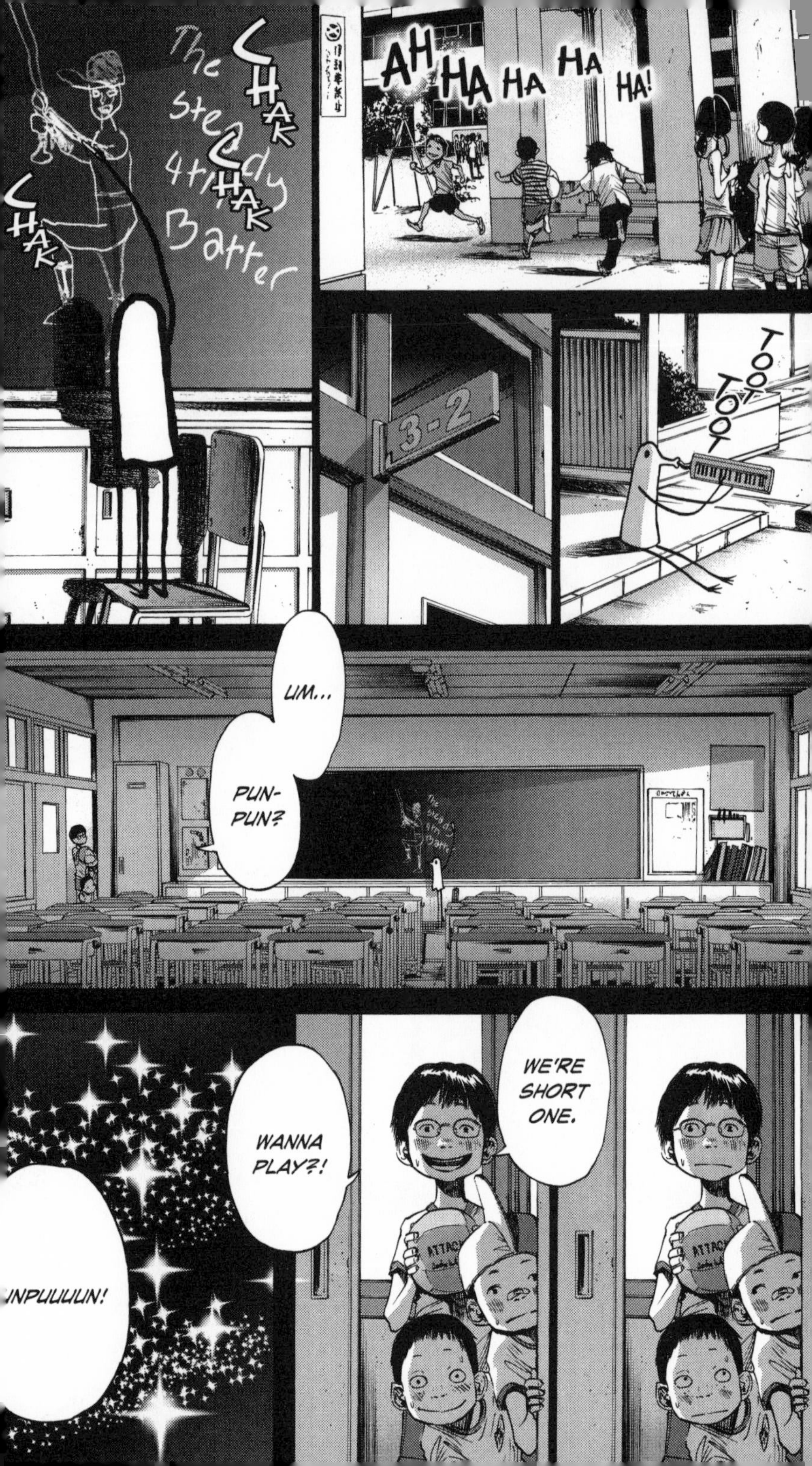
AH HA HA HA HA HA!
TOOT TOOT TOOT
3-2
CHAK CHAK CHAK
The steady 4th Batter
UM...
PUN-PUN?
WE'RE SHORT ONE.
WANNA PLAY?!
UNPUUUUN!

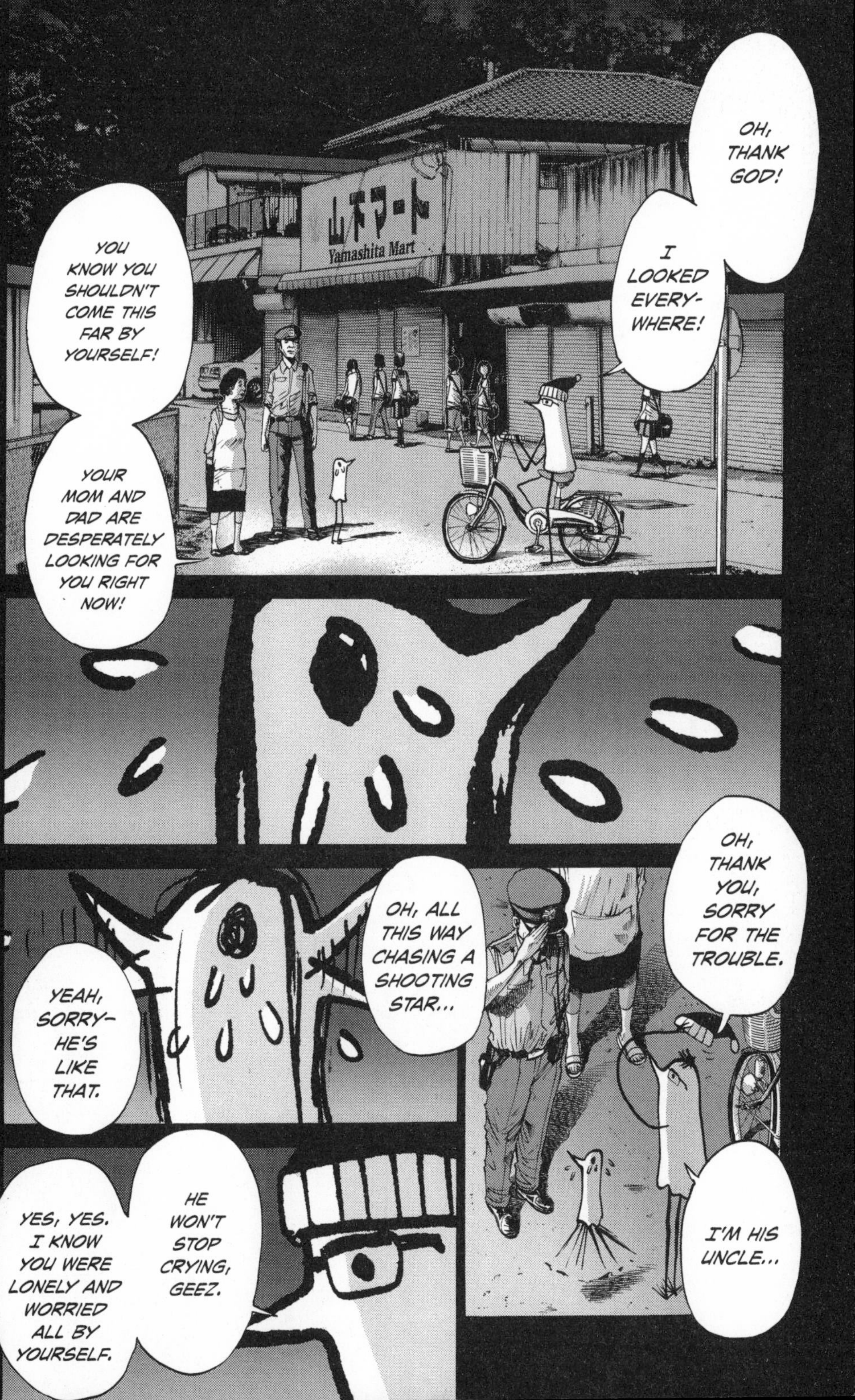
OH, THANK GOD!
I LOOKED EVERY-WHERE!
Yamashita Mart
YOU KNOW YOU SHOULDN'T COME THIS FAR BY YOURSELF!
YOUR MOM AND DAD ARE DESPERATELY LOOKING FOR YOU RIGHT NOW!
OH, THANK YOU, SORRY FOR THE TROUBLE.
OH, ALL THIS WAY CHASING A SHOOTING STAR...
I'M HIS UNCLE...
YEAH, SORRY— HE'S LIKE THAT.
HE WON'T STOP CRYING, GEEZ.
YES, YES. I KNOW YOU WERE LONELY AND WORRIED ALL BY YOURSELF.

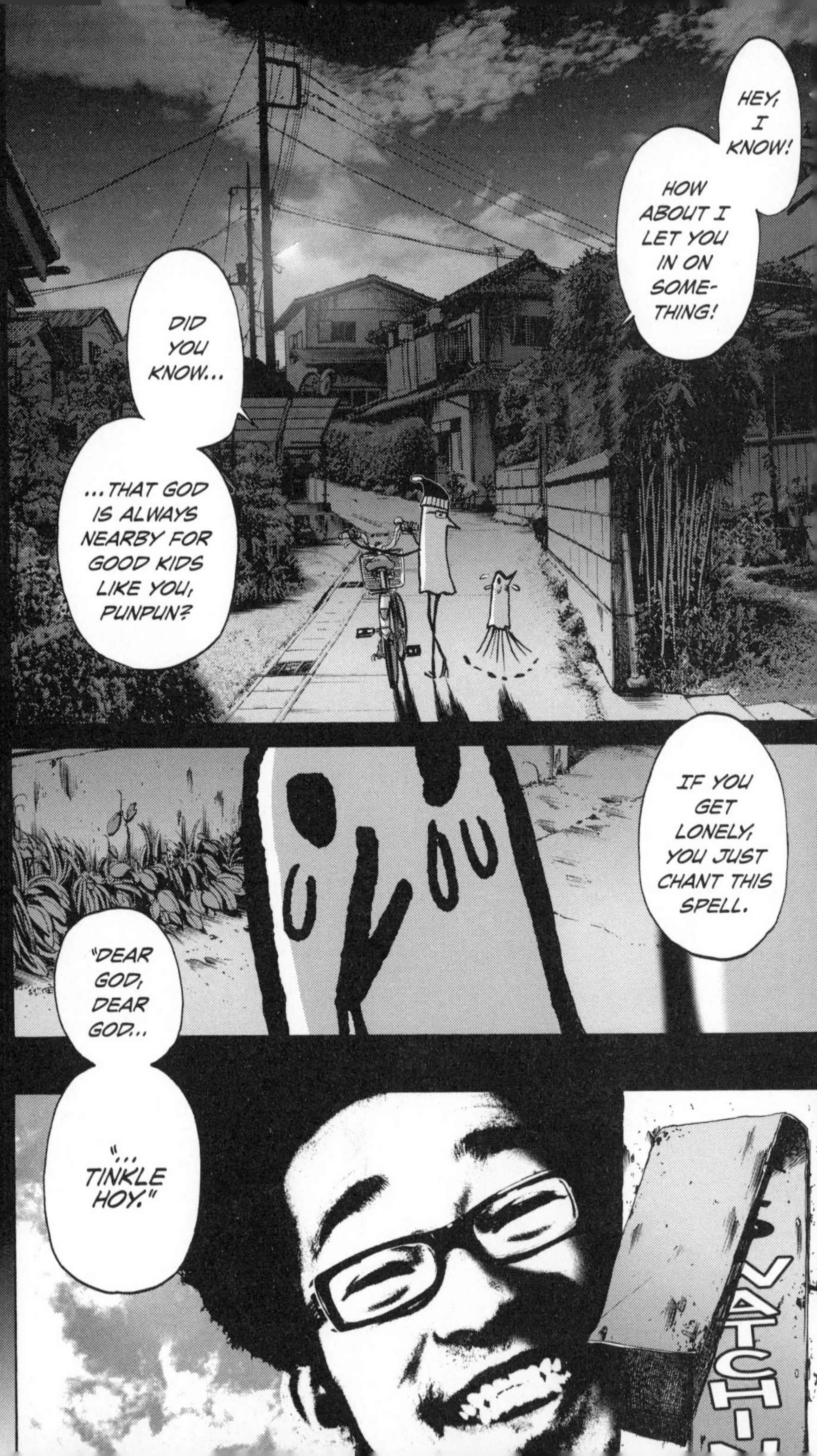
HEY, I KNOW!
HOW ABOUT I LET YOU IN ON SOME-THING!
DID YOU KNOW...
...THAT GOD IS ALWAYS NEARBY FOR GOOD KIDS LIKE YOU, PUNPUN?
IF YOU GET LONELY, YOU JUST CHANT THIS SPELL.
"DEAR GOD, DEAR GOD...
"... TINKLE HOY."
VATCHI

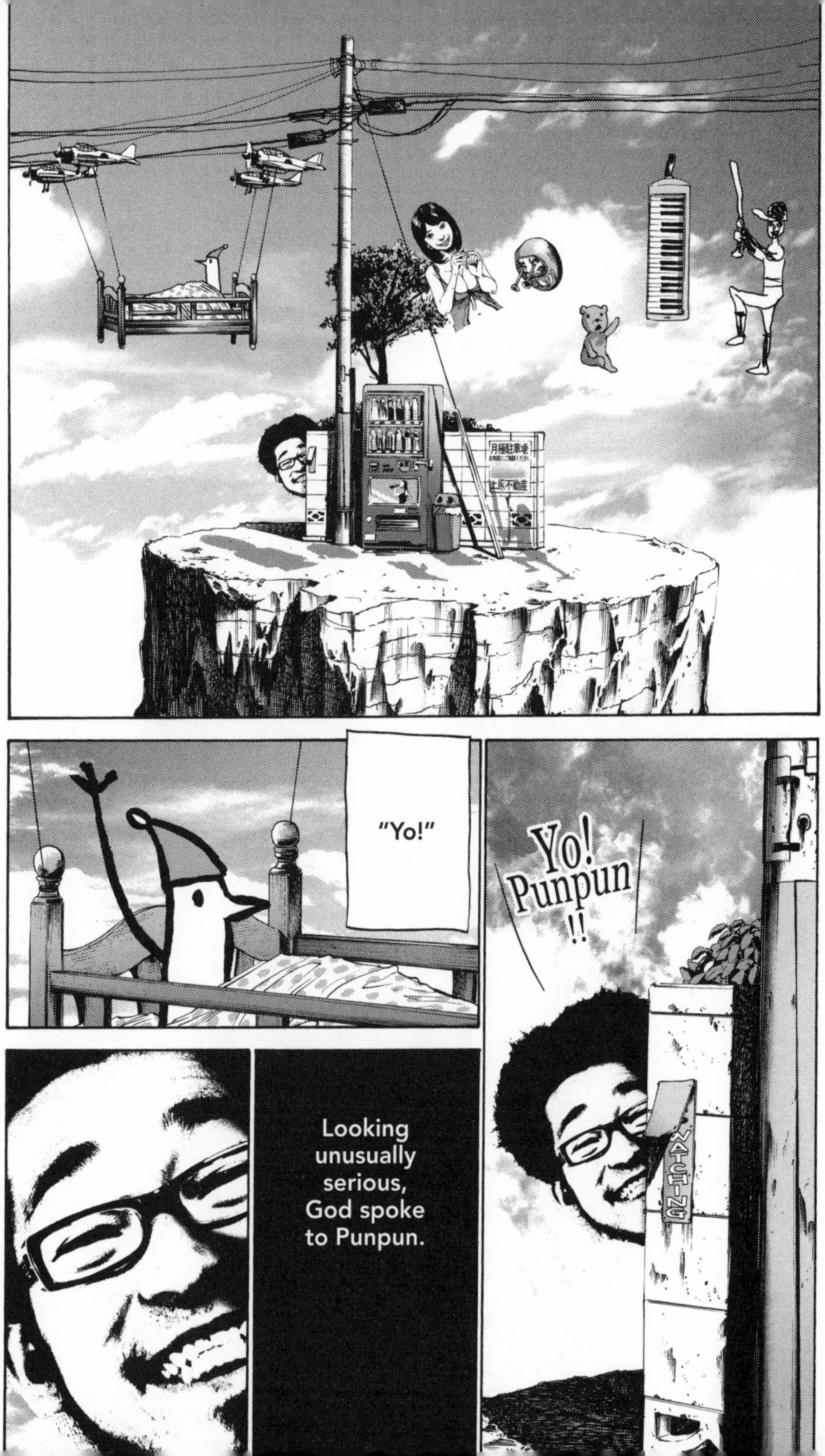

Yo! Punpun!!
WATCHING
"Yo!"
Looking unusually serious, God spoke to Punpun.

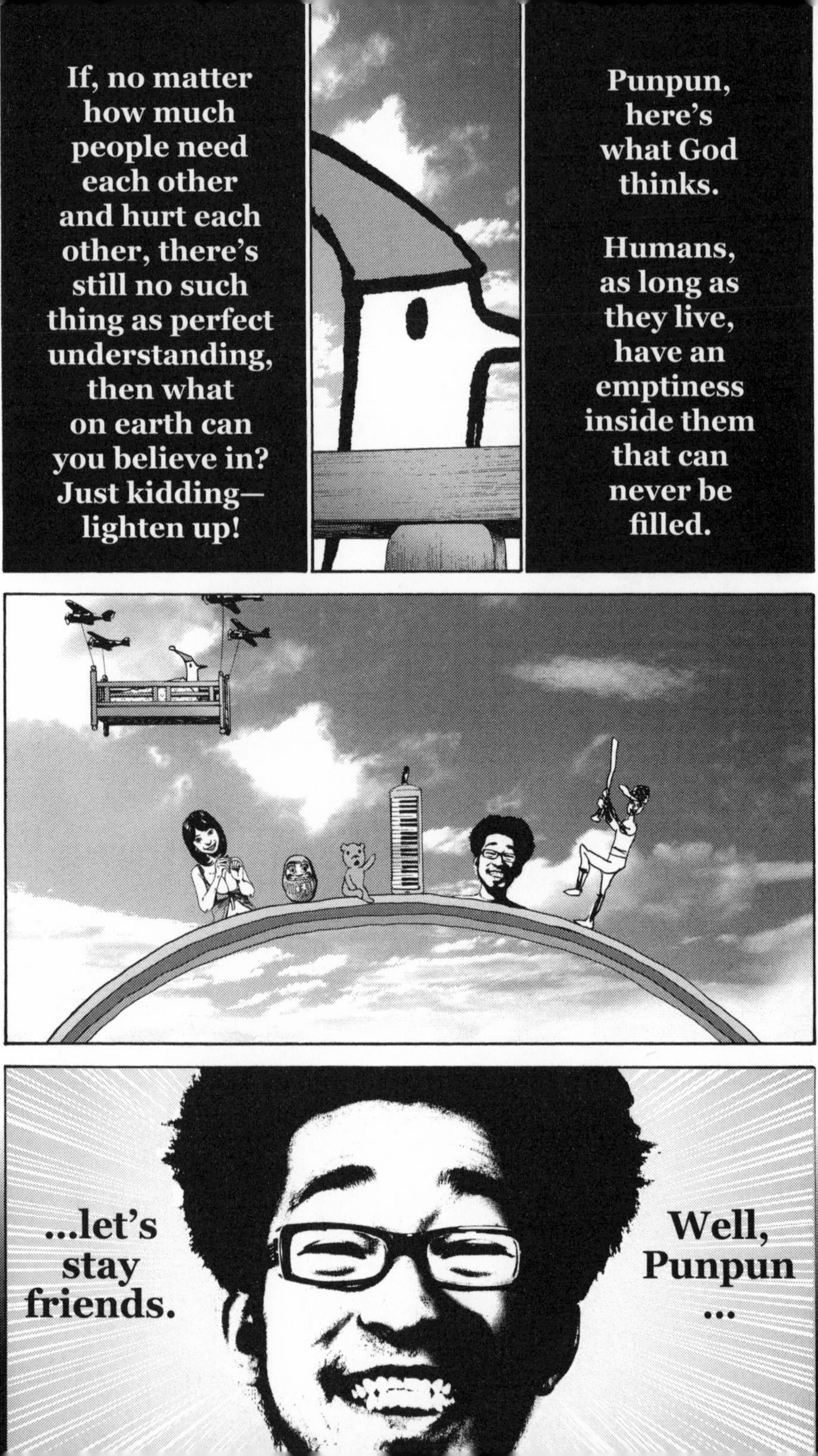
Punpun, here's what God thinks.
Humans, as long as they live, have an emptiness inside them that can never be filled.
If, no matter how much people need each other and hurt each other, there's still no such thing as perfect understanding, then what on earth can you believe in? Just kidding—lighten up!
Well, Punpun ...
...let's stay friends.

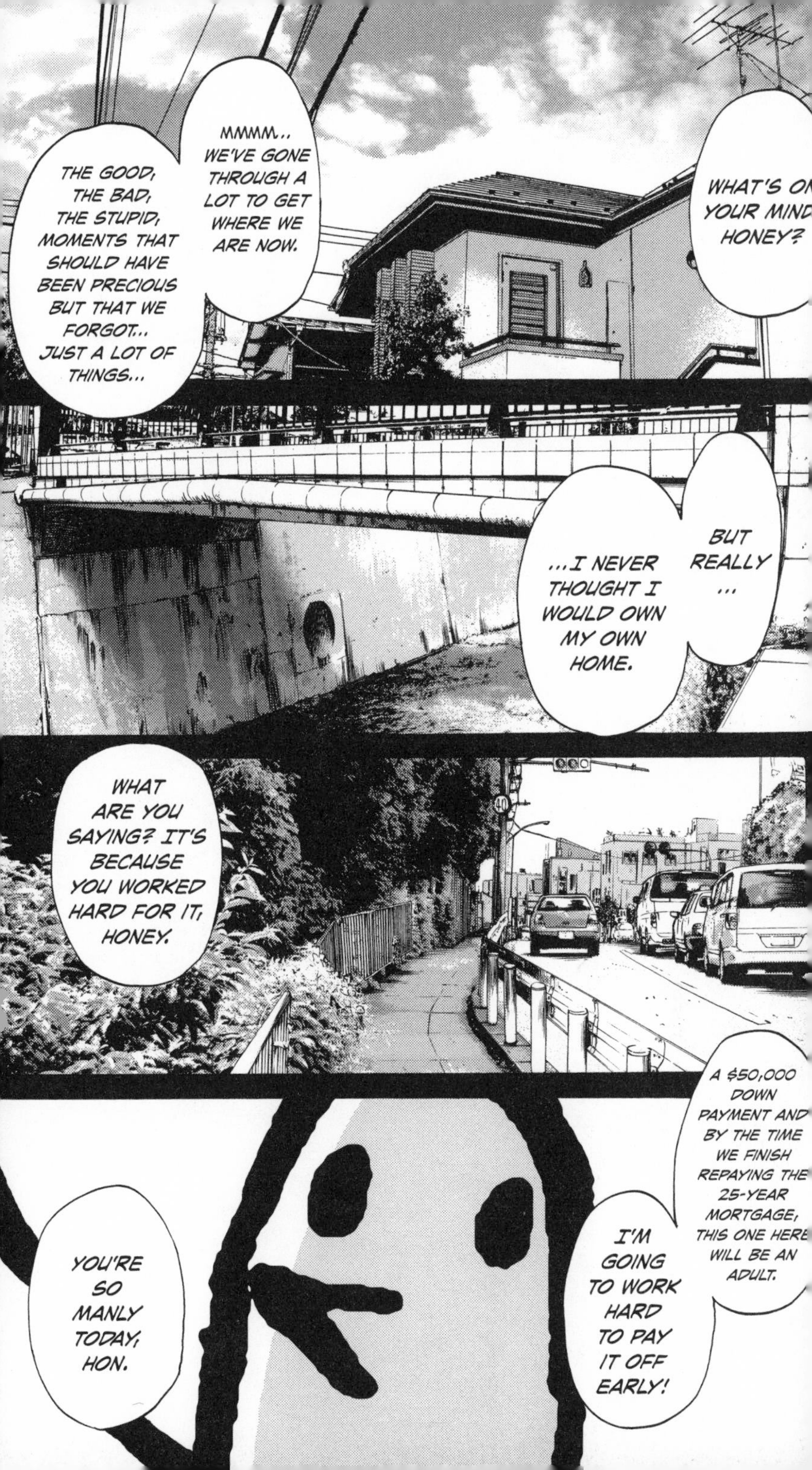
WHAT'S ON YOUR MIND HONEY?
MMMM... WE'VE GONE THROUGH A LOT TO GET WHERE WE ARE NOW.
THE GOOD, THE BAD, THE STUPID, MOMENTS THAT SHOULD HAVE BEEN PRECIOUS BUT THAT WE FORGOT... JUST A LOT OF THINGS...
BUT REALLY ...
...I NEVER THOUGHT I WOULD OWN MY OWN HOME.
WHAT ARE YOU SAYING? IT'S BECAUSE YOU WORKED HARD FOR IT, HONEY.
A $50,000 DOWN PAYMENT AND BY THE TIME WE FINISH REPAYING THE 25-YEAR MORTGAGE, THIS ONE HERE WILL BE AN ADULT.
I'M GOING TO WORK HARD TO PAY IT OFF EARLY!
YOU'RE SO MANLY TODAY, HON.

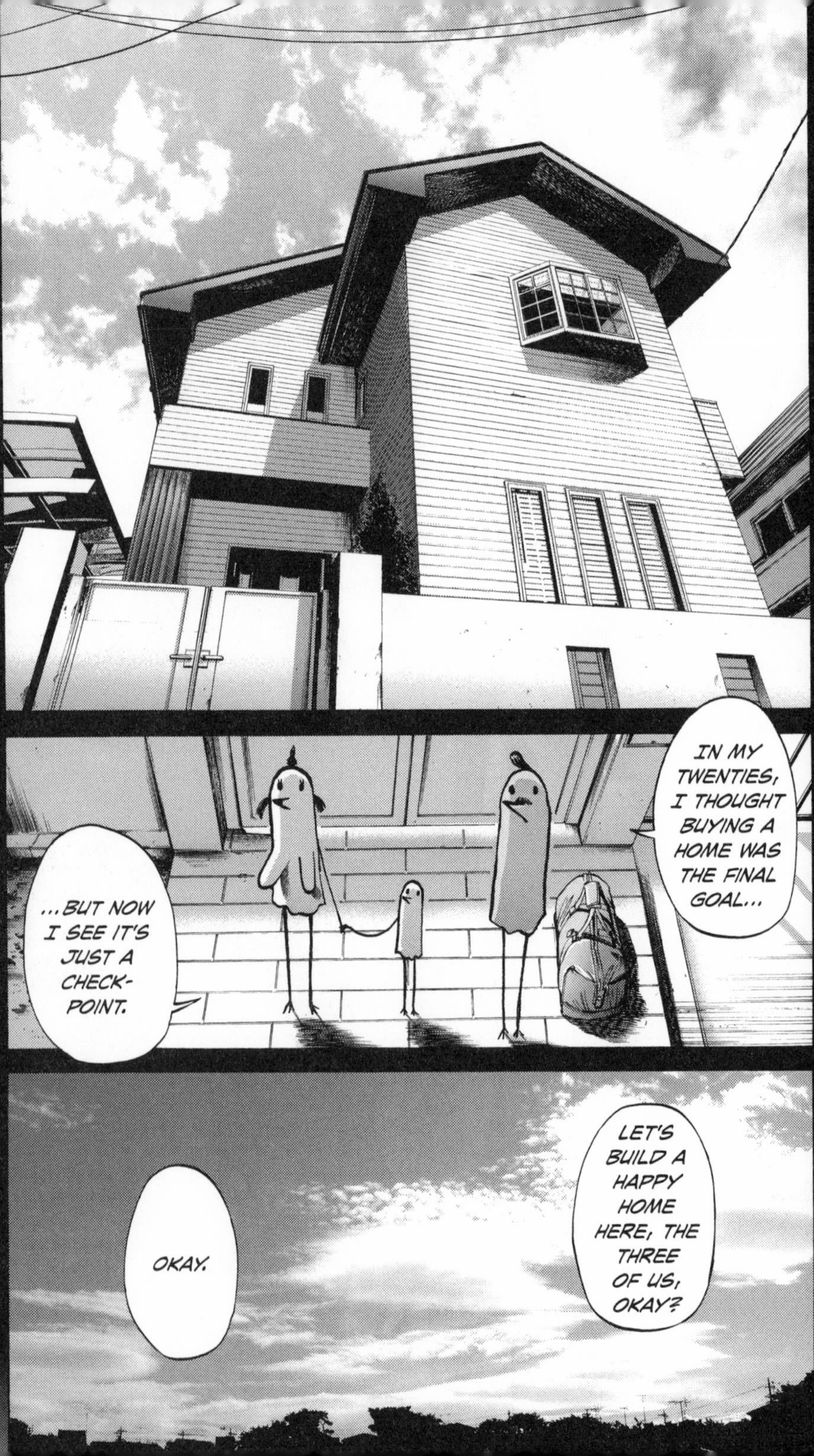
IN MY TWENTIES, I THOUGHT BUYING A HOME WAS THE FINAL GOAL...
...BUT NOW I SEE IT'S JUST A CHECK-POINT.
LET'S BUILD A HAPPY HOME HERE, THE THREE OF US, OKAY?
OKAY.

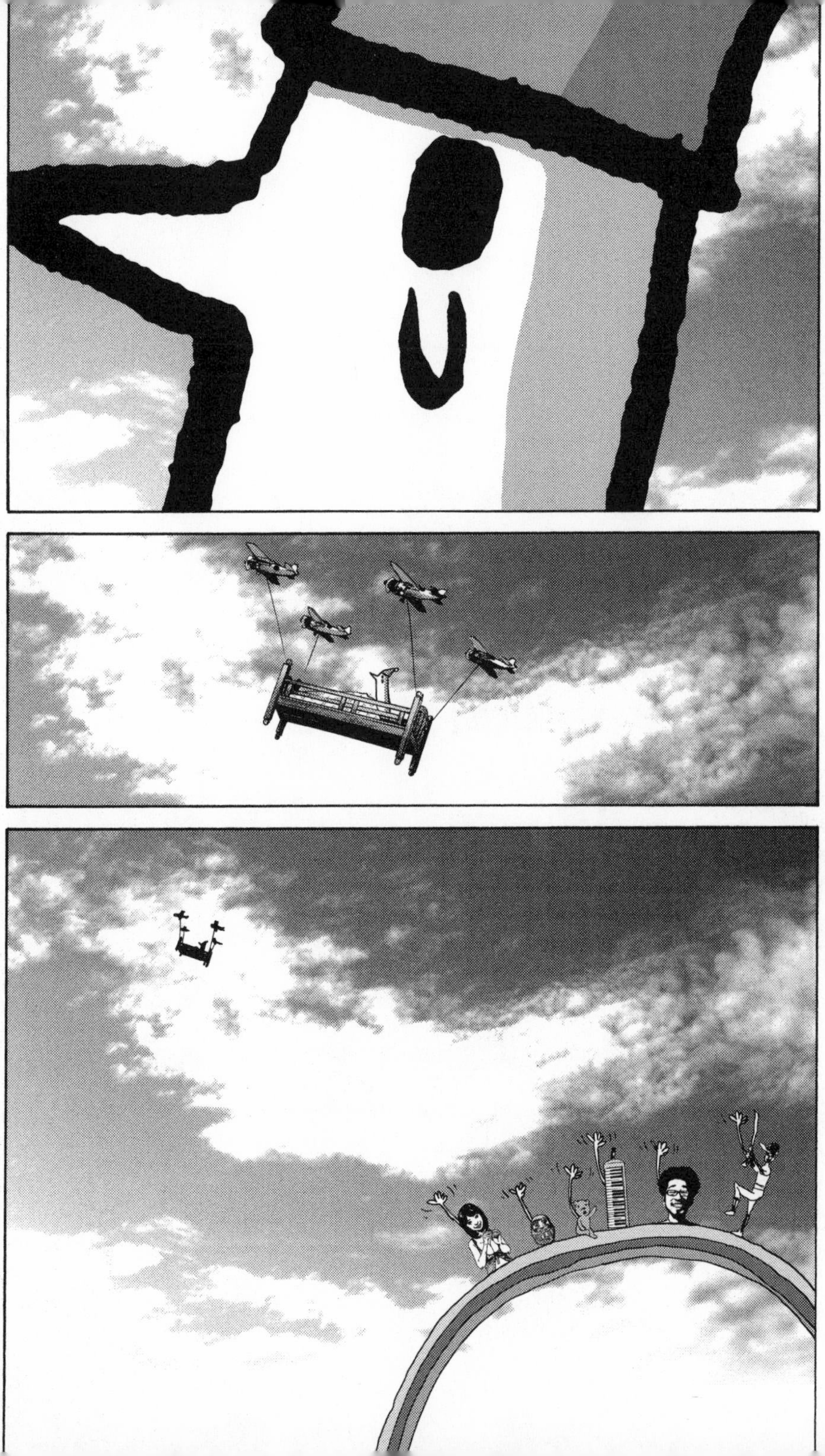

Chapter 17

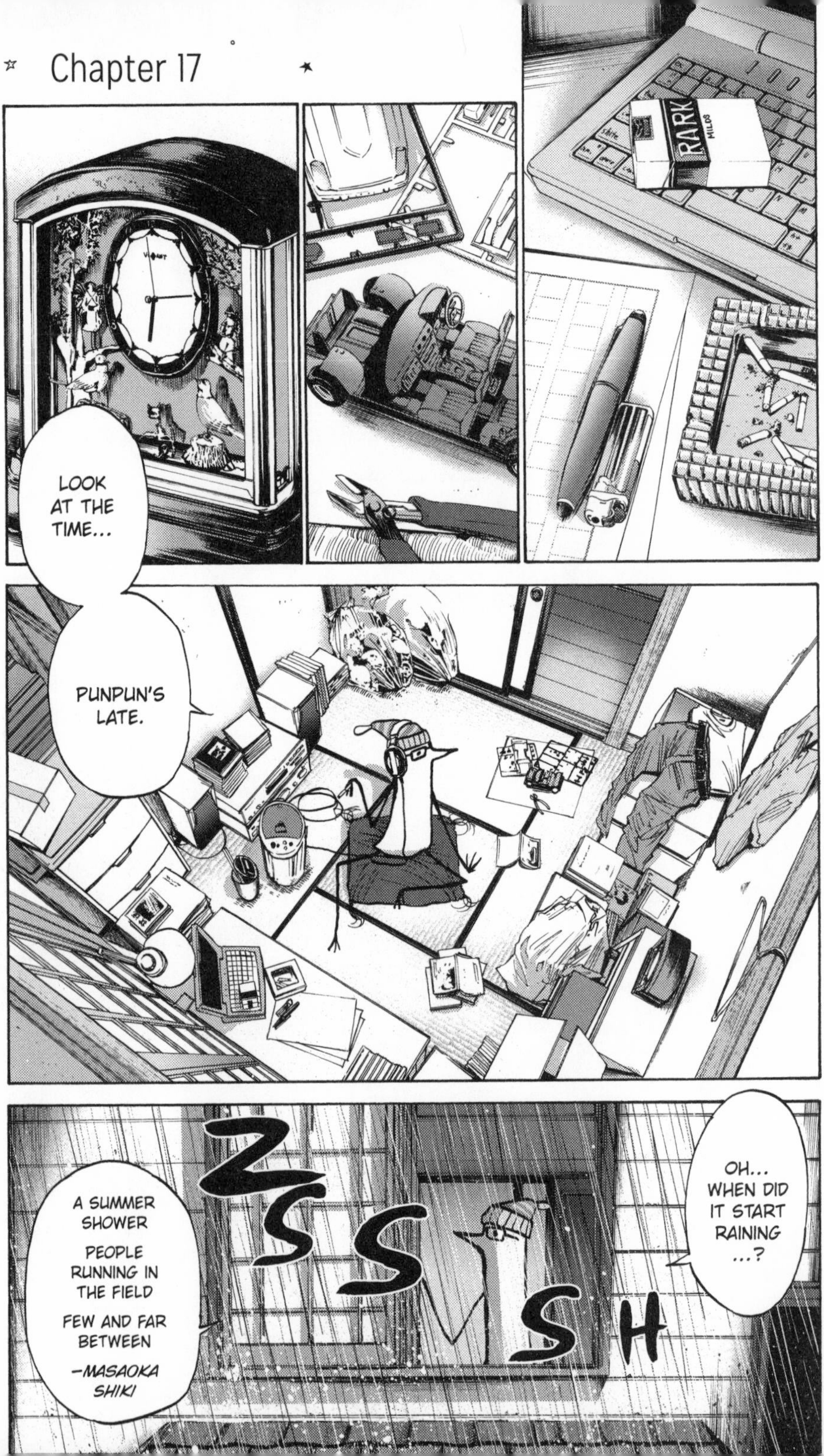
RARK
MILOS
LOOK AT THE TIME...
PUNPUN'S LATE.
OH... WHEN DID IT START RAINING ...?
ZSSSH
A SUMMER SHOWER
PEOPLE RUNNING IN THE FIELD
FEW AND FAR BETWEEN
—MASAOKA SHIKI

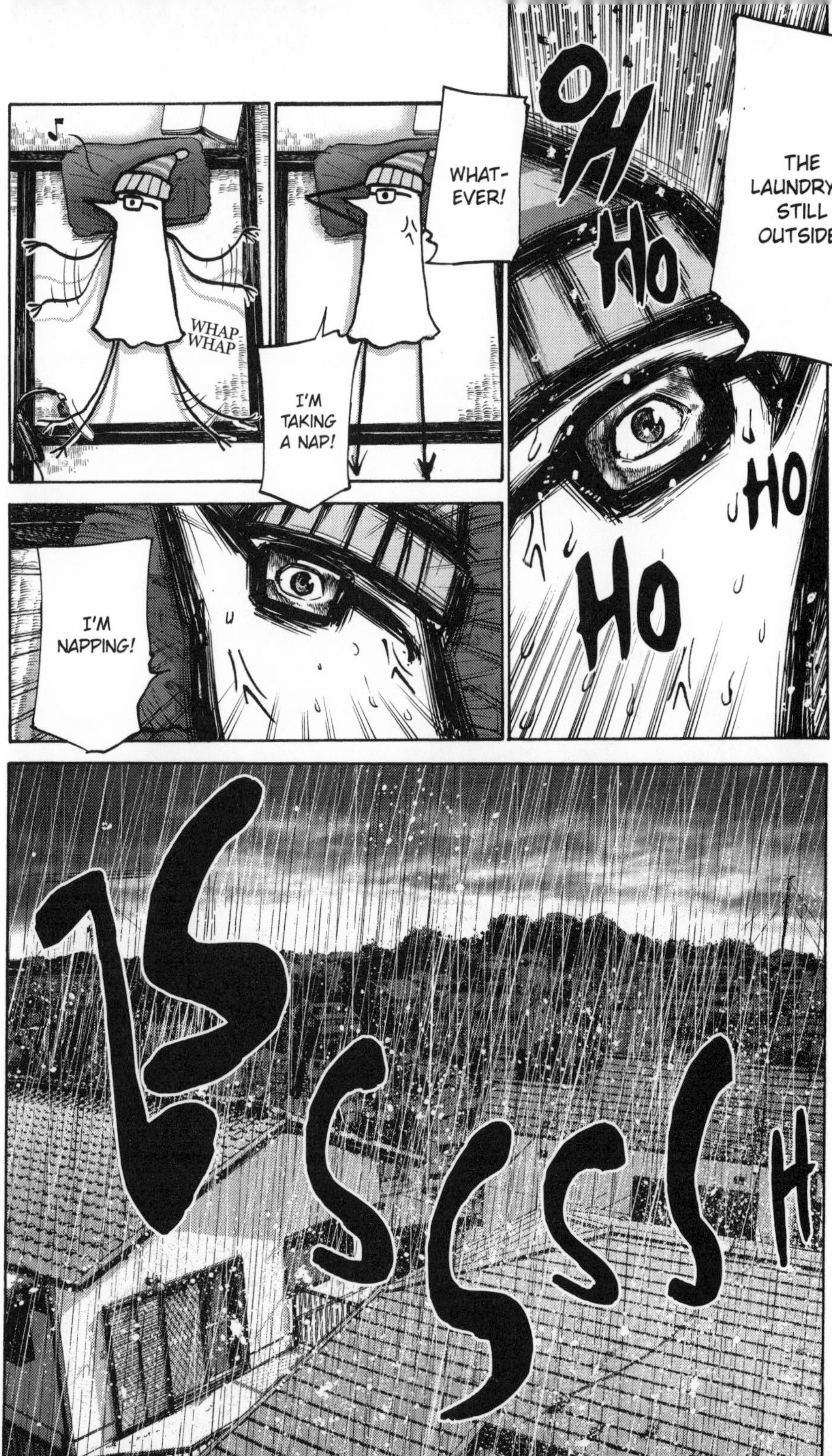
THE LAUNDRY'S STILL OUTSIDE!
OH HO HO HO
WHAT-EVER!
I'M TAKING A NAP!
WHAP WHAP
I'M NAPPING!
SSSSSH

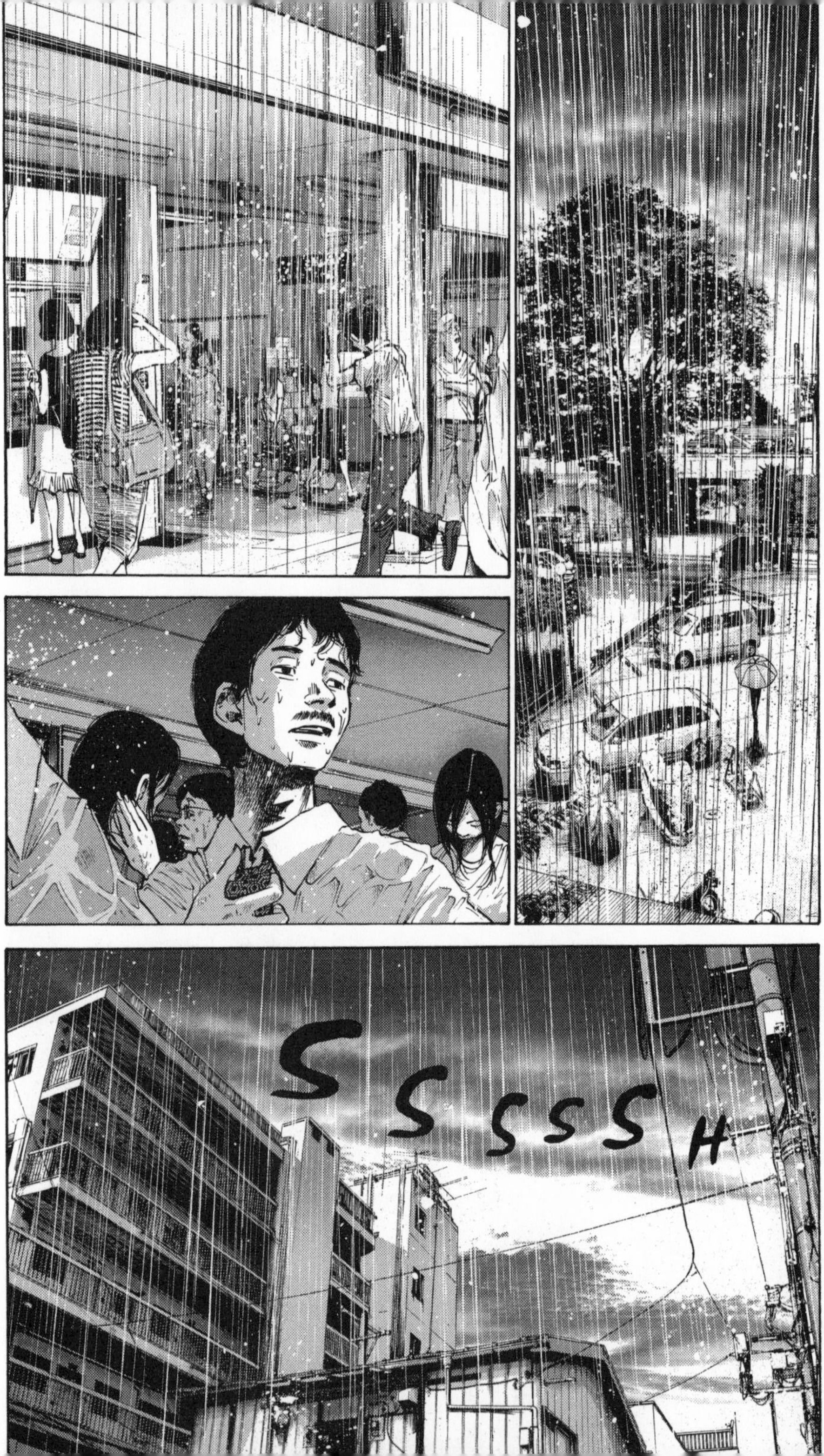
SSSSSH

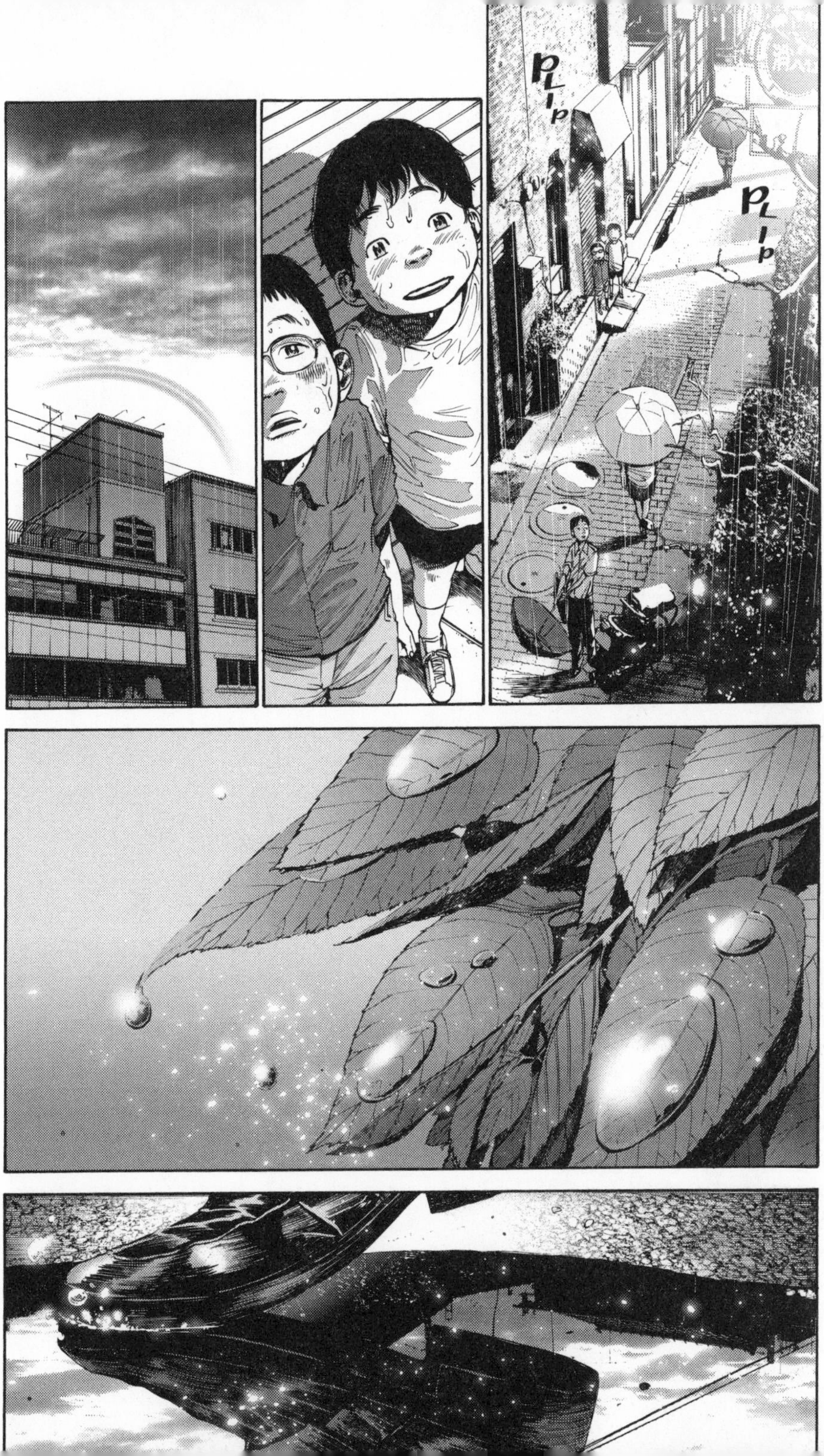
PLIP
PLIP

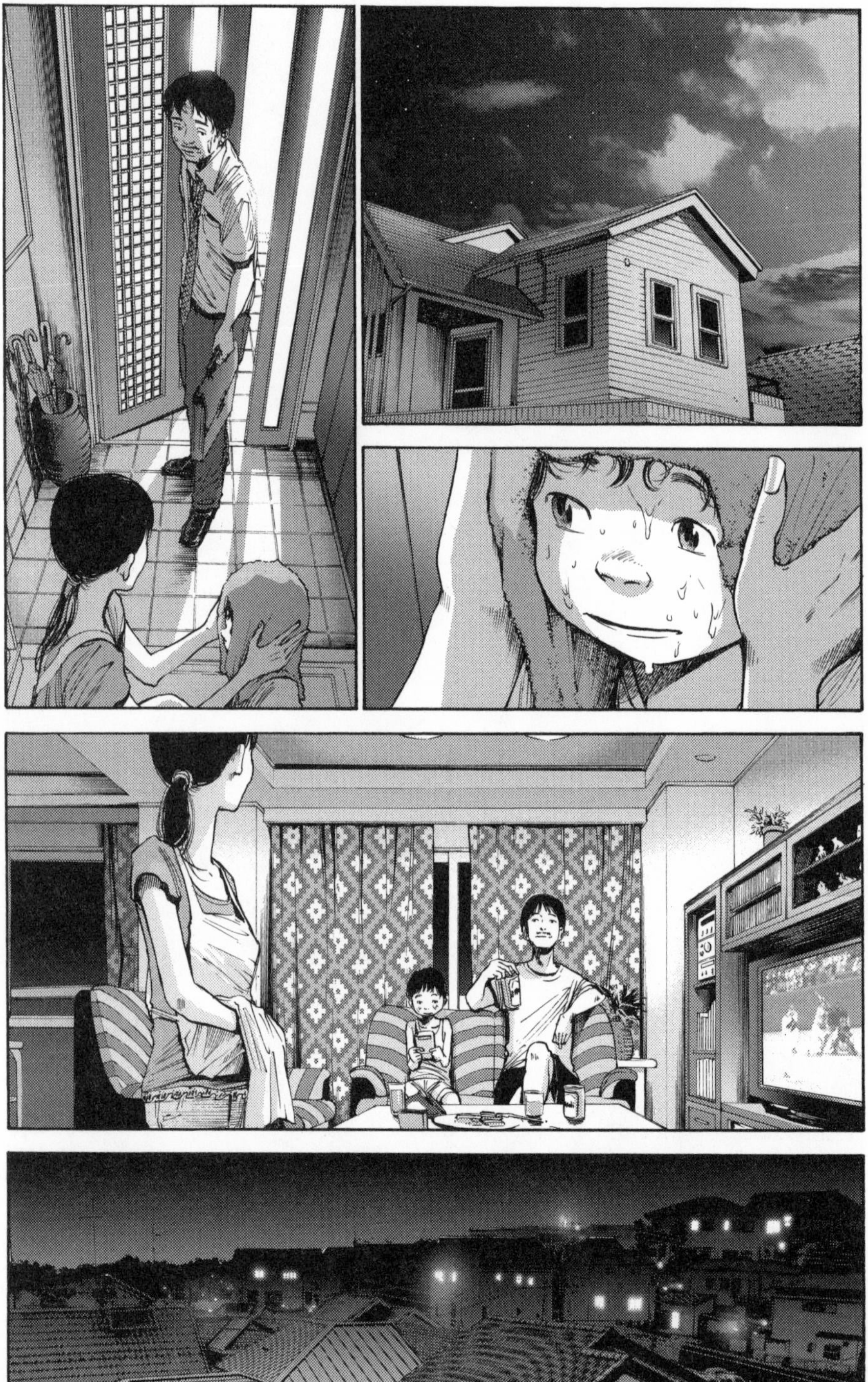

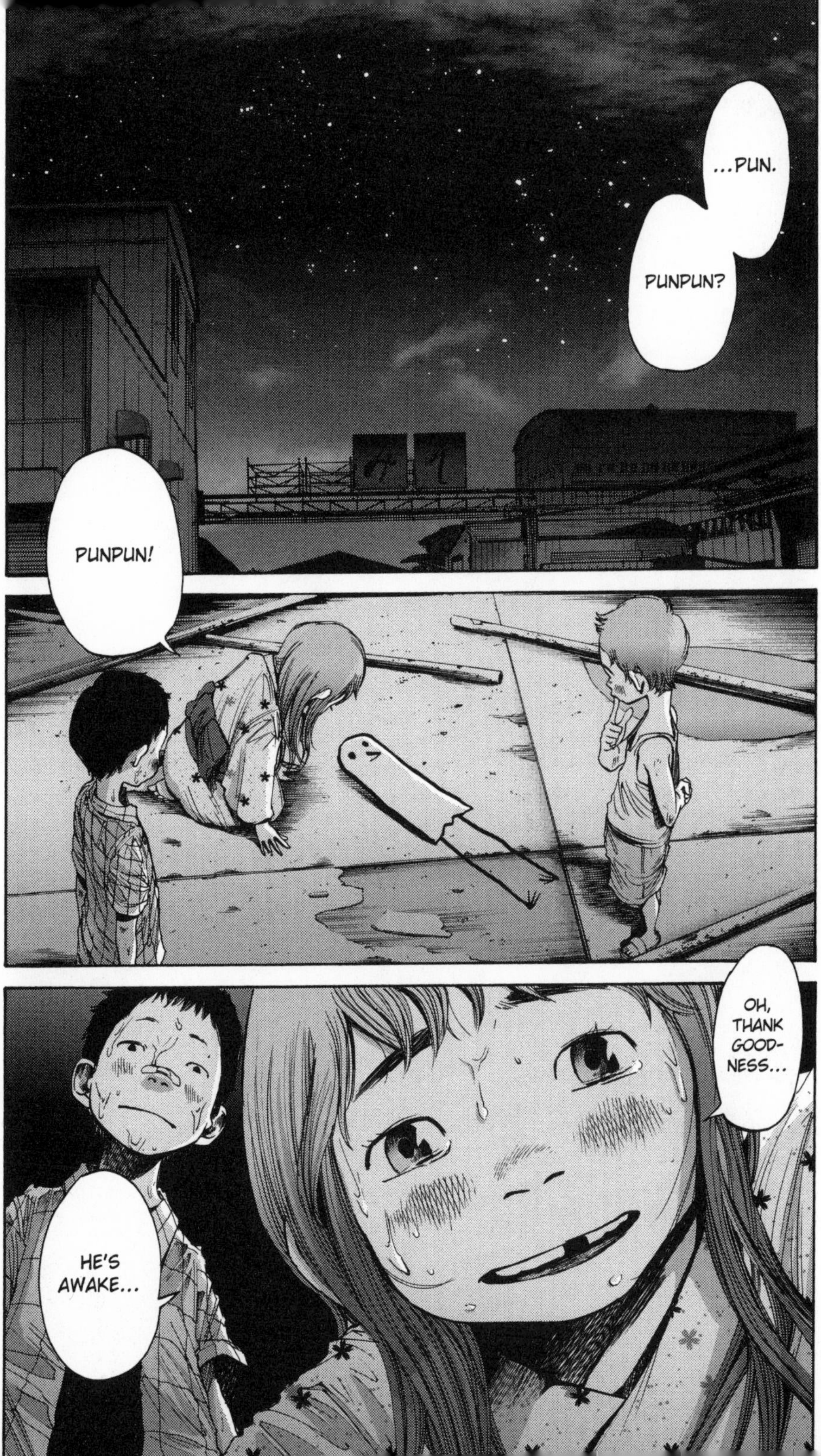
...PUN.
PUNPUN?
PUNPUN!
OH, THANK GOOD-NESS...
HE'S AWAKE...

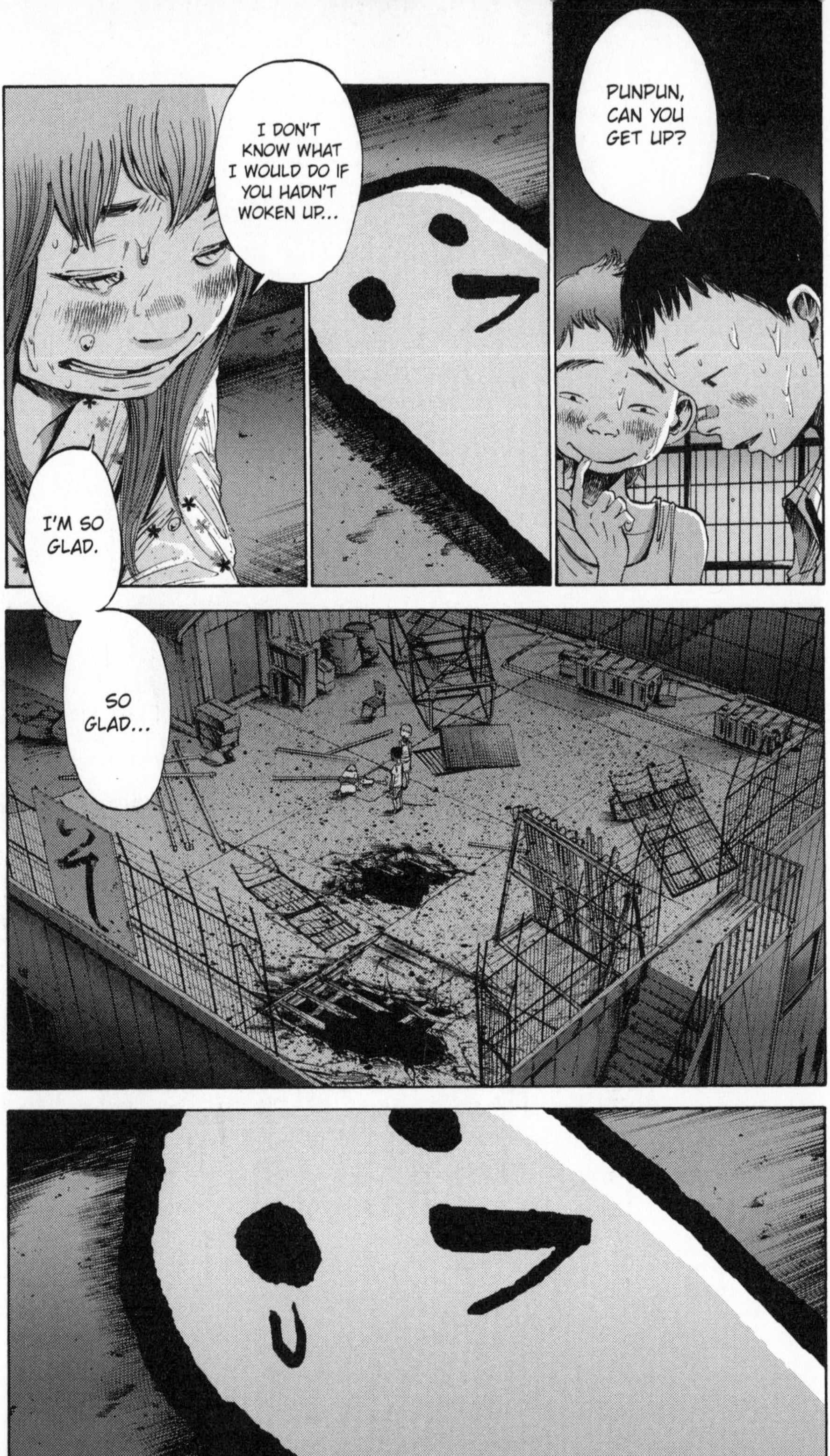
PUNPUN, CAN YOU GET UP?
I DON'T KNOW WHAT I WOULD DO IF YOU HADN'T WOKEN UP...
I'M SO GLAD.
SO GLAD...

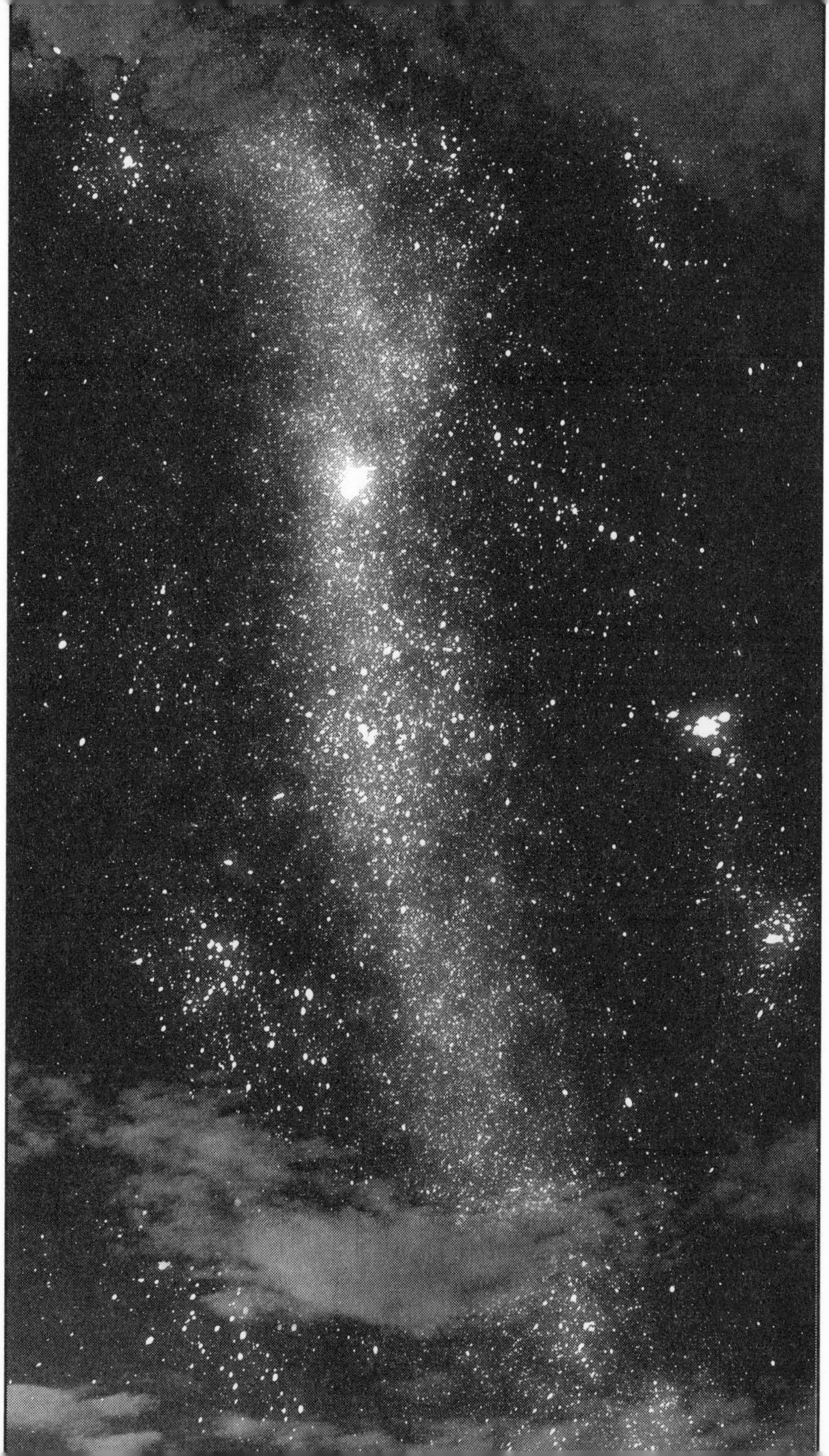

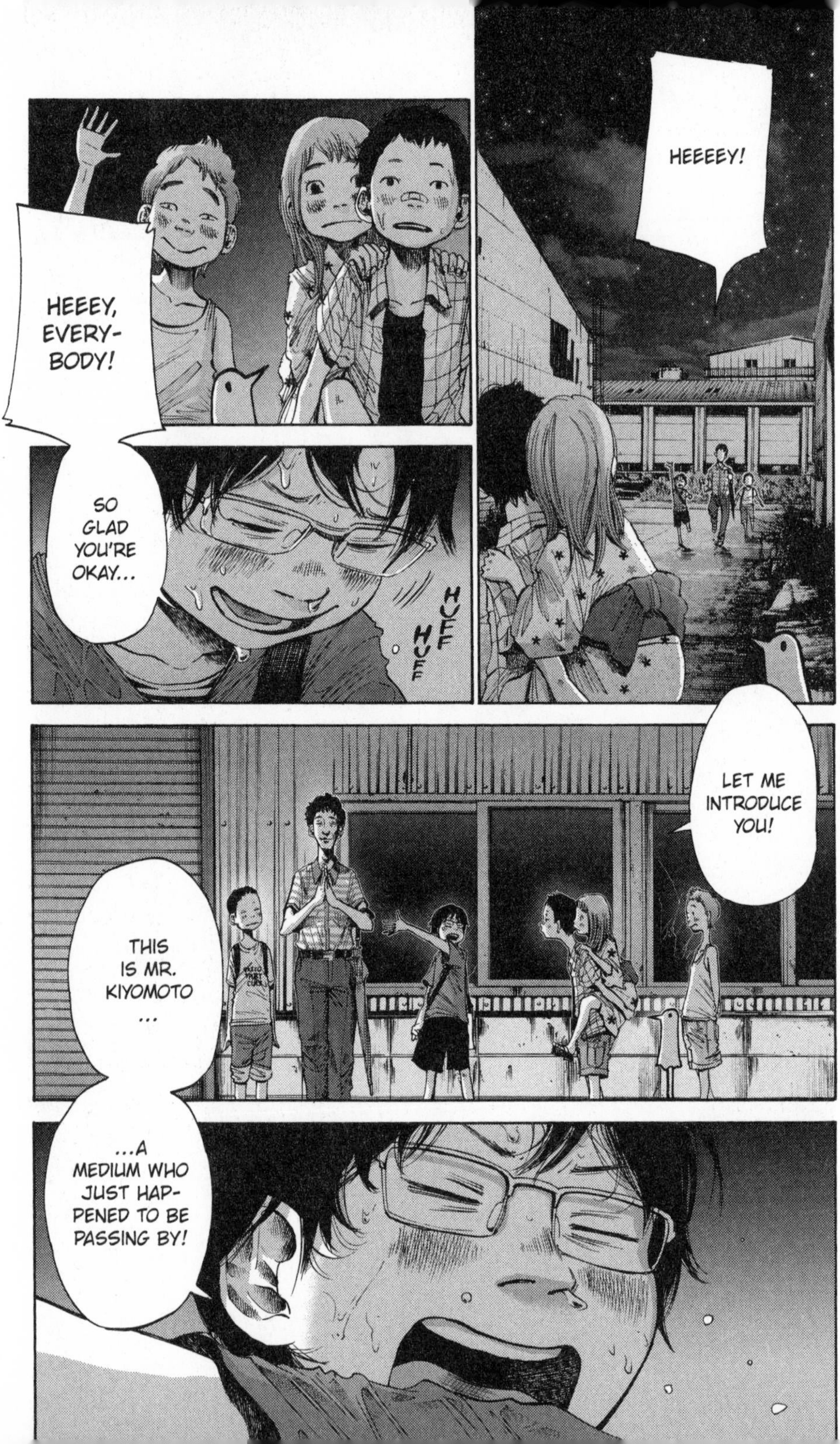
HEEEEY!
HEEEY, EVERY-BODY!
SO GLAD YOU'RE OKAY...
HUFF HUFF
LET ME INTRODUCE YOU!
THIS IS MR. KIYOMOTO ...
...A MEDIUM WHO JUST HAPPENED TO BE PASSING BY!

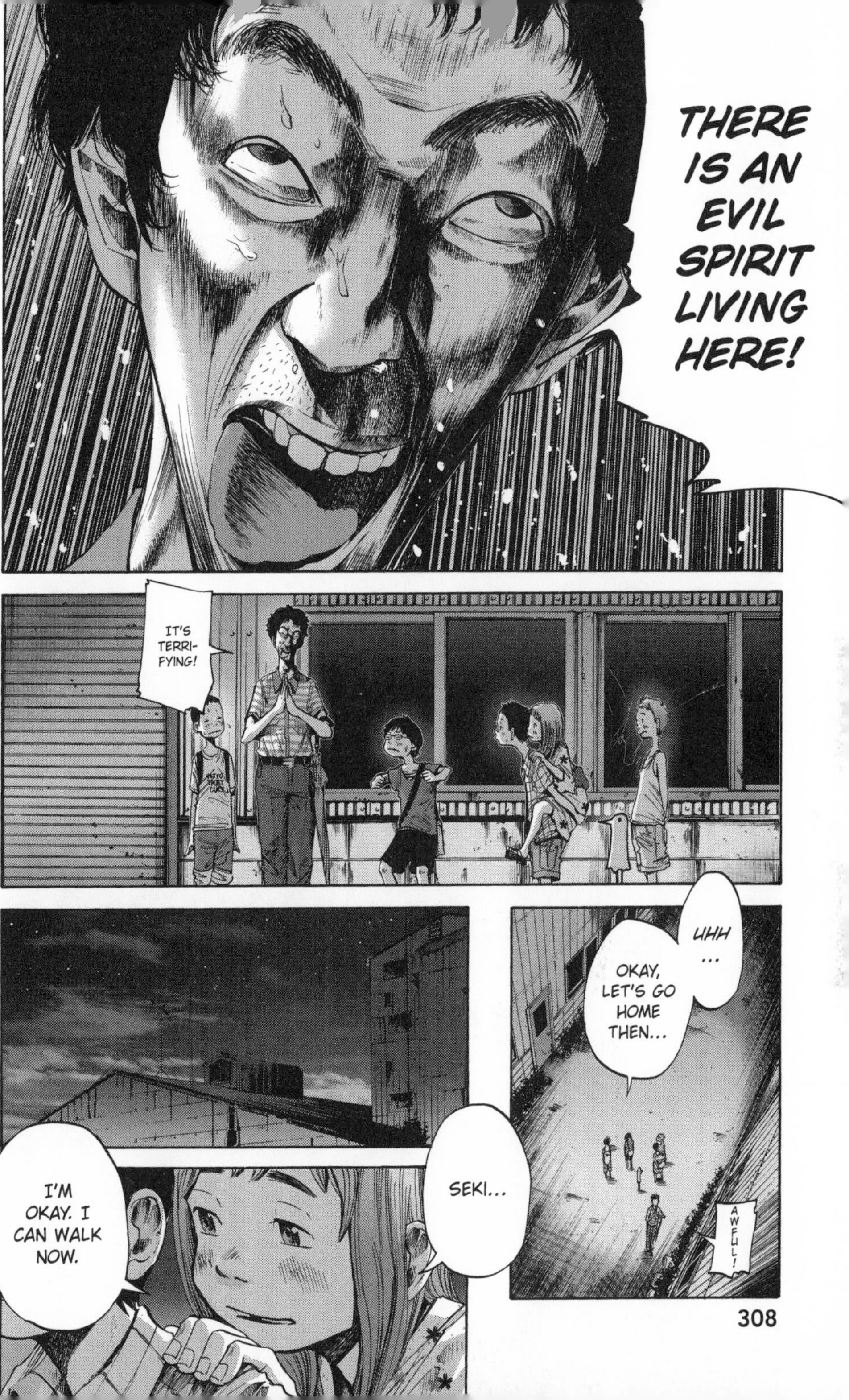
THERE IS AN EVIL SPIRIT LIVING HERE!
IT'S TERRI-FYING!
UHH ...
OKAY, LET'S GO HOME THEN...
AWFUL!
SEKI...
I'M OKAY. I CAN WALK NOW.

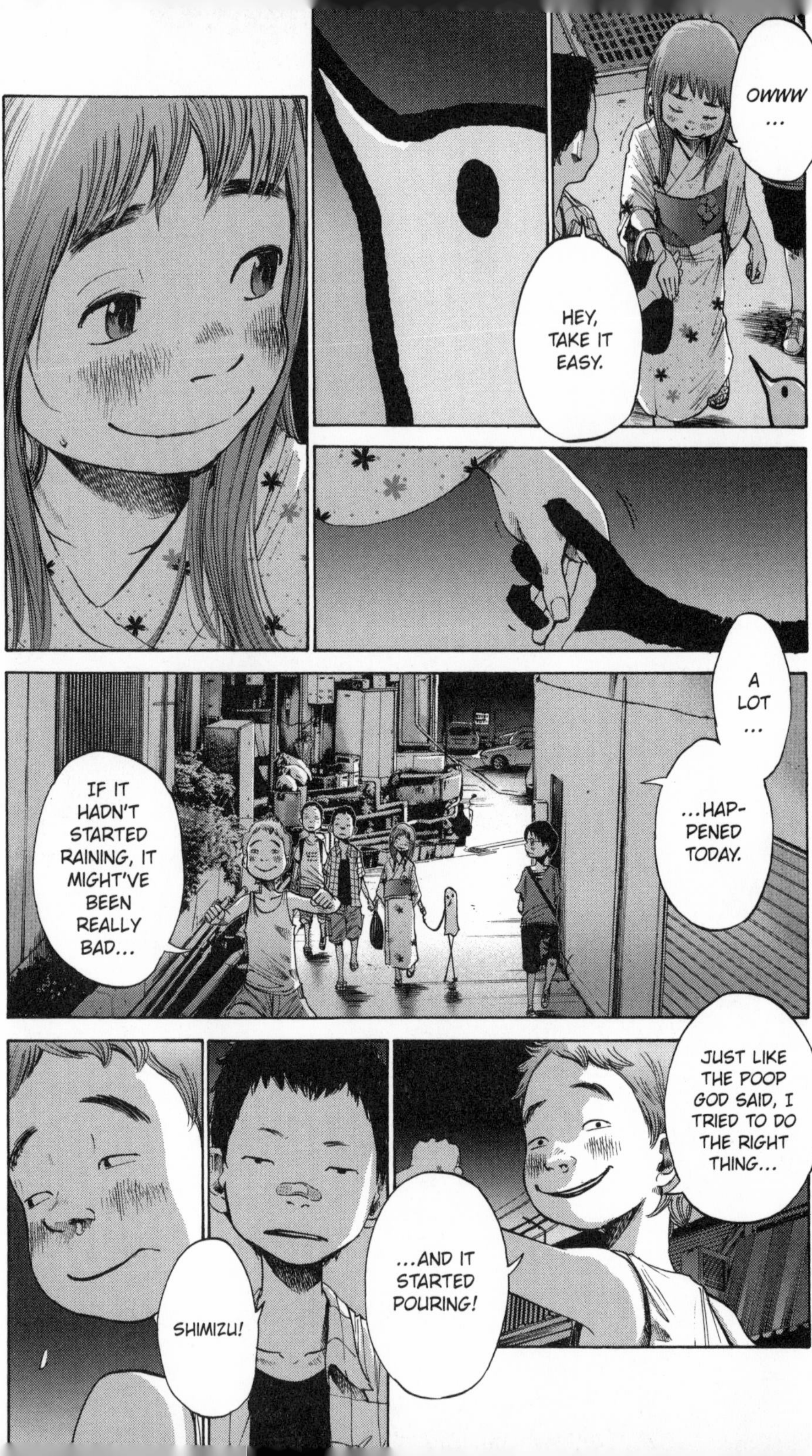
OWWW ...
HEY, TAKE IT EASY.
A LOT ...
...HAP-PENED TODAY.
IF IT HADN'T STARTED RAINING, IT MIGHT'VE BEEN REALLY BAD...
JUST LIKE THE POOP GOD SAID, I TRIED TO DO THE RIGHT THING...
...AND IT STARTED POURING!
SHIMIZU!

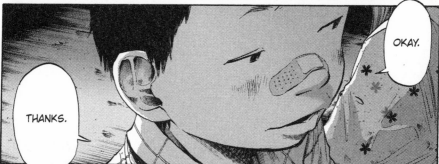

OKAY.

THANKS.

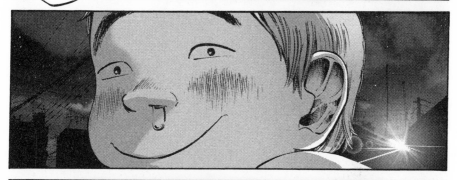

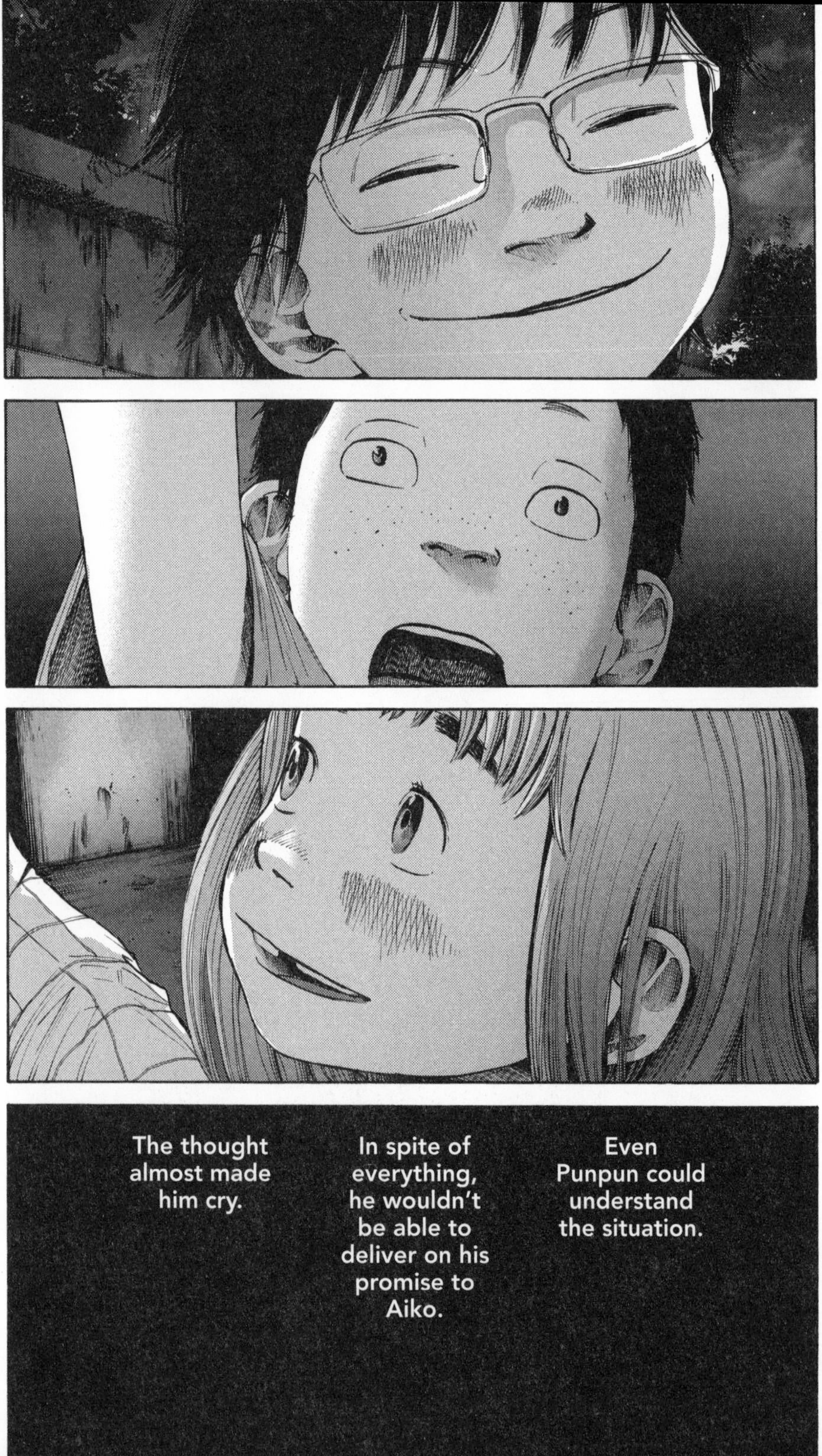
Even Punpun could understand the situation.
In spite of everything, he wouldn't be able to deliver on his promise to Aiko.
The thought almost made him cry.

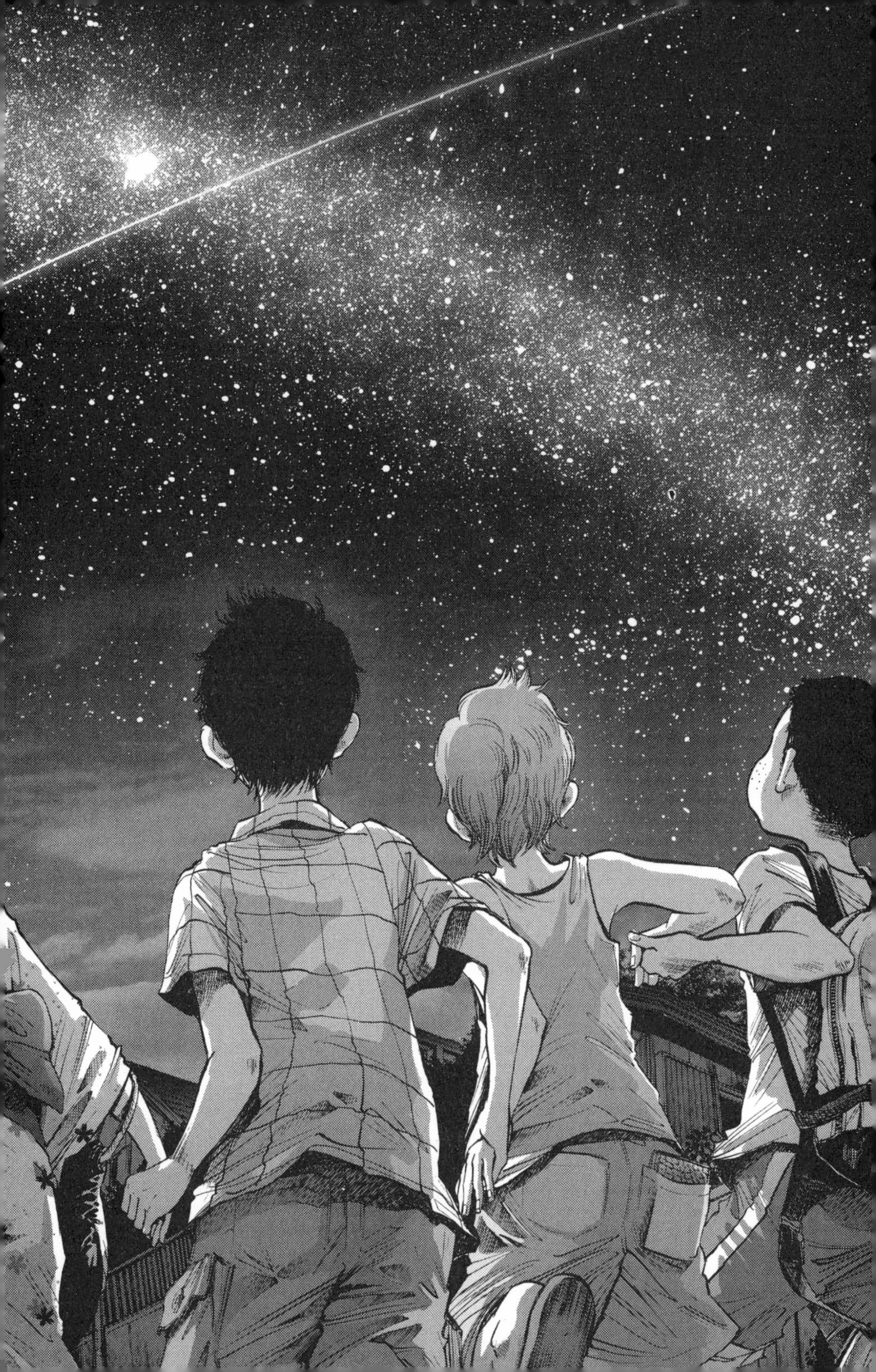

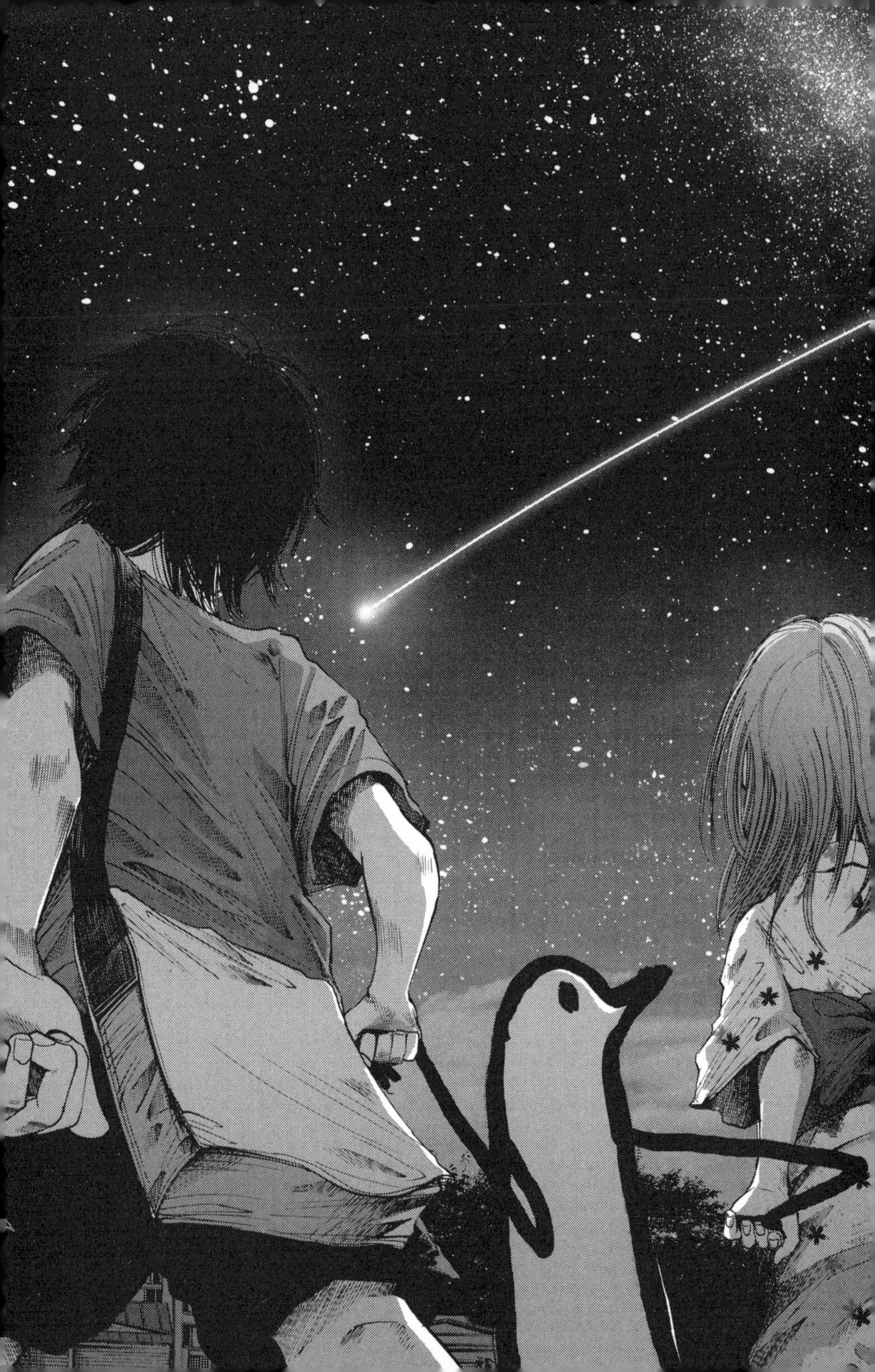

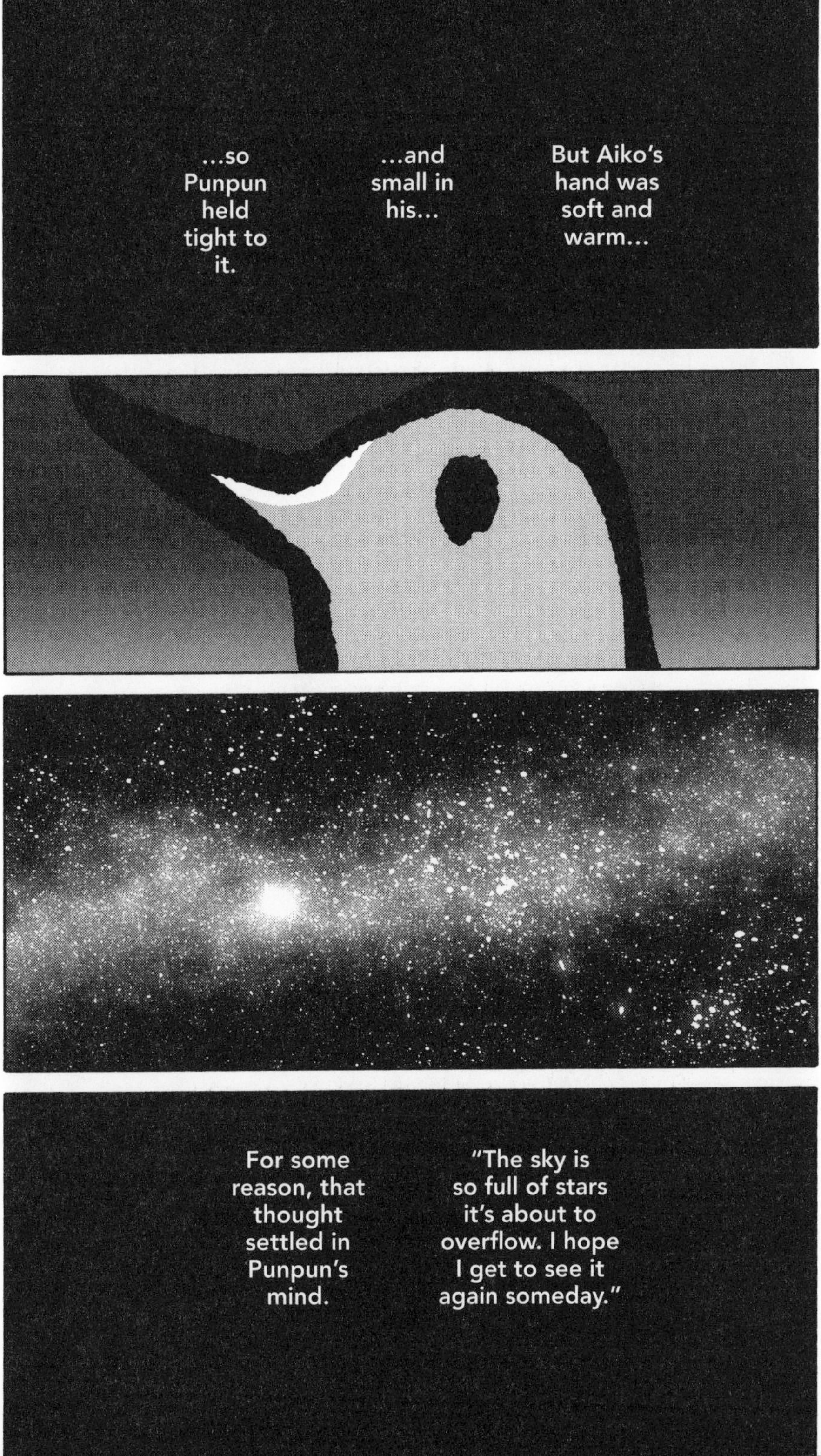
But Aiko's hand was soft and warm...
...and small in his...
...so Punpun held tight to it.
"The sky is so full of stars it's about to overflow. I hope I get to see it again someday."
For some reason, that thought settled in Punpun's mind.

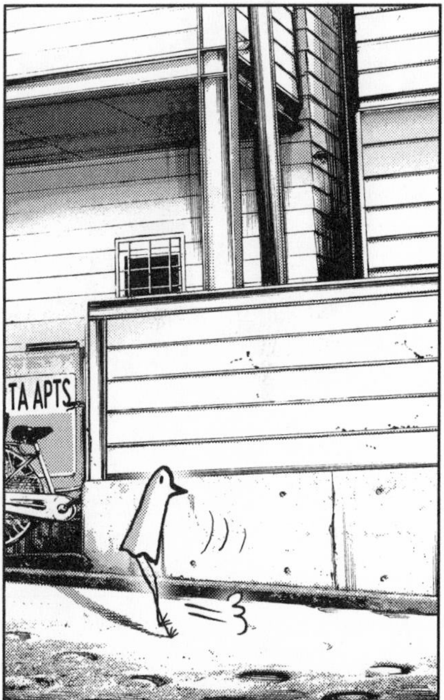
TA APTS

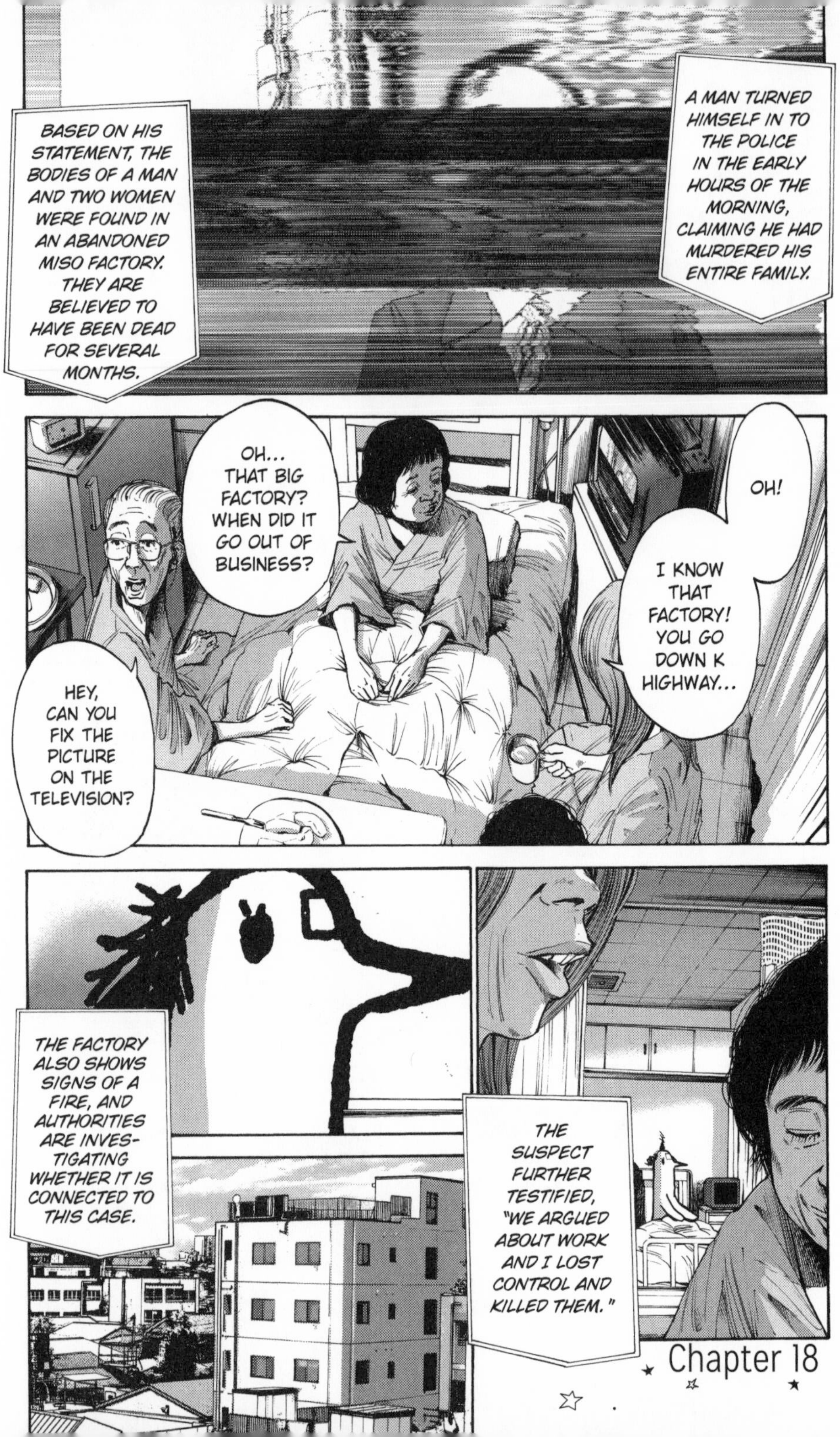
A MAN TURNED HIMSELF IN TO THE POLICE IN THE EARLY HOURS OF THE MORNING, CLAIMING HE HAD MURDERED HIS ENTIRE FAMILY.
BASED ON HIS STATEMENT, THE BODIES OF A MAN AND TWO WOMEN WERE FOUND IN AN ABANDONED MISO FACTORY. THEY ARE BELIEVED TO HAVE BEEN DEAD FOR SEVERAL MONTHS.
OH!
I KNOW THAT FACTORY! YOU GO DOWN K HIGHWAY...
OH... THAT BIG FACTORY? WHEN DID IT GO OUT OF BUSINESS?
HEY, CAN YOU FIX THE PICTURE ON THE TELEVISION?
THE SUSPECT FURTHER TESTIFIED, "WE ARGUED ABOUT WORK AND I LOST CONTROL AND KILLED THEM."
THE FACTORY ALSO SHOWS SIGNS OF A FIRE, AND AUTHORITIES ARE INVES-TIGATING WHETHER IT IS CONNECTED TO THIS CASE.

Chapter 18

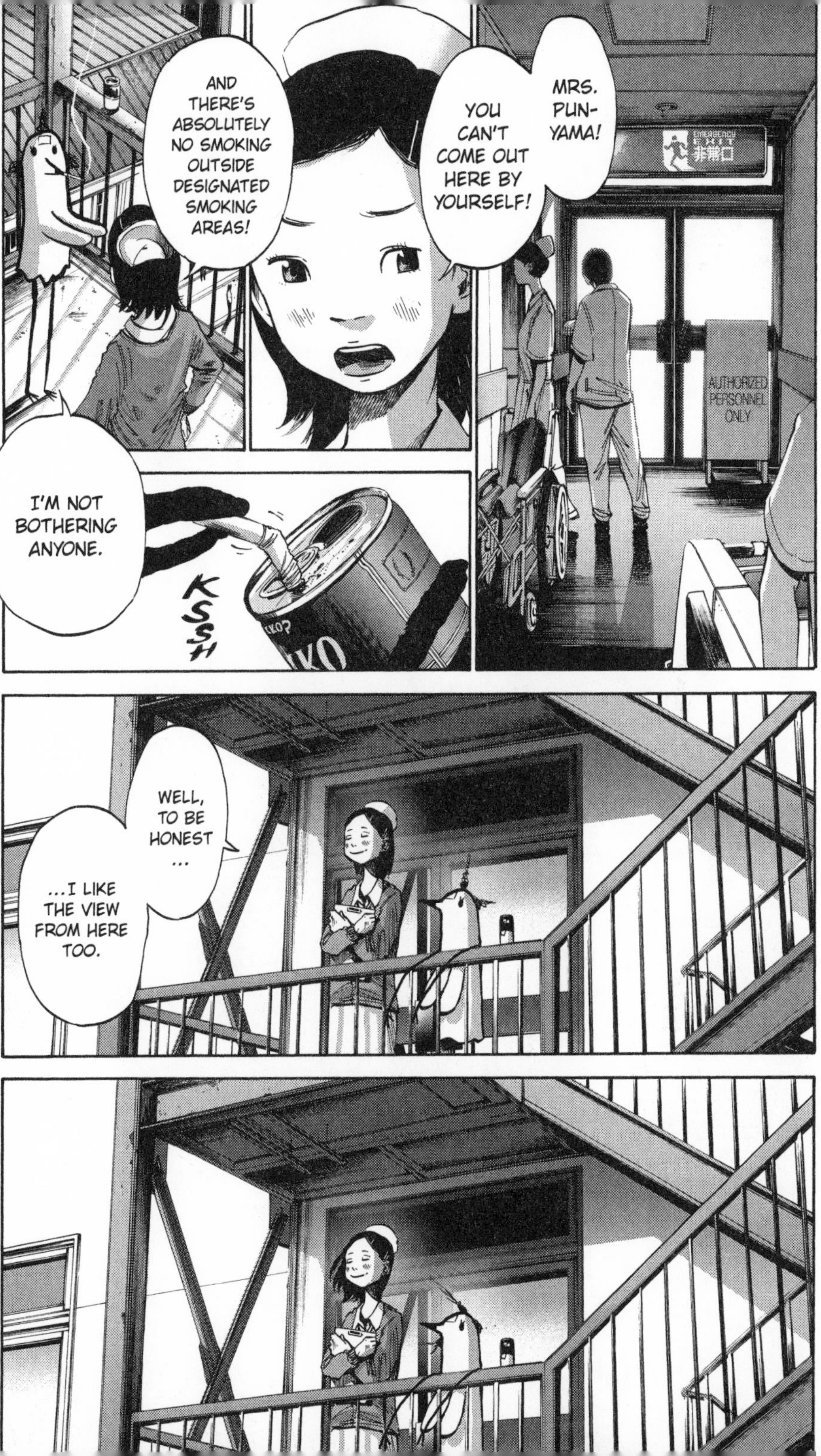
MRS. PUN-YAMA!
YOU CAN'T COME OUT HERE BY YOURSELF!
EMERGENCY EXIT 非常口
AUTHORIZED PERSONNEL ONLY
AND THERE'S ABSOLUTELY NO SMOKING OUTSIDE DESIGNATED SMOKING AREAS!
I'M NOT BOTHERING ANYONE.
KSSH
WELL, TO BE HONEST ...
...I LIKE THE VIEW FROM HERE TOO.

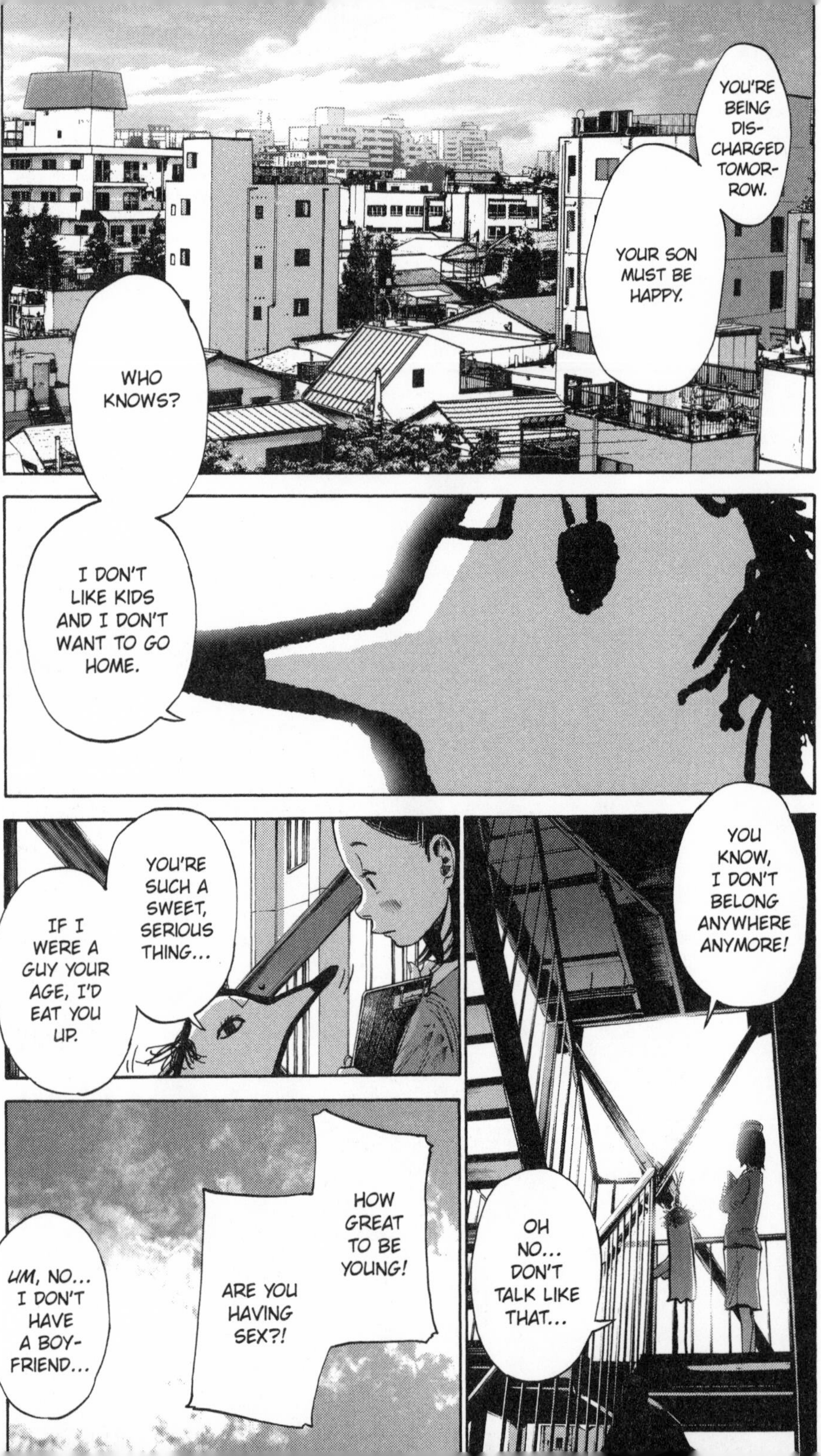
YOU'RE BEING DIS-CHARGED TOMOR-ROW.
YOUR SON MUST BE HAPPY.
WHO KNOWS?
I DON'T LIKE KIDS AND I DON'T WANT TO GO HOME.
YOU KNOW, I DON'T BELONG ANYWHERE ANYMORE!
OH NO... DON'T TALK LIKE THAT...
YOU'RE SUCH A SWEET, SERIOUS THING...
IF I WERE A GUY YOUR AGE, I'D EAT YOU UP.
HOW GREAT TO BE YOUNG!
ARE YOU HAVING SEX?!
UM, NO... I DON'T HAVE A BOY-FRIEND...

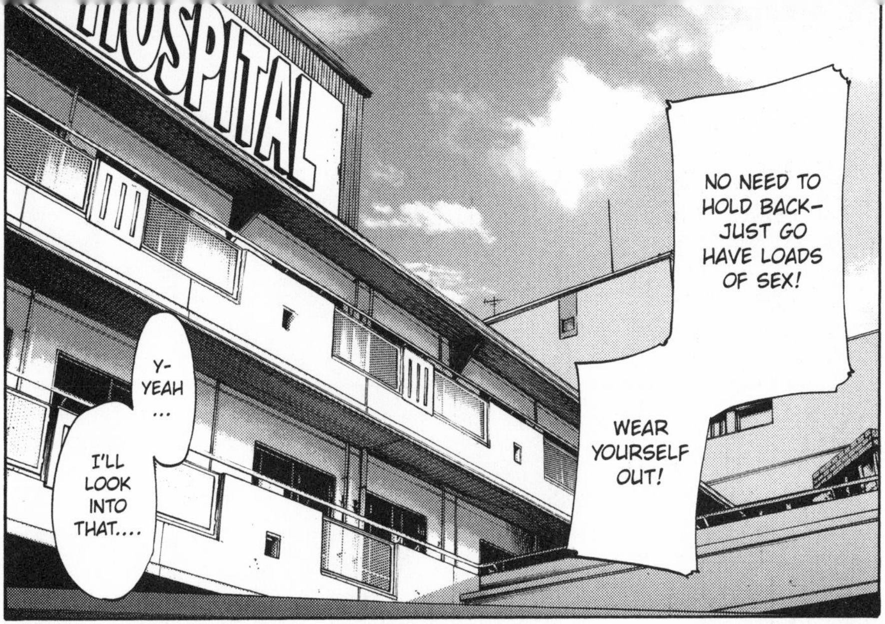
HOSPITAL
NO NEED TO HOLD BACK– JUST GO HAVE LOADS OF SEX!
WEAR YOURSELF OUT!
Y-YEAH …
I'LL LOOK INTO THAT….

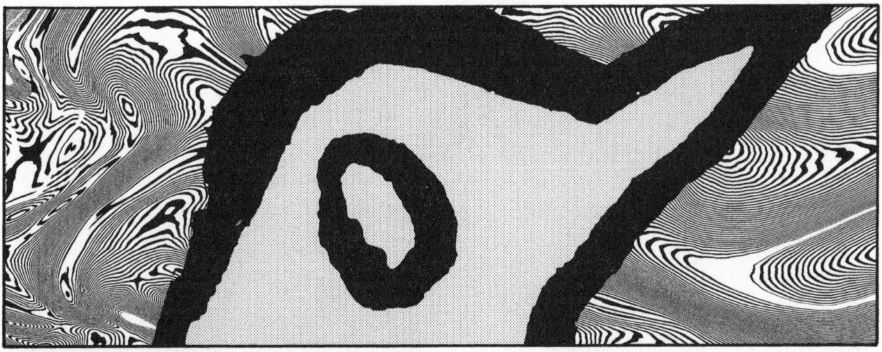

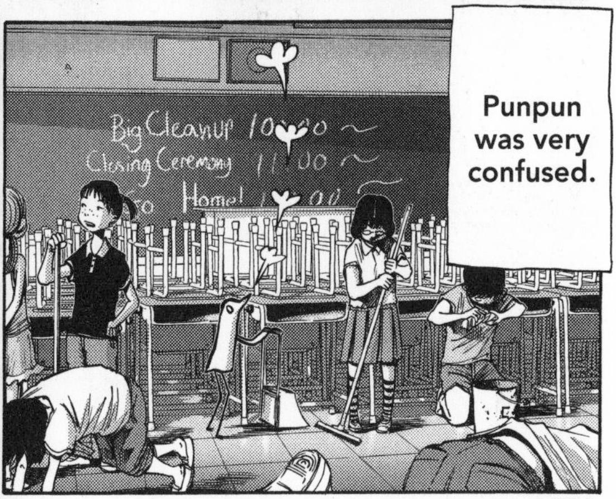
Punpun was very confused.
Big Cleanup
Closing Ceremony
Home!

But he knew that no matter how confused he was, it wouldn't solve anything, and he was even a little angry that he couldn't be anything but confused.

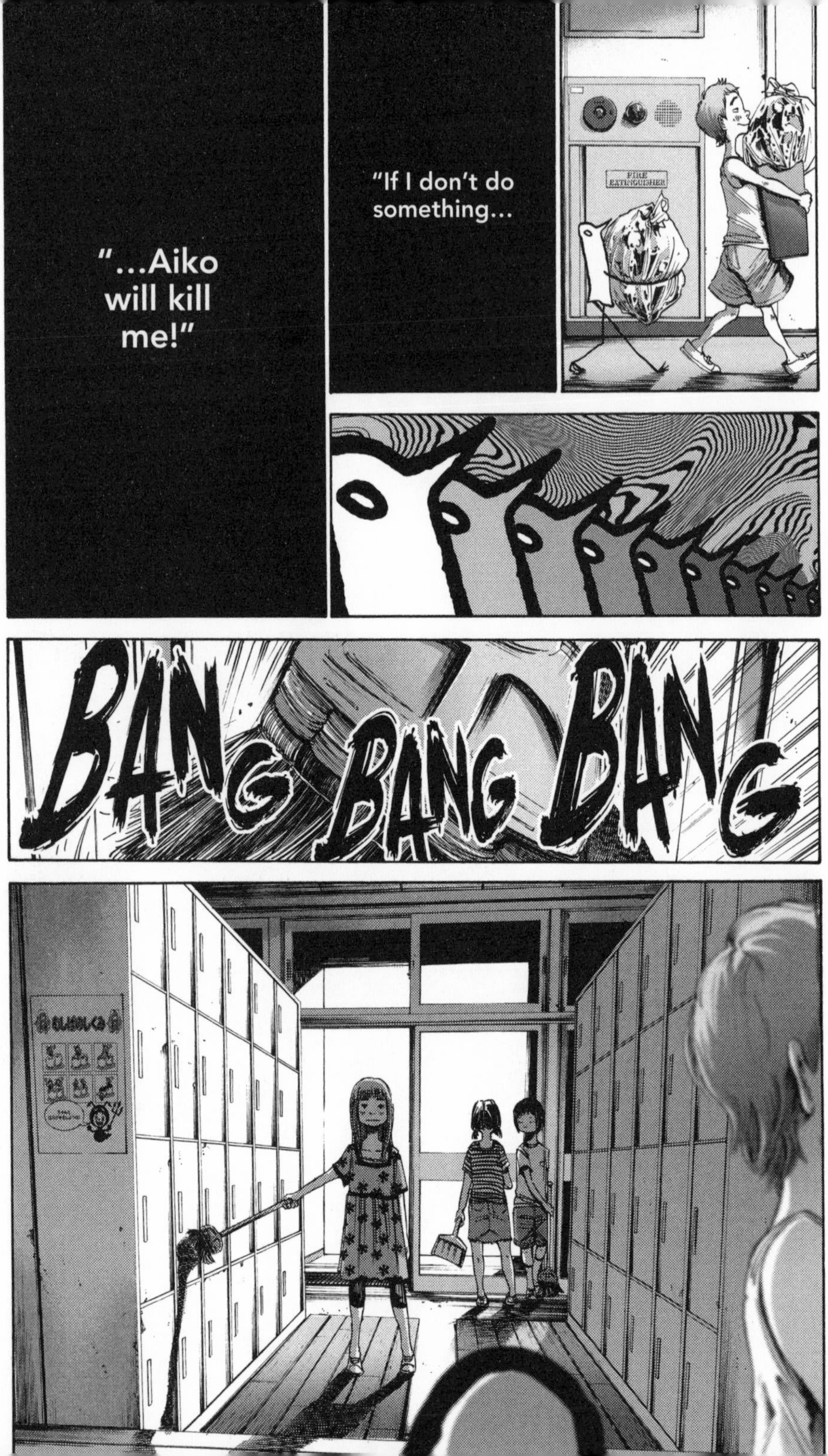
FIRE EXTINGUISHER
"If I don't do something...
"...Aiko will kill me!"
BANG BANG BANG

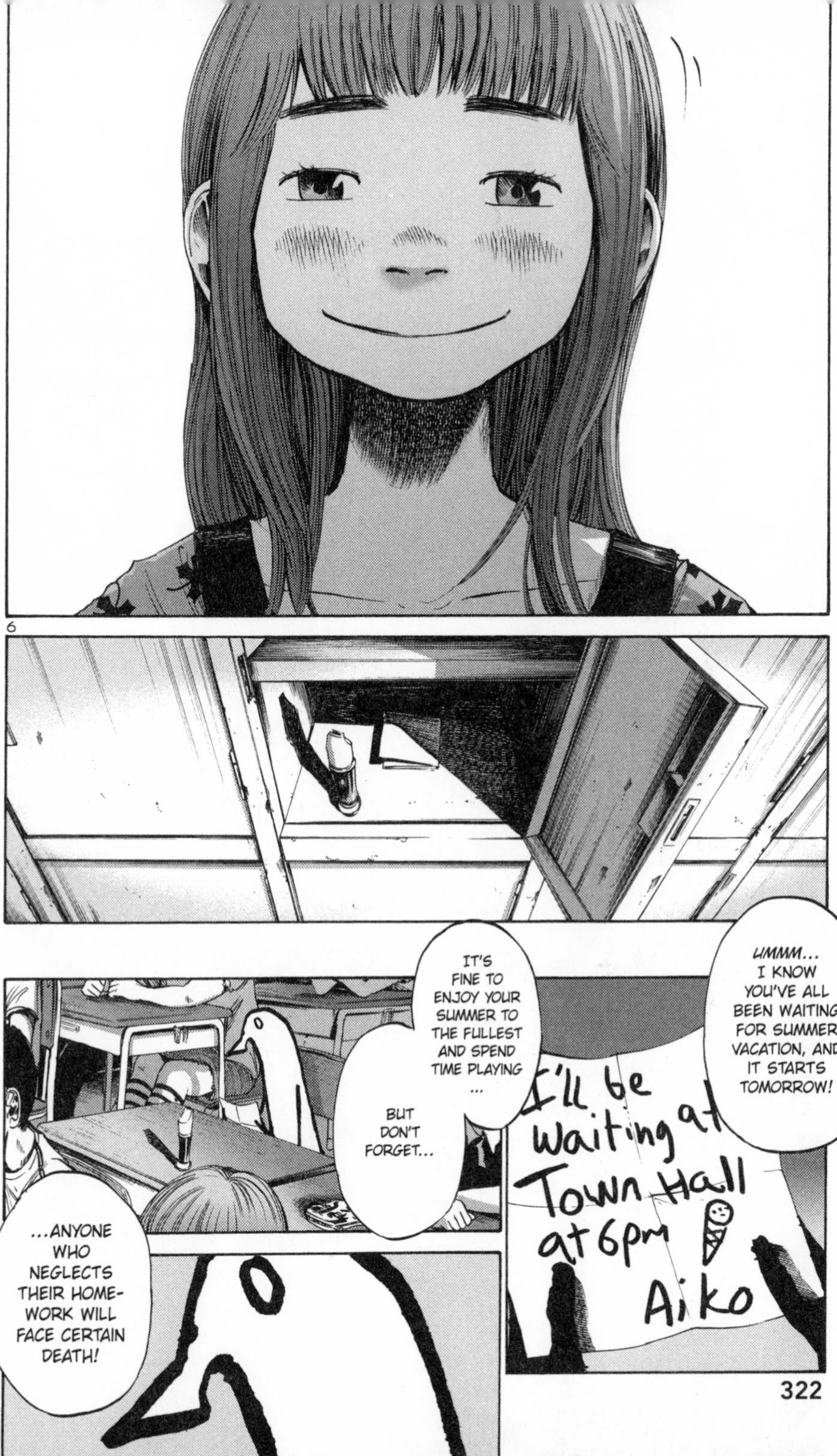
UMMM... I KNOW YOU'VE ALL BEEN WAITING FOR SUMMER VACATION, AND IT STARTS TOMORROW!
I'll be waiting at Town Hall at 6pm Aiko
IT'S FINE TO ENJOY YOUR SUMMER TO THE FULLEST AND SPEND TIME PLAYING ...
BUT DON'T FORGET...
...ANYONE WHO NEGLECTS THEIR HOME-WORK WILL FACE CERTAIN DEATH!

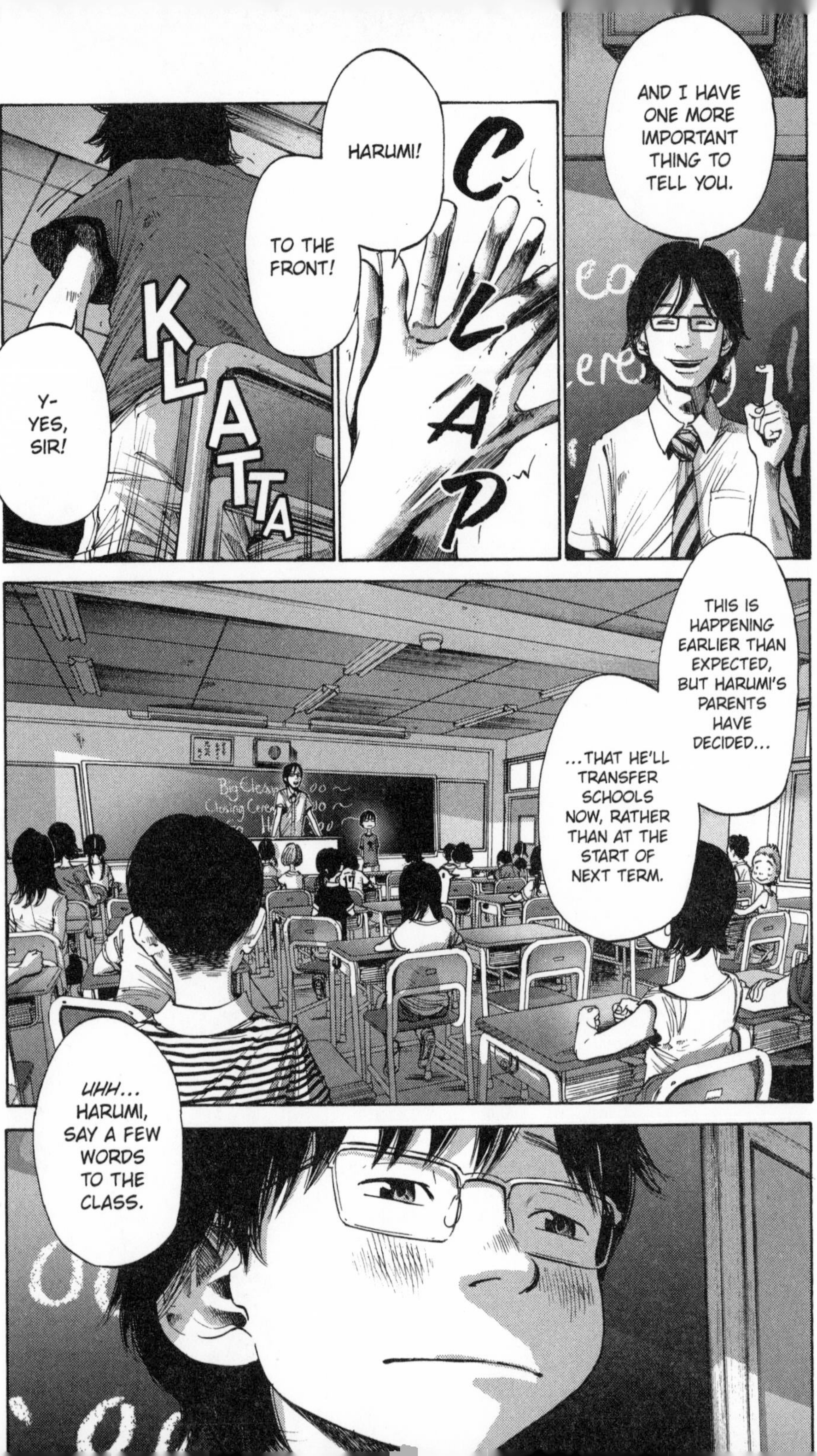
AND I HAVE ONE MORE IMPORTANT THING TO TELL YOU.
CLAP
HARUMI!
TO THE FRONT!
KLATTA
Y- YES, SIR!
THIS IS HAPPENING EARLIER THAN EXPECTED, BUT HARUMI'S PARENTS HAVE DECIDED...
...THAT HE'LL TRANSFER SCHOOLS NOW, RATHER THAN AT THE START OF NEXT TERM.
UHH... HARUMI, SAY A FEW WORDS TO THE CLASS.

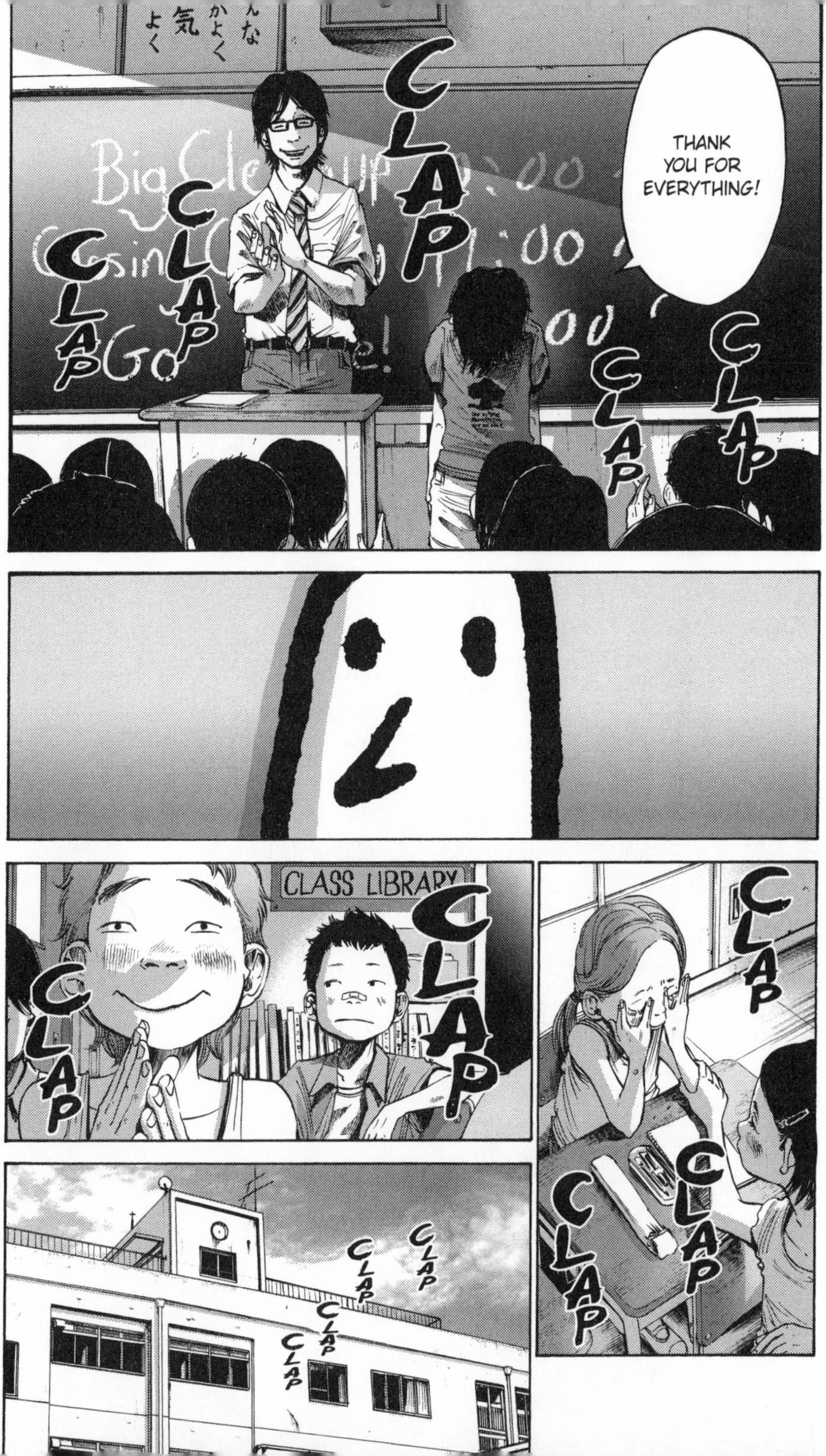
THANK YOU FOR EVERYTHING!
CLAP
CLAP
CLAP
CLAP
CLAP
CLAP
CLAP
CLAP
CLAP
CLASS LIBRARY
CLAP
CLAP
CLAP
CLAP
CLAP
CLAP

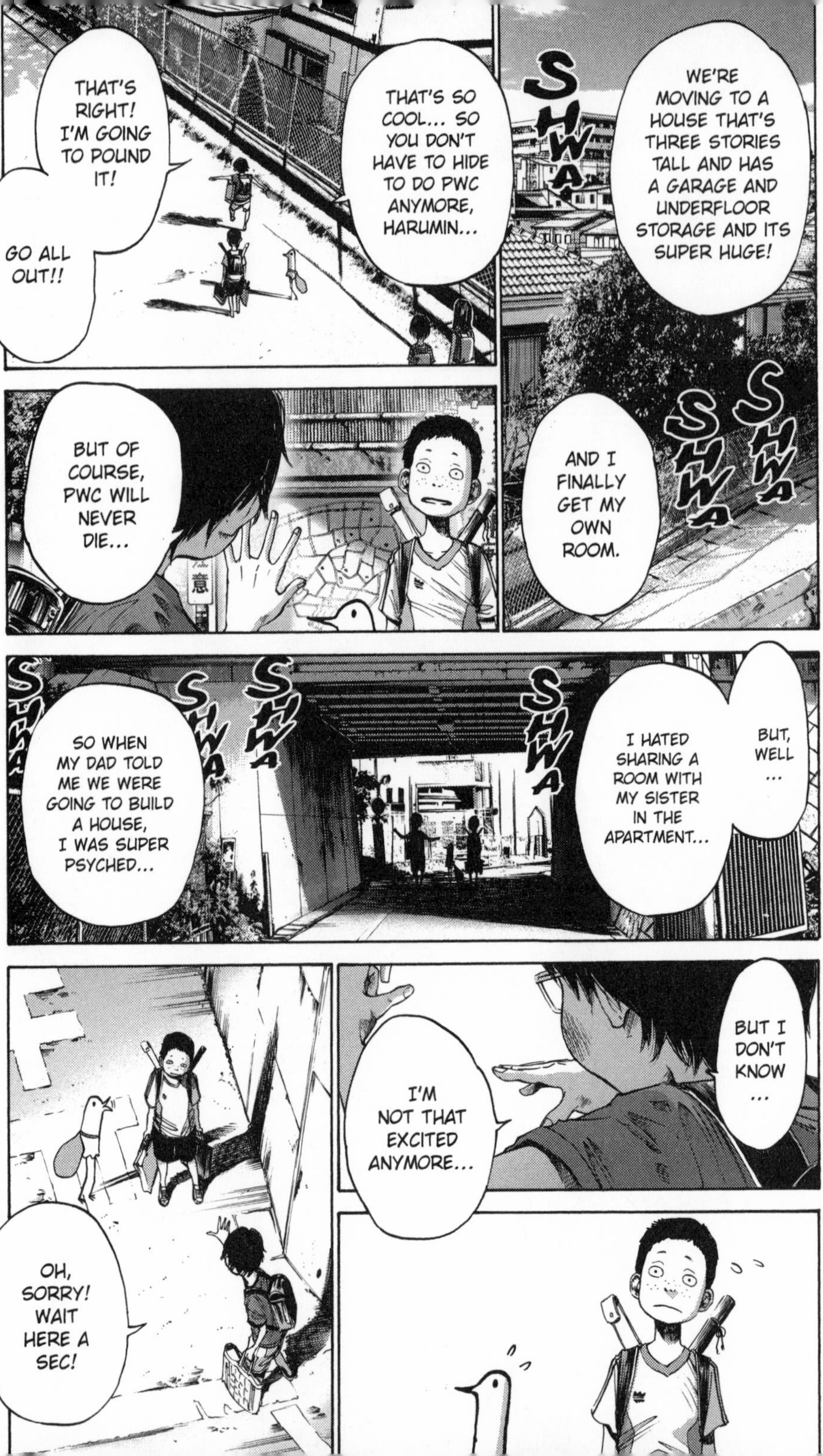
WE'RE MOVING TO A HOUSE THAT'S THREE STORIES TALL AND HAS A GARAGE AND UNDERFLOOR STORAGE AND ITS SUPER HUGE!
SHWA
AND I FINALLY GET MY OWN ROOM.
SHWA
SHWA
THAT'S SO COOL... SO YOU DON'T HAVE TO HIDE TO DO PWC ANYMORE, HARUMIN...
THAT'S RIGHT! I'M GOING TO POUND IT!
GO ALL OUT!!
BUT OF COURSE, PWC WILL NEVER DIE...
BUT, WELL...
I HATED SHARING A ROOM WITH MY SISTER IN THE APARTMENT...
SHWA
SHWA
SHWA
SO WHEN MY DAD TOLD ME WE WERE GOING TO BUILD A HOUSE, I WAS SUPER PSYCHED...
SHWA
BUT I DON'T KNOW...
I'M NOT THAT EXCITED ANYMORE...
OH, SORRY! WAIT HERE A SEC!

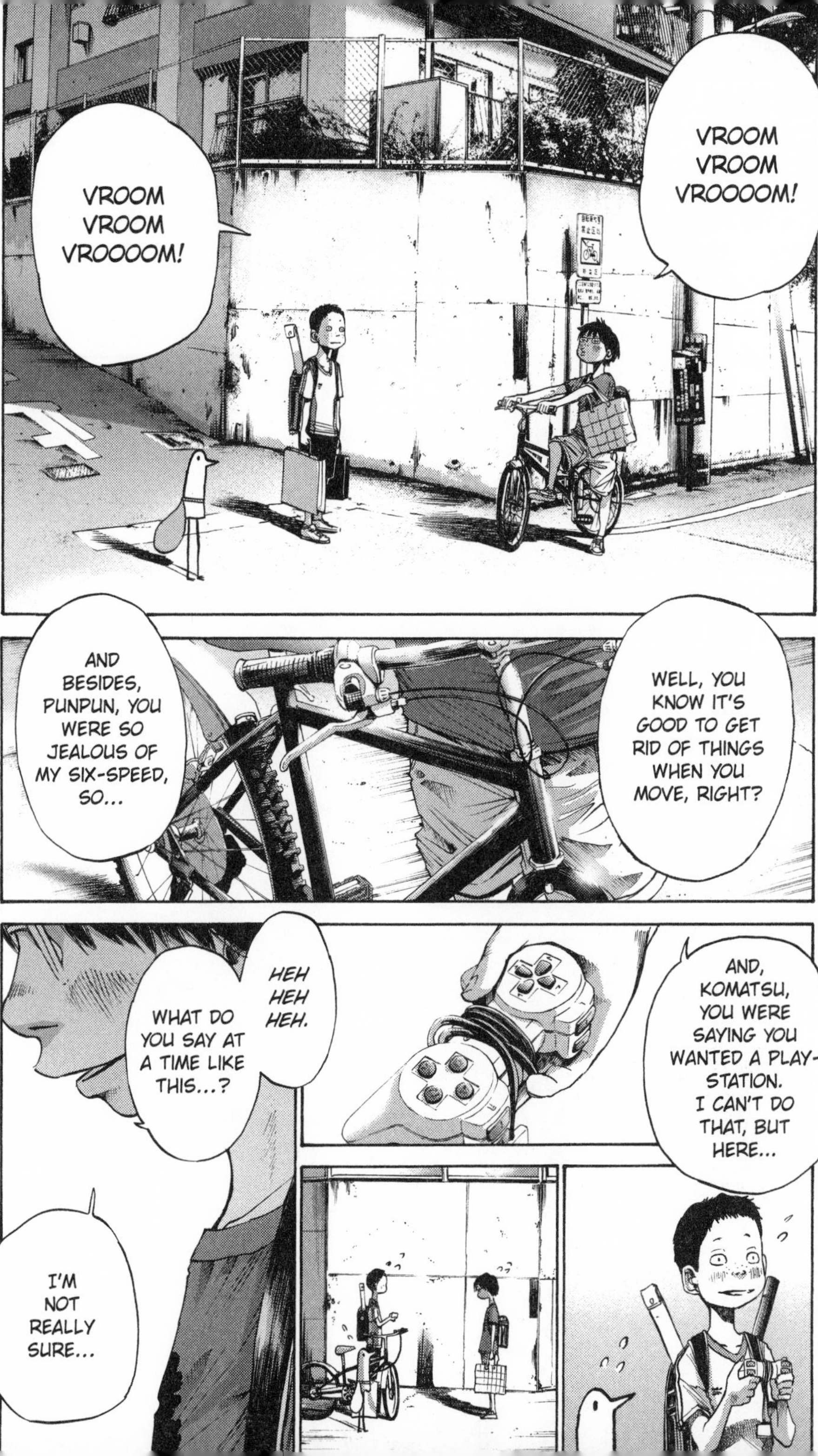
VROOM VROOM VROOOOM!
VROOM VROOM VROOOOM!
WELL, YOU KNOW IT'S GOOD TO GET RID OF THINGS WHEN YOU MOVE, RIGHT?
AND BESIDES, PUNPUN, YOU WERE SO JEALOUS OF MY SIX-SPEED, SO...
AND, KOMATSU, YOU WERE SAYING YOU WANTED A PLAY-STATION. I CAN'T DO THAT, BUT HERE...
HEH HEH HEH.
WHAT DO YOU SAY AT A TIME LIKE THIS...?
I'M NOT REALLY SURE...

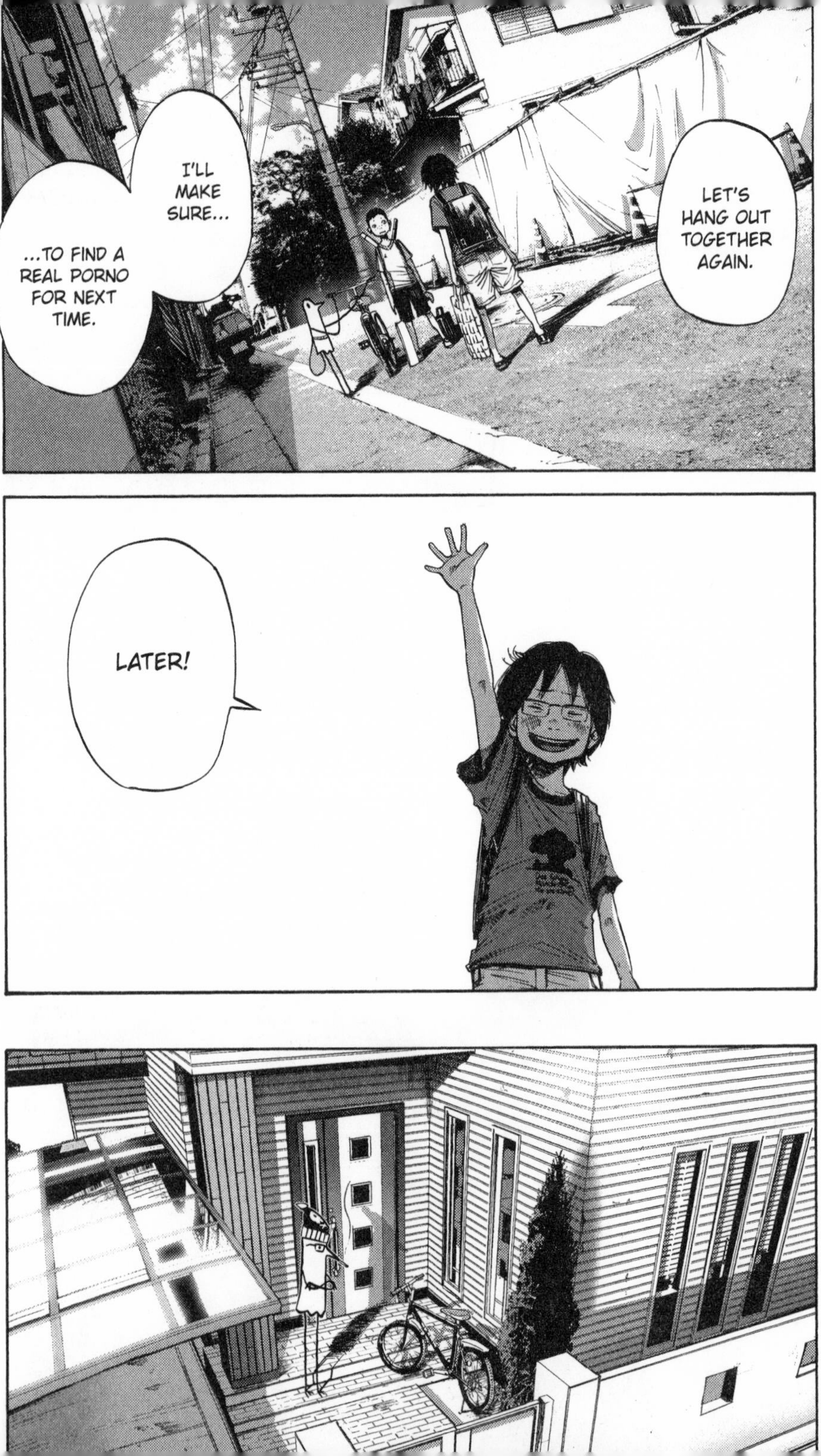
LET'S HANG OUT TOGETHER AGAIN.
I'LL MAKE SURE...
...TO FIND A REAL PORNO FOR NEXT TIME.
LATER!

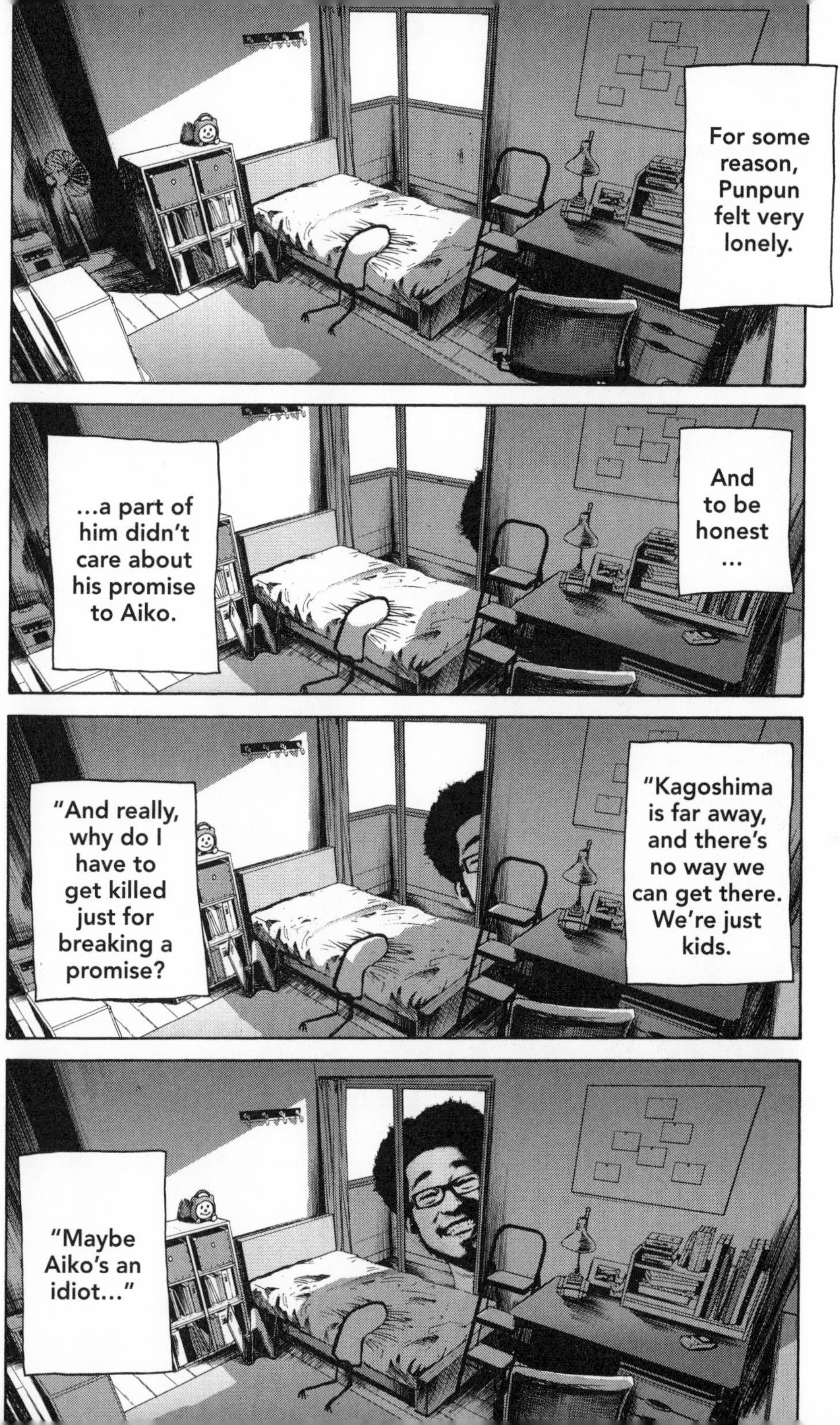
For some reason, Punpun felt very lonely.
And to be honest ...
...a part of him didn't care about his promise to Aiko.
"Kagoshima is far away, and there's no way we can get there. We're just kids.
"And really, why do I have to get killed just for breaking a promise?
"Maybe Aiko's an idiot..."

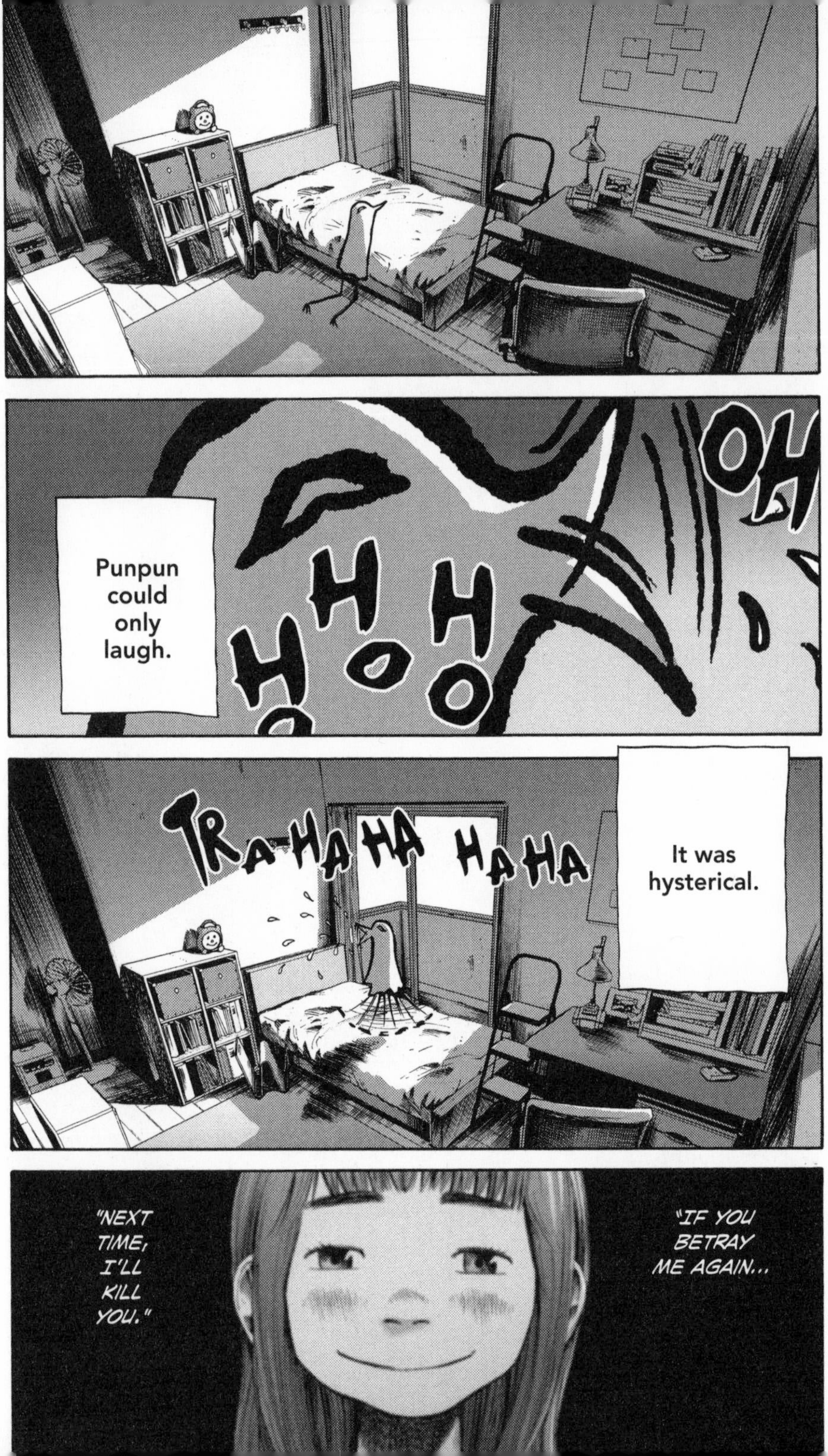
OH
Punpun could only laugh.
It was hysterical.
TRAHAHAHA HAHAHA
"IF YOU BETRAY ME AGAIN...
"NEXT TIME, I'LL KILL YOU."

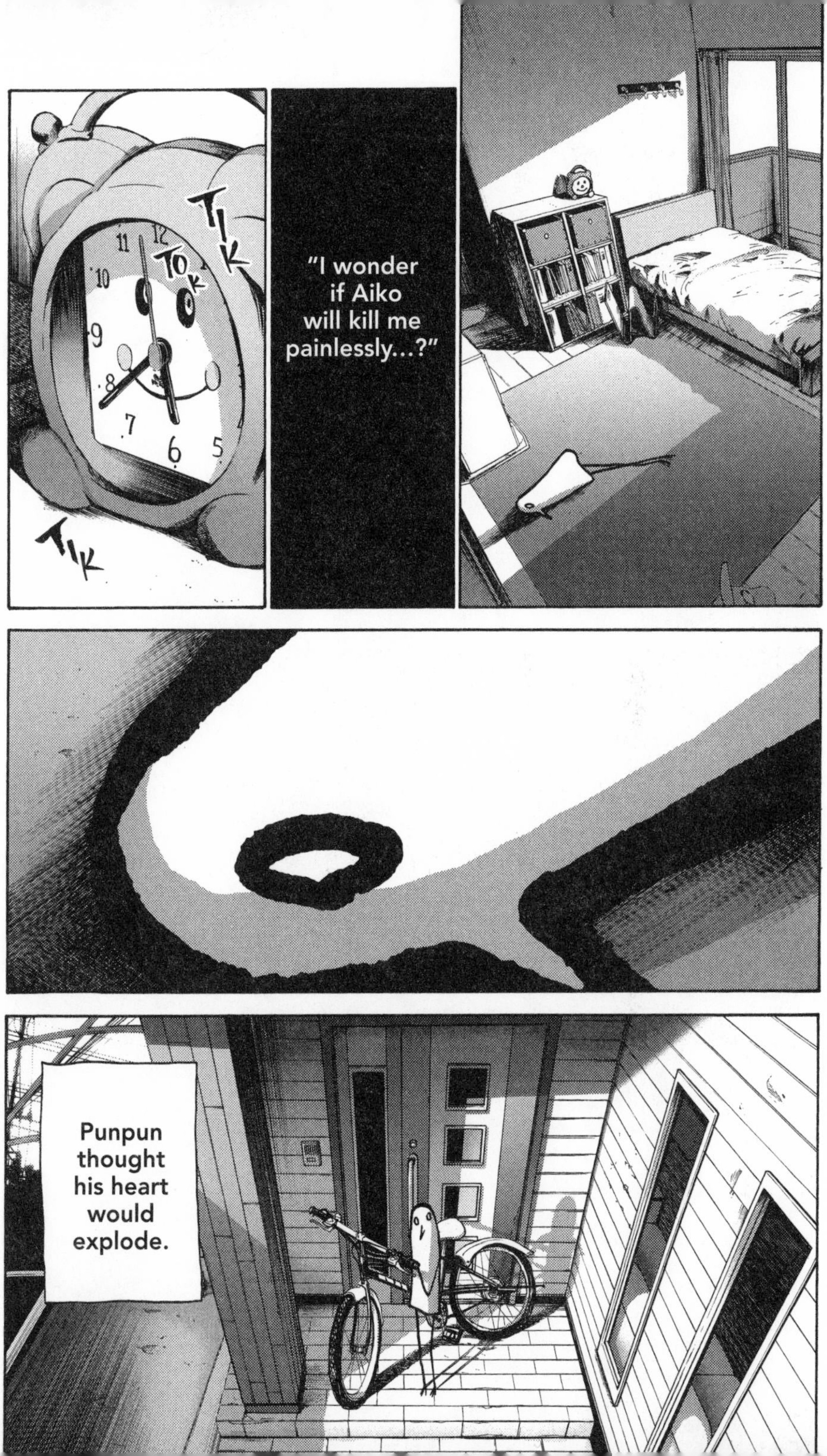
"I wonder if Aiko will kill me painlessly...?"
TIK
TOK
TIK
Punpun thought his heart would explode.

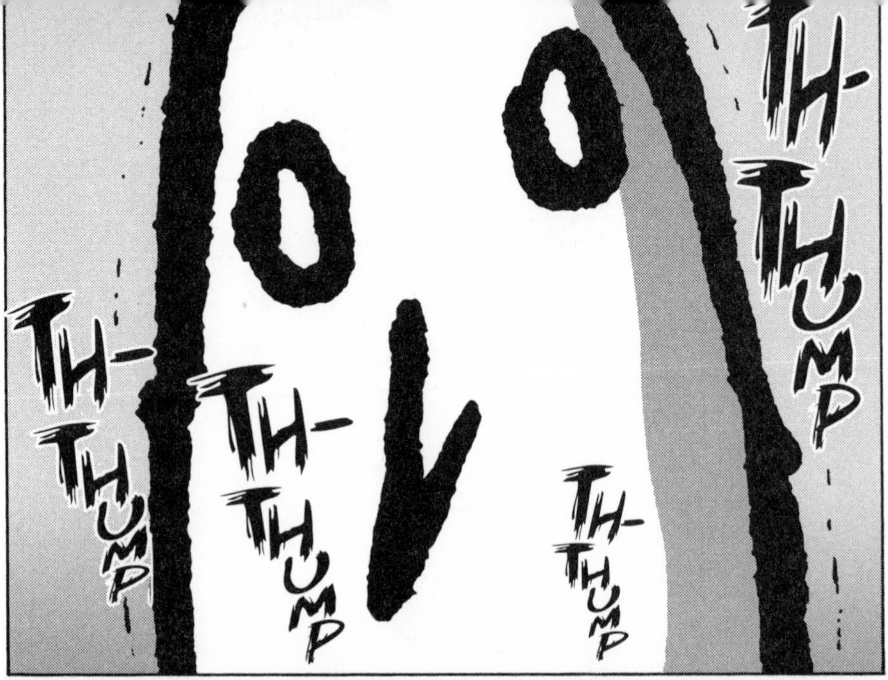
TH-THUMP
TH-THUMP
TH-THUMP
TH-THUMP

"On a six-speed,
we might make
it to Kagoshima..."

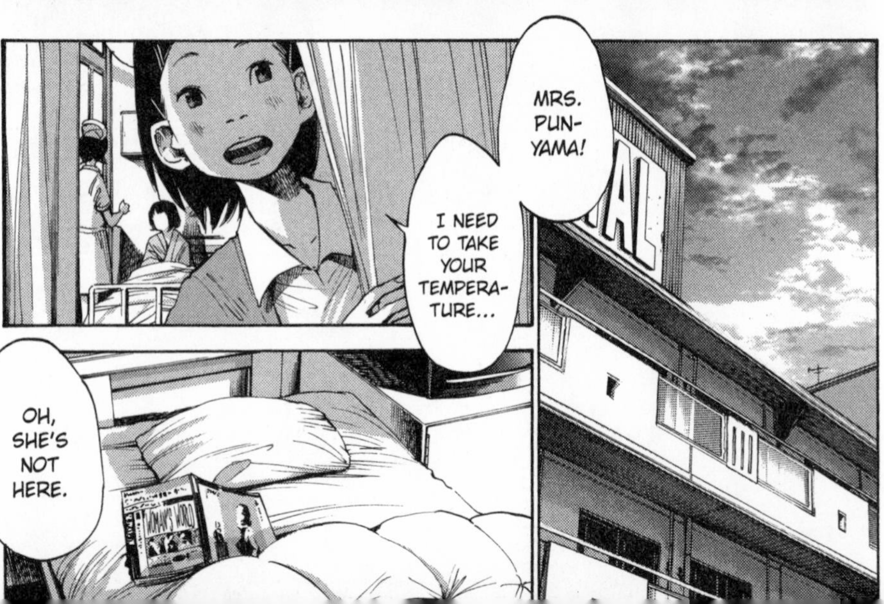
MRS. PUN-YAMA!
I NEED TO TAKE YOUR TEMPERATURE...
OH, SHE'S NOT HERE.

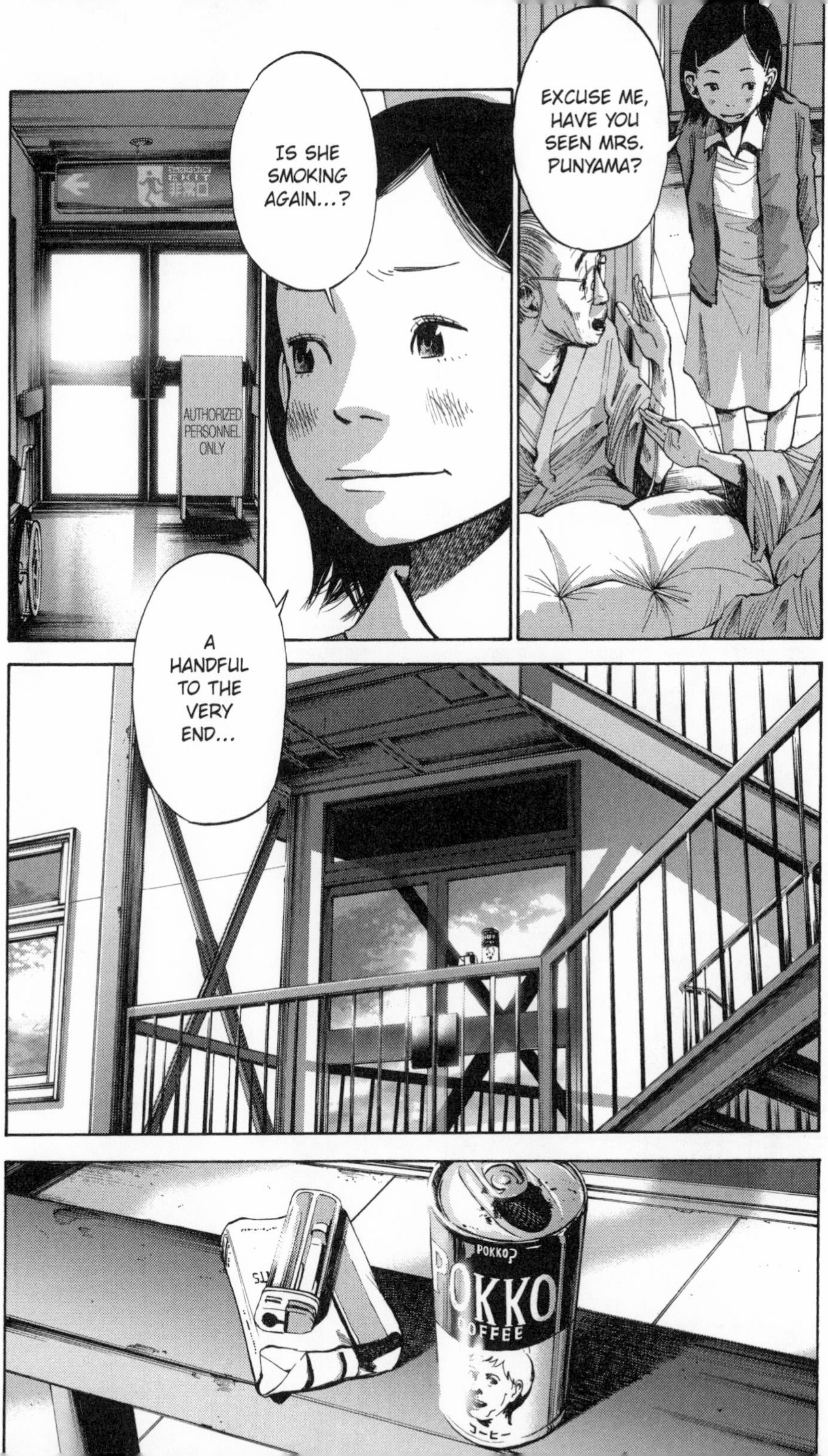
EXCUSE ME, HAVE YOU SEEN MRS. PUNYAMA?
IS SHE SMOKING AGAIN...?
A HANDFUL TO THE VERY END...
AUTHORIZED PERSONNEL ONLY

HELL

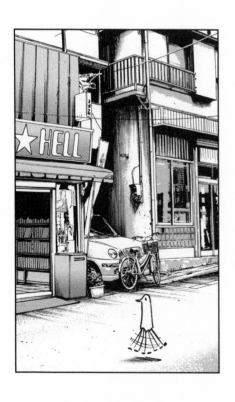

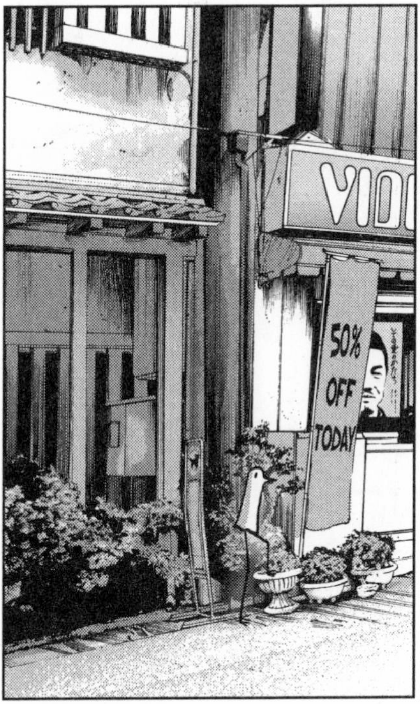
50% OFF TODAY

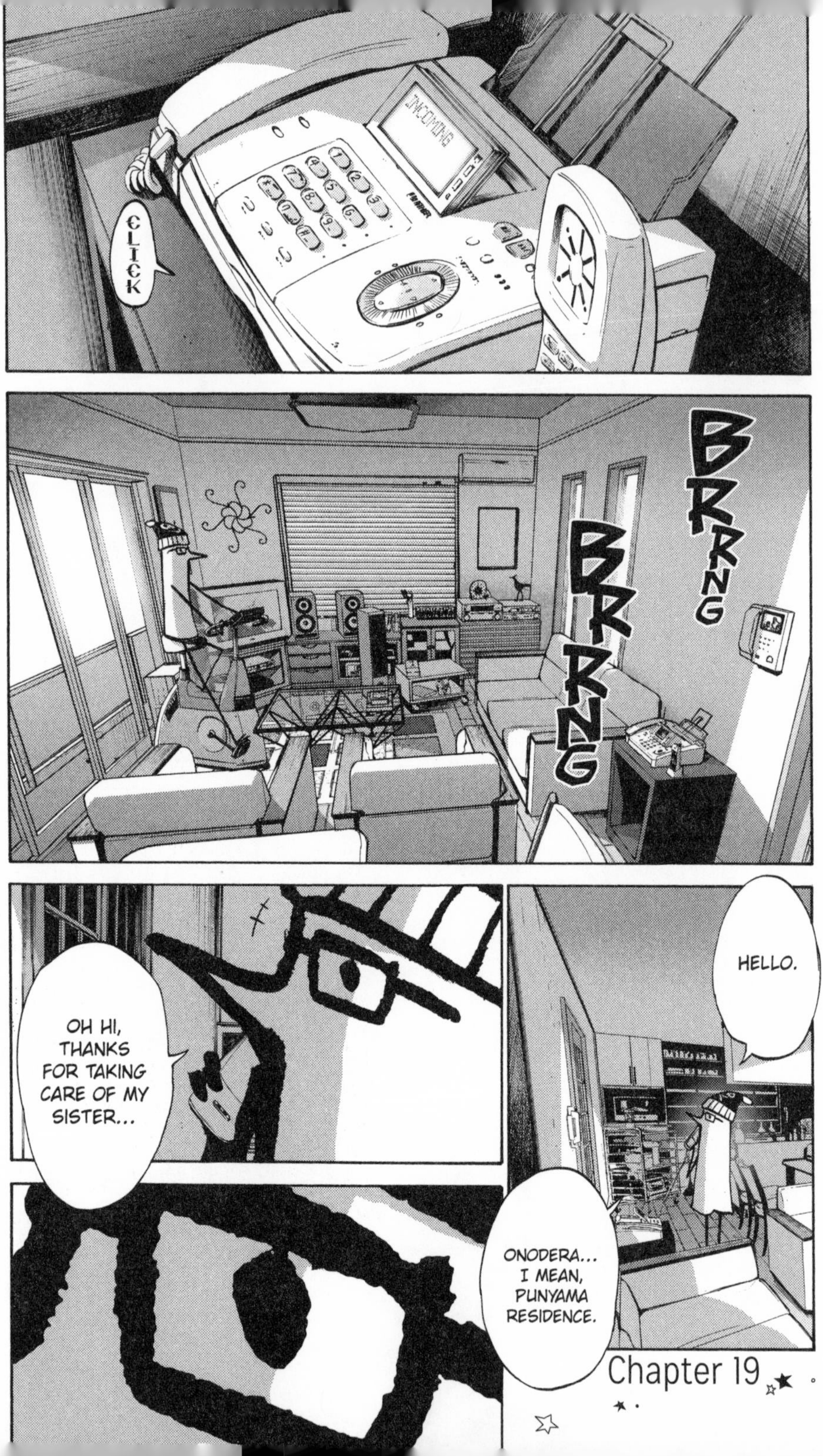
INCOMING
CLICK
BRRRNG
BRRRNG
HELLO.
ONODERA... I MEAN, PUNYAMA RESIDENCE.
Chapter 19
OH HI, THANKS FOR TAKING CARE OF MY SISTER...

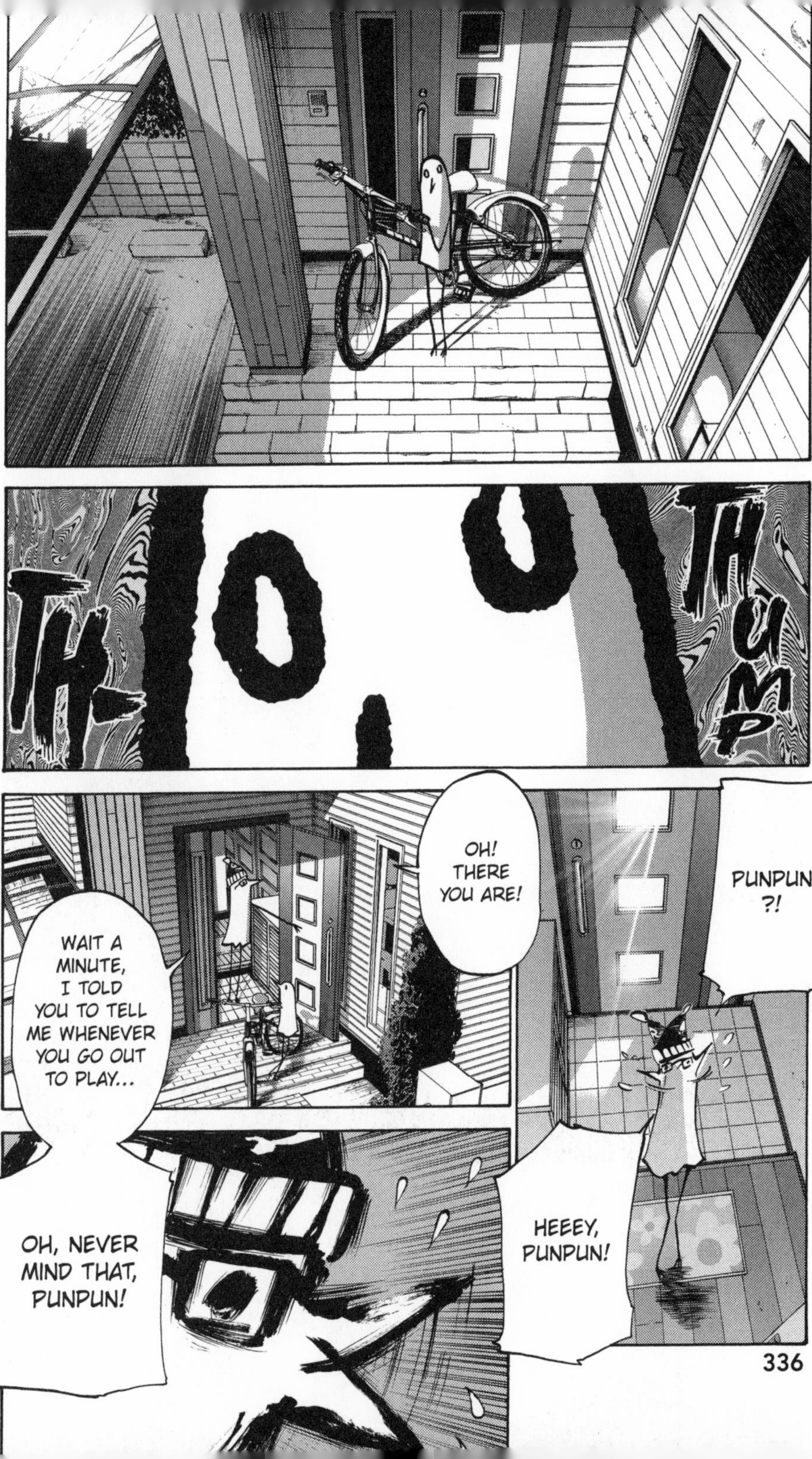
THUMP
TH-
PUNPUN?!
OH! THERE YOU ARE!
WAIT A MINUTE, I TOLD YOU TO TELL ME WHENEVER YOU GO OUT TO PLAY...
HEEEY, PUNPUN!
OH, NEVER MIND THAT, PUNPUN!

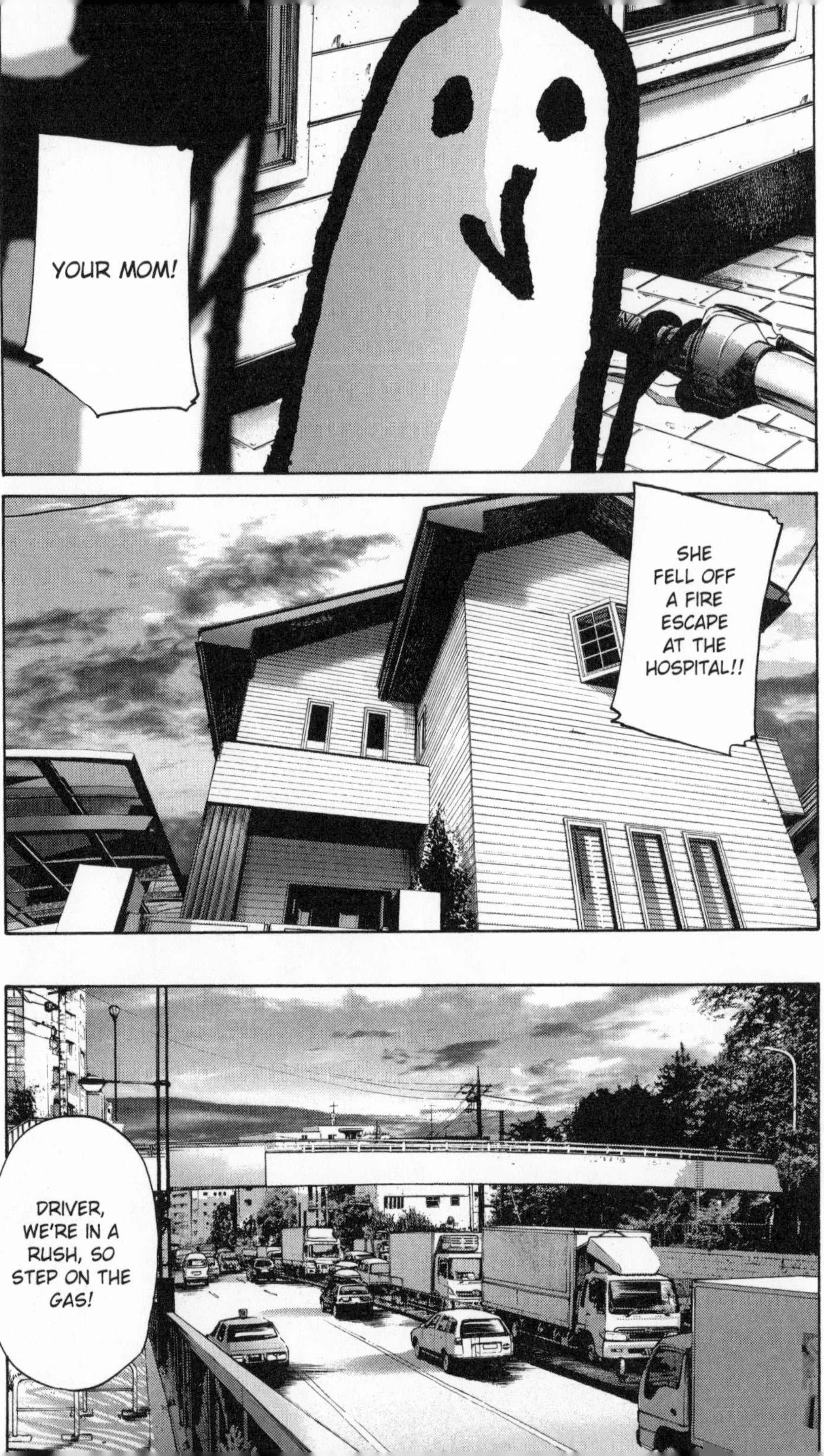
YOUR MOM!
SHE FELL OFF A FIRE ESCAPE AT THE HOSPITAL!!
DRIVER, WE'RE IN A RUSH, SO STEP ON THE GAS!

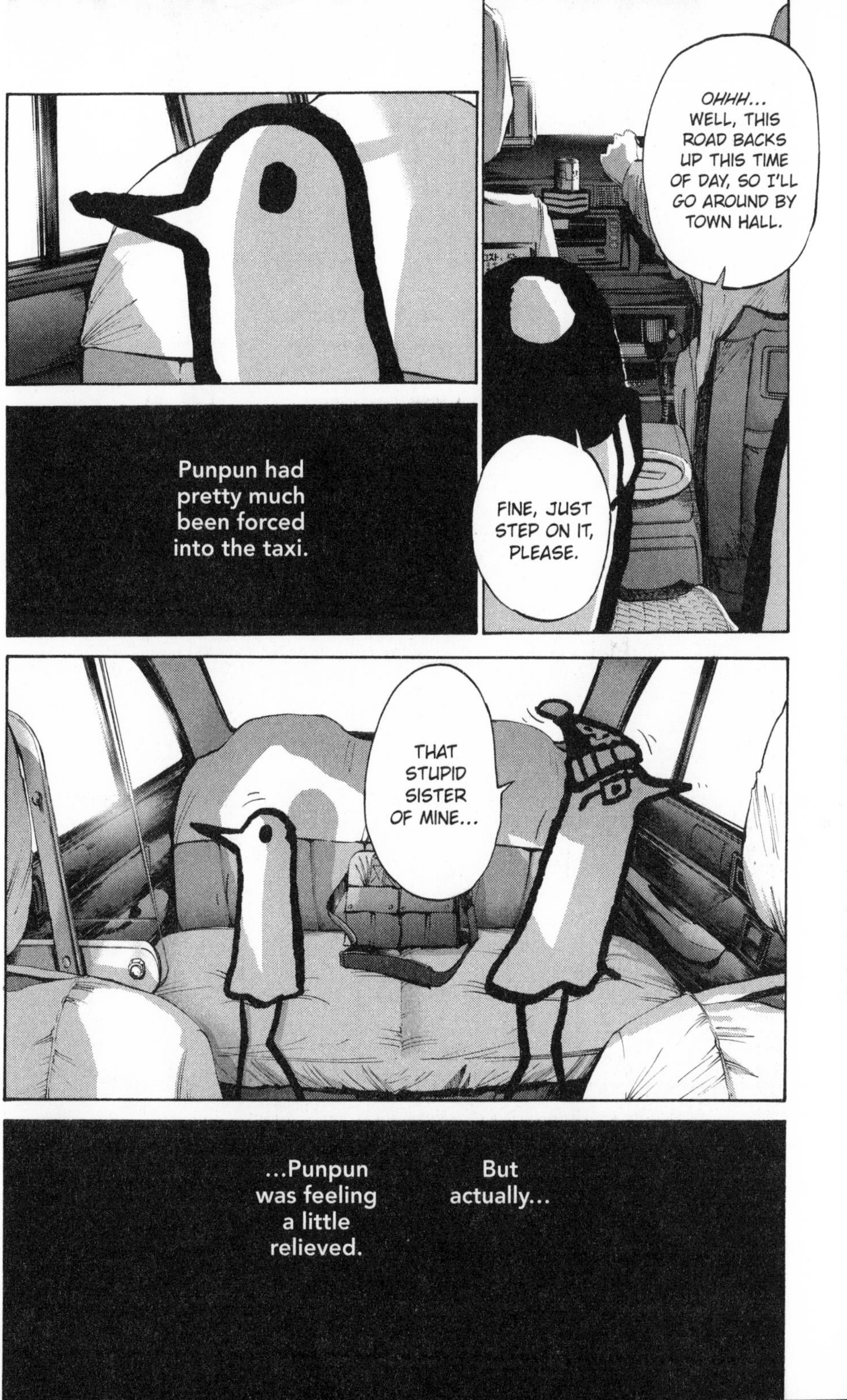
OHHH... WELL, THIS ROAD BACKS UP THIS TIME OF DAY, SO I'LL GO AROUND BY TOWN HALL.
FINE, JUST STEP ON IT, PLEASE.
Punpun had pretty much been forced into the taxi.
THAT STUPID SISTER OF MINE...
But actually...
...Punpun was feeling a little relieved.

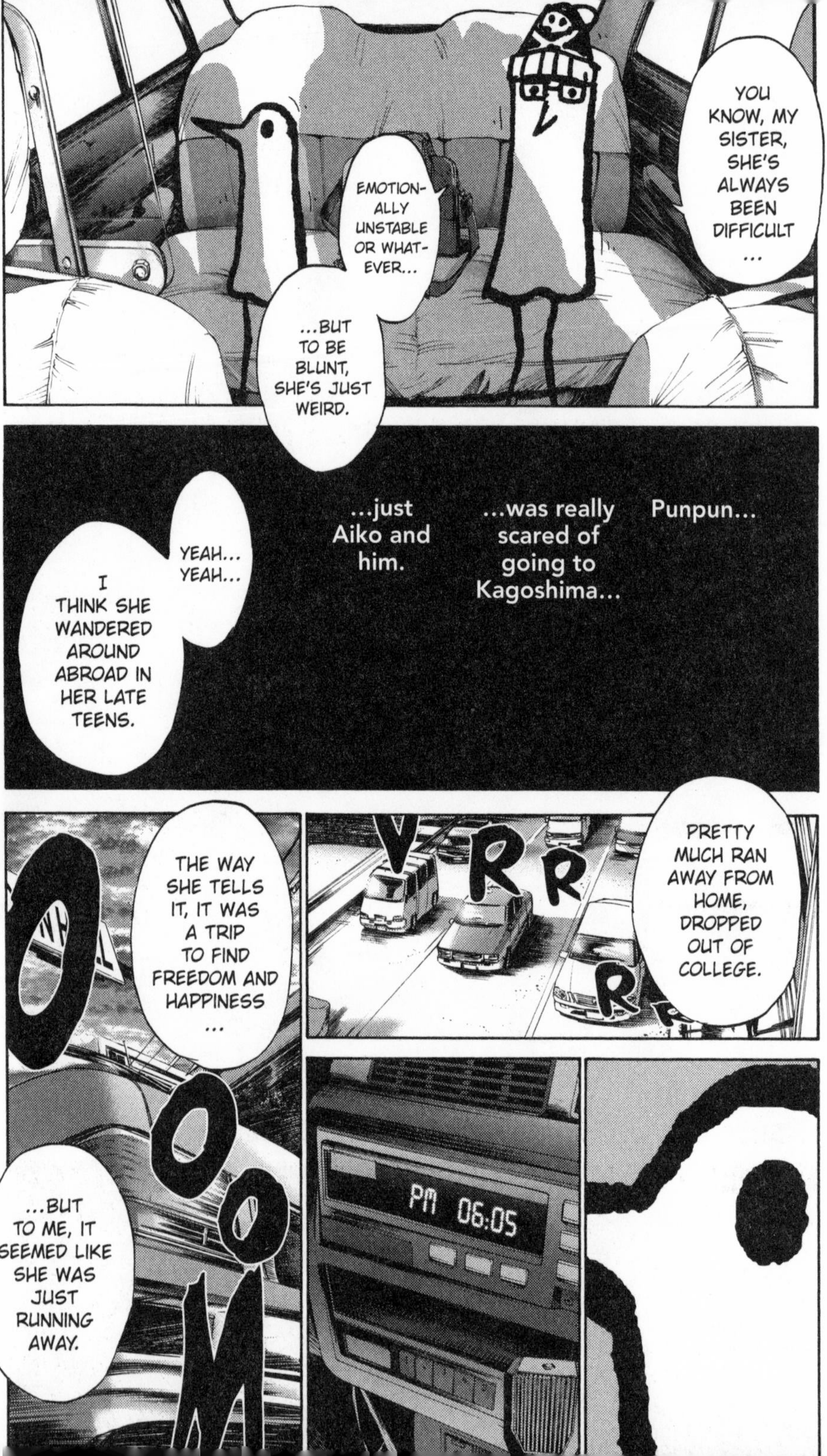

YOU KNOW, MY SISTER, SHE'S ALWAYS BEEN DIFFICULT...
EMOTIONALLY UNSTABLE OR WHATEVER...
...BUT TO BE BLUNT, SHE'S JUST WEIRD.
Punpun...
...was really scared of going to Kagoshima...
...just Aiko and him.
YEAH... YEAH...
I THINK SHE WANDERED AROUND ABROAD IN HER LATE TEENS.
VRRR
PRETTY MUCH RAN AWAY FROM HOME, DROPPED OUT OF COLLEGE.
PM 06:05
THE WAY SHE TELLS IT, IT WAS A TRIP TO FIND FREEDOM AND HAPPINESS...
OOOOM
...BUT TO ME, IT SEEMED LIKE SHE WAS JUST RUNNING AWAY.

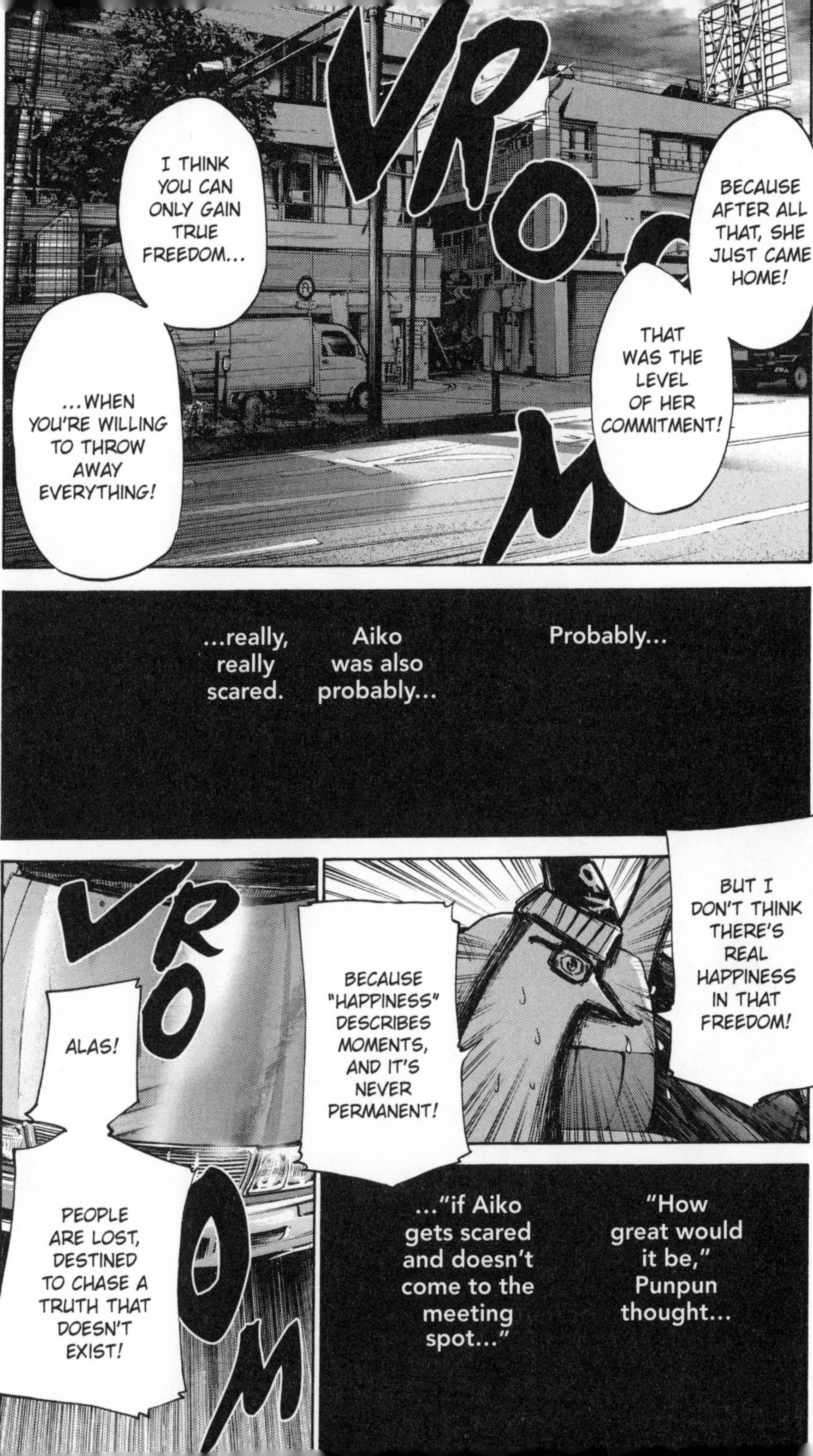

BECAUSE AFTER ALL THAT, SHE JUST CAME HOME!
THAT WAS THE LEVEL OF HER COMMITMENT!
VROOOM
I THINK YOU CAN ONLY GAIN TRUE FREEDOM...
...WHEN YOU'RE WILLING TO THROW AWAY EVERYTHING!
Probably...
Aiko was also probably...
...really, really scared.
BUT I DON'T THINK THERE'S REAL HAPPINESS IN THAT FREEDOM!
BECAUSE "HAPPINESS" DESCRIBES MOMENTS, AND IT'S NEVER PERMANENT!
"How great would it be," Punpun thought...
..."if Aiko gets scared and doesn't come to the meeting spot..."
VROOOM
ALAS!
PEOPLE ARE LOST, DESTINED TO CHASE A TRUTH THAT DOESN'T EXIST!

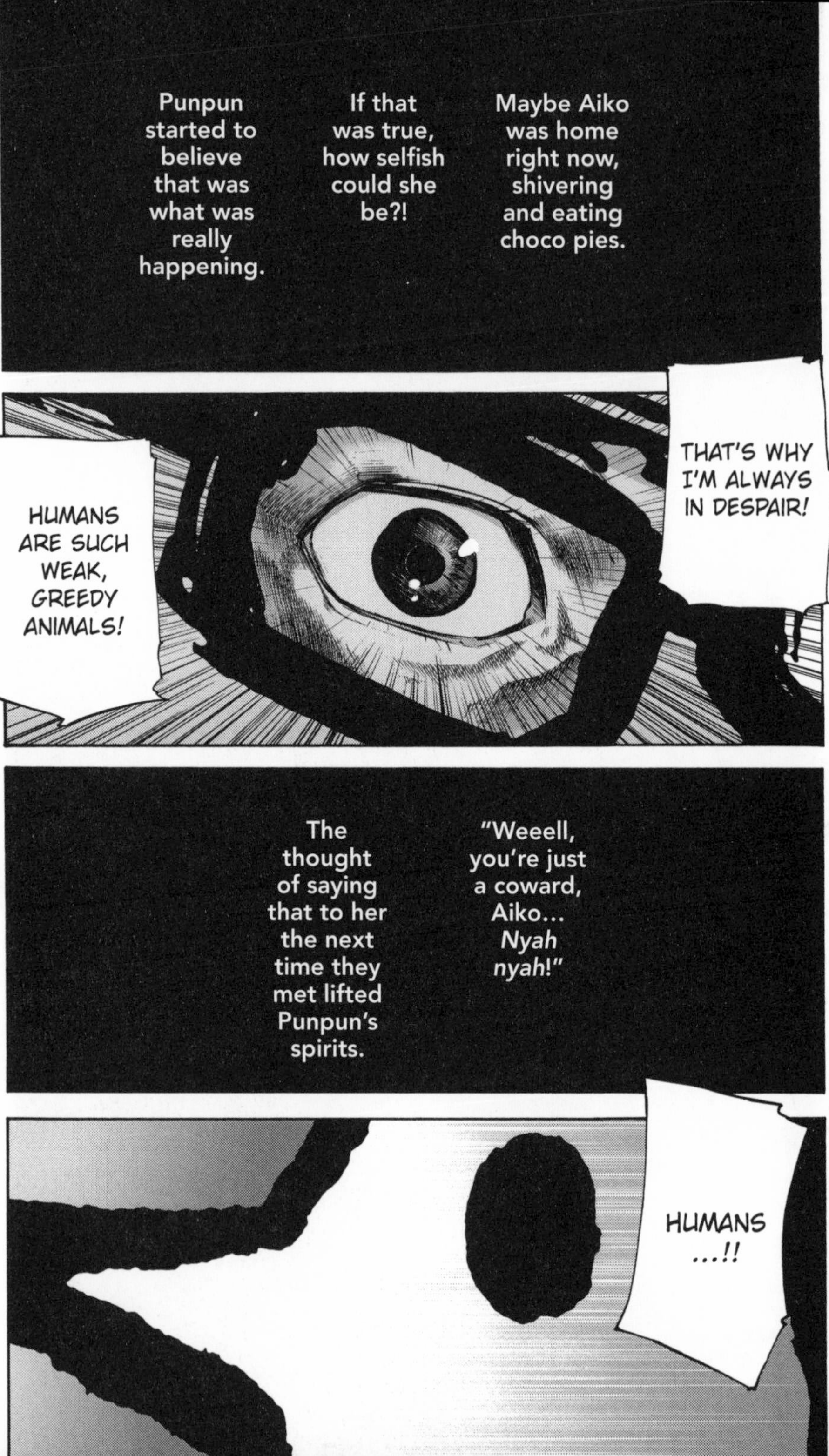
Maybe Aiko was home right now, shivering and eating choco pies.
If that was true, how selfish could she be?!
Punpun started to believe that was what was really happening.
THAT'S WHY I'M ALWAYS IN DESPAIR!
HUMANS ARE SUCH WEAK, GREEDY ANIMALS!
"Weeell, you're just a coward, Aiko... *Nyah nyah*!"
The thought of saying that to her the next time they met lifted Punpun's spirits.
HUMANS ...!!

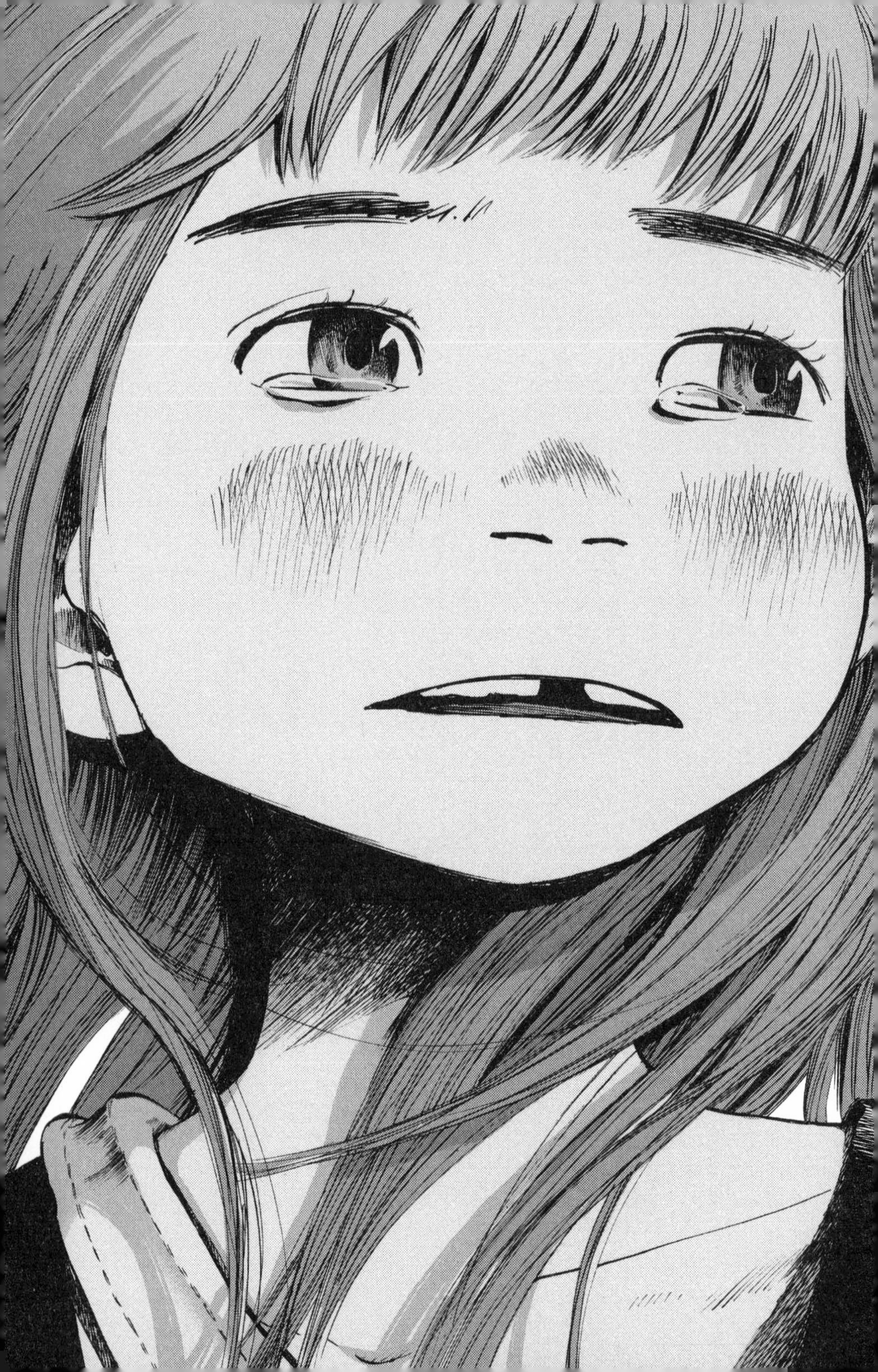

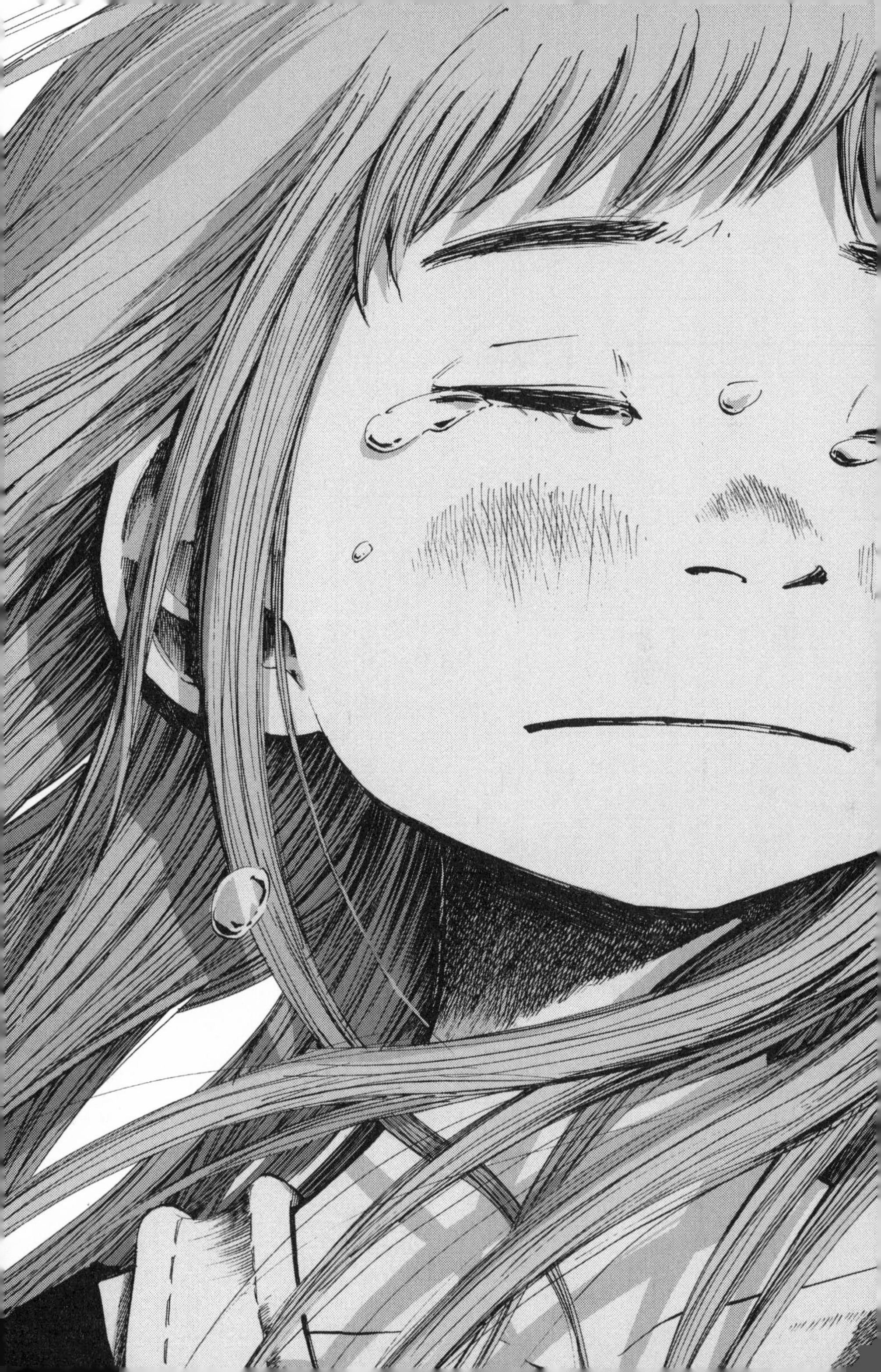

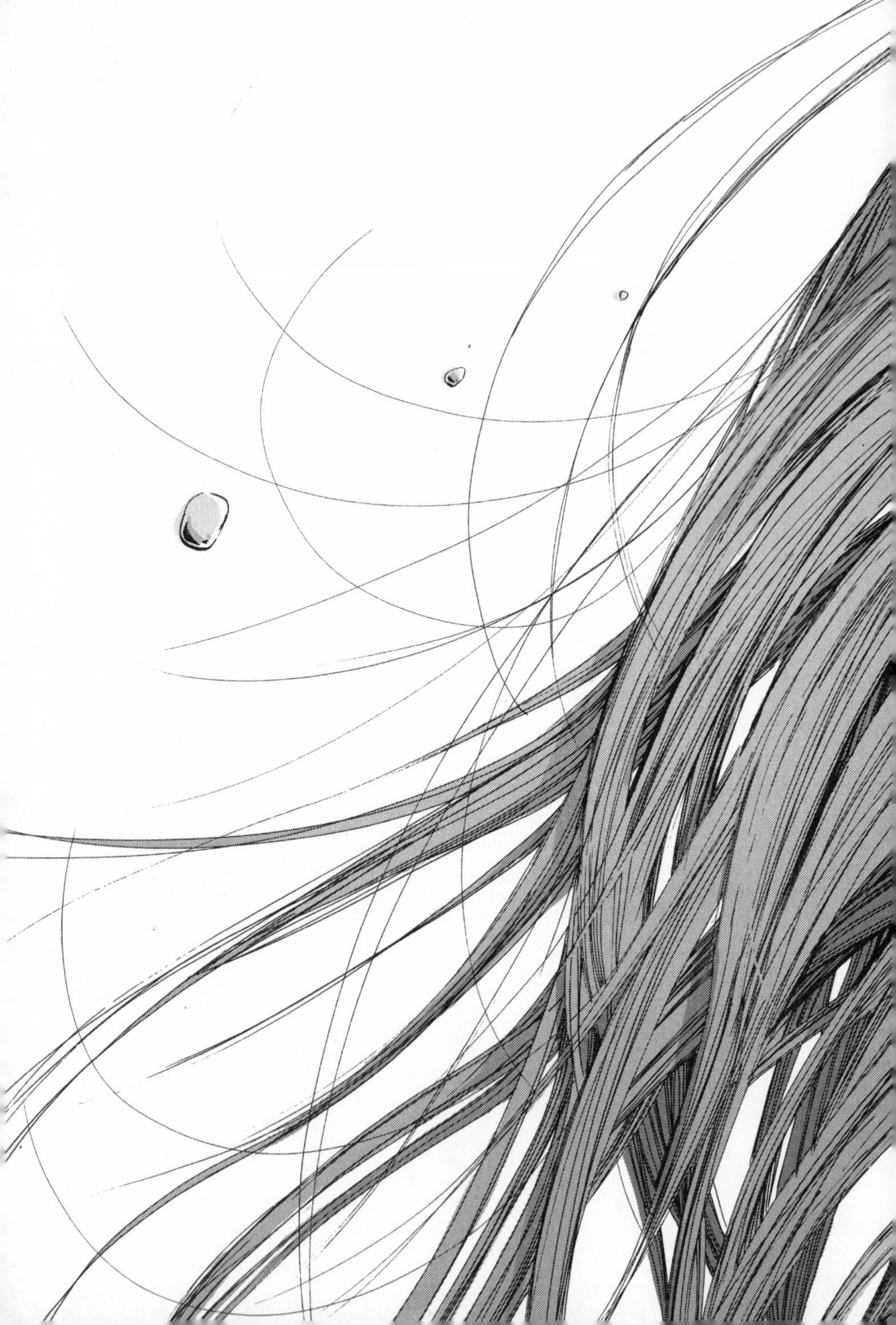

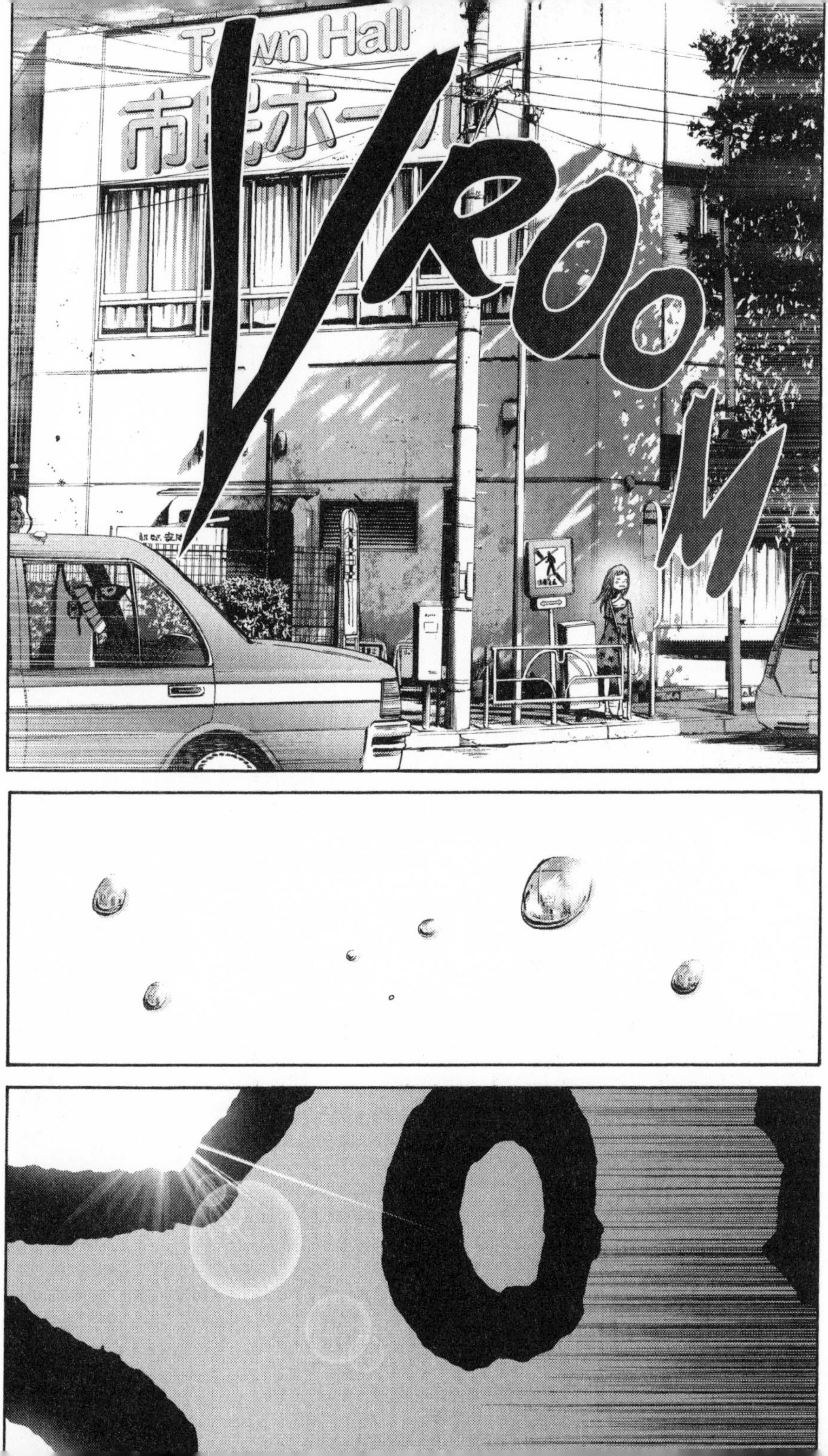
VROOM

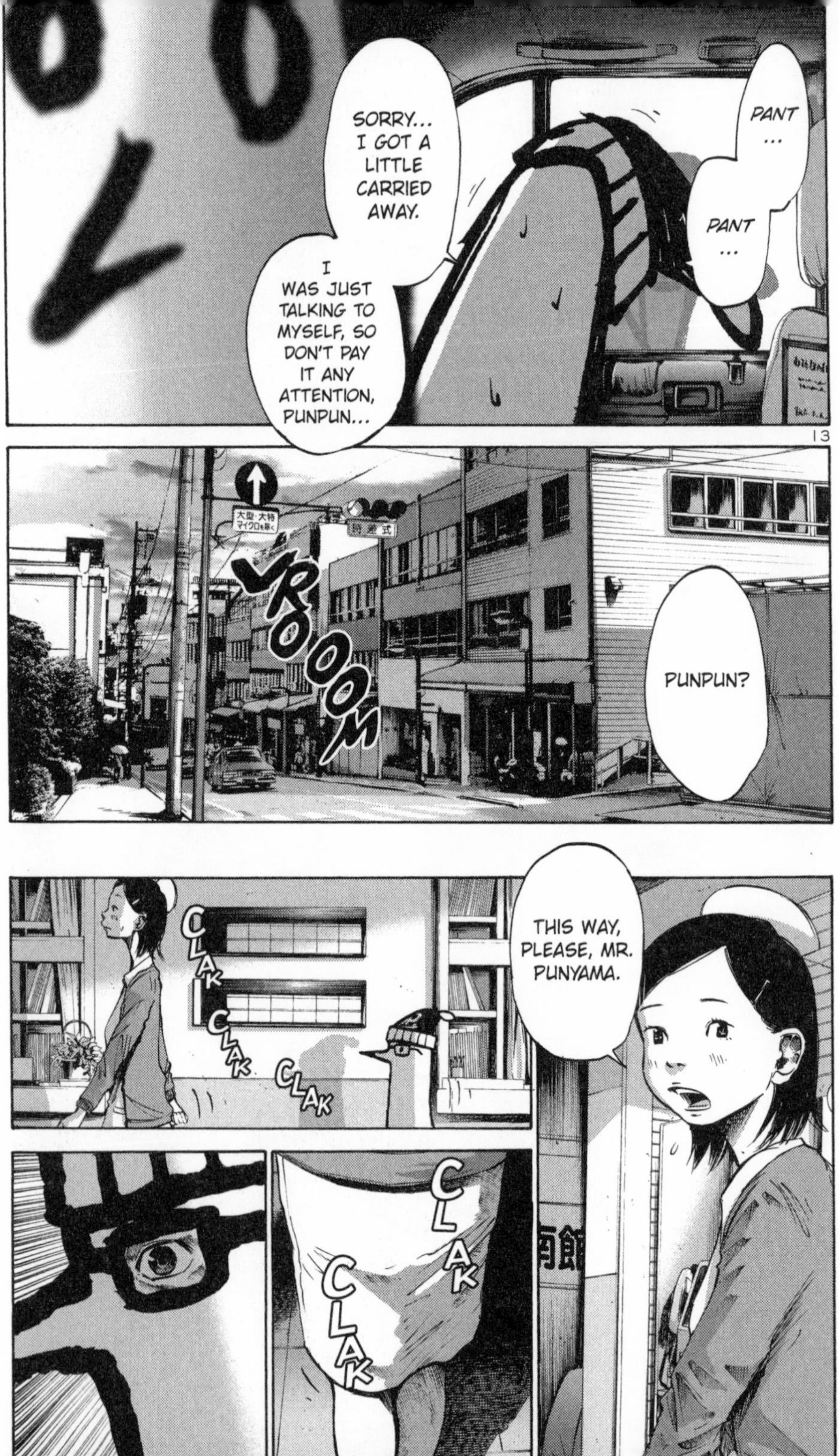
PANT ...
PANT ...
SORRY... I GOT A LITTLE CARRIED AWAY.
I WAS JUST TALKING TO MYSELF, SO DON'T PAY IT ANY ATTENTION, PUNPUN...
13
PUNPUN?
VROOOOM
THIS WAY, PLEASE, MR. PUNYAMA.
CLAK CLAK CLAK CLAK
CLAK CLAK

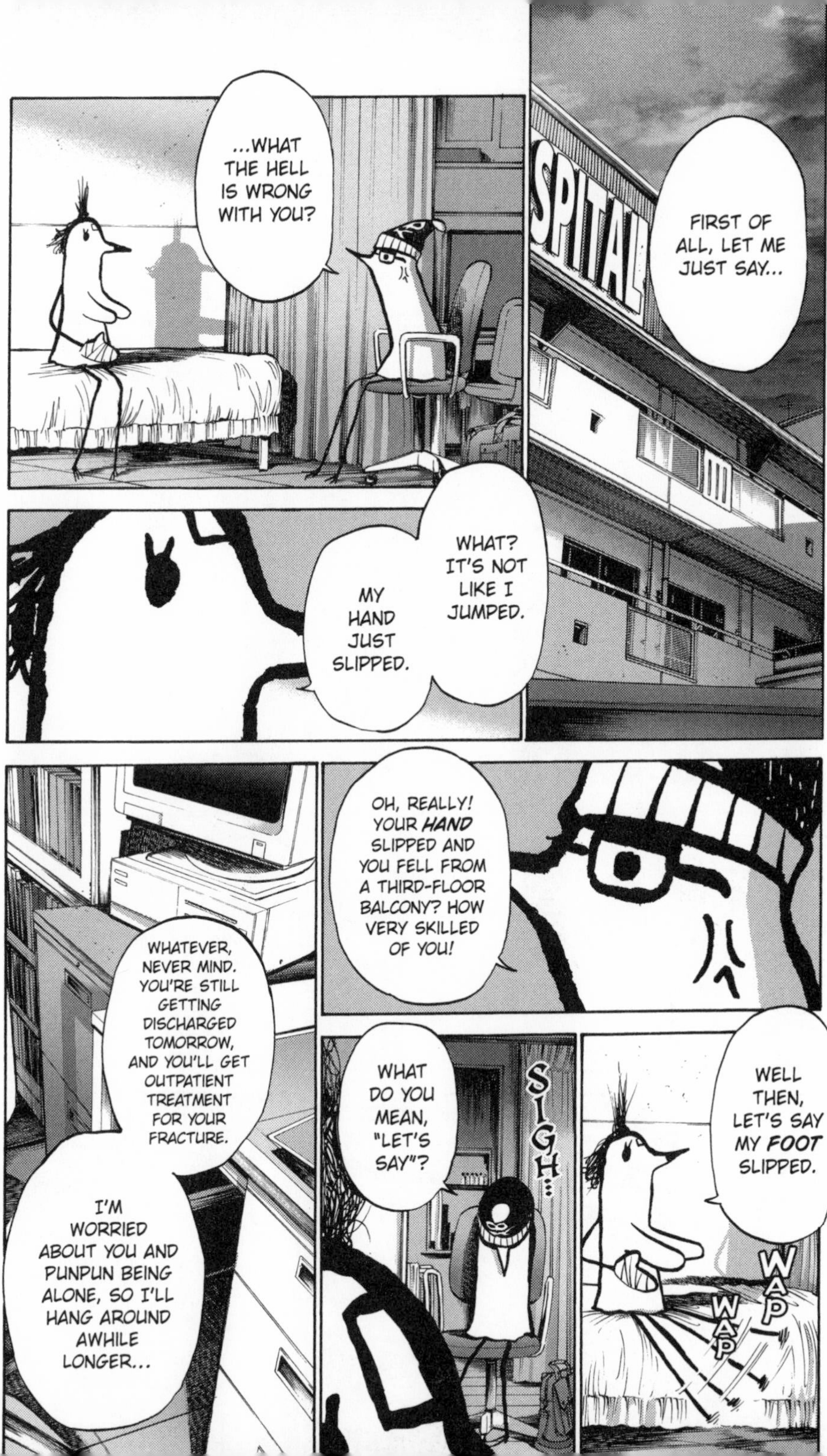
FIRST OF ALL, LET ME JUST SAY...
SPITAL
...WHAT THE HELL IS WRONG WITH YOU?
WHAT? IT'S NOT LIKE I JUMPED.
MY HAND JUST SLIPPED.
OH, REALLY! YOUR ***HAND*** SLIPPED AND YOU FELL FROM A THIRD-FLOOR BALCONY? HOW VERY SKILLED OF YOU!
WELL THEN, LET'S SAY MY ***FOOT*** SLIPPED.
WAP
WAP
WHAT DO YOU MEAN, "LET'S SAY"?
SIGH...
WHATEVER, NEVER MIND. YOU'RE STILL GETTING DISCHARGED TOMORROW, AND YOU'LL GET OUTPATIENT TREATMENT FOR YOUR FRACTURE.
I'M WORRIED ABOUT YOU AND PUNPUN BEING ALONE, SO I'LL HANG AROUND AWHILE LONGER...

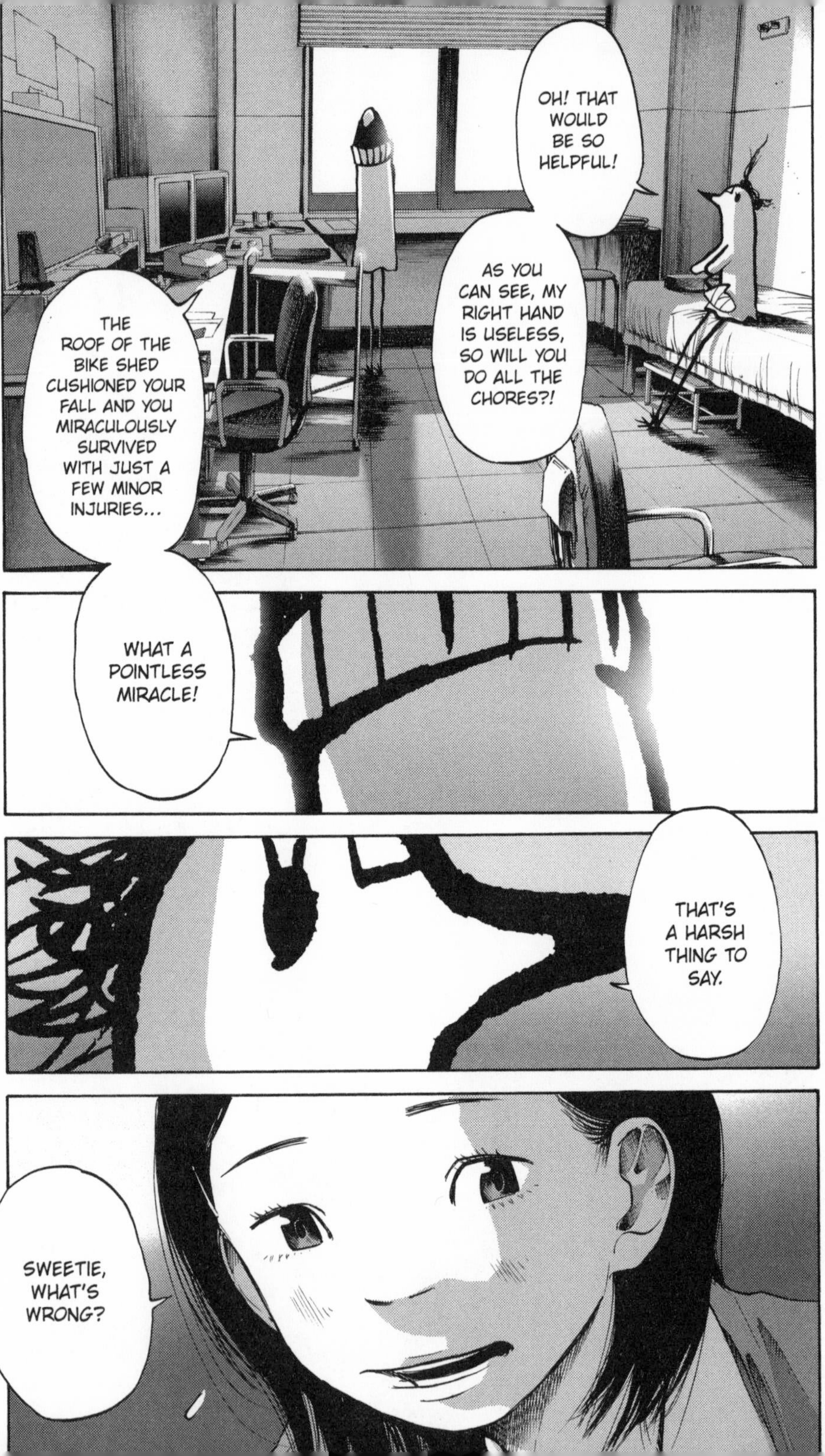
OH! THAT WOULD BE SO HELPFUL!
AS YOU CAN SEE, MY RIGHT HAND IS USELESS, SO WILL YOU DO ALL THE CHORES?!
THE ROOF OF THE BIKE SHED CUSHIONED YOUR FALL AND YOU MIRACULOUSLY SURVIVED WITH JUST A FEW MINOR INJURIES...
WHAT A POINTLESS MIRACLE!
THAT'S A HARSH THING TO SAY.
SWEETIE, WHAT'S WRONG?

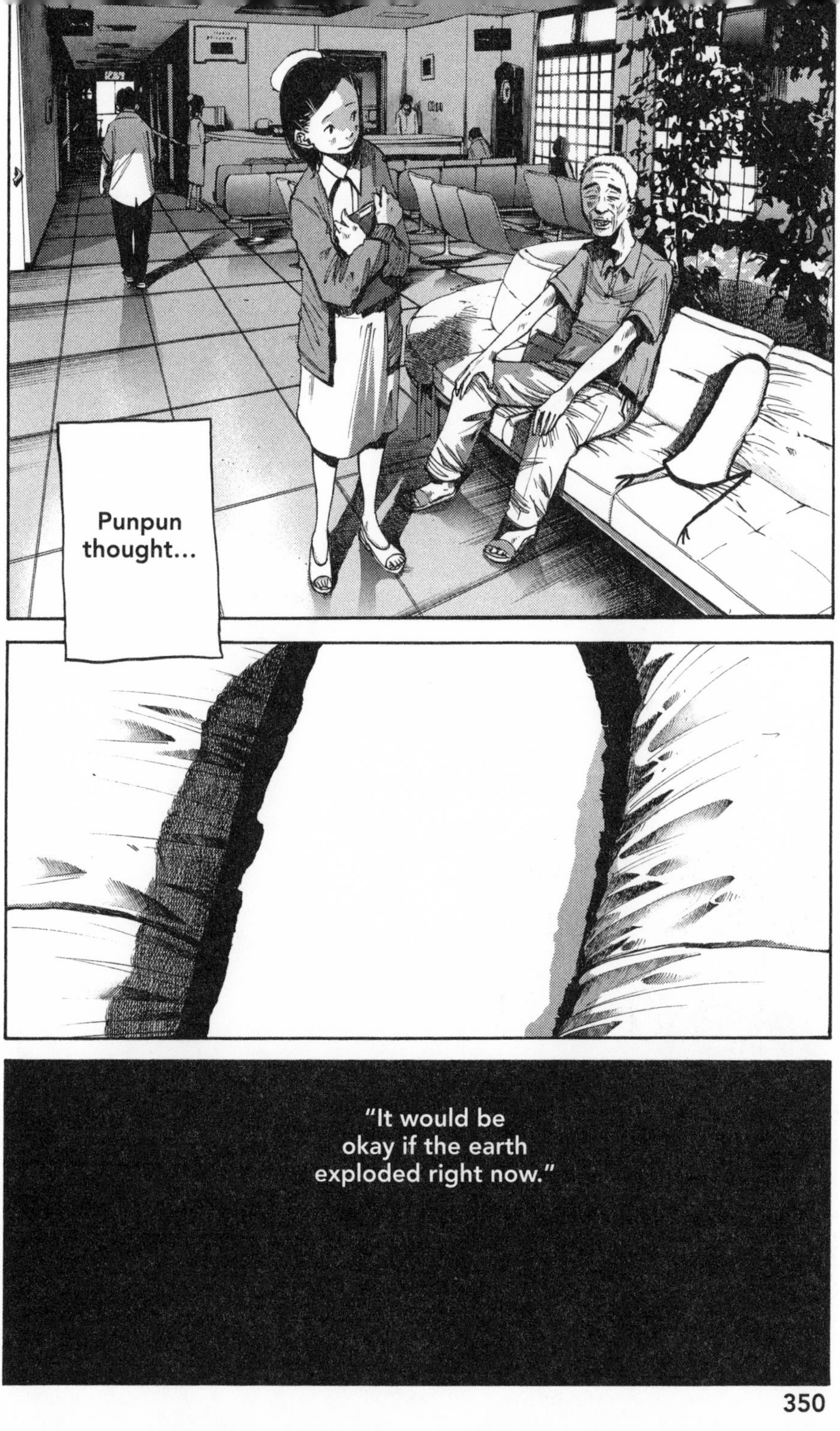
Punpun thought...
"It would be okay if the earth exploded right now."

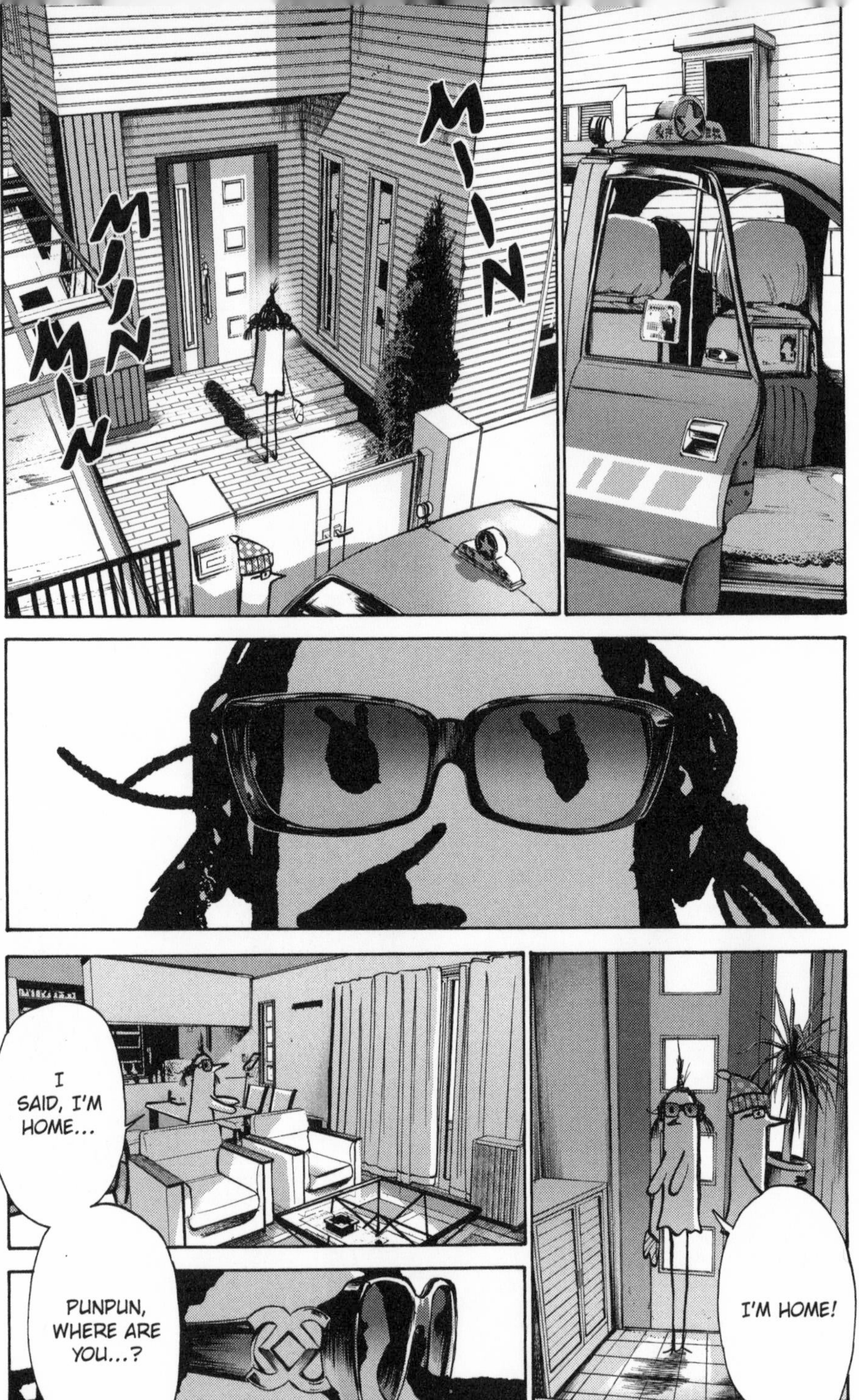
MIIN
MIN
MIN
I'M HOME!
I SAID, I'M HOME...
PUNPUN, WHERE ARE YOU...?

Chapter 20

I SAID, I'M HOME!

OH, THERE YOU ARE.

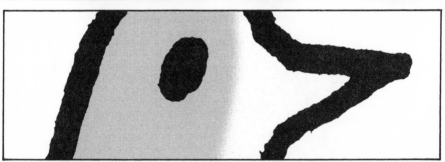

SAY SOME-THING!

WHACK

354

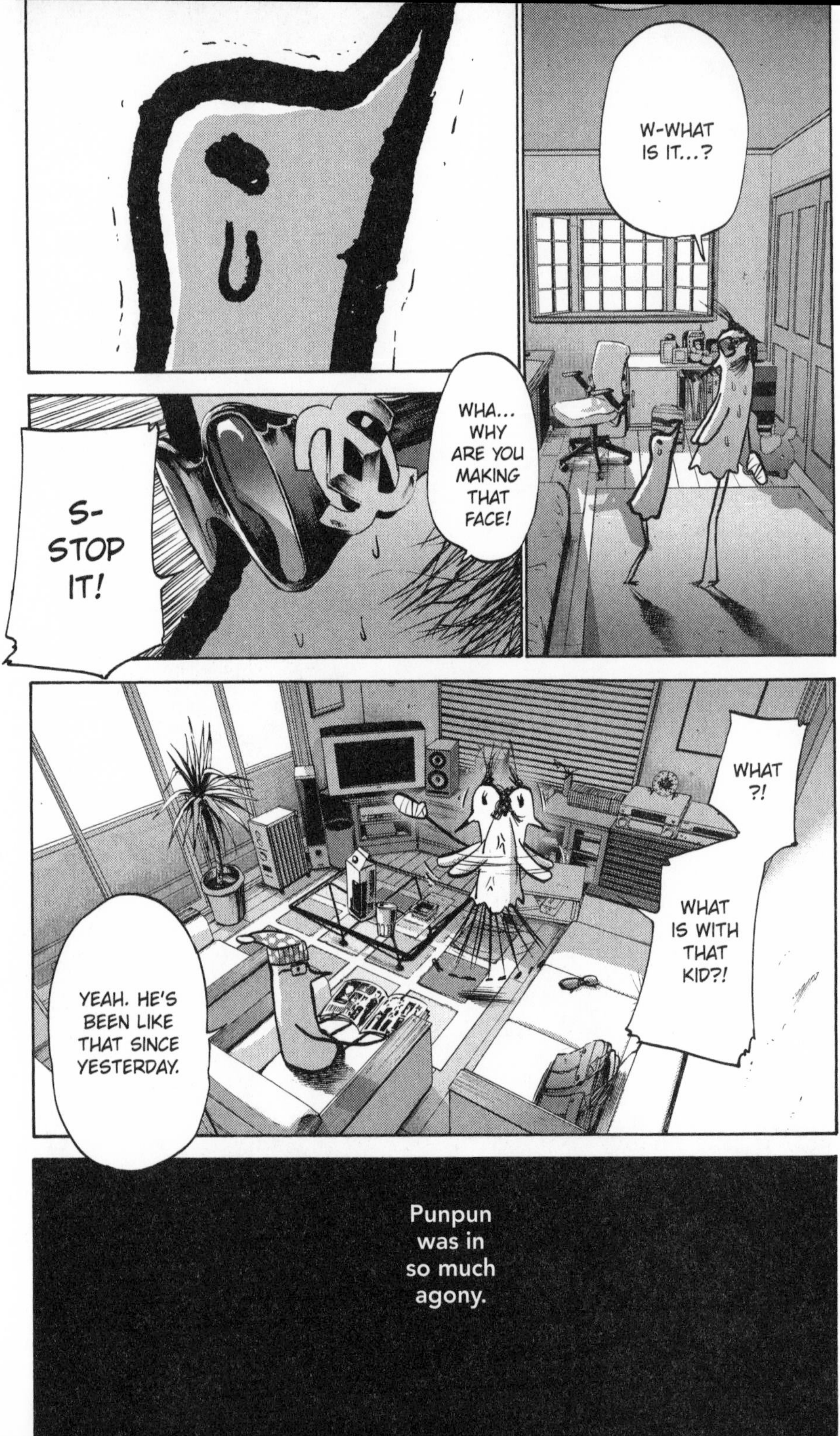
W-WHAT IS IT...?
WHA... WHY ARE YOU MAKING THAT FACE!
S-STOP IT!
WHAT ?!
WHAT IS WITH THAT KID?!
YEAH. HE'S BEEN LIKE THAT SINCE YESTERDAY.
Punpun was in so much agony.

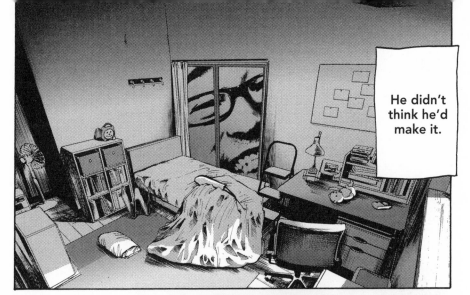

He didn't think he'd make it.

Do you feel better now that you've taken it out on her?

God loves the despicable Mr. Punyama!

It felt bad.

Not at all.

356

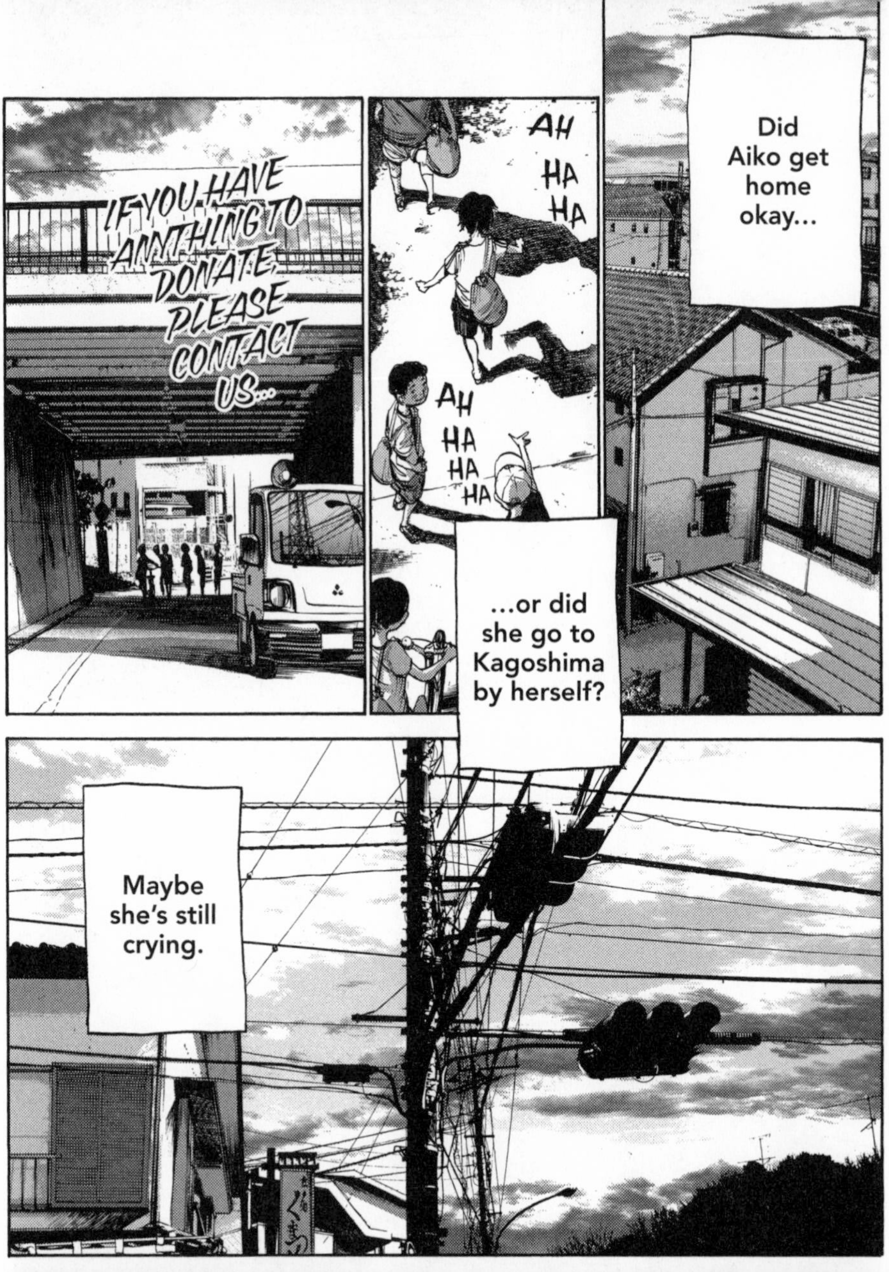
Did Aiko get home okay...
...or did she go to Kagoshima by herself?
AH HA HA
AH HA HA HA
IF YOU HAVE ANYTHING TO DONATE, PLEASE CONTACT US...
Maybe she's still crying.

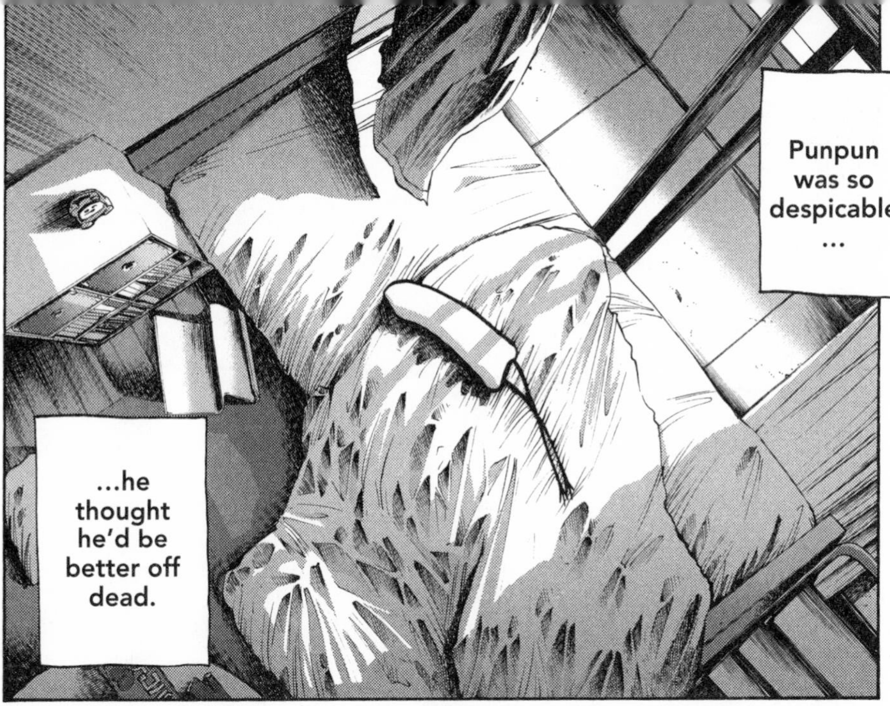
Punpun was so despicable ...
...he thought he'd be better off dead.

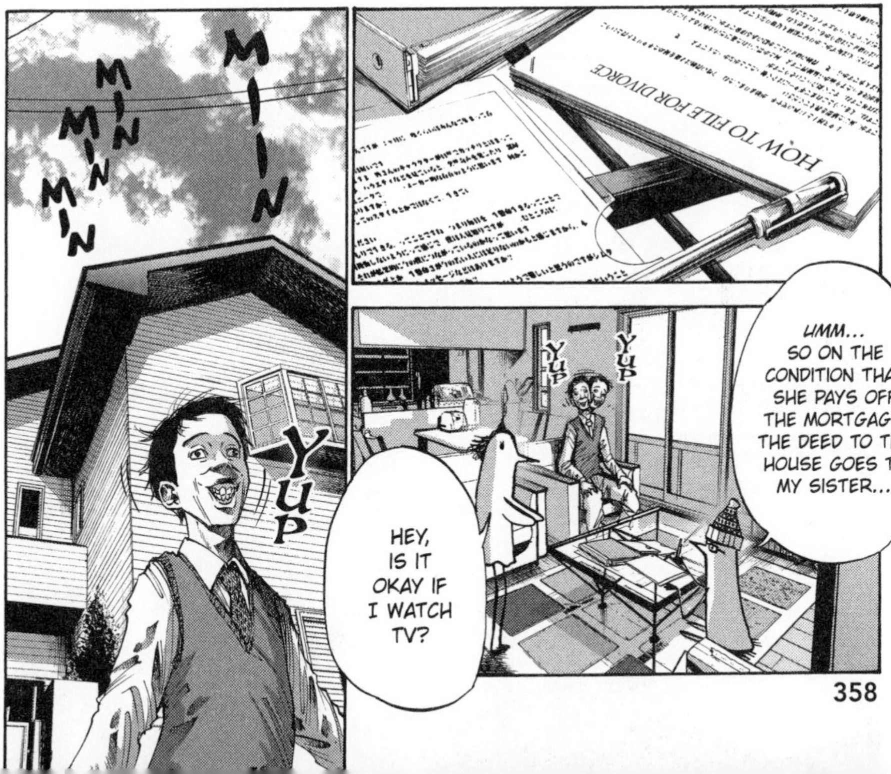
HOW TO FILE FOR DIVORCE
UMM... SO ON THE CONDITION THAT SHE PAYS OFF THE MORTGAGE, THE DEED TO THE HOUSE GOES TO MY SISTER...
YUP
YUP
HEY, IS IT OKAY IF I WATCH TV?
MIN MIN MIN
MI—N
YUP YUP

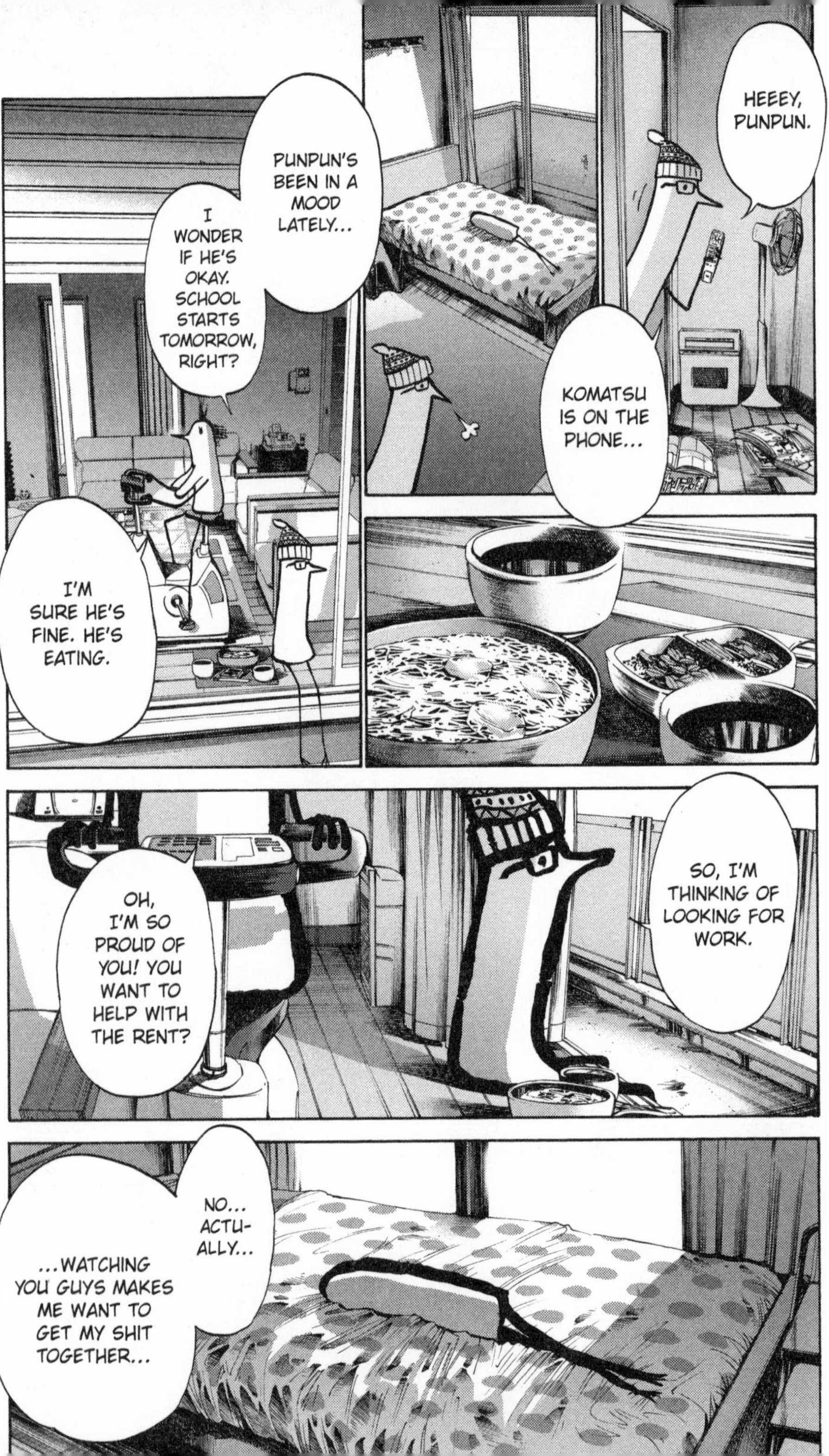
HEEEY, PUNPUN.
KOMATSU IS ON THE PHONE...
PUNPUN'S BEEN IN A MOOD LATELY...
I WONDER IF HE'S OKAY. SCHOOL STARTS TOMORROW, RIGHT?
I'M SURE HE'S FINE. HE'S EATING.
SO, I'M THINKING OF LOOKING FOR WORK.
OH, I'M SO PROUD OF YOU! YOU WANT TO HELP WITH THE RENT?
NO... ACTU-ALLY...
...WATCHING YOU GUYS MAKES ME WANT TO GET MY SHIT TOGETHER...

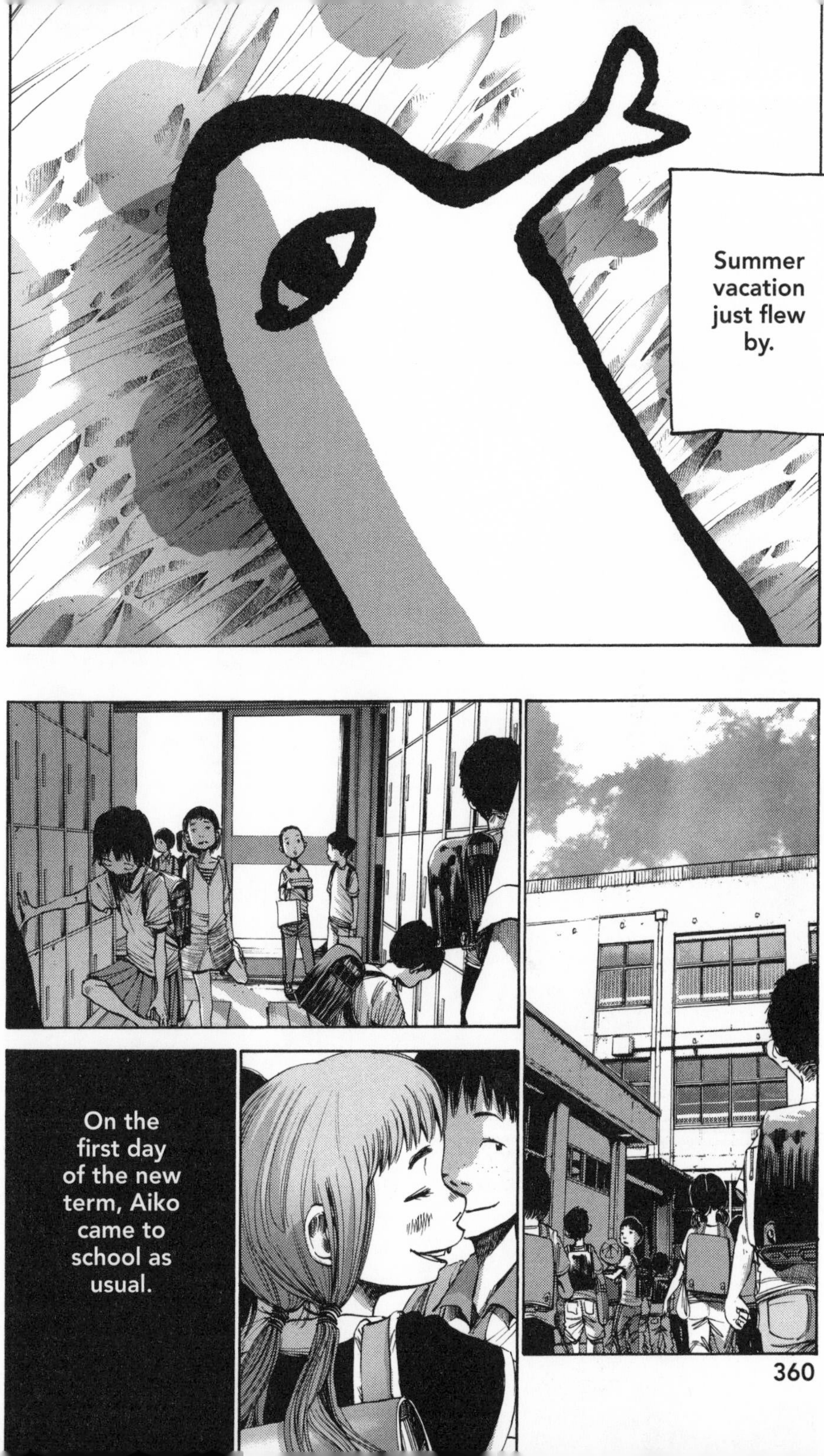
Summer vacation just flew by.
On the first day of the new term, Aiko came to school as usual.

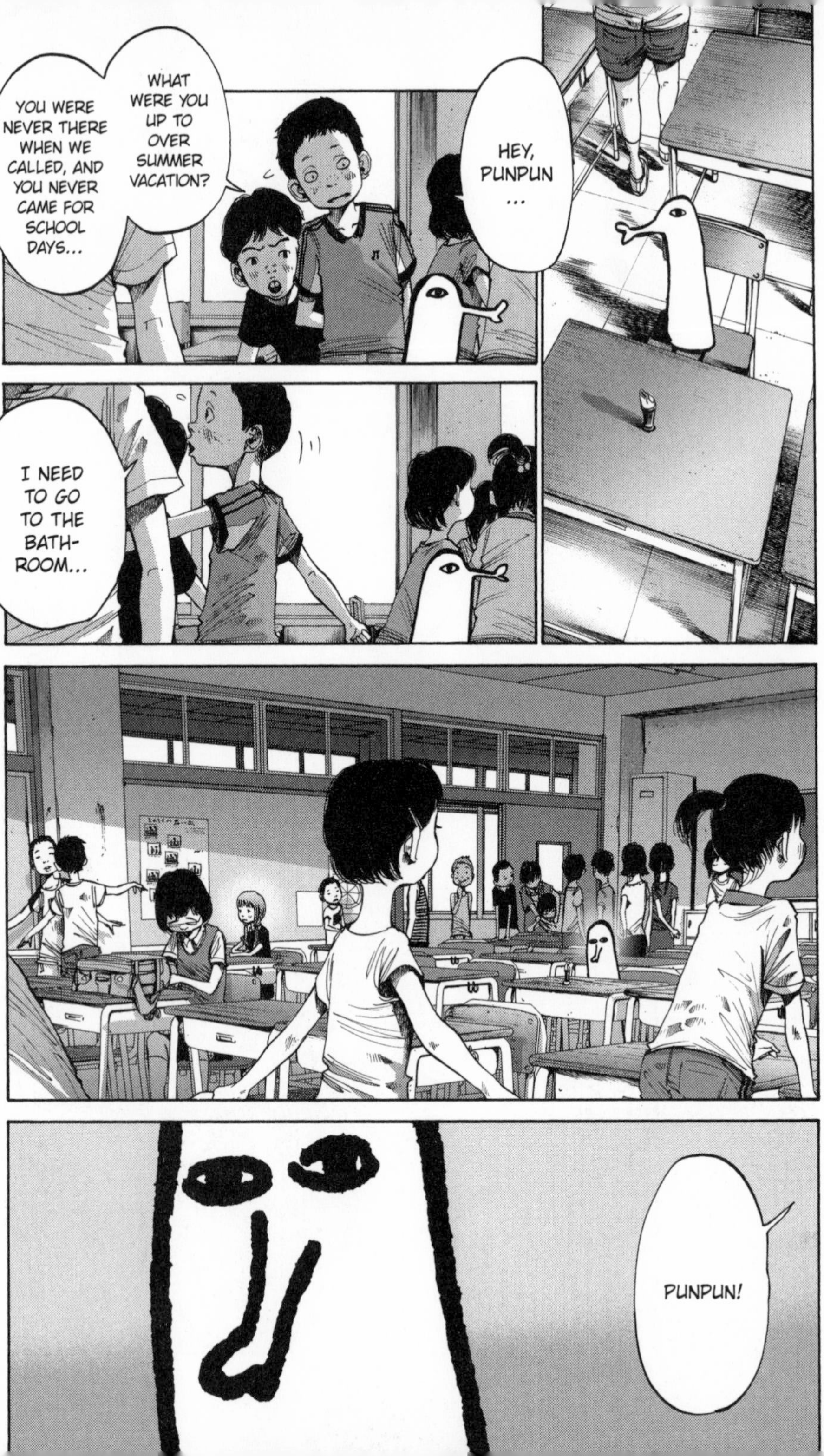
HEY, PUNPUN ...
WHAT WERE YOU UP TO OVER SUMMER VACATION?
YOU WERE NEVER THERE WHEN WE CALLED, AND YOU NEVER CAME FOR SCHOOL DAYS...
I NEED TO GO TO THE BATHROOM...
PUNPUN!

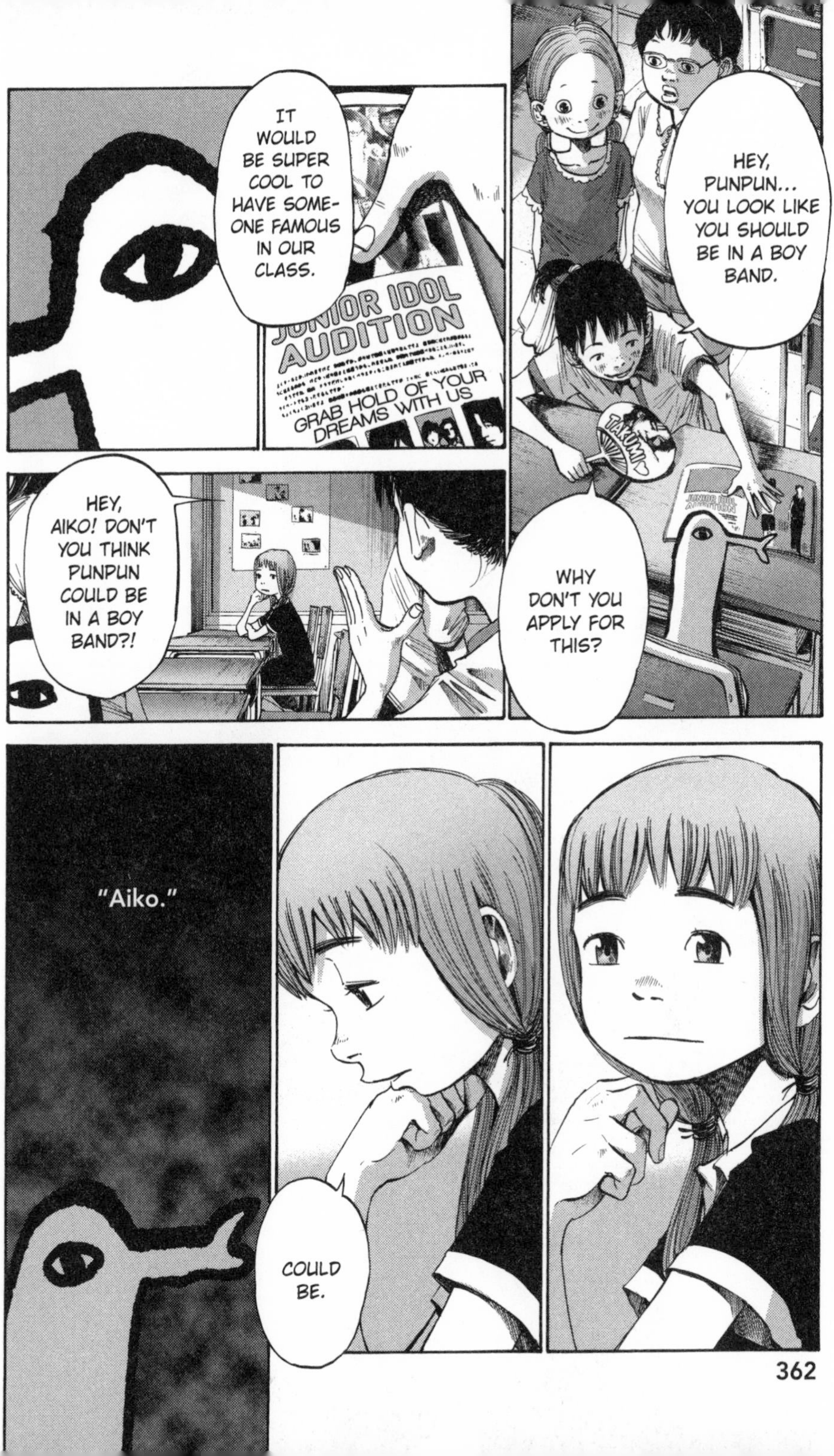
HEY, PUNPUN... YOU LOOK LIKE YOU SHOULD BE IN A BOY BAND.
TAKUMI
WHY DON'T YOU APPLY FOR THIS?
IT WOULD BE SUPER COOL TO HAVE SOME-ONE FAMOUS IN OUR CLASS.
JUNIOR IDOL AUDITION
GRAB HOLD OF YOUR DREAMS WITH US
HEY, AIKO! DON'T YOU THINK PUNPUN COULD BE IN A BOY BAND?!
COULD BE.
"Aiko."

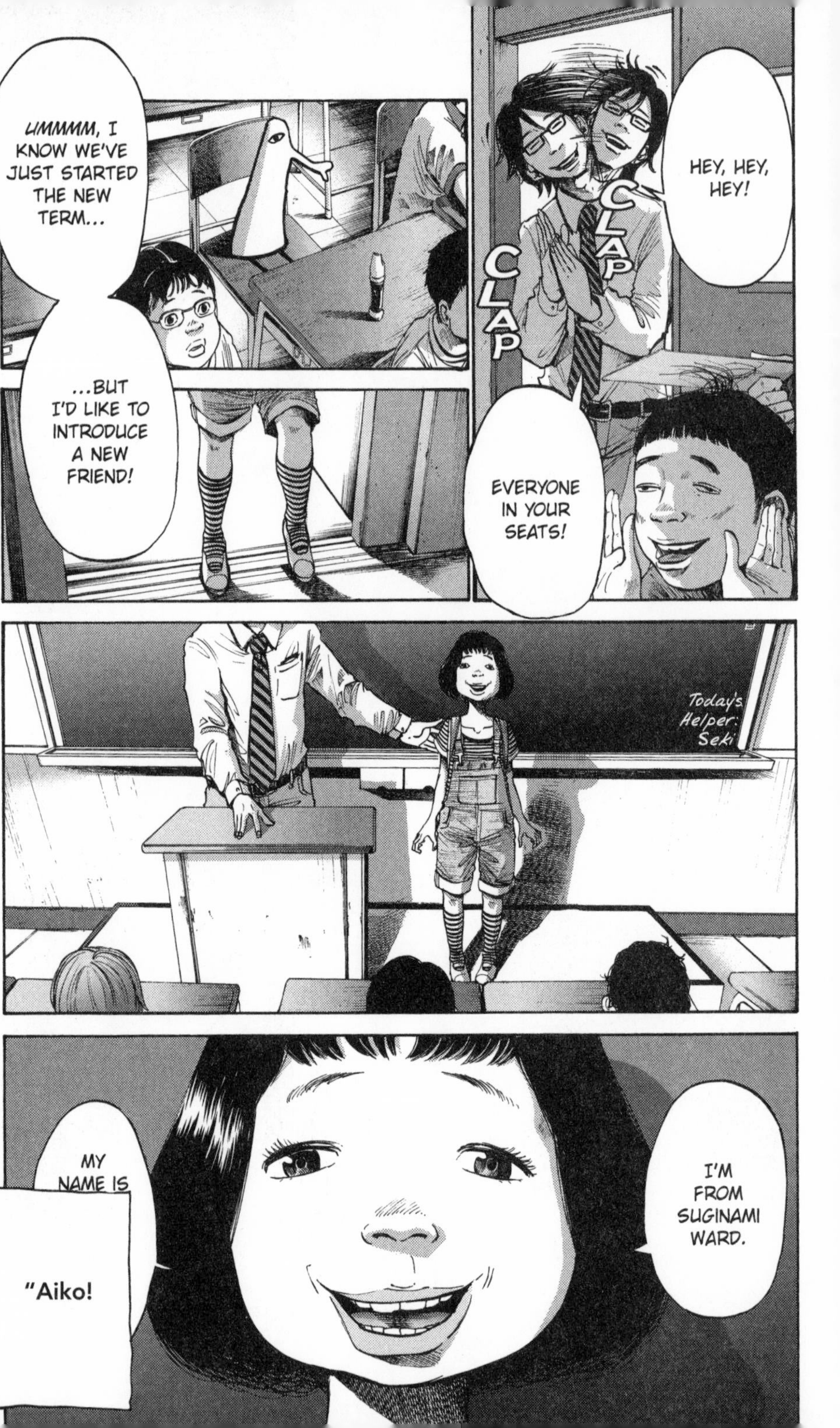
HEY, HEY, HEY!
CLAP
CLAP
EVERYONE IN YOUR SEATS!
UMMMM, I KNOW WE'VE JUST STARTED THE NEW TERM...
...BUT I'D LIKE TO INTRODUCE A NEW FRIEND!
Today's Helper: Seki
MY NAME IS
"Aiko!
I'M FROM SUGINAMI WARD.

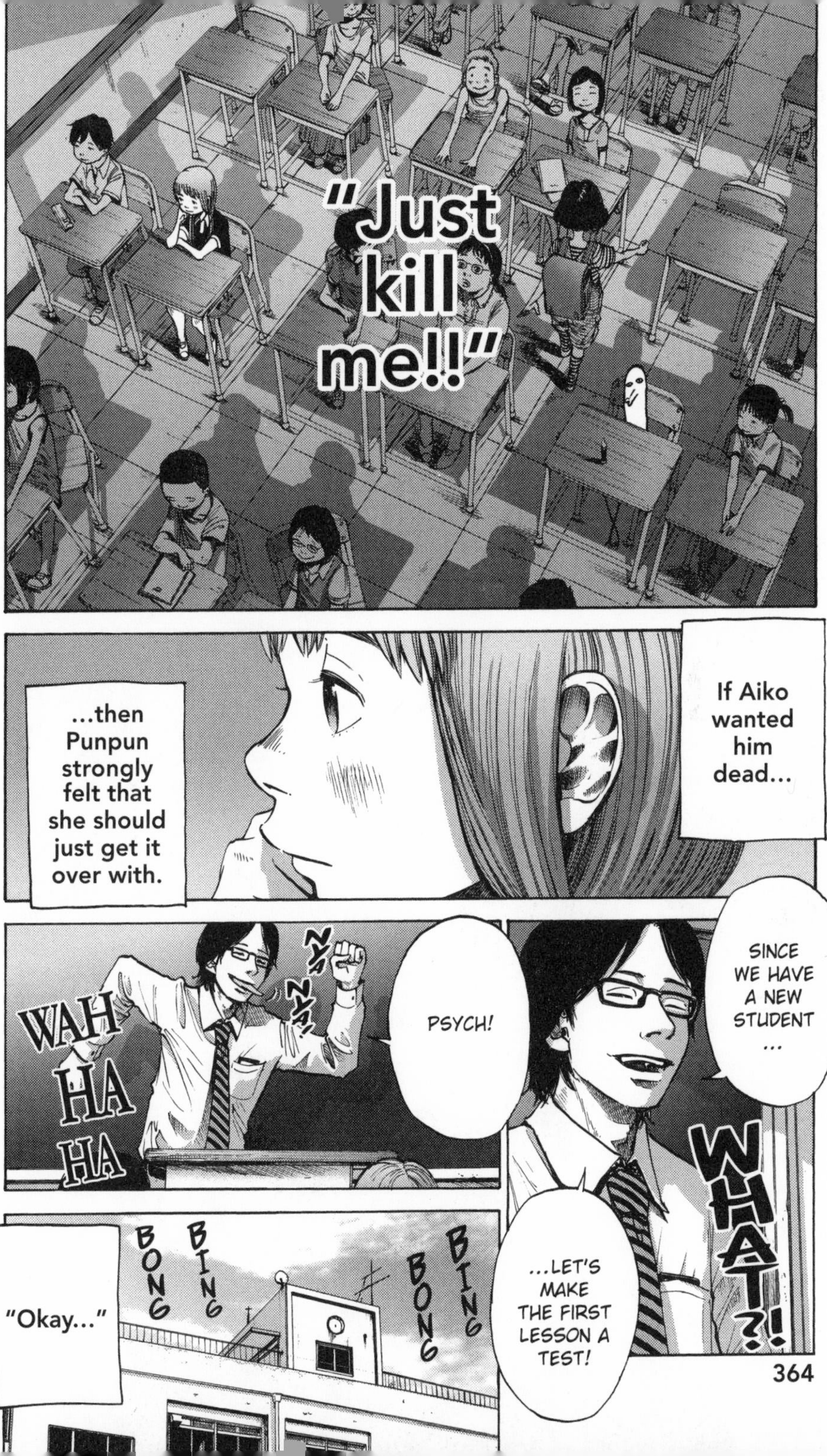

"Just kill me!!"
If Aiko wanted him dead...
...then Punpun strongly felt that she should just get it over with.
SINCE WE HAVE A NEW STUDENT ...
WHAT?!
...LET'S MAKE THE FIRST LESSON A TEST!
PSYCH!
NYA NYA
WAH HA HA
BING BONG
BING BONG
"Okay..."

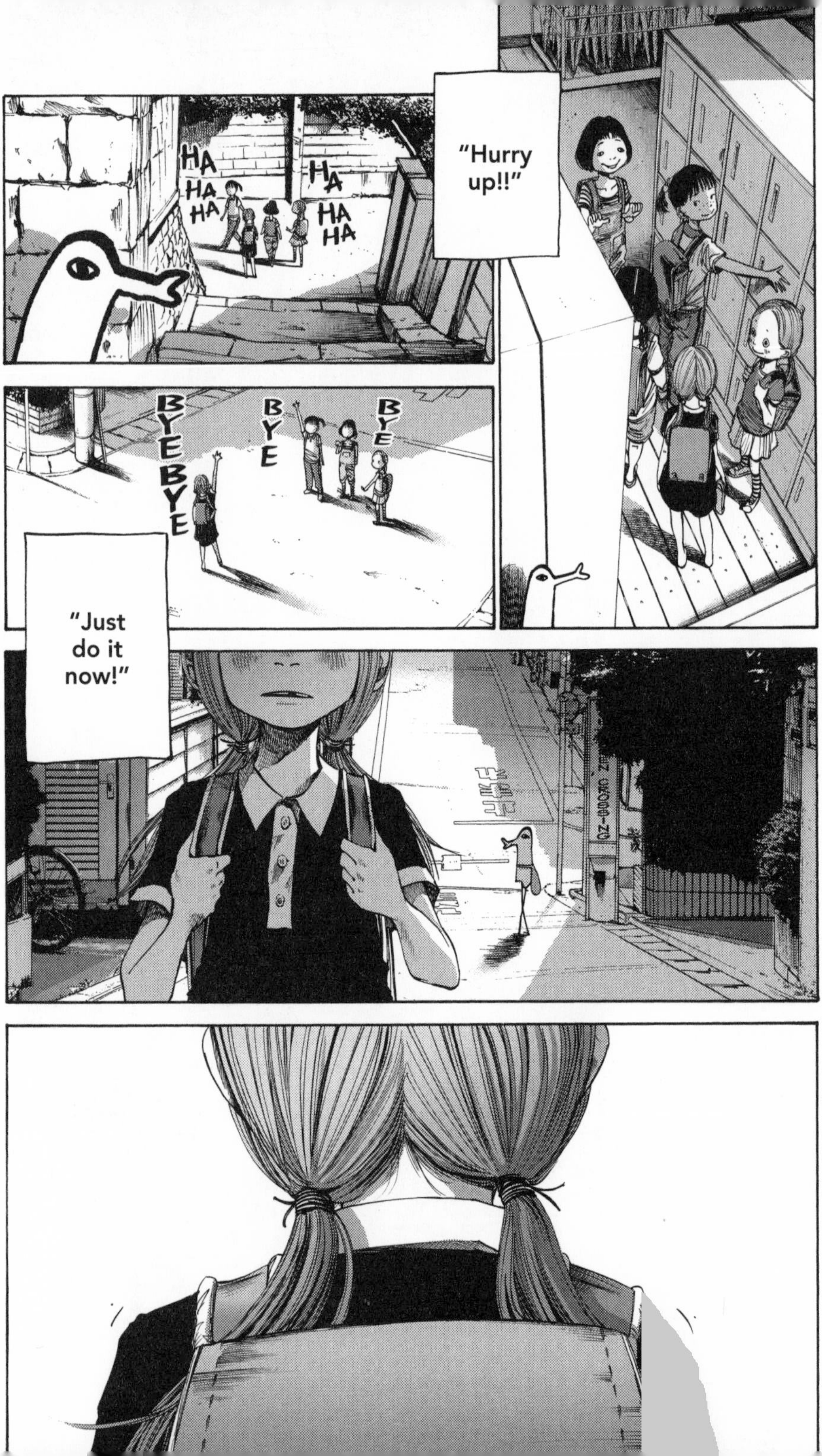
"Hurry up!!"
HA HA HA
HA HA HA
BYE BYE
BYE
BYE
"Just do it now!"

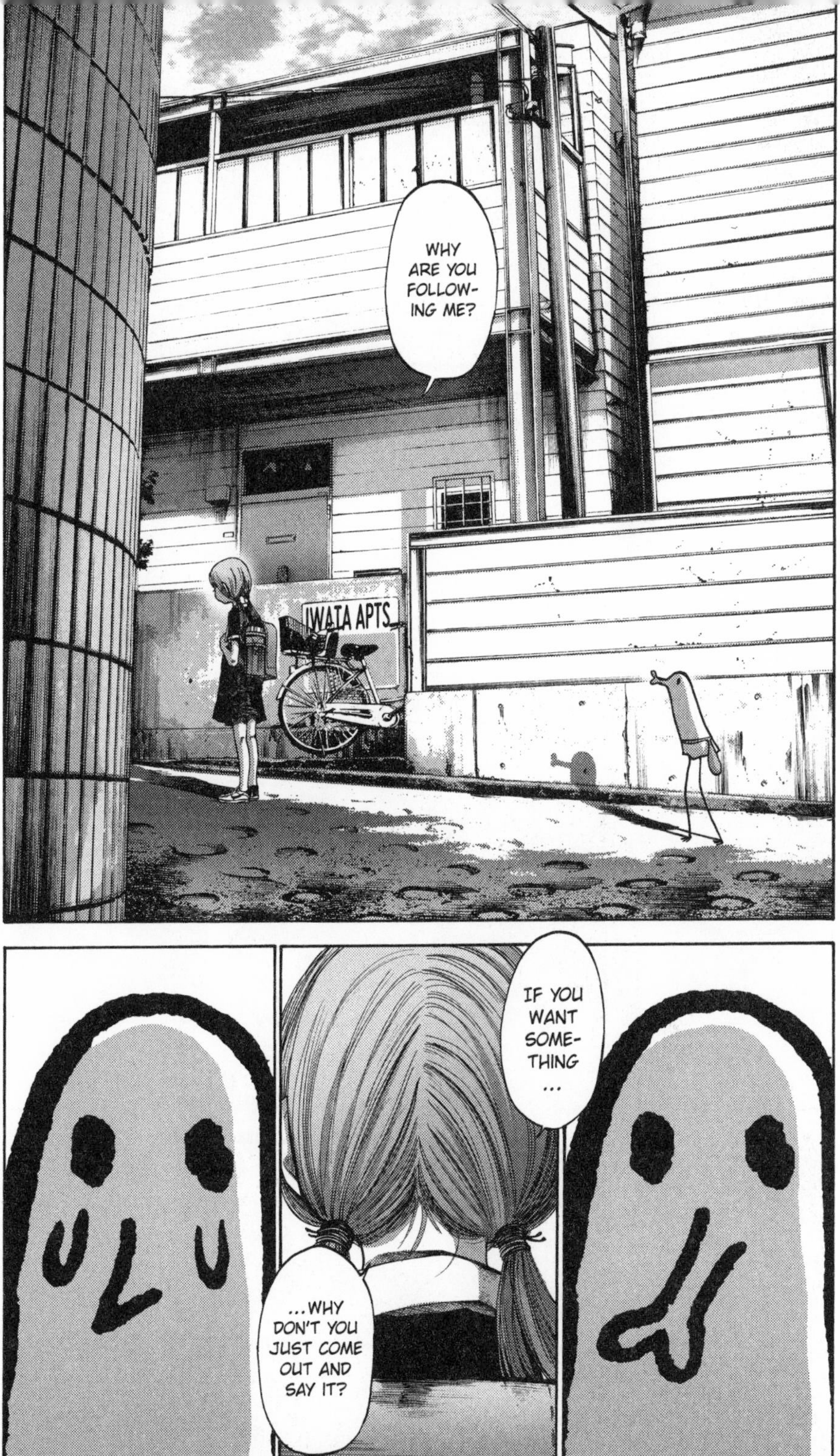
WHY ARE YOU FOLLOWING ME?
IWAIA APTS
IF YOU WANT SOMETHING...
...WHY DON'T YOU JUST COME OUT AND SAY IT?

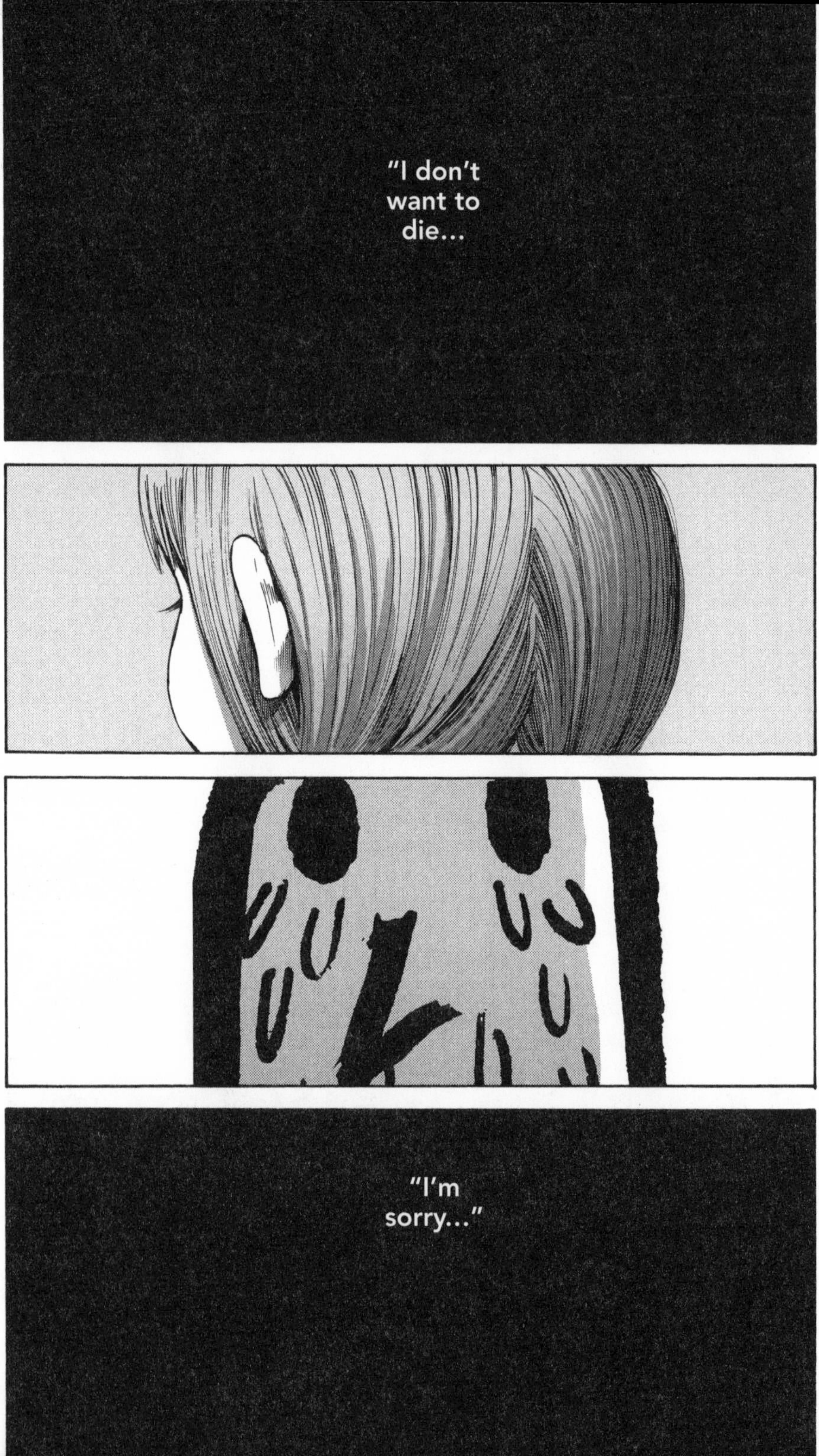

"I don't
want to
die...

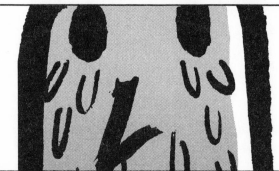

"I'm
sorry..."

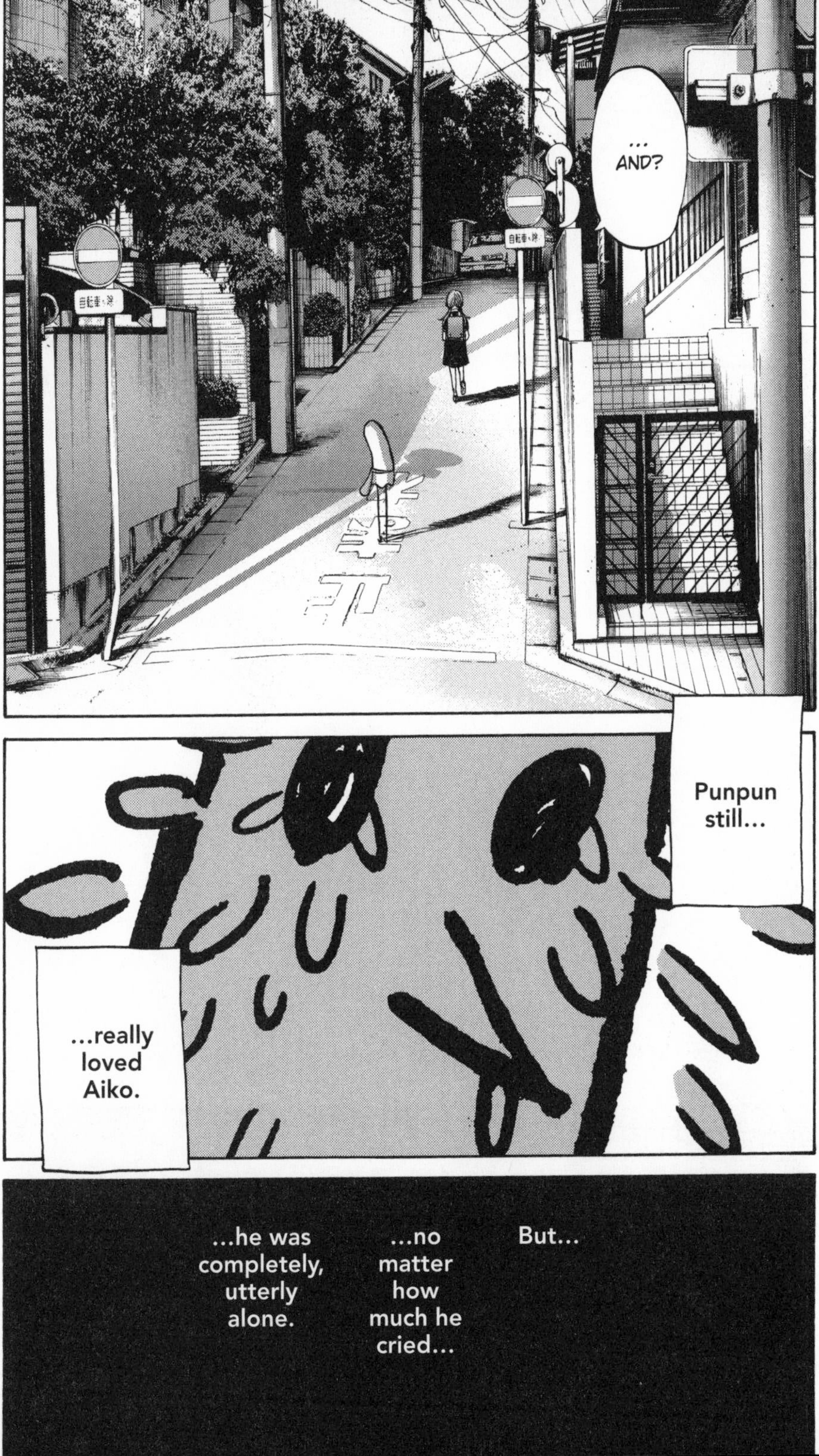
... AND?
Punpun still...
...really loved Aiko.
But...
...no matter how much he cried...
...he was completely, utterly alone.

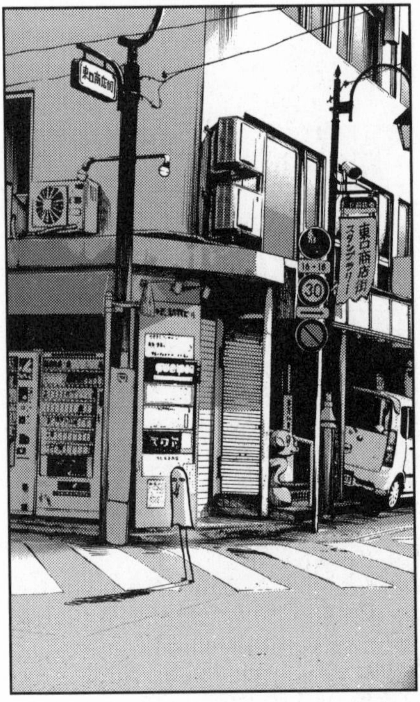
東口商店街
東口商店街
スタンプラリー
30

ELEVEN

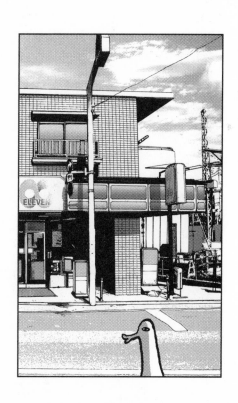

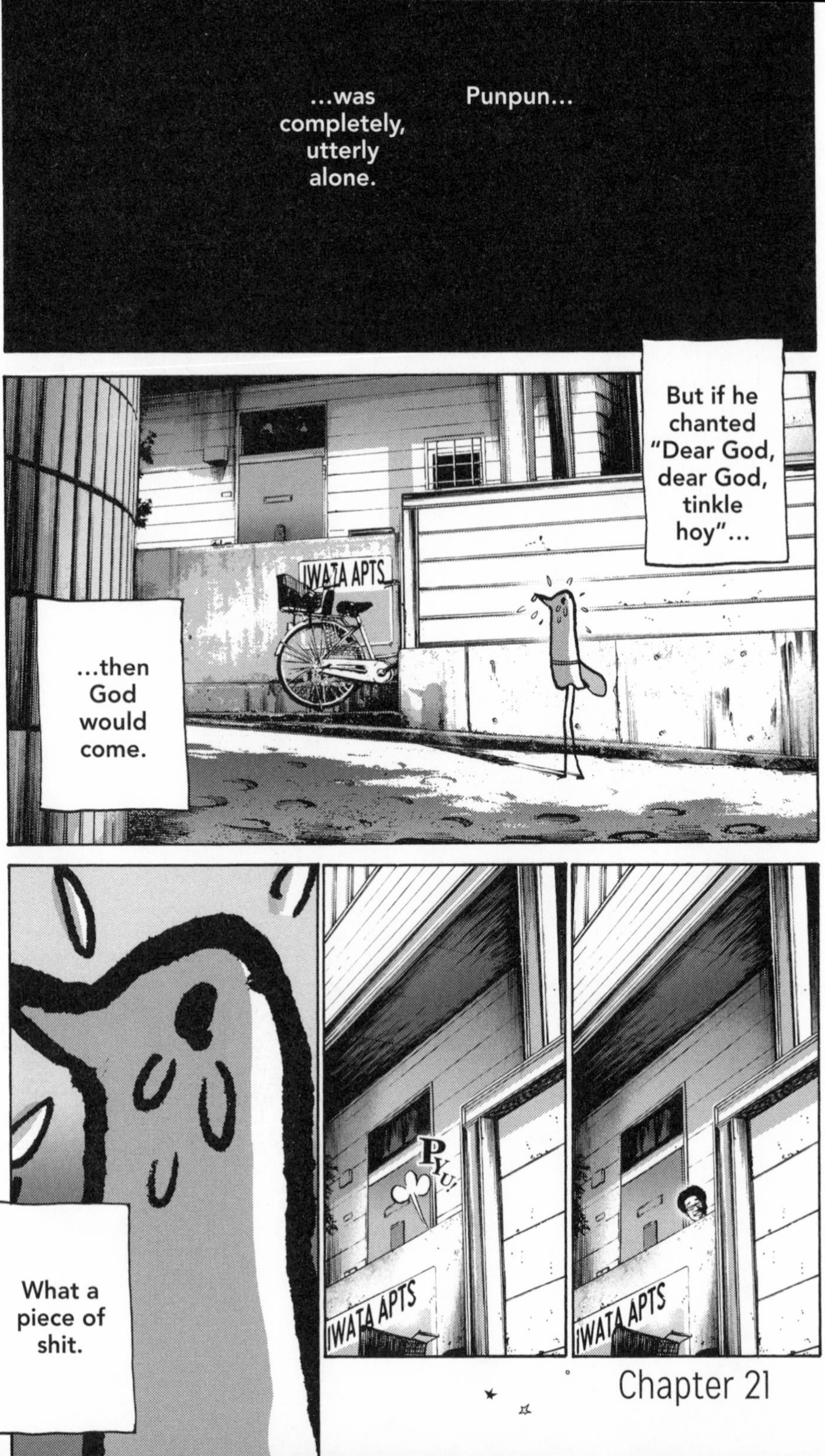
Punpun...
...was completely, utterly alone.
But if he chanted "Dear God, dear God, tinkle hoy"...
...then God would come.
IWATA APTS
IWATA APTS
IWATA APTS
PYU!
What a piece of shit.

Chapter 21

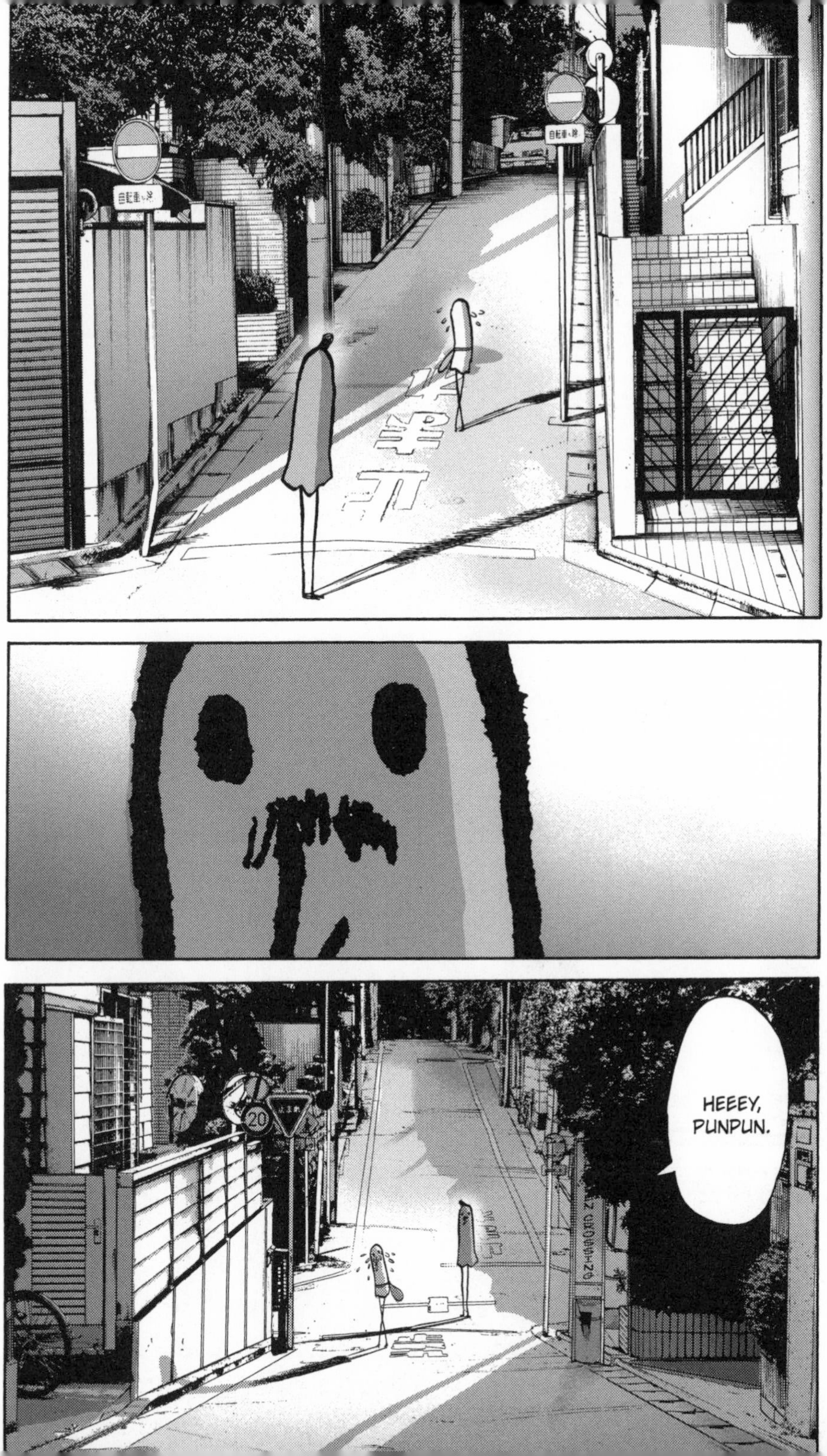
HEEEY, PUNPUN.

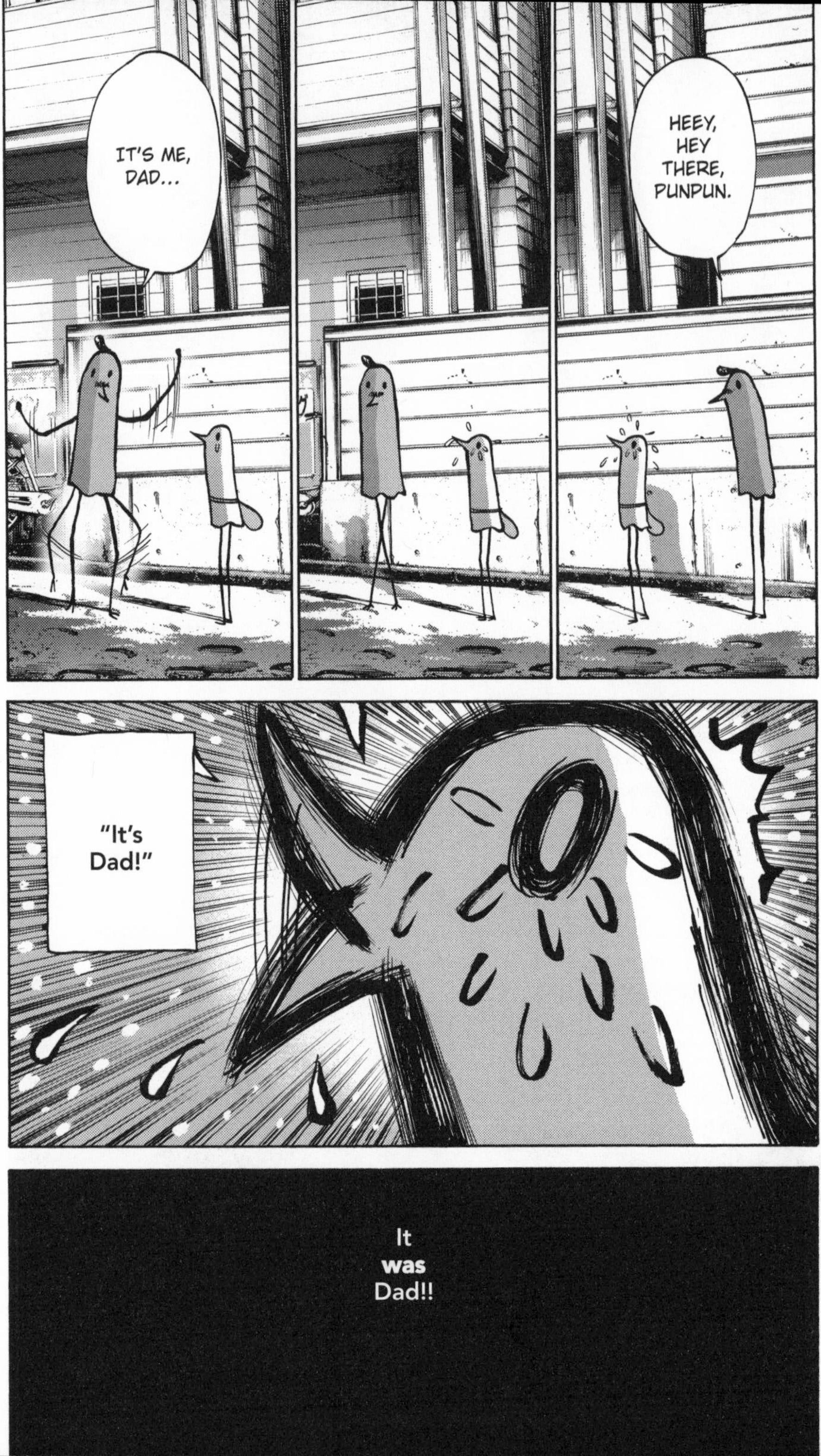
HEEY, HEY THERE, PUNPUN.
IT'S ME, DAD...
"It's Dad!"
It was Dad!!

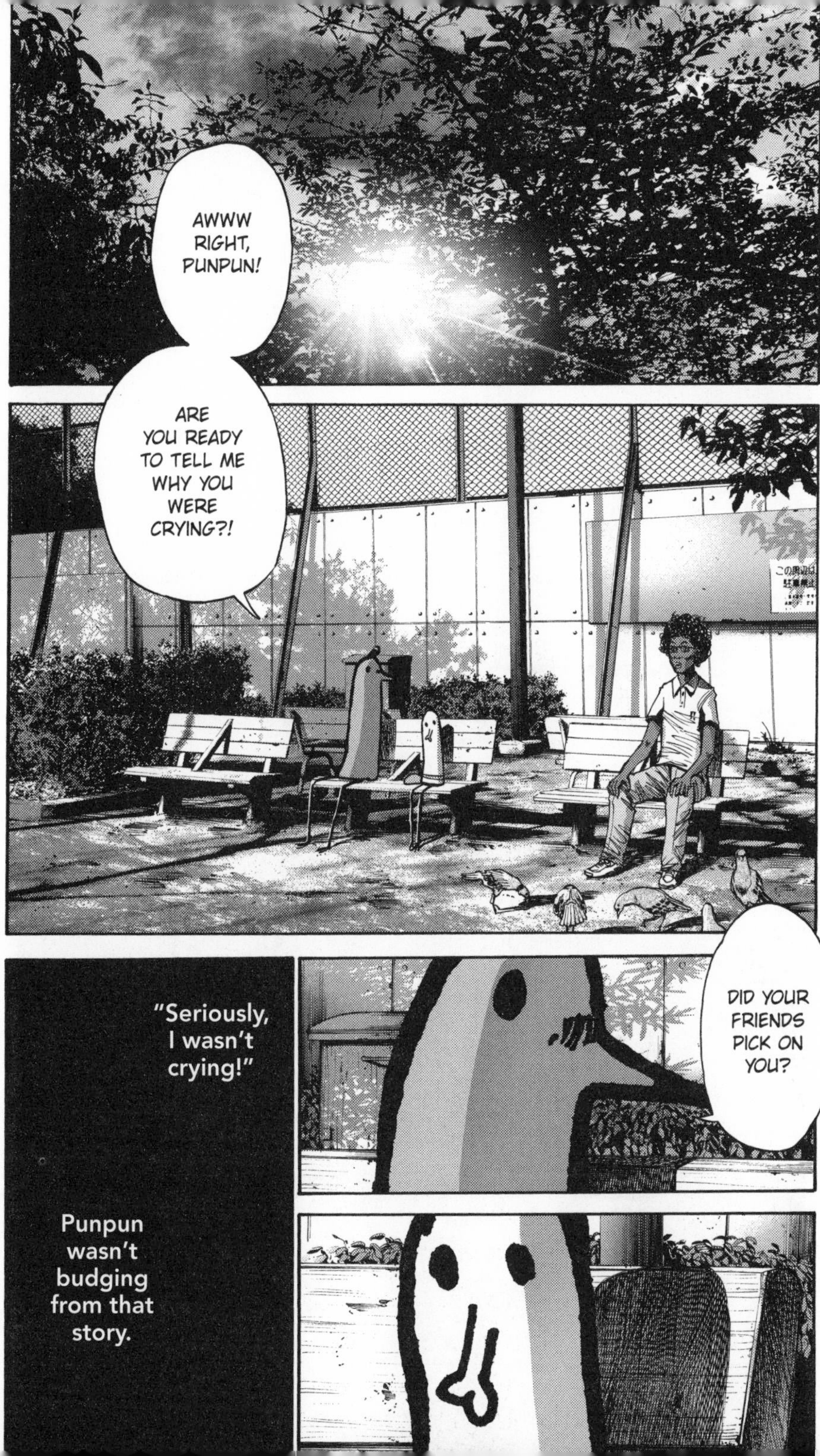
AWWW RIGHT, PUNPUN!
ARE YOU READY TO TELL ME WHY YOU WERE CRYING?!
DID YOUR FRIENDS PICK ON YOU?
"Seriously, I wasn't crying!"
Punpun wasn't budging from that story.

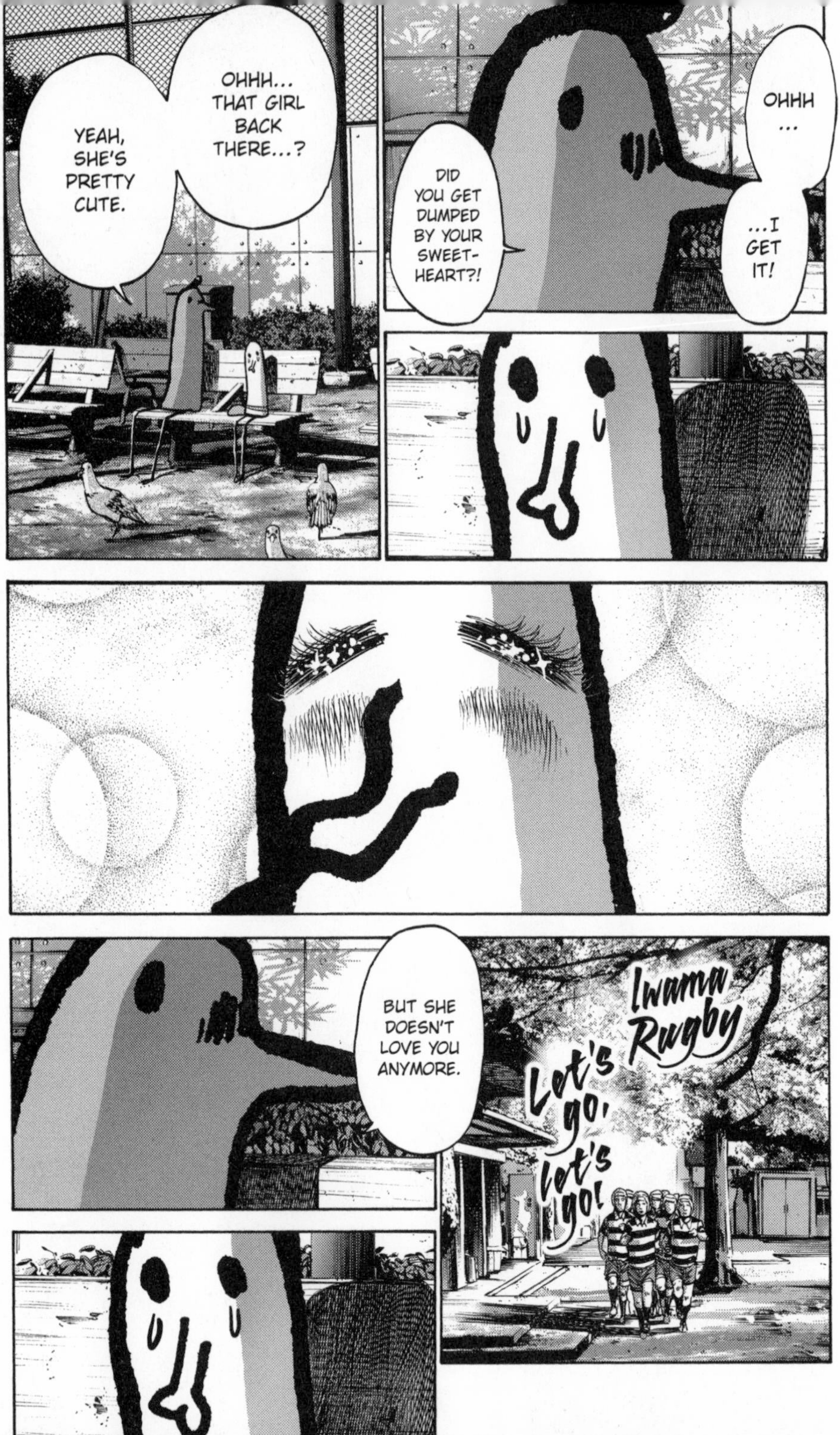
OHHH ...
...I GET IT!
DID YOU GET DUMPED BY YOUR SWEET-HEART?!
OHHH... THAT GIRL BACK THERE...?
YEAH, SHE'S PRETTY CUTE.
Iwama Rugby
Let's go, let's go!
BUT SHE DOESN'T LOVE YOU ANYMORE.

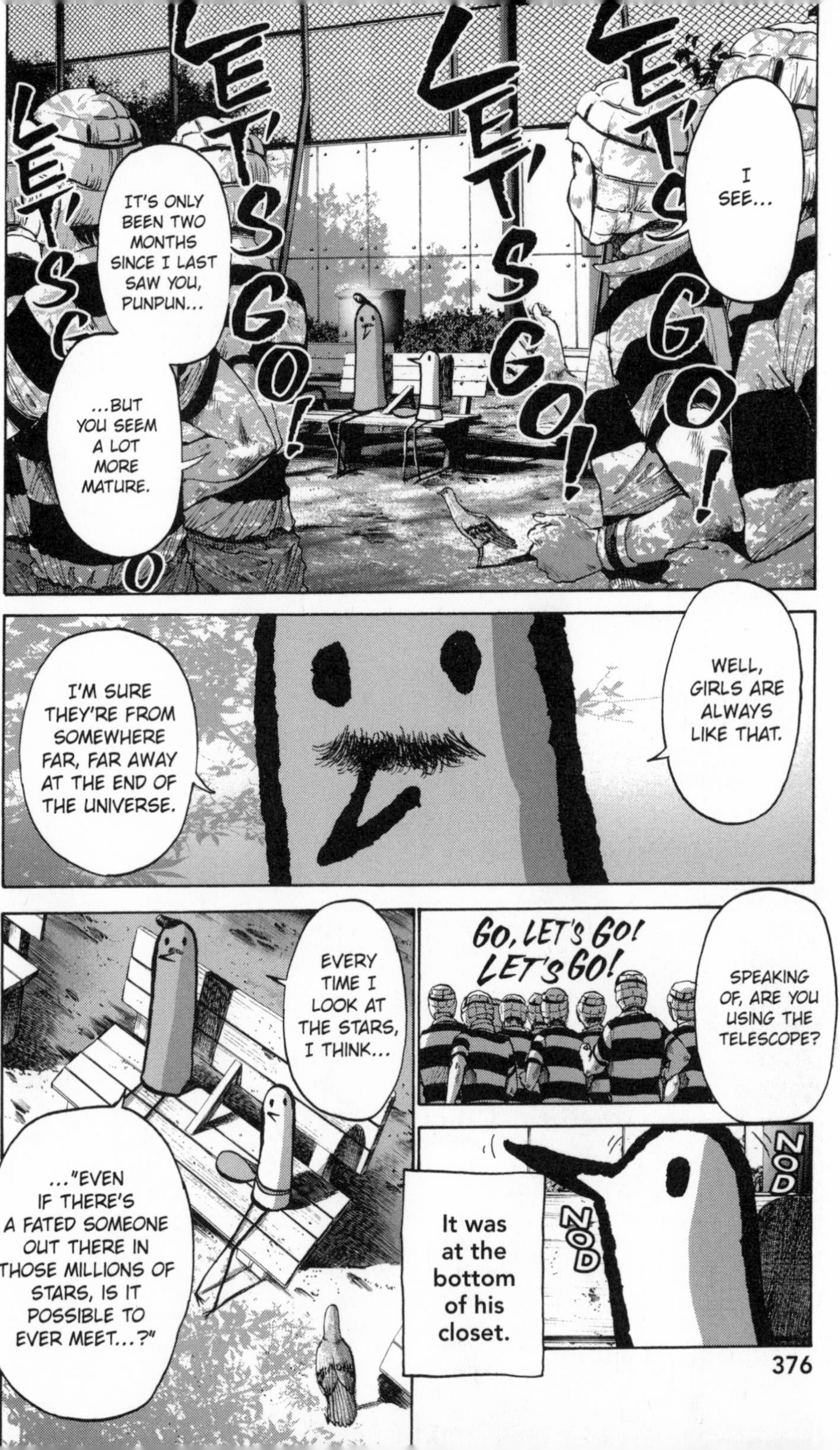
LET'S GO!
I SEE...
LET'S GO!
LET'S GO!
IT'S ONLY BEEN TWO MONTHS SINCE I LAST SAW YOU, PUNPUN...
...BUT YOU SEEM A LOT MORE MATURE.
WELL, GIRLS ARE ALWAYS LIKE THAT.
I'M SURE THEY'RE FROM SOMEWHERE FAR, FAR AWAY AT THE END OF THE UNIVERSE.
SPEAKING OF, ARE YOU USING THE TELESCOPE?
GO, LET'S GO! LET'S GO!
NOD
NOD
It was at the bottom of his closet.
EVERY TIME I LOOK AT THE STARS, I THINK...
..."EVEN IF THERE'S A FATED SOMEONE OUT THERE IN THOSE MILLIONS OF STARS, IS IT POSSIBLE TO EVER MEET...?"

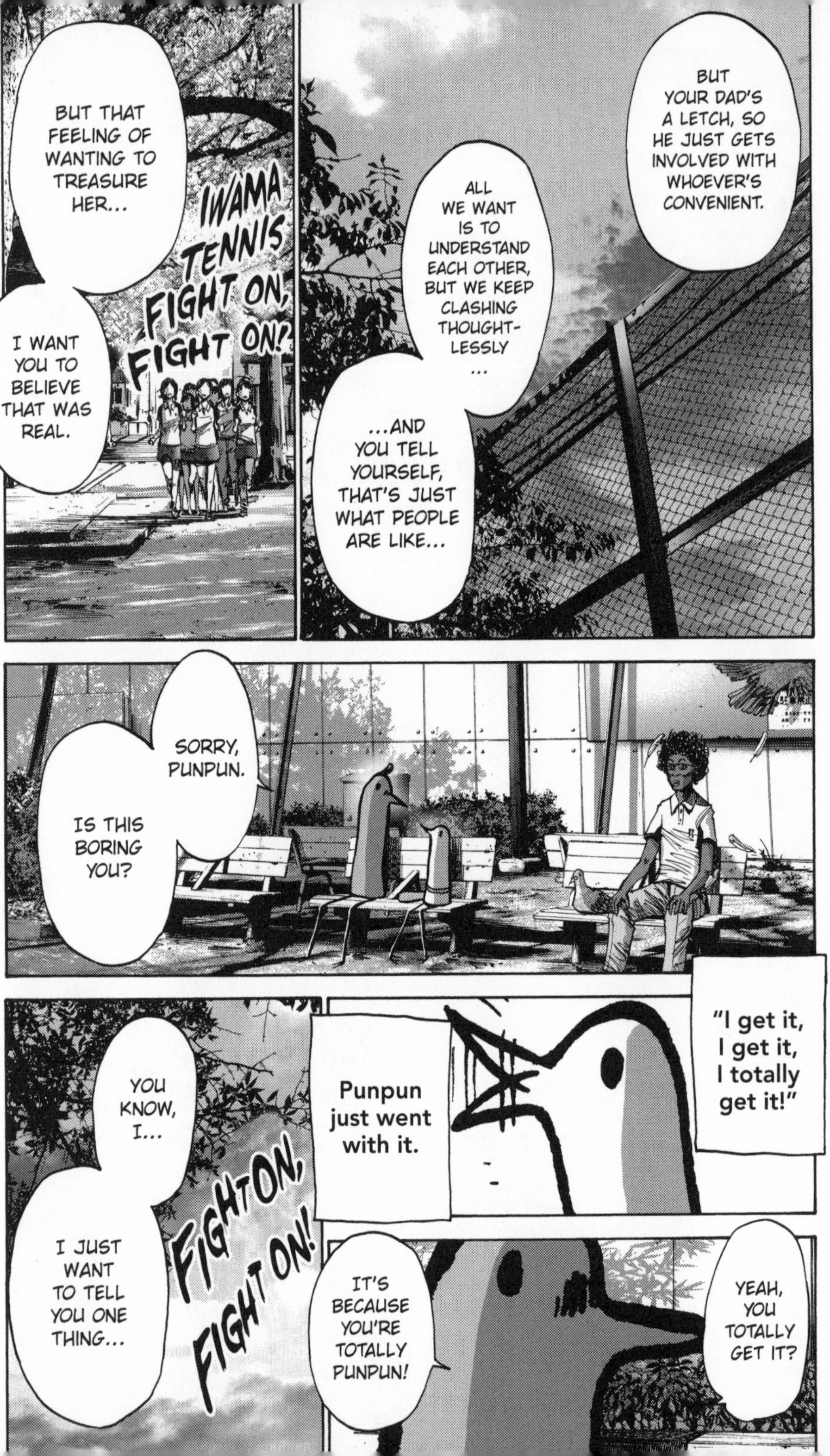
BUT YOUR DAD'S A LETCH, SO HE JUST GETS INVOLVED WITH WHOEVER'S CONVENIENT.
ALL WE WANT IS TO UNDERSTAND EACH OTHER, BUT WE KEEP CLASHING THOUGHT-LESSLY...
...AND YOU TELL YOURSELF, THAT'S JUST WHAT PEOPLE ARE LIKE...
BUT THAT FEELING OF WANTING TO TREASURE HER...
IWAMA TENNIS FIGHT ON, FIGHT ON!
I WANT YOU TO BELIEVE THAT WAS REAL.
SORRY, PUNPUN.
IS THIS BORING YOU?
"I get it, I get it, I totally get it!"
Punpun just went with it.
YEAH, YOU TOTALLY GET IT?
IT'S BECAUSE YOU'RE TOTALLY PUNPUN!
YOU KNOW, I...
I JUST WANT TO TELL YOU ONE THING...
FIGHT ON, FIGHT ON!

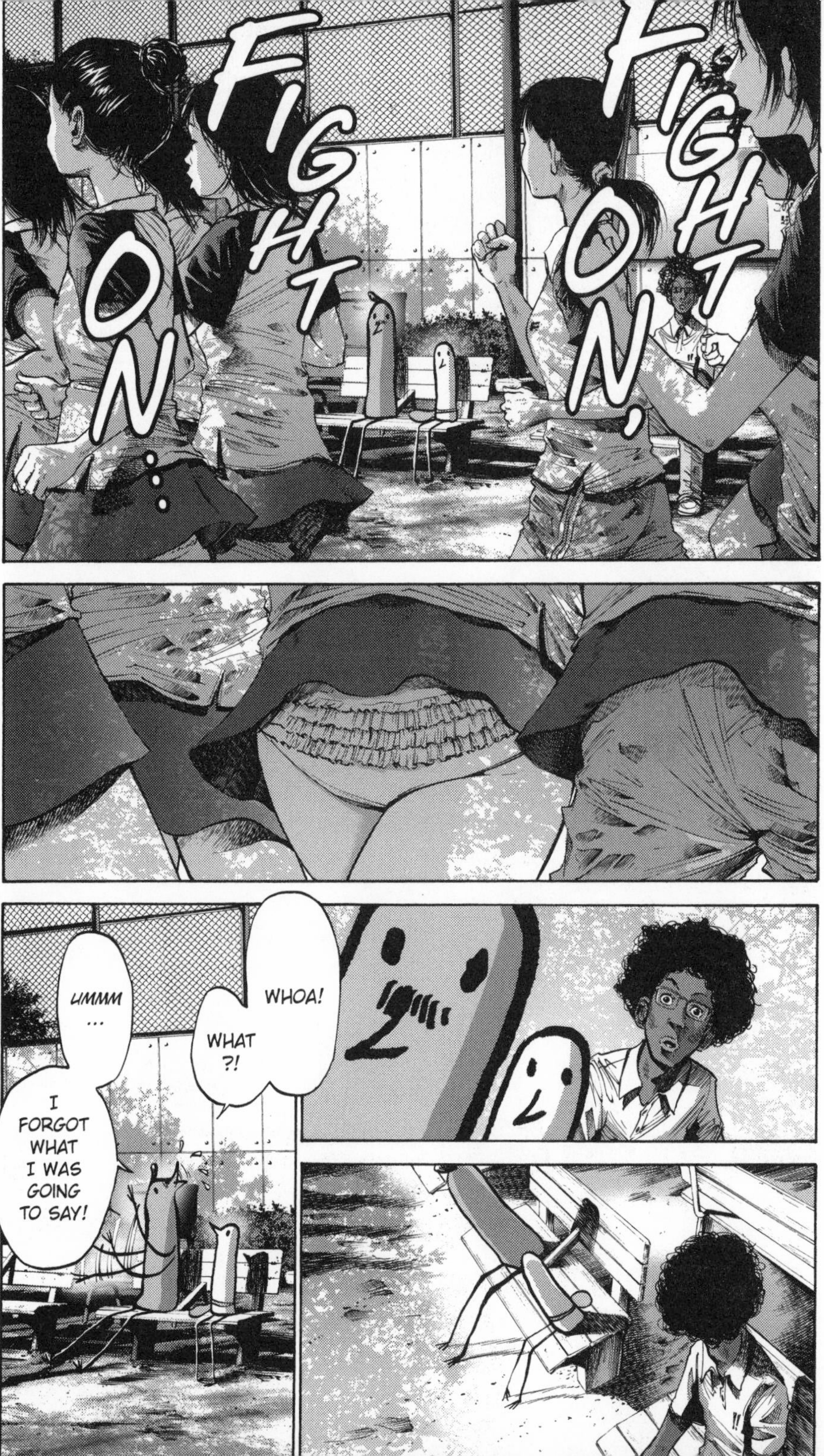
FIGHT ON,
FIGHT ON...
WHOA!
WHAT ?!
UMMM ...
I FORGOT WHAT I WAS GOING TO SAY!
!!

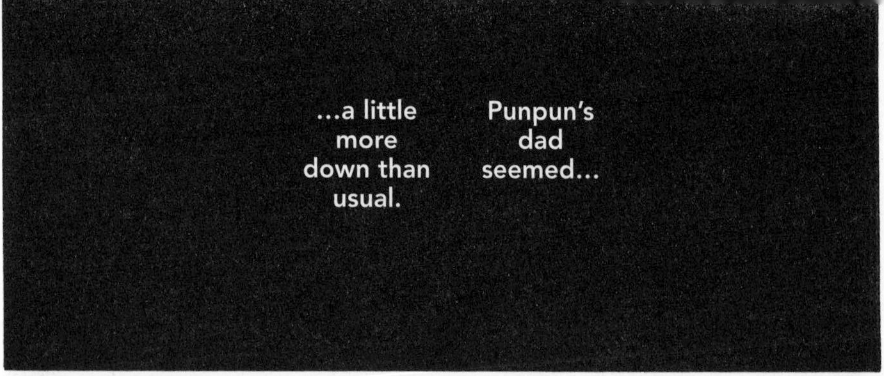
Punpun's dad seemed...
...a little more down than usual.

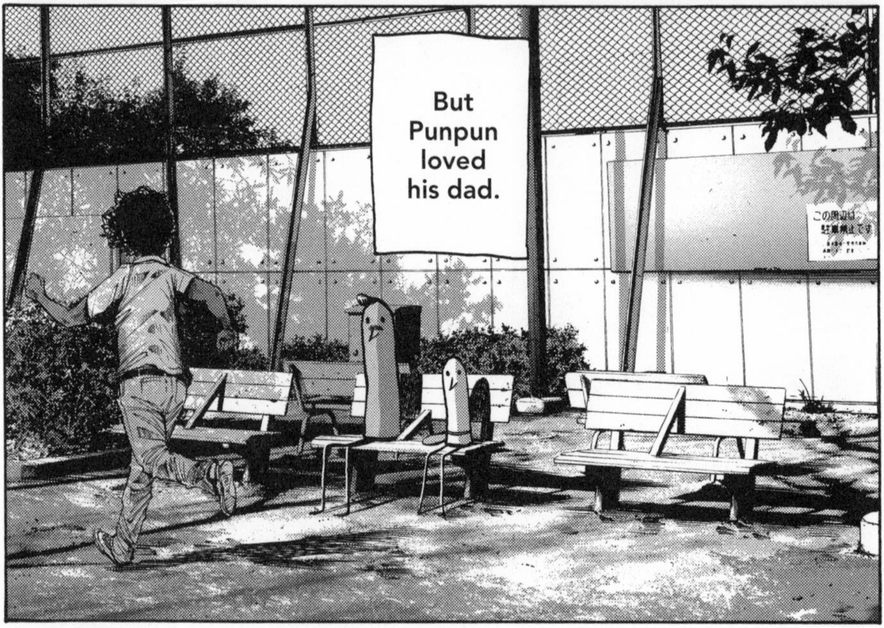
But Punpun loved his dad.

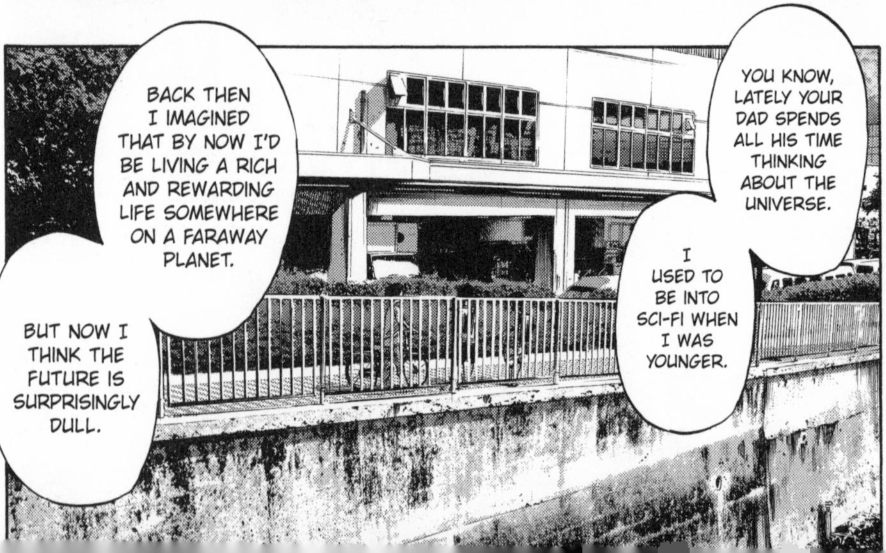
YOU KNOW, LATELY YOUR DAD SPENDS ALL HIS TIME THINKING ABOUT THE UNIVERSE.
I USED TO BE INTO SCI-FI WHEN I WAS YOUNGER.
BACK THEN I IMAGINED THAT BY NOW I'D BE LIVING A RICH AND REWARDING LIFE SOMEWHERE ON A FARAWAY PLANET.
BUT NOW I THINK THE FUTURE IS SURPRISINGLY DULL.

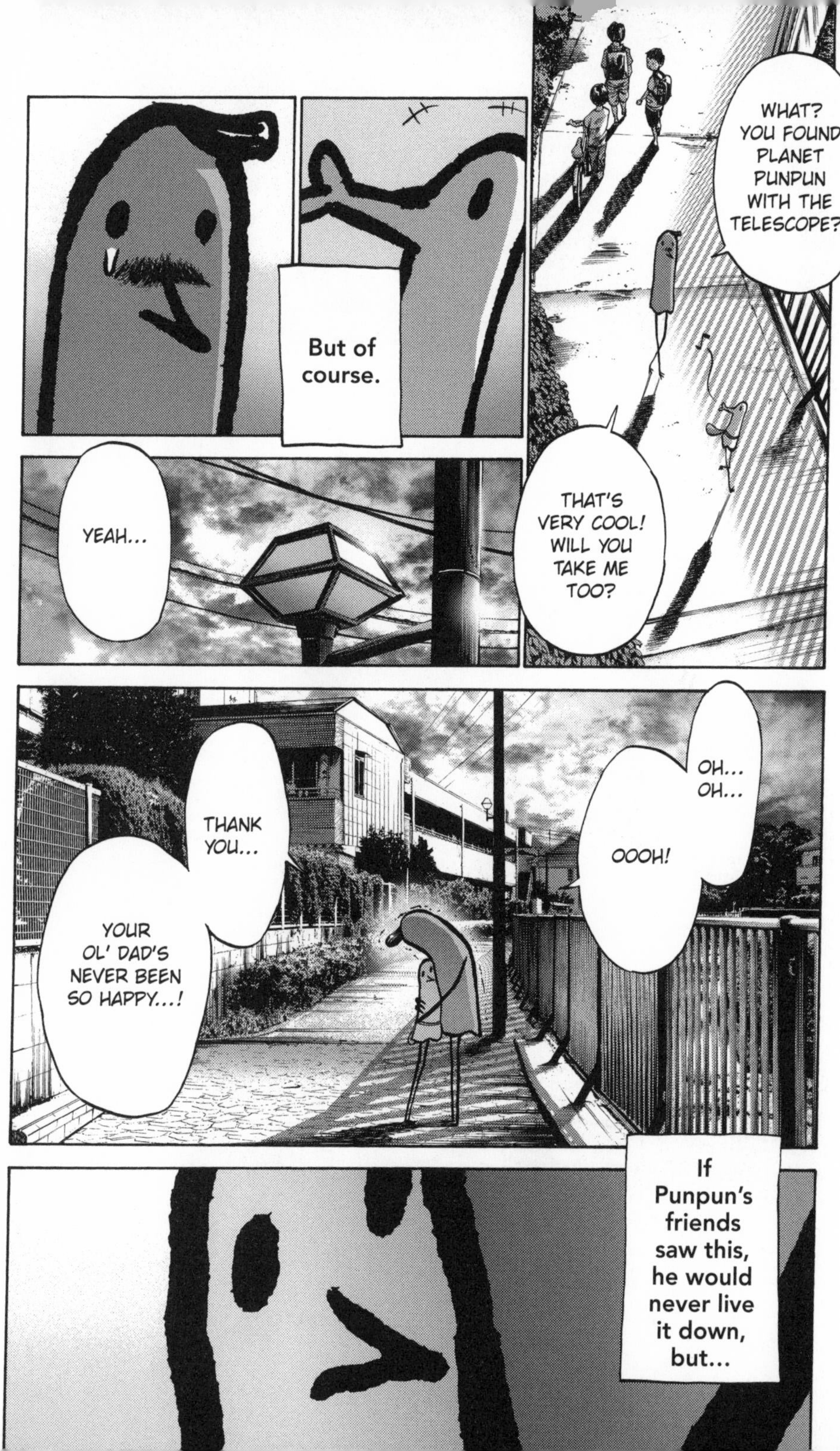

WHAT? YOU FOUND PLANET PUNPUN WITH THE TELESCOPE?!
THAT'S VERY COOL! WILL YOU TAKE ME TOO?
But of course.
YEAH...
OH... OH...
OOOH!
THANK YOU...
YOUR OL' DAD'S NEVER BEEN SO HAPPY...!
If Punpun's friends saw this, he would never live it down, but...

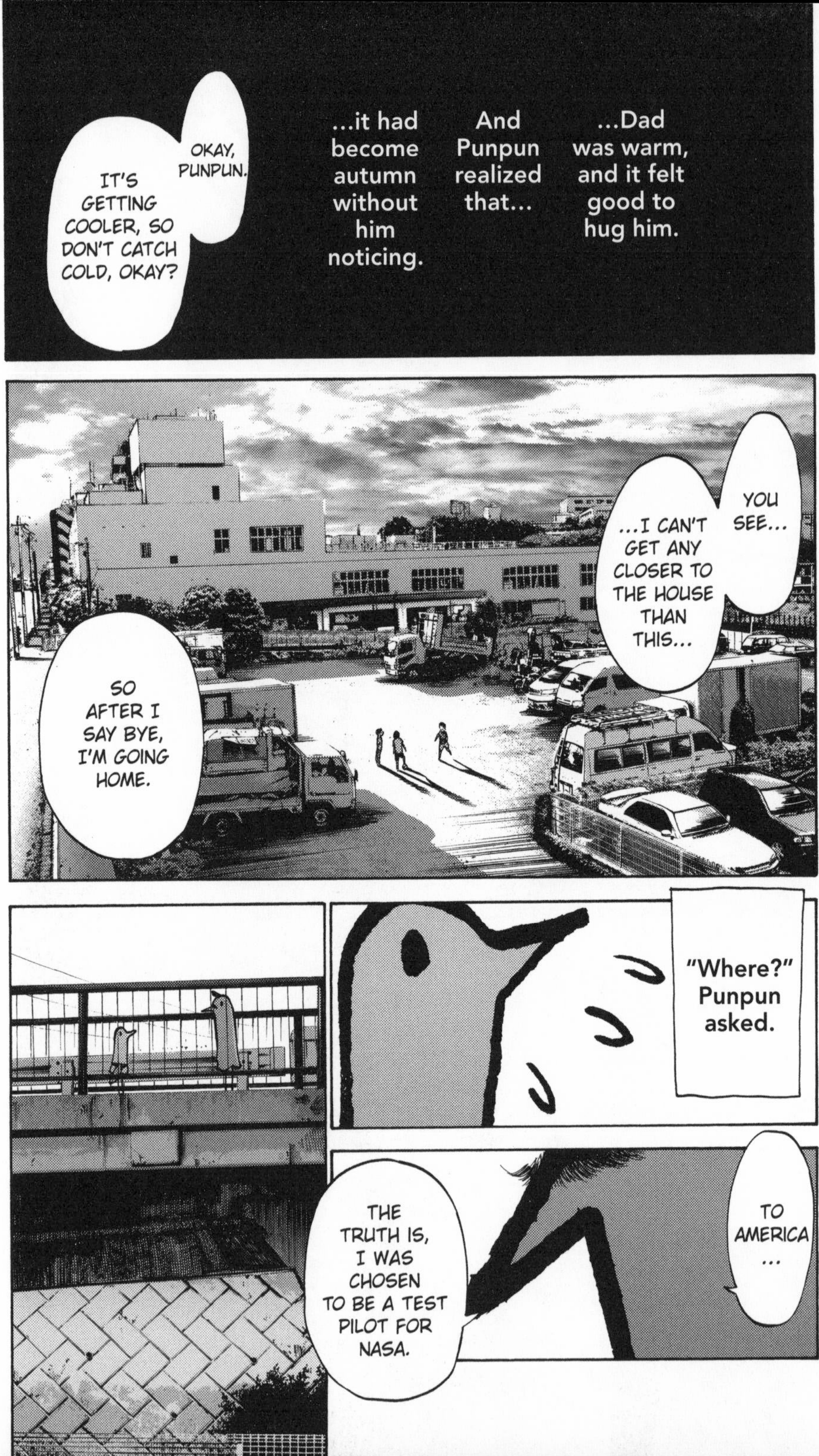
...Dad was warm, and it felt good to hug him.
And Punpun realized that...
...it had become autumn without him noticing.
OKAY, PUNPUN.
IT'S GETTING COOLER, SO DON'T CATCH COLD, OKAY?
YOU SEE...
...I CAN'T GET ANY CLOSER TO THE HOUSE THAN THIS...
SO AFTER I SAY BYE, I'M GOING HOME.
"Where?" Punpun asked.
TO AMERICA...
THE TRUTH IS, I WAS CHOSEN TO BE A TEST PILOT FOR NASA.

GO ON! GET GOING!

YOUR MOM MUST BE WORRIED!

IF SHE FOUND OUT I WAS WAITING FOR YOU AFTER SCHOOL, WE'D HAVE ANOTHER ARGUMENT! HA HA HA HA!

"When will I see you again?"

...Punpun asked his dad.

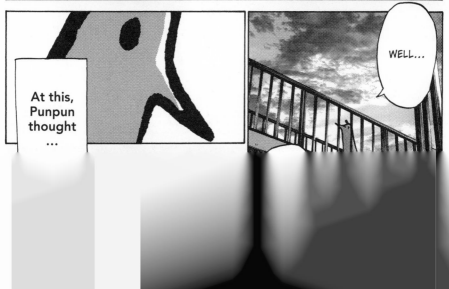

At this, Punpun thought ...

WELL...

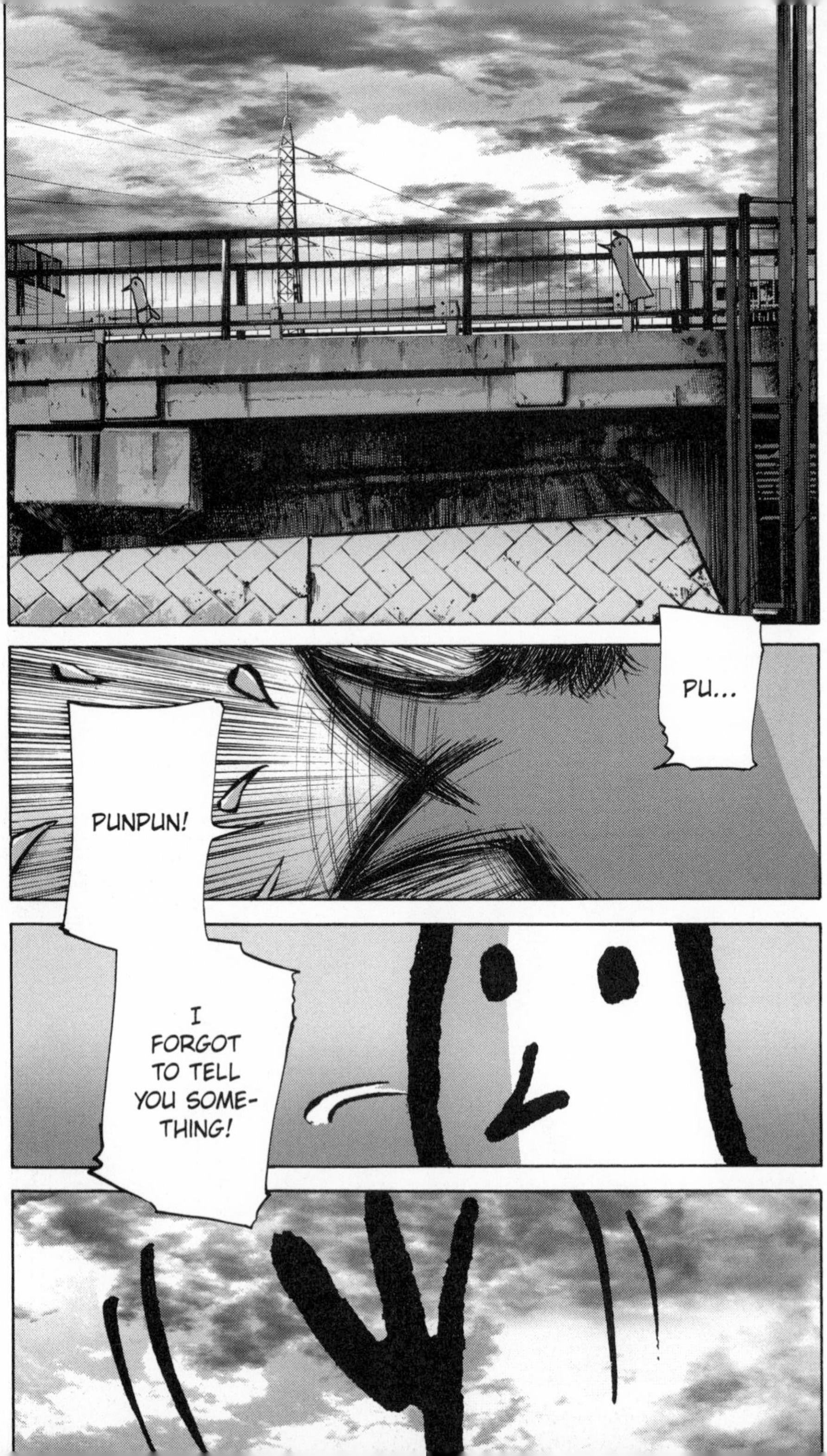
PU...
PUNPUN!
I FORGOT TO TELL YOU SOME-THING!

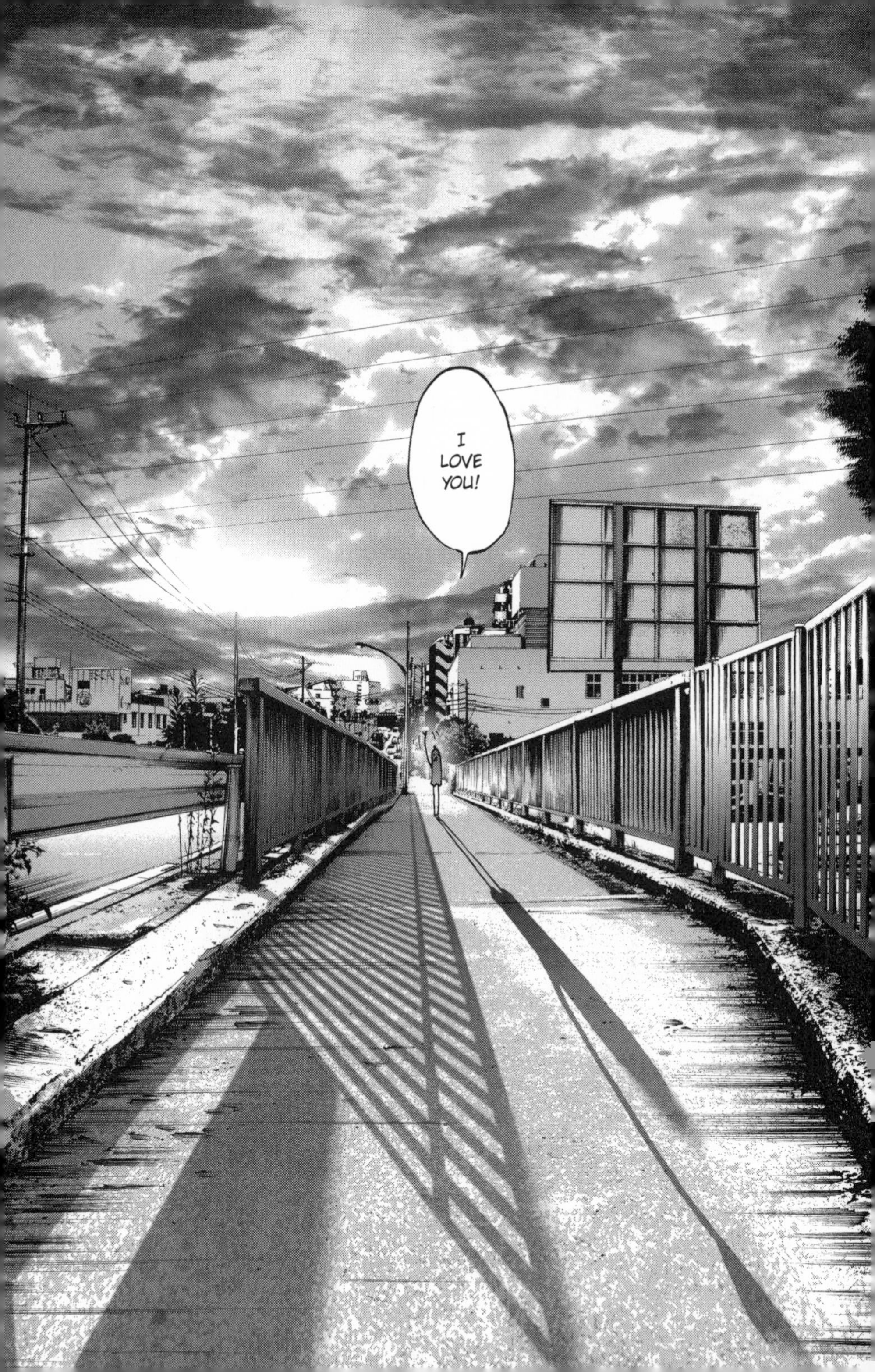
I LOVE YOU!

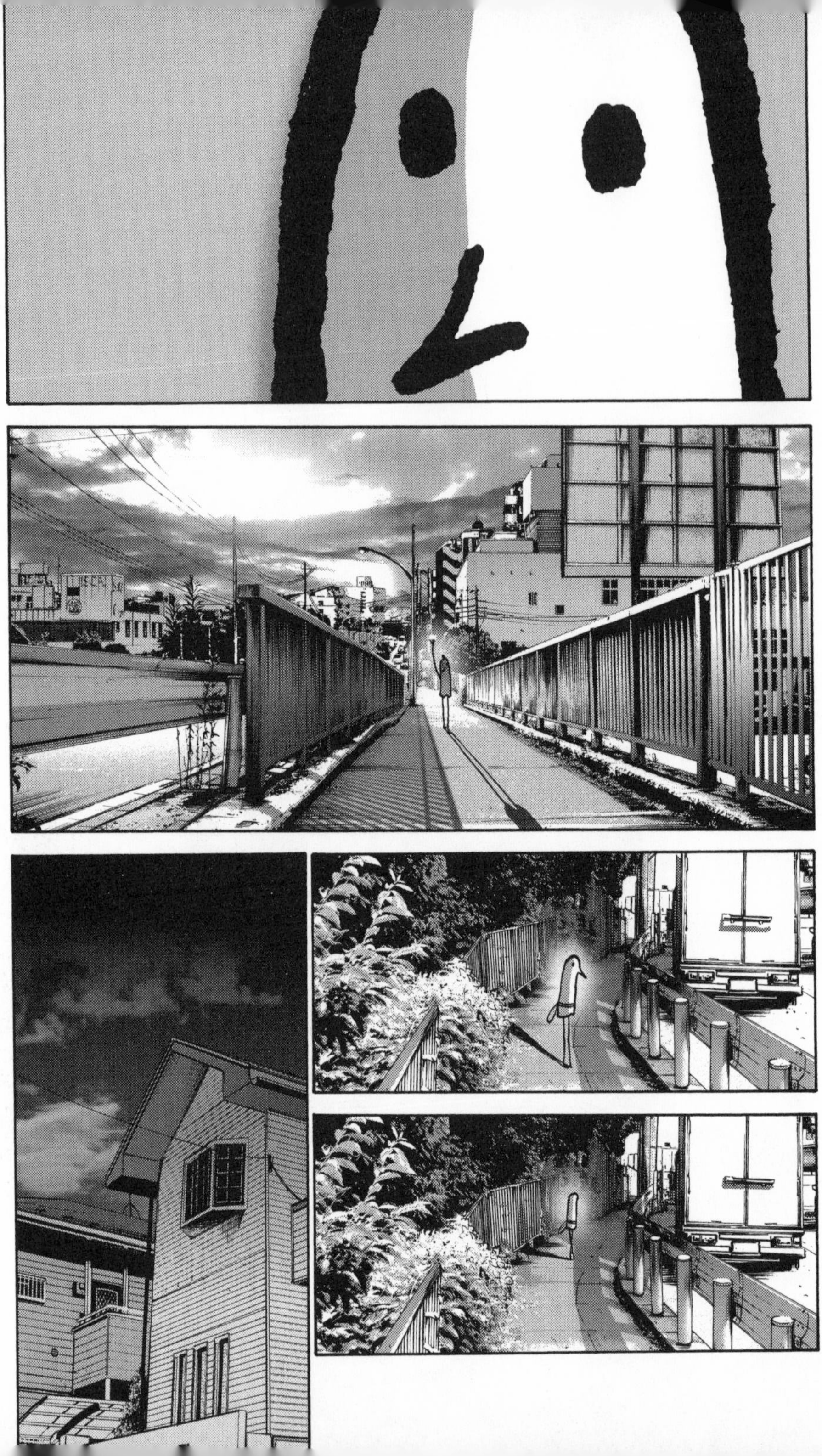

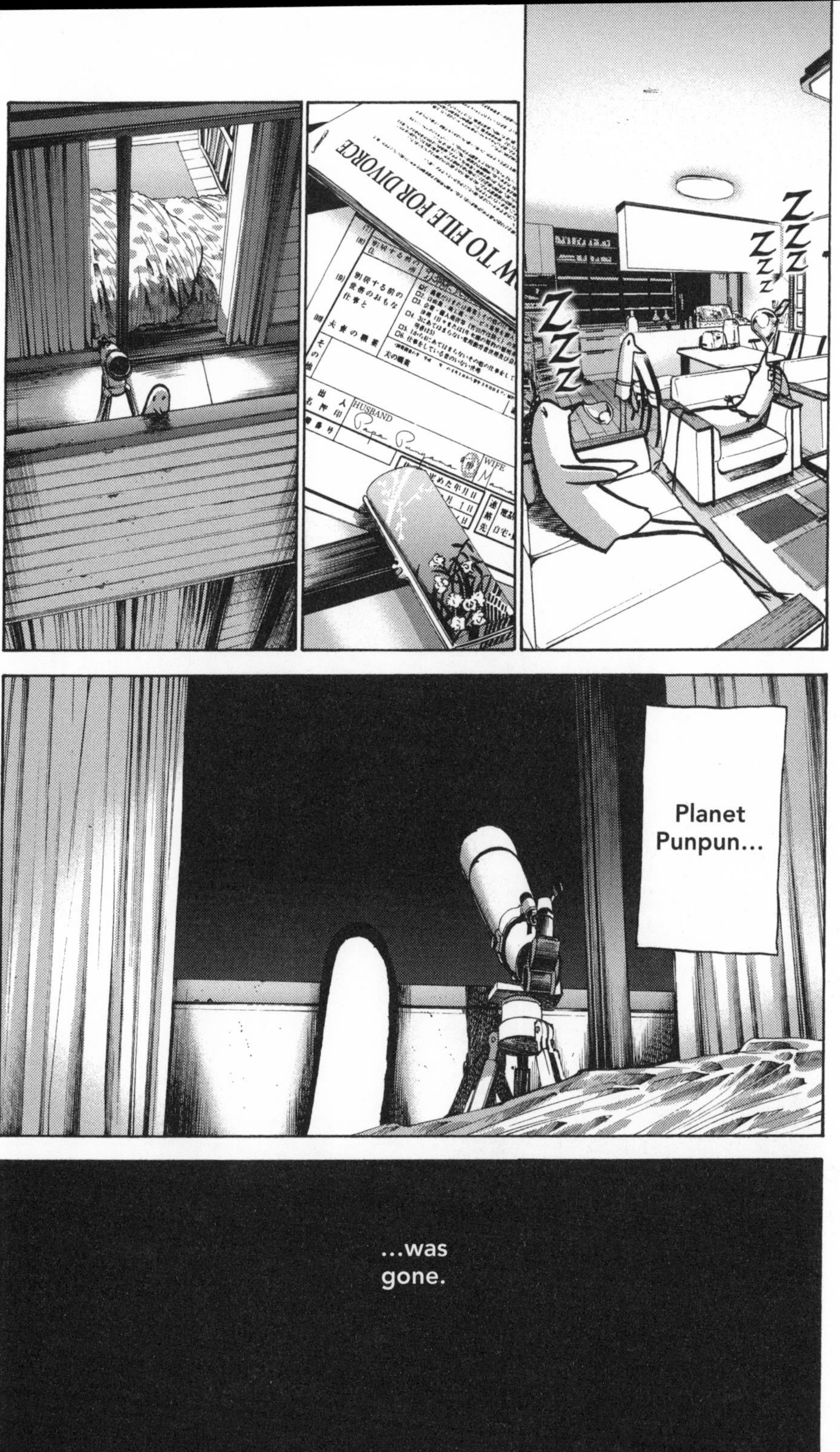
ZZZ
ZZZ
W TO FILE FOR DIVORCE
HUSBAND
WIFE
Planet Punpun...
...was gone.

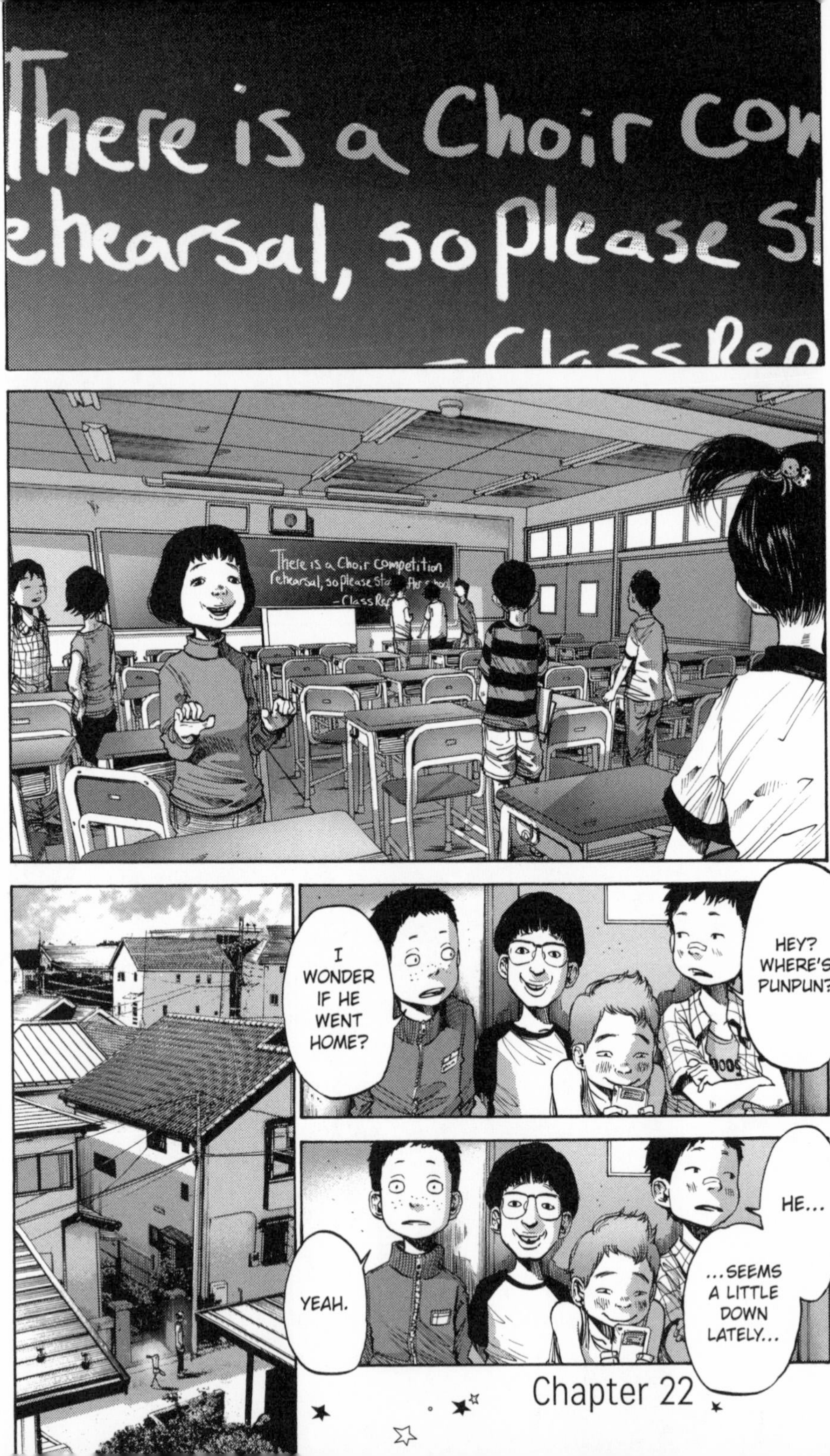
There is a Choir Com
ehearsal, so please st
Class Rep
HEY? WHERE'S PUNPUN?
I WONDER IF HE WENT HOME?
HE...
...SEEMS A LITTLE DOWN LATELY...
YEAH.

Chapter 22

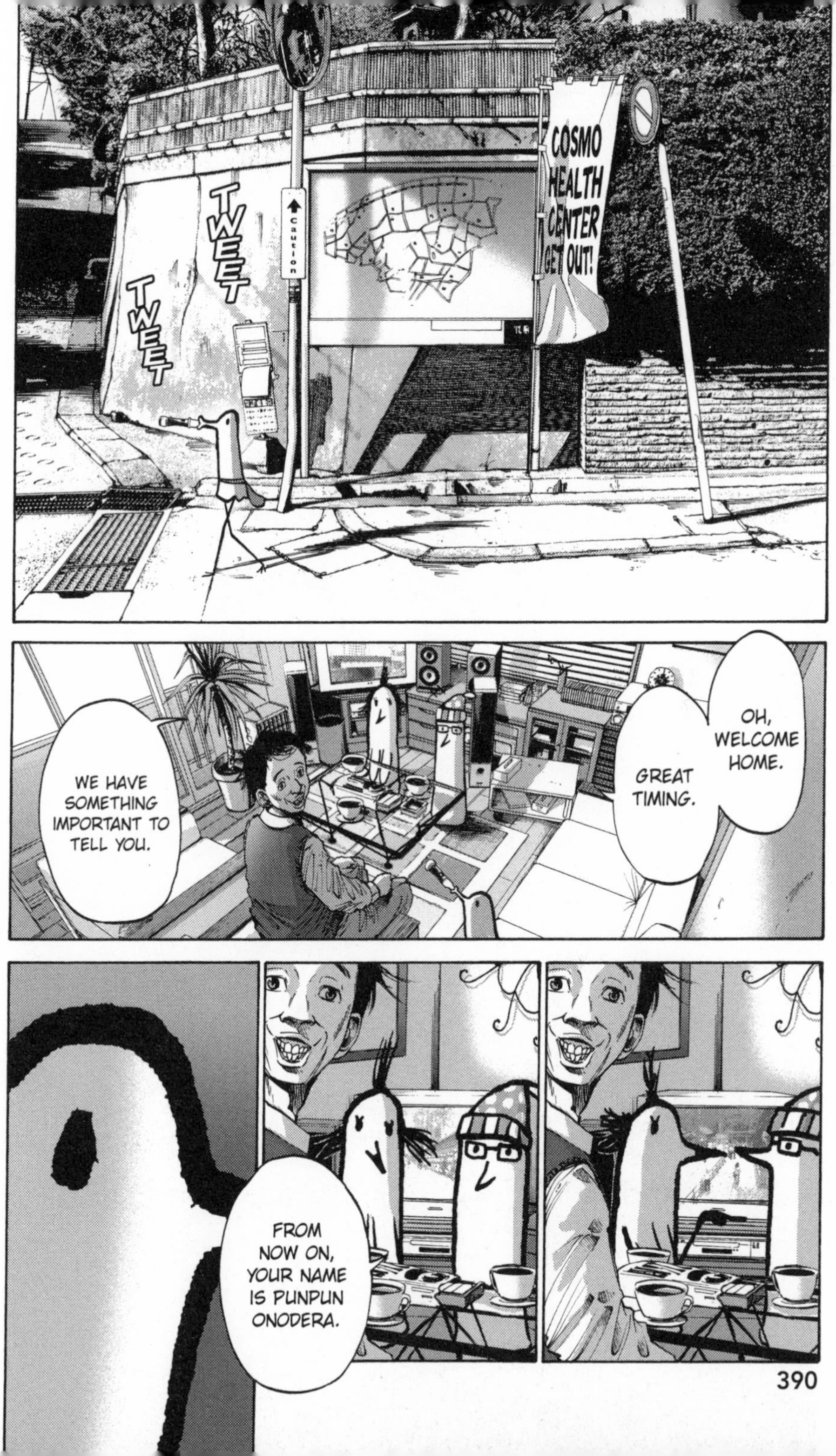
TWEET
TWEET
caution
COSMO HEALTH CENTER GET OUT!
OH, WELCOME HOME.
GREAT TIMING.
WE HAVE SOMETHING IMPORTANT TO TELL YOU.
FROM NOW ON, YOUR NAME IS PUNPUN ONODERA.

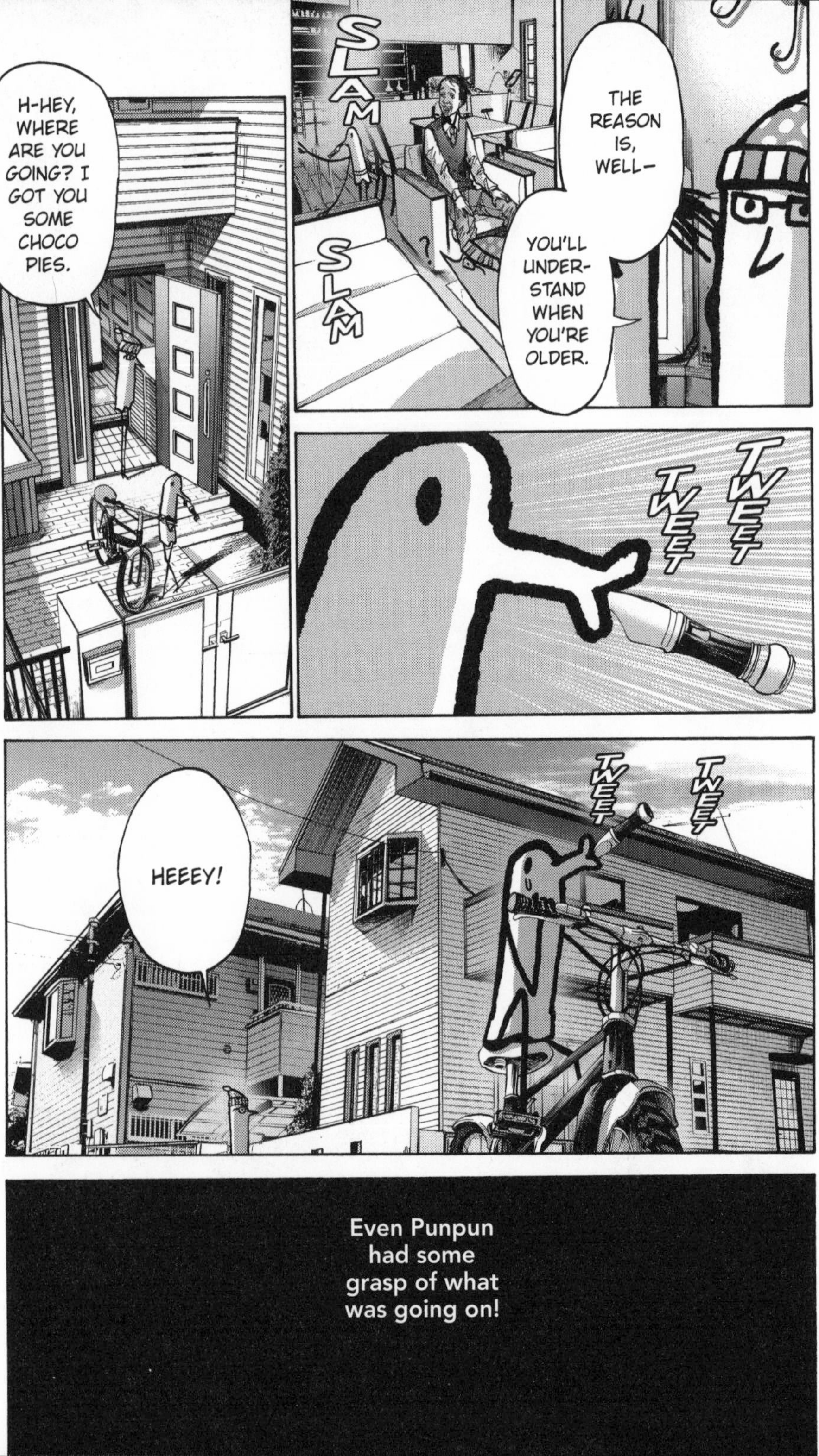
THE REASON IS, WELL—
YOU'LL UNDERSTAND WHEN YOU'RE OLDER.
SLAM
SLAM
TWEET
TWEET
H-HEY, WHERE ARE YOU GOING? I GOT YOU SOME CHOCO PIES.
TWEET
TWEET
HEEEY!
Even Punpun had some grasp of what was going on!

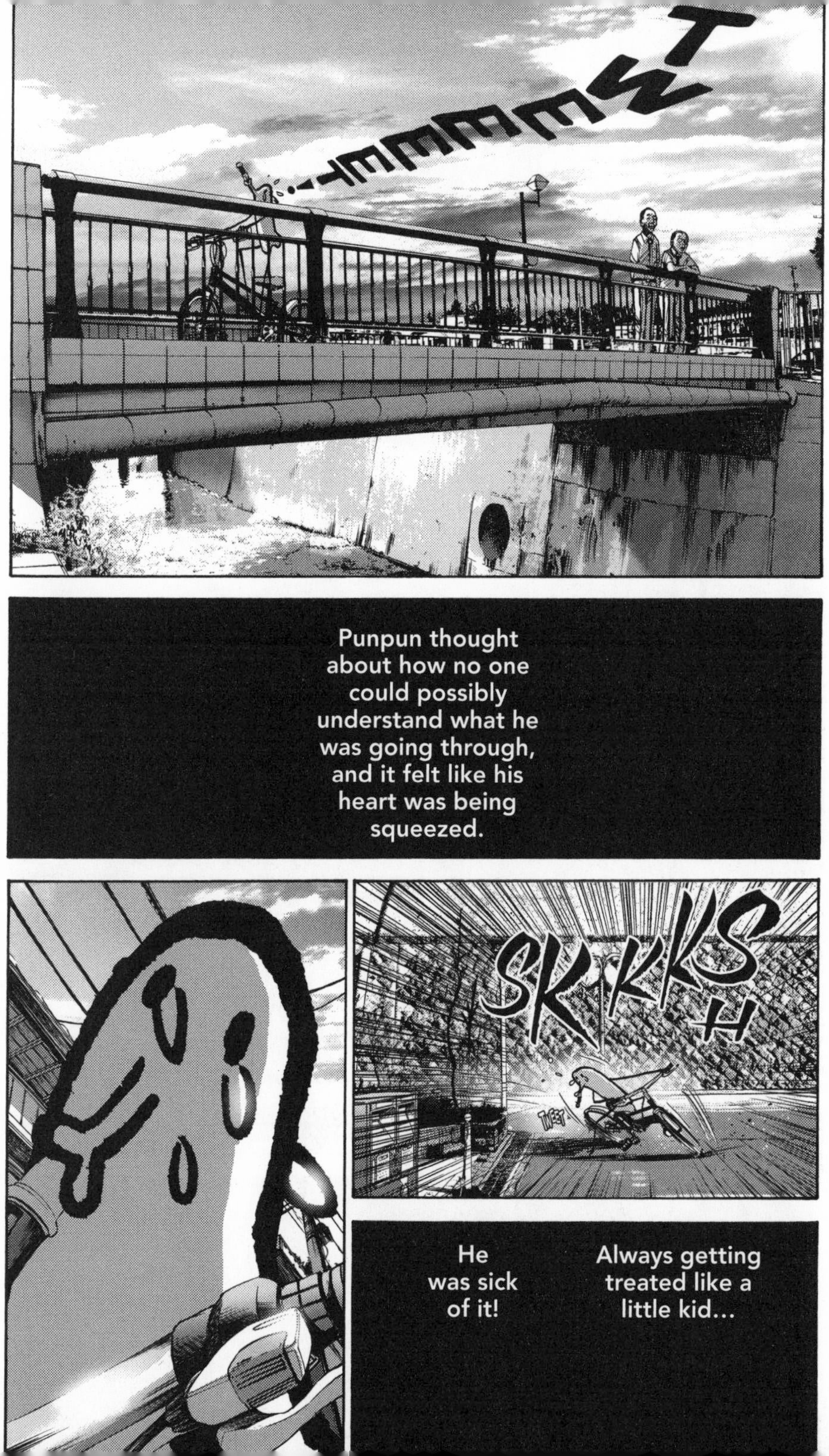
Punpun thought about how no one could possibly understand what he was going through, and it felt like his heart was being squeezed.
SKKKSH
TWEET
Always getting treated like a little kid...
He was sick of it!

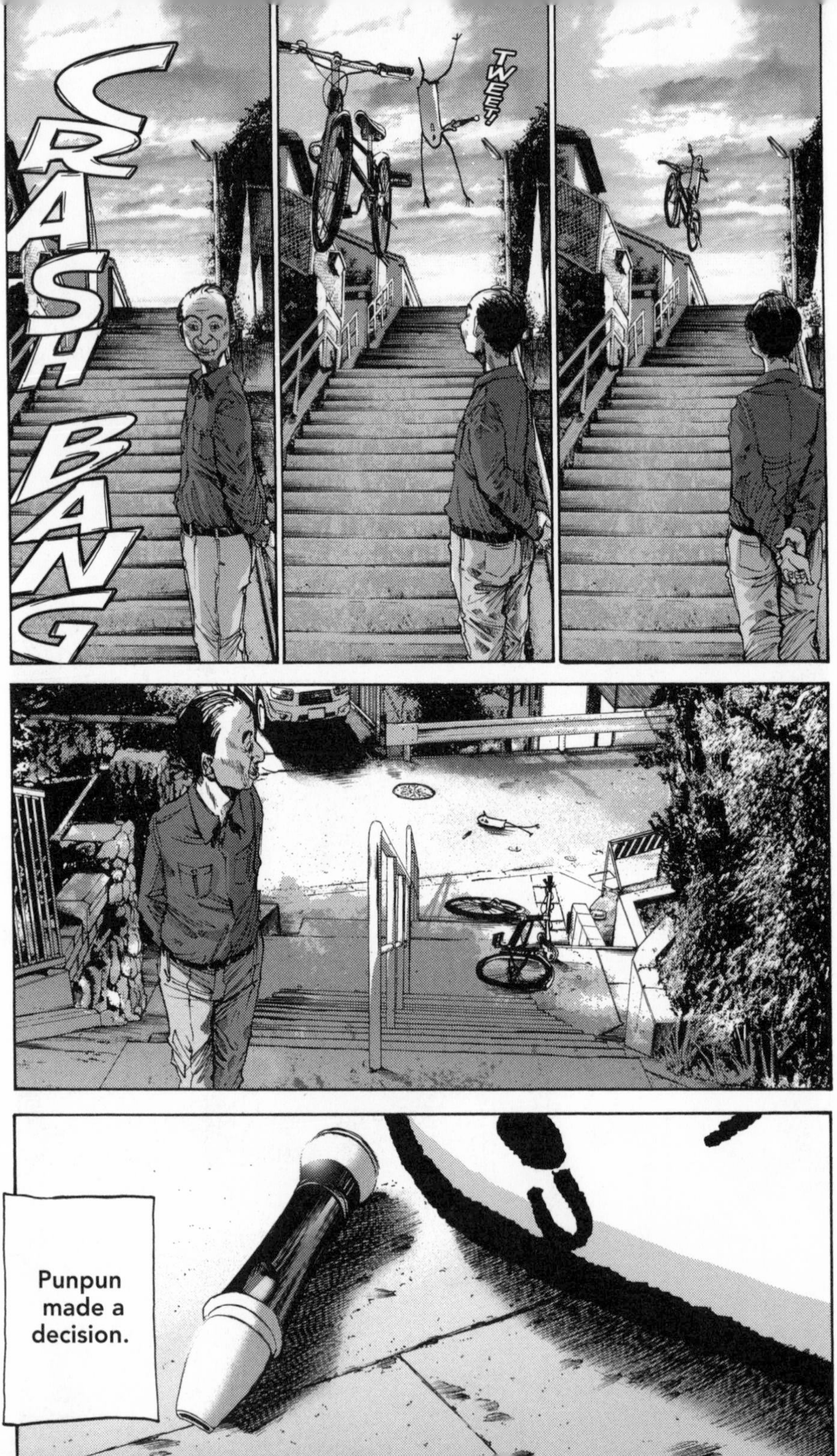
TWEET!
CRASH
BANG
Punpun made a decision.

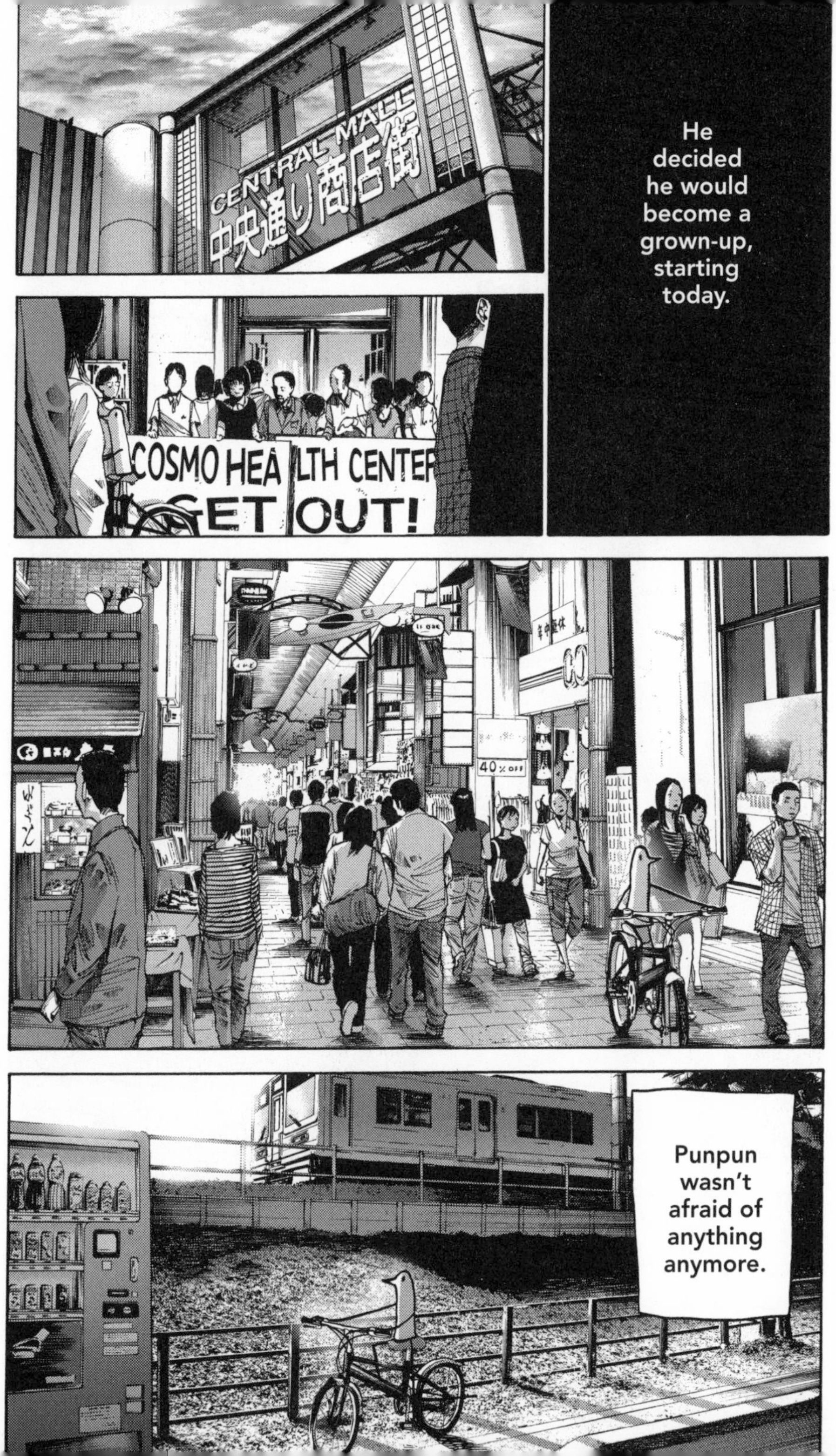
He decided he would become a grown-up, starting today.
CENTRAL MALL
中央通り商店街
COSMO HEALTH CENTER
GET OUT!
40% OFF
Punpun wasn't afraid of anything anymore.

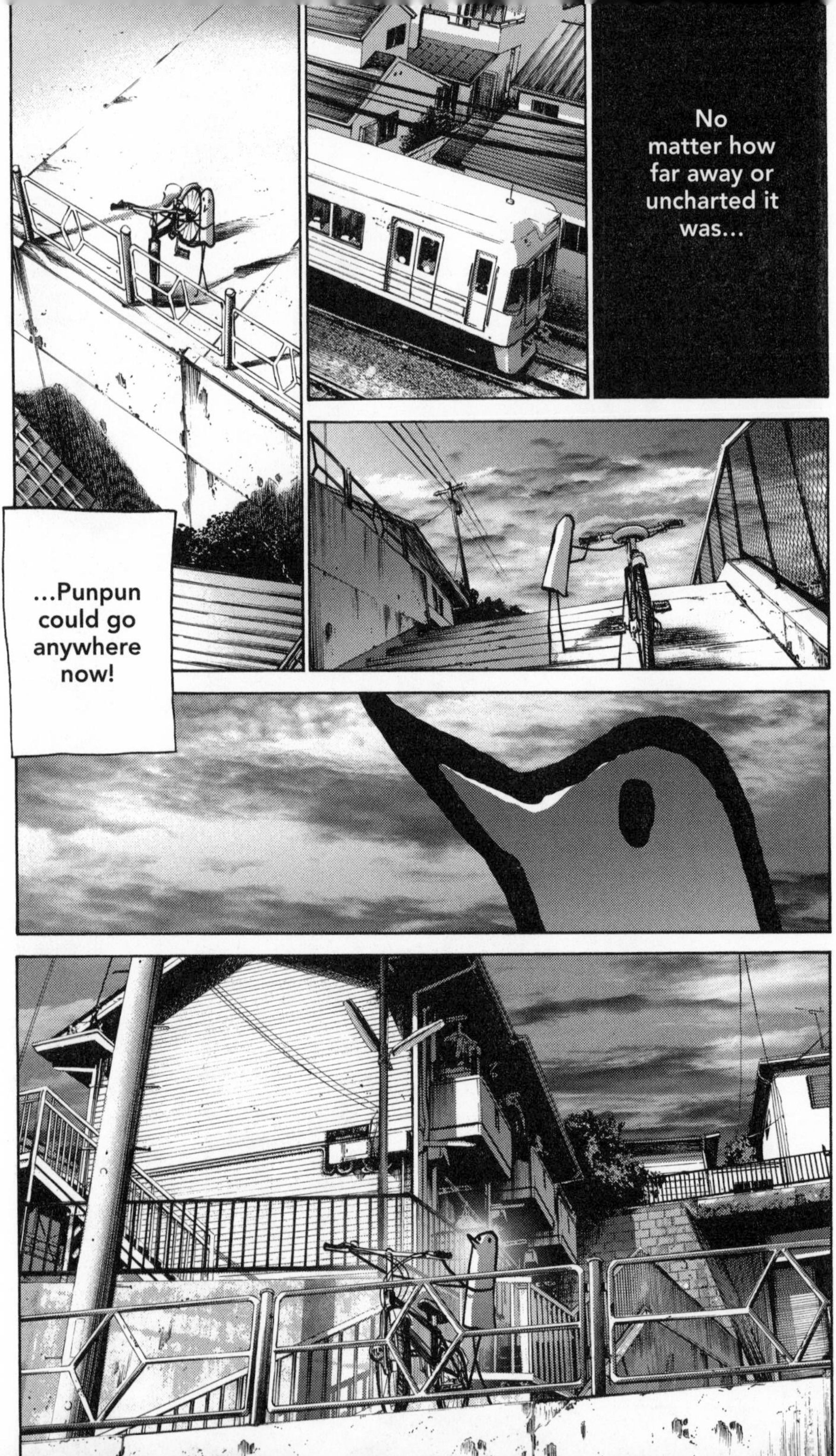
No matter how far away or uncharted it was...
...Punpun could go anywhere now!

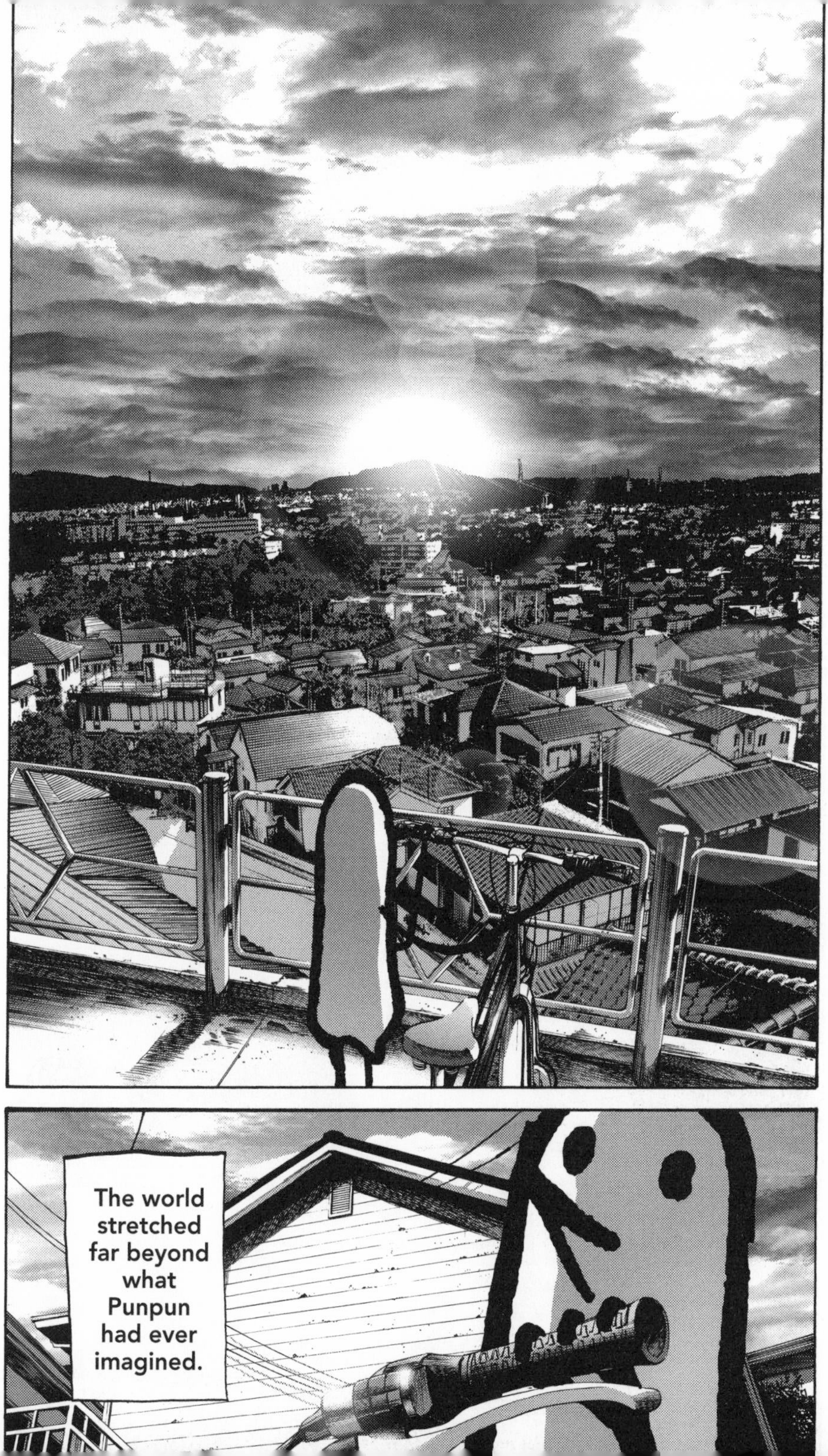
The world stretched far beyond what Punpun had ever imagined.

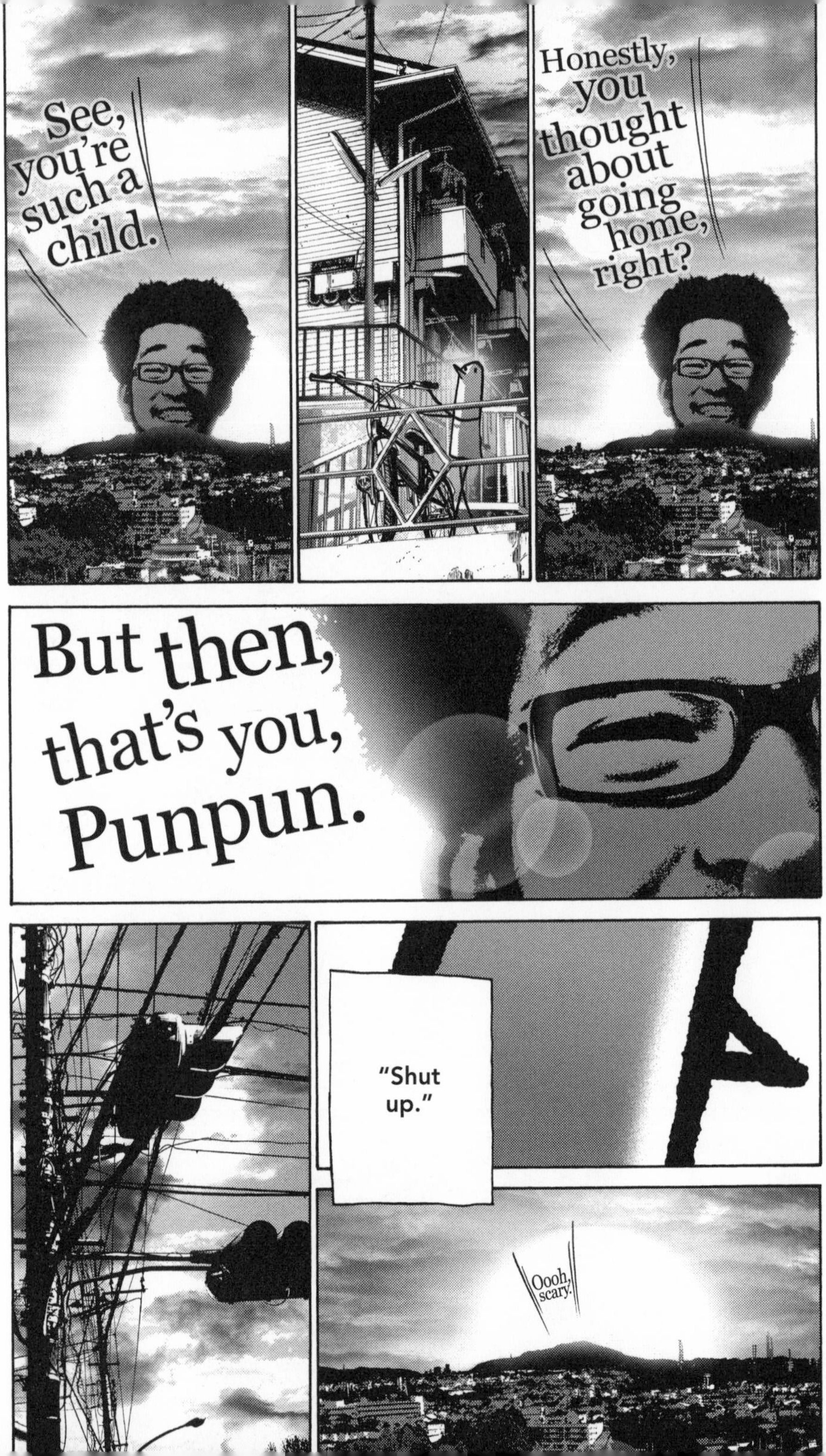
Honestly, you thought about going home, right?
See, you're such a child.
But then, that's you, Punpun.
"Shut up."
Oooh, scary.

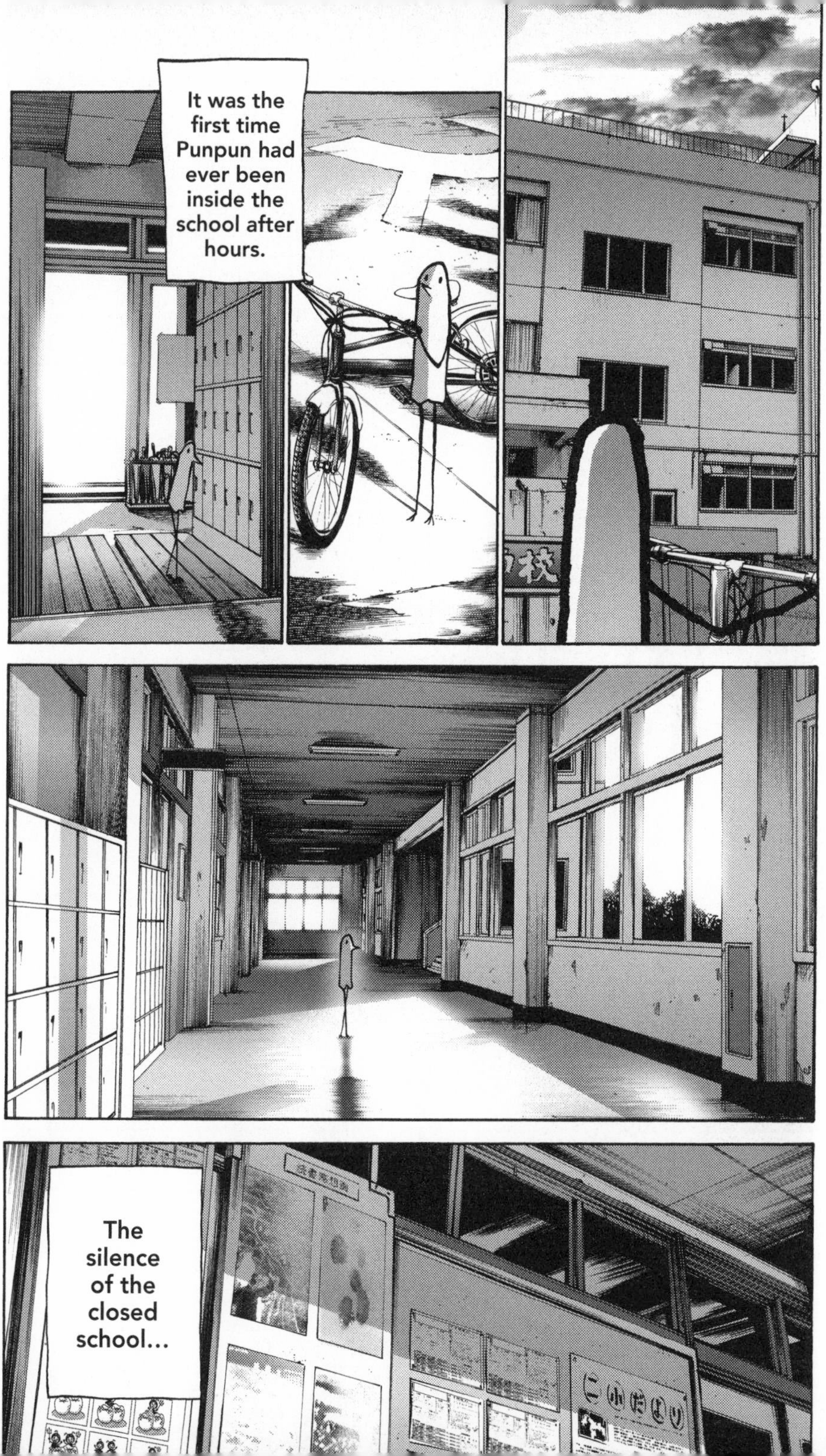
It was the first time Punpun had ever been inside the school after hours.
The silence of the closed school...

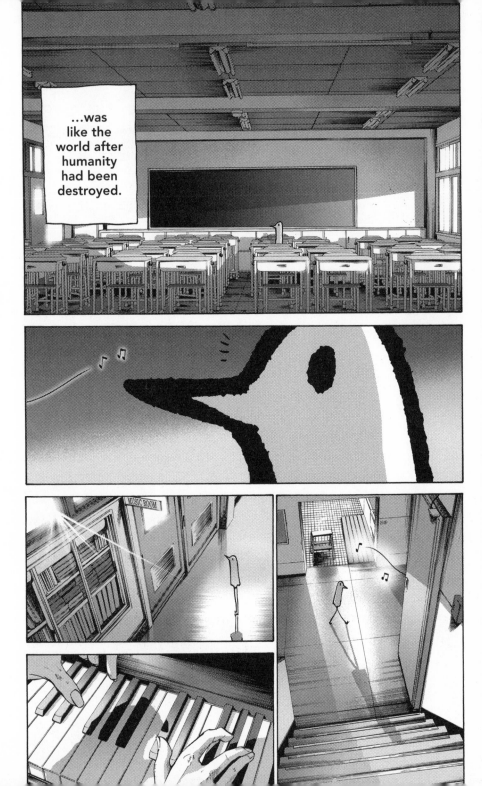

...was like the world after humanity had been destroyed.

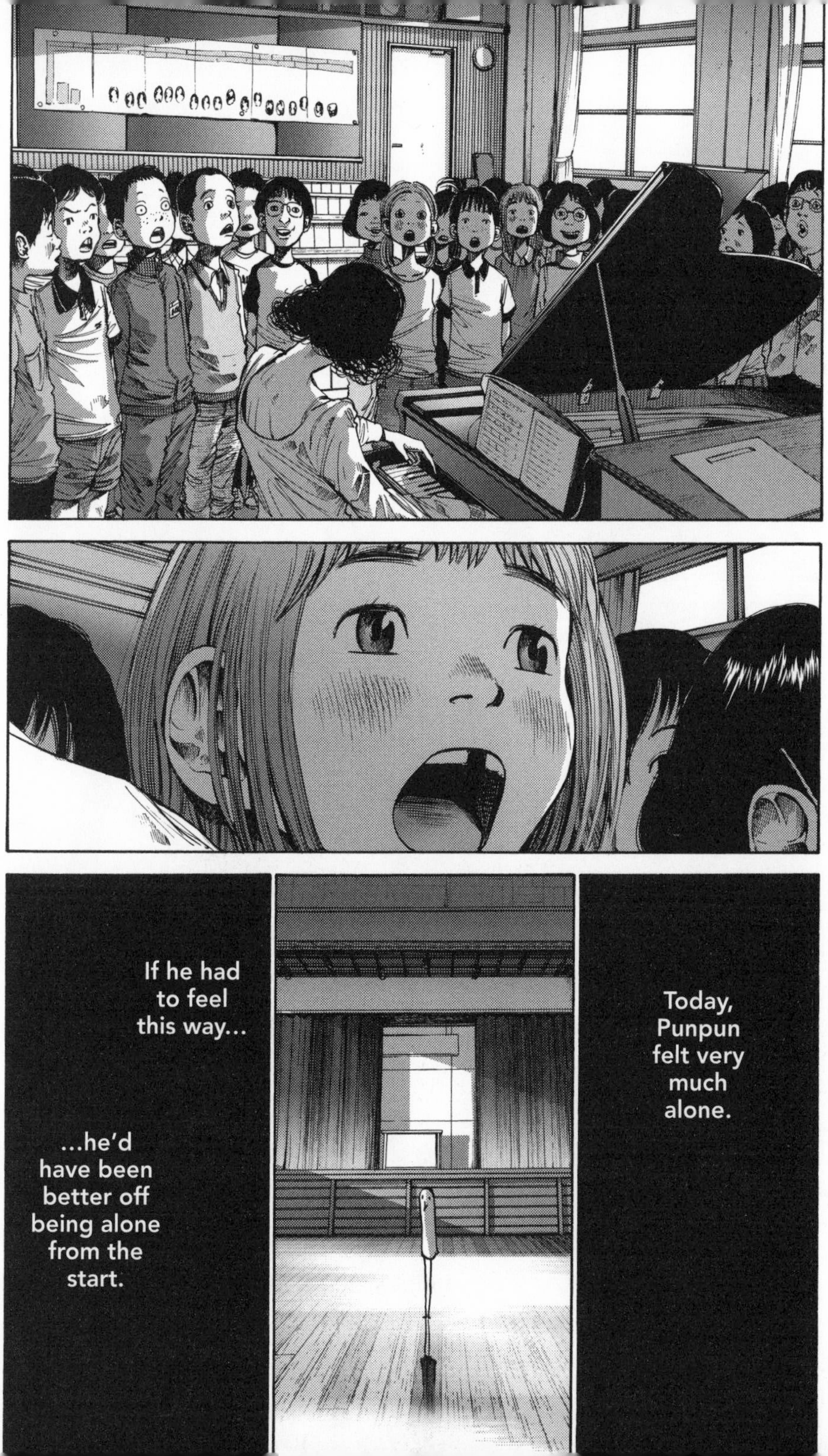
Today, Punpun felt very much alone.
If he had to feel this way...
...he'd have been better off being alone from the start.

Today, the autumn light seemed very soft.

And if he stayed like that with his eyes closed...

...maybe he'd evaporate like water, and then he could fly wherever he wanted.

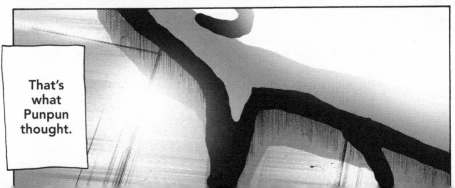

That's what Punpun thought.

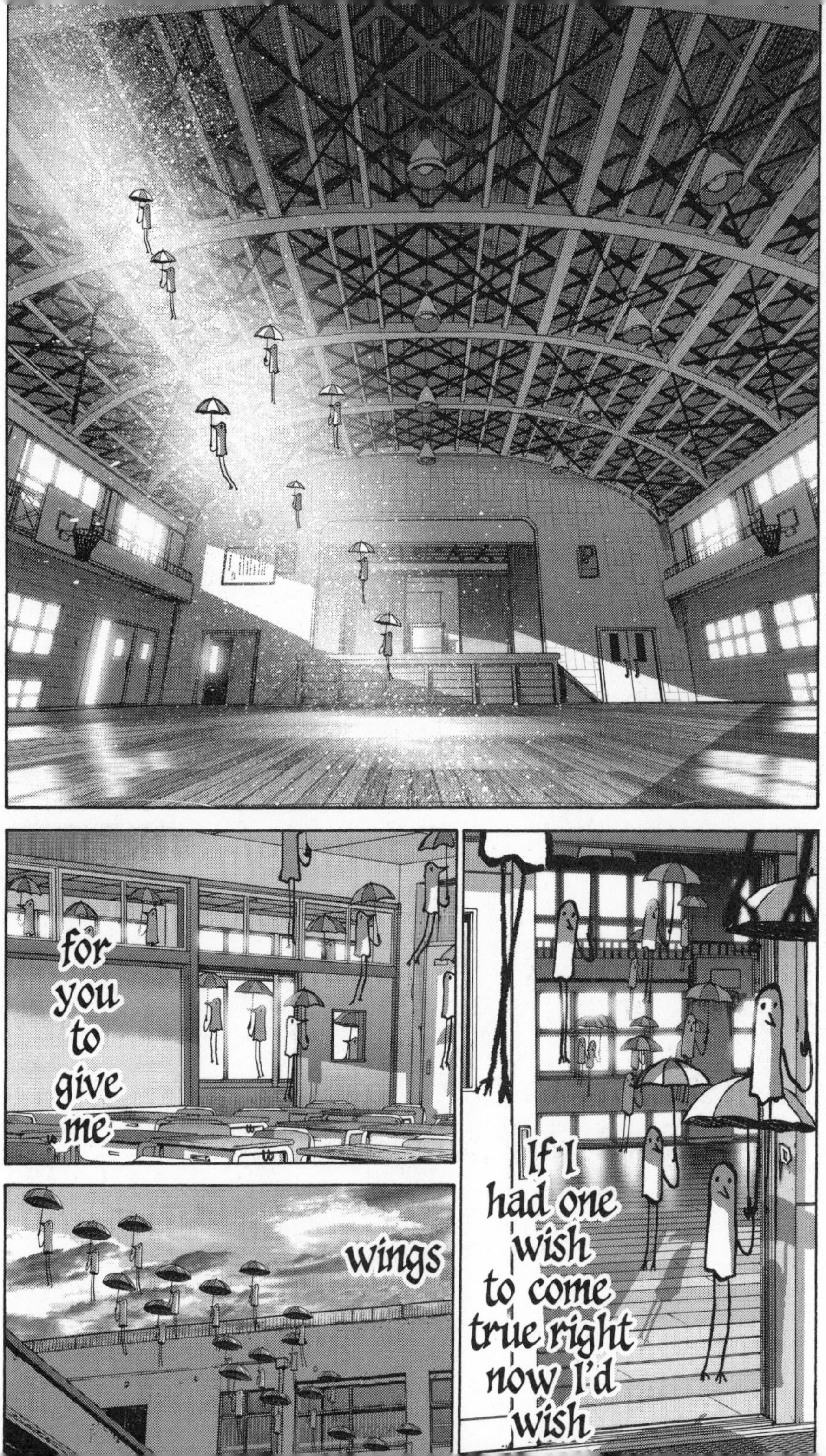
If I had one wish to come true right now I'd wish
for you to give me
wings

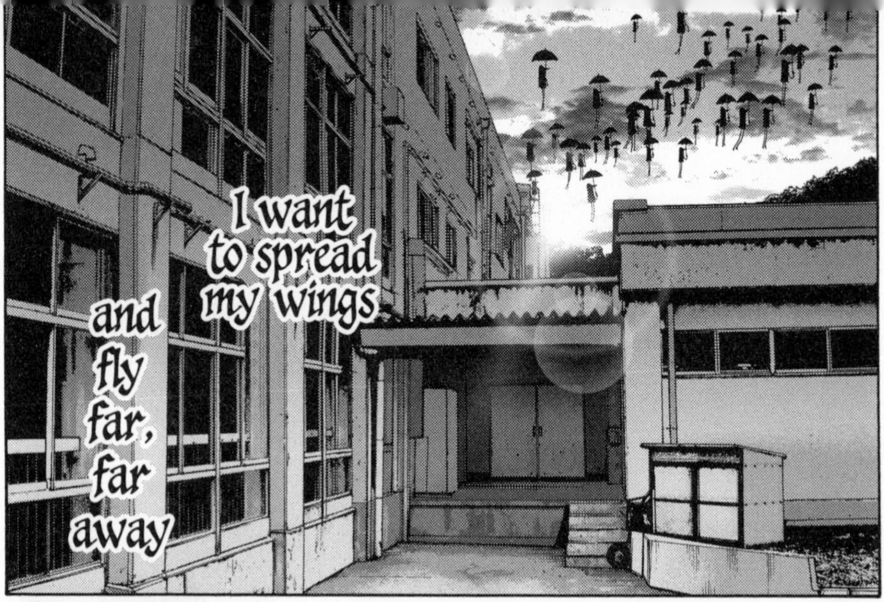
I want to spread my wings
and fly far, far away

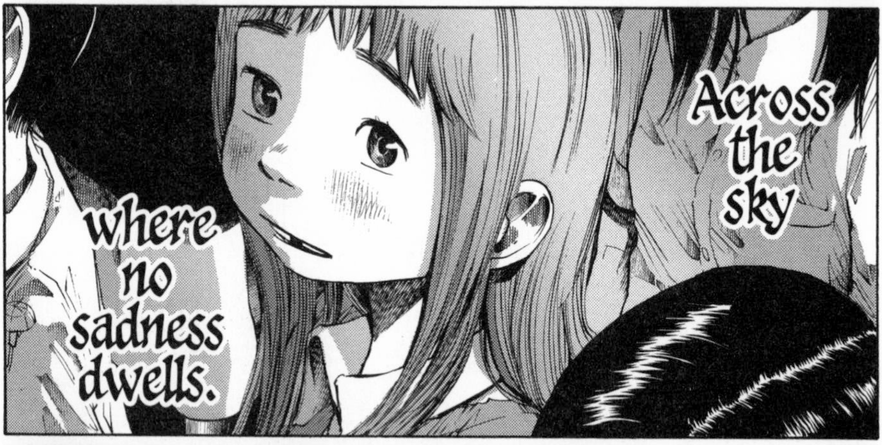
Across the sky
where no sadness dwells.

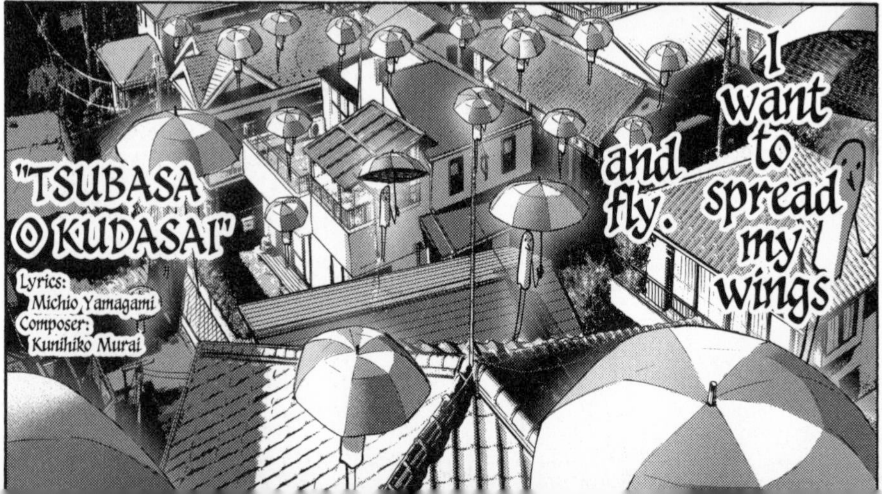
I want to spread my wings
and fly.
"TSUBASA O KUDASAI"
Lyrics: Michio Yamagami
Composer: Kunihiko Murai

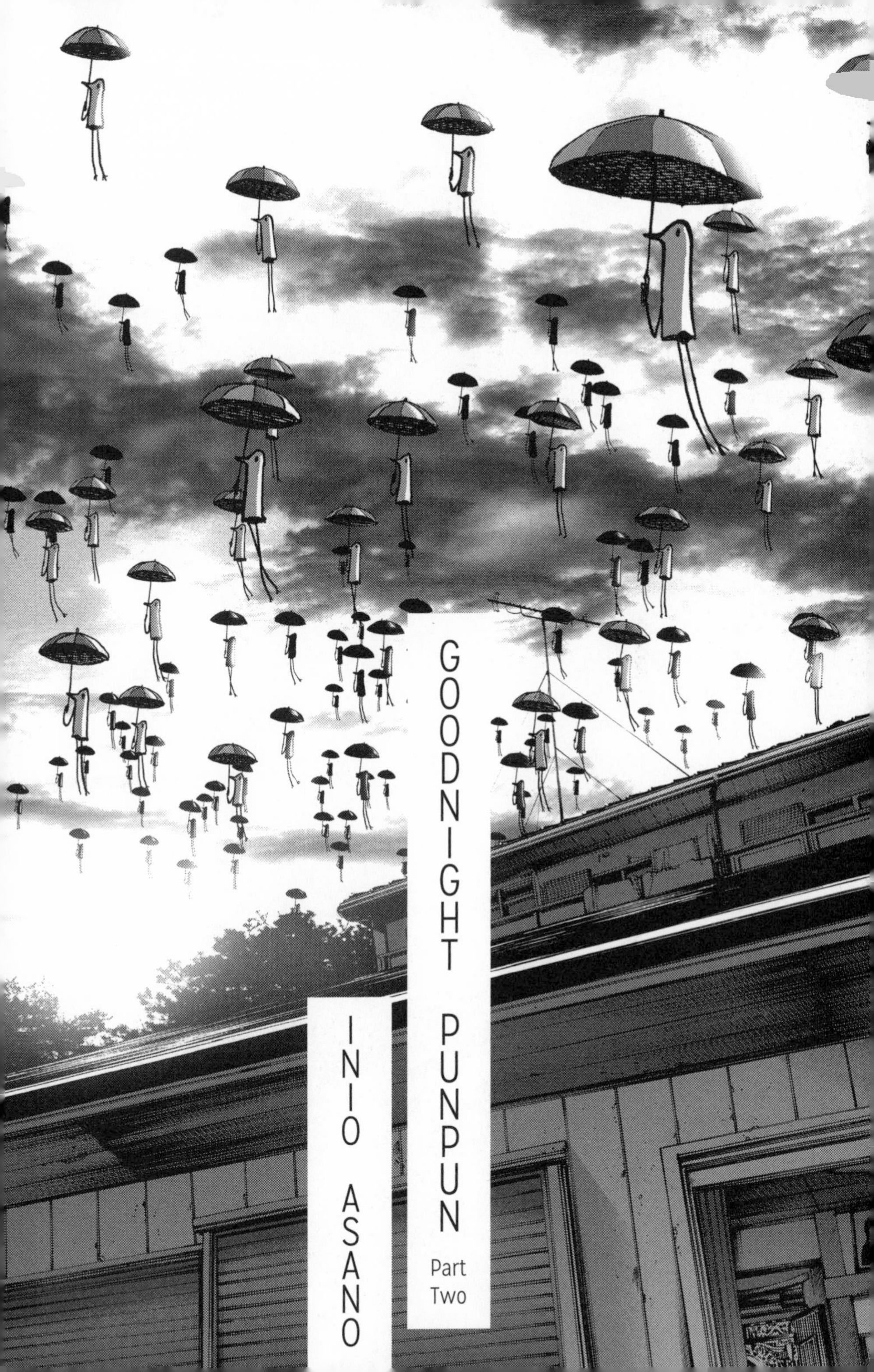
GOODNIGHT PUNPUN
Part Two
INIO ASANO

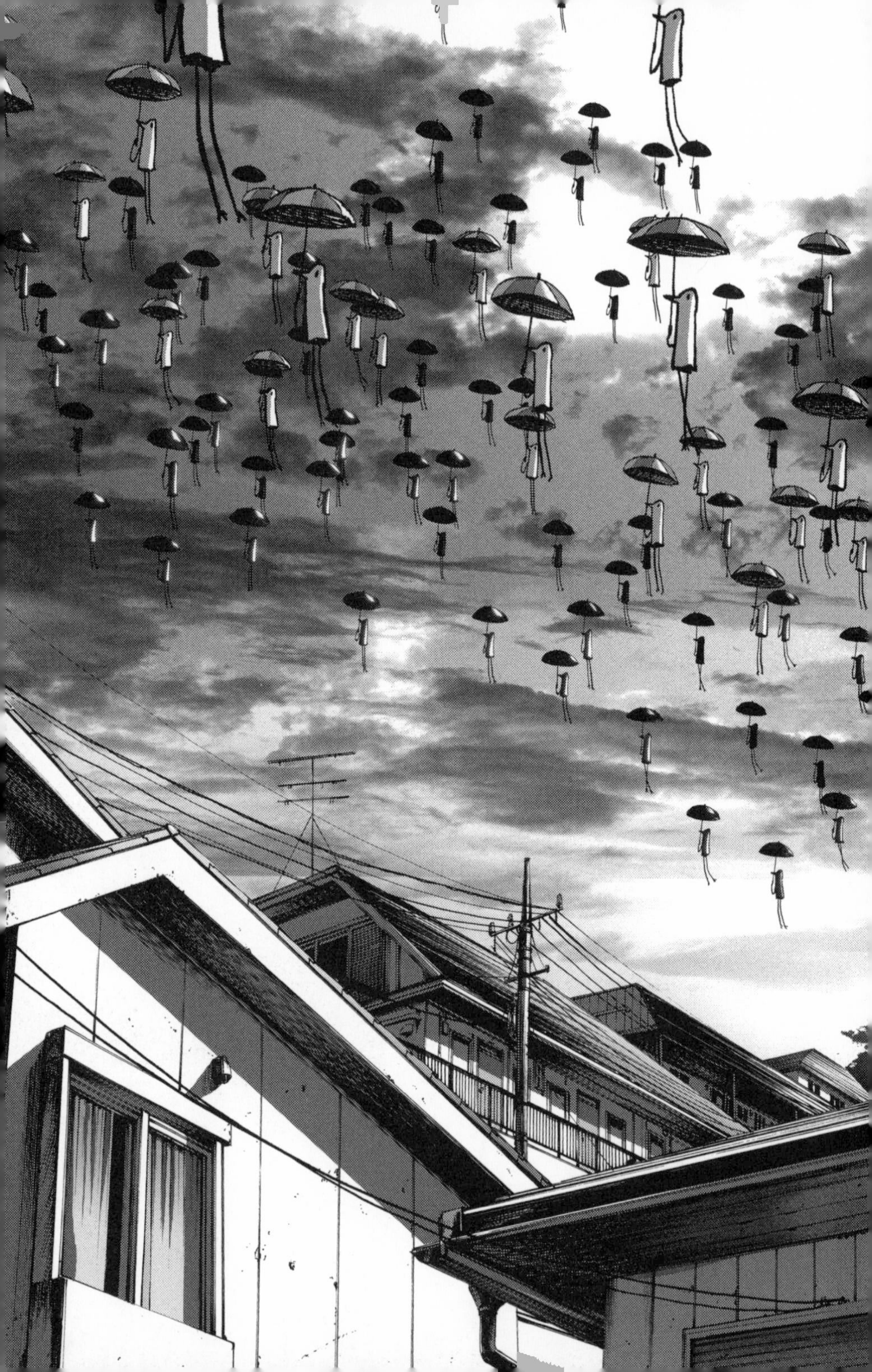

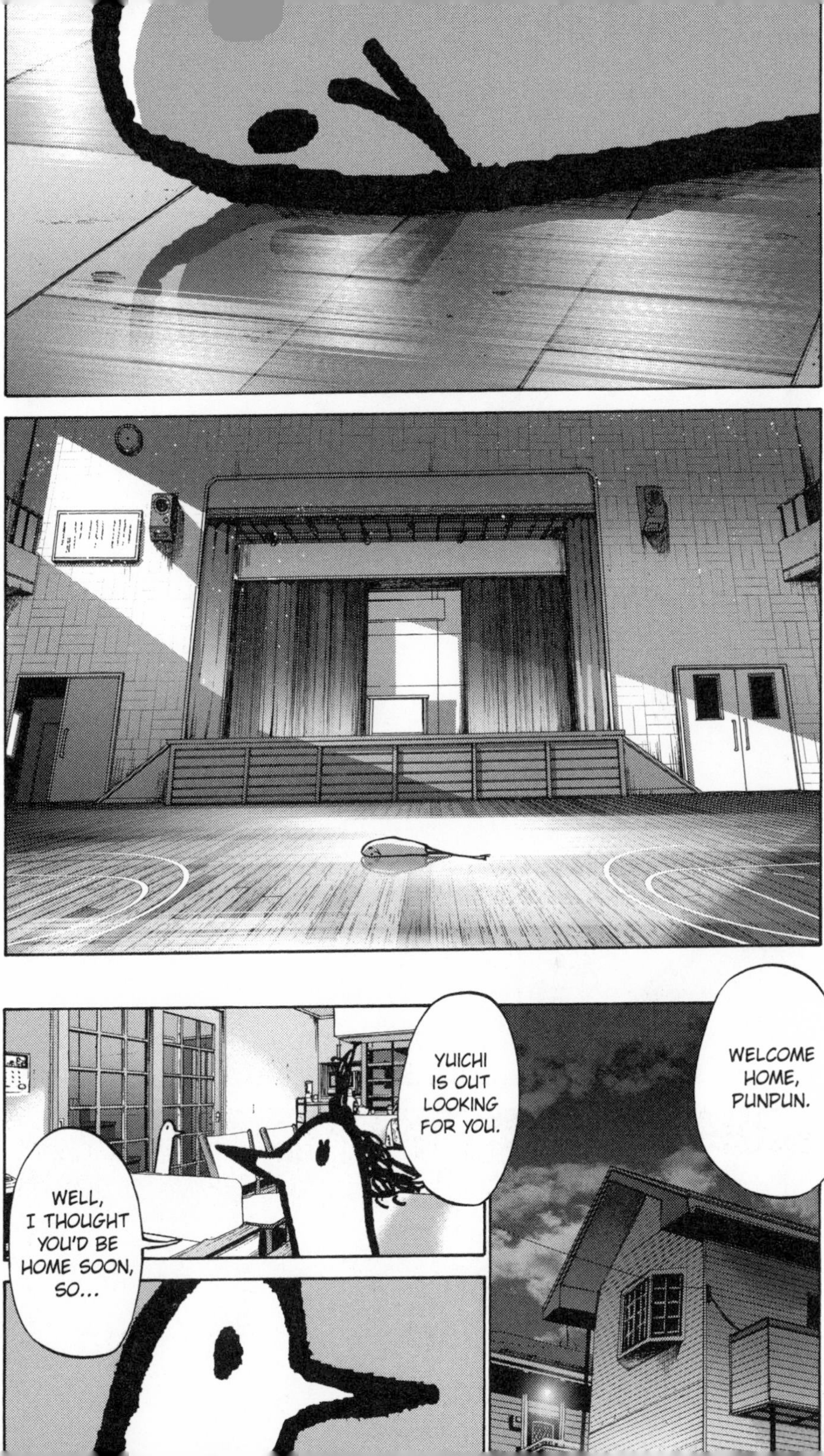
WELCOME HOME, PUNPUN.
YUICHI IS OUT LOOKING FOR YOU.
WELL, I THOUGHT YOU'D BE HOME SOON, SO...

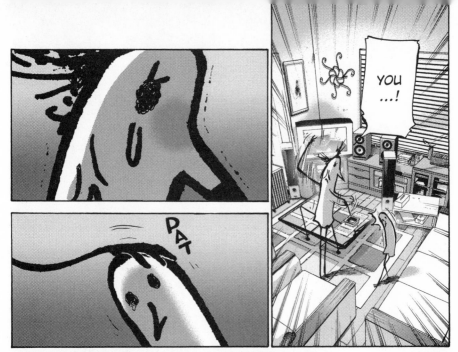

YOU
...!

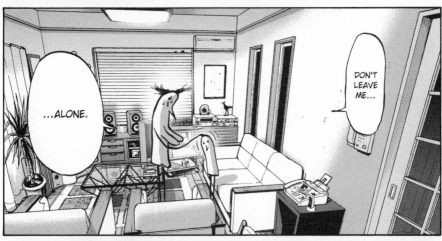

...ALONE.

DON'T
LEAVE
ME...

Punpun...

...had no
idea why,
but the tears
wouldn't
stop.

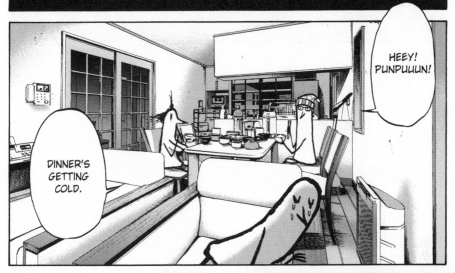

HEEY!
PUNPUUUN!

DINNER'S
GETTING
COLD.

Goodnight,
Punpun.

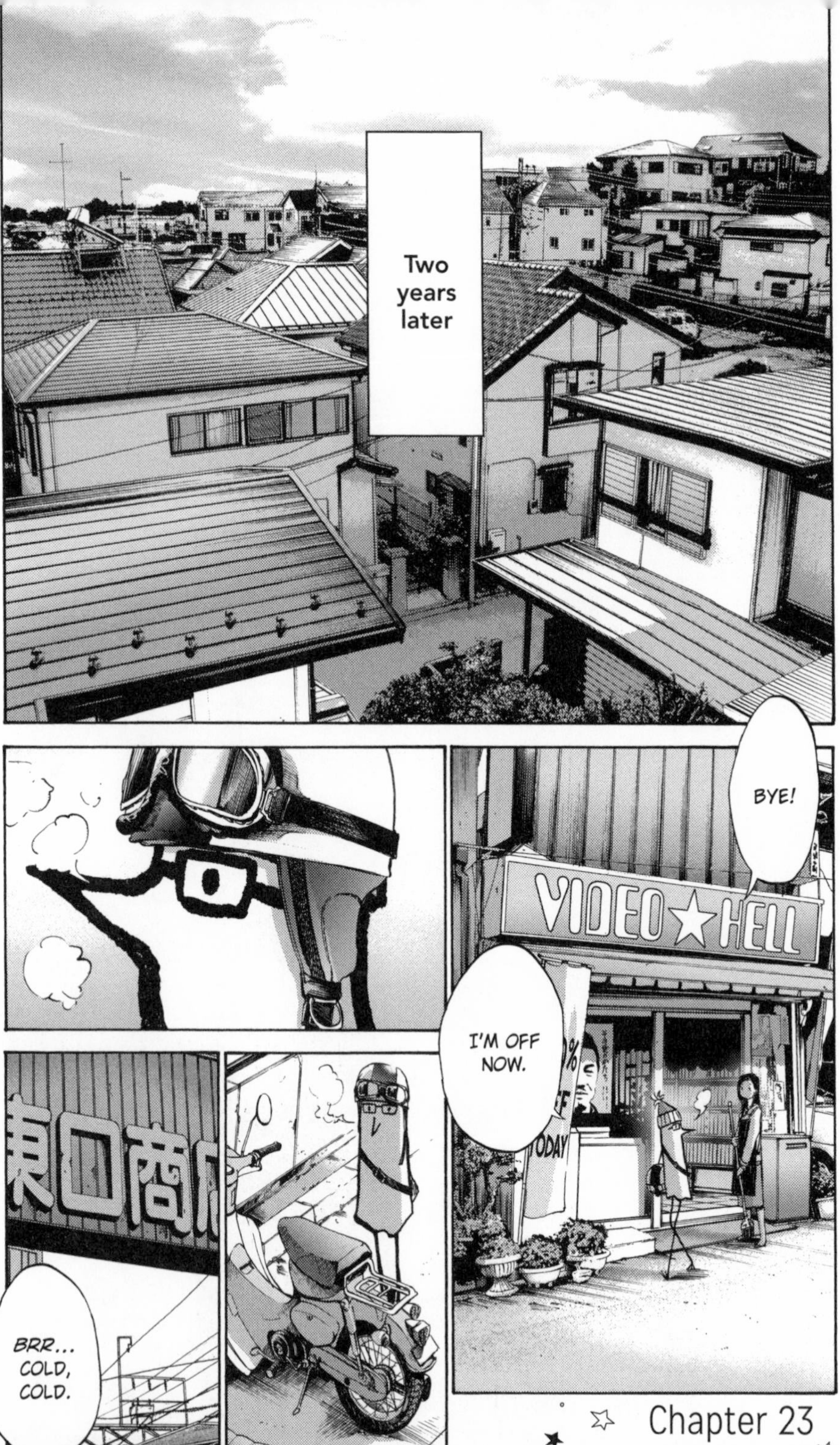
Two years later
BYE!
VIDEO★HELL
I'M OFF NOW.
TODAY
BRR... COLD, COLD.
東口商

Chapter 23

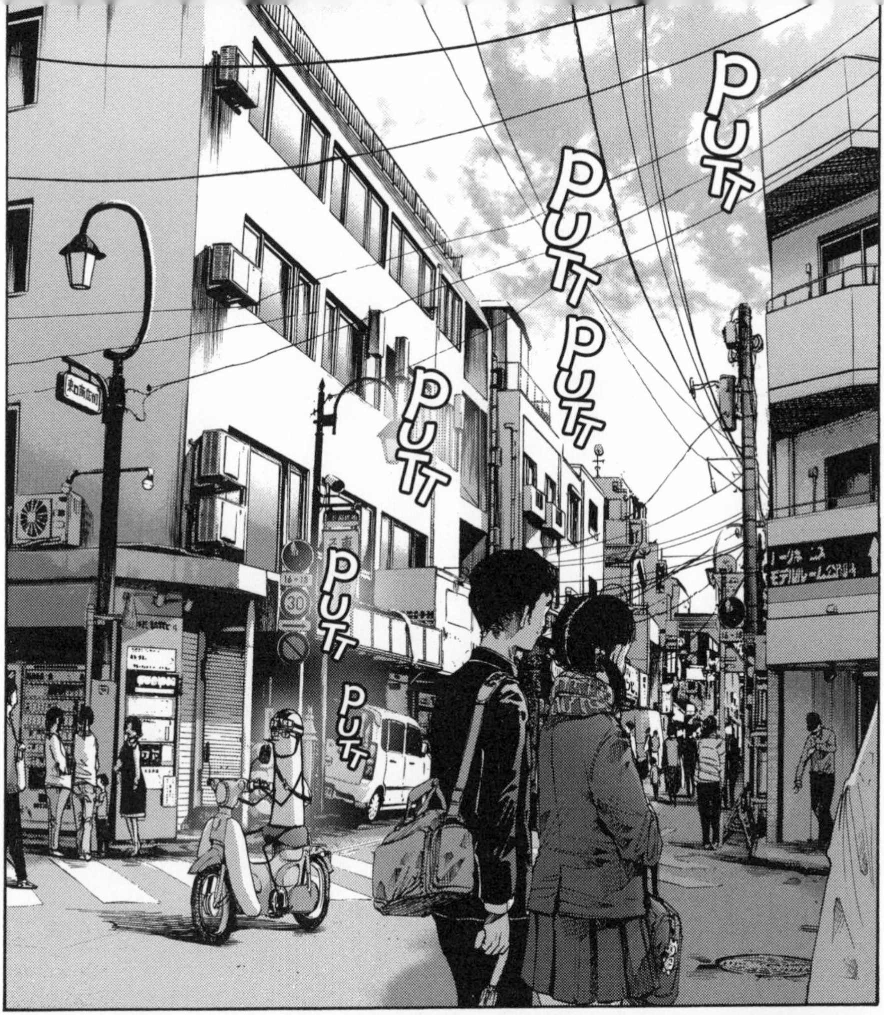
PUTT
PUTT
PUTT
PUTT
PUTT
PUTT

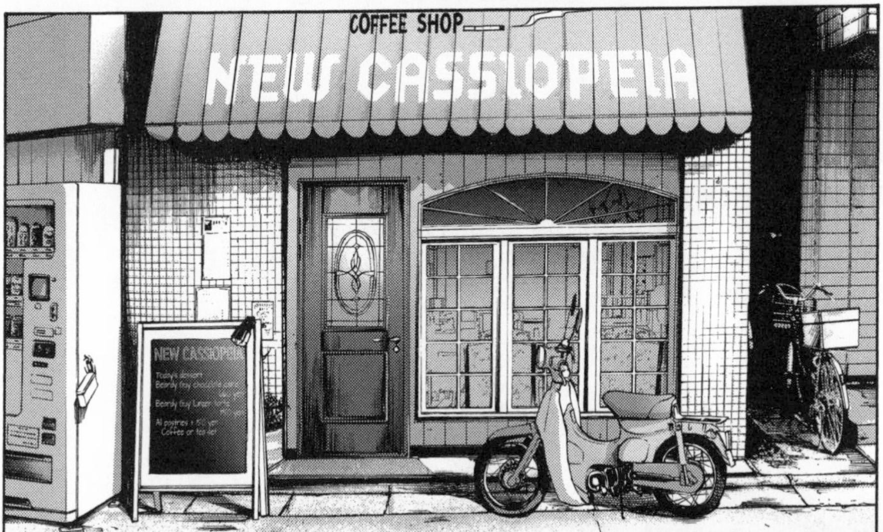
COFFEE SHOP
NEW CASSIOPEIA

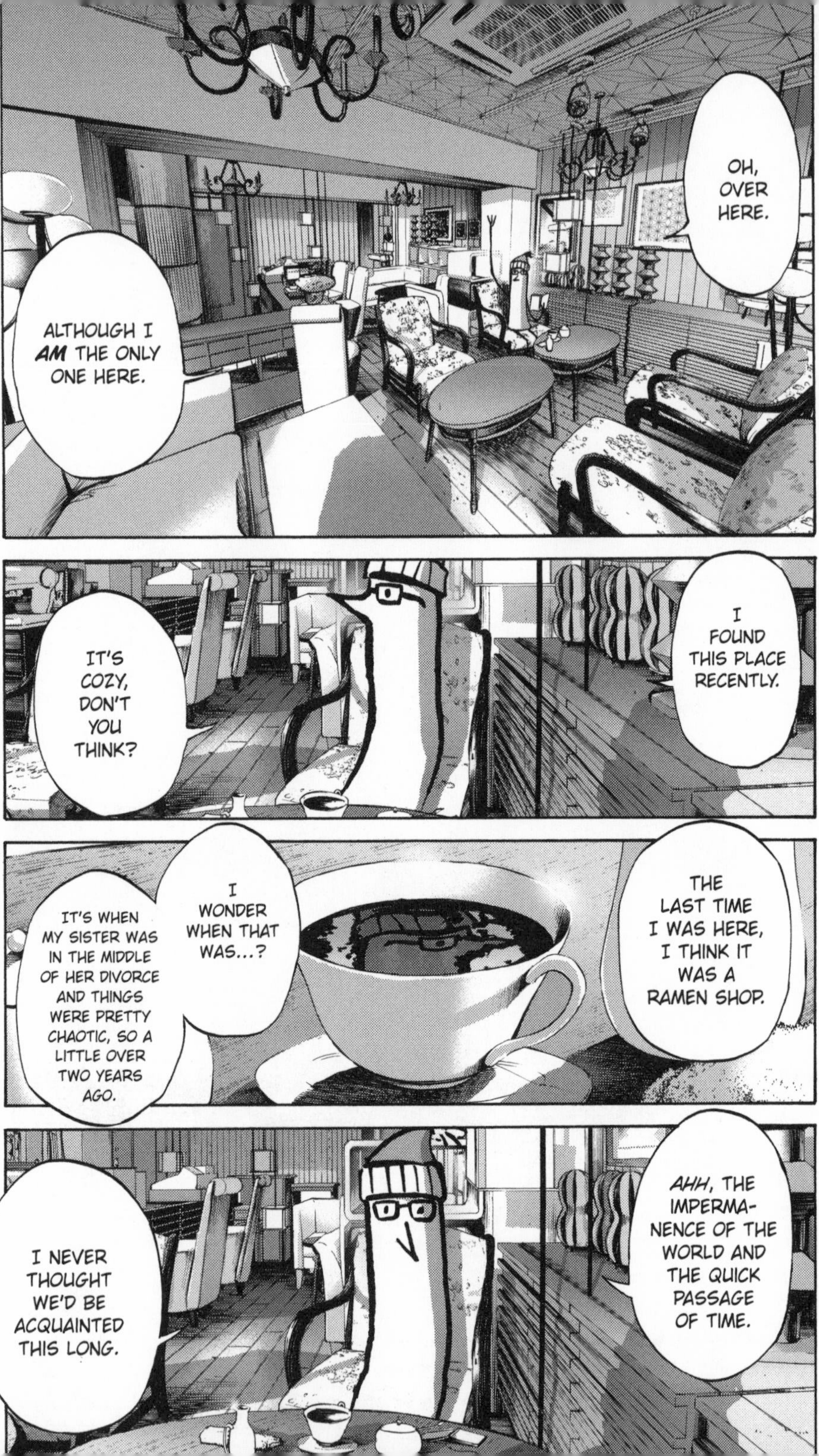
OH, OVER HERE.
ALTHOUGH I *AM* THE ONLY ONE HERE.
I FOUND THIS PLACE RECENTLY.
IT'S COZY, DON'T YOU THINK?
THE LAST TIME I WAS HERE, I THINK IT WAS A RAMEN SHOP.
I WONDER WHEN THAT WAS...?
IT'S WHEN MY SISTER WAS IN THE MIDDLE OF HER DIVORCE AND THINGS WERE PRETTY CHAOTIC, SO A LITTLE OVER TWO YEARS AGO.
AHH, THE IMPERMA-NENCE OF THE WORLD AND THE QUICK PASSAGE OF TIME.
I NEVER THOUGHT WE'D BE ACQUAINTED THIS LONG.

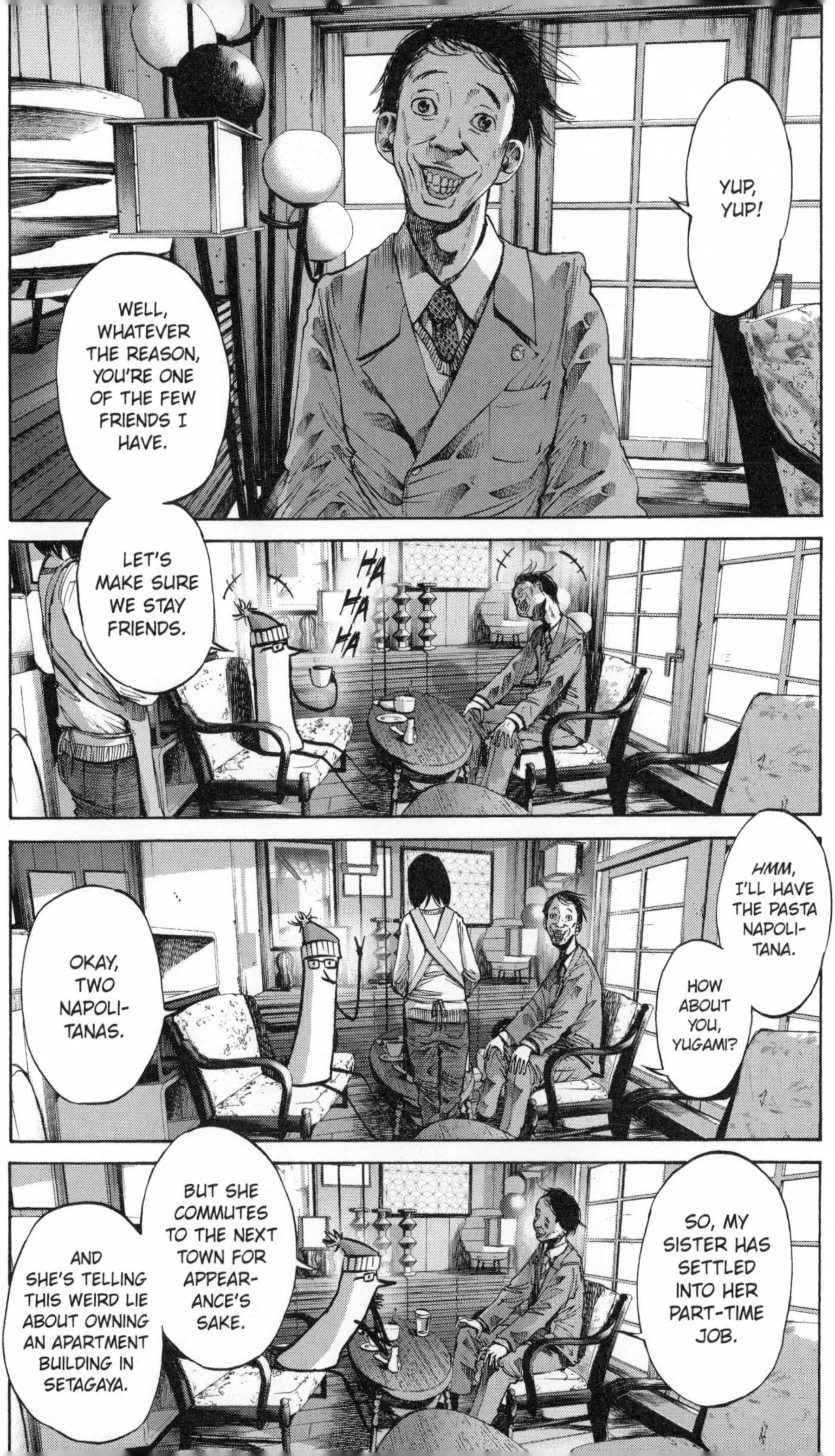
YUP, YUP!
WELL, WHATEVER THE REASON, YOU'RE ONE OF THE FEW FRIENDS I HAVE.
LET'S MAKE SURE WE STAY FRIENDS.
HA HA HA HA
HMM, I'LL HAVE THE PASTA NAPOLI-TANA.
HOW ABOUT YOU, YUGAMI?
OKAY, TWO NAPOLI-TANAS.
SO, MY SISTER HAS SETTLED INTO HER PART-TIME JOB.
BUT SHE COMMUTES TO THE NEXT TOWN FOR APPEAR-ANCE'S SAKE.
AND SHE'S TELLING THIS WEIRD LIE ABOUT OWNING AN APARTMENT BUILDING IN SETAGAYA.

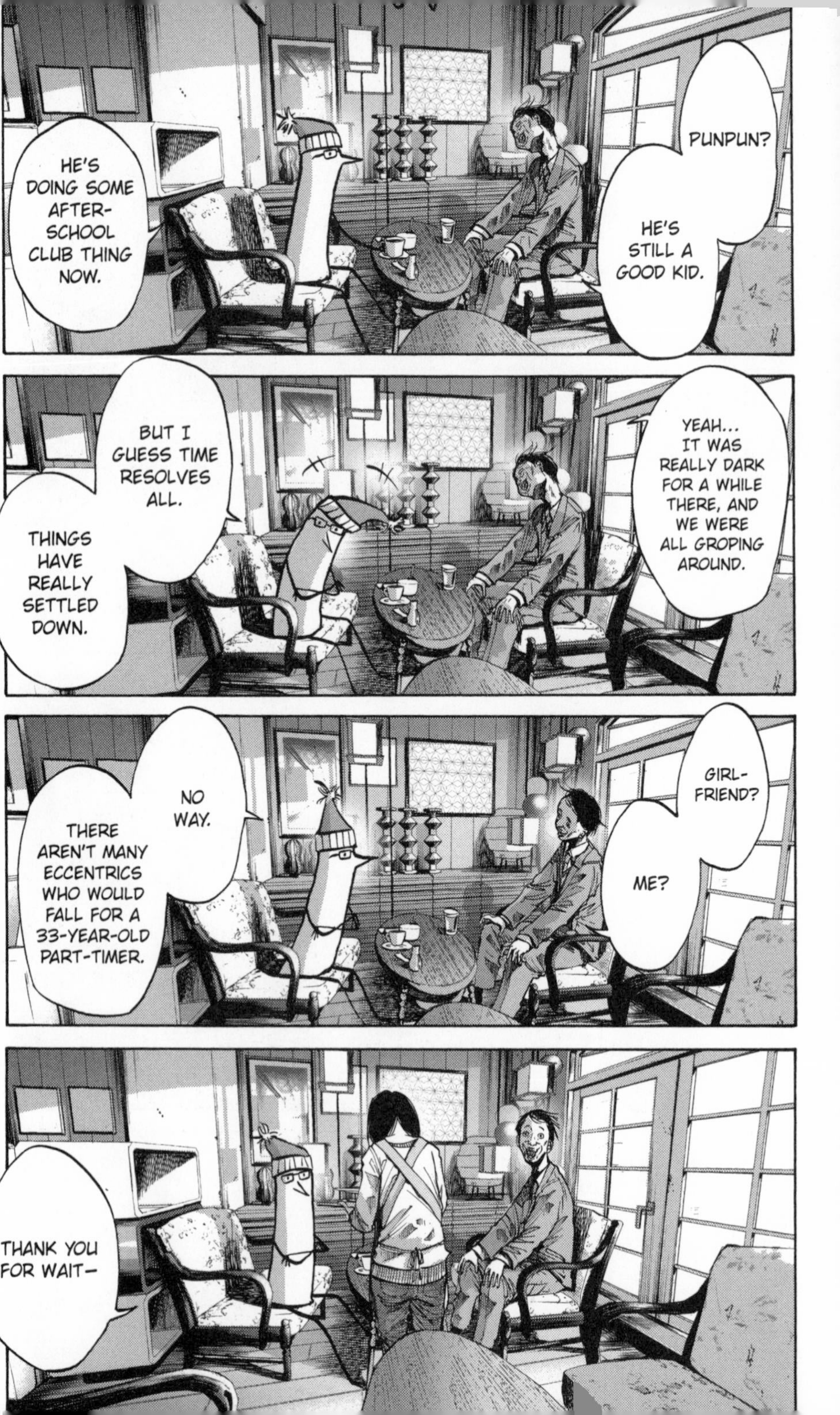
PUNPUN?
HE'S STILL A GOOD KID.
HE'S DOING SOME AFTER-SCHOOL CLUB THING NOW.
YEAH... IT WAS REALLY DARK FOR A WHILE THERE, AND WE WERE ALL GROPING AROUND.
BUT I GUESS TIME RESOLVES ALL.
THINGS HAVE REALLY SETTLED DOWN.
GIRL-FRIEND?
ME?
NO WAY.
THERE AREN'T MANY ECCENTRICS WHO WOULD FALL FOR A 33-YEAR-OLD PART-TIMER.
THANK YOU FOR WAIT—

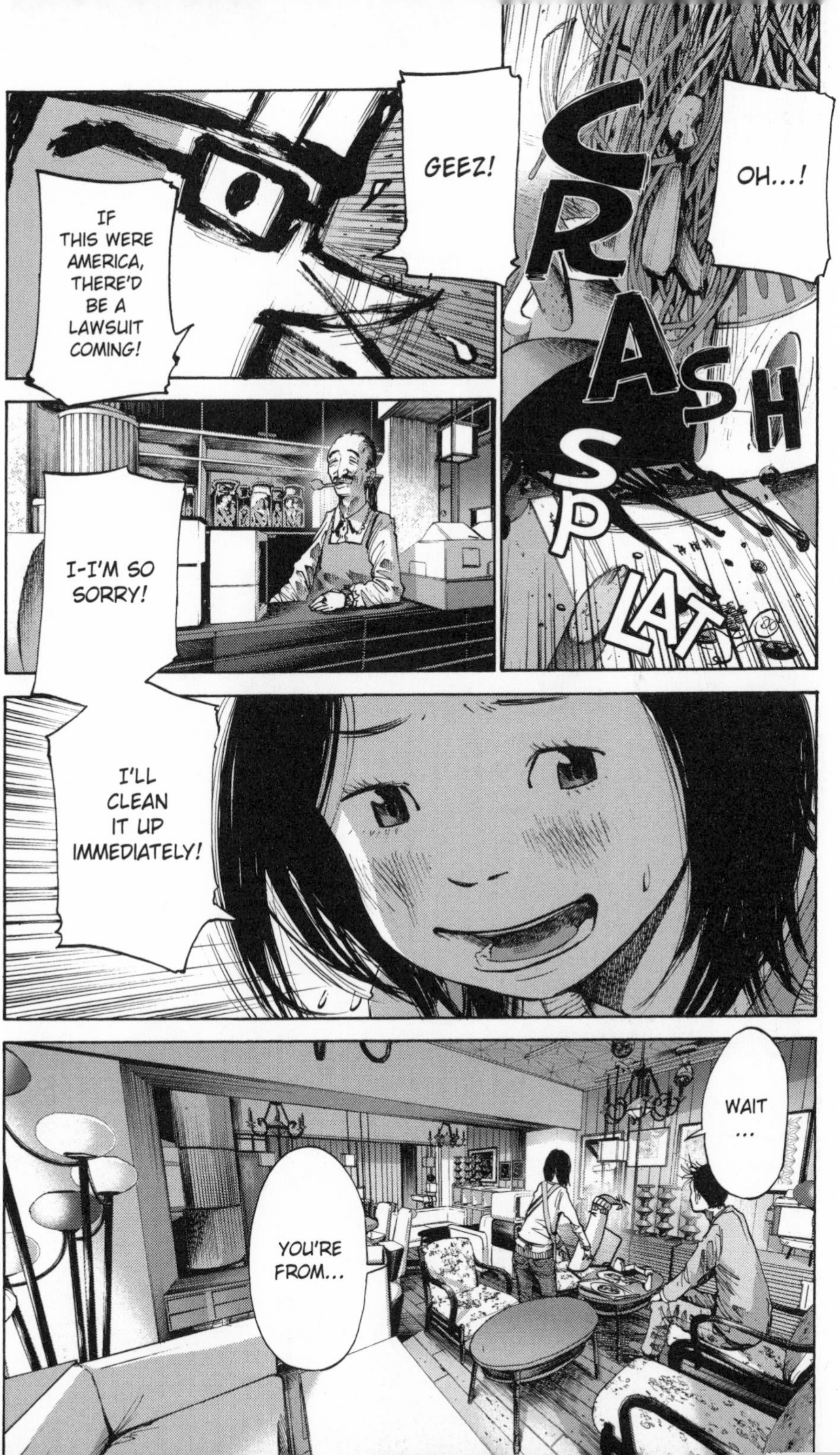
OH...!
CRASH
SPLAT
GEEZ!
IF THIS WERE AMERICA, THERE'D BE A LAWSUIT COMING!
I-I'M SO SORRY!
I'LL CLEAN IT UP IMMEDIATELY!
WAIT ...
YOU'RE FROM...

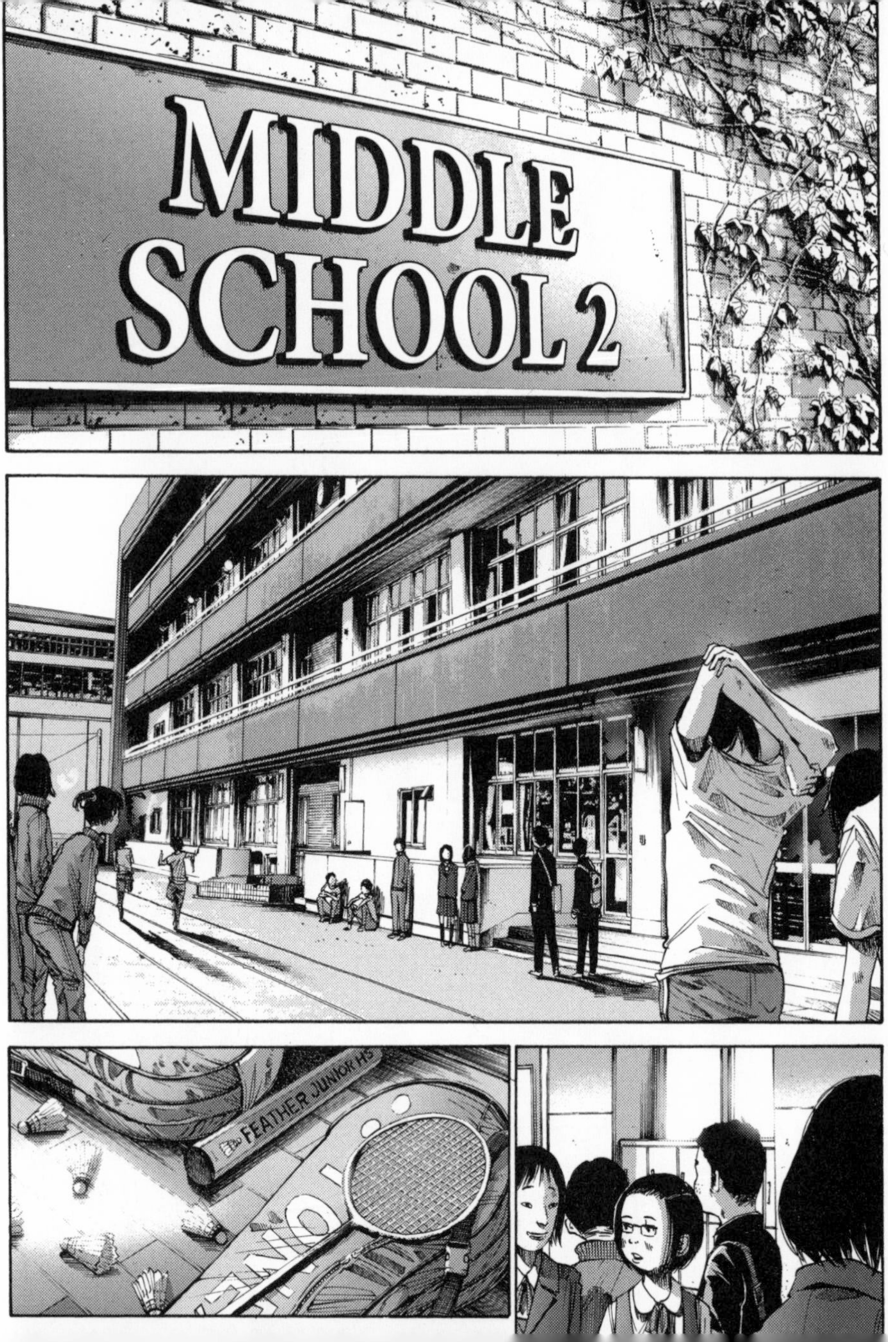
MIDDLE SCHOOL 2
FEATHER JUNIOR HS

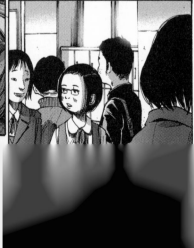

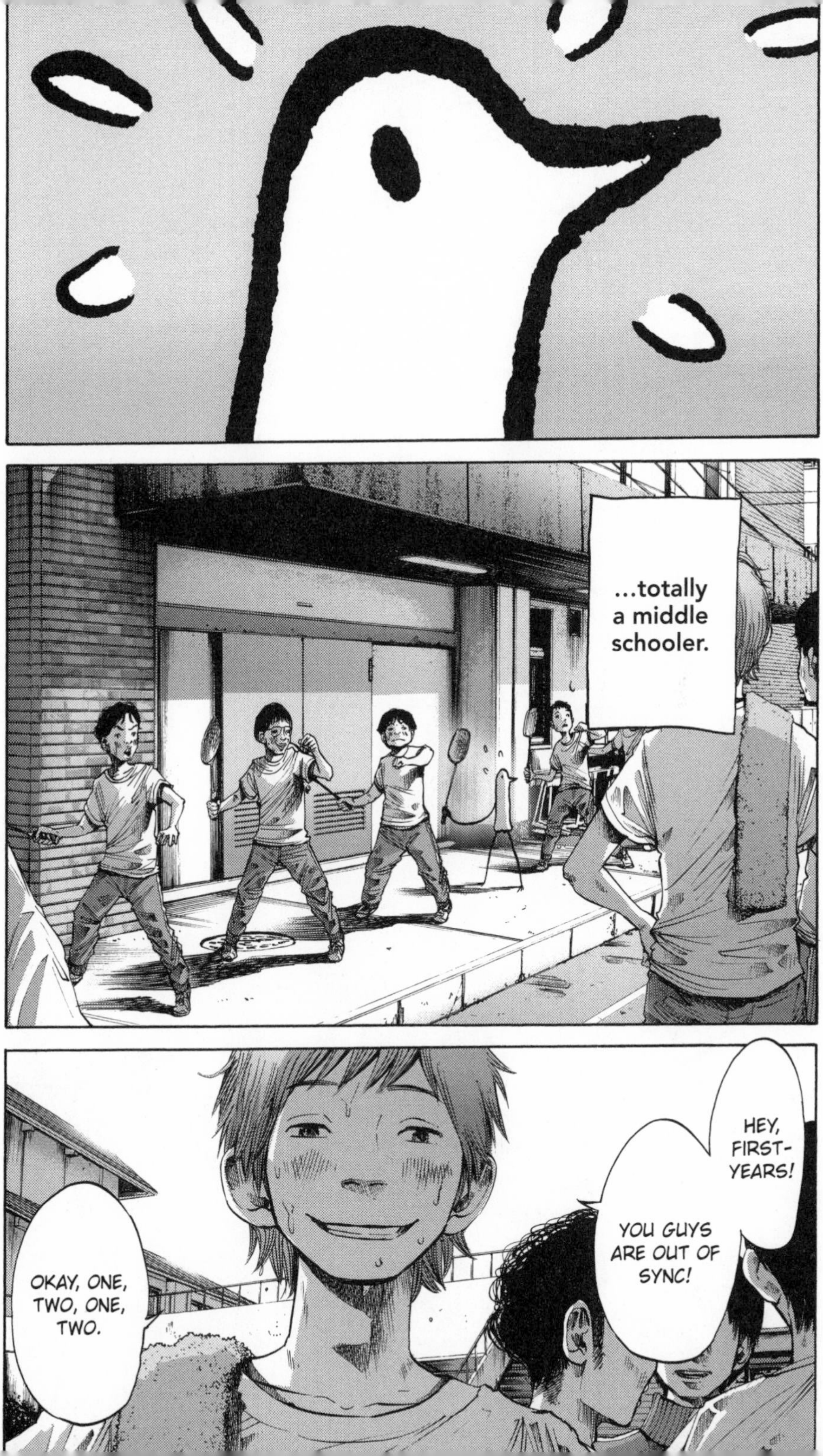
...totally a middle schooler.
HEY, FIRST-YEARS!
YOU GUYS ARE OUT OF SYNC!
OKAY, ONE, TWO, ONE, TWO.

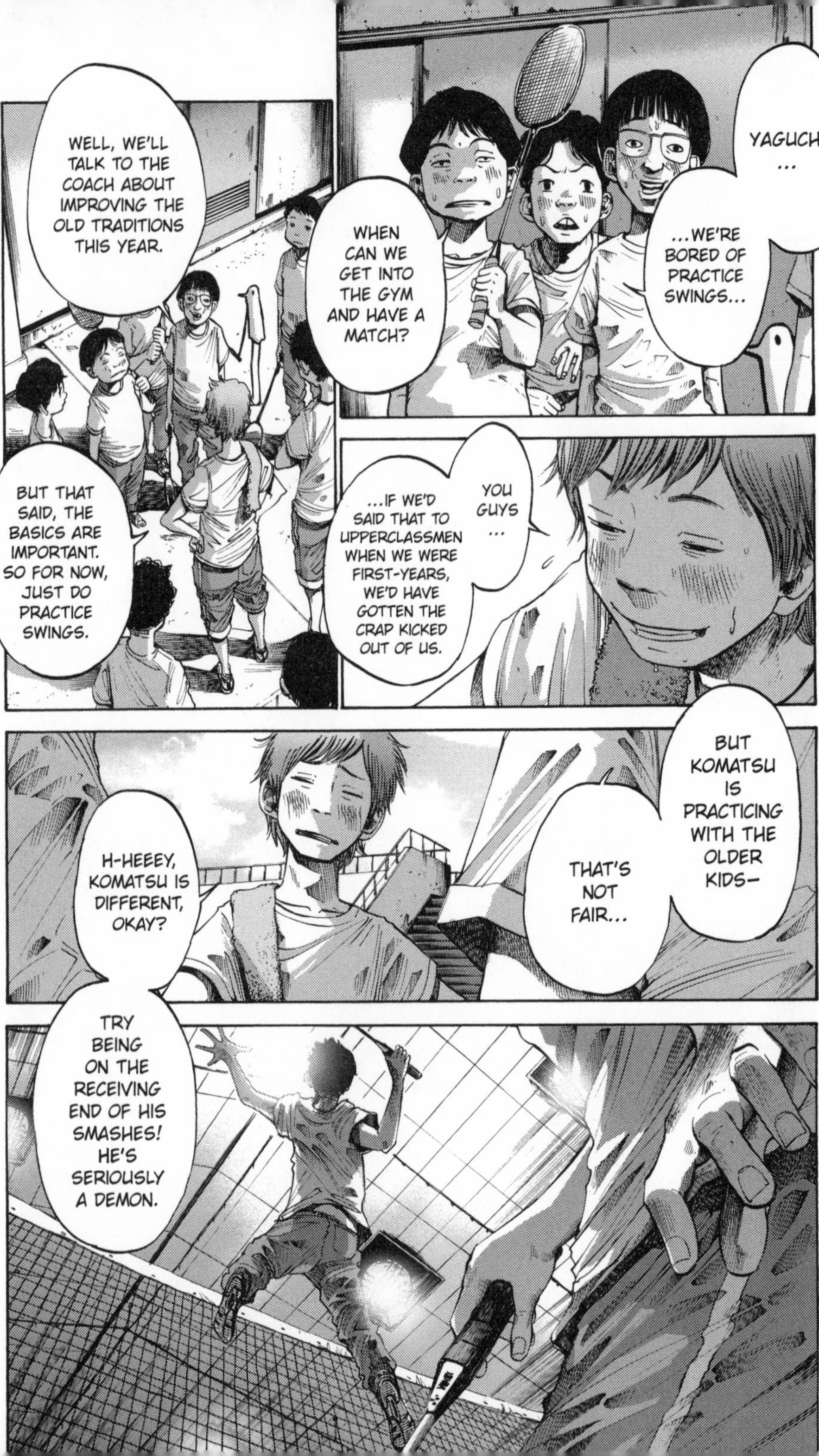
YAGUCHI ...
...WE'RE BORED OF PRACTICE SWINGS...
WHEN CAN WE GET INTO THE GYM AND HAVE A MATCH?
YOU GUYS ...
...IF WE'D SAID THAT TO UPPERCLASSMEN WHEN WE WERE FIRST-YEARS, WE'D HAVE GOTTEN THE CRAP KICKED OUT OF US.
WELL, WE'LL TALK TO THE COACH ABOUT IMPROVING THE OLD TRADITIONS THIS YEAR.
BUT THAT SAID, THE BASICS ARE IMPORTANT. SO FOR NOW, JUST DO PRACTICE SWINGS.
BUT KOMATSU IS PRACTICING WITH THE OLDER KIDS—
THAT'S NOT FAIR...
H-HEEEY, KOMATSU IS DIFFERENT, OKAY?
TRY BEING ON THE RECEIVING END OF HIS SMASHES! HE'S SERIOUSLY A DEMON.

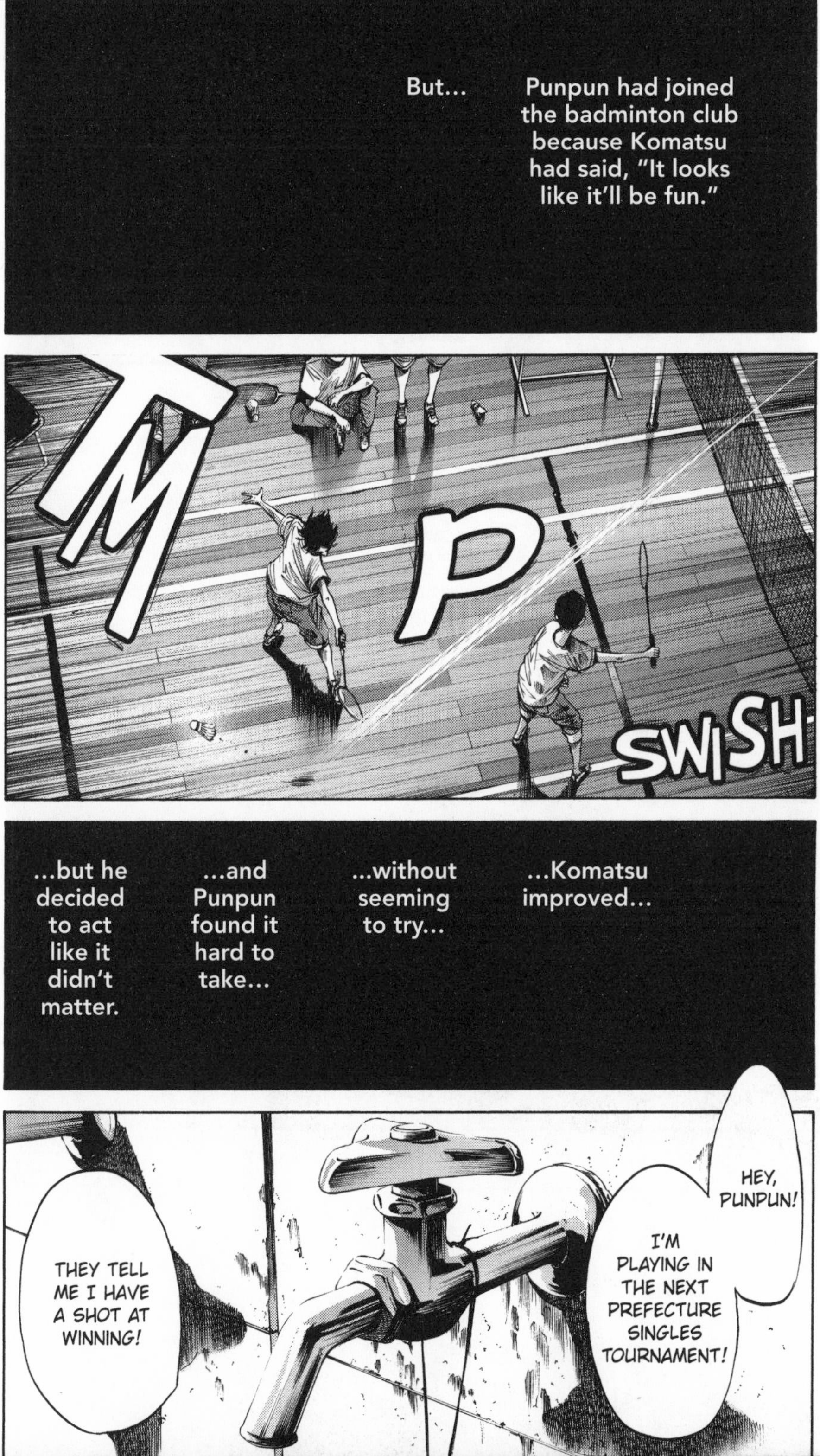

Punpun had joined the badminton club because Komatsu had said, "It looks like it'll be fun."
But...
TMP
SWISH
...Komatsu improved...
...without seeming to try...
...and Punpun found it hard to take...
...but he decided to act like it didn't matter.
HEY, PUNPUN!
I'M PLAYING IN THE NEXT PREFECTURE SINGLES TOURNAMENT!
THEY TELL ME I HAVE A SHOT AT WINNING!

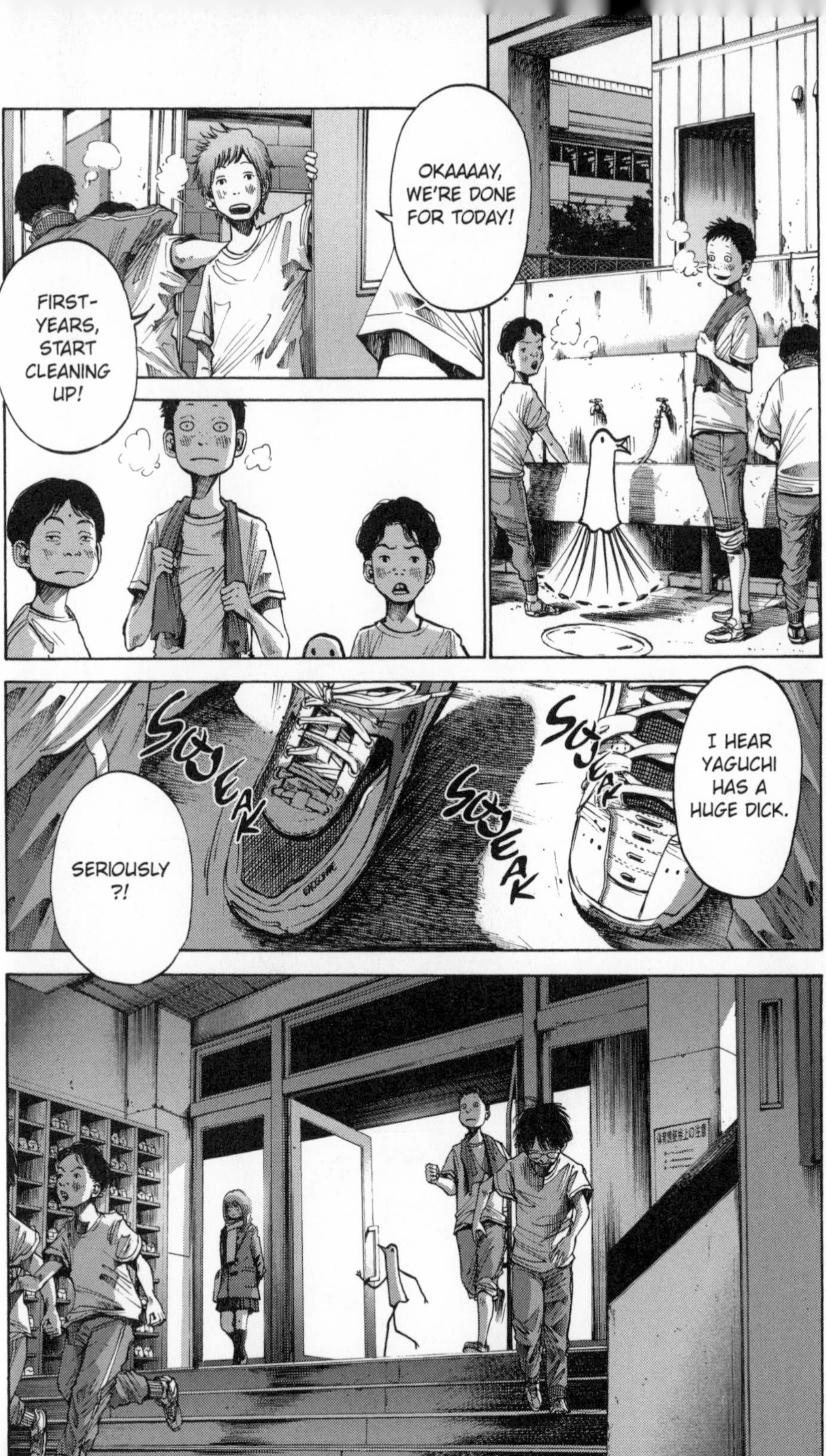
OKAAAAY, WE'RE DONE FOR TODAY!
FIRST-YEARS, START CLEANING UP!
I HEAR YAGUCHI HAS A HUGE DICK.
SQUEAK
SQUEAK
SQUEAK
SERIOUSLY?!

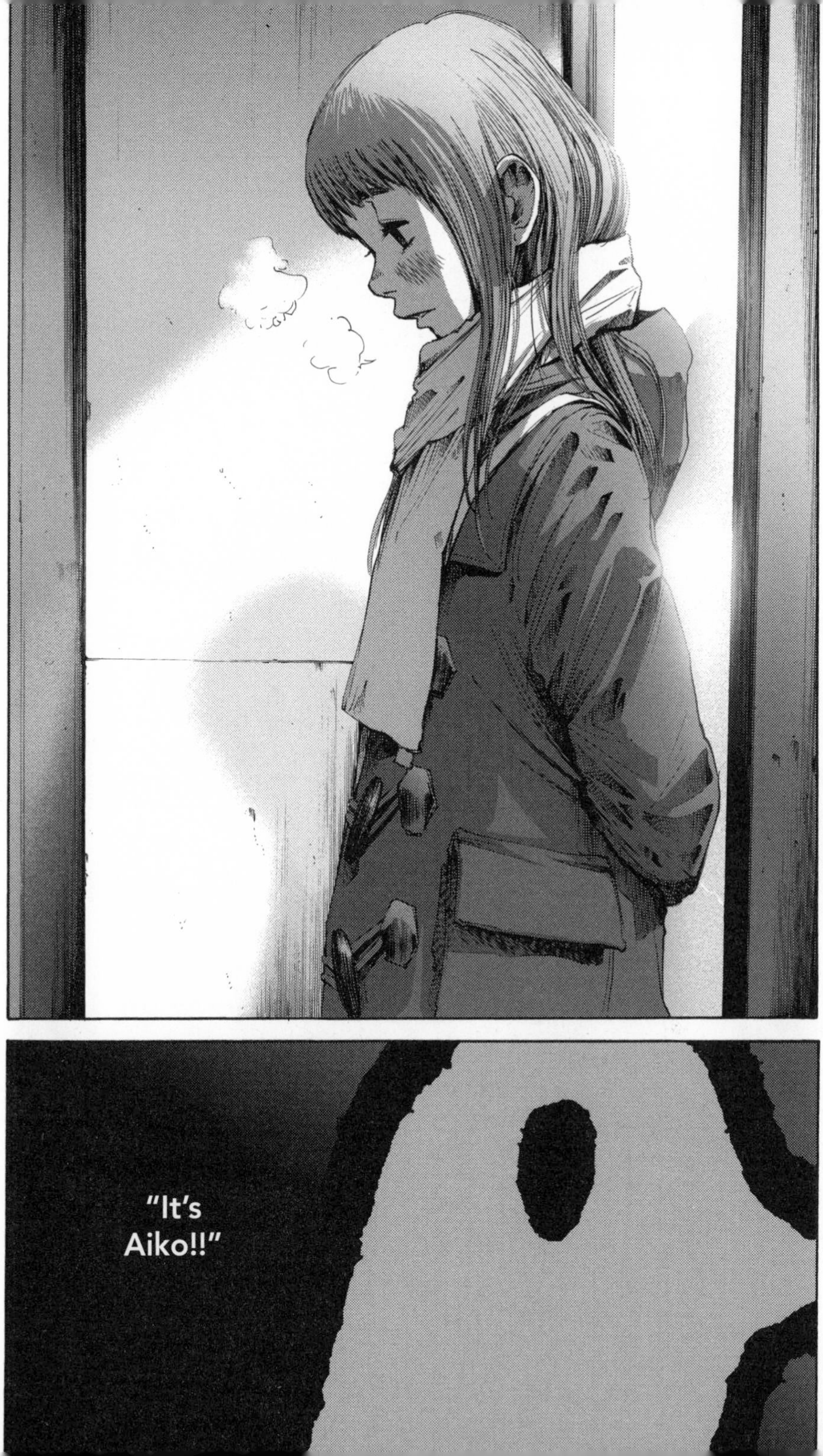
"It's
Aiko!!"

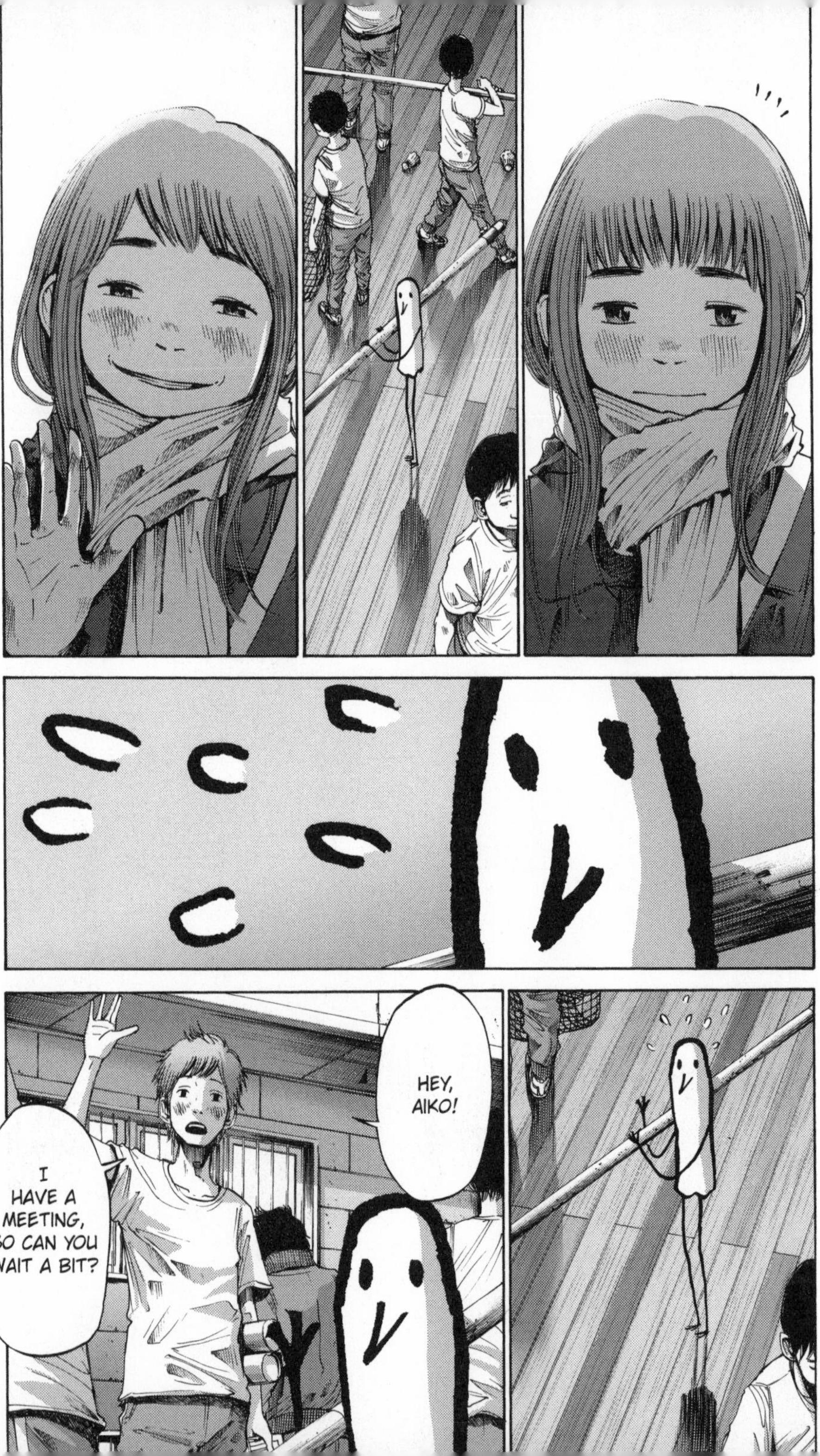
HEY, AIKO!
I HAVE A MEETING, SO CAN YOU WAIT A BIT?

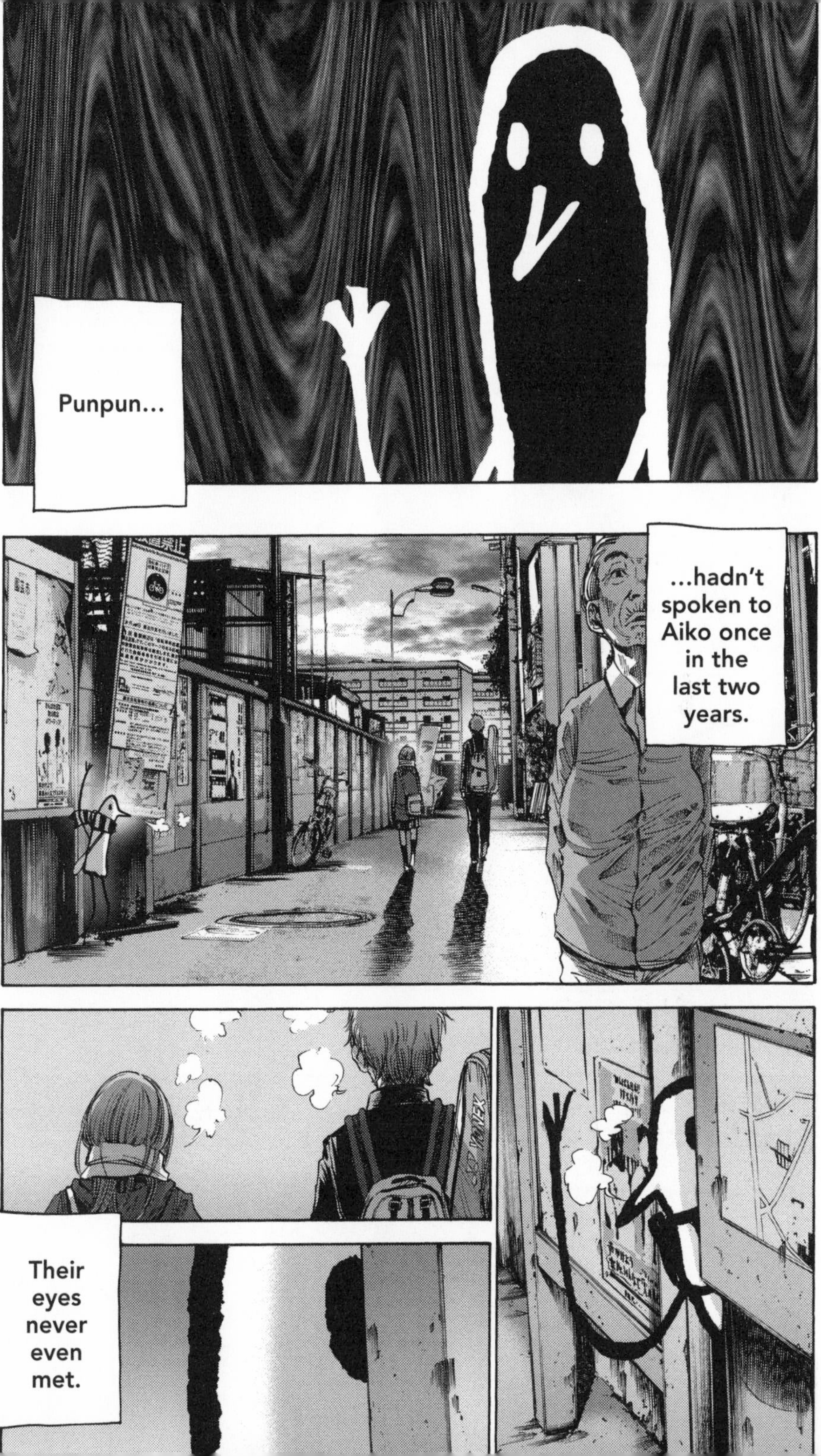
Punpun...
...hadn't spoken to Aiko once in the last two years.
Their eyes never even met.

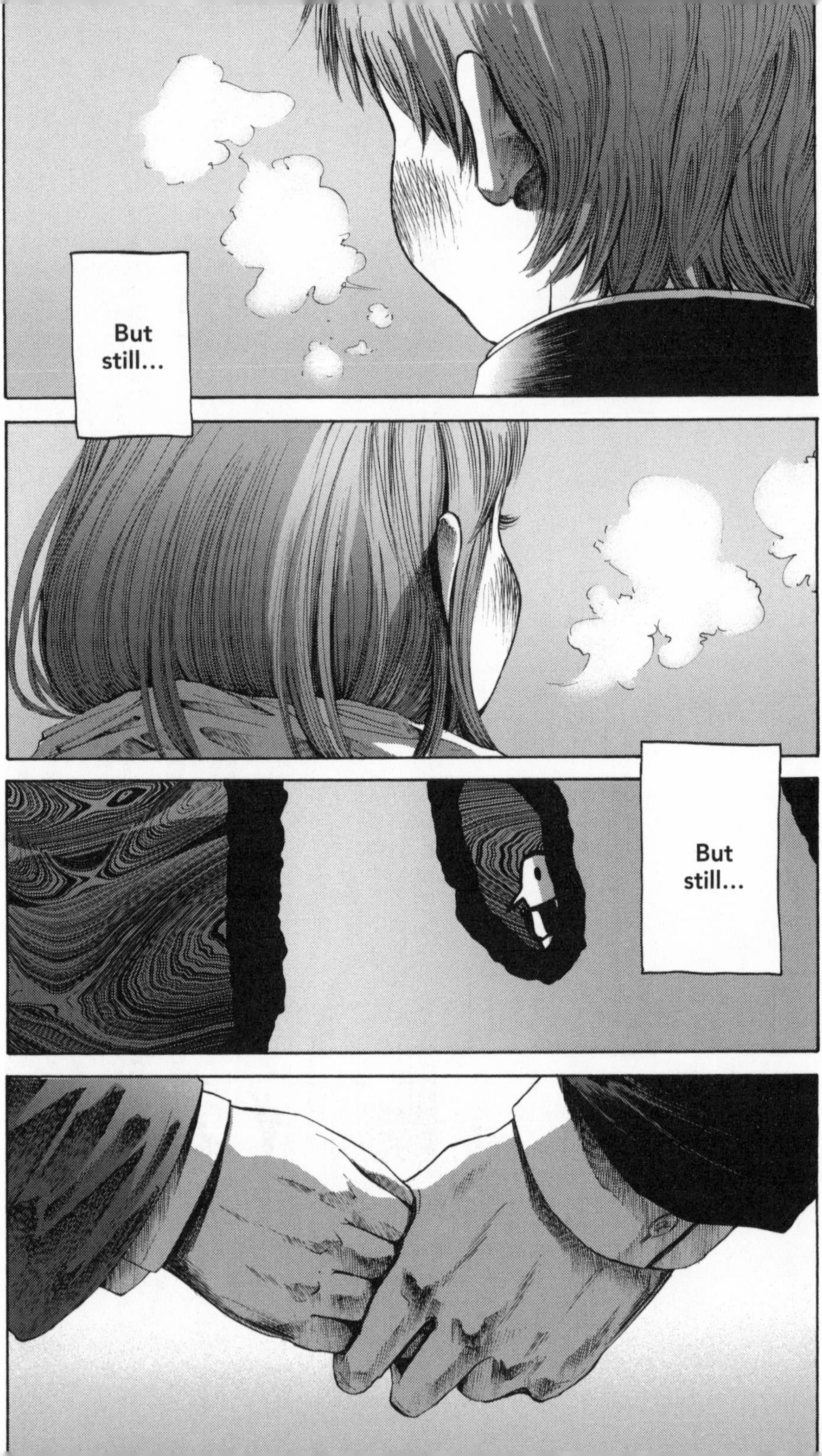
But still...
But still...

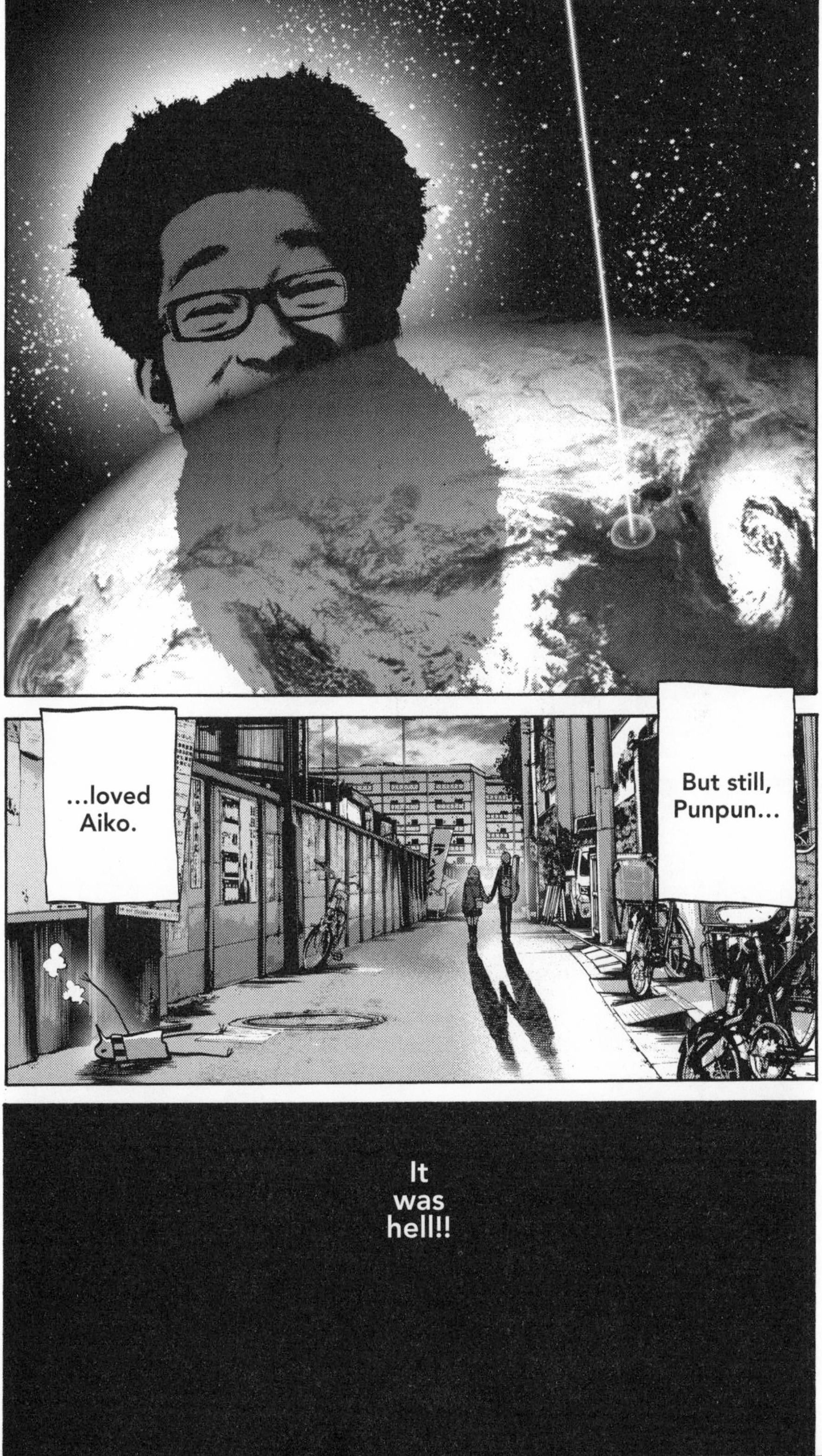
But still, Punpun...
...loved Aiko.
It was hell!!

GOODNIGHT PUNPUN INIO ASANO
Part Two

BACKGROUND ASSISTANTS: Yuki Toribuchi
                        Satsuki Sato
CG ASSISTANT: Hisashi Saito
COOPERATION: Kumatsuto
              Yasumasa Iwama

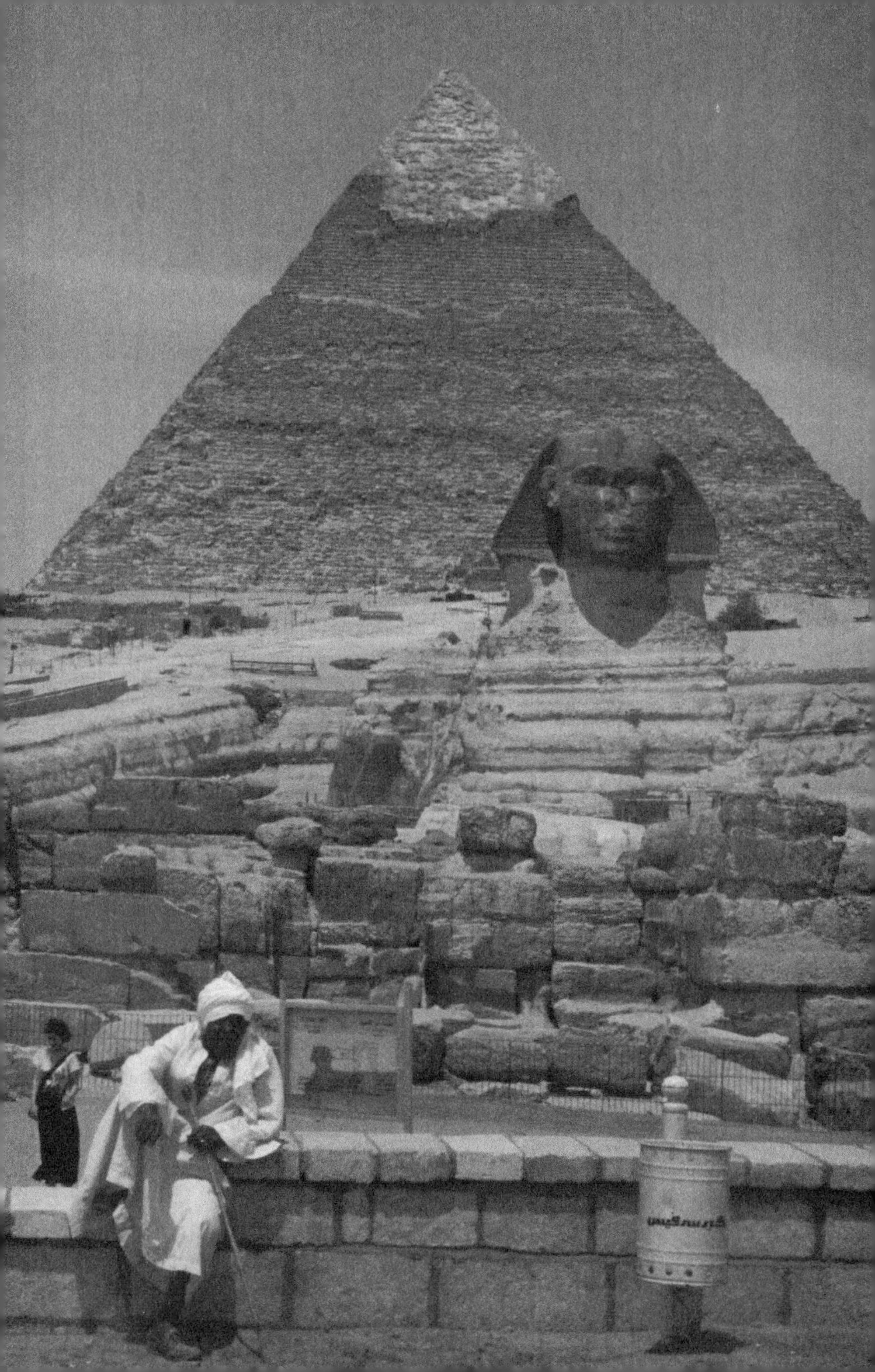

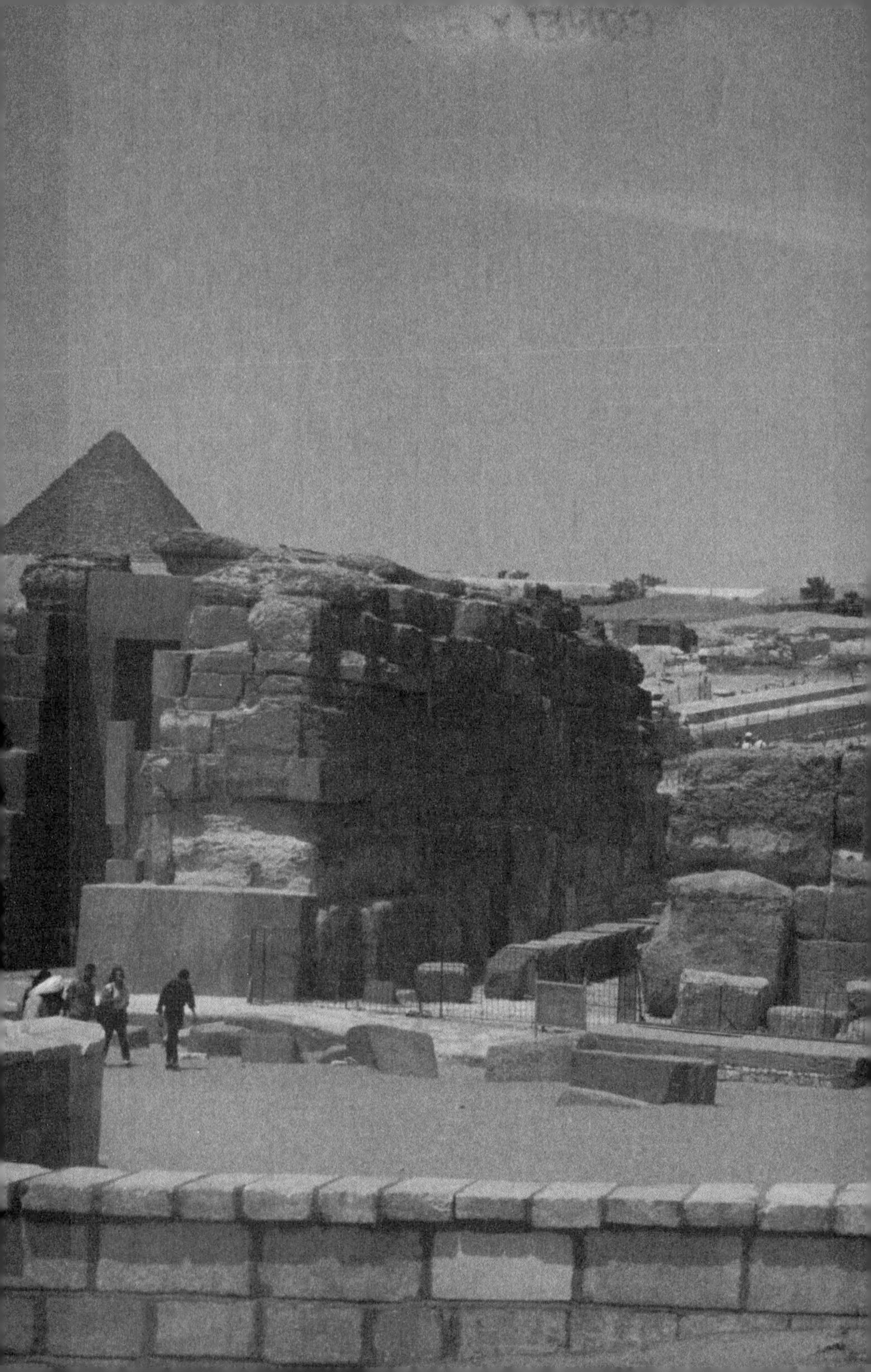

INIO ASANO, a bona fide earthling, was born in Ibaraki, Japan, in 1980. In 2001, his short story "Uchu kara Konnichiwa" (Hello from Outer Space) won the first Sunday GX Rookie Prize. Later, GX published his series *Subarashi Sekai*, available in English from VIZ Media as *What a Wonderful World!* His other works include *Hikari no Machi* (City of Light), *Nijigahara Holograph* and *Umibe no Onna no Ko* (A Girl on the Shore), as well as *solanin*, also available from VIZ Media.

GOODNIGHT PUNPUN
Volume 1
VIZ Signature Edition

Story and Art by INIO ASANO

OYASUMI PUNPUN Vol. 1, 2
by Inio ASANO
© 2007 Inio ASANO
All rights reserved.
Original Japanese edition published by SHOGAKUKAN.
English translation rights in the United States of America,
Canada, the United Kingdom and Ireland arranged with
SHOGAKUKAN.

Translation ☆ JN PRODUCTIONS
Touch-Up Art & Lettering ✧ ANNALIESE CHRISTMAN
Design ✦ FAWN LAU
Editor ✧ PANCHA DIAZ

Printed in the U.S.A.

Published by VIZ Media, LLC
P.O. Box 77010
San Francisco, CA 94107

10 9 8 7 6 5 4 3 2
First printing, March 2016
Second printing, November 2016

www.viz.com

DEC - 2017

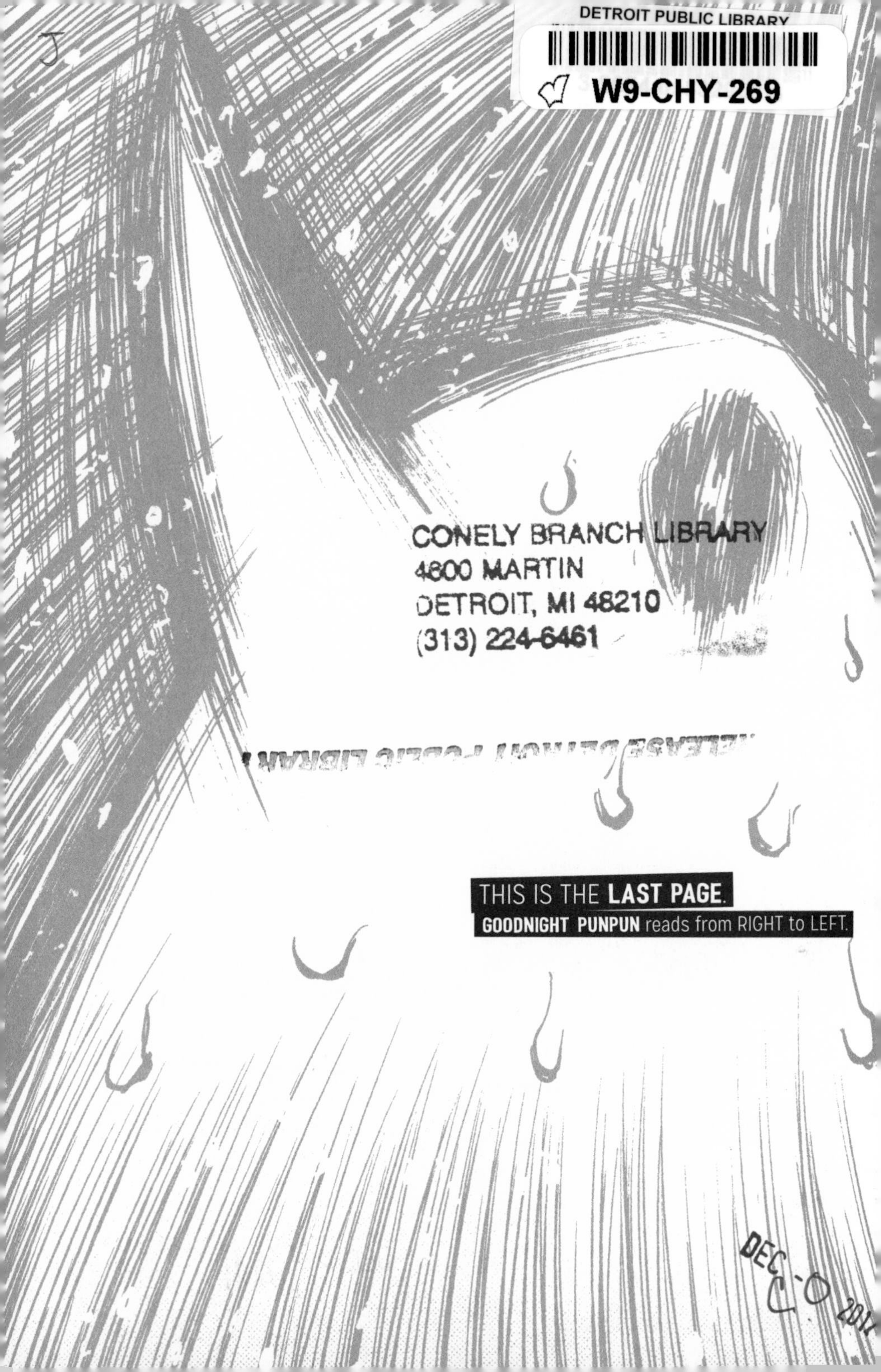

THIS IS THE **LAST PAGE**.

GOODNIGHT PUNPUN reads from RIGHT to LEFT.